DEFENDING THE ROCK

Gibraltar and the Second World War

NICHOLAS RANKIN

FABER & FABER

First published in 2017
by Faber & Faber Limited
Bloomsbury House,
74–77 Great Russell Street,
London WC1B 3DA
This paperback edition first published in 2019

Typeset by Faber & Faber Ltd
Printed in the UK by CPI Group (UK) Ltd, Croydon, CR0 4YY

The right of Nicholas Rankin to be identified as author of this work
has been asserted in accordance with Section 77 of the Copyright,
Designs and Patents Act 1988

A CIP record for this book
is available from the British Library

ISBN 978-0-571-30772-2

2 4 6 8 10 9 7 5 3 1

DEFENDING THE ROCK

Nicholas Rankin worked for twenty years for the BBC World Service, winning two UN awards and becoming Chief Producer. His previous books include biographies of Robert Louis Stevenson and the war correspondent George Steer, *Churchill's Wizards*, a study of camouflage, deception and black propaganda in both world wars, and *Ian Fleming's Commandos*, the history of a WWII naval intelligence unit. He is a Fellow of the Royal Society of Literature and lives in Ramsgate, Kent.

Further praise for *Defending the Rock*:

'Rankin has researched his theme thoroughly, and his book goes far beyond military history to take in the active spy war fought in the Rock's shadows, along with the colourful characters who peopled Gibraltar in the war years.' Nigel Jones, *Times Literary Supplement*

'Fascinating . . . Meticulously researched.' Jules Stewart, *BBC History Magazine*

'Rankin has chosen an unusual vantage point to view the wider war, and told his story well.' Richard Overy, *Guardian*

'Masterly . . . Refreshingly bold and ambitious, never scared to tackle controversial topics, Rankin takes us to places where historians have never been before . . . It is a book crammed with incident and anecdote, with a cast of characters worthy of a Shakespearean dramatis personae . . . This is an unimpeachably objective and well-resea   h.' M.G. Sanchez,

'[Rankin] pinpoints a moment in history, sets it into its broader context, then dives down deep into intimate detail . . . This is fertile ground for a skilful storyteller like Rankin, who combines a scholarly command of his subject with a reporter's eye for the smaller details that help tell a bigger story. This is a book filled with tales of military heroism and tragedy, of diplomatic wrangling, espionage and subterfuge, peopled with a cast of colourful characters . . . whose stories are carefully crafted onto the page. Rankin's depth of knowledge shines effortlessly throughout the 600-plus pages of this formidable book.'
Brian Reyes, *Gibraltar Chronicle*

'A splendid book, peppered with fascinating stories.' Francis Ghilès, *esglobal.org*

by the same author

DEAD MAN'S CHEST:
TRAVELS AFTER ROBERT LOUIS STEVENSON

TELEGRAM FROM GUERNICA:
THE EXTRAORDINARY LIFE OF GEORGE STEER, WAR CORRESPONDENT

CHURCHILL'S WIZARDS:
THE BRITISH GENIUS FOR DECEPTION 1914–1945

IAN FLEMING'S COMMANDOS:
THE STORY OF 30 ASSAULT UNIT IN WWII

This Rock is a wonderful place, with a population infinitely diversified. Moors with costumes radiant as a rainbow or an Eastern melodrama; Jews with gaberdines and skull-caps; Genoese, Highlanders, and Spaniards . . .

Benjamin Disraeli, 1 July 1830

Gibraltar is soon seen . . . There is neither letters nor fine art, the arts of making money and war excepted.

Richard Ford, *A Handbook for Travellers in Spain* (1845)

The value of Gibraltar harbour and base to us is so great . . .

Winston Churchill to Franklin Roosevelt, 16 December 1941

Contents

Illustrations

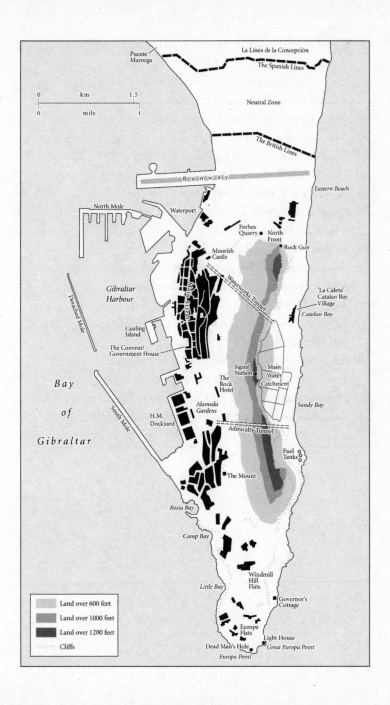

I

Enemies in the Dark

May and June 1940 were blazing, July thundery. Fortress Gibraltar sweltered, waiting for war's *Donner und Blitzen* to split the sky. The Battle of France was lost, and with the German air force now bombing ships in the English Channel and strafing south coast towns, the Battle of Britain was just beginning.

'Upon this battle depends the survival of Christian civilisation,' Winston Churchill declared on 18 June. 'Upon it depends our own British life . . . and our Empire. The whole fury and might of the enemy must very soon be turned upon us. Hitler knows he will have to break us in this island or lose the war.' On 14 July, Churchill added: 'We await undismayed the impending assault. Perhaps it will come tonight. Perhaps it will come next week . . . We must show ourselves equally capable of meeting a sudden violent shock, or . . . a prolonged vigil.'

The Battle of Britain was also the battle of the British Empire. The Dominions – Australia, Canada, New Zealand, South Africa – the Indian Raj and Burma, as well as the Colonial Empire of fifty-odd crown colonies, dependencies, mandates, overseas territories and protectorates, which included the faraway Gilbert and Ellice Islands as well as Guyana, the Gold Coast and Gibraltar, had all rallied to the mother country in September 1939 and joined in declaring war on Germany. Only Ireland/Éire, a self-governing dominion within the British Commonwealth of Nations, chose neutrality. The distinctive Rock of Gibraltar, three miles long and 1400 feet high, hanging off southern Spain by a sandy isthmus, was a tiny but significant part of the empire, waiting to do its duty. As the last Allied toehold remaining on the continent of Europe, everyone knew that the

Rock would be a target for attack, but no one could say how, when or where it would come. Insect-buzzing aircraft had passed in daylight reconnaissance, and early one morning some bombs had been dropped harmlessly in the sea. But the sound of droning aeroplanes in the middle of a summer night was unusual, ominous. The air-raid sirens sounded. Was this it, then? Was the match about to kick off at the western end of the Mediterranean?

In the early hours of Thursday 18 July 1940 a full moon silvered the Sphinx-like profile of the Rock. All except the uniformed men on duty were indoors or at home during the curfew from 11.30 p.m. to 5.30 a.m. As the siren wailed, young John Porral, in his cotton summer pyjamas, went downstairs with his sister to the ground-floor sitting room of their house on Main Street. The aeroplane engines crescendoed above and the upward searchlight beams criss-crossed nervously, searching for a target so the anti-aircraft 'ack-ack' guns could pump explosive shells up into the sky. The gunners were not wholly proficient at this, having only practised in daylight with limited ammunition on drogues, known as 'sleeves', towed behind old-fashioned biplanes. The novelist Thackeray once called Fortress Gibraltar 'this great blunderbuss', but it was now somewhat rusty, and the Rock clogged with supernumeraries.

Two months earlier, the military authorities had ordered the decks cleared of all 'useless mouths' – the dismal phrase for civilians who were too young (under sixteen), too old (over sixty) or too female to be combatants. The great exodus had begun well, with the first shipload of women and children leaving Gibraltar on 21 May 1940. The nearest and safest place for non-combatants was thought to be the French Empire in North Africa, and so thirteen thousand Gibraltarians had been compulsorily evacuated by ship to Casablanca in Morocco. Then the evacuation plan was forced into reverse, so Gibraltar was again packed to the gunwales with returned civilians.

These 'chattels of the military, slaves of the fortress' were a small part of larger wartime movements of people. 'Evacuation', as the British Cabinet Secretary drily remarked, 'is becoming our greatest national industry.' The German *Blitzkrieg* made millions of Europeans refugees, and over half a million Allied soldiers had to be rescued by the Royal Navy as Britain's main ally, France, surrendered.

The Fortress braced for its first bombing in this new Great War. But whose bombers were heading for the Rock? Which air force was about to drop its ordnance? At that moment of history, in the middle of July 1940, there were multiple possibilities, because Gibraltar was confronting not one but *four* potential enemies.

First among them was Nazi Germany. The attacking aeroplanes might be from the German air force, whose northern cohorts were now probing British airspace. Adolf Hitler's armed forces had already conquered Czechoslovakia, Poland, Denmark, Norway, Holland, Belgium, Luxembourg and the Channel Islands. France had capitulated to Nazi *Blitzkrieg* on 22 June, and the Wehrmacht had parked their Panzers at the Pyrenees, with some officers crossing the Spanish frontier to celebrate in the hotels of San Sebastián. The German military was familiar with Spain: nineteen thousand volunteers from *das Heer*, *die Luftwaffe* and *die Kriegsmarine* had served there with the Condor Legion between 1936 and 1939, helping Franco's Nationalist rebels to win the Spanish Civil War.

The peninsula of Gibraltar lay five hundred miles south of the nearest German airfield in occupied France. Perhaps this night raid was the first step of a coming German attempt to rub out the British enclave and close off the mouth of the Mediterranean. The Germans had been intriguing in Morocco for four decades and their espionage in the area was proficient. If controlling the Strait of Gibraltar was the next step in the *Führer*'s strategic push westward across Europe, tonight's exploratory raid might be followed by a full artillery 'stonking', Stuka dive-bombing and parachutists dropping from the sky, as had worked so well in the German invasion of the Low Countries.

The second possible enemy was Fascist Italy, which had joined the war only five weeks before. Eighty thousand Italian regulars and

Fascist militiamen had served on Franco's Nationalist side in the Spanish Civil War. Benito Mussolini wanted a new Roman Empire in the Mediterranean – '*Mare Nostrum*', 'our sea' – and the Italian navy was developing new kinds of submarine to attack the British fleets that controlled its surface and its exits. Mussolini had declaimed: 'The guards of this prison are Gibraltar and Suez', and on 9 June 1940 he wrote to Franco, 'In the new reorganisation of the Mediterranean which will result from the war, Gibraltar will be returned to Spain.' When he declared war the next day, the Fascist leader said: 'We want to break the territorial and military chains which are strangling us in our sea.' Italian aircraft immediately started bombing British Malta, carrying out more than fifty air raids in June 1940. Perhaps a raid on Gibraltar in the west presaged the Italian fleet breaking out into the Atlantic to help the Germans throttle British sea lanes.

Gibraltar's third possible enemy was its next-door neighbour: Falangist Spain. Spain was brutalised and impoverished by the three-year civil war that had left a million dead and tens of thousands jailed or exiled. The date of the bombing attack, 18 July 1940, could be significant. It was the fourth anniversary of General Franco's military uprising. Perhaps Franco was abandoning his country's peculiar status of 'non-belligerence' to join forces with the 'Axis' of Nazi Germany and Fascist Italy, the same totalitarian powers which had helped his military *coup d'état* against the elected Spanish Republic. He had declared the Rock a legacy of the fifteenth-century Queen Isabel *la Católica*, which it was Spain's 'duty and mission' to recapture. When Britain's new ambassador had arrived on 1 June, Falangists shouting '*¡Gibraltar español!*' had mobbed the British Embassy in Madrid.

Franco's military had indeed been working on a secret plan to take back *el Peñon de Gibraltar*, mapping the entire peninsula through photographs in order to direct artillery fire on all its installations and defences. From 1939, up to fifteen thousand Republican prisoners of war, organised in 'Disciplinary Battalions', had begun slave labour, widening roads and building gun sites in the Spanish hinterland north of the Rock, *el Campo de Gibraltar*. The Spanish said publicly that the 'southern border fortifications' conducted by General Pedro Jevenois were purely defensive, but admitted privately that 'the planned use of artillery has the clearly offensive aim of destroying the English garrison'. The British press and parliament had been worried for some time about 'Guns over Gibraltar', the heavy artillery gun barrels pointed straight at the peninsula.

Gibraltar's fourth potential attacker was Vichy France. The military defeat of the French Third Republic in June 1940 had been a tremendous shock to the British as the bulwark on which Allied defence relied fell apart like wet cardboard. France's huge army, navy and air force, with more than enough guns and tanks and ships and planes to match the Germans, had disintegrated. The western part of France was now occupied by German troops, and the new right-wing government of *l'État français*, established in the spa town of Vichy, was collaborating with the Nazis.

On 3 July 1940, British Royal Navy ships from Gibraltar had been ordered by Winston Churchill to bombard the French fleet in Algeria to stop its battleships falling into German hands. This desperate action killed nearly 1300 French sailors and started a blood feud between the former allies. Admiral François Darlan, the head of the French navy, who already resented the Royal Navy for killing his great-grandfather at Trafalgar in 1805, was enraged, and on Bastille Day, Sunday 14 July, persuaded his new president, Marshal Philippe Pétain, to strike back. Smiting the treacherous English would be a pleasure as well as a duty.

Following the killing of the French sailors at Mers-el-Kébir, life had been made intolerable for the Gibraltarian evacuees so recently arrived in Vichy France-controlled Morocco. The British refugees were expelled from French territory in the filthy holds of cargo boats that had just brought back to the Maghreb thousands of not very clean French soldiers who favoured Vichy rather than Charles de Gaulle's Free French.

This was why, from 10 July 1940, up to twenty-two thousand Gibraltarian civilians, women, children, aged and infirm, chattering away in Yanito, their Rock Spanish idiolect, were back home again in Gibraltar's narrow streets, crammed hugger-mugger wherever they could fit in spaces not yet requisitioned by the military. Their menfolk – insultingly dubbed 'Rock Scorpions' by the soldiers – had had to make a mass demonstration, threatening the governor with paralysing strikes, before he allowed their families off the beshitten boats bringing them back from Morocco.

At two o'clock in the morning of 18 July 1940, bombs started dropping from a pair of aircraft whose identities were unclear. No one was quite sure whether they were German Heinkel He 111s or Italian Piaggio P.2s or French Glenn Martin 167s, although the targets of the air raid were most likely the high-ranking British admirals based at Gibraltar. Since the late eighteenth century, Royal Navy flag officers had occupied a large house with extensive grounds off Europa Road on the western slope of the Rock overlooking the dockyard, the bay and the strait. This shuttered house, the Mount, was guarded by Royal Navy personnel and was well known to all visiting dignitaries and naval attachés. The pilots were probably aiming to kill or wound Admiral Sir Dudley North, Flag Officer Commanding North Atlantic Squadron, and his colleague Vice Admiral Sir James Somerville, the Commander-in-Chief of Force 'H'.

Bombing was imprecise in 1940. A 'surgical strike' was as likely as a successful operation with a lump hammer. The only military fatality of the first air raid on Gibraltar was Gunner Percy Leonard, a twenty-year-old serving high on the Rock with 4 Battery, Royal Artillery, who now lies buried in the North Front cemetery. Although a stick of bombs did run up Gibraltar's western slope, the Royal Navy's villa was unscathed. One bomb missed the northern gateway and guardhouse of the Mount by a few yards. It shot through the downstairs wall of 13 Europa Road, which was the home of the Loreto Convent School, founded by Irish nuns from the Institute of the Blessed Virgin Mary.

The projectile exploded by the school laundry. The body of seventy-one-year-old Sister Lorcan O'Connor, a blameless, smiling nun who had spent fifty years of her life teaching in Gibraltar and was now awaiting re-evacuation to England with her schoolgirls, became lodged in the rafters: a fireman called Sheehan had to bring down the remains. Two more wounded nuns, Sister Milagrosa McGovern and Sister Thomas More Devaney, were taken to hospital. Nearby, rescuers found more 'collateral damage' among the innocent: the corpses of the school's caretaker-cum-gardener, Luis Dallia, and his wife, Maria.

Who did this? On balance of probability they were Vichy planes on a vengeance mission for the sinking of the French ships. The Germans had too far to fly, the Italians were occupied elsewhere and the Spanish would not have dared. But whoever struck that first blow, in July 1940 the Rock of Gibraltar was threatened on four sides by imperial powers, and not too well protected by the fifth, Great Britain.

The paradox of bombing is that it often stiffens resolve rather than breaking morale. John Porral, sitting it out in the downstairs shelter of his home in Main Street, was now even more determined to join the Gibraltar Defence Force. Although he would not turn seventeen until mid-September, he and his friend Hector Sheppard-Capurro soon went together to Fortress Headquarters in Line Wall Road to sign up and get into uniform. Their fathers had served together in Sam Browne's Cavalry in the First World War, and were now honorary *aides-de-camp* (ADCs) to the governor. When the aeroplanes came back in full force in late September 1940, the boys would be serving the pair of three-inch twenty-hundredweight ack-ack guns that the Gibraltar Defence Force had hauled and manhandled high up to the top of Signal Hill. The two young Gibraltarians would do their bit defending the Rock.

2

Web of Empire

The British Empire – described by Ashley Jackson as 'the world's largest political entity, a powerful military and strategic alliance, and an economic bloc' – could not help making enemies. Gibraltar was a key imperial fortress and its four foes in 1940 – France, Spain, Italy, Germany – had their own empires and their own imperial ambitions. Britons had been fighting Frenchmen and Spaniards for centuries and were now confronting Germans and Italians too.

A look at the map explains why the British were here, and why other empires wanted to drive them out. The peninsula of Gibraltar is at the key maritime choke point where two huge continental land masses almost meet and two great bodies of water do not quite mingle. This location, on what an eighteenth-century commentator called 'the greatest Thoroughfare of Trade and Commerce in the World', at the crossroads of traffic between Europe and Africa, between the Atlantic and the Mediterranean, has given a very small spur of land great strategic significance in imperial power play.

The actual Rock of Gibraltar is a chunk of Jurassic limestone, folded by such tectonic violence that some geologists thought it might be upside down. It stands on the north side of a fissure probably carved over five million years ago by what is termed the Zanclean Deluge, when the western ocean poured through the gap between Europe and Africa to fill up the desiccated basin of the middle sea. The mouth formed by this cataclysm has a southern as well as a northern lip: in the ancient world the two promontories were known as the Pillars of Melkart to the Phoenicians, the Pillars of Herakles to the Greeks and Romans. In the latter story, the mythical hero and strongman Herakles, or Hercules, pulled Africa and Europe apart with his bare hands. In tearing open the Fretum Herculeum, the 'Herculean Channel', he squeezed up Mons Abyla with one fist and formed Mons Calpe with the other. Today we call these two headlands Ceuta and Gibraltar, and the turbulent channel between them the Strait of Gibraltar or *el Estrecho de Gibraltar*.

The Rock has seen the ebb and flow of many empires over thousands of human (and hominin) lifetimes. 'Neanderthal Man' should really be 'Gibraltar Woman', because the very first known skull of our human ancestor was found in Forbes Quarry in Gibraltar, eight years before another similar cranium was discovered in 1856 in Germany's Neander Valley, which gained the honour of naming the Neanderthals. A rock engraving found in 2012 in Gorham's Cave at the southern end of Gibraltar, with lines carefully scored into rock and cross-hatched, seems to prove the Neanderthals' capacity for abstract thought. Gibraltar may have been the last European redoubt of Neanderthal hominins fleeing southward from the ice around forty thousand years ago.

The Phoenician and Roman name for the limestone peninsula was Calpe. The name 'Gibraltar' resulted from the Moorish conquest of Spain that began in AD 711. Landing there from Africa, the Berber chief Tarik ibn Zeyad called the prominent Rock after himself, Jebel-el-Tarik (Tarik's Mountain). The Moors held Gibraltar for 750 years, but the twelfth-century Moorish castle that still stands on the northwest shoulder is all that now remains of their 'City of Victory'. When the Spanish took the rocky outcrop back in the fifteenth century they hispanicised the place name to 'Gibraltar', though the earliest English seamen through the strait tacked closer to the Arabic version of the name, spelling it 'Jerbolter' or 'Jubalterra'.

George Macaulay Trevelyan considered that AD 711 was when Gibraltar's human history began, summarising thus:

The Phoenicians, when they first sailed into history, used the Rock as a seamark, but their trading stations were on the mainland. For two thousand years the northern Pillar of Hercules was famous in the talk of seafaring folk, but was seldom trodden by the foot of man. The Roman saw no use in it. Even the Viking passed it by. Wild beasts roamed its steep jungle, and spirits were said to haunt there.

That 'jungle' was evergreen oak, pine and Mediterranean scrub of wild olive, buckthorn and turpentine. The 'beasts' included wild boar, red deer, foxes, rabbits, snakes and lizards. Gibraltar's 'Barbary apes' are actually tailless monkeys, *Macaca sylvanus*, introduced by humans from Morocco.* In the eighteenth century, macaques warred with the raptors who also nested on the Rock. The monkeys stole eagle eggs and the eagles feasted on baby monkey. Humans cut down most of the trees for firewood and fuel in their sieges, and goats and cattle scavenged the rest of the aromatic shrubbery.

British strategic interest in the Strait of Gibraltar began some nine hundred years after Tarik ibn Zeyad, with sea battles in the Anglo-Spanish War of the 1590s. In the seventeenth century, Barbary pirates out of Algiers and Tunis (some of them English renegades) played havoc with Mediterranean trade routes, threatening London's supply of coffee. James I sent out a punitive expedition in 1620, and the Protector Oliver Cromwell considered seizing Gibraltar from Spain.

Actual taking of territory in the area began after the Restoration of King Charles II, when the nearby Atlantic port of Tangier came into English possession in the dowry of the Portuguese Catherine of Braganza on her marriage to Charles in 1661. English occupation of Moroccan soil was brief, although 'TANGIER 1662–1680' became the earliest 'battle honour' of the standing army, and the word 'tangerine' crept into the English language. The English abandoned the port of Tangier itself in 1685 – but not before the Admiralty had glimpsed the strategic potential of Gibraltar as the key to the Mediterranean.

---

* The Mediterranean 'Barbary Coast' stretches west from Egypt to the Atlantic. The Arabs conquering North Africa called the people who lived in the Maghreb before them 'Berbers', following the Roman name '*barbari*', barbarians. 'Barbary apes' and 'Barbary steeds' are essentially Moroccan.

In 1700, Carlos II, the last Habsburg king of Spain, died disabled, deranged and devoid of issue. The War of the Spanish Succession (1702–13) followed over who was to inherit his global empire, a dynastic fight between two royal cousins, an Austrian Habsburg, Archduke Charles, and a French Bourbon, Philippe d'Anjou, who was backed by his grandfather, the 'Sun King' Louis XIV of France. The prospect of France and Spain uniting as a Catholic superpower threatened Protestant England and Holland, so they joined an alliance supporting the Austrian claim.

The commander-in-chief of the combined Dutch and English forces in Europe was John Churchill, who was made the first Duke of Marlborough in 1702. Although the French and the Spanish had the largest land armies in Europe, Marlborough outmanoeuvred them to achieve four great victories in five years – Blenheim, Ramillies, Oudenarde and Malplaquet.

Early in 1704, the testy English admiral Sir George Rooke sailed his second task force into the Mediterranean. Rooke had reasons to be grumpy: his wife had just died, he was a martyr to gout and his mission was going wrong. Finding Cádiz too well defended to attack, Rooke decided to capture Gibraltar, which was manned by a tiny Spanish garrison.

On Friday 21 July 1704 (OS)* a squadron of sixteen English and six Dutch warships under Admiral Sir George Byng sailed into the bay and anchored in line abreast opposite Gibraltar's western seafront defences. At the same time, nineteen hundred English and four hundred Dutch marines under Prince George of Hesse were landed on the sandy isthmus in the north. The prince summoned the Spanish governor, Don Diego de Salinas, to surrender. He defiantly declined to do so, although he had only a few score fighting men and several

---

* The Old Style (OS) Julian calendar, used in England until 1752, was eleven days earlier than the New Style (NS) Gregorian calendar used on the continent. The Royal Navy at sea tended to follow the Old Style of home, whereas the British army, in land wars abroad, used New Style to conform with local allies. Thus 21 July 1704 (OS) was also 1 August (NS). Whichever date you prefer, it was summer, and searingly hot.

hundred civilian militia who were already beginning to melt away like the morning dew.

At five o'clock in the bright blue morning of Sunday 23 July Admiral Byng's ships began bombarding the city's fortifications, although the gunners often could not see through the voluminous white clouds of gunpowder smoke. Then Byng sent in two naval landing parties in longboats, rowing through a vile slick of effluent from the ships' heads and the town's sewers to storm the breached castle by the southern mole. The party under Captain William Jumper took the southern fortification and ran up the Union Jack; it is called Jumper's Bastion to this day.

By Monday, the situation of the besieged defenders was untenable. Gibraltar was under marine musket fire from the north and naval bombardment from the west. Many Gibraltarian civilians had retreated to the Upper Rock, out of range of the shelling, while some wives and children fled to the Catholic shrine of Our Lady of Europa at the flatter southern end of the peninsula. There, in English accounts, the officers held their men back from rape and robbery, but according to the Spaniard Ignacio López de Ayala there was no such restraint, and Gibraltarians had to avenge their womenfolk by knifing English rapists and dropping their bodies down wells or sewers. The governor, Don Diego, was forced to capitulate and make terms.

Under these, there was to be no change in the religion or laws of Gibraltar. Those who swore allegiance to Charles III could stay, with the same privileges and rights as before. Only two dozen Gibraltarian families, some seventy people, chose to remain. About four thousand refugees left, decamping to San Roque nearby and other parts of Spain, led by priests who assured them that the French would soon drive the heretics out. The English looted all their Catholic churches save one, and despoiled their sacred shrines. The statue of Our Lady of Europa, which every passing Catholic ship dipped its colours to, was thrown unceremoniously into the surf, together with the beheaded baby Jesus. English imperialism of the day meant Protestantism and plunder.

The War of the Spanish Succession rolled on. In August, there was an all-day sea battle between the English and French fleets off Vélez-Málaga, the largest naval engagement of the war. Battleships and war galleys pounded each other into an exhausted stalemate; hundreds of sailors died before both fleets retreated.

Gibraltar had fallen to Anglo-Dutch forces and now the Mediterranean started to become a British lake. After previous raids on Spanish territory, the English 'pirates' usually went home. Not this time. The enclave on the Rock would grow into a gall on Andalusia: a citadel, a foreign colony, a nest of commerce and capitalism, a port of free trade. As Thackeray put it: 'Gibraltar is the great British depot for smuggling goods into the Peninsula.'

Spain made ferocious assaults to take the place back in 1704 and 1705, but the defences, sometimes manned by Royal Marines, held.* The French won the War of the Spanish Succession in the sense that the Bourbon Philippe d'Anjou got the crown and became *Su Majestad* Felipe V, *Rey Católica de España*, but they also lost. The spoils of war were sorted out in the 1713–14 Treaties of Utrecht. Following the 1706–7 Acts of Union the now united 'Kingdom of Great Britain' legally acquired 'the full and entire propriety of the Town and Castle of Gibraltar, together with the Port, Fortifications and Forts thereunto belonging . . .'

Article X of the Treaty of Peace and Friendship between Great Britain and Spain, signed in Utrecht on 13 July 1713, stated: 'Her Britannic Majesty [Queen Anne], at the request of the Catholic King, does consent and agree, that no leave shall be given under any pretence whatsoever, either to Jews or Moors, to reside or have their dwelling in the said Town of Gibraltar . . .' London would keep asking if this condition was being met and Gibraltar would keep demurring.

---

* Since 1827 the Royal Marines' insignia has included GIBRALTAR as their sole battle honour above the globe and laurel and the motto *per mare per terram*, by sea and by land. For the three hundred and fiftieth anniversary of the Corps in October 2014, Gibraltar gave a chunk of the Rock to stand as a memorial near the Royal Marines' main training base at Lympstone in Devon.

The reality was that the garrison and fortress could not keep going without both Jews and Moors. They were under the protection of the Emperor of Fez and Morocco, who only allowed besieged Gibraltar to import fresh food, provisions and building materials like timber and bricks from the Barbary Shore on the proviso that the place be open to all his subjects. From 1712 to 1717, the Jews from Tetuán had a synagogue in what is now Gibraltar's Bomb House Lane. A 1721 treaty with the emperor granted his subjects, 'whether Moors or Jews', exactly the same privileges in British dominions as those 'granted to the English residing in Barbary'. The fact that this directly contradicted the Treaty of Utrecht was an anomaly that Gibraltar was happy to live with. Other dissidents escaping from intolerance also began gravitating to Gibraltar, 'the asylum of people of all nations who expatriate themselves for their country's good', as the nineteenth-century traveller Richard Ford tartly remarked.

Secure on the territory it had seized, Britain could now open the door to the Mediterranean. Gibraltar, as the journalist Tommy Bowles quipped, was the hook on which the key hung. The Rock became the portal for the Royal Navy's expansion of the British Empire eastwards through space and time: Gibraltar in 1704, Minorca in 1708, Malta in 1800, Corfu in 1814, Cyprus in 1878, and Egypt with the Suez Canal in 1882.

The American War of Independence, which began in 1775, was a military disaster for the British Empire. Among all the setbacks and surrenders, Gibraltar remained invincible, withstanding what is still called 'the Great Siege', actually its fourteenth, between 21 June 1779 and 3 February 1783. French and Spanish forces assailed the Rock for an incredible three years, seven months and twelve days, and the defending governor, General Eliott, proved an outstanding leader. 'Stout old Eliott' (as G. M. Trevelyan called him) inspired his garrison of 7500 men and 3000 civilians while holding off at least 35,000 French and Spanish soldiers, who attacked Gibraltar with fireships, bombardments and infantry.

Initially finding Gibraltar's civilian engineers 'indolent, drunken, disorderly and over-paid', teetotal Eliott created a company of 'soldier artificers' drawn from willing volunteers in the Gibraltar garrison. These forefathers of the British army's Royal Engineers built the King's Bastion, a blunt arrowhead of a fortress jutting west into the Bay of Gibraltar, and during the siege, under their top NCO, the Cornish ex-miner Sergeant Major Henry Ince, dug tunnels through the limestone to shoot down on the enemy from halfway up the great limestone bluff at the northern end of the Rock.

When peace came early in 1783 Governor Eliott was given the Order of the Bath and elevated to the peerage as first Baron Heathfield of Gibraltar. Seagulls now perch on the head of his noble bust that stands prominent in Gibraltar's Alameda Gardens. Eliott had ensured that Spain did not become a French province nor the Mediterranean a French lake. Captain John Drinkwater's non-fiction *History of the Late Siege of Gibraltar*, first published in 1785, went through four editions in five years and made its author a small fortune. Drinkwater returned to Gibraltar and started building the Garrison Library in 1793. (This was for British officers only: Gibraltarian civilians had to found their own Exchange and Commercial Library in 1817.)

In the years after the Great Siege, Gibraltar's population swelled. The place became an entrepôt for legitimate trade and illicit smuggling as well as a byword for squalor, drunkenness and disease. 'Yellow Jack' and malaria raged intermittently. Ill-disciplined soldiers stupefied themselves with 'blackstrap' or other raw drink in the ninety or so grogshops crammed into the wynds, alleys and steep 'ramps' of the Upper Town. Corruption ruled. Governor O'Hara – 'the Cock of the Rock' – ignored public intoxication because he received a major cut of all alcohol sold.

The Duke of Kent (Queen Victoria's father) began unpopular but much-needed reforms when he became governor in 1802, but the poet Samuel Taylor Coleridge, en route to Malta in April 1804, still recoiled from the stink of the drains, the 'degraded' Spaniards and

Moorish 'wretches'. (He did enjoy the yellow broom in flower and the 'perfect Gothic Extravaganza' of the stalactites in St Michael's Cave, reminding him of the 'caverns measureless to man' he had already written about in 'Kubla Khan'.) Lord Byron, spotted scowling in the Garrison Library by John Galt in 1809, found Gibraltar 'the dirtiest and most detestable spot in existence'.

When Napoleon made his foolish decision to invade Spain, Gibraltar did very well out of it. In the Peninsular War of 1807–14, British and Portuguese forces under the Duke of Wellington eventually drove the French Grande Armée out, assisted by bandit armies of Spanish *guerrilleros* who ambushed French convoys, with all the atrocious cruelties that Francisco Goya depicted in *Los Desastres de la Guerra*. Genoese entrepreneurs fleeing the French armies set up shop in the British peninsula, bypassing Cádiz and trading with Spain's disaffected American colonies. There was serious money to be made from prize ships captured in naval warfare, and work in the Royal Navy dockyards.

Some of Admiral Horatio Nelson's fleet resupplied at Gibraltar before sailing out to do battle with the Napoleonic navy off the Spanish coast on 21 October 1805. His last signal read 'Engage the enemy more closely' as he led his twenty-seven ships head on against thirty-three French and Spanish vessels off Cape Trafalgar. As he walked on the quarterdeck of *Victory* in the pell-mell battle, one-eyed, one-armed Nelson was shot by a sniper firing down from the mizzen-top of the French ship *Redoubtable* grappled alongside. He died painfully about three hours later, saying: 'Thank God, I have done my duty.' His grieving crew transported his corpse back to Rosia Bay in Gibraltar in a barrel of Spanish brandy. Nelson's final triumph at Trafalgar was a world scoop for the *Gibraltar Chronicle*, and marked the start of his posthumous celebrity.*

---

* A Miss Mdingane, a school teacher in the Eastern Cape of South Africa, gave a small boy called Rolihlahla the Christian name 'Nelson' on his first day of school in 1923. Perhaps she foresaw that young Nelson Mandela would become a heroic leader (see http://www.nelsonmandela.org/content/page/names).

In Victorian and Edwardian days Gibraltar became well known as 'the Rock'. Other nicknames – the Gate, the Key, the Lock, the Keeper, the Watchdog, the Guardian, the Sentinel of the Mediterranean – marked it as a pillar of empire. Its profile appeared on colourful tea-towels, tin trays and china plates. Many troopships called in at Gibraltar on their way to and from imperial wars. Between 1815 and 1904, the British army took part in thirty-three overseas campaigns, fighting Abyssinians and Afghans, Boers and Burmese, Ceylonese and Chinese, violently pacifying Maoris, Tibetans and Zulus. A hundred Gibraltarian muleteers earned the Anglo-Egyptian medal with 'Suakin 1885' clasp for their work as porters of military equipment in the fight against Sudanese Dervishes.

In 1855, the dauntless Jamaican-born sutler Mary Seacole was surprised to hear her name called out in the marketplace in Gibraltar. 'Why, bless my soul, old fellow, if this is not our good old Mother Seacole!' She turned to find two invalided officers from the 48th Regiment of Foot who had often been fed at her house in Kingston in the Caribbean, now hard to recognise beneath the thick beards they had grown in the Crimean War. Mrs Seacole was en route to the front in order to set up the British Hotel near Balaclava, 'a mess-table and comfortable quarters for sick and convalescent officers'. In her next stopover in Malta, a British doctor would give her an introduction to Florence Nightingale at Scutari.

Mark Twain arrived in a party of North American tourists on board SS *Quaker City* in 1867 and described the Rock in chapter 7 of *The Innocents Abroad*: 'everywhere you choose to look, Gibraltar is clad with masonry and bristling with guns'.

There is an English garrison at Gibraltar of 6000 or 7000 men, and so uniforms of flaming red are plenty; and red and blue, and undress costumes of snowy white, and also the queer uniform of the bare-kneed Highlander; and one sees soft-eyed Spanish girls from San Roque, and veiled Moorish beauties (I suppose they are beauties) from Tarifa, and turbaned, sashed and trousered Moorish merchants from Fez, and long-robed, bare-legged, ragged Mohammedan vagabonds from Tetouan and Tangier, some brown, some yellow and some as black as virgin ink – and Jews from all around, in gaberdine, skull-cap and slippers, just as they are in pictures and theatres and just as they were three thousand years ago, no doubt.

Gibraltar saw every kind of sea-going vessel because by the end of the nineteenth century Britannia did indeed rule the waves. The Royal Navy – 'the shield of Empire' to popular newspapers – was then the world's largest; British merchant shipping carried 60 per cent of world trade; and Gibraltar became an important coaling station for steamships whose engineered propulsion meant they could ignore the peninsula's peculiar winds that caused problems in the age of sail. By the 1880s, between fifteen and twenty vessels a day were bunkering in Gibraltar, refuelled by Maltese coalheavers. Common names in Gibraltar like Azzopardi, Borg, Caruana, Mifsud and Zammit attest to Maltese ancestry.

The Suez Canal opened at the end of 1869 and was a boon to the British. By Queen Victoria's Golden Jubilee year, 1887, the British India Steam Navigation Company (BI) and the Peninsular & Oriental Steam Navigation Company (P&O) were among the shipping lines carrying thousands of passengers along 'all-red routes', named after the colour that marked British territories on the map of the world. The British Empire covered nine million square miles and contained over 300 million people. One key British-controlled all-red route was broken into passages of roughly a thousand nautical miles each: Portsmouth to Gibraltar; Gibraltar to Malta; Malta to Port Said, and then, via the Suez Canal which Prime Minister Anthony Eden once described as 'the swing door of the British Empire', another thousand nautical miles to Aden. From there, the itinerary either dropped south towards British East Africa and Cape Colony in South Africa or led east towards India, Ceylon, Burma, and the trading ports of Singapore and Hong Kong, as well as the white settler dominions of Australasia. Travellers on this route always looked out for the Rock.

Entrepreneurs took advantage of the new opportunities and markets that easier travel opened up. Few were as enterprising as the

Hindu merchants from the city of Hyderabad, ninety miles northeast of Karachi in Sind, then in British India and now part of Pakistan. These adaptable *bania* saw the whole world as their market. Family firms sent out hawker-scouts on long-distance voyages from Bombay to find niches along the shipping routes where small businesses could establish a foothold, and then sent stock and staff to make them flourish in places like Aden, Port Said, Alexandria, Cyprus, Malta and, of course, Gibraltar.

By March 1938 there were 129 British Indians living on the Rock, running twenty-six shops along Main Street. It is possible that the very first Sindwork shop opened in Waterport Street as far back as the 1860s. Other Hyderabad family firms such as D. Chellaram, J. T. Chandia and Pohoomull Brothers followed in the 1870s and 1880s, selling silks, shawls, lace, oriental curios and brass and silver knick-knacks to tourists. In 1916, Bulchand & Sons and Khemchand & Sons were the first 'Indian Bazaar and Curio Stores' to join the Gibraltar Chamber of Commerce. But by then, the merchants' legal status had changed. From the beginning of the twentieth century, as British subjects not born in Gibraltar but only allowed to reside there, the Indians were deemed 'Statutory Aliens' and suffered the same sort of prejudices here as Jews did elsewhere. Stephen Constantine has pointed out that 'Statutory Alien' was the lawyerly term used to soften the frankly racist Aliens Order Extension Order of June 1900 which allowed the governor to expel any person judged 'undesirable'. Why was this happening? As the Rock was growing in naval and military importance, Whitehall was on the lookout for possible threats to that development. 'We take it as an admitted principle', said an 1889 British government report, 'that no person, whether British subject or an alien, has an absolute right to enter or remain in the Fortress of Gibraltar contrary to the wishes and commands of the Crown and its Officers.'

The pound sterling became legal tender in Gibraltar on 1 October 1898, replacing Spanish coinage; the money that HM Government invested is further evidence of the strategic importance of the Rock. Between 1895 and 1905, a great new harbour and dockyard was constructed, covering over three hundred acres of Gibraltar Bay. There were three new moles, with piers and moorings, as well as three graving docks for the Royal Navy's biggest battleships, with cranes, workshops and forges. It was pointed out that this £11,000,000 investment (approximately £1.2 billion today) was vulnerable to hostile shelling from the hills on the Spanish mainland, but the objection was confidently overruled. As a concession, the oil tanks were moved to the eastern side of the Rock and the thousand-yard Admiralty Tunnel was cut straight through the limestone to link Sandy Bay on the east side of the peninsula to the works.

Gibraltar is parched in summer, so between 1898 and 1928 six huge water reservoirs were also carved inside the limestone rock. On the eastern slope of scree breccia and windblown dunes above Sandy Bay they constructed a 'water catchment area' covering fourteen acres. Timber piles driven deep into the steep slope held a wooden framework to which hundreds of sheets of galvanised corrugated iron were screwed. (When ants ate the timber, they imported British Empire teak.) Fresh rainwater could then run down the sheets, whitened with slaked lime, into a channel feeding the giant tanks inside. The four reservoirs holding five million gallons of water were impressive enough for King George V and Queen Mary to pay them a dutiful visit on 30 January 1912, returning from the Coronation Durbar in India.

Bad drains had plagued Gibraltar: improving its public health raised its status. An attempt at moral cleansing, also, followed the Great War (in which seventy-six Gibraltarians joined the British armed forces, half a dozen died on active service and some four hundred patrolled the Rock in the Gibraltar Volunteer Corps). In January 1922, Governor Smith-Dorrien expelled over a hundred Spanish prostitutes from Serruya's Lane (a name whitewashed to New Passage in modern Gibraltar). The women were pushed across the Spanish border to La Línea, to ply their trade in the brothels on Calle Gibraltar or 'Gib Street'.*

When the British Empire pioneered telecommunications, Gibraltar was at the heart of it. By 1870, Birmingham could communicate with Bombay by telegraph, in messages pulsed in Morse code along undersea trunk lines of copper wires sheathed in gutta percha. The cable ran from Cornwall to Portugal and then onwards via the Rock of Gibraltar through the Mediterranean, the Suez Canal, the Red Sea and across the Indian Ocean. By 1887, the year after Gibraltar got its first telephone exchange, the Rock was one of sixty-four stations along the Eastern Telegraph's 22,400-mile cable network.

In December 1901, Guglielmo Marconi bounced the first radio signal (three dots: 'S' in Morse code) 1700 miles over the Atlantic, from Poldhu in Cornwall to Signal Hill in Newfoundland. By 1903, a wireless-equipped warship could steam from Portsmouth to Gibraltar receiving Poldhu transmissions all the way. In 1906, the Admiralty set up Morse radio transmitters with a thousand-mile range at Gibraltar, Portsmouth and Cleethorpes. On the Rock, the Royal Navy took over the ship monitoring and signal station of Lloyd's Register of Shipping at Windmill Hill, just north of Europa Point, four hundred feet above sea level. The transmitters were converted to high power in 1909, so the Admiralty in London could directly control the fleet at sea.

The exercise of sea power, as the narrative historian Barbara Tuchman pointed out, can be as unconscious an activity as breathing oxygen or speaking prose. It took an American naval officer, Captain Alfred Thayer Mahan, to formulate the process. The impact of his classic book, *The Influence of Sea Power on History 1660–1783*, pub-

---

* 1922 also saw the publication of *Ulysses* by James Joyce, a book which ends with Molly Bloom, born Marion Tweedy in Gibraltar, remembering the fig trees in the Alameda Gardens 'and the jessamine and geraniums and cactuses and Gibraltar as a girl where I was a Flower of the mountain yes', and under the Moorish wall the lingering memory of an erotic kiss.

lished in 1890, was enormous in his day. The book stated the obvious
– who masters the sea commands the stage – but said it so persua-
sively that it affected global geopolitics. 'In isolating and describing
a great historical fact,' Tuchman observed, '[Mahan] himself made
history.'

Admiral Mahan's big idea galvanised imperialism. It boosted the
USA's turn to empire in the 1890s, and provided the rationale behind
the annexation of Hawaii, the development of the Panama Canal
and the seizure of Cuba and the Philippines in the 1898 Spanish-
American War. 'Take up the White Man's burden –', exhorted the
imperialist Rudyard Kipling in a poem for the Americans soon after,

> And reap his old reward:
> The blame of those ye better,
> The hate of those ye guard –

The Influence of Sea Power on History was also avidly studied in
East Asia. Imperial Japan built a powerful fleet to strike at Imperial
Russia in 1904. Although China was occupied and fragmented, Chi-
nese nationalists like Sun Yat Sen dreamed of a maritime strategy
for the future, only now being achieved in the twenty-first century
with China's creation of a 'blue water' fleet for the People's Liber-
ation Army (Navy) and huge new island bases in the South China
Sea. 'Seapower is the lifeline of China's market economy,' wrote a
Chinese academic in an article on Mahan in 2011, and President Xi
Jinping has pledged to make China a global naval power.

In the nineteenth century, Imperial Britain was mad for Mahan
because the admiral flattered British pride in their maritime empire.
In 1893, Mahan dined with Queen Victoria and the British Prime
Minister, William Gladstone, and he was awarded honorary degrees
by both Oxford and Cambridge in the same week. 'Command of the
sea is everything,' young Winston Churchill told his mother in 1896.

Early in the book, Captain Mahan pointed out the importance
of the seizure of Gibraltar in 1704. The severing of Spain's Atlantic

naval base at Cádiz in the west from its Mediterranean naval base at Cartagena in the east effectively crippled Spanish sea power. 'It is a bridle in the mouth of Spain and Barbary,' Richard Ford had observed of Gibraltar fifty years before Mahan.

At the end of the nineteenth century, however, a new power was rising. Imperial Germany emerged in 1871 from the unification of twenty-seven German-speaking territories as a vigorous industrial prodigy under its Iron Chancellor, Otto von Bismarck. But when the mentally unstable Wilhelm II unexpectedly became Kaiser in 1888 he wanted to run things his own impetuous way, especially abroad. Captain Mahan's ideas inspired Wilhelm to think globally: he was fascinated by the growth of the United States and Japan, and coined '*die gelbe Gefahr*', 'the yellow peril', a racist term for the Chinese. A grandson of Queen Victoria, the big-moustached Kaiser wanted to emulate Britain by having a large navy and lots of faraway colonies in the Pacific and Africa. Wilhelm II ordered copies of Mahan's book for every ship in the German fleet, and started building three dozen battleships. In 1906, Britain produced HMS *Dreadnought*, the new 'all big gun' battleship armed with ten twelve-inch guns and fast turbine engines, starting 'the dreadnought race' for giant warships.

A dispute over the Strait of Gibraltar had nearly ignited the Great War of 1914–18 ten years earlier. Germany wanted a colony on the shores of the Mediterranean and objected strongly to France being given a free hand in Morocco, seeing it as a conspiracy by existing members of the imperial club to block its own ambitions there. It was as though the Italians and the British had agreed that the French could put their towels on all the Moroccan loungers, which the Germans hoped would be their 'place in the sun'.

At the end of March 1905, Kaiser Wilhelm II made an inflammatory speech in Tangier in favour of Moroccan independence, and Germany threatened war against France. No one wanted another Franco-Prussian War like that of 1870–1 when Paris was besieged and so much blood was shed. At the beginning of 1906, twelve nations gathered in the south of Spain for a three-month peace conference at Algeciras, actually just 'a milestone on the road to Armageddon', as Winston Churchill later remarked.

The delegates all met in the brand new, British-designed-and-owned Reina Cristina Hotel in Algeciras, looking across to the leonine silhouette of Gibraltar. In the bay in between, the great, grey warships of the Royal Navy's Atlantic and Mediterranean Fleets lay at anchor. As Nelson's old dictum put it: 'A fleet of British ships of war are the greatest negotiators in Europe.' Representatives of the future 'Entente Alliance' of France, Britain, Russia, the United States and their supporters (which included Spain and Italy) squared up to diplomats from the future 'Central Powers' of Germany and Austro-Hungary. The Allies won. After US President Teddy Roosevelt leaned on him, the German emperor backed down; the Sultanate of Morocco would henceforth be policed and 'protected' by France and Spain.

In March 1912, France established a protectorate over the whole of Morocco, conceding to Spain in November of that year a small northern coastal strip, 'the bone of the Moroccan cutlet', henceforth known as Spanish Morocco. In 1923, British diplomats ensured that Tangier became an 'international zone' run by a committee drawn from six nations – Belgium, Britain, France, Italy, Portugal and Spain – so no single foreign power could plant its guns at the mouth of the Mediterranean and threaten the Strait of Gibraltar.

3

Rifts in the Rock

Hierarchies of caste, class and race have been the scaffolding of empire. Monarchy and aristocracy tend to be at the top, trumping nationality, and producing curious effects over time. John Churchill became the Duke of Marlborough during the War of the Spanish Succession when Gibraltar was acquired for the British Empire. The duke's most famous descendant was Sir Winston Churchill (who wrote his ancestor's biography, *Marlborough: His Life and Times*, in the 1930s), and Marlborough's most famous enemy, a brilliant general on the opposing Franco-Spanish side, was his own nephew, the first Duke of Berwick, illegitimate son of his sister Arabella and King James II of England. One descendant of this liaison, Don Jacobo Fitz-James Stuart y Falcó, tenth Duke of Berwick and seventeenth Duke of Alba, became General Franco's ambassador to Great Britain from 1937 to 1945. Churchill's personal relationship with the person he referred to as 'my kinsman – Jimmy Alba' tempered British policy towards Spain in the Second World War.

On 31 May 1906, in the year of the Algeciras Treaty, King Alfonso XIII of Spain married the niece of King Edward VII of England, Princess Victoria Eugenie of Battenburg (known in Britain as Princess Ena). From a window, a Catalan anarchist called Mateu Morral lobbed a bomb in a bouquet of flowers down on the coach transporting the king and his new British bride along the crowded Calle Mayor in Madrid. Ena's pearls and silk were spattered with the blood of horses and humans.

★

No such revolutionaries were allowed in Gibraltar, a smaller and more tightly controlled society where the hierarchies of class, caste and race were rigidly observed. A fortress first and a colony second, Gibraltar replicated the military and social mores of the British Empire. Gareth Stockey has described the virtual apartheid between the 'English' Gibraltar of the army and navy and the 'Spanish' Gibraltar of the civilian working class, with the two leading utterly separate lives and speaking different languages. But his history also describes Gibraltar's 'moneyed class', who evaded this simple dichotomy. The millionaires rose to the top, of course. And wealthy Gibraltarians of varied Mediterranean ancestry, people who owned land and houses, made money from business, trade and industry and ran banking, shipping and other services, also bridged the great divide. The merchant class were allowed into 'English' society initially through Freemasonry (the first Masonic Lodge on Gibraltar was established in 1727), the Gibraltar Yacht Club (founded 1829), and through the extraordinary fox-hunting organisation which the *Naval Review* once called '*the* great institution of Gibraltar'.

The Calpe Hunt, whose name derives from the Roman term for the Rock, dated back to Napoleonic times. It was founded in 1812 by the chaplain to the governor, Reverend Mackereth, and his lawyer friend Mr Relph, who used two hounds – Rockwood and Ranter – to flush the foxes out of the scrubby thickets of the Upper Rock. After French troops withdrew in 1813 from the Peninsular War, it became possible for Gibraltarians to extend the hunt northward, on horseback, deeper into Spain, in that part of the province of Cádiz known as *el Campo de Gibraltar*.* Blue-jacketed civilians were joined by army officers from the garrison and visiting naval officers in scarlet riding coats. They also invited their brother officers from the Spanish military based at Algeciras and San Roque to ride with them.

---

* *El campo* means 'the country' or 'the countryside' in Spanish. In some Spanish-speaking places where the British have settled, like the Argentine and the Falkland Islands, the word is anglicised to 'the camp', as in 'Do come to our place in the camp this weekend.'

The Campo was rough, dry country, with the added spice of bandits and robbers. There were pine woods, cork oak forests, crags and crannies, gorse and scrub. One rider said it was 'full of 'ills and 'oles and very 'ard on 'orses'. The American war correspondent Richard Harding Davies told his mother in 1893: 'There are no fences but the ground is one mass of rocks and cactus and ravines down which these English go with an ease that makes me tremble with admiration.' As the Campo saw increased cultivation during the nineteenth century, the Calpe Hunt needed to negotiate with Spanish-speaking landowners and farmers. This is where the remarkable Larios dynasty of Gibraltar enters the story.

Gibraltar has always owed a lot to its enemies, who invigorate its economy with new blood. Among the unintentional gifts of Napoleon were waves of refugees from Genoa and Spain who saw the economic possibilities of a free port with access to the Atlantic and the Mediterranean. When Pablo Larios y las Héras (1755–1814) settled in Gibraltar in 1809 he started trading with Spain's South American colonies, who were breaking away and becoming independent republics. The first Larios made a lot of money, which the next generation of the Larios family invested in other Andalusian businesses – gin and cotton in Málaga, sugar in Cádiz, cork in La Línea.

Larios's sons Manuel, Pablo and Martin started buying thousands of hectares in the Campo de Gibraltar, stretching into the cork oak forests of Almoraima and set up a large processing factory at La Línea, where a thousand workers produced sheets of cork and 100 million wine-bottle stoppers a year.

Pablo Larios's grandson, Pablo Antonio Larios y Tashara, spent the family's wealth living large in Gibraltar. In 1875, he bought the Club House Hotel in the centre of town and transformed it into the grand Connaught House so Queen Victoria's son Prince Arthur could live there for four months. He also hosted Arthur's elder brother, the future King Edward VII, when he visited in April 1876. Three years later, the third Pablo Larios was killed by an out-of-control horse.

The fourth Pablo, the original Pablo Larios's great-grandson, Pablo Jerónimo Larios Sánchez de Piña (1865–1938), was horse-mad; jockey-racing at ten, hunting at eleven, taking up polo brilliantly at twenty, winning the Barcelona Derby at twenty-two and the Calpe Hunt Cup ten times. Pablo Larios shot boar, chamois, ibex, lynx, red deer, roe deer and wolf with a rifle, blasted red-legged partridge with a shotgun, chanced his arm at pig-sticking in Almoraima and was the first man to catch tunny with rod and line in the Strait of Gibraltar. His *Ríos salmoneros de Asturias* (1927) is authoritative on Spanish fly-fishing. Aged only twenty-six, he was elected Master of the Calpe Hunt in 1891. This was most unusual because by tradition the Master was a garrison officer and the hounds were kennelled in Gibraltar, but wealthy Pablo Larios owned vast tracts of land over which the hunt could flow.

In August 1901, thirty-six-year-old Pablo Larios married Pepita, his second cousin once removed, whose full name was Josefa Fernández de Villavicencio Crooke Corral y Larios. In 1910, she inherited a family title, Marchioness of Marzales. In the Spanish way, Larios as her husband now styled himself 'Marqués de Marzales'. In 1903 the Larioses built a British-style, Queen Anne revival house at *el cortijo de Guadacorte*, their 750-hectare estate overlooking the Strait of Gibraltar. The family grafted the society and lifestyle of the British Rock onto the southern Spanish landowning aristocracy. When Edward VII became the first British monarch ever to visit Gibraltar in April 1903, Pablo and Pepita dined with him at the Convent,* the governor's house, a former Franciscan convent in the middle of the city, and lunched on the royal yacht *Victoria and Albert*. The king (in field marshal's uniform) was driven round the town and out to the North Front to see the Calpe Hunt hounds out at exercise from their kennels.

* After a Protestant bigot complained that the king should not grace a Papist establishment, in April 1908 Edward VII ordered the name changed to 'Government House'; George VI rescinded the command in June 1943 and the governor's home is once again 'The Convent'.

In 1906, Pablo Larios achieved a unique double: he managed to get both King Alfonso XII of Spain and King Edward VII of England to agree to become joint patrons of the Gibraltar fox hunt. So, on 9 April 1906, with new silver buttons sporting double crowns, the Calpe Hunt became the *Royal* Calpe Hunt.

The social glory lingered, but in the downturn after the First World War, the Larios money leaked away. Lavish overspending and a disastrous series of fires at the factory in La Línea, in which thousands of tons of cork went up in smoke, meant that Connaught House had to be sold in 1920. (It is now Gibraltar's City Hall.) The Guadacorte *cortijo* was sold in 1929, and the Larios landholding company, Sociedad Industrial y Agrícola de Guadiaro, was snapped up by the ruthless millionaire Juan March.* Although Pablo Larios retired to his house in Algeciras, he refused to resign as Master of the Royal Calpe Hunt even when he turned sixty-five in 1930 and his eyesight and hearing were going.

Larios's refusal to stand down infuriated the Governor of Gibraltar, General Sir Alexander Godley, also known as 'Lord God', a teetotal stickler with a face as gaunt as a drainage spade. Stiff-necked Godley annoyed the navy by ordering all attending race meetings at North Front to wear bowler hats, though few naval officers packed such headgear to go to sea. He was not amused when sailors came ashore in cut-out pretend bowlers of every shape and size.

After a disastrous farmers' lunch at a point-to-point when everybody wanted to sit at Larios's table rather than his, the governor conceived a violent antipathy to Pablo Larios, and plotted to remove him as Master of Fox Hounds in 1932. The Royal Calpe Hunt followers then split into two camps, known as 'the Godley' and 'the

* Juan March Ordinas (1880–1962) came from Mallorca and made his initial fortune from contraband and legal tobacco before diversifying into shipping, banking, etc. During the First World War he made money from both sides. After March escaped from a Spanish jail in 1933 he brought his two prison officers with him to Gibraltar in his Rolls-Royce and lived at the Rock Hotel.

Un-Godley', and Godley wrote a poisonous letter about Larios to King George V.

The king had heard the other side of the Royal Calpe Hunt dispute, so General Sir Charles Harington arrived as the new governor in October 1933 with royal instructions 'to put it right'. For the first season, he did nothing and the hunt had few places to go because Larios and his farmer friends forbade access to their lands. 'Gibraltar is a most difficult place to handle,' Harington wrote miserably. 'No man will ever lead it. It is all in little cliques who are jealous of each other and fight about everything . . . I have certainly spent the unhappiest year of my career here. Everyone could be so happy but they just won't be. They prefer to quarrel.'

It took a sensible woman, Mrs Peatt, married to the hunt's vet, to come up with a brilliant solution to this war of male *amour propre*. Why not make the new governor's cheerful wife, Gladys Harington – a jolly, banjo-playing, red-haired Irishwoman whom everyone called 'Paddy' – the joint Master of Fox Hounds with sixty-nine-year-old Pablo Larios? This was agreed and honour was finally satisfied.

Gibraltar was far too small to sustain the military/aristocratic lifestyle on its own; the rocky peninsula could not even feed itself as the good land all lay to the north in the Campo de Gibraltar on the Spanish mainland. The need for flat ground had led the British garrison to expand into the 1500-yard sandy isthmus that lies between the Rock and the Campo. This was where the British marines had landed to seize Gibraltar in July 1704; according to the Treaty of Utrecht the isthmus was meant to be neutral. The British had pushed slowly pushed their line northward, starting with a yellow-fever quarantine camp in 1815, then a rubbish dump in 1845. Mark Twain wrote in 1869 that Gibraltar was

. . . pushed out into the sea on the end of a flat, narrow strip of land, and is suggestive of a 'gob' of mud on the end of a shingle. A few hundred yards of this flat ground at its base belongs to the English, and then, extending across the strip from the Atlantic to the Mediterranean, a distance of a quarter of a mile, comes the 'Neutral Ground', a space two or three hundred yards wide, which is free to both parties.

But to protect their gain of half a mile, in 1908 the British erected a nine-foot-high iron fence across the isthmus, with a gate.

Gibraltar's isthmus was a peaceful, even bucolic place in the 1930s, with cows grazing in Governor's Meadow, and shady trees in Victoria Gardens. It was the Rock's place of recreation. The North Front was not fortified; it had no siege lines, entrenchments or gun pits, because there had been no warfare here for more than a century and a half. Below the sheer face of Devil's Tower, beyond the cemeteries, lay the sports grounds for cricket and rugby and football, the cattle sheds, the Calpe Hunt kennels and the Gibraltar Jockey Club's horse-racing track and grandstand.

Beyond the British Lines, a well-trodden road led across a bare patch of neutral ground to the Spanish frontier and the border town, La Línea de la Concepción, which had grown in symbiosis with Gibraltar. It took its name from *la línea de contravalación*, the chain of eighteenth-century fortifications in the early anti-British sieges, but La Línea's economy had become entwined with Gibraltar's. When Henry Buckley, the *Daily Telegraph* correspondent in Spain, drove down to the Rock in 1935, he collected on the way his American journalist friend Jay Allen of the *Chicago Daily Tribune*, then living up the coast in the village of Torremolinos, trying to write books. Buckley observed:

Gibraltar is a strange place, and so English. Tea rooms everywhere. Steak-and-kidney pudding, with the temperature at ninety in the shade . . . There is nothing Spanish about Gibraltar; it is just a small transplanted bit of England. Jay wanted to know how the soldiers amused themselves and were there any licensed houses on the Rock where they could go. But we were told for that purpose leave was given to go to the small town of La Linea.

However, in the 1930s La Línea was not just where British soldiers and matelots went for sex in the brothels of 'Gib Street', Calle Gibraltar. There was much greater legitimate traffic heading the other way. La Línea evolved as the working-class district of Gibraltar, home to people who worked on the Rock every day but could not actually live there because of overcrowding in the slummy 'ramps' of the Upper Town. Every morning, thousands of Andalusian men and women walked from Spain across the Neutral Ground and the isthmus to go and work in British territory. There were no great formalities at the border, little paperwork to impede the regular ebb and flow of Spanish people in solid employment with regular wages in Gibraltar. Hundreds went to the docks to work as labourers, and other tradesmen for jobs with the army or branches of the colonial government. There were leathery men driving donkey carts carrying milk and water, fruit and vegetables, fish and meat. Many women worked as cleaners, cooks, seamstresses, shop assistants, maids and waitresses. La Línea and Gibraltar depended on each other like an old married couple. The Spanish town and country fed and watered the British colony of Gibraltar, and many Gibraltarians had property in the Campo, where there was room to breathe and grow things. 'Spain was open,' wrote Governor Harington of the peaceful years, 'and everyone was able to ride and motor in that beautiful country: the greater part of Gibraltar used to go into Spain on Sundays for bathing and picnics.'

La Línea was very much a working-class Republican town: 98.6 per cent had voted for the Republican–Socialist coalition in June 1931, and 90 per cent for the left-wing Popular Front in the Spanish general election of February 1936. La Línea's workers were strongly unionised and felt class solidarity with their 'brothers' in the Transport and General Workers' Union in Gibraltar. La Línea was also home to some four thousand British citizens, many of whom had bought land in Spain before the Republic curtailed the practice, and there were many progressive Freemasons, inheritors of the liberal ideas of the Enlightenment, with seventeen lodges in the Campo de

Gibraltar alone. Across the frontier, the Gibraltar Masonic Institute was in Cornwall's Parade. The long tradition of Freemasonry in Gibraltar meant that strongly Catholic and fiercely anti-Masonic Spaniards tended to portray the Rock as a satanic inferno of liberal conspiracies. However, leftist Spaniards demonised it in similar fashion, as a bolt-hole for rebellious right-wing generals like José Sanjurjo and crooked financiers like Juan March, making dastardly plans with British arms dealers.

The Campo itself was starkly divided on class lines. Pablo and Pepita Larios's eight children (one son and seven daughters) all married into the Spanish aristocracy, the landed gentry and the political elite. After the proclamation of a republic in Spain on 14 April 1931 and the fall of the monarchy, this ruling class felt the lower orders had been encouraged in dangerous hopes that threatened its own privileges. Poorer people, on the other hand, rejoiced that the rule of Spain by kings, priests, soldiers, industrialists and wealthy landowners might be crumbling, giving them the chance of education, agrarian reform and social progress.

Not long after the advent of the Republic, Pablo Larios's sleek-headed twenty-one-year-old son José, *el señorito Pepito*, was driving around La Línea in a motor-car, tearing down every Republican tricolour he could find while loudly shouting '*¡Viva el rey!*' ('Long live the king!'). As young José strolled arrogantly through La Línea the next day, some young Republicans grabbed him and tried to throw him in the town drain. During the fist fight that followed, the Guardia Civil arrested José Larios and took him to the police station, followed by a shouting lynch mob. 'My ancestors were called unprintable names,' he remembered. 'I don't think I have ever been so scared in my life.'

The age of deference was not quite over; Spain was still a poor country dominated by rich people. The new mayor of La Línea was persuaded to let José Larios go, quietly, and he was smuggled across the border into Gibraltar at night. The next day, he attended a reception at the governor's residence to bid farewell to Alfonso XIII's youngest surviving son, seventeen-year-old Prince Juan de Borbón y Battenburg, who was going into exile in England on board a British warship to study at the Royal Naval College at Dartmouth in Devon. When he died over sixty years later, Juan de Bórbon, the grandfather of the present Spanish monarch, Felipe VI, was Captain General of the Armada Española, the Spanish navy, with tattoos he got in the British Royal Navy.

José Larios was not the only member of his family caught up in the polarising politics of 1930s Spain. Pablo Larios's fourth daughter, Margarita, married Miguel Primo de Rivera,* the brother of José Antonio Primo de Rivera, who founded the Spanish Fascist Party, *la Falange Española*, in 1933. Its initials (which can be pronounced *fé*, meaning 'faith' in Spanish) originally stood for *Fascismo Español*. The Falangists believed in terror and violence, insulted and broke the windows of the right, and beat up or murdered the left. They wanted to create chaos so that the people would demand a change of government, and then the Falange would march in to put an end to the reign of terror they had started.

Class hatred was virulent in southern Spain in the 1930s because of the enormous disparity between the rich and the poor. The Larioses' second daughter, Mercedes, married into the Domecq family. She was a soft-hearted person who once sheltered a fox escaping from the Royal Calpe Hunt and let it live in the house for a month. But personal characteristics are irrelevant in group conflict. At a right-wing political meeting in San Fernando on Sunday 11 November 1933, a left-wing gunman or *pistolero* opened fire. One of the rounds hit Mercedes in the head, severing the optic nerve. Brain surgery saved her, but she was blinded for life.

---

* Sir Martin Gilbert identified Miguel Primo de Rivera, Marqués de Estella, as the 'Spanish friend' of the Duke of Windsor involved in what Churchill called 'a Nazi-German intrigue to entangle and compromise a Royal Prince' in Lisbon in July 1940. The potentially traitorous ex-king was then parked safely in the Bahamas for the duration. See Martin Gilbert, *Finest Hour* (Heinemann, 1983), pp. 706–7.

4

The Abyssinian Crisis

The official history of MI5 states that when war broke out in September 1939 'the permanent establishment of the Security Service overseas consisted of six officers located at Gibraltar, Malta, Cairo, Aden, Singapore and Hong Kong'. MI5, the Security Service, which employs around four thousand people today, was a small organisation in the 1930s, with about thirty officers, a hundred secretarial staff and half a dozen 'watchers' in the surveillance section, but it aspired to a global reach. 'Our Security Service is more than national, it is Imperial,' wrote its deputy director general in 1934. 'We have official agencies cooperating with us, under the direct instructions of the Dominion and Colonial Offices and the supervision of the local Governors, and their chiefs of police, for enforcing local Security Laws in every British Community overseas.'

During the First World War, MI5's man in Gibraltar was called a 'Military Control Officer'. Then the term 'Defence Security Officer' (DSO) came into use. Gibraltar and Malta were among the first to get them because they were key naval bases targeted by enemy spies. By March 1936 the Gibraltar Defence Security Office was established in Gunners Parade and had its own headed writing-paper.

On 28 November 1935, Sir Vernon Kell, the head of MI5, wrote to the Defence Security Officer c/o Fortress Headquarters, Gibraltar, giving further details about a suspicious German called Charles or Carlos or Karl Baum from Valencia in Spain, who had been placed on an MI5 Black List as far back as November 1918 for being a 'naval enemy agent'. Code-named 'Martha' by the Germans, Baum was still the German navy's main spy in Catalonia.

The Defence Security Officer to whom Vernon Kell was writing in late 1935, Captain Kenneth Strong of the Royal Scots Fusiliers, was a sharp young intelligence officer who had held the same role in Malta in 1930, and was now in Gibraltar on attachment from what he called in his autobiography 'the German Intelligence Section at the War Office', also known as MI14, although an October 1935 continuity-page note by the Colonial Secretary refers to him as 'Captain Strong of MI5 on temporary duty at Gibraltar'. Strong was a fluent German speaker from the British Army of the Rhine who went on to become assistant military attaché in Berlin from 1937 to 1939. In time, he rose to become General Eisenhower's intelligence chief, and finally the Director General of Intelligence at the Ministry of Defence in the 1960s.

Noel Annan described Strong as looking like a beaver, '– an eager beaver bursting out of his uniform, with dark hair, a fine forehead, clever, shifty eyes and so chinless he came to be known as the hangman's dilemma'. Throughout the 1930s Kenneth Strong was wholly dedicated to studying German forces and strategy. In his three months on the Rock, he surveyed the situation for the Imperial Security Service – MI5 in its pith helmet – and set up an elementary security organisation to be run by Captain 'Tim' Airy. The 1936 *Gibraltar Directory*'s list of officers in the command includes under Special Appointments: 'Defence Security Officer – Capt A. E. Airy, The Buffs'.

There was continuing concern about German espionage from Ceuta, the city right across the strait in Spanish Morocco. This spying became noticeable in 1934 when a German national called Hermann Paege, using an inordinate amount of concrete, built two houses at a site overlooking the Strait, where it seemed that the masters of every German ship calling at Ceuta regularly stayed. The General Staff Officer, Gibraltar, had reported this to MI3 (operational intelligence) in London, who in turn alerted Naval Intelligence at the Admiralty. They thought that the houses might be intended to report ship movements in the event of hostilities; the thick concrete foundations could be designed to carry heavy wireless transmitting gear. Was electrical equipment being installed?

On 25 April 1935, Colonel Beattie, the Colonial Secretary in

Gibraltar, forwarded to the head of MI5 a five-page memorandum which detailed the activities of three Germans, Hermann Paege, Alfred Busch and Engelbert Pratz, including all the dates of their visits to the Rock, compiled from immigration data and old hotel lists going back to 1931. Several visits coincided with the arrival of the combined British fleets. There were only ten Germans actually residing in Gibraltar, and no system for keeping German visitors under observation.

Why was there a spike of German foreign intelligence interest in the Strait of Gibraltar in 1935? The first reason was that the Abwehr, Germany's foreign intelligence organisation, had a new head that year, Admiral Wilhelm Canaris, who was besotted with Spain. Born into a Rhineland family who made their money from Ruhr coal and iron, Canaris was smitten by the warm south as a boy on a visit to Athens, where he saw a statue of Admiral Konstantinos Kanaris (1793–1877), five times Prime Minister of Greece. The story of Kanaris, the orphan who became the hero of the Greek war of independence when he sailed fire-ships against the Turkish fleet, sparked ambition in young Wilhelm Canaris, the German boy with almost the same surname. He joined Kaiser Wilhelm II's navy, the iron-clad fleet then undergoing massive expansion at the beginning of the twentieth century.

Canaris was good at languages and became fluent in Spanish while serving on the German navy's East American station. When the Great War broke out in 1914, his ship joined the German Pacific squadron, and information from Canaris's Chilean agents enabled them to surprise and defeat the Royal Navy at the battle of Coronel on 10 November 1914. Eventually Canaris was caught and interned by the Chileans. He escaped from Quiraquina island by bribing a fisherman, made his way by horse through the winter Andes and then crossed the pampas to report to the German naval attaché in Buenos Aires. Back in Europe, Canaris successfully talked his way through British immigration control at Plymouth and finally got home to Germany on 4 October 1915. Two months later, he was in Spain, setting up another network to spy on Allied shipping movements. When his cover was blown, Canaris had to be evacuated by submarine. He next saw Gibraltar in January 1918, through the periscope of *U-34*, which he was commanding.

After Imperial Germany's defeat, Canaris mixed with right-wingers and became caught up in secret German naval rearmament, selling German U-boat designs abroad and ensuring German personnel helped construct them. He arrived back in Spain early in 1925, also aiming to resuscitate the German espionage network of the Great War. By 1926, Canaris had arranged for the building of German submarines, torpedoes and torpedo boats at Cádiz, and was well in with senior Spanish naval and military figures like Lieutenant Colonel Kindelán (who let German aviators observe Spanish air force activities in the Moroccan wars), General Conde de Jordana, the Minister of the Colonies, and General Bazan, *jefe de seguridad*, the head of the Spanish secret police, with whom Canaris concluded an anti-communist pact in February 1928. Canaris also courted the circle around the Spanish king Alfonso XIII.

Canaris became a convinced Nazi in the early 1930s: loyalty to the Kaiser transferred naturally to loyalty to the *Führer*. When he became head of the Amt Ausland/Abwehr, the foreign political and military intelligence organisation, in early 1935, Canaris had achieved his dream job. He moved swiftly to co-operate with Heinrich Himmler's SS who were expanding state powers through the secret police, but he retained his intense interest in Spain, his favourite *Ausland*.

The second reason for the renewed German interest in the Strait of Gibraltar in the late summer of 1935 was the massive naval movements taking place. Britain was reinforcing its Mediterranean Fleet in response to one of the biggest international crises of the 1930s, the Italian invasion of Ethiopia, also known as Abyssinia.* What

---

* The proper name of the East African country is Ethiopia (in Amharic, *Ityopya*) but the name Abyssinia (derived from Arabic *habash*, 'mixture') was commonly used then. Abyssinia joined the League of Nations in September 1923; Ethiopia joined the United Nations in November 1945.

Stanley Baldwin recalled as 'that wonderful Jubilee summer' at home in Britain in 1935 was a season of sabre-rattling on the continent.

Adolf Hitler had stunned Europe in the spring by introducing compulsory military service in Germany and claiming to have an air force of 2500 planes, as large as Britain's. It was, in fact, just a useful bluff to gain some leverage in that summer's Anglo-German Naval Agreement, which relaxed the terms of German disarmament imposed in the 1919 Versailles Treaty. To arrange the new deal in London, Joachim von Ribbentrop's forty-strong party, equipped with five Mercedes-Benz limousines, took over two floors of the Carlton House hotel and draped a large swastika over its Haymarket entrance.

Ribbentrop, the 'Extraordinary Ambassador of the German Reich on Special Mission', met the Prince of Wales and his mistress, Mrs Wallis Simpson. Ribbentrop, a former champagne salesman and later German ambassador in London, would send her bouquets, always (mysteriously) of seventeen roses or carnations, which was rumoured to refer to the number of their assignations, though Anne Sebba says 'there is no evidence of an affair'. At the Silver Jubilee Parade for King George V and Queen Mary on 3 June, the guests standing on the German Embassy balcony all raised their right arms in the Hitler salute as the royal carriage passed.

Joachim von Ribbentrop bullied through the signing of the Anglo-German Naval Agreement before Britain had finished consulting all its friends and allies. Ribbentrop threatened that discussions would end if the British Foreign Secretary did not agree immediately to the formula that Nazi Germany be allowed to build thirty-five tons of warship for every hundred tons that Britain's navy had. The next day, 18 June, the British signed the agreement. 'Its effects upon the Continent were disastrous,' wrote the diplomat Walford Selby, then head of the British Legation at Vienna. Russia, France and Italy were all unhappy, and Hitler promptly commissioned two new pocket battleships.

The Conservative Stanley Baldwin had become prime minister again on 7 June 1935, after the resignation of Ramsay MacDonald. His reshuffle of the coalition government put two ministers into the Cabinet to handle foreign affairs: smooth Anthony Eden, whom *Tatler* called 'the Beau Brummell of British politics', as Minister without Portfolio for League of Nations affairs, and the fastidious Sir Samuel Hoare, 'the last in a long line of maiden aunts' according to F. E. Smith, as Foreign Secretary.

This arrangement allowed England to double-deal. As G. T. Garratt wrote in *The Shadow of the Swastika*: 'Mr Eden, in charge of League Affairs, was the Dr Jekyll to the Mr Hyde of Sir Samuel Hoare . . . Mr Eden['s] . . . job was to give the appearance in England of pushing the League [of Nations] forward . . . to pose as the young man terribly in earnest for peace.' Meanwhile, Sir Samuel Hoare was quietly working with Pierre Laval of France to help Italy achieve its imperial ambitions in Africa. In this way the British government maintained, as Daniel Waley put it, 'a mistress in Paris as well as a legal wife in Geneva'.

Fascist Italy had two colonies in the Horn of Africa: Eritrea and Italian Somalia. Now the Italian dictator Benito Mussolini wanted to conquer Ethiopia, the independent country that lay in between them. The dictator responded vociferously to international criticisms: 'We will imitate to the letter those who wish to give us a lesson,' Mussolini said in Sardinia on 8 June. '[Britain and France] have shown that, when it was a question of creating an empire or defending it, they never took any notice of world opinion.'

Both Italy and Ethiopia were members of the League of Nations, set up in 1919 after the Great War as a talking shop to prevent war through 'collective security', which meant that if one member state was attacked the others would rally to defend it. The powerful USA was not a member (which was a pity), and Germany and Japan had left (which was a problem).

The British government was well aware that Mussolini was planning to annex Ethiopia, and was not overly concerned. The confidential report by Sir John Maffey concluded in June 1935: 'There are no vital British interests in Abyssinia or adjoining countries such as to necessitate British resistance to an Italian conquest of Abyssinia.' Mussolini was able to enjoy this secret report fresh from the British Embassy in Rome because a Chancery servant there, Secondo Constantini, long trusted as a 'friend of the family' by naïve British diplomats, was regularly stealing all the classified documents from the safe of the ambassador and handing them straight over to Italian intelligence to photograph before putting them back. The Italians later embarrassed the British by leaking the Maffey report's contents to the international press in February 1936.

There was a considerable anti-war movement in the UK in the 1930s still calling for everyone to lay down their weapons, even after the failure of the World Disarmament Conference, which had run in Geneva from October 1932 to June 1934.* In June 1935 there was a second reading in Parliament of the Liberal-sponsored Peace Bill that would make it 'unlawful to use the armed forces of the Crown in any manner' contrary to the Covenant of the League of Nations. The League of Nations Union, led by Robert Cecil, held a 'Peace Ballot' in which an astonishing eleven and a half million people, nearly a third of the entire British electorate, cast their votes. The crucial question was the fifth. 'Do you consider that, if a nation insists on attacking another, the other nations should combine to compel it to stop by (a) Economic and non-military measures? (b) If necessary, military measures?' Eighty-six per cent said yes to question (a), but, rather surprisingly for a peace ballot to believers, in answer to (b) 58 per cent said yes to the use of force –'military measures' – to stop an aggressor. That blip aside, the general impression given was that Britain was for peace at any price.

Both the political right and left had ideological reasons to dislike

---

* When the Afghan delegates were asked why they were there, not being members of the League, they said if everyone else was disarming they might pick up some guns on the cheap.

the League of Nations. The *Daily Mail* and the *Morning Post* organised ballots in which their readers voted robustly against membership of the League and for massive rearmament now, while on the left, Sir Stafford Cripps of the Socialist League in the almost entirely pacifist Labour Party saw the League of Nations as nothing but 'the tool of the satiated imperialist powers'.

In the big picture of European strategy in 1935, both the French and British governments wanted Italy as a possible ally against the greater threat of Nazi Germany. Anthony Eden went to see Benito Mussolini at the end of June 1935, trying by personal diplomacy to negotiate some kind of settlement over Ethiopia. They spoke in French. Mussolini knew all the British positions from his spy in the embassy. Eden saw Mussolini as a coarse bully with appalling table manners, while the Italian press saw the Old Etonian minister as a 'well-dressed fool' trying to thwart Italy's legitimate ambitions.

In his first speech about the Ethiopian crisis on 11 July 1935, the British Foreign Secretary Sir Samuel Hoare bent over backwards to admit 'the need of Italian expansion' and 'the justice of some of the criticisms that have been made against the Abyssinian government'. He cited the 'old and valued tradition of amity with Italy . . . our friend since the Risorgimiento', and so on. But in that same month, Mussolini boomed: 'We have decided upon a struggle . . . Remember the Italians have always defeated black races'. The voice of the Emperor of Ethiopia, the Negus Haile Selassie I, sounded out clearly, calling on his people to 'unite against the invader . . . Soldiers, it is better to die free than live as slaves.'

In the Three Power Conference of August 1935, Britain, France and Italy failed to agree about Ethiopia because of Mussolini's arrogant stance. Italy ordered all its sixty-nine submarines into the main shipping lanes towards the Suez Canal and Mussolini depicted the Mediterranean – *Mare Nostrum* ('Our Sea') of the old Roman Empire – as now caged in by Britain and France: 'The bars of this prison are Corsica, Tunisia . . . The guards of this prison are Gibraltar and Suez.'

Italian intelligence was certainly interested in the Rock. In September 1935, the Spanish police in La Línea tipped off their colleagues across the border in Gibraltar that two Italians, Alfredo Rabaglietti and Giorgio Bedin, were coming to the Rock from Tangier on an espionage mission. A detective in Gibraltar saw them taking notes on the harbour from Line Wall Road, then trying to hide a piece of paper. They were searched at the police station and were found to be using a crude code in which weapons and equipment were logged as sacks of potatoes or bags of rice. The Spanish police searched Rabaglietti's room in La Línea, but without enough evidence to charge them the two men were released and expelled from the Fortress. Three Italians working at the Reina Cristina Hotel in Algeciras were believed to be Italian spies, as well as an engineer called Giulio Pistono who built a house at Campamento with a suspiciously good view of the Bay of Gibraltar.

As war came nearer, anxious civilians looked to the League of Nations. An idealistic young American, Helen Hiett, working at the Geneva Research Centre, recorded ten thousand worried telegrams arriving over three days. In Geneva, on 11 September 1935, Sir Samuel Hoare told the Assembly of the League that the British people and government stood firmly 'for steady and collective resistance to all acts of unprovoked aggression'. Winston Churchill observed that Sir Samuel 'received the rapturous applause of all the small States at Geneva', adding: 'The Abyssinians were encouraged to a desperate resistance by the feeling that almost the whole world, and, above all, Great Britain, were behind them.'

The British lion seemed to have woken up. In the Mediterranean, the Royal Navy reinforced its fleet to achieve a tonnage of warships greater than the entire Italian navy. The heavyweight battle cruisers *Hood* and *Renown* glowered from Gibraltar in the west, while fifty more British warships were concentrated in the east, at Alexandria and Haifa and Port Said by the Suez Canal. Admiral Cunningham believed there was an effective plan to cripple the Italian fleet on the first day of any fighting, and enough ships to do the job: four battleships, three heavy cruisers, five light cruisers, two aircraft carriers and thirty-six destroyers organised in four flotillas, plus a dozen submarines.

If Italy attacked Ethiopia (a breach of Article 12 of the League of Nations Covenant), then, under Article 16, Britain's Royal Navy could block further Italian troops and supplies traversing the Suez Canal. This would have stopped the war in Abyssinia dead in its tracks; the British fleet, with greater experience and higher morale, could have handled any response by Mussolini without much difficulty.

But from the jaws of a collective victory, Britain snatched only moral defeat. On 3 October 1935, Italian forces bombed and invaded Ethiopia; the League declared Italy 'an aggressor nation' on the 7th, but there was no subsequent blockade of Italian shipping by the British. They failed to prevent Italian ammunition, bombs and poison gas canisters travelling through the Suez Canal which they controlled. Not a single Italian soldier or airman was impeded on his way to conquer an independent country that was a fellow member of the League of Nations. The rhetoric bore no relationship to the reality. Yet through a posture of support for the Covenant of the League of Nations, Stanley Baldwin's party managed to win the general election on 14 November 1935 with a greatly increased majority.

'The most charitable account of their conduct', Professor Arnold Toynbee wrote soon afterwards, 'would be that they were bluffing, while, on a harsher interpretation, they were deliberately throwing dust in the eyes of the electorate of the United Kingdom and of the Governments and peoples of all the states members of the League.' John Dill, the Director of Military Operations at the War Office, wrote: 'I have a feeling that *morally* we are wrong, and that we shall suffer for it.'

Sir Samuel Hoare attempted to resolve the Ethiopian crisis via a secret peace plan with the French premier (and Foreign Minister),

Pierre Laval.* Hoare later wrote of Laval: 'Whilst his greasy hair, dirty white tie and shifty look did not prepossess me, I could not help admiring the quickness of his versatile mind.' The Hoare–Laval plan, provisionally cobbled together in two days at the Quai d'Orsay in Paris, involved Ethiopia handing over to the Italians sixty thousand square miles of its territory, in return for access to a tiny port in Eritrea.

When news of this broke prematurely in December 1935, 'There arose a howl of indignation from the people of Great Britain,' Duff Cooper, then War Secretary, wrote in his memoirs. 'During my experience of politics I have never witnessed so devastating a wave of public opinion . . . That outburst swept Sir Samuel Hoare from office.' Anthony Eden became Foreign Secretary instead and on 19 December 1935, the prime minister, Stanley Baldwin, said the Hoare–Laval proposals were now 'absolutely and completely dead'. Three days later, the Italians first used their modern air force to drop chemical weapons, yperite mustard-gas bombs, on Haile Selassie's essentially mediaeval army, and the Italo-Abyssinian war began in earnest.

'Seared and suffocated by poison gas, mown down by machine guns, battered by artillery, bombed from the air, the primitive military organisation of the Ethiopians is in fearful disarray,' wrote Winston Churchill. Chaos and looting broke out in the Ethiopian capital. The Italians took Addis Ababa on 5 May 1936 and the emperor fled, escaping from the port of Djibouti on a British warship.

HMS *Enterprise* carried Haile Selassie up the Red Sea and through the Suez Canal to Haifa in Palestine. The same British cruiser had in 1928 rescued the Prince of Wales, later Edward VIII, from an East African safari when his father, George V, was thought to be dying, getting the prince home from Tanganyika in a record nine days.

---

* The crafty peasant lawyer Pierre Laval (1883–1946) rose and fell in a hail of bullets. He became French Foreign Minister in October 1934 after Louis Barthou was killed by a Bulgarian terrorist in the fusillade that assassinated King Alexander I of Yugoslavia, and twelve years later to the month he himself died by firing squad, shot for his treasonous wartime Vichy government collaboration with the Germans.

HMS *Enterprise* now left behind the emperor's two live pet lions and a hundred Ethiopian courtiers in French Somaliland, and sailed on to Palestine with an escort destroyer, HMS *Diana*, and a party of forty that included the emperor's family with fifteen tons of baggage and many boxes containing some three hundred thousand Maria Theresa silver dollars. *Enterprise*'s captain said the emperor was exhausted and afraid, with 'a hunted look in his eyes'. When Captain Morgan assured him that once he stepped on the gangway he would be 'as safe as the Bank of England', Haile Selassie smiled, unforgettably, and the naval officer commented, 'You are always hoping that you will say something of which he approves or do some little thing that will please him, so that you can see him smile.'*

The royal family, Ethiopian Christians, wanted to make a pilgrimage to Jerusalem. They prayed for their country's salvation in its round Ethiopian Orthodox church, Debra Gannet. Then, leaving his empress and courtiers behind in Jerusalem, Haile Selassie set sail for Gibraltar on 23 May aboard the cruiser HMS *Capetown*. As he crossed the Mediterranean with a reduced suite of eight, Haile Selassie did not know that he was the subject of British secret cipher messages flashing between the civil and naval authorities in London, Malta, Palestine and Gibraltar. When the emperor asked if HMS *Capetown*, already heading home, could take him all the way to London, the request was passed up the chain and denied. He was told that the warship required 'urgent repairs' in Gibraltar. He would have to change ship at the Rock to the passenger liner SS *Orford*.

On Monday 25 May, with Haile Selassie due to arrive in Gibraltar on the Friday, the governor, Sir Charles Harington, asked London for instructions. Harington had experience of handling distinguished foreign exiles, having helped Mehmed Vehideddin, the last Sultan of Turkey, in 1922, and the ex-King Ammanullah of Afghanistan in 1929.

Governor Harington cabled three questions about Haile Selassie:

---

* Lieutenant Peter Gretton saw Haile Selassie passing through Port Said and wrote, nearly fifty years later, that the emperor's dignity in tragedy was still vivid to him.

Please inform me (1) Is he travelling as Emperor and entitled to salutes and guard of honour? (2) Am I to accommodate him and suite at Rock Hotel as British government guests, or is he on his own after arrival here? (3) Am I to entertain him officially? Am quite prepared to do anything but would like to know wishes of HMG.

The swift reply from London was brusque:

No. 318. SECRET. The Negus travels incognito. You should not accord him any salutes nor provide him with a guard of honour but a representative of yours should meet him on arrival; whether or not he should be given hospitality while in the Colony is entirely within your own discretion.

This cool telegram was signed 'Secretary of State'.

In fact, in that particular week, there was no Secretary of State for the Colonies in post because Jim Thomas (Labour) had been forced to resign on 22 May for giving away Budget secrets on the golf course. It was almost certainly Foreign Secretary Anthony Eden who decided that the exiled Ethiopian emperor should travel 'incognito', literally 'unknown'. This meant that the usual protocol could be downgraded to mere politeness.

HMS *Capetown* passed the Northern Entrance of Gibraltar at 9.00 a.m. on Friday 29 May 1936 and was safely moored near the Admiralty Tower by 9.30. Gibraltar's top civil servant, the Colonial Secretary, Lieutenant Colonel Alexander Beattie, accompanied by an aide in morning dress, slipped aboard the Royal Navy cruiser to welcome the royal visitors in the name of the governor.

The emperor disembarked at half past one. A small man with weighty Ethiopian titles, His Imperial Majesty Haile Selassie the First, Elect of God, the Power of the Trinity, the Lion of Judah and *Negusa Nagast*, the King of Kings, descended with dignity to Gun Wharf. He had a pointed beard and sad eyes in a dark face made paler by seasickness. His East African country, the last independent nation in a continent of colonies, had been brutally invaded by Mussolini's tanks and aeroplanes, and his armies had all been smashed, but Haile Selassie in exile was not dishevelled. He was wearing a grey homburg hat, a suit and tie with a white silk scarf under a black woollen travel cape, and his tiny shoes (not quite size 6), peeping out from under grey spats, were lustrously polished.

A pair of gleaming cars waited to ferry the emperor's party through Ragged Staff Gates to luncheon with the Governor and Commander-in-Chief of Gibraltar. Three of Haile Selassie's gawky, adolescent children were travelling with him into exile: Crown Prince Asfa Wossen, who was nearly twenty, twelve-year-old Prince Makonnen, the *Mesfin* or Duke of Harar, and Princess Tsehai, a spirited sixteen-year-old girl in a blue frock with white gloves, wearing a wide straw hat whose brim she could skilfully tilt to conceal or reveal her doe eyes. Behind her was a heavyweight, grizzled figure in black, Ras Kassa Hailu, once Haile Selassie's potential rival but now his staunchest support, the man who had led the emperor's northern army, until it was scattered by Italian aeroplanes dropping blast bombs and yperite poison gas.

Now Ras Kassa Hailu stared up at the Moorish castle and the high scrubby spine of the Rock with its circling seabirds, recalling for the others present how once upon a time his delegation had visited Gibraltar on their way to the coronation in London of King George V, where the world's rulers had gathered. A quarter of a century later and King George was in his grave. Fuad of Egypt, the richest king in the world, son of Ismail the Magnificent, was also dead. Now the schoolboy Farouk and the playboy Edward sat on their thrones in Cairo and London. Back then in Gibraltar, Ras Kassa informed the others, we Ethiopian delegates had to break our religious fast, because the permitted Lenten foods were hard to find. There were 'awesome' passages through this mountain, he added, remembering the Admiralty Tunnel. 'In six minutes we got somewhere that would have taken us six hours going over the top.'

A large crowd was waiting in Main Street outside Government House to catch a glimpse of Haile Selassie. The man was world famous: for the last seven months, the global press, including the local newspapers, the *Gibraltar Chronicle*, *El Calpense* and *El Anunciador*, had been following events in the Horn of Africa. The Emperor of Abyssinia nodded and smiled in acknowledgement of the people.

The Governor of Gibraltar was a spare-looking, highly strung soldier with a neat moustache and a chestful of medals. On the eve of his sixty-fourth birthday, sports-mad General Harington was still fit: he had swum across the Hellespont and back in his fifties, and in his last cricket match in Gibraltar hit a six right out of the ground. Harington had been the chief of staff to General Plumer in the First World War, brilliantly co-ordinating the Second Army's successful attack on Messines Ridge in June 1917. In the 1922 'Chanak crisis' he averted a disastrous war with Turkey by talking to the Kemalist Turks rather than shooting at them.

After lunch, the imperial entourage were driven up Mount Road to the snow-white Rock Hotel, Gibraltar's newest and grandest, built four years earlier by the wealthy Marquess of Bute to match his El Minzah Hotel in Tangier. The Swiss manager greeted the party to cheers and clapping from another crowd outside, and staff escorted them to the eight rooms that had been reserved. Hotels marked the *via dolorosa* of Haile Selassie's exile: in Jerusalem, the King David; in Gibraltar, the Rock; in London, Brown's and the Langham; in Geneva, the Beau-Rivage; in Bath, the Spa; in Malvern, the Abbey.

From his Rock Hotel balcony in the late afternoon, Haile Selassie could look westward over the palmy Alameda Gardens towards Algeciras and hear the tinkling bells of nanny goats going down Europa Road for milking. He could also see the warships at anchor in the five-mile arc of Gibraltar Bay and feel the melancholy of a deposed monarch at the very end of the age of kings. To the left, low on the horizon, lay his own continent of Africa and the reddish mountains of Morocco where Sultan Muhammad V reigned over a land of six hundred tribes now divided between the armed 'protectorates' of Spain and France, with a peculiar little 'international zone' around Tangier. Straight ahead, the sun was going down in a blaze of red behind a sierra in Spain, a turbulent republic run by middle-class intellectuals since the deposition of Bourbon King Alfonso XIII in 1931. Winston Churchill wrote poignantly of Alfonso: 'To be born a king; never to have been anything else but a king; to have reigned for forty-six years, and then to be dethroned!'

On Saturday 30 May, His Imperial Majesty sent the Crown Prince down with a £1 note for the charwoman washing the steps of the Rock Hotel. Then, after breakfast on his balcony, he received local and foreign journalists and walked with them in the gardens. Speaking in French and English, the emperor said he was most grateful for the warm welcome in Gibraltar and that he had come to Europe to plead Ethiopia's cause before the League of Nations in Geneva. The *Gibraltar Chronicle* reported that although he was indebted to the British government for the facilities afforded him, the emperor had no wish to be 'an embarrassment'.

Later that morning, he was offered a demonstration of how Britain ruled the waves. He was piped aboard HMS *Hood*, then the world's largest battle cruiser, a forty-five-thousand-ton steel behemoth over eight hundred feet long with monstrous guns that could fire a one-ton shell every four seconds, followed by lunch aboard HMS *Rodney*, a thirty-five-thousand-ton Nelson-class battleship that was the flagship of the Commander-in-Chief of the Home Fleet, Admiral Sir Roger Backhouse, who stood six foot four in his socks.

(The British always seemed to send out their tallest men to tower over foreigners they wished to dominate. At his coronation in Addis Ababa on 2 November 1930 the five-foot-four-inch emperor had seen a British delegation led by King George V's youngest son, Prince Henry, Duke of Gloucester, with men who all seemed to be giants in their uniforms and medals, plumed hats and white gloves: Kittermaster of Somaliland was six foot seven inches tall, Maffey of Sudan six foot five and Admiral Fullerton from Aden six foot three.)

On Saturday afternoon, the Ethiopians were driven to the Mount, by tradition the home of the senior naval officer in charge of Gibraltar, then Rear Admiral Sir James Murray Pipon, a 'Champagne

Charlie' brimming with bonhomie and risqué jokes but with ante-diluvian political views. Stewards in whites served tea in a garden with a commanding view westward over the harbour and the seaway towards Tangier. At 'the Gut', the narrowest stretch of the thirty-six-mile-long Strait of Gibraltar, there was a gap not quite nine miles wide between Europe and Africa. The sea traffic, hundreds of ships criss-crossing and passing every day, was a continual reminder of Gibraltar's strategic location and its importance to the mighty British Empire.

It was designed to awe, but the display of British sea power could not have been more galling to Haile Selassie. The Royal Navy vessels were only there because Italy's illegal war on Ethiopia had made Britain reinforce its Mediterranean Fleet. Yet what had this great armada done? Nothing. The whole show of force was an imperial pantomime. The exiled Emperor of Ethiopia was a source of shame to the British government; 'travelling incognito' was a diplomatic fiction cooked up to save face. It was a lie that *HMS Capetown* had 'urgent repairs' which required docking at Gibraltar. The Rock was simply a convenient place for Haile Selassie's entourage to be shuf-fled off to the Orient liner SS *Orford* on its regular commercial voy-age from Sydney to Southampton. The British government did not want the emperor to be seen arriving in the UK on a Royal Navy vessel.*

Governor Harington made personal efforts to do the decent thing by Haile Selassie, whom he later described as 'exceedingly courte-ous, dignified and grateful'. Although London had ordered Haring-ton not to accord guards of honour, the emperor was treated with respect and piped aboard the battleships. On his last evening in Gibraltar, Haile Selassie was driven with Harington to Governor's Cottage, his personal retreat tucked away at the southeast corner of the peninsula. Suddenly the chauffeur had to brake. The road was

* Unlike October 1954, when the British cruiser HMS *Nigeria* with Admiral Lord Mountbatten aboard would happily carry the restored Emperor Haile Selassie I past Gibraltar on his state visit to the newly crowned Queen Elizabeth II of England.

full of fox hounds. The governor explained to the emperor that these dogs were used to chase and kill foxes, while being followed by ladies and gentlemen on horseback.

The Emperor of Ethiopia said he was familiar with English chase-mania in Addis Ababa. The British Legation there had a club of young men called 'The Plughole' whose members used to pursue the British acting vice consul, Mr Trapman, through eucalyptus groves, while he rode ahead on a fast pony dropping a trail of torn paper behind him, and the 'Huntsman', Mr Lee of the Secret Intelligence Service, blew calls on a copper horn.

Harington smiled happily upon his real pack of hounds who chased genuine foxes, patting his black spaniel, Bunty, and remembering how the Royal Calpe Hunt had been 'the first big problem' of his governorship, three years before, until he reached the happy compromise of making his own wife the joint Master of Fox Hounds.

Haile Selassie I sailed on from Gibraltar on the ordinary passenger liner and docked at Southampton on 3 June 1936. No minister of the national government was there to greet the 'incognito' emperor when he arrived by train at London's Waterloo Station. Instead, Foreign Secretary Eden's private secretary, Oliver Harvey, met him, along with the usual sympathisers from the left: ardent Mrs Sylvia Pankhurst, Norman Angell, the MPs Vyvyan Adams and Eleanor Rathbone. When Eden suggested to King Edward VIII that it would be 'a popular gesture' if HM were to receive Haile Selassie at Buckingham Palace, the monarch replied sharply, 'Popular with whom? Certainly not with the Italians.'

The government's policy of appeasing Mussolini became clearer the day after Haile Selassie's arrival, when it was announced that Sir Samuel Hoare, who had been Foreign Secretary at the outbreak of the Italo-Abyssinian War and made the unpopular peace plan with the Frenchman Pierre Laval, was returning to the Cabinet as First Lord of the Admiralty. Tory MP 'Chips' Channon wrote in his diary:

Sam Hoare is now back at the Admiralty as First Lord . . . Six months ago Hoare was ignominiously turned out . . . The Government simply bowed to public opinion and chucked him overboard . . . Now he is back, and the newspapers predict . . . that the Government will become less anti-Italian, pro-realist, less Geneva-ist, less visionary.

Neville Chamberlain now said it would be 'the very midsummer of madness' to think an independent Ethiopia could be restored. On 18 June 1936, Anthony Eden apologetically informed the House of Commons that Britain was abandoning sanctions against Italy, because they had failed to achieve anything. No Abyssinian government could be restored except by military action from outside. To preserve peace, retreat was best.

'Shame!' 'Resign!' 'Sabotage!' cried some MPs. David Lloyd George, the former prime minister, spoke scathingly:

The Government dared not advance because they were afraid of Mussolini. They dared not retreat because they were afraid of public opinion . . . The worst of it is that 50 nations ranged themselves behind Mr Baldwin. The Abyssinians believed him. The vast majority of people in this country believed him. The Government had not been in for more than a few weeks before that torch was hidden. Tonight it is quenched – with a hiss which will re-echo throughout the whole world.

5

Rebellion of the Right

With the lifting of sanctions against Italy, Sir Samuel Hoare ordered the Home Fleet home again after ten months of Mediterranean patrols, and they steamed back from Alexandria via Gibraltar. By Saturday 18 July 1936, the Rock had already waved goodbye to battleships, cruisers and the aircraft carrier *Furious*, as well as flotillas of destroyers and submarines returning from Egypt.

That Saturday, the hot sun beat down on the isthmus at North Front. Across the way, the Spanish border town of La Línea de la Concepción was opening its annual *feria de julio*. Over the next seven days there would be stalls and sideshows, fireworks, food and football, a fancy dress competition for children, the Municipal Band oompahing every evening and a first-class *novillada* at the bullring on the final Sunday, with Torerito de Triana and Pascual Márquez matched against large, fierce Miura bulls from Seville.

But this year it went wrong from the start. There was 'trouble at the Fair', they said, but it wasn't quite clear what was happening at first over there by the bullring. Shooting, explosions. Someone said sticks of dynamite were among the fireworks that traditionally opened the *feria* with a bang. Someone else said no, the gunfire began just as the string of firecrackers called *la traca* were going off, masking a shoot-out between Falangists and Anarchists. Another said the fighting was at the barracks and the whole fair had been called off. By the evening of Saturday 18th, rumours were flying thick and fast. The Spanish regular army had risen in Morocco, they said; someone had heard it on the radio. They said Moors and Legionnaires, the terrifying soldiers who took no prisoners in the Moroccan Rif and then were used to smash the Asturian miners in 1934, were crossing the strait from Ceuta in the ferries. *¡Moros en la costa!* ('Moors on the coast!') is an old Spanish phrase from the days of the Barbary pirates, meaning watch out, danger is looming – best stay at home and lock the door.

Phil and Mary 'Mabs' Bower, on honeymoon from Cheshire, innocently went across the bay from Gibraltar to Spain by the Algeciras ferry that Saturday in order to have tea at the smart Reina Cristina Hotel. Afterwards they tried to get the ferry back to Gibraltar but there was a soldier reading a proclamation and troops on the quay. Then the new Mr and Mrs Bower bumped into the British vice consul, who told them they should get back to the Rock forthwith. A Spanish army officer in uniform offered to escort them to the frontier and they were bundled into a car full of weapons and ammunition. At La Línea, gala-festooned for the *feria del pueblo*, there was a barricade, men with rifles, shooting. The Spanish soldiers jumped from the car and returned fire. Mabs clutched her shoulder, shocked, shot. Phil dragged her from the car and they ran over to a block of flats. A woman leaned out of a window. On hearing they were English she waved them up and sent down her daughter to lead the way. The *señora* dressed the wound and eventually the Bowers made their way to the frontier to British territory.

At the Four Corners gate Gibraltarian bobbies in absurd British police helmets were trying to filter the crowds of Britons and Spaniards fleeing from the fair. With them, 'in support of the civil power', were British soldiers, baggy-shorted, pith-helmeted picquets from the 1st Battalion, King's Own Yorkshire Light Infantry, with bayonets on their *bundooks* or rifles. When the gate opened for a motor car, the Bowers ran behind it to reach the safety of Gibraltar. They left for England the next day on the Anchor Line's SS *Elysia*, and their story was squabbled over by the British press: the London *Evening Standard* offering £10, the *Daily Express* £15, for an exclusive.

A nine-year-old girl called Mariola, dressed in her best, waited for her Gibraltarian policeman father, Gustavo Benavente, to finish his

Saturday shift and take her with her two younger brothers to the opening parade in La Línea as he usually did. This year, he came home very late and did not take them to the fair. She heard him say those were not fireworks, but gunshots, and the grown-ups talked sombrely of *revolución* and *guerra*.

What was going on? At 2.13 p.m. on Saturday 18 July 1936, the Senior Officer (Intelligence) at Gibraltar sent a signal marked 'IMPORTANT' to the Admiralty and the Commander-in-Chief, Home Forces in London, and the C-in-C, Mediterranean in Malta:

The Military Commander in Chief of Spanish Morocco announced by wireless from CEUTA at 12.00 today in essence that the Military forces both Spanish and Native, in Spanish Morocco and the Canary Islands have revolted against the government, and are in control of those areas.

Reports claim that Spanish Navy and Air Force are with them. This is supported by rumours reaching here from TANGIER. Fighting reported in vicinity of CEUTA and transport has been ordered to ALGECIRAS to embark troops for that port today. Unconfirmed report from CARTAGENA states that warships there have refused to proceed to Morocco.

All quiet at present in GIBRALTAR area.

It should not be forgotten – whatever justifications and lies were offered afterwards – that what we now call the Spanish Civil War began with an attempted *coup d'état* or military rebellion by General Franco's forces against the democratically elected government of the Spanish Republic. Franco's military insurgents justified their coup on the spurious grounds that the February 1936 elections which brought in the Popular Front government had been corrupt. The military uprising was led by three Spanish army generals – Franco, Mola and Sanjurjo – who had got to know each other in brutal campaigns suppressing the Berber tribespeople of Spanish Morocco. Colonial warfare there was atrocious, with no quarter given on either side. In 1921, in their stunning victory at Annual, the Rifian guerrillas led by

Muhammad Abdel Krim and his brother M'hemmed had managed to kill up to twelve thousand Spanish soldiers, but the Berbers were crushed in 1926 by combined French and Spanish armies using air power and illegal poison gas manufactured with German help.

The formerly incompetent, underpaid Spanish army had reinvented itself in North Africa, creating two new and ferocious units: the Regulares, formed in 1911 from Moroccan volunteers and so always known as *moros* – the Moors – and *el Tercio de Extranjeros*, the foreigners' regiment, founded in 1920. The Tercio or Legion was modelled on the French Foreign Legion, and their berserker war-cry was '*¡Viva la Muerte!*' ('Long live Death!'). When the 1936 military uprising began, these two units made up Spain's most professional fighting force, the African Army, *el ejército de África*, with eighteen thousand Spaniards and sixteen thousand Moroccans.

Generals Franco, Mola and Sanjurjo began their violent insurrection against the Popular Front government in Madrid on the evening of Friday 17 July with garrison risings in Spanish Morocco, shooting dead 225 loyalist soldiers and citizens who resisted them. On Saturday morning in Andalusia, four thousand men led by the right-wing General Gonzalo Queipo de Llano seized Seville and its radio station, where he broadcast regularly for the next eighteen months. In Navarre, General Emilio Mola took Pamplona.

Other rebellious officers failed to take key cities like Madrid and Barcelona because the workers resisted or those in uniform stayed loyal to the elected government, so the uprising's outcome hung in the balance. Barely a third of Spain's territory was in insurgent hands at this stage: they controlled over half the army, 60 per cent of the artillery and almost half the Guardia Civil, but only a third of the air force, the Carabineros, the Republican Assault Guards and, most worryingly for them, the navy. For the *coup d'état* to succeed, the military rebellion needed to get their toughest fighting force, the Army of Africa, back to Europe by air or by sea. If they could stop them at the Strait of Gibraltar, the Spanish navy might nip this rebellion in the bud.

The Spanish Republican navy, which does not seem to have been significantly involved in planning the army-led coup, had twenty thousand men and around eighty vessels, including two battleships, seven cruisers, seventeen destroyers, five gunboats, nine coastguard vessels, eleven torpedo boats and a dozen submarines. It operated from three main bases: El Ferrol, looking to the north and the Bay of Biscay, Cádiz facing the Atlantic and Cartagena in the Mediterranean. But how reliable was the navy, how loyal to the Republic's current government? On 14 July, a signal had gone out from the Ministry of Marine in Madrid to the heads of the three naval bases, admirals of squadrons and all flotilla leaders, warning them to take precautions 'to prevent extremists of one side or other from spreading propaganda among personnel under your command' and to signal back whether 'personnel of all classes and categories can be trusted to obey your orders'. Naval officers thought to be of dubious loyalty were asked to resign.

Anyone with foresight could have seen that the Strait of Gibraltar was key to a military coup. José Giral, the Republic's Minister of Marine, a mild-mannered chemistry professor, certainly understood its strategic importance and acted swiftly on 16 July by ordering four warships to Spain's southern waters, but events overtook him. On 19 July, President Azaña asked Giral to become prime minister and, fatally, no one replaced him as Minister of Marine.

The Spanish navy may have had more conservative and reactionary officers than the army and air force, but there were also radicals with opposing views. In March 1936, the Republican Popular Front government had passed a law allowing people dismissed for their left-wing political views to rejoin the armed forces. The existence of La Unión Militar Republicana y Antifascista (UMRA), the Republican and Antifascist Military Union, within the navy, indicates that not every naval person was conservative.

One UMRA member was a strongly Republican warrant officer from Galicia called Benjamin Balboa López, a radio operator who worked at the Spanish Admiralty's central telecommunications centre at Ciudad Lineal in the pine forest of Chamartín, north of Madrid. A command-centre radio operator is better informed than most people. Balboa worried that the crews of ships at sea, cut off from events on land, might be stopped from hearing what was going on by officers intending to join the right-wing revolt.

The first radio messages about uprisings against the Republican government in Morocco came through to Madrid on the afternoon of Friday 17 July. Early next morning, General Franco sent two messages for re-transmission to all garrisons. Radio operator Balboa acted swiftly. Instead of passing on Franco's messages he alerted the Galician prime minister, Santiago Casares, and José Giral, then still Minister of Marine. When Balboa's commanding officer, Captain Castor Ibáñez Aldecoa, learned of this act of disobedience he snatched Franco's messages and telephoned their contents himself to Vice Admiral Javier de Salas, higher up the chain of command, who was in on the right-wing plot. Salas told Ibáñez to send Franco's message to all garrisons. Back in the radio room, Ibáñez ordered Balboa to his quarters, under arrest.

But Balboa stood his ground. 'I will not comply with that order . . . I am here to defend the Republic against those people who are, as you well know, betraying it. And from right now it's you, not me, who's barred from the radio room.' With that, Balboa drew his nine-shot .22 Luger pistol and pointed it at his superior officer's abdomen. Balboa locked his commanding officer up, and the police later drove him and Admiral Salas away to prison. (Ibáñez later got away to a friendly embassy, but Salas was taken out of jail and shot by leftists in August.)

Loyalists now occupied the Ministry of Marine building in Madrid. From the telecommunications centre at Ciudad Lineal, Balboa and his team started sending a stream of messages to the men of the fleet. Every ship was to report its position every two hours and listen for instructions; all communications were to be 'in clear' or using current language, since conspirators were hiding behind ciphers. Balboa wanted to reach every radio operator in the fleet, because he believed that every ship had at least one loyal Republican among the operators who could spread the message horizontally to the crew, bypassing the vertical chain of command.

On Saturday afternoon, 18 July, Minister of Marine José Giral signed official telegrams which Balboa sent out in Morse code to the commanding officers of the four Spanish destroyers and one gunboat at Ceuta and Melilla, ordering them to stop any ships bringing troops across the Strait of Gibraltar from Africa. In addition, they were to open fire on rebel camps, barracks or gatherings. 'The Spanish Republic expects that the loyalty and discipline of the crew will honour the shining tradition of the Navy.'

At Melilla, some officers disregarded this command. Captain Fernando Bastarreche tried to persuade the crew that he was right to do so. He waved a copy of Franco's message:

I'm not going to read it but to tell you that a military uprising has broken out across Spain, the whole army has risen . . . Heading the movement is a glorious Spaniard, General Franco, a man who is worthy of your trust, a good and patriotic Spaniard who has never meddled in politics . . . There is a government in Madrid that is no kind of a government. You will have read about the series of murders that are staining our land with blood, and for this reason General Franco is calling on all good Spaniards to help save our homeland. We have received an order to bombard Melilla . . . Tell me: which of you would open fire on our brothers?

A hoarse voice broke the tense silence. 'So why did the army start shooting in Asturias in '34? Is it because miners, being miners, aren't our brothers?'

'I wouldn't have fired,' said Bastarreche.

'That may be true. But someone on your side did.'

Then Guevara from the engine room spoke up. He praised the Republic and said he would accept no orders except those from the legitimate government. Enraged, Bastarreche told him to leave the ship and telegraph Madrid. Guevara refused. 'Sir, I am someone you kill from the front, not in the back, like a dog.' The crews clamoured to return to Cartagena, and the two destroyers blundered out to sea, almost colliding. However, they carried no insurgent troops across from Melilla to mainland Spain.

It was a different story along the African coast at Ceuta. In the dark of Saturday night, the destroyer *Churruca* embarked four hundred Moorish soldiers loyal to Franco, and together with the passenger/cargo ship *Ciudad de Algeciras* (owned by Juan March), also carrying insurgent military personnel, set off for Cádiz. The mail steam-packet *Cabo Espartel*, carrying a further battalion of Regulares, headed for Algeciras. As they crossed the strait, a radio operator on *Churruca* managed to tell Balboa what was happening and swore that Republican loyalists would later take over the rebel ship, and if necessary sink her in the strait.

Now the Spanish Republican navy was in turmoil, caught in a tragedy of loyalties. Officers rebelling against the state they were pledged to serve provoked mutiny among men whose duty was to follow orders. In one ship, an officer argued passionately to his crew that the military rebellion was not to import fascism but to stop communism taking over the country. A sailor replied that they wanted neither fascism nor communism, but in order to defend the Republic from both extremes they were prepared to shed their blood. And bloodshed there was, as loyalists and rebels fought for control of ships and bases. Rebels took El Ferrol, La Coruña, San Fernando near Cádiz and Palma de Mallorca. The northern Biscay coast from Gijon to San Sebastián stayed loyal to the government, as did the whole Mediterranean littoral from Málaga to Barcelona. Urged on by Balboa in Madrid and radio operators on other ships, loyal crew members seized the cruisers *Libertad* and *Miguel de Cervantes* from officers who wished to join the insurgency. Hugh Thomas says the pro-Franco officers on the *Cervantes* resisted to the last man and that other officers were imprisoned and then shot at Cartagena in August. The worst atrocities and murders happened on prison ships afterwards, not during the initial fighting. George Steer records how 'drunk and dirty sailors' from a left-wing Republican warship crept aboard the prison ship *Cabo de Quilates* in Bilbao waters and murdered forty-two Francoist prisoners in early October. Overall, more than a third of the Spanish navy's officers perished.

These events had consequences in Gibraltar. On 19 July, somewhere at sea off the coast of Portugal, there was a brief gunfight for control of the España-class battleship *Jaime I*, a dreadnought with eight twelve-inch guns. Sailors loyal to the Republican government acquired pistols, stormed the defended bridge and killed two rebel officers, Captain Aguilar and Lieutenant Cañas. Both sides were guilty of opposing lawful authority; but which of them was in the right?

It being high summer, the loyalist sailors asked the Marine Ministry in Madrid for instructions about what to do with the dead bodies of the officers. The reply, to this specific question, was brief: '*Con sobriedad respetuosa den fondo a los cadáveres, anotando situación*' ('With respectful solemnity, commit their bodies to the deep, noting position'). Franco's rebels later dishonestly portrayed this message as a general government mandate to murder officers by throwing them overboard.

General Franco broadcast by radio from Tenerife his first manifesto, claiming he was saving Spain from anarchy and foreign subversion. Then he flew from the Canary Islands to Spanish Morocco in a British-owned and British-piloted Dragon Rapide aeroplane, hired with £2000 of Juan March's money. A right-wing 'adventurer' called Major Hugh Pollard, who did odd jobs for SIS, brought the aircraft out to him. When he landed at Tetuán early on Sunday 19 July, Franco learned that the colonels supporting him had managed to send some Moorish Regulares (commanded by Spanish officers) to Algeciras on the Spanish mainland aboard three small ships. Thus the city across the bay from Gibraltar became the beachhead for rebel troops from Morocco to disembark.

The Senior Naval Officer (Intelligence) in Gibraltar reported to the Admiralty on Sunday 19 July that 'Martial law was declared in

ALGECIRAS when Communist leader was shot last night.' Algeciras had fallen to the rebels straight away on 18 July; its newly arrived military commandant, Colonel Emilio March, was swift to join the conspiracy. As the *Gibraltar Chronicle and Official Gazette* approvingly put it in its front-page lead on Monday 20 July: 'The military assumed power at Algeciras on Saturday afternoon in the quietest possible manner.' Among the leading civilian supporters of the rebellion were the conservative Larios family. Pablo Larios's house, San Bernardo, became a barracks for young right-wingers, eager to shed Red blood.

What happened in La Línea over the same two days was very different. The *carabineros*, the armed corps that patrolled coasts and borders, remained largely loyal to the government. NCOs at the Ballesteros barracks disarmed those officers who wished to rebel and pushed some across the border into Gibraltar late on Saturday, before the gate at Four Corners closed at midnight. The next day the fighting continued.

After hearing the first radio reports of military turbulence, the American reporter Jay Allen left his house in Torremolinos to see what was happening further south down the coast. He arrived in La Línea on the morning of Sunday 19 July in a rich man's limousine. Nervous Anarcho-Syndicalists opened fire on what they thought was a right-winger's vehicle, wounding Allen's Spanish driver. A mob of men seized the reporter but he talked his way out in fluent Spanish. He went home, said goodbye to his writer friends, Gerald Brenan and Gamel Woolsey, and got a fisherman to take him with his typewriter and suitcase from Estepona to Gibraltar to hunt out good stories for the *News Chronicle*.

At eleven o'clock that morning, the rebel torpedo boat *T-19* shelled La Línea's Ballesteros barracks. When 170 Moorish Regulares who had disembarked in Algeciras joined the attack, the defenders could not withstand the assault. 'Loyal troops there have capitulated,' signalled the Gibraltar Staff Officer (Intelligence), 'and both LINEA and ALGECIRAS are in the hands of revolutionaries.' Among those rebel attackers, one of Pablo Larios's sons-in-law, Fernando Povar, took a bullet in the shoulder and nearly lost his arm to gangrene later.

After the Sunday lunchtime battle in La Línea, the Moorish Regulares, seeing signs of hostility in the crowds outside the barracks, started shooting into them too, killing and wounding scores of civilians. Estimates of the number of dead range from ninety to over 150.

On Tuesday 21 July, the Gibraltar government cabled a report to the Colonial Office:

Situation in Spain where as you will be aware Army in conjunction with Fascist party has rebelled against Socialist government is very obscure. Algeciras in hands of rebels. Malaga reported still held by Government but burning in many places. Neighbouring town of La Linea occupied by rebel troops from Morocco and there have been clashes there with Communist mob. Reaction in Gibraltar has been that Colony has been inundated with over 2000 of the 4000 British subjects living there [*in La Línea*]. Also considerable influx of terror-stricken Spanish including many women and children. Entry of Spaniards however being strictly controlled. Some inconveniences through lack of Spanish labour but not yet serious. Similarly a shortage of fresh vegetables etc, but supplies expected from Tangier. British tourists and others have been collected from Algeciras by Port Department launch and from Torremolinos west of Malaga by War Department tug. Telephone communication with Spain suspended, train services not running, travel by road impossible or risky. No overland mails received since Saturday. Please repeat to General Harington, 94 Piccadilly.

The sporty Governor of Gibraltar, General Sir Charles Harington, was on leave in England, happily watching the cricket at Lord's, having taken a little flat nearby so as not to miss a stroke of the batting, and picked up messages at his club, the Naval and Military, known as the 'In and Out', at 94 Piccadilly. The Acting Governor and Commander-in-Chief of Gibraltar was Brigadier W. T. Brooks.

The Rock was a very long way from Lord's Cricket Ground. There had been an enormous stampede of people out of La Línea. Those who could not get through the gate rowed or even swam across to Gibraltar's Eastern Beach, seeking shelter with friends and family or among kindly strangers. Fishing boats from La Atunera ferried refugees to Catalan Bay. The wounded were taken to the Colonial Hospital and the semi-naked, hungry children clothed and fed. No one knows exactly how many refugees there were, but Harington later estimated up to ten thousand. He wrote: 'Gibraltar was at once dangerously overcrowded. These people lived in caves, on hulks, in hovels of every kind, many in the streets, in taxis, in gardens and in a camp we prepared for them.'

This was an army tent-camp rigged up for twelve hundred people on the racecourse at North Front, where the Gibraltar Soup Kitchen provided many thousands of hot meals and hundreds of tins of milk for babies. The CO of the Gordon Highlanders complained in mid-August that refugees were freely defecating by the hedge round the manège (riding school), but others set up a subscription fund to help the destitute. The Indian Merchants' Association, while worried about 'our people and property' in Spanish territories, were 'deeply touched' by the influx of frightened civilians pouring into Gibraltar, and wrote to the Colonial Secretary generously offering 'advice, help and co-operation, any time we are called upon'. Over a hundred new Special Constables were recruited to help with the refugees, many of whom were poor working-class Spaniards who feared going back because they might be shot for their left-wing views. (Although in British official eyes only 'prominent persons e.g. of ministerial status' counted as 'political refugees'.)

Flies, dust and filth led Lieutenant Colonel Allnutt, the Medical Officer of Health, to call for improvements in sanitation and three-times-a-day emptying of the thirty-four bucket-latrines provided. Seven young children and two old people died in the camp, but when the governor closed the place in mid-September, the refugees resisted, scuffling with the police in Irish Town. The National Council of Civil Liberties in London sent a telegram to the Secretary of State for the Colonies, Major Ormsby-Gore, on 19 September:

Gravely disturbed at reports that Spanish refugee camp in Gibraltar closed down and refugees camping in streets and refugees without money liable to be sent over border to rebel territory where they would be exposed to risk of torture or death . . . These reports causing widespread feeling in this country and regarded as violations of British tradition on right of asylum stop We earnestly beg you make immediate investigation and prevent grievous injustice being done ends.

Among those who signed the letter were the liberal Tory MP Vyvyan Adams, the lawyer and MP Dingle Foot, Professor Julian Huxley, the campaigning journalist Henry Nevinson, the progressive MP Eleanor Rathbone and the novelist H. G. Wells. The Gibraltar government replied that no one was being sent by force anywhere they did not want to go: fifteen hundred refugees had been shipped to Málaga, still under Republican government control, while another two hundred had drifted back to La Línea.

In late July 1936, General Franco's whole strategy hinged on the Strait of Gibraltar. His rebel army was mostly cut off in Africa; he was desperate to get them across the water to Europe, and he had to stop the loyalist navy from blocking their way. In the Mediterranean and the Strait of Gibraltar, the Republic still ruled the waves, retaining a battleship and two cruisers, as well as nine destroyers, eight submarines, four torpedo boats and some smaller craft. Franco used every aeroplane he could muster at Tetuán in Spanish Morocco, mainly Breguet biplanes but also half a dozen small trainers from the Seville Aero Club, to bomb these ships and drive them away. Nearly all the Francoist attacks missed, but since several targets were British-flagged vessels, including the *Gibel Dersa*, the regular Bland Line ferry to Tangier, the British government sent warnings via the British consul in Tetuán that any more such incidents would be met by force.

A squadron of Spanish Republican ships – the cruisers *Libertad* and *Cervantes*, the destroyer *Churruca* and three gunboats – converged on the port of Tangier in Morocco, seeking water and fuel.

Tangier was a law unto itself, run by a Control Commission of six European nations: Belgium, Britain, France, Italy, Portugal and Spain. Under Article 3 of the 1923 Convention establishing Tangier as a neutral 'international zone', all military activity was prohibited. On these grounds, Shell refused to sell the Spanish government ships any bunker oil, although refuelling was not strictly 'military'. Forty kilometres away in Tetuán, General Franco was outraged that the Republican ships were in Tangier at all, breaching neutrality, he claimed, by using the international zone as a base for potential attacks on Ceuta and Melilla and Gibraltar. When Franco threatened to bomb the Republican vessels, an international incident began brewing.

Gibraltar cabled the Admiralty on 20 July: 'Tangier reports that Spanish warships in harbour have placed their officers under arrest and have constituted a Soviet . . . They are awaiting oil fuel from Malaga and then propose to bombard Cadiz and Algeciras.' The next day the Republican flotilla moved across the strait. Led by the battleship *Jaime I*, which arrived on 21 July, and the cruisers *Libertad* and *Miguel de Cervantes*, the fuel-starved ships started arriving in Gibraltar Bay on the evening of Tuesday 21 July. By Wednesday 22 July 1936, they had all dropped anchor among the commercial shipping outside the naval harbour.

This worried General Franco. From Tetuán he sent a telegram addressed to the Governor of Gibraltar, trying to persuade him that the Republican navy was no longer legitimate and should not be refuelled or resupplied. This is how his 21 July message was translated from the Spanish, with the original ink underlinings of key phrases:

General Staff in Chief of Expeditionary Force and High Commissioner of Spain in Morocco triumphant in Spanish general rising against communism can assure you that Government no longer exists and is only obeyed by scattered groups and <u>mobs in a state of anarchism</u> and one or two capital ships of Spanish navy from Tangier to your port intending to refuel. <u>The state of their crews is fully communistic.</u> The staff and officers have been made prisoners when not killed or wounded as has happened to battleship JAIME

I which establishes <u>characteristics of pirate ships</u> to the extreme so that an inspection on board will satisfy you. Having assumed responsibility of this command to bring peace to the nation and as it is not in the interest of Spain that fuel oil be supplied to them or that they be allowed to fuel in English waters I pray Your Excellency to <u>transmit to His Majesty's Government</u> these circumstances with the object that the anarchist influence of these ships in the Mediterranean be terminated ends.

In Gibraltar Bay, the British boarding officers and the naval visiting officer came to visit the Republican vessels but could not immediately see Commander Fernando Navarro Capdevila, who was said to be in charge of the cruiser *Libertad*. Then an unshaven person appeared. He was dressed in the correct officer's uniform with the right insignia denoting *Capitán de Fragata*, but he was not wearing socks.

Did this shocking aberration indicate the collapse of decency and the rise of communism? Or was he perhaps a member of the lower orders impersonating an officer? In fact, the cruiser had run out of fresh water to wash with, and Commander Navarro had been racing pillar to post for four days without a change of clothes. This loyal officer had taken an emergency flight from the Ministry of Marine in Madrid; narrowly escaped execution by rebels in Cartagena and, once freed, had sailed via Tangier to Gibraltar, where he was finally able to take his socks off.

The Francoist rebel command were trying to recapture the narrative by making the legitimate Spanish government seem illegitimate. Colonel Emilio March, the Francoist Military Commandant of Algeciras, sent a mildly threatening message to the Acting Governor of Gibraltar, Brigadier Brooks:

Governments can treat with warships of other nations if they are legal and their officers genuine. But if they are prisoners on board or they have been shot, the ships should be considered as pirate ships and should not be helped in any way ... [T]here may be consequences.

Brooks later telexed the Colonial Office in London about the Republican ships, telling them that he had received a visit from a rather junior officer, Lieutenant José Paz, claiming to be the acting chief of staff, accompanied by the Consul of the Spanish Republic. Paz, who was not in uniform, admitted there were very few officers on board his ship: 'they had left when the trouble broke out.' The Republican flotilla had then applied to the local commercial bunkering firms for coal and fuel oil, the Gibraltar firms had refused to supply them without reference to their principals in London. Meanwhile the Spanish government oiler *Ophir* was supplying the flotilla with five hundred tons, enough for them to get to Málaga. Brooks thought the Republican ships wanted 'to use Gibraltar if possible as a fuelling and supply base and to bring the neighbouring towns under fire'. He pointed out that General Franco in Morocco had warned that 'he will be forced to fight the Government Fleet with his aeroplanes and that British ships in the straits should carry distinctive signs in order to prevent mistakes'. In view of this, Brooks asked the Republicans 'to move their anchorage to the north end of the bay near the Spanish shore . . . I consider it is most desirable that this Fleet should depart from British waters as soon as possible and be discouraged from returning.'

All the Gibraltar bunkering firms were situated in the central street called Irish Town and almost all refused to sell fuel to the Republican ships. (Were they 'squared' by the rebels? Or the Gibraltar government? Possibly; no evidence remains.) Their representative, Lionel Imossi, claimed that he told Lieutenant José Paz there would be no coal unless imprisoned officers were handed over to the judicial authorities; Paz denied that he held any prisoners. Official Gibraltar was suspicious and fearful of the Republican sailors, with the Royal Navy in particular seeing revolutionary fervour as a dangerous contagion. Acting Governor Brooks soon sent a cable that is further evidence of shallow analysis.

I am not satisfied that the ships mentioned belong to the Spanish government although they fly the Spanish national flag. My definite opinion is that

Communists are commanding and manning them. Sailors have landed here and have given publicly in Gibraltar the Communist salute. A young officer off one of the ships . . . says that all the officers on board are locked up. All Gibraltar coal merchants except one state that they are unable to give coal to Spanish ships on account of lack of stocks. The remaining one will supply it if it receives definite orders from Government so to do and payment guaranteed. Immediate instructions are required.

Official Gibraltar did not ask the right questions and made no mention of the salient fact that the Franco-favouring rebel officers were disobeying the orders of the legitimate Spanish government. The spectre of 'Communism' was enough to frighten the class- and caste-bound British, horrified by scruffy crews and breaches of decorum. They also believed that naval officers were imprisoned below decks, murdered and thrown overboard, perhaps even, as the anti-communist Francis Yeats-Brown later alleged, 'crucified . . . on the quarter-deck'.

The Royal Navy – the Senior Service – had always feared insurrection from below and repressed it fiercely. 'What are the traditions of the navy, pray?' Churchill is said to have expostulated: 'Rum, sodomy and the lash!' The late King George V, most punctilious of naval monarchs, once rebuked Claude Elliott, the head master of Eton, for allowing Eisenstein's 1925 silent film *Battleship Potemkin* to be shown at the school. Told that it was good for the boys to see new cinematic techniques like montage even if they did come from Soviet Russia, the king said, 'Nonsense! It is certainly not good for the boys to witness mutinies, especially naval mutinies.'

In the end, no Gibraltarian oil or coal was sold. The Republican ships got just enough fuel from their own oil tanker to make it to Málaga.

The Admiralty Tower at Gibraltar was alive with signals as the Royal Navy was galvanised for action all round the coast of Spain. From Vigo in northwest Spain, far off from the British Embassy and the Foreign Office, came a request for a fast warship to protect

'British lives and property in case needed. All business closed since July 13th. General strike now in progress and disturbances at San Pedro hourly. Town and district virtually in hands of proletariat.'

The Royal Navy's policy was to rescue all Britons and other respectable persons from the chaos caused by dangerously over-excited foreigners. Rear Admiral James Murray Pipon at Gibraltar committed the S-class destroyer HMS *Shamrock* to evacuations from Málaga, Marbella and then Sevilla; he sent HMS *Whitehall* to Tangier, the ageing sloop HMS *Cormorant* to patrol the Eastern Beach of Gibraltar, and the dockyard tug *Energetic* to pick up 130 British nationals and various foreigners and take them away from Algeciras.

All through the Mediterranean, screws were churning: six B-class destroyers arrived from Malta to help; the battle cruiser HMS *Repulse* brought the 2nd Battalion Gordon Highlanders at high speed back from Egypt, and after disembarking them in Gibraltar on the 25th, headed for Palma de Mallorca to evacuate over five hundred foreigners. *Basilisk* went to Almería, *Boadicea* to Alicante, *Devonshire* to Palma, *Keith* to Valencia, *Keppel* and *Whitshed* to Vigo, and five more British warships to Barcelona.

The reporter George Steer was sardonic about the evacuations, which he witnessed in the autonomous Basque country in northwest Spain even though it had remained orderly: 'There was no social revolution at Bilbao . . . political murder and destruction of property (the very thought of which was horrible to the Basque farmer-bourgeoisie) were suppressed at once.' Nevertheless, Steer said, foreign navies, including the British Royal Navy, were insisting that all their citizens be immediately evacuated, which in effect helped the Francoist rebels, because the loss of foreign technicians, businessmen, bankers, managers, etc., caused severe economic damage to the Republic. Steer wrote in his 1938 book *The Tree of Gernika* that 'the official naval attitude to the Civil War was summed up colourfully in the *Official Gazette* of Gibraltar, which described the Spanish Government with which its own Government maintained normal diplomatic relations as – The Reds.' Indeed, 'Malaga in Hands of Reds' and 'Warships Turn Red' were the front-page headlines of the *Gibraltar Chronicle and Official Gazette* on Tuesday 21 and Wednesday 22 July 1936.*

Gibraltar's prejudices distorted London's policy towards Spain because the British government had nowhere else to get its information. The best British correspondent in Spain, Henry Buckley of the *Daily Telegraph*, pointed out in his exemplary book *The Life and Death of the Spanish Republic* (1940) that British officials were absent from Madrid. The ambassador, Sir Henry Chilton, was away summering at San Sebastián with the *corps diplomatique*; the British consul, George Ogilvie-Forbes, was on holiday for a whole month until the middle of August. No one was *en poste* throughout to tell HMG what was really going on.

In Madrid and Barcelona, an ill-armed citizenry had managed to thwart the military uprising against a democratic state, and there was still a moderate, middle-class Spanish government, however precarious: Don Manuel Azaña was president and Don José Giral, the bespectacled pharmaceutical chemistry professor, was still prime minister. Henry Buckley's view was that the British government did not want to know in precise detail what was happening, they were just waiting (and hoping?) for Franco to win. The reporter thought the complete lack of 'fresh and accurate material' from diplomats, analysts and 'unofficial observers of insight and experience' during the dramatic events of mid-July set the entire course of subsequent British policy, which began in ignorance. Carl von Clausewitz said that the first and 'the most far-reaching act of judgement' that commanders have to make is to establish what *kind* of war is being embarked on. Calling Franco's rebellion 'the Spanish Civil War' was a category error. The file that the Gibraltar government started

---

* When George Orwell visited Gibraltar en route to Morocco on 7 and 8 September 1938, he described the paper thus: 'Local English daily, *Gibraltar Chronicle & Official Gazette*, 8 pages of which 2½ advertisements, 1d. Current number, 31,251. More or less pro-Fascist.'

on the events did at least have a more accurate title: 'Military Rising in Spain, July 1936'.

England's rulers assumed their class interest was the same thing as the national interest. By standing back, refusing to help or arm another democracy, they yielded the ground to totalitarian powers to fight their proxy wars. Henry Buckley regretted that British Empire policy was shaped too much by prejudice. 'Well, I suppose all empires grow old,' Buckley concluded. 'But it is not much fun to be a young man in an old empire.'

Andalusia in 1936 was as unequal as Ireland in 1836. Five per cent of the landowners in some provinces had three quarters of the total agricultural wealth, and the landless got a few pesetas a day for seasonal work. This bred anger and resentment, and when the serious shooting started in the summer of 1936, it allowed the different classes to start murdering each other in a *furia española*.

One of the first buildings set on fire in Málaga in July 1936 was the Casa Larios, the headquarters of Málaga's principal industries. Its reduction to an 'ugly, smoking shell' was witnessed by Gamel Woolsey, the melancholy poet from South Carolina who had fallen in love with another writer, Gerald Brenan. In July 1936 she was happily living with him in their thick-walled old farmhouse in the village of Churriana, south of Málaga on the road to Torremolinos – a property Brenan had bought from Don Carlos Crooke Larios.

Gerald Brenan, a self-described rebel against middle-class English life, knew and loved Spain and the Spanish people. After winning the Military Cross as a captain in the Great War, he left England 'to discover new and more breathable atmospheres' in Spain, an experience memorably evoked in his book *South from Granada*. Brenan's account of the social and political background of the civil war, *The Spanish Labyrinth* (1943), is a classic which the historian Hugh Trevor-Roper said 'made everything else written on Spain seem pitifully shoddy'.

Gamel Woolsey's own book, *Death's Other Kingdom: a Spanish village on the eve of the Civil War* (1939), tracks the emotional and psychological effects of fanaticism and political murder on ordinary life. Looking at the torched Casa Larios, she wondered if arson wasn't 'a vice of the nature of an erotic crime': rape on the grand scale. 'The mad faces in the streets of Málaga seemed drugged with the lust of burning; and all the queer creatures of the gutter and the cellar, the twisted, the perverse and the maimed had crawled up into the light of the flames.'*

Ingenious methods were used to rescue people from 'Red' Málaga. The Ruggeroni brothers, Angel and Ernest, who acted as the Mexican consul and vice consul in Gibraltar, used blank Mexican passports to help give the persecuted new identities. They usually took the bogus passports off people when they got to the Rock, but when someone travelled further with one, Mexico closed the scheme down.

As humane, educated people, Woolsey and Brenan felt it was their duty to protect their neighbour, Carlos Crooke Larios, from roaming Anarchist death squads looking for any 'Fascists' to shoot. Brenan described Don Carlos as full of optimism and good cheer, but with a cruel and destructive streak. They hid him with his sons in their house for a month even though he was a most annoying and dangerous guest. During a Francoist air raid on Málaga he was seen jumping about on the roof and shouting '¡Viva España!' which could have led to the whole household being shot by a renegade leftist *camarilla*. Eventually, with the help of a Spanish Liberal called Don Francisco, Brenan got Don Carlos the right papers to board an American warship evacuating people to Gibraltar.

Ten days later, Brenan and Woolsey followed him into exile. Among the rich Spanish refugees on the Rock they found Don Carlos Crooke Larios again, now working for General Franco's intelligence service.

---

* Just before his evacuation by British destroyer to Gibraltar in July 1936, the young Laurie Lee felt something similar after the villagers burned down the pseudo-Moorish casino in Almuñecar, 'an air of orgiastic gloom . . . a sour and desolate sadness'.

I asked him when he returned to Malaga to protect Don Francisco, to whom he owed his life and who was in any case not a Red but a harmless liberal, trapped in a situation which he hated.

'He'll be shot all right,' Don Carlos answered breezily. 'We are going to shoot everyone who worked for the Reds.'

On Wednesday 22 July, between 4.30 and 7.00 p.m., Franco's insurgent aircraft flew over the strait from Ceuta in Africa to bomb the five Republican warships that were anchored at the north end of Gibraltar Bay. The Fortress told the War Office that the Republican ships 'engaged aircraft actively with all available guns. Several unexploded shells and many fragments fell in Gibraltar but little damage, no casualties. Situation complicated by presence of Spanish Government aircraft flying low and dropping bomb on neutral ground and machine-gunning troops in La Linea. Strongest possible protest lodged with both sides.' Some shrapnel fell on the roof of the Rock Hotel and other bits went right over the top of the Rock and landed on Catalan Bay village.

Gibraltar's Colonial Secretary, Colonel Beattie, addressed 'the strongest possible protest against this outrage and contravention of international law' to the Republican Commander Fernando Navarro on the *Libertad*, reminding him that his ships were 'admitted to port only for supplies and they must not jeopardize life by actions of this kind'. If any similar incidents occurred, the ships would have to leave. In a gesture towards even-handedness, he also informed Navarro that 'a protest is being lodged with the [Francoist] authorities responsible for the despatch of the aircraft'.

Captain Navarro replied straight away:

We respectfully beg to state to Your Excellency that in view of the attitude of the subversive aviation against the legitimate Govt. of Spain we have been compelled to bombard this aviation which repeatedly violates international treaties and put themselves outside the law and which I respectfully put forward for Your Excellency's information in case Your Excellency should deem it expedient to act in defence of the international treaties. We respectfully offer our respects to the representative of His Britannic Majesty's Government.

General Franco also responded to the protest note, sending an insincere telegram via the Algeciras commandant Colonel March to the Colonial Secretary, to let 'His Excellency the Governor of that Fortress' know just how 'extraordinarily' annoyed he was by bombs falling in the wrong places. Franco would issue 'the strictest orders' against any repetition. Nevertheless, any shrapnel that fell was all the fault of 'the state of anarchism of the Spanish fleet'. The message ended with a stiff reassurance: 'It is the greatest interest and desire of General Franco to avoid by all means any inconvenience, danger and juridical infringement to the British nation and its inhabitants . . .'

Over the telephone from Algeciras, the rebel Colonel March continued to argue that Republican ships were effectively pirate ships. He thought 'the proper thing' for British naval forces to do was to disarm such warships and intern their crews in the fortress, citing the authority of General Franco as the '*de facto* chief of the Spanish government, since his forces have possession of ¾ of Spanish territory, and there is in fact no government in our capital'.

Around midnight on Wednesday 22 July, the Republican flotilla left Gibraltar and headed to Málaga for fuel. Franco's planes repeatedly bombed all ships in the strait. At 10 a.m. on Thursday, a rebel plane dropped a bomb near the British destroyer HMS *Beagle*, and around noon the civilian *Gibel Dersa* ferry was bombed at the entrance to Tangier harbour. HMS *Whitehall* opened fire, and the aircraft went away. When the *Gibel Dersa* was bombed again on the way back to Gibraltar at 18.20, George Gaggero, the chairman of Bland Line, protested by telegram. Franco's disingenuous, comic-opera response was to award the *Gibel Dersa*'s captain, José Silva García, the Cross of Military Merit.

6

Death from the Air

A new attempt by the Francoists to ingratiate themselves with Gibraltar began on Thursday 23 July 1936 with another telephone message from Colonel March in Algeciras to the Colonial Secretary on the Rock, to say 'General Kinderlin [*sic*] requests permission to call on the General and Governor of Gibraltar and says he has a motorboat to cross over.' The Colonial Secretary sent back a cautious request for more information.

General Alfredo Kindelán Duany was the founder of the Spanish air force, a tall, incorruptible monarchist who had gone into exile in 1931 rather than live under a republic. A key figure in the 1936 military conspiracy, he had come down to Cádiz to act as General Mola's liaison with the naval command whose help they needed to ship the rebel army over from Africa. Now Kindelán had linked up with the ground forces in Algeciras, where his two sons, Ultano and Alfredo, were staying with the Larios family. After Franco arrived in Spanish Morocco, he spoke by telephone across the strait with Kindelán and appointed him the head of his fledgling air force, which both men agreed was vital to the success of the rebellion.

At 2.30 p.m., siesta time, on Thursday 23 July, Colonial Secretary Alex Beattie had an unexpected and glamorous visitor at his house, Pablo Larios's eldest daughter Natalia (more usually called Talia), bearing a message from General Franco about the purpose of General Kindelán's visit. Talia was married to the aristocrat Fernando Povar, who had been wounded by the Republicans in the shooting at La Línea on 19 July and was now in the Colonial Hospital in Gibraltar. The Marquesa de Povar was an attractive woman, and she and her sister Mercedes had 'countless admirers' on the Rock, according to the overexcited historian of the Royal Calpe Hunt: 'They were vivacious, happy, exquisitely beautiful, and polished horsewomen.' Talia, who was now living in a flat in Gibraltar during her husband's treatment, told Colonel Beattie that General Kindelán wanted to convey in person to the British authorities General Franco's own explanation of the bombing incidents.

Beattie telephoned the acting governor, Brigadier Brooks, who said he was prepared to see General Kindelán at 5 p.m. at Government House, on the understanding that their talk was in connection with recent 'incidents of contravention by Spanish aeroplanes of the International Air Convention'. The Gibraltar Port Launch was sent over to Algeciras to pick him up.

The visit was a diplomatic ploy, for Kindelán had plans elsewhere. On the same day he crossed over to Gibraltar, his chief of staff, Captain Francisco Arranz Monasterio, was aboard a commandeered German Deutsche-Lufthansa Junkers Ju 52 passenger plane, the *Max von Müller*, together with a German businessman, Johannes Bernhardt, and the Nazi Party 'group leader' in Morocco, Adolf Langenheim, flying to Nazi Germany to chase up Franco's request for German transport planes.

Meanwhile, Kindelán arrived in Gibraltar accompanied by a laughing group of upper-class Spanish ladies and gentlemen. Brigadier Brooks and Colonel Beattie started their meeting with Kindelán at 5.30, with the honorary ADC, Captain F. J. W 'Paco' Porral, acting as their interpreter. The ex-cavalryman Porral, the father of twelve-year-old John Porral, was, with his friend Bobby Capurro, a long-serving aide-de-camp to several governors. Being Gibraltarians, they were fluent in Spanish, which most senior British officers never managed to master.

General Kindelán said he had come to express General Franco's great regret at his aeroplanes flying over Gibraltar and dropping bombs in the vicinity, but of course some of the fliers were inexperienced. As for the shrapnel which fell on the Rock, the general said that the blame for that lay entirely with the Spanish government warships. Since their crews had murdered or imprisoned their officers, the Gibraltar authorities should have interned them all when they entered Gibraltarian waters. No Spanish Republican ships should be allowed to operate freely in the Strait.

The real nub of the meeting was the threat posed by the 'pirate' Republican navy to Franco's urgent plans to get his army across the water. Beattie made two further cryptic notes at the bottom left of his handwritten summary of the meeting. One read: 'Three requests: searchlights, ship patrol, British transport ship.' Presumably this means Kindelán asked for the Republican ships to be illuminated with searchlights and kept under observation, and for some kind of direct help from the British to transport Francoist troops and supplies across the strait.

Beattie's second cryptic note, scribbled at the bottom of the page, is interesting: 'T. Povar saw B & myself re Br w'ships convoying Franco's transports.'

My reading of this is 'Talia Povar saw Brooks and myself to ask about British warships convoying Franco's transports.' Franco was deploying a charm offensive, using an alluring and confident woman to get what he wanted. Talia, Marquesa de Povar, was zealous in his cause. She was the eldest sister of José Larios, who later became a pilot in Franco's air force. In his memoir *Combat over Spain* he wrote that Talia 'remained at Gibraltar for the remainder of the war, working with our [Francoist] Intelligence Service and relaying much useful information concerning the movement of the Red fleet and the passage of war material for unloading at Red ports'.

Both Beattie and Brooks resisted her seductions, however. Would British warships escort the vessels transporting Franco's troops across the Strait of Gibraltar? 'Nothing doing', wrote tight-lipped Beattie in his notes. (German warships and German and Italian aircraft would eventually escort Franco's 'convoy of victory' over from Africa on 5 August.)

It was after 7 p.m. when General Kindelán left Government House and went with his upper-class pals up to the Rock Hotel to join the

Spanish monarchists and aristocrats who had flooded there in recent months. One of the reasons why Kindelán came to Gibraltar was so he could use the Gibraltar telephone exchange to place three international calls: to Franco's Morocco, to Fascist Rome and, crucially, to Arranz at the embassy in Berlin, where his emissaries had flown on their urgent quest for transport planes from Nazi Germany.

Two of the Francoist delegation – Bernhardt and Langenheim – eventually met Adolf Hitler on Saturday night, 25 July, at the Villa Wahnfried in Bayreuth, where the German chancellor was attending the Wagner festival. They found the *Führer* in a state of ecstatic elation after a performance of the third opera in *Der Ring des Nibelungen* cycle, *Siegfried*, conducted by Wilhelm Furtwängler. They asked Hitler to supply ten transport aircraft, with pilots and crew, in order to help Franco's army get across the Strait of Gibraltar. Hitler summoned Hermann Göring, the head of the air force, and Werner von Blomberg, the Minister of War, for a conference. Göring was initially reluctant, then, seeing Hitler's excitement, changed tack and joined in the romantic fantasy. An unnamed German admiral was also present at the meeting. Was he Wilhelm Canaris, the head of the Abwehr, the foreign intelligence service? Paul Preston thinks it 'unlikely', Ian Colvin 'probable'. Spain was Canaris's old stamping ground, and he would become a key link between Germany and Iberia. At gone one in the morning, Hitler agreed to supply double the number of planes asked for, and Göring came up with the theatrical code-name *Unternehmen Feuerzauber*, 'Operation *Magic Fire*', after the flames that the Germanic hero Siegfried has to pass through in order to free the fair maiden Brünnhilde. In a week's time, at the opening of the 1936 Berlin Olympic Games, Hitler would be publicly accepting an olive branch from a Greek marathon runner while thirty-five thousand white doves of peace whooshed up into the air. But now, in secret joy, he was brandishing Siegfried's sword.

★

Franco and Kindelán used what aircraft they had to harry Republican forces at sea and on land, but found they could not rely on all their pilots. On 25 July, two days after Kindelán's visit to Gibraltar, the Basque-born Sergeant Félix Urtubi was flying a Breguet Bre-19 from Tetuán to bomb and strafe a column of Republican government soldiers approaching La Línea when he changed sides in mid-air. 'At an altitude of 1000 feet over the Strait of Gibraltar I turned to the lieutenant and shot him four times – in the forehead, in the chest and through the mouth. I didn't give the traitor time to look at me in dismay and cry "No! No!"'

With the corpse of Lieutenant Juan Miguel de Castro Gutiérrez beside him, Sergeant Urtubi flew halfway across Spain to land at Getafe airfield, Madrid. He then pointed his pistol at his own head and asked the men surrounding his plane if the capital was in Republican hands. 'If not, I'd have shot myself rather than surrender,' he later told journalists. Urtubi did sacrifice himself not long afterwards, by deliberately crashing his plane headlong into a Francoist aircraft when he ran out of ammunition defending the skies above Madrid.

The enterprising American journalist Jay Allen made his way to Spanish Morocco, where, on 27 July 1936, he became the first foreign correspondent to interview Francisco Franco, ensconced in the Spanish High Commissioner's house in Tetuán. One of Franco's first actions there had been to set up a concentration camp outside the city at El Mogote, the first of four Francoist camps in the Protectorate to hold leftists, Republicans, Freemasons and other subversives in appalling conditions, with regular executions by firing squad. Allen noticed several copies of the ultra right-wing, anti-Semitic and anti-Bolshevik *Bulletin de L'Entente Internationale contre la Troisième Internationale* on the general's desk. Franco said he found the journal 'valuable'.

'There can be no compromise, no truce,' Franco declared to Allen. 'I shall go on preparing my advance to Madrid. I shall advance. I shall take the capital. I shall save Spain from Marxism at whatever cost . . . Shortly, very shortly, my troops will have pacified the country and all of this will soon seem like a nightmare.'

'This means that you will have to shoot half Spain?'

'I said whatever the cost.'

In La Línea, a stone's throw from Gibraltar, Franco's repression soon started, with the local Falange and other right-wingers helping to hunt down anarchists, communists, leftists, liberals, socialists, and troublemaking freethinkers of the Republican persuasion. Interrogated and convicted of 'military rebellion' by those who were the real military rebels, they were shot in batches by the bullring. One man was condemned to death because a pair of shoes on their way to the cobbler's was wrapped in an old sheet of the pro-Republican newspaper *El Calpense*. Among the many Freemasons executed in La Línea were *señores* Cayo, Moya, Ruíz and Troyano, the bookseller Gamboa, the chemist Autor and Dr Juan García Rodríguez, a much-loved paediatrician at the Municipal Hospital, who was killed on 27 July 1936. He was known as 'Don Juanito el Médico' to his poorer patients, whom, communistically, he often omitted to charge.

On 28 July, General Sir Charles Harington finally returned to his post, travelling with his wife, Gladys, on the P&O liner SS *Narkunda*. A fellow passenger on the four-day voyage was José Larios, Talia's brother and son of the Joint Master of the Royal Calpe Hunt. Young Larios was hurrying back to join Franco's rebellion. Answering General Kindelán's appeal for volunteers, he crossed the strait from Algeciras in an old Dornier flying boat and started training as a pilot at Tetuán. When José Larios came back to Gibraltar to visit pals in the army, his good friend from the Royal Calpe Hunt, Lieutenant Hector Lorenzo Christie of the Gordon Highlanders, 'drowned' him in whisky toasts, and a British officers' mess drank to 'a quick victory' by Franco's forces.

The Francoist emissaries to Germany, Bernhardt, Langenheim and Arranz, returned to Morocco in the same stripped-down commandeered Junkers Ju 52 passenger plane in which they had flown to

Nazi Germany. They landed at Tetuán on 28 July and reported that more aeroplanes were on their way from Hermann Göring. Flight Captain Alfred Henke, their pilot, also co-opted from Lufthansa, was now ardent for the cause. After removing its German identification, he and his crew readied the aircraft to fly a larger contingent of Franco's African Army across the Strait of Gibraltar to Seville. With the seats stripped out and no heavy cargo, a Ju 52 could carry a platoon of Moors at a time, twenty-five men with their personal weapons, on the one-hour flight. The following day, a second Lufthansa plane arrived to speed up the shuttle. In the last days of July 1936, over a hundred flights of small planes and transports carried barely nine hundred men over; but in August, with the help of the planes that Hitler had promised, more than three times the number of flights airlifted 4800 soldiers together with their heavy weapons and kit.

Meanwhile, Benito Mussolini was also responding to Franco's appeal for help. On 30 July he sent a dozen Savoia-Marchetti SM.81 Pipistrello or 'Bat' bomber/ transport planes with crews and technicians from Sardinia to Spanish Morocco. Three planes crashed on the way, but the surviving crew members were enrolled in the Spanish Foreign Legion. A dozen Italian Fiat CR.32 fighter biplanes arrived by sea in mid-August, and a dozen more by 3 September.

In Nazi Germany, Sonderstab (Special Staff) W worked fast inside Göring's Air Ministry, acquiring, sometimes straight off the production line, twenty new Junkers Ju 52 bomber or transport planes, half a dozen Heinkel He 51 fighter biplanes with maintenance kit and spare parts, and twenty 20 mm anti-aircraft cannons plus munitions. The Junkers firm at Dessau was instructed to remove the German markings from the six fighters and from ten bombers, and to dismantle and pack them in camouflaged crates for shipping to Spain from Hamburg. The Gestapo handled security. Sonderstab W also organised a full complement of air and ground crews, all single men, compulsorily 'volunteered' from their units and sworn to secrecy: twenty-five officers and sixty-six NCOs, soldiers and technicians who were capable pilots, navigators, gunners, engineers, mechanics and instructors. In civilian clothes, with identical cheap suitcases, posing as 'Tourist Group Union', they boarded the Woermann Line cargo ship *Usaramo* in Hamburg, and with 773 heavy crates of dismantled aeroplanes stowed safely on board, sailed for Spain around midnight on 31 July.

Naval support for Franco's rebellion was proceeding. A week earlier, two modern German *Panzerschiffen* or pocket battleships, the *Deutschland* and the *Admiral Scheer*, had sailed from Wilhelmshaven for Spanish waters, followed not long after by the cruiser *Köln* and four German destroyers. The Germans were very gung-ho, but did not get it all their own way. Captain Thomas Aubrey of HMS *Veteran* went to greet the *Deutschland* early on Sunday morning, 26 July, at San Sebastián in the Basque province of Guipuzcoa and managed to stop the captain marching fifty fully armed Nazi marines into what was now a very left-wing city. He suggested that the Republicans might well misinterpret any big-gun salutes as a hostile bombardment. *Deutschland* eventually put into Ceuta in Spanish Morocco on 3 August. There, German Vice Admiral Rolf Carls dined with Langenheim and Bernhardt, the two German emissaries from Morocco who had gone to meet Hitler, together with General Franco and Juan Beigbeder Atienza, a Spanish colonel who spoke fluent Arabic and good German. Beigbeder had been the military attaché in Berlin who acted as interpreter for General Sanjurjo on his visit to Nazi Germany's arms factories in February 1936.

At the beginning of August, British Rear Admiral James Somerville arrived in the port of Tangier aboard his flagship, the light cruiser HMS *Galatea*. Somerville, a son of Somerset squires, was a remarkable sailor. When he first entered Britannia Royal Naval College at Dartmouth in January 1897, an officer remarked of the slight-looking cadet: 'Poor little blighter. He won't last long!' But on VE Day 1945, that shrimp reached Admiral of the Fleet, the highest rank in the Royal Navy. HMS *Galatea* in 1936 carried an Osprey seaplane which the vigorous admiral liked to go up in, acting as his own radio operator because he was schooled in signals. Like his friend Vice Admiral Andrew Cunningham who had led the Mediterranean destroyer flotillas before him, Somerville was a no-nonsense, decisive admiral and an uncomplicated political thinker: 'The trouble is that the Spanish Navy – Communists – are using Tangier as a base and preventing Franco from taking troops across to Spain.'

Nevertheless, if General Franco did open hostilities, Somerville was prepared to defend the neutrality of Tangier and uphold international law. 'We are getting the anti-aircraft guns ready in case any of the Spanish aircraft attack us or ships in the vicinity,' Somerville wrote to his wife Mollie. 'I wish they would as we would learn them a lesson all right but I'm afraid they won't.' The consuls of the six nations who ran neutral Interzone Tangier struck Somerville as a 'weak-kneed lot of rats', dithering unnecessarily. 'It's high time we took a strong line with these bloody Spaniards. If anyone drops a brick near me, he'll certainly know about it . . .'

Franco wanted to get men and munitions across the Strait of Gibraltar from Morocco to Spain to prove that the rebels were capable of breaking the Republican government blockade. The eventual 'Convoy of Victory' was as much a propaganda exercise as a practical operation. Franco chose a day of religious significance – 5 August, the feast day of Our Lady of Africa in Ceuta – a stormy day when much of the Republican fleet was refuelling. The convoy crossed by daylight because his twenty-six aircraft needed to see enough to chase off any Republican warship trying to block their passage. From early in the day they maintained constant patrols of aggressive aircraft.

At 7 a.m., three Francoist aeroplanes attacked the Republican destroyer *Lepanto* and a bomb exploded on the port side, killing one man and wounding five more. The ship limped into Gibraltar to unload the wounded, and Franco telephoned the British Fortress to demand its immediate expulsion. *Lepanto* left for Málaga to bury the dead man, escorted by *Churruca*; both destroyers exhausted their anti-aircraft ammunition shooting back wildly at more Francoist planes. (Most ammunition used by the Republican navy throughout the civil war was fired against aeroplanes.) The Republican destroyer *Almirante Valdés* was hit by a 100 kg bomb dropped by an Italian Savoia-Marchetti SM.81. British, Dutch and Italian vessels were also bombed, but without great harm.

The Spanish Republic's failure to use all its available ships and aircraft to stop the rebels crossing the Strait of Gibraltar to establish their bridgehead in southern Spain was the strategic error that probably cost them the war. The initial tactic of taking command of navy vessels before Francoist insurgents could use them for their ends was a good move, but purging most of the officers was not so wise, because the fleet was then deprived of the drive, skills and experience of several hundred executives and engineers. Just as the French may have lost the battle of Trafalgar because the toll the Revolution had taken on the higher ranks crippled the fleet's effectiveness, so the officerless ships of *la armada española* may have doomed the Spanish Republic. Orders that needed the approval of a democratic 'soviet' of the crew (what Robert Louis Stevenson's *Treasure Island* pirates called a 'fo'c'sle council') slowed proceedings. Those on the bridge did not always know what was best. Aeroplanes in particular caused them to panic.

The Francoist armada that eventually set sail from Ceuta to Algeciras through a heavy sea and faint mist at 4.30 on the afternoon of Wednesday 5 August was not large. There were two medium-sized cargo ships belonging to Juan March, *Ciudad de Cádiz* and *Ciudad de Algeciras*, a sea-going tug, *Benot*, the auxiliary ship *Araujo*, escorted by the gunboat *Eduardo Dato*, the torpedo-ship *T-19* and the coastguard cutter *Uad-Kert*. But the convoy was carrying three thousand soldiers with their transport vehicles, six 105 mm howitzers plus shells, four mortars, twelve hundred grenades and two million rounds of rifle ammunition. Stopping them would have been a devastating coup, and Admiral Somerville thought the Republican failure to do so 'just shows what a feeble lot they are, as they ought to have made mincemeat of Franco's party'.

The rebel flotilla had almost reached the Bay of Algeciras when the Republican destroyer *Alcalá Galiano* appeared from the west at high speed with her forward guns firing. *Eduardo Dato* peeled off to port to engage her and the rebel big guns at Carnero Point also opened up on the Republican destroyer. Then Italian aircraft arrived to bomb the ship: *Alcalá Galiano* suffered eighteen dead and twenty-eight badly wounded. Anti-aircraft shrapnel from the battle rained down on the playing fields at Gibraltar's North Front and the batters and bowlers were forced to pull stumps. War was not cricket.

In Berlin, the Eleventh Olympiad was under way. Jesse Owens was winning the third of his four gold medals and African Americans were triumphing in track and field, infuriating the Nazis. However, German athletes did top the final medal league, which prompted them to claim Aryan racial supremacy. In the Olympic village at Döberitz (afterwards turned into a giant infantry barracks), the German hosts showed films of athletes blending into warriors: 'the long jumper was transformed in mid-air into a soldier leaping over barbed-wire, the hammer became a stick grenade . . .' International sportspeople watched the martial propaganda in silence.

The next day, Thursday 6 August, the German cargo ship *Usaramo*, escorted from Portuguese waters by the heavy cruiser *Deutschland*, docked at Cádiz to unload German aircrews in mufti and their many aeroplanes in crates. In Gibraltar, Governor Harington called a meeting of the civil and military authorities to compose a letter to the Secretary of State for the Colonies about what needed to be done. Rear Admiral Pipon of the Royal Navy, the man who had entertained Haile Selassie to tea in Gibraltar, wrote a revealing draft memo, asking for 'this so-called rebellion to be classed as a civil war and both sides be declared to be belligerents by the Powers'.

This was exactly the status that the rebel Franco craved, because until proper war was declared he had no legal right to object to Spanish government ships using Tangier as a base and preventing his troops being shipped across the strait. The British government did not want to award Franco belligerent rights because that would give him the right to stop and search neutral British merchant ships. Belligerent rights were never, in the end, awarded, but Admiral Pipon, who feared that Gibraltar was becoming 'the sanctuary . . . of . . . Spanish government Communist refugees and agents', parroted the line of the right-wing English press:

The so-called Spanish Government is being over-ridden by Communists whose avowed object is the establishment of an extreme Soviet State. The anti-Government forces are not Monarchists or extreme Fascists . . . and the provinces they now occupy are being governed in an orderly manner.

On Friday 7 August, the Republicans brought the war back to the Bay of Gibraltar. Having failed to stop Franco's convoy of victory, they arrived to punish the ships that had participated and Algeciras itself. At 6.30 a.m. Algeciras was bombed from the air and at 8.30 the battleship *Jaime I*, the cruiser *Libertad* and two destroyers arrived to shell its coastal batteries at Punto Carnero. The rebel gunboat *Eduardo Dato* was hit and caught fire, the cutter *Uad-Kert* was incapacitated, and the town was battered for three hours. From their rooftops and windows, Gibraltarians watched the shelling across the bay.

John Porral was a month short of his thirteenth birthday when he stood with his father on Europa Road, just across from the Casino, a couple of hundred yards south of the Rock Hotel, looking out over the South Mole and the waters of Gibraltar Bay towards Spain. The grey Republican battleship *Jaime I* was broadside on, a mile and a half away. They could see the flash of its big guns before they heard the boom. In the shelling of Algeciras, the British-owned Reina Cristina Hotel was badly damaged, as was the Larios town house nearby. Two shells hit the home of the British vice consul, Mr E. G. Beckinsale, bringing down half the roof and forcing Mrs Beckinsale to take shelter in a cell at the police station. Many public buildings were damaged and one eyewitness told *The*

Times's stringer that Algeciras looked like a town 'devastated by earthquake'.

On 3 August, Governor Harington had banned the civilian ownership of firearms in Gibraltar. A week later, on 10 August, he issued a Special Warning, the first 'Impartiality Ordinance', intended to quell political arguments among the population of Gibraltar. It ordered people 'to refrain from either acting or speaking publicly in such a manner as to display marked partiality or partisanship to either of the contending parties to the present Spanish dispute', or risk expulsion from the Fortress. This was rich, coming from an establishment that refused to sell coal or fuel to the Republican navy serving the legitimate government, while complying, or so German sources alleged, with formal requests from the Francoist military commandant at Algeciras for items including ammunition. After an HM Dockyard painter called Juan Villa was detained for twenty-one days for saying 'Franco will never take Madrid' while drinking in a Calle Gibraltar bar, all British subjects living in La Línea were warned against 'disloyal and disobedient indiscretions' concerning the 'Junta authorities'. Villa was lucky to be British: if Spanish, he would have got six months digging trenches.

No 'Impartiality Ordinance' was going to stop Gibraltarians of different classes having different beliefs. Generally speaking, the bourgeoisie supported Franco's rebels and the working class were for the Republican government. Already there were divisions in the social life of the street; pro-Republicans gathered at Café Imperial, Petit Bar and Amar's Bakery, while the pro-Francoists, who were going to call themselves 'Nationalists', met at a tobacconist's shop in Market Lane and at the Café Universal, situated at 153 Main Street. The Café was a large, hot, high room with a stage at one side and a long bar at the end; upstairs was the Embassy nightclub. Both businesses were run by two brothers from Malta, Angelo and Biagio D'Amato, a pair of entrepreneurs who were soon supplying Franco's forces. Many prominent Gibraltarians were ardent for Franco, and some even wore Carlist or Falangist uniforms when they were across the frontier in Spain. Other partisans might sport the five-arrow Falangist symbol or a hammer-and-sickle communist brooch.

The Gibraltar City Council election in late 1936 showed the polarisation: two councillors were elected from the pro-Republican left – Agustín Huart and Anthony Baldorino – and two from the pro-Francoist right – Peter Russo and Carlos Pou. The Catholic Church split the sheep from the goats too. The better-off Gibraltarian families sent their boys to Roman Catholic schools in England, such as Ampleforth, Downside and Stonyhurst, where they thought Franco was saintly and the Republic satanic. But not everybody well-to-do was like that. Joshua Hassan, for example, the son of a Jewish cloth merchant, was descended from Sephardi families established on the Rock since the 1720s. Although he went to the bullfights in Spain with the other young Gibraltarians, the young Hassan – known as Salvador – was not sent abroad to school and the inequalities and injustices that he saw closer to home made him left-wing politically, and an ardent supporter of the Republican cause.

A punch-up between a monarchist and a syndicalist was small beer; uglier scenes marked Gibraltar's divisions. Five men got six months in jail for unlawful wounding after they beat up the right-wing cousin of Pablo Larios, Carlos Crooke Larios. On the day they assaulted him, there had been a fresh round of Francoist executions in La Línea; one of those shot was a child. In their defence, the five men said that Carlos Crooke Larios was the man who had signed the death warrants. That may or may not have been correct; it was an unpleasant Gibraltarian named Emilio Griffiths who usually enforced General Queipo de Llano's edicts in La Línea. But Carlos Crooke Larios was certainly working for Nationalist intelligence. He told Gerald Brenan, approvingly, that three Carlist soldiers were following the reporter Jay Allen, hoping to bump him off in some lonely street in Gibraltar or Tangier, and that Allen was a target because his reporting of the massacre at Badajoz had embarrassed Franco's side. (Allen escaped his pursuers.)

*

Another US reporter, Frank L. Kluckhohn from Minnesota (a cousin of Clyde Kluckhohn, the anthropologist of the Navaho), got the scoop on German activities in Spain. Frank happened to be sitting in the lobby of the Cristina Hotel in Seville when the first contingent of German aviators arrived, so he could start putting together the story he eventually sent by courier to Gibraltar for dispatch by wireless across the Atlantic. 'FOREIGN PLANES AT SEVILLE' appeared on the front page of the *New York Times* on 12 August 1936.

Twenty heavy German Junker bombing planes and five German pursuit planes manned by German military pilots arrived at Rebel headquarters in Seville today. The airplanes had been landed from a ship at the Rebel port of Cadiz and were then flown here.

With these and seven Italian Caproni bombers, which arrived during the past few days piloted by Italians, the Rebels are in a position . . . to bomb strategic points, the Loyalist fleet or anything else they wish to attack . . .

General Francisco Franco, leader of the revolt, conferred until a late hour tonight with the chief of the Rebel aviation service, working out details of campaign plans.

The writer saw some of the new German planes. The German Consul here privately admits they were flown by German military aviators.

GERMANS TO BE INSTRUCTORS

The Italian and German aviators are living at the Hotel Cristina here. Neither group is in military uniforms. The Germans are wearing white caps. According to official German sources here, the Nazi aviators will not fly the planes, but will instruct Spanish aviators how to use them.

That initial reticence did not last long. The German air force was going into action, testing its wings. By 13 August, a pair of Ju 52s had been converted into bombers, each carrying six 250 kg bombs in three double magazines. With Flight Captain Henke flying one of the planes, his bombardier Oberleutnant Graf Hoyos managed to land a bomb on the bow of the dreadnought battleship *Jaime I* off Málaga. Then they dropped some aluminium chests of supplies with a message of encouragement from Franco into the Alcázar fortress and military academy at Toledo, then in the midst of a heroic two-month siege.

Meanwhile, on the ground, the Army of Africa, headed by Lieutenant Colonel Juan Yagüe Blanco, became the column of death. Once they had been flown across the Strait of Gibraltar, the thousands of regulars and mercenaries headed north through Spain, killing, mutilating, raping and robbing. When a town or village was taken, the Moorish soldiers were given two hours' licence to do whatever they wanted. The Army of Africa massacred hundreds after Badajoz resisted on 14 August. 'The blood was supposed to be palm deep on the far side of the lane,' Jay Allen reported ten days later. His story of what happened in the bullring – 'It was a hot night. There was a smell. I can't describe and won't describe it' – was so horrific the *Chicago Daily Tribune* would not print it; they later sacked him for being too left-wing.

The German military operation in Spain was camouflaged as a commercial enterprise. Bernhardt, one of the three original emissaries, set up a private Spanish–German company which Franco named HISMA (Compañía Hispano-Marroquí de Transportes SA), with offices in Ceuta and Sevilla, to monopolise the import of 'goods' and the export of raw materials to Germany. With Hermann Göring's assistance, a second holding company, ROWAK (Rohstoffe und Waren Einkaufsgesellschaft) was set up as cover at the German end. Later, other businesses with the same aim were grouped into a new holding company, SOFINDUS (Sociedad Financiera Industrial).

The rearmament of Nazi Germany required 'raw stuff and stock' from Spain and its protectorate in Morocco. Minerals like copper, iron ore and tungsten (then often called wolfram) were vital for military industries. Since Roman times, the colony of Hispania, later España or Spain, had been a source of gold and other valuable metals. The Basque mountains are made of iron; Catalonia holds potash; Almadén in central Spain has a huge mercury mine.

In 1873, during the Second Carlist War, a largely British consortium had bought the freehold to the richest ancient mines in Spain from a desperate government at the bargain price of £3.5 million sterling. These mines were thirty miles from the Gulf of Cádiz at a place called Río Tinto, so named because the copper leachings had stained the local river wine-dark. The Rio Tinto Company went on to create a British enclave, a kind of mini-Gibraltar, in their corner of Andalusia, investing millions to develop a port and jetty at Huelva and build a three-foot-six-inch narrow-gauge railway up to the mines in the hills. About a fifth of all foreign investment in Spain was British, and that mainly in mining. After the Francoist military uprising in July 1936, the Royal Navy destroyer HMS *Boreas* evacuated 130 British women and children from Huelva, taking them the 175 miles to Gibraltar. Some fifty British men stayed behind.

At that time, Rio Tinto employed 8500 Spanish people as miners, digging out pyrites, the valuable ore made of sulphur, iron and copper, or as processors, extracting from the rock sulphuric acid (useful for high explosives) or the iron and copper derivatives that industry so needed. These Spanish miners armed themselves to defend their communities. In late August they were crushed by General Queipo de Llano, commanding Franco's Army of the South, who called the miners 'savages' and 'Marxist scum' and treated them atrociously. He sent the Tercio – the Spanish Foreign Legion – into Huelva, where they left hundreds of slaughtered bodies in the gutters. Other small mining villages were attacked. In Nerva, 288 people were summarily shot after they surrendered; in Aroche, 143 men and women were executed.

On 28 August 1936, Franco's headquarters at Burgos in northern Spain requisitioned all the products of the Rio Tinto mines, under 'Nationalist Decree No. 70'. (The anti-Republicans were now calling themselves Nationalists.) A colonel from Sevilla informed the mine manager, Mr Alexander Hall, that 'the tremendous amount of help from Germany had to be paid partly in Rio Tinto copper and pyrites'. The company also had 'to hand over the sterling proceeds of its deliveries to other countries', in return for pesetas of unpredictable value. The April 1938 Report stated that by this means more than £1,750,000 had passed from the Rio Tinto Company to General Franco's administration.

From late August 1936, Germany was supplying guns and ammunition to Franco's Spain in return for ore. Having unloaded eight thousand rifles, eight million rounds of ammunition and ten thousand stick grenades at La Coruña for General Mola, the German ship *Girgenti* proceeded to Huelva to load up with Rio Tinto copper. In 1937, Nazi Germany got 2.58 million tons of iron ore, pyrites and other minerals from Spain. Speaking in Würzburg in June that year, Adolf Hitler said, 'Germany needs to import ore. That is why we want a Nationalist government in Spain.'

From the beginning, the Germans wanted their support of Franco to be clandestine. Frank Kluckhohn, who had broken the story of the German aircraft for the *New York Times*, had rather better luck than the writer Arthur Koestler, then thirty years old, who found himself on 28 August having a lonely lunch in Seville's Cristina Hotel. Through Franco's brother Nicolás, Koestler had arranged to interview General Queipo de Llano, who had recently issued an edict saying that anyone in the Campo de Gibraltar indulging in 'economic crimes' like smuggling would be shot 'without trial'. When Koestler asked Queipo where he got his foreign war planes, the drunken old general veered off to describe in spittle-flecked detail the atrocities which he claimed were committed by government troops – disembowelling pregnant women, violating children in front of their fathers and then setting them on fire with petrol – which Koestler diagnosed as 'a perfect clinical demonstration in sexual psychopathology'.

The reporter now sat quietly observing the winged swastikas (the Nazi 'Emblem of Distinction') embroidered on the snowy breasts of four German pilots at a nearby table. Their white uniforms and caps – which had also been worn by the security staff at the Berlin Olympics – made the Germans stand out in Seville. Then Koestler was recognised by the Nazi journalist Hans Strindberg (son of the playwright August), who knew him of old in Berlin as a communist. There was a noisy and dramatic row, and Koestler only just managed to bluff his way out and escape to Gibraltar.*

That day, 28 August, in Berlin, Adolf Hitler gave permission for German military personnel in Spain to engage in active combat. (They had already started: Hannes Trautloft in a Heinkel He 51 shot down his first Republican plane, a Breguet XIX, on 25 August.) Lieutenant Colonel Walter Warlimont, a brilliant staff officer from the German Ministry of War, was sent to Spain to take charge of military operations, supporting and advising Franco's Nationalists and co-operating with the Italians. Having visited Franco's headquarters in early September 1936, Warlimont (code-named 'Guido') asked for a force of German ground troops with artillery and armoured vehicles, who arrived by sea in Cádiz on 7 October.

The German ground forces in Spain were code-named Imker or 'beekeeper'. The initial Gruppe Drohne of ten officers and 225 men arrived with forty-one Krupp-manufactured Panzer Mark I tanks, the first of 122 German tanks eventually deployed in Spain. The Imker team wore black berets with a silver death's-head badge to which some added the Nazi swastika, and their leader was the Bavarian tank pioneer Major Wilhelm Ritter von Thoma, who would later lead Panzer tanks in Poland and Russia. After the Second World War, von Thoma told the military commentator Basil Liddell Hart that he had always seen Spain as a training ground, 'the European Aldershot', and the ideal place to field-test new weapons.

In 1937, the most versatile of these was the 8.8 cm FlaK 18 *Flugabwehrkanone* or anti-aircraft gun, later to be feared by experienced Allied infantry more than any other Axis weapon. Originally, the '88'

---

* The Nationalists caught Koestler in Málaga in February 1937. Imprisoned in Seville, he lived under daily threat of execution for three months, before being exchanged in a prisoner swap. Released in La Línea, the French-and-German-speaking Hungarian Jew wrote in his first book in English, *Spanish Testament*: 'On May 14th I trod British soil as a free man.'

was secretly designed and built by Krupp engineers who had evaded the restrictions of the Treaty of Versailles by working for Bofors in Sweden before returning to Essen in Germany in 1931. The '88' had an ingenious sliding breech mechanism and with a good crew could fire fifteen high explosive shells per minute; the gun rested on a pedestal, supported by a four-legged stabilising platform, which gave it a 360-degree traverse. Most important of all, the barrel could be elevated to +85 degrees and lowered to −3 degrees, which widened its capacities. What the Germans discovered in Spain, early in 1937, was the importance of thinking laterally. 'Anti-aircraft gun' was only a category; the '88' could also be an *anti-tank weapon* of great precision, range and power. By the final Spanish Civil War campaigns in 1939, only 7 per cent of the ammunition used by the '88s' was expended on air targets, 93 per cent on ground targets. Only German personnel handled these guns – no Spaniards were allowed near them.

British military intelligence should have been paying more attention; although a sub-committee's report to the Joint Intelligence Committee in October 1937 gave the German anti-aircraft gun high marks, they seemed unaware of its field artillery role. It came as a shock, when the British Army first clashed with the German Afrika Korps in June 1941, to find that the '88' could penetrate a Matilda tank at two thousand yards. And early in 1943 the Americans found that the '88' easily outranged their Sherman tanks' 75 mm guns.

Nazi Germany additionally supplied Spain with thirty-nine more fighter planes, forty-five trucks, twelve thousand cannon shells, twenty thousand 2 cm grenades, eighty million rounds of rifle and machine-gun ammunition, eighty-six thousand kilos of bombs and battlefield communications kit, including radios, telephones, switchboards, five hundred kilometres of field wire and twenty-seven electromechanical Enigma enciphering machines. The secretive Imker Horch-Kompanie or 'beekeeper listening company' not only encrypted communications but intercepted the radio transmissions of the Republican army. (The Republic would fight back: in September 1939 a seven-man team of exiled Spanish Republican cryptologists were working on Enigma machines with Polish and French intelligence.)

Right-wing commentators assert that the Francoist uprising was to foil a Communist International plot to take over Spain. But it is clear that German and Italian military personnel were in Spain first, helping the rebel generals soon after the military *coup d'état* in July 1936. Soviet Russia did not start supplying tanks, guns and planes to help the Spanish Republic until three months later, in October 1936. Joseph Stalin got the opportunity to supply weapons and take Spain's gold reserves in return because the democratic countries – hostile Britain, reluctant France and, crucially, the misinformed USA – refused to help arm the elected government of a sister democracy in case it was 'Red'.

In August 1935 an isolationist US Congress had passed the first Neutrality Act, prohibiting the export of 'arms, ammunition, and implements of war' from the USA to foreign nations at war, but that did not prevent American companies like Texaco, Standard Oil and Socony supplying Franco's rebels with 3.5 million tons of oil on credit. Meanwhile, Ford, Studebaker and General Motors were exporting twelve thousand trucks to the Nationalists, while Dupont evaded the law by cleverly rerouting forty thousand bombs for Spain via Germany. Some of these foodstuffs, fuel and other supplies came through Gibraltar: the Bland Line ships *Gibel Dersa*, *Gibel Zerjon* and *Gibel Kebir* frequently carried goods to and from Seville, Ceuta and Melilla for the Francoists. The M. H. Bland & Co. bicentennial history glides silently over this very profitable period.

In vain did the Spanish Republic's ambassador in London, Pablo de Azcárate, explain that the best way to stop a liberal and democratic regime falling into disorder was to offer moral help to the Republic, as Britain had in the nineteenth century, when it had supported the constitutionalists against the absolutists.

'No British statesman can rise to office without knowing that our

Empire safety must always depend on the existence of a friendly Spain,' wrote Henry Buckley in *The Life and Death of the Spanish Republic*:

At the bottom, the question for them to decide was not as to whether Sr. Giral was a 'nice person' or a 'red hooligan', or whether the Duke of This had been murdered and the Countess of That tortured and imprisoned. No, the sacred duty of Mr Baldwin and of Mr Eden was to decide which Spain better served the needs of our Empire, that of Sr. Giral or that of the Junta of Generals.

And Buckley thought that 'Mr Baldwin and his Ministers' were not paying nearly enough attention to 'the active intervention of Berlin in affairs in Spain' on the side of the junta.

7

Deutschland über Alles

'Non-Intervention' was the new watchword as the British government declared itself neutral in the Spanish conflict. In the summer
of 1936, an increasingly tired Stanley Baldwin was dealing with the
growing constitutional crisis of the selfish and petulant new monarch
Edward VIII, who wanted to marry the American divorcée, Wallis
Warfield Simpson. So the prime minister left foreign policy mostly to
Anthony Eden. Cosy, tweedy, moderately conservative Britain preferred to sit out a Spanish scrap between 'Reds' and 'Whites'. At
the same time Britain was carefully enforcing an arms embargo that
actually favoured those who already had weapons, the Francoists.
The left-wing journalist G. T. Garratt saw a direct continuation of
the British policy towards Ethiopia: 'disarm the weak, and spare the
strong as much trouble as possible'. Neville Chamberlain, the Chancellor of the Exchequer, said Non-Intervention helped 'to maintain
the peace of Europe by confining the war to Spain'. A cheerfully
complacent (and not very well informed) Winston Churchill told the
House of Commons on 8 January 1937 that 'We are equally opposed
both to Nazism and Communism':

When I read of large numbers of German Nazis and Italian Fascists travelling to the Spanish arena to slay large numbers of Russian Bolshevists and
French Communists, I deplore these savage excursions. But when I search
my heart I cannot feel, that if all these armed tourists to Spain were to trans-
fix each other with the simultaneous efficiency of Ivan and Bulbul Amir till
there was no one left, except the Press representatives to tell the tale, the
interests and safety of Britain would be in any way endangered.

The International Supervisory Committee of Non-Intervention, set up by Britain and France and supported by two dozen countries, met over a hundred times in London from 9 September 1936 until early 1939. It was an elaborate farce from the start because the main perpetrators of violent interference also sat on it. Yet in the eyes of Lord Halifax, Foreign Secretary from 1938, its very make-believe and hypocrisy were a useful safety valve, keeping any actual intervention 'entirely non-official, to be denied or at least deprecated by the responsible spokesman of the nation concerned, so that there was neither need nor occasion for any action by Governments to support their nationals'.

The policy, dubbed by its detractors 'malevolent neutrality', confirms what J. B. Priestley wrote of the English then: 'What the rest of the world often fails to realise is that we are a nation of idealistic simpletons frequently governed and manipulated by cynics.'

The Governor of Gibraltar is by definition an agent of HM Government. In his memoirs, Sir Charles Harington explains why he felt it necessary to placate General Franco:

People in this country have never realised our position in Gibraltar. They have never understood how dependent we are on Spain, and how vital it is for us to be friends with our neighbours in Spain whatever their politics . . . Whites, or Reds, or whatever they might be.

The Gibraltarian is not a technical man. Nearly all our carpenters and masons, and many other tradesmen are Spaniards. We depend on Spain also for all our vegetables, fruit, flowers, etc; nothing is grown in Gibraltar. The coaling of ships is all done by Spanish labour. Gibraltar depends on being able to get some 6,000 Spanish workmen in through her gates daily and out again at night.

Ever since the Spanish War started there were difficulties. At one moment Spain closed the frontier; at the next, she opened it with all sorts of reservations. The difficulties over passes were never ending . . . At the same time I am quite prepared to state that the country administered by General Franco was much better administered than it had been before the war. There was at any rate a system . . .

Indeed, there was a system: the reign of terror. Franco's forces took the province of Cádiz by September 1936, executing over three thousand people in the process. In the first week after the city of Málaga fell on 8 February 1937, another 3500 people were shot, and many thousands more were locked up all across Andalusia. Civilians fleeing the repression along the road to Almería were bombed and machine-gunned by Italian aircraft and shelled from the sea; several thousand more were killed.

'I was never privileged to meet General Franco,' wrote General Harington, 'but I had many dealings with him, and I shall always be grateful to him for numerous matters in connection with Gibraltar, and especially for his consideration regarding the Royal Calpe Hunt . . . [I]n both my last seasons General Franco was good enough to grant permission [to hunt in Spain], and this will ever be gratefully remembered in Gibraltar.'

So the British officers and ladies and gentlemen of the Royal Calpe Hunt could once again ride freely, away from the confinement of the Rock and its oppressive 'Levanters', the muggy turbans of cloud that can settle on the Rock like a headache. The Larios acres were now purged of left-wing troublemakers, and the Francoist *¡ARRIBA ESPAÑA!* was painted in white on the Campo de Gibraltar roads. Near Los Barrios, Lady Harington once saw a man come out of his house waving his arms. She felt he must be glad to see the hounds once again, but discovered he was furious, because 'he thought all those in pink coats must be Reds!' On another day that winter, a Spanish sentry snatched the red ribbon warning that a horse was a 'kicker' off its tail and ground it into the sand with his heel. After that, kicking horses had to be identified by yellow ribbons, rather than red.

General Harington left Gibraltar on 24 October 1938. In retirement he continued to speak up for General Franco after the civil war had ended, telling twelve hundred ex-servicemen in Eastbourne on 25 June 1939: 'I think General Franco's main idea is to be a friend of England . . . I am sure there is no hostile intention towards Gibraltar.'

Harington died in Cheltenham on 22 October 1940, not long after the publication of his memoir *Tim Harington Looks Back*. Things had changed. 'As I write,' he says on page 207, 'air attacks are being made on the Rock.'

The women and children have been evacuated and Gibraltar is prepared for whatever may happen. Gibraltar may, I fear, have a bad time . . .

The danger to my mind is from guns mounted in Spain, which might make the harbour and dockyard untenable. In the Spanish War Franco mounted some heavy howitzers at Pelayo, not far from Algeciras . . . [T]hey could have reached our harbour and so could guns if mounted near San Roque or the Queen of Spain's Chair.

Harington said the Francoist guns were first placed in response to the shelling of Algeciras by the government battleship *Jaime I* on 7 August 1936.

General Franco started to put guns to defend the Bay, and he mounted a number of approximately 6-inch guns at Carnero and at various other points, and some 12-inch howitzers near Pelayo . . . Our Press made a certain amount of copy in respect of these guns and the danger to Gibraltar.

One of the first press men to see those guns in March 1937 was Noel Monks of the *Daily Express*. The big genial blond Australian had just endured an unpleasant encounter with paunchy, flabby-faced *Generalísimo* Franco, 'the most unmilitary figure I have ever seen', in his military headquarters in Seville. Franco was shouting in Spanish and banging his fist on a copy of the *Daily Express* while his bullying press chief, Captain Luís Bolín, threatened Monks with a firing squad for evading censorship. 'You can't shoot me, I'm British,' protested Monks, while desperately trying to read Franco's newspaper upside down. 'ANOTHER ITALIAN ROUT IN SPAIN', he saw, and his own byline, '*by Noel Monks*', even though when he had telephoned in the story from the Bar Basque in St-Jean-de-Luz he had emphasised: 'My name not, repeat, NOT to be used', knowing that any mention of the foreign forces helping Franco was forbidden by the Nationalist censors. His story was quite true: the Republicans and the International Brigades had indeed ignominiously thrashed the Italians at the battle of Guadalajara. Monks felt that 'to write about the Spanish Civil War without being able to mention Italians and Germans was making oneself a party to Franco's hoodwinking the world into believing that his revolt against the democratic government of Spain was an all-Spanish affair, opposed to a gang of Moscow-led thugs'.

Monks was duly expelled from Nationalist Spain. The *Express* sent their Gibraltar stringer, Pepe, up to Seville to drive Monks the five hours back to the Rock, and the two men gave a friendly lift in their car to twenty-five-year-old Randolph Churchill, Winston's ebullient son. Young Churchill, who had dropped out of Oxford to become a journalist, was unimpressed by Spain's internal conflict, seeing it as 'just a lot of bloody dagoes killing each other'. But as they drove from Tarifa towards Algeciras, at a point overlooking the Rock they came across hundreds of sun-tanned Germans, wearing only shorts, boots and peaked caps, toiling in the sun, building emplacements for gigantic field guns. One artillery piece was already in position, pointing straight at Gibraltar. Monks asked Pepe how long this had been going on.

'Some weeks. We don't mention it – if we want to come and go between Gib and Spain.'

'By Christ, I'm going to mention it!' roared Randolph Churchill. 'I'm going to cable the old man as soon as I get to Gib.'

Young Churchill soon found himself banned too.

Noel Monks's own expulsion from Franco's Spain meant the *Daily Express* could send him back to France's Pays Basque in pursuit of 'Potato' Jones, a colourful character among the British sea captains who were trying to get food into the Spanish Basque country, then blockaded by Franco's navy. Monks arrived in Bilbao on 23 April 1937. Three days later, he was one of the five foreign reporters who covered one of the most controversial stories of the civil war, telling the world about the destruction of the Basque town of Gernika or Guernica by a fleet of German and Italian aeroplanes flying for Franco.

Admiral Canaris negotiated a deal that put all the military support for Spain under General Franco's command and control. The Condor Legion (*die Legion Condor* in German, *la Legión Cóndor* in Spanish) was an independent *Fliegerkorps* or air corps, led by the bulldog-faced *Generalmajor* Hugo Sperrle, who was code-named 'Sander'. Adolf Hitler himself described Sperrle as 'one of my two most brutal-looking generals', and he sometimes used him at meetings not to talk, but just to sit there, massive, scowling, glaring through his monocle, to intimidate any opposition. Sperrle's aggressive chief of staff was Colonel Wolfram von Richthofen, a cousin of the Red Baron. In April 1937, the Condor Legion was hovering over northern Spain and the tiny Basque republic called Euzkadi, which had been granted autonomy on 7 October 1936 by the Spanish Republic on condition that it fought on their side.

The Condor Legion field-tested weapons of war for Hermann Göring's Luftwaffe; Spain was their laboratory or live firing range. All the new German bombers and fighter planes went through their paces in Spain: the Dornier Do 17, the Heinkel He 111, the Messerschmitt Bf 109, and the Junkers Ju 87 Stuka. About 125 Luftwaffe officers and 280 NCOs gained their spurs in Condor Legion fighters.

In the spring of 1937, Condor Legion aircraft were being used as mobile artillery in close support operations for the Spanish and Italian infantry advancing against the Basques, testing the efficacy of different mixes of incendiary and blast bombs and even 'devil's eggs' – a drop-tank of petrol fitted with two 10 kg explosives – to destroy infrastructure and terrorise ground troops. The Basques had no air force to speak of, just six fighter planes and one outstanding pilot, Captain Felipe del Río Crespo, who shot down seven planes before the Condor Legion downed him on 22 April 1937 near Lamiako.

In the raid on Gernika on Monday 26 April, twenty-seven Axis bombers dropped around twenty-five tons of explosives (the largest bombs weighed 250 kg) and some ten tons of thermite incendiaries on the undefended town, while up to three dozen fighter planes swooped down to scatter smaller ordnance and to strafe the running people. The German bomber aircraft included the VB/88 experimental flight of one Dornier Do 17 and two Heinkel He 111s, led by Lieutenant Rudolf Freiherr von Moreau, as well as twenty-one Junkers Ju 52s in three squadrons. The Italian Aviazione Legionaria contributed three Savoia-Marchetti SM.79 bombers. As for the fighter planes, in addition to Lieutenant Harro Harder's seven Heinkel He 51 biplanes, there were six brand-new Messerschmitt Bf 109 monoplanes led by Lieutenant Colonel Günther Lützow, and twenty or more Fiat CR.32 fighters, flown by Italian aviators.

In an air raid which lasted for nearly three and a half hours, the bomber planes first dropped a few bombs to drive everyone into the air-raid shelters, then devastated three quarters of the town with waves of heavy bombing while the chasers circled the town to harry and machine-gun people fleeing from their burning homes. One of the witnesses was a Basque priest, Father Alberto de Onaindia. 'Through the streets wandered the animals brought to market, donkeys, pigs, chickens. In the midst of that conflagration we saw people who fled screaming, praying or gesticulating against the attackers.' The town's mayor said that in just one air-raid shelter that was buried, 450 citizens died. Franco's forces captured the town soon afterwards and claimed that the 'Reds' had blown up their own town with dynamite and petrol. The Francoists said only eight people perished; the Basque government asserted that 1684 died. Bombing worked as an instrument of terror: mass evacuations of civilians followed.

The event inspired an international propaganda war that included Pablo Picasso's masterpiece *Guernica*, whose cry of pain on behalf of the victims of war was heard around the world. The destruction of Gernika finally proved to those who believed G. L. Steer's reports in *The Times* and the *New York Times* that Germany and Italy were intervening violently in Spain, whatever the appeasing

British government was saying. It showed the ruthlessness of modern warfare against civilians. Ordinary people everywhere realised that they too could be hit by blast bombs, or machine-gunned from the air as they ran from homes set alight by incendiary bombs. This was war today; not professional soldiers killing each other in muddy trenches, but civilians at home, cowering under the stairs while the roof of the house came tumbling down to bury them.

April 1937 saw two British technological advances in the art of war. On the 13th, the aircraft carrier HMS *Ark Royal* was launched at Birkenhead before a cheering crowd of twenty thousand. Maud Lygon, Sir Samuel Hoare's wife, fresh off the newly recommissioned Admiralty yacht *Enchantress*, broke the bottle on the bows. Two thousand men had taken three and a half years to build the ship, at a cost of £2.33 million, the largest Admiralty contract since the end of the Great War. The *Ark* would carry nearly sixteen hundred men and sixty aircraft that could rise from hangar to flight deck in giant double-decker lifts. A Blackburn Skua flying off the *Ark* would be the first plane to shoot down an enemy aircraft in the Second World War. Britain was slowly rearming and strengthening the fleet; the 1937 naval construction programme included five capital ships, two aircraft carriers, seven cruisers, sixteen destroyers, seven submarines and forty-five miscellaneous vessels including minesweepers and depot ships. Naval construction spending had risen from £12 million in the disarmament years of 1931–4 to £62 million in 1937.

Also in April 1937, British signals intelligence made a great breakthrough. Everyone knows that Bletchley Park – the war station of GCCS, the Government Code and Cipher School* – did sterling code-breaking in the Second World War, but wide-ranging decryption work of a high standard had continued between the world wars as well. Since 1926, GCCS had been sharing Broadway Buildings

---

* It was originally spelled 'Cypher', but we have modernised to 'cipher' throughout this book.

in London with its controlling organisation, the Secret Intelligence Service. Between 1934 and 1937, during the Ethiopian crisis and afterwards, GCCS increased the staff of the Italian sub-unit of its Naval Section from five to eighteen members. By 1935, the cryptographers had broken some of the high-grade ciphers of the Italian armed forces and were also making progress with Italy's encrypted diplomatic telegrams.

In 1936, the classical scholar and cryptographer Dillwyn 'Dilly' Knox was working on Italian naval and military messages. He had cracked the superenciphered codebooks the Italians used during the Abyssinian crisis but now, in the Spanish Civil War, he found that both the Italians and the Spanish had bought electromechanical Enigma enciphering machines from their German allies, and all three naval forces were using them for their messages. The codebook was named *DEI*, an acronym of Deutschland, España, Italia.

The first Enigma machines looked like elaborate boxed typewriters. They had no plugboard, but used the machines' complicated wiring and movable wheels to scramble the alphabetic letters many, many times, although following certain rules through all their multiple permutations. One rule is that no letter can encipher as itself. So 'A' pressed on the keyboard can never light up as 'A' on the enciphered lampboard. This can be very helpful to the unscrambler. Dilly Knox waited for an operator to make a mistake, and in April 1937, the same month that the Germans and the Italians bombed Gernika, twenty naval messages were sent out on the same setting, strictly against the standard procedure that operators were trained in. Knox pounced. Through familiarity with Italian naval procedures and vocabulary, letter frequencies and guesswork of probable words and standard phrases, he was able to read the messages coherently and then from them to reconstruct the way the machine and its wheels had been wired, through the reverse-engineering process that he called 'buttoning up'. Knox soon found that the rotors and reflectors of all Franco's machines were wired up in exactly the same way and were never changed, probably in order to ease communications with the Italians and Germans. He got a Spanish expert, Wilfred Bodsworth, to take over decrypting in that language.

To intercept coded wireless messages for the cryptographers, you need a good wireless intercept, a so-called WI (pronounced 'Y') listening service to capture exactly what is sent over the airwaves, and a radio direction-finding or RDF service to pinpoint where it is coming from. Windmill Hill in Gibraltar, known as 'Windy', played an important part in picking up Italian and Spanish signals. In the Mediterranean, there was also Dingli in Malta, and Britain and France shared a wireless station on the Île Sainte-Marguerite off the Pointe de la Croisette at Cannes in southern France. In September 1939, 'Windy' caught a new wireless station reporting shipping movements to Madrid, and pinpointed it near Algeciras railway station.

One of Britain's failures in the First World War was that naval intelligence could not communicate properly in real time with naval operations. To make these systems cohere, Commander Norman Denning set up a new Operational Intelligence Centre inside the Admiralty in 1937, with a tracking room that co-ordinated information about ship movements from wireless intercept and radio direction finding. Denning's idea was to link the navy's brain with its limbs by creating a centre to take in and assess information and then transmit it to the right place at the right time. The Operational Intelligence Centre or OIC, which grew Mediterranean branches at Malta and later Alexandria, was a crucial reconfiguration of naval intelligence, and like the newly co-ordinated British air defence system, would more than earn its keep when war came.

'Can the Powers Bring Peace to Spain?' Winston Churchill asked the House of Commons on 2 April 1937. The picture he painted of the left in Spain was as lurid as one of his sunset oil paintings:

[B]lood, alas, continues to flow, not only on the fighting fronts, but far behind them. The odious cruelties and murders by the Communists and

Anarchists of helpless people belonging to classes for whose extermination they thirst, still persist at Barcelona. The revelations of what occurred at during the Red Terror at Malaga, where perhaps ten thousand unoffending persons were foully slaughtered, have recently been confirmed by a credible British witness, Major Yeats-Brown, well-known as 'Bengal Lancer'. The bound corpses of butchered hostages, which the sea casts up upon the French coast, bring home to French people the horrible realities of the Spanish conflict.

This piece of rhetoric is numerically exaggerated; the death toll in 'Red' Málaga was actually around eleven hundred murdered, not ten thousand. The *'incontrolados'* of the Republican left murdered many, but the Nationalist right killed many more, deliberately, as policy, and told a lot of lies about it. In his 1939 book, *Memoirs of a Spanish Nationalist*, the Catholic publisher Antonio Bahamonde y Sánchez de Castro (who defected from Franco's side, appalled by what he witnessed) confessed to earlier fabricating atrocities by the left in the course of his work as General Queipo de Llano's Commissioner for Propaganda:

I had the duty of propagandizing in Badajoz that in Málaga [the Republicans] had assassinated during the seven months of 'red' domination some fifteen thousand persons, of rightist tendencies, that they had murdered all the nuns after raping them . . . Of Málaga we said the priests had been killed and hung on meat hooks in the butcher shops with a card attached on which was written: 'Pork for Sale' . . .

The 'credible British witness' cited by Churchill, Major Francis Yeats-Brown, was a fellow alumnus of Harrow and a member of Oswald Mosley's right-wing January Club, an officer who openly supported Franco, Mussolini and Hitler. Adolf Hitler said that the 1935 Hollywood movie *The Lives of a Bengal Lancer*, loosely adapted from Yeats-Brown's memoir *Bengal Lancer* and starring Gary Cooper, was one of his favourite films. He saw it three times and liked it 'because it depicted a handful of Britons holding a continent in thrall. That was how a superior race must behave and the film was compulsory viewing for the S.S.'*

Churchill, like many aristocratic or bourgeois conservatives, feared and loathed communism, seeing the Russian Revolution much as Edmund Burke saw the French. Hence his dwelling on the atrocities of the Republican side, while, in his view, the Francoist Nationalists practised only 'grim retaliation': 'Peace and order reign over the broad areas of Nationalist Spain, and industry and agriculture pursue their course. Trains run. Food and petrol can be freely purchased. All the decencies of civilised life appear upon the surface, but the slightest signs of disaffection are repressed with prompt and ruthless executions.'

Gibraltar was a fount of stories about Republican atrocities. The Rock was where foreign journalists often met English-speaking upper-class refugees who justified their panicked flight from Spain with alarming tales of frightfulness. On 21 August 1936, Robert Neville of the *New York Herald Tribune* noted: 'In Gibraltar I found to my surprise that most of the newspapermen had been sending only "horror" stories. They do not seem to be awake to the terrible international implications in this story.'

In her book *Death's Other Kingdom*, Gamel Woolsey wrote that after she and Gerald Brenan were evacuated from Málaga to Gibraltar by British warship during the civil war, 'safe' Gibraltar seemed more unpleasant than 'Red' Málaga. Refugees of every class and party had carried their fears and hatreds into neutral territory where their anxious excitement was contagious, making everyone feel insecure. The rich refugees in the Rock Hotel were particularly disagreeable; one lunch in the dining room would make anyone a communist, she thought. 'You felt concentrated there all the

---

* General Franco also enjoyed *The Lives of a Bengal Lancer*. In the anti-Semitic 'Children of Israel' chapter of *European Jungle* (1939) Yeats-Brown says the film was financed and produced by Jews, and that a Jewish stockbroker and a Jewish accountant helped with his earnings from it. 'So the Jews have never done me any harm.' Some of his best friends . . .

irresponsible stupidity of modern wealth. The sort of conversation you would hear from the tables around you, smug, self-complacent, secure in the power of unearned money . . . made me, for one, long for a cataclysm.' Ignorant deprecation of the Spanish people and indifference to their sufferings were combined with violent prejudices and 'an embarrassingly erotic lust for preposterous atrocity stories'.

They were generally not so much *for* the Nationalists . . . as *against* the Reds. And it would have been amusing, if it had not been so discouraging to anyone who would like to think well of the human intelligence, to listen to some stalwart Englishman or Englishwoman holding forth about the 'Communists' and their extraordinary atrocities, then, sometimes, to see a look of doubt and hesitation come over their faces, and the uncertain question 'Which side *are* the Moors fighting on?'

Gerald Brenan was questioned about one story being spread by Governor Sir Charles Harington himself. Was it true that the Reds in Málaga had laid naked nuns in the roadway and then squashed them flat with a road-levelling steam-roller? Brenan said Málaga did not possess a steam-roller and no nuns had been squashed. Gamel Woolsey came to realise 'what atrocity stories really are: they are the pornography of violence. The dreamy lustful look that accompanies them, the full enjoyment of horror (especially noticeable in respectable elderly Englishmen speaking of the rape or torture of naked nuns: it is significant that they are always *naked* in such stories), show only too plainly their erotic source.'

Sir Charles Harington's vision was, like that of other expats on the Rock, limited, though he did not lack a sense of humour. In his memoir of Gibraltar he described his 'worst crisis' as that moment when he had one hand on a tricky yacht tiller, and the other holding a hard-boiled egg in which his false teeth were wedged. Harington once walked down a street so engrossed in a newspaper's sports reports that he collided with a circus elephant. Similarly, in his time on the Rock, the white-moustached Governor of Gibraltar was busy with his cricket, his yachting and his riding to hounds, and he failed to see the German elephant in the room.

May 1937 was a critical month in British constitutional history. First there was the coronation of King George VI on 10 May, replacing his brother Edward VIII, who had abdicated in December 1936. Then, on 28 May, Neville Chamberlain took over as prime minister from an exhausted Stanley Baldwin. It was also a bad month for the German Reich. On 6 May 1937, the hydrogen airship LZ 129 *Hindenburg* caught fire in New Jersey and crashed in flames, killing thirty-six people. Then, at the end of the month, the Spanish Republicans bombed a German pocket battleship.

The powers – Britain, France, Italy and Germany – had divided up the Spanish coastline to police for breaches of Non-Intervention; Germany's patrol area lay between Murcia and the Balearics, and two Spanish Republican aircraft flown by Russian pilots attacked the *Deutschland* in the late afternoon of 29 May, off Ibiza. The Tupolev SB-2 high-speed bombers allegedly mistook the neutral German *Panzerschiff* for the Francoist cruiser *Canarias* and dropped a dozen bombs, two of which struck the *Deutschland*. The most effective punched through the foredeck and exploded in the seamen's mess, killing twenty-three sailors, seriously injuring nineteen and wounding three score more. The German sailors tried to fight a fire made worse by aviation fuel combusting, but their medical facilities were overwhelmed.

The *Deutschland* radioed ahead and limped towards Gibraltar. The battleship arrived, with her Kriegsmarine flag at half-mast, at sunset on Sunday 30 May 1937. It was Corpus Christi, the day when boys and girls dressed in white process along Gibraltar's Main Street in the Roman Catholic religious festival celebrating the Solemnity of the Most Holy Body and Blood of Christ. Most Gibraltarians are Catholic and the then Catholic Bishop of Gibraltar, Richard Fitzgerald, described by Admiral Evans as 'a southern Irishman, soaked in intrigue and as untrustworthy and, in my opinion, as disloyal as can be', was virulently pro-Franco, seeing him as 'fighting for the cause of God'. Now, at the end of this sacred day, fifty-three wounded, burned and dying men on Franco's side were being stretchered to the military hospital. A request for more help was flashed to England, and four nurses from Queen Alexandra's Imperial Military Nursing Service were flown out by RAF flying boat. Gibraltar was galvanised: Codali Funeral Services in Devil's Tower Road worked flat out through the night and most of the next day preparing coffins for the dead; a mass grave was dug at the eastern end of North Front Cemetery; the garrison spruced itself up for a funeral parade.

The *Daily Express* reporter Alan Moorehead had also arrived in Gibraltar that day and saw the *Deutschland* tie up in the twilight. It was a solemn and ominous scene as the sailors struggled to get the first coffin silently down the gangplank. In their nervousness, they dropped it on the dock:

Then suddenly a curious thing happened. The hundreds of young Nazis standing on the deck broke their ranks and scrambled over the side. In scores and dozens they dropped on to the wharf and there was a kind of panic – a sort of mass fear among them. That bomb, falling so unexpectedly and fatally among them, had broken their nerve. All they wanted was to get onto dry land again and get away from the sight of the wounded and the dead.

Most of them were fair-haired boys of eighteen or so and this was their first experience of war – real war – not the war of parades and bands.

The panic only lasted half an hour or so. The officers snapped orders to the sailors, and you could see how they pulled themselves together and a hard set look came into their faces . . .

At 11 a.m. on Monday 31 May, the *Deutschland* mysteriously headed out to sea again, leaving behind only the German chaplain and an interpreter. At 5 p.m., a dozen small lorries from the Royal Army Service Corps drove slowly out of the Dockyard North Gate. Each vehicle carried a pair of coffins, draped in the 1935 red, black and white *Reichskriegflagge* with the Nazi *Hakenkreuz* or swastika at the heart, and each vehicle was escorted by four British sailors in whites or four pith-helmeted Royal Marines from HMS *Arethusa*, together with a solemn blue-uniformed Gibraltar policeman. They drove slowly along Reclamation Road and the Causeway and then turned right along Devil's Tower Road. Some civilians watching the procession took off their hats or lowered their heads as the swasti-ka'ed coffins went past. Others resented this partisan demonstration of respect, remembering that nine months earlier when the Repub-lican destroyer *Lepanto*, bombed by a German plane, brought in its dead and wounded, the bodies had been hurried off and the ship sent packing after Franco sent a threatening telegram to the governor.

This time Governor Harington gave full ceremonial to the Ger-man dead. The silent cortège was preceded by a Royal Navy detach-ment of sailors in immaculate whites with webbing belt and leather gaiters, followed by the buglers of the King's Own Yorkshire Light Infantry and the band of the Royal Marines. Harington himself was on parade in his bemedalled white tropical dress uniform and a Wolseley-pattern pith helmet with swan plumes, attended by aides, the senior naval and military officers of the Fortress, the civil digni-taries and foreign consuls. Every vessel in the harbour lowered its flag at half-mast and sent a detachment, so there were American, British, Dutch and Turkish sailors also present.

At the cemetery gates under the great white bluff of greyish lime-stone, the RN Destroyer Squadron formed a guard of honour. *Are-thusa*'s matelots carried the coffins of fellow seamen to the graveside accompanied by solemn music from the Royal Marines. The Dean of the Anglican Cathedral intoned the opening prayer, and the German chaplain read the committal. As the mass grave was closed, a firing party from HMS *Despatch* saluted with three volleys. The Yorkshire buglers sounded a poignant Last Post and Reveille.

When Hitler received the news, around Sunday lunchtime, that the *Deutschland* – the name of the Fatherland! – had been bombed, he flew into one of his terrible screaming rages. At first he wanted to shell Valencia, the seat of the Spanish government, and to declare war on the Spanish Republic, but the army and navy chiefs restrained him, although both Germany and Italy withdrew from all Non-Intervention talks and patrols. His revenge came early on Monday 31 May, the day of the mass funerals in Gibraltar. The pocket battleship *Admiral Scheer*, accompanied by four German destroyers, *Seeadler*, *Albatros*, *Leopard* and *Luch*, rounded Cape Gata and lined up seven miles offshore from the port of Almería. At 5.30 a.m., they opened fire.

When the Moors ruled Spain, says Gerald Brenan, Almería was 'the Manchester of Europe', a city inhabited by a quarter of a million people who produced and exported exquisite gold and silk tissue, pottery and glass. Around fifty-four thousand people were still living in the Andalusian port when the German warships started lobbing the first of some 275 shells at them. The Germans claimed they only shelled 'the harbour works' and 'hostile batteries'. In fact, their one-hour bombardment knocked out the telephone and electrical systems and hit the cathedral, the railway station, the park, the bullring, the Credit Bank, a church and the office of the newspaper *Adelante*, in a series of violent explosions which completely destroyed seventy buildings and damaged hundreds more. Thirty-one people were killed, scores wounded and thousands left homeless.

At the same time as the German sailors were being buried in Gibraltar, 180 miles away in Almería there was grief and tears for the victims of Hitler's reprisals. The US newsman William L. Shirer wrote in his *Berlin Diary* that he felt like screaming himself: 'Thus Hitler has his cheap revenge and a few more Spanish women and children are dead.' Alan Moorehead, who visited the town, called it 'one of the most calculated and cruel acts of modern times'. The Spanish Republic's Minister of Defence, Indalecio Prieto, wanted to attack the German fleet even at the cost of starting a world war, but President Manuel Azaña restrained him, remembering the disasters of 1898 when Spain lost Cuba to the USA. The British reporter Henry Buckley attended the funeral of a trade unionist who had died of his injuries in the attack on Almería. He watched the working men following the coffin, dressed in their best, looking clumsy and out of place, clumping along behind the hearse. Looking at their worn faces and gnarled hands he wondered why so few middle-class people cared how much the working masses suffered.

Hitler, ever volatile, then changed his mind about the Gibraltar burials. Gallant German war dead should not lie in foreign soil, but must be brought back to the homeland for ceremonial honouring of their noble sacrifice, in full view of Joseph Goebbels's Propaganda Ministry.

On 11 June 1937, the *Deutschland* returned to Gibraltar to pick up the twenty German sailors discharged from hospital and the dead bodies. News of the German shelling of Almería had outraged supporters of the Spanish Republic in Gibraltar, so this time there were no parades, and no opportunities for demonstrations by workers in the dockyard. The disinterment of the German corpses took place in the dark, by torchlight. The lead-lined coffins were taken in their crates to Stone Jetty at Bayside, the closest landing place to the cemetery, from where a lighter ferried them out to the battleship. The ghastly process took all night. The *Deutschland* returned to Wilhelmshaven on 16 June with the Non-Intervention Patrol identification stripes of red, white and black still painted over her eleven-inch gun turrets and with her gangways draped in black. In Germany, Hitler himself came on board in his brown uniform to address the crew. There were now thirty-two dead; all the Nazi top brass attended the packed, flower-laden funeral at Kiel the next day.

The Times reported the funeral on Friday 18 June. In the same issue, the paper ran an interview with General Franco obtained by the Burgos correspondent James Holburn just before Nationalist soldiers took Bilbao in the Basque country. Among other things, Franco denied that Gibraltar could ever be the cause of 'an anti-British policy in Spain. For England, Gibraltar has lost much of its importance,' he said, ominously, incorrectly.

8

Guns over Gibraltar

In Parliament in June and July 1937, the Labour opposition, as well as asking awkward questions about the bombing of Gernika, pressed the national government about what the newspapers were calling 'Guns over Gibraltar', the heavy artillery trained on the Rock and seen by Noel Monks and Randolph Churchill. Foreign Secretary Anthony Eden, who had earlier stated that 'the existence of German heavy guns at Ceuta has not been confirmed', gave a guarded response:

I understand that it is the case that General Franco has installed batteries on the coast between Algeciras and Tarifa. My information does not, however, bear out the Press reports to the effect that German experts have assisted in mounting these batteries. The position is naturally being kept under close review . . .

The next day, Leslie Hore-Belisha (the man who got 'Belisha beacons' placed at pedestrian crossings, and now the Secretary of State for War) stonewalled all technical military queries.

Mr Seymour Cocks (Broxtowe, Lab): Can the Minister say whether these guns include 16-inch Krupp guns and 12-inch howitzers; and is it not a fact that we have always had a friendly understanding with the Spanish government that these heights facing Gibraltar shall not be fortified?

Mr Leslie Hore-Belisha (Plymouth, Devonport, L. Nat): That may or may not be the case. (Laughter.)

On Monday 19 July Winston Churchill reiterated that the heavy howitzers mounted near Gibraltar represented a genuine threat.

A 12-inch howitzer properly mounted could hurl a projectile 10 or 12 miles, and within range they could quickly destroy the dockyard at Gibraltar and render the bay untenable to His Majesty's ships . . . Could they obstruct or close the Straits? Where were they sited and at whose instigation had they been erected? ('Hear, hear' said the MPs.) . . . [N]o such guns existed before the outbreak of the civil war. Where, then, had they come from? Were they from the [German] foundries of Krupp or [the Italian foundries] of Ansaldo? . . . Were these weapons the price which General Franco had to pay to certain Powers for their assistance?

Then David Lloyd George weighed in:

Why were these very astute rulers, Mussolini and Hitler, throwing themselves with such energy into this contest? It was not their sympathies with the political principles of General Franco that had made them send 80,000 troops, hundreds of aeroplanes, and heavy guns to Spain . . . Spain was in the most vital strategic position for us of almost any country in Europe . . . [Hitler and Mussolini] wanted Spain with its great population, natural resources of copper and iron, and with its immense strategic opportunities.

Finally, the Foreign Office sent Viscount Cranborne, its parliamentary under-secretary, out to bat. He played the Harington defence, that the guns in the neighbourhood of Gibraltar were only mounted to fend off future bombardments:

VISCOUNT CRANBORNE – That is all I have to say.

Mr. CHURCHILL – It is not nearly enough. Are they 12-inch guns or howitzers?

VISCOUNT CRANBORNE – It would not be in the public interest to give the information. They are of smallish calibre, and we are confident they constitute no menace to Gibraltar. There is no truth in the story of any 12-inch howitzers dominating the fort of Gibraltar or the harbour . . .

Mr. ATTLEE – Do these guns dominate the passage of the Mediterranean by ships? Are they endangered by these guns?

VISCOUNT CRANBORNE – These guns fire from Spain across the Straits, but in the view of the military experts they do not constitute a military menace.

In fact, between March and June 1937 Whitehall had requested three reports about Nationalist gun emplacements facing Gibraltar. The reports stated the awkward facts: 'German and Italian artillery experts have . . . advise[d] and assist[ed] in mounting the Spanish defences of the Straits', and 'the 12-inch guns being mounted near Mount Bujeo are howitzers not ordinarily designed for use against warships . . . it is quite possible that they be so placed as to be invulnerable from the 9.2-inch guns on the Rock and at the same time be able to throw their projectiles onto the Dockyard.'

Churchill returned to the theme on 6 August:

Large howitzers and many secondary guns have been mounted on both sides of the Straits of Gibraltar at Algeciras and Ceuta. The fire of these guns interlaces across the waterway . . . It is one thing for a fortress to fire at a gun and quite another for a gun to fire at a harbour. The anchorage of Gibraltar might at any time be rendered unusable by the British fleet.

The threat to Gibraltar even entered popular fiction. J. M. Walsh, a prolific Australian author of middlebrow espionage novels, published *Spies in Spain*, set during the Spanish Civil War, in 1937. Four intrepid heroes, led by Colonel Ormiston of the Secret Service, discover a tunnel, started by the Republic and continued by the Francoist rebels, being excavated from Algeciras to Ceuta under the Strait of Gibraltar, infiltrate the workings and blow up the spur leading off towards Gibraltar. The moral of the book seems to be that though the civil war is a Spanish matter, they touch anything British at their peril.

In reality, the 'Guns over Gibraltar' issue would divide opinion for the rest of the Spanish Civil War. Pro-Francoists pooh-poohed their very existence; pro-Republicans stressed the danger to British strategic interests. The Spanish-language newspaper *Madrid*, published in Paris, splashed a big story on Thursday 17 March 1938, 'A SECRET GERMAN PLAN to capture Gibraltar in six hours'. Accompanied by a dramatic black-and-white map of the Strait of Gibraltar showing a swarm of planes and ships and arrows targeting the Rock, the story said the coast from Tarifa to Algeciras was armed with long-range German guns, and Ceuta, Málaga and Mallorca would act as bases for German and Italian submarines. A German colonel was quoted as saying that 'When the war starts, not a British, French or allied ship will get through the strait of Gibraltar.' The unnamed author of the article says he does not know when the surprise attack will take place, but draws attention to the recent arrival of a German general '*que se llama Zander o Zanner*'. ('Sander' was the code-name of the first commandant of the Condor Legion in Spain, General Hugo Sperrle.)

The September 1938 edition of the fourth 'Penguin Special', *Searchlight on Spain*, written by the so-called 'Red Duchess', Katharine Stewart-Murray, Duchess of Atholl, an elected MP, carried a dramatic new map opposite the title page 'giving a general idea of the guns threatening Gibraltar and the Straits'. And in March 1939, Jonathan Cape published *Gibraltar and the Mediterranean*, a polemic by G. T. Garratt. Geoffrey Garratt had covered the Abyssinian War for the *Manchester Guardian* and spent much of 1937 and 1938 working in eastern Spain with Eleanor Rathbone's National Joint Committee for Spanish Relief. In 1938 he had published two books: *Mussolini's Roman Empire*, a 'Penguin Special' which sold an astonishing three hundred thousand copies, and *The Shadow of the Swastika*, dedicated to 'the Englishmen of the International Brigade, who died in what may well be the last fight for English freedom', a bracingly partisan study of how fascism was infecting English society while its people hid their heads in the sand.

In the third part of *Gibraltar and the Mediterranean*, 'The Era of Imperial Decline', Garratt argued that the democracies were trying to placate the totalitarians at the cost of their principles. *Gibraltar and the Mediterranean* was a slashing argument designed to embarrass the British government for its policy of appeasement and neglect of defence. It was so widely reviewed and discussed that in *The Rock*, Warren Tute's novel of wartime Gibraltar, it could be referred to simply as 'that book'.

Gibraltar and the Mediterranean's last chapters argued that Germany was not only the dominant Axis partner but also the greatest threat to British interests, because it had managed to encircle Gibraltar in both northern Morocco and southern Spain. A conservative naval officer writing under the pseudonym 'Holdfast' in the *Naval Review* in May 1939 considered the book's 'political bias' typical of 'that ideological medley of professors, duchesses, young intellectuals and "experts in foreign affairs" whose politics range from faint pink to crimson red'. The reviewer continued, 'Those who believe that Lord Baldwin, Lord Halifax and Mr Chamberlain, for instance, are incapable of chicanery and double-dealing will find these latter chapters very irritating' – which rings hollow in retrospect.

Major Geoffrey Garratt died in the Second World War. Aged more than fifty, he had joined the Pioneer Corps and was commanding 87 (Alien) Company, which had Austrians, Germans and German Jews in its ranks (including Private Walter Freud, the grandson of the psychiatrist), tasked with clearing landmines. On 28 April 1942, he was in Wales, attending a demonstration at Pembroke Dock Defensible Barracks of how to defuse a German-made Teller anti-tank mine. In theory, it needed about 200 lb of direct pressure to set off its stone of TNT, but the Teller was also fitted with anti-handling devices which made it dangerous to unscrew the pressure plate. When this example exploded, it killed all nineteen soldiers in the basement room, including G. T. Garratt.

Like the arguments over the destruction of Gernika, the 'Guns over Gibraltar' polemic continued for decades. In 1974, for example, George Hills (author of the 1967 hagiography *Franco: the Man and His Nation*) published a history of Gibraltar called *Rock of Contention* which concluded that Britain should negotiate the return of the peninsula to Spain; buried in the book's 510 pages is an extraordinarily vitriolic attack on Geoffrey Garratt, by then long dead, whom he smears as a perniciously anti-Catholic, Communist stooge seeking 'to convince British journalists that Gibraltar was surrounded by heavy guns and howitzers manned by Germans and ready to fire at a moment's notice'. Hills concludes: 'There were no howitzers, guns or Germans.'

On Tuesday 17 August 1937, the Panzerschiff *Admiral Scheer* came into Gibraltar harbour carrying Fleet Commander Admiral Rolf Carls, whom Admiral Erich Raeder hoped would succeed him as head of the German navy. Carls was bringing medals and thanks from the *Führer* for the help that Gibraltar had given to Germany's sailors on the *Deutschland*, and was welcomed with Gibraltar's finest ceremonial. At eleven o'clock sharp, Brigadier Curry invited Carls to inspect the King's Own Yorkshire Light Infantry parade outside Government House, to the music of a military band and the distant booms of a seventeen-gun salute in the bay. At a governor's reception in the Convent, the German admiral thanked the Executive Council and the gathered civic and military dignitaries, and at noon, Governor Harington, booted and spurred, in his beribboned parade tunic with polished Sam Browne belt and khaki barathea jodhpurs, was piped aboard the *Admiral Scheer* for a quick tour by German naval officers in double-breasted dark blue frock-coats. Then it was off to Governor's Cottage for luncheon. That evening, Rear Admiral Alfred Evans, the Rear Admiral-in-Charge and Admiral Superintendent HM Dockyard Gibraltar, gave a dinner at his residence, the Mount. The following day, Admiral Carls reciprocated with a luncheon aboard his battleship, and the visit ended with a cocktail party hosted by the German consul, George Imossi, at the Rock Hotel. From its terrace, Franco's followers could smile approvingly on the *Admiral Scheer*, bathed in evening sunlight, congratulating themselves on how it had punished the 'Reds' of Almería.

In his memoir, Harington rather oddly chooses to reprint the fulsome letter he wrote to Admiral Carls before he left:

... to thank you most sincerely for the way in which you have conveyed the thanks of Der Fuhrer and your great nation, and your great Navy for the help given by the Staff and medical Services in Gibraltar to your sailors in the *Deutschland* . . . I hope that you will express to Der Fuhrer my deepest thanks for this great honour which has been bestowed upon myself and on those under me . . .

Admiral Carls had awarded Governor Harington and Admiral Evans the Star of the Order of the German Red Cross. Lesser medals went to a dozen others, and twenty-one women were awarded the *Damenkreuz* or Ladies' Cross. Each medal came with a Gothic black-letter certificate whose largest typeface was reserved for the name of Adolf Hitler.

Just over a year later, in September 1938, Admiral Rolf Carls would be contributing to the German 'Draft Study of Naval Warfare against England': 'War against England means at the same time war against the [British] Empire, against France, probably against Russia as well, and a large number of countries overseas; in fact, against one half to one third of the whole world.'

In September 1937, fifty-seven-year-old General Sir Edmund Ironside, the burly Scottish soldier who would succeed Harington as Governor of Gibraltar, got a closer look at *der Führer*. Ironside was nicknamed 'Tiny' because he was six foot four inches tall and weighed fifteen and a half stone, but he was more than just a bruiser, having a working knowledge of fourteen languages. Once the youngest major general in the British army, he was widely credited as the model for John Buchan's tenacious fictional character Richard Hannay. Ironside's real-life adventures included one as a young lieutenant when he disguised himself as an Afrikaner and, using his fluent *taal* or Cape Dutch, went to southwest Africa to spy on the Germans in their war on the Herero people. Ironside served bravely on the Western Front all through the First World War, commanded the Allied expedition to Archangel to support the White Russians against the Bolsheviks or 'Bolos', and then undertook missions to Hungary, Turkey, Persia and Iraq, where he specialised in extricating British troops from tight corners. As commandant of the Staff College from 1922 to 1926, he had been a moderniser, embracing new ideas of creating a mechanised army with close air support to fight global 'small wars'.

Invited to witness the Reichswehr's autumn manoeuvres at Mecklenburg in the north German plain, Ironside took the ferry across the North Sea on 21 September 1937. Earlier that month, at the annual congress and rally of the Nazi Party at Nuremberg, Adolf Hitler had loudly stated three facts: the Treaty of Versailles was dead; Germany was free; the guarantor of that freedom was the German army.

On his first night in Germany Ironside dined with the enthusiastic Nazi General Walter von Reichenau, organiser of the 1936 Olympic Games, and Marshal Pietro Badoglio of Italy, conqueror of Libya and instigator of poison gas attacks in Ethiopia. The next day he met Field Marshal von Blomberg, in overall command of all three German fighting services, and General von Fritsch, commander-in-chief of the army. Ironside reckoned the Germans were going fast but were not yet ready for war. 'If I were to hazard a guess', he wrote in his contemporaneous diary, 'I might say 1940 . . .' On the Friday night before the manoeuvres, Ironside fed the same three German generals a lot of whisky. 'They were silly to think that they, who had never tasted it, could compete with an old Scotsman like me.' General von Reichenau – who would boast in a lecture that 'two years' real war experience' in Spain was of more use to the still 'immature' German armed forces than 'ten years of peaceful training', and who, as commander of the German Sixth Army in Russia in 1941, would order the extermination of 'Jewish sub-humanity' – drank a toast to 'brotherhood with England, but only for two years'.

Nursing their hangovers the next day, the generals and other guests watched the German navy go through their paces – deploying submarines, smoke-screens, aeroplane torpedo attacks, the shelling and bombing of convoys. Around midday, Ironside saw a column of twenty cars come up the road:

In the leading one, an enormous open grey six-wheeler, sat the Führer in light brown – almost biscuit colour – with a cap with a brown leather peak.

On his right was Mussolini in his greyish field kit, almost a light blue. His great black face and big jaw stuck out fiercely. Then he raised his hand in a fascist salute as did Hitler with his. The German seems less theatrical. Mussolini gave the impression of trying to look fierce. He stalked up the hill with the Führer almost hurrying beside him.

Mussolini, the junior partner in the Rome–Berlin alliance that he christened 'the Axis', was on a five-day state visit to Nazi Germany, and Hitler had laid on several spectacular shows designed to impress and overawe him. The two dictators awarded each other grandiose medals. The foreign visitors gaped at a jaw-dropping demonstration of Teutonic firepower at Mecklenburg. Aeroplanes were already part of many national displays – 460 British aircraft at the Hendon Air Parade in June, five hundred French planes over Paris on Bastille Day – but now hundreds of German bombers and fighters were swarming in close support of six hundred tanks on the ground, attacking in co-ordinated waves, refuelling and returning in the shuttle tactics evolved on the battlefields of Spain. And for the first time ever in public, German parachutists dropped from the sky.

The elephantine Hermann Göring arrived, late, in his air force uniform, 'a youngish but immensely fat man,' wrote Ironside, 'with simply enormous legs, a fair unlined face and a few longish hairs hanging down under his cap', who panted badly coming up the hill. Ironside watched the crowd of toadies around him, 'all frightfully enthusiastic at being in the train of such a great man'. The British delegation were ushered into a tent to meet the *Führer*, who made a poor impression on Ironside:

I was at once struck by his vacuous-looking grin – one could hardly call it a smile – and his watery, weak-looking eye . . . Reichenau told Hitler that I could speak German, and I chatted for a minute with him in German. He complimented me and told me I spoke it like a German. The man struck me not at all. His voice was soft and his German of the south.

To Ironside, Hitler seemed like a mild professor with a drink problem. In fact, Hitler had simply not switched on his charisma. This was not the pumped-up, red-faced orator who had ranted about 'Jewish Bolshevism' at the closing of the Nuremberg rally two weeks before, furiously scorning 'the claim of an uncivilised Jewish-Bolshevik guild of criminals to rule Germany from Moscow'.

But the Mecklenburg military show greatly impressed Ironside, especially in the co-operation it demonstrated between the German armed forces, so unlike Britain where the air force saw supporting army or navy operations as 'prostitution'. 'The German Army, Navy and Air Force are all united . . . They have one direction and as far as I could see no jealousies . . . no watertight compartments. They have thus a great advantage over us.'

Colonel Noel Mason-MacFarlane, like Ironside a future Governor of Gibraltar, soon got a closer look at the armed forces of Adolf Hitler's Third Reich. Mason-MacFarlane arrived in Berlin as the British military attaché in January 1938. He was an energetic regular gunner who had won three Military Crosses and the Croix de Guerre in the First World War. His father had been a fanatical Scottish Territorial colonel and his younger brother was killed on active service with the Imperial Camel Corps in Libya. 'Mason-Mac' (as he was commonly known) spoke fluent French and German, wrote sharp satirical verses, enjoyed theatre and had a sense of humour, in his case a mark of intelligence. At the same time, Mason-MacFarlane 'did not suffer fools gladly'. His forthrightness was often rudeness and his irascibility was not helped by pain from sporting and motoring injuries. But according to MI3, the European section of military intelligence at the War Office, he combined 'a first-class brain with a remarkable flair for intelligence work . . . Full of mental and physical energy and with great initiative . . . he should go far.'

The idea of the military attaché – a uniformed serviceman working in an embassy or with a diplomatic mission abroad – was an early nineteenth-century Prussian invention. An attaché's role was not espionage as generally understood but the gathering of 'open source' intelligence through contacts with the host nation's military, observing their exercises and manoeuvres, studying their manuals and organisation, mingling with other countries' attachés, reading the press and keeping his eyes and ears open. An attaché had to be up to speed on all the latest military technology, have a grasp of economics and politics, and understand the changes a country might be going through. A major British embassy like the one in Berlin had three military attachés, one from each service. As Ironside had noted, there was little co-ordination between them, because the sailor (Captain Tom Troubridge RN), the soldier (Colonel Mason-MacFarlane) and the airman (Group Captain J. L. Vachell) each reported to his own separate director of intelligence back in Whitehall.

A military attaché had a dual allegiance: he was both a serviceman and a member of the ambassador's staff whose views and rules he was supposed to respect.* This was difficult for the attachés in Nazi Germany from 1937 to 1939. On his arrival in Berlin at the start of 1938, Mason-MacFarlane was glad to find an able assistant military attaché, the 'eager beaver' Major Kenneth Strong. In his own post-war memoirs, Strong wrote, with suave understatement: 'The policy of the British Embassy under [Ambassador] Sir Nevile Henderson did not always seem to the attachés to be consistent with the available military information.'

The trouble was that sixty-nine-year-old Prime Minister Neville Chamberlain was now in the driving seat of foreign policy, and still believed in the sunlit uplands of a pan-European settlement that would bring peace to the entire continent. He took to foreign affairs, said Malcolm Muggeridge, 'with a beginner's passion and recklessness, though not luck'. The somewhat prim, vain and unworldly

---

* 'It is a commonplace of diplomatic observation that all military attachés are inclined to meddle with what does not concern their duties, and as long as military attachés are allowed to have their own cipher and communicate with the War Office they will be subject to this temptation.' Compton Mackenzie, *First Athenian Memories* (Cassell, 1931), p. 57.

prime minister could not see through the ruthless lies of the European dictators and was, as the diplomat Ivone Kirkpatrick said, 'determined to tame Hitler by kindness'.

It was Chamberlain who selected Sir Nevile Henderson as ambassador to Berlin, and Henderson took up his post on 1 May 1937 'resolved', in his own words, 'to do my utmost to see the good side of the Nazi régime as well as the bad' and 'to labour for an honourable peace'. Henderson, who described the 'superb' Nuremberg rally he attended as 'a triumph of mass organisation combined with beauty', replaced a far more cynical ambassador, Sir Eric Phipps. (When Hermann Göring once explained he was late because he had been out shooting, Phipps remarked acidly, 'Animals, I trust'; by contrast, Henderson, hearing Göring criticised as 'a butcher', defended him by saying, 'Absolute rubbish! He's a charming man. I went shooting with him only last week.')

General Hermann Göring, a man of gargantuan appetite and ambition (and a secret morphine addict), carried more medals on his capacious chest than anyone else in the Third Reich, and the full list of his posts – Head of the Air Force, Prime Minister of Prussia, Supreme Head of the Ministry of Economy and Commissioner of the Four-Year Plan, etc., etc. – took minutes to read aloud. As Game Warden of the Third Reich, Göring had prohibited snares and steel traps and was trying to restore the European bison and the original wild horse. He had introduced elk onto his ten-thousand-acre estate in East Prussia for sporting purposes and he invited Sir Nevile Henderson to come stag shooting. Henderson was proud to drop a fourteen-pointer with a single shot through the heart. Göring loved all shooting. When *Homes & Gardens* profiled 'Hitler's Mountain Home' in 1938, the reporter saw the archery butts behind the Bavarian chalet. 'It is strange to watch the burly Field-Marshal Göring, as chief of the most formidable air force in Europe, taking a turn with the bow and arrow at straw targets of twenty-five yards range. There is as much to-do about those scarlet bulls'-eyes as though the fate of nations depended on a full score.'

It was Henderson who arranged British participation in the huge hunting exhibition that Göring organised in Berlin in November 1937, where a selection of stuffed animals (including a giant panda) that had enjoyed the honour of being shot dead in every corner of the empire by British royalty and aristocracy duly won first prize for 'Overseas Collection'. Neville Chamberlain used the bizarre event as a way of establishing personal contact with the Nazis. He arranged that his ally Lord Halifax, then Lord President of the (Privy) Council, be privately invited to the exhibition in his capacity as Joint Master of Fox Hounds of the Middleton Hunt in Yorkshire. Afterwards, Halifax went south by special train to meet Adolf Hitler at Berchtesgaden. The whole mission almost collapsed when tall and patrician Halifax got out of the car and was on the point of handing his bowler hat and overcoat to a nondescript little man with greasy hair. Von Neurath, the German Foreign Minister, hissed urgently, '*Der Führer! der Führer!*'

Hitler got the message from Halifax that parts of the Versailles Treaty could be peacefully renegotiated in his favour, including Danzig, Austria and Czechoslovakia, and in return offered a solution for the British Empire's troubles in India: 'Shoot Gandhi, and if that does not suffice, shoot a dozen leading members of Congress; and if that does not suffice, shoot two hundred and so on until order is restored.'

The next day, Halifax travelled to Karinhall and was deceived by the charm of fat Hermann Göring in his big-feathered hat – 'frankly attractive, like a great schoolboy . . . a composite personality – film star, great landowner interested in his estate, Prime Minister, party manager, head gamekeeper at Chatsworth'.

Early in 1938, the top army men whom Ironside had met were framed for sexual deviancy by the Gestapo and swept away. Adolf Hitler took complete command of the German armed forces and elevated Göring to field marshal. The Ministry of War was abolished on 4 February and the Oberkommando der Wehrmacht (OKW), the High Command of the Armed Forces, was set up as Hitler's personal staff. In his memoir *Lost Victories*, Field Marshal Erich von Manstein said that reducing OKW to a mere military secretariat meant that there was no proper chief of staff to think about grand strategy. Unlike Roosevelt or Churchill, Hitler had no strong figure to stand up and wrestle with his ideas. He relied on his own instinct, his genius for opportunism and his absolute power to issue directives from the *Führer*.

Meanwhile, Neville Chamberlain, an inveterate intriguer, bypassed his Foreign Secretary Anthony Eden and set up back-channels to the Italian Fascist regime, conducting 'unofficial diplomacy' with the *Duce* himself in Rome through Dame Ivy Chamberlain, the widow of his half-brother Sir Austen Chamberlain.* The appeasing Chamberlain wanted legal recognition of the Italian conquest of Ethiopia, whereas Anthony Eden pressed for a *quid pro quo* in the Mediterranean: he wanted Italy to withdraw four thousand 'volunteers' fighting for Franco in Spain and an end to Italian submarine attacks. But Eden was squeezed out, and on 20 February 1938, Chamberlain replaced him as Foreign Secretary with Lord Halifax.

The day that Eden resigned, Hitler made a raging speech to the Reichstag, presenting territorial aggression as self-defence. He promised to protect the ten million Germans living outside Germany's borders, seven million of them in Austria, and three million in Czechoslovakia. They had the right to what he called 'racial self-determination'.

---

* Sir Austen Chamberlain (1863–1937) became a Knight of the Garter and won the Nobel Peace Prize for negotiating the Locarno Pact in 1925. The monocle-wearing Conservative exchanged Christmas cards and went on family holiday with Benito Mussolini.

9

Scrabbling on the Brink

At La Línea, so close to Gibraltar, on Sunday 27 February 1938, the Francoist General Queipo de Llano provoked controversy by arriving, according to the *Daily Herald*, with an escort of goosestepping German soldiers in Reichswehr uniforms, and making an inflammatory speech at a mass rally with loudspeakers pointing towards the Rock. According to the *Daily Telegraph*, the garrulous Spanish soldier declared: 'We shall soon incorporate Gibraltar in our motherland. Then Gibraltar will be free from the grip of the smuggler bandits who now control it.' A correspondent of *The Times* in Bayonne picked up a broadcast from Seville on 28 February which said that 'General Queipo de Llano, in a speech, had referred to Gibraltar as having been stolen from Spain by treason', adding that it would 'soon be back in the hands of the Mother Country'.

Nationalist Spain hurried to whitewash over what seemed like a diplomatic gaffe. The Duke of Alba, General Franco's agent in London, went to the Foreign Office to protest 'in the strongest terms against what he called "the misrepresentation by irresponsible correspondents in Gibraltar" of a speech given by General Queipo de Llano on the future of Gibraltar'. The duke said such reports were entirely false; the general had only said that Spain should always be strong, and that her moments of weakness had always had fatal consequences for her 'as happened in the War of Succession which deprived her of Gibraltar, and again now in the case of Bolshevist designs to acquire control of Spain'.

In reply to British government queries, Governor Harington also maintained that Queipo de Llano had not said what he was reported as saying, citing the British vice consul of La Línea as a witness, together with several prominent Gibraltarian citizens of the merchant class. He added that the speech was at the swearing-in ceremony of five hundred new NCOs at the infantry barracks in San Roque, but chose not to mention that the goosestepping German soldiers who escorted Queipo de Llano were the German military instructors at the barracks, who were training thousands of Spaniards for combat, using German weapons, ammunition and equipment.

The wife of Major General Sir Walter Maxwell Scott, attending the event as Queipo de Llano's personal guest, sent indignant telegrams to the press baron Lord Beaverbrook and his *Daily Express*, complaining about 'disgraceful Red propaganda continually coming from Gibraltar' and Queipo de Llano himself dismissed the negative reports of his speech as 'a typically foul Marxist trick'.

In early March 1938, the Royal Navy held their customary spring naval exercises off Gibraltar and General Harington had sixteen British admirals to dine at Government House, recording it with an official photo. In the black-and-white picture, the six senior admirals are seated with the governor and the other ten stand behind, all in black tie and medals, the elite flag ranks from the Home and Mediterranean Fleets gathered at the Rock. James Somerville, Rear Admiral (Destroyers), and Andrew Browne Cunningham, Vice Admiral (Battlecruisers), both from the Mediterranean Fleet, were leading the opposed sides in the war games; in the photograph they are sitting together on the left. Next to them is Admiral Sir Roger Backhouse, Commander-in-Chief of the Home Fleet, and next to him the head of the whole Royal Navy, the First Sea Lord, Admiral of the Fleet Sir Ernle Chatfield. On the other side of Harington sits Admiral Sir Dudley Pound, Commander-in-Chief of the Mediterranean Fleet (who would become First Sea Lord in June 1939), and Vice Admiral Charles Kennedy-Purvis of the 1st Cruiser Squadron.

At dinner they discussed the extent of the threat Fascist Italy posed to the Mediterranean. Cargo ships of all nationalities trading to Republican ports had been bombed by Italian aeroplanes and sunk by the Italian submarine fleet (then the largest in the world), although the Non-Intervention Committee always pretended the attackers were of 'unknown' origin. Following the Italian submarine *Iride*'s attack on the British destroyer HMS *Havock*, Anthony Eden had organised a conference at Nyon to end submarine warfare. As part of the elaborate diplomatic make-believe, Italy the aggressor was later formally invited to play a part in the peacekeeping force.

The Spanish Civil War was not a happy period for the Royal Navy. 'How I loathe this damn Spain and all the doings here,' Admiral Somerville wrote to his wife. 'It is all indescribably filthy.' Policing Non-Intervention and enforcing the Nyon Agreement's interdiction of submarine warfare meant too many time-wasting tasks for the fleet. The Royal Navy was involved in protecting British merchant ships entering and leaving ports from the Bay of Biscay to the Costa Brava, in blockade work – stopping and searching for contraband and smuggled weaponry – evacuating civilians, minesweeping, and seeing off threats by Nationalist warships, hostile aircraft or submarines that were torpedoing ships, as well as simply flying the flag in trouble spots. Valencia and Barcelona were grateful when a British capital ship put in, because the Italians would not bomb them while the British ships were in port. Deployment on all these tedious tasks meant that the Admiralty could not refit and repair the ships, a real concern for those who wished to rearm while the politicians and diplomats bought time.

One unpleasant but necessary job for the Royal Navy was rescuing crews of sunken ships. On 6 March 1938, while the combined British fleet exercise was under way, there was a Spanish sea battle off Cape Palos near Cartagena. The Republican destroyer *Lepanto*, which had once limped damaged into Gibraltar, fired two torpedoes which hit the Nationalist heavy cruiser *Baleares* on the starboard side, detonating the forward magazine. (British rumour had it that a Republican who was once a torpedo rating in the Royal Navy fired the torpedoes.)

Two British destroyers on Non-Intervention patrol, HMS *Kempenfelt* and HMS *Boreas*, came to the rescue of the *Baleares* in the early hours of the morning. Captain Rhoderick McGrigor tried to get *Kempenfelt* close enough so men could jump across from the cruiser's quarterdeck, but sharp girders and uplifted propellers made the manoeuvre impossible and *Baleares* went down at 5.08 a.m., taking Admiral Manuel Vierna and 765 officers and men with her. *Kempenfelt* and *Boreas* immediately moved into the mass of figures struggling in the black waters and British officers and men went overboard to help rescue Spanish survivors. It was dark and cold, and thick engine oil choked men's lungs and made hands, ropes and boats slimy and slippery. Nevertheless, they saved over 440 Nationalist *marineros*.

Events in Europe were moving fast. On 11 March 1938, the British Embassy in Berlin learned that German troops and police were advancing through Munich eastwards towards Austria. Colonel Mason-MacFarlane went to see the Director of Military Intelligence at the German High Command to find out what was going on. A senior staff officer insisted the Britisher was misinformed. Mason-MacFarlane did not believe him and set off on a recce, soon finding himself among armed police and SS moving towards Austria in buses, vans, lorries and miscellaneous requisitioned vehicles. Adolf Hitler's demand on the first page of *Mein Kampf* was finally being fulfilled: 'German-Austria must return to the great German mother country . . . One blood demands one Reich.'

Meanwhile, Kenneth Strong was summoned to the German High Command where an embarrassed staff officer explained that Mason-MacFarlane had been wrongly briefed and there was indeed 'a strong demonstration' on the Austrian border to prevent disorders 'of Marxist origin' spreading into Germany. Mason-MacFarlane made his way to Vienna the next day. At Aspern airport, Ju 52s full of German troops were landing at the rate of one a minute; the attaché had to duck down to avoid being seen by the German Director of Military Intelligence. The Austrians, like the British, drove on the left side of the road, but the German SS were ignoring that, going helter-skelter on the right. Finally, the German military attaché in Vienna, General von Muff, gave Mason-MacFarlane, an old friend, a full account of what was going on. It was *der Anschluss*, the 'connecting up' of Austria with Nazi Germany.

In Vienna that evening, the American CBS reporter William Shirer, temporarily forbidden to broadcast on the day of the annexation, got caught up on the Kärntnerstrasse among crowds singing Nazi songs. He noticed Austrian policemen now wore swastika armbands. 'Young toughs were heaving paving blocks into the windows of the Jewish shops. The crowd roared with delight.' Soon elderly Jewish people, including rich women in their fur coats, would be forced to clean the streets on their hands and knees while 'good Germans' spat on them. Eleven hundred Viennese Jews killed themselves after the *Anschluss*.

Europe was shocked by the annexation. 'Violence has triumphed,' said *Le Figaro*; 'Austria has lost her sovereignty,' said *Le Journal de Genève*; 'All the dreams of collective guarantees are illusory,' said *Gazeta Polska*. In Britain, the *Daily Telegraph and Morning Post* deplored 'the mailed fist' and the *Manchester Guardian* said, 'No propaganda can disguise and no ignorance fail to understand so unconcealed a threat of armed force.'

Mason-MacFarlane watched Austrian-born Adolf Hitler drive from his home-town of Linz towards Vienna: 'There was something terribly sinister about that string of shining black Mercedes, rolling along inexorably . . . with the impassive figure with the black cowlick and toothbrush moustache gazing fixedly ahead and taking no account whatever of his surroundings.' 'Easy rifle-shot,' Mason-MacFarlane remarked to Ewan Butler, *The Times*'s correspondent in Berlin, looking out from his drawing-room window to where they were building the reviewing stand for Hitler's fiftieth birthday parade on 20 April 1939. 'I could pick the bastard off from here easy as winking, and what's more I'm thinking of doing it.'

Ewan Butler demurred politely on moral grounds. 'Besides, think of the backlash when they discovered he'd been potted by a British officer!'

'Oh I know . . . I'd be finished in every sense of the word. Still, I doubt if they'd declare war, and with that lunatic out of the way we might be able to get some sense into things.'

Many others felt the same way. George Orwell, reviewing *Mein Kampf*, said 'I would certainly kill him if I could get within reach of him.' Geoffrey Household wrote of Hitler: 'The man had to be dealt with, and I began to think how much I would love to kill him.' Household dramatised those thoughts – 'my feeling for Nazi Germany had the savagery of a personal vendetta' – in his classic 1939 pursuit thriller, *Rogue Male*, in which the failed assassin of an unnamed European tyrant escapes from his torturers and is hunted down, deep in the English countryside. In another 1939 novel, *The Man Who Killed Hitler*, by 'Anonymous', the maddened Austrian psychiatrist hero only succeeds in murdering – with a heavy bust of Hindenburg – one of the *Führer*'s four doubles.*

One fatality of the torpedoing of the Nationalist cruiser *Baleares* was Fernando, Marqués de Povar, Talia Larios's husband. In mournful respect, the Royal Calpe Hunt cancelled the meet on 10 March. A congregation of eight hundred attended the memorial service for the *Baleares* crewmen, arranged by the Anti-Communist Association of Gibraltar, an offshoot of Oswald Mosley's British Union of Fascists, headed by Luis Bertuchi. A Mass was held in the Sacred Heart parish church, up behind the Garrison Library, on 26 March 1938, presided over by Luciano López Ferrer, the Nationalist sub-agent on the Rock, and his deputy Leopold Yome, with the Italian and German consuls sitting just behind. The right-wing Bishop Fitzgerald and his confederate, Father Paul Murphy of the Christian Brothers, were there among prominent Gibraltarian citizens and businessmen.

---

* The saga continues. James MacManus's novel *Midnight in Berlin* (Duckworth Overlook, 2016) is dedicated to the memory of Colonel Noel Mason-MacFarlane 'whose courage and vision inspired a story woven round the plan to assassinate Hitler in Berlin in 1939 and the Gestapo's efforts to compromise the British diplomat who intended to be the assassin'.

Afterwards, López Ferrer took the fascist salute from the crowd in Main Street outside the Catholic cathedral, and a small group of Gibraltarian fascists took a wreath across the frontier to La Línea to place it at *la cruz de los caídos*, the Nationalists' Cross of the Fallen.

The left in Gibraltar were not going to take this sort of thing lying down, and held their own large rally five days later. Bishop Fitzgerald tried to get the Colonial Secretary to ban it on the grounds that the mob might attack his Catholic churches. The Transport and General Workers' Union put out a manifesto declaring the support of Gibraltar's workers for Spanish democracy, condemning both the moneyed classes and British colonial officers for their support of the Nationalists. Three thousand people gathered at Gibraltar's Assembly Rooms (today the site of the Queen's Cinema and Theatre) where Spanish Republican flags were pinned to the walls and the 'Internationale' was played. The councillor and union man Agustín Huart gave the final speech, throwing down the gauntlet to the right-wingers on the Rock: 'If General Franco wins the war with the aid of Italy and Germany, where would we stand, and which steps would the fascists of Gibraltar take, they who call themselves British?'

The question went to the heart of Gibraltarian identity; the right had no monopoly on patriotism and loyalty to the Crown. The elaborate service for the drowned *Baleares* sailors was a deliberate provocation, Agustín Huart continued. Where was the church service for the ten Gibraltarian seamen who died in January on the Gibraltar-registered SS *Endymion*, torpedoed by the Nationalist submarine *General Sanjurjo*? How come the police arrested workers for using the clenched-fist salute when no one did anything about the fascist salute outside the church? And what about the rich, 'who would not lower themselves to talk to the working man but would do so with pride to the Marquesa de Povar'? The meeting ended in a blaze of leftist patriotism. People sang both the 'Marseillaise' and 'God Save the King' with clenched fists aloft.

The widow Talia Larios, *la Marquesa viuda de Povar*, suffered a further blow when her father, Don Pablo Larios Sánchez de Piña,

Marqués de Marzales, died just a few weeks after her husband, at home in Algeciras on Sunday 3 April 1938. A launch brought his coffin to Stone Jetty at Bayside in Gibraltar and the Joint Master of the Royal Calpe Hunt was buried in the family vault at Gibraltar's North Front Cemetery on the same day. Governor Harington was there, with members of the hunt in full hunting uniform. The Pablo Larios Memorial Fund was set up to keep hunting going, and ex-King Alfonso XIII sent £5 from his £35 million fortune.

The Defence Security Officer in Gibraltar was Captain A. E. Airy, now assisted by Staff Sergeant Holden, confidential clerk in charge of the files and index. Airy had to liaise with MI6 about foreign espionage from Spain or Tangier, but he was keeping an eye on the Marquesa de Povar on behalf of MI5, who had first opened a personal file (PF. 458/8) on her in June 1937, interested in her links to German intelligence. Airy told them in a letter dated 19 June 1938 that 'any general Intelligence about Gibraltar collected locally, including local defences, details of Warships, etc., is freely exchanged between Germany, Italy and Nationalist Spain'. A month later Airy reported to MI5: 'I know for a fact that the German instructors at the Military School at San Roque, for instance, have been to her people's house in Algeciras.'

Airy described the Marquesa de Povar as 'a very jealous woman' with a lot of information about British officers 'at her finger-tips' which she would readily share with Nationalist and foreign intelligence officers. She and her attractive young aunt, Isabel Fernández Villavicencio y Crooke, Marquesa de Nájera, had been making a 'dead set' at the junior officers of the Welsh Guards, recently arrived on the Rock. In July 1938, as British MPs were asking more questions about the German guns facing Gibraltar, Airy was following up a British officer (well known to the 'exceedingly friendly' pair of marquesas) who had gone to Casablanca to see a Dane called Karl or Charles Cabos, believed to be working for German intelligence in French Morocco.

The suspect British officer was revealed to be Second Lieutenant Richard C. Sharples of the 1st Battalion, Welsh Guards.* He was questioned at GHQ in Gibraltar and his innocent explanation was that Cabos knew his father – both had worked for the Shell Oil Company – and had invited him over to Casablanca on local leave. Sharples said he had been lavishly entertained but had told Cabos nothing of interest or importance.

Airy made further enquiries about the two women: he discovered the Marquesa de Povar held a Spanish (Nationalist) passport, no. 220, issued in Cádiz in June 1937 and renewed for one year by the Spanish (Nationalist) Consulate in Gibraltar in June 1938. She lived in a large flat in Gibraltar and had a house near Algeciras, but her resident's permit had not been traced. She had contracted heavy debts in Gibraltar and was 'thought to be financially embarrassed'. Airy also recorded that her aunt, the Marquesa de Nájera, was the guest of a British resident of Gibraltar and was believed to be sleeping with the Marquis Cittadini Cesi, former Italian consul in Tangier, now temporarily Italian consul in Gibraltar, and an associate of the Italian spy Dante Brancolini. The marquesas were giving their all for Franco. *Todo por la patria*, as the saying went.

In September 1938, the Czech crisis blew up. The Third Reich bullied its way into the so-called Sudetenland of Czechoslovakia, ten thousand square miles of territory in Bohemia and Moravia where most of Czechoslovakia's three and a half million German-speaking inhabitants lived. This 23 per cent of the population listened solely to the German radio station RRG, Reichs-Rundfunk-Gesellschaft, run since 1933 by the Propaganda Minister, Dr Joseph Goebbels, a man who saw radio as the most modern and important way to influence

* Sir Richard Sharples (1916–73) later became a Conservative politician and Cabinet minister. When Governor of Bermuda, he was assassinated on 10 March 1973 by a Black Power militant who also shot dead his Great Dane dog, Horsa, and his aide-de-camp, Captain Hugh Sayers. The murderer, Erskine Burrows, was hanged on 2 December 1977, one of the last judicial executions conducted under British rule.

the masses. 'While others build up troops and organise armies, we want to mobilise the army of public opinion. The army of spiritual unification.'

The Nazi Party rally at Nuremberg in September 1938 was widely broadcast on radio. Goebbels denounced the communist menace in Czechoslovakia, saying that 'Bolshevism is the rude child of democracy'. Field Marshal Göring boasted that Germany had never been stronger: tremendous fortifications in the west were overflown by the planet's most powerful air force, yet 'We love peace more than anyone in the world,' he declared. 'The only countries working for peace in Europe are Germany and Italy.' Hitler also spoke, and his broadcast was listened to in dread by millions across the continent. In a truculent and paranoid speech, he attacked the Versailles Treaty that created Czechoslovakia, saying it had denied 3.5 million Germans living there their right to self-determination. These brothers were being oppressed and tortured, and Hitler would no longer tolerate it. He drew a parallel with Palestine. 'The poor Arabs are deserted and perhaps defenceless. The Germans of Czechoslovakia, however, are neither defenceless nor deserted.' Encouraged by these words, German-speakers in Bohemia attacked Czech and Jewish property. Martial law was declared. Refugees fled to Silesia.

Sir Nevile Henderson, the British ambassador, said in his memoir that he spent his time at the Nuremberg rally warning senior Nazis that 'If Germany makes an aggressive attack on Czechoslovakia, France is in honour bound to come to the aid of the Czechs, and if France is engaged in war, Great Britain will inevitably be drawn in also.' But he took a hint from Göring that personal diplomacy might help to avoid a conflagration. On 15 September 1938, Neville Chamberlain flew (the first time he had ever been in an aeroplane) from London to Munich and then took a train south to Berchtesgaden.

The *Führer*, in Nazi uniform at the top of the steps, gave his *Hitlergrüss* arm-salute. Chamberlain, dressed like an undertaker, his black umbrella hooked over his left arm, raised his homburg with his right hand and gave it a little wave. The British prime minister was eager to help persuade the Czechs to cede a chunk of territory peacefully to the Germans. Hitler promised not to attack while Chamberlain put pressure on Edvard Beneš, the Czechoslovak head of state, to give Germans in southern Czechoslovakia the right to secede.

Things got worse. The Poles and Hungarians wanted gobbets of Czechoslovakia too. Chamberlain flew to Cologne for a meeting on 22 September. He was put up in the Petersberg Hotel, which belonged to the man who owned Eau de Cologne. (The rooms had lavish displays of different bottles, which members of the British team discreetly pocketed for their wives.) Hitler was staying at the Dreesen Hotel on the other side of the river, tense and twitchy, living on his nerves. The German economy was in trouble, the generals were conspiring against him and he feigned terrifying tantrums to get his way. '*Teppichfresser*' ('Carpet-chewer'), muttered a German editor to the reporter William Shirer, referring to an incident where Hitler had rolled raging on the floor. Chamberlain patiently explained to Hitler that the French and the British had persuaded the Czechs to cede the Sudetenland to Germany without a plebiscite. It was to no avail. Hitler said it was no longer enough – '*das geht nicht mehr*'. German troops must occupy the Sudetenland straight away. Chamberlain flushed in shock; Hitler had moved the goal-posts once more.

The next day, the 23rd, Hitler produced a map with a great crescent of all the territory he wanted from Czechoslovakia drawn on it in thick blue crayon. If he did not get it by 28 September, he would invade. After Chamberlain gained a tiny concession – the deadline was pushed on three days to 1 October – he agreed to convey Hitler's ultimatum/'memorandum' plus the map to the Czech government. The man who volunteered to take the documents by hand to Prague was the Berlin military attaché and future Governor of Gibraltar, Colonel Noel Mason-MacFarlane.

This was no easy task. The Czech frontier was closed and policed on both sides by jumpy men with guns. On the 23rd, Mason-Mac-Farlane flew in an elderly Breguet east from Cologne to Templehof airfield at Berlin, where he was met by a car with a driver and the

Czech assistant military attaché. The three men drove fast to Zinn-wald on the Czech border, arriving at dusk, but German border guards said the road was impassable, a fact confirmed by Czech frontier guards. Mason-MacFarlane sent the car and driver back to Dresden, telling him to return next morning. Meanwhile, Mason-MacFarlane and the Czech officer sat in the guard post and worked out a plan.

They could hear gunfire from the 'Sudeten Free Corps', hoping to ambush Czech patrols, but there was still a phone line open to Teplitz-Schönau, a few miles further inside Czechoslovakia, and the attaché rang the commanding officer of the regiment there to say that he and a British military attaché would be making their way on foot through the woods, bringing a vital document for delivery to Prague. Could he arrange for a car to meet them and get them to the capital? After two hours of scrambling in the dark sodden forest, where pro-Nazi vigilantes were roaming with guns, the two men, their clothes soaked and hands and faces bloody from bramble scratches and barbed wire, met a Czech picquet. They eventually drove to Prague on a cratered road, through many roadblocks. When he got to the British Legation at one in the morning, Mason-MacFarlane found they had given him up for lost and gone to bed. He handed over Hitler's map and memorandum to the dressing-gowned ambassa-dor and then got some sleep. Back at the German border next day he found the faithful driver waiting and a parade of eager Nazis – Army, SS and Freikorps – drawn up to salute *der Englander* for hav-ing helped *der Führer* in a dangerous mission. Mason-MacFarlane felt humiliated at being thanked for doing Hitler's dirty work and slipped away as soon as possible.

Back in Berlin, Mason-MacFarlane learned the Czechs had rejected the ultimatum he had carried, and Europe was cascading towards war. The French mobilised half a million men and reaf-firmed their military commitment to the Czechs. President Roosevelt and a clutch of South American leaders appealed for calm; the Pope asked the faithful to pray for peace.

*

British 'precautionary measures' on 25, 26 and 27 September 1938 included mobilising the fleet, distributing forty million gas masks, digging air-raid trenches in park flowerbeds, evacuating schoolchildren, instituting rationing, fixing food prices and sandbagging key London buildings against possible bombing. The Territorial anti-aircraft and coastal defence forces were called up, as well as the entire Auxiliary Air Force. The War Office instituted a new non-combatant organisation for women, the ATS, Auxiliary Territorial Service, to help the armed forces with cooking, clerking and driving. The Czech crisis galvanised the nation. The forty-eight-page HMSO booklet *National Service*, distributed free to every British household in January 1939, lists what Anthony James calls 'an amazing array of organisations clearly already in place for offensive, defensive and support activities', plus two pull-out, official-paid Application for Enrolment forms. By the summer of 1939, this would raise three hundred thousand men for the armed forces and 1.5 million people for civil defence.

In Gibraltar, security was tightened, especially as regarded the eight thousand people who crossed the frontier from Spain every day. Dockyard Identity Cards were issued to all civilian employees, the Defence Security Officer issued new Military Permits and the Civil Police carefully controlled other Spaniards entering Gibraltar daily to work. All cards carried a photograph of the bearer, and a duplicate went into the card index. Foreign visitors and tourists had to leave their passports at Four Corners or Waterport on arrival, to collect on leaving; these too were discreetly copied and filed.

Mason-MacFarlane had flown back to London to brief General Lord Gort, the Chief of the Imperial General Staff, and the entire Cabinet (with Neville Chamberlain not paying attention, but riffling unconcernedly through a pile of papers). After Mason-MacFarlane painted his gloomy picture of Czech morale, Alec Cadogan of the Foreign Office wrote crossly in his diary, 'What does he know about it?' Mason-MacFarlane felt the primary aim of HM Government was still to avoid war, at all costs, because the ill-equipped armed forces were not ready to fight.

At eight o'clock that night, 27 September, Neville Chamberlain took to the airwaves, using the medium of radio like Hitler, but in a very different tone. He spoke on the BBC Home and Empire Services, to 'you, men and women of Britain and the Empire, and perhaps to others as well', describing the letters of gratitude for his efforts and the prayers for his success that he and his wife had received:

Most of these letters have come from women – mothers or sisters of our own countrymen. But there are countless others besides, from France, from Belgium, from Italy, even from Germany, and it has been heartbreaking to read of the growing anxiety they reveal . . .

How horrible, fantastic, incredible it is that we should be digging trenches and trying on gas-masks here because of a quarrel in a far-away country between people of whom we know nothing . . .

The next morning, Chamberlain was just telling the House of Commons that he was willing to make one final effort, when his speech was interrupted by the delivery of a letter from Herr Hitler, inviting the prime minister to meet him at Munich the next day, together with Signor Mussolini and Monsieur Daladier. This news provoked a storm of cheering.

Chamberlain flew out once again, this time to the Four Power conference – Britain, France, Germany and Italy – at the Nazi Brown House in Munich. The Czechoslovaks were not invited to discuss their own fate. On the same day, 29 September, the rolled-up canvas of Picasso's *Guernica* arrived in London, care of the National Joint Committee for Spanish Relief, to display the agonies of the casualties of Nazi bombing first at the New Burlington Galleries off Regent Street, and then at the Whitechapel Art Gallery in the East End (where the price of admission was a pair of boots for Spanish Republican soldiers).

In the early hours of 30 September, the Four Powers agreed that the Sudetenland would be ceded to Germany, Teschen to Poland and Ruthenia to Hungary. Seven million Czechs saw their country, only created two decades earlier by Britain and France at the Treaty of

Versailles, dismembered by the same two countries, because their leaders thought yielding was more politic than fighting. The Munich agreement also doomed the hopes of the Spanish Republic to join Britain and France in an international war against totalitarianism.

Neville Chamberlain had another early morning meeting with Adolf Hitler and flew back to London waving a meaningless piece of paper with a bland declaration 'symbolic of the desire of our two peoples never to go to war with one another again'. There were hysterical scenes in the capital, weeping, shouting crowds of people giving thanks that bloodshed was averted. The gaunt, sixty-nine-year-old prime minister was thrilled at his tumultuous reception, addressing the crowd outside No. 10 Downing Street as 'my very good friends', and saying: 'I believe it is peace for our time. We thank you from the bottom of our hearts. And now I recommend you to go home and sleep quietly in your beds.'

When the more realistic French Prime Minister Edouard Daladier arrived back in France from Munich he thought the great crowds assembled were there to lynch him; their cheers and tears amazed him. '*Ah, les cons!*' he exclaimed (delicately translated by the BBC as 'These people are mad!'). Another Frenchman said that Munich offered the democracies all the relief of an urgent defecation, followed by the realisation that they had not managed to drop their trousers in time.

'Isn't this splendid?' said Ambassador Sir Nevile Henderson to blackly depressed Mason-MacFarlane on the latter's return to Berlin. 'If only you soldiers can produce a plan to get the Czechs out of the Sudetenland and the Germans into it without a fight we shall have peace in Europe for ten years!'

Winston Churchill, however, in a superb jeremiad on 5 October, described the disastrous Munich agreement as 'a total and unmitigated defeat'. All sides of the House of Commons howled him down.

That autumn, Edmund Ironside replaced Charles Harington as Governor and Commander-in-Chief of Gibraltar. He arrived with his wife and daughter aboard the SS *Orford*, the ship that had taken Haile Selassie to the UK, on 9 November 1938. General Ironside was met on the Rock with a ceremonial seventeen-gun salute at Ragged Staff steps, two honour guards in review order with medals, and a motor route lined with sailors, gunners and engineers smartly at attention. In the ballroom of Government House, the Chief Justice administered the oaths of allegiance and office and Ironside received the keys to the city. Among the speeches of 'hearty welcome' was one ('following an ancient and pleasant custom') from the Managing Board of the Hebrew Community of Gibraltar, who pointed out that the Jews were:

... among the first in point of time to have become residents of this Colony under British Rule and are second to none in their unswerving loyalty to all you represent ... Your Excellency will always find this community individually or as a body, ready and willing to cooperate, wholeheartedly and unstintingly, towards everything that might be needed for the welfare of the Empire, in general, and of Gibraltar, in particular.

How much better to be a Jew in Gibraltar than in Germany! That very date, 9 November 1938, marked the start of *Kristallnacht*, the violent two-day Nazi pogrom in which the windows of 7500 Jewish shops were smashed, some four hundred German Jews were killed, thousands more beaten and abused, thirty thousand locked up or sent to concentration camps, and over a thousand synagogues burned. Kenneth Strong, once the DSO in Gibraltar and now the assistant British military attaché in Berlin, worked near the British Passport Control Office. He recalled seeing 'a long line of distressed Jews, weeping, waiting, hoping and begging to be given passports to leave Germany. They grabbed at me as I passed, old men and women, young children, all desperate to get out of Germany.'

Ironside's initial brief from the Secretary of State for War, Leslie Hore-Belisha, and the Chief of the Imperial General Staff, John Gort, was to prepare to be commander-in-chief for the entire Mediterranean area, which forced him to take the big strategic view. He saw clearly from the world map that Britain could 'not afford to give up this Mediterranean route. We need it as an Imperial artery.' The Middle East had to be reinforced, with reserves of stores in case of trouble. He also saw that 'None of our Imperial stations such as Gibraltar, Malta, Cyprus, Alexandria and Haifa is safe – or shall I say immune? – from heavy air attack in the early stages of a war with Italy and Germany.'

One glaring fact was that Gibraltar itself had no airfield. The RAF detachment relied on Fairey seaplanes with buoyancy floats touching down on the waters of Gibraltar Bay. A system of 'Emergency Landings Only' on the grass racecourse was jealously policed by the old buffers of the Gibraltar Jockey Club and was hardly the ideal situation for a modern air force. The racecourse on the sandy isthmus north of Devil's Tower Road was the only place on the peninsula where an aerodrome could go, but Foreign Office lawyers were worried about the legal ownership of this strip of terrain, as it was not actually specified in the Treaty of Utrecht, and the Spanish were (with justice) complaining about encroachment from the Gibraltar side. The working agreement with Spain had been that only temporary buildings, such as tents for sick people during epidemics, could ever go up there; by tradition the ground was reserved for parks, sports and recreational facilities only.

Ironside started cracking the whip. The Colonial Office had approved a budget of £500 a year to set up an anti-aircraft unit, but Ironside told the War Office in February 1939 that should war break out, he wanted a locally recruited Gibraltar Defence Force of nearly four hundred men, with anti-aircraft, artillery, signals, transport and medical sections. In 1939, however, there was not enough money for this as well as the Air Raid Precautions (ARP) that Ironside had determined were needed. To protect the civilian population against bombing he instituted the building of a series of 'Ironside Air Raid Shelters'. Right in the middle of town, City Council of Gibraltar workers dug up the entire piazza of Commercial Square to make an underground reinforced-concrete shelter for many hundreds. The square was resurfaced afterwards, but the market did not return and the ugly concrete entrances remained as a reminder of the brutalism of modern war.

The Marquesa de Povar, clad in widow's weeds, was helping Nationalist intelligence with even greater determination in revenge for her husband's death. When the damaged Republican government destroyer *José Luis Diez* arrived in Gibraltar for repairs, there was a flurry of activity by other Nationalist agents too, like the Spanish naval intelligence officer Fausto Saavedra, Marqués de Viana, hoping either to sabotage the destroyer for good or to make sure she did not get away. The Yome brothers, the Burgos delegate López Ferrer, his plain-clothes policeman, Horacio Soler, and the clerk Chicluna kept a twenty-four-hour watch on the Republican destroyer. When the *José Luis Diez* did escape from Gibraltar at 1 a.m. on 30 December, the Marquesa de Povar was said to be one of those who fired rockets (from, reportedly, the Royal Gibraltar Yacht Club) to alert Nationalist naval patrols. After a sharp fire-fight with the Nationalist gunboat *Calvo Sotelo* and the minelayers *Júpiter* and *Vulcano*, the Republican destroyer was run aground off the eastern fishing village of Catalan Bay, where several mis-directed shells landed and small-arms fire ricocheted. Gibraltar Police Constable Joseph Baglietto received a medal for saving cit-izens in this chaos, even though he himself was bleeding copiously from a jagged lump of shrapnel that struck him on the left breast, narrowly missing his heart.

A few days later, in January 1939, the editor of the *Gibraltar Chron-icle* received a vigorous letter from a group of Spanish Nationalists:

The great Spain of FRANCO demands the immediate deliverance of Gibraltar which was stolen from us by English pirates. By force of arms we demand it. Your sea-power is finished. Today we are the ones who give the orders. We sink your ships, we burn your flag, we shoot up Catalan Bay, we arrest your consular spies, we take possession of the Mediterranean, and we

defile your mothers. What do you do? Nothing. You are like your CHAM-
BERLAIN who goes from time to time to kiss the buttocks of the Dictators
who today govern the world. We will build a secure and strong empire. We
will destroy England . . . and only MUSSOLINI and HITLER will give
orders in Asia, Africa and everywhere.

The hour of revenge has come!! Our Gibraltar will be freed!! If
you refuse to give us our Gibraltar, we will massacre you as we did at
Guernica!!

English pirates and cowards, flee from Gibraltar, or Ceuta will blow you
up and no one will be left alive to abandon the Rock!!

Long live Franco.

Death to England.

Long live Fascism.

GIBRALTAR FOR SPAIN

On 27 January 1939, the Marquesa de Povar was among those
who celebrated the fall of Republican Barcelona to Franco's forces
with a drunken party at the 'Burgos Offices', the Nationalist sub-
agency at 2–4 College Lane, just where the narrow street curves west
off Main Street, opposite the offices of *El Calpense* newspaper. With
the windows open, the Spanish and Gibraltarian guests inside sang
triumphant Nationalist songs while an angry pro-Republican crowd
crammed the street outside. The Francoists taunted them with slogans shouted down from the windows. '*Un, dos, tres . . . ¡Barcelona
nuestra es!*' ('One, two, three . . . Barcelona belongs to me!') A man in
a Guardia Civil uniform gave the fascist salute, and there were *vivas*
for Franco, Hitler, *Italia* and *Alemania*, which agitated the crowd
even more. Then the overexcited Marquesa de Povar shouted from
the window, '*¡Muera Inglaterra!*' ('Death to England!'). The crowd
boiled over and only the police with truncheons stopped them battering down the thick door and storming the place. There were some
fights as the guests departed, but most of the crowd outside left to
follow a Gibraltarian called Richard Balloqui, waving a Union Jack,
just north along Main Street to El Martillo, the Commercial Square.
Balloqui then asked the 'brothers' to go home, without shouting and

making more noise, in a touching declaration of loyalty to the crown: 'We are all British subjects and very proud to be, God Bless our King. We are all working-class people, and know how to behave ourselves, and defend our flag, that flag, that we are under, and has been insulted by the bad fascists.'

The Spanish Republic was dying. In freezing February 1939, the Republican political leaders – Aguirre, Azaña, Companys, Martínez Barrio, Negrín – and thousands of refugees were escaping across the snowy Pyrenees from Catalonia into France, while seventy Condor Legion aircraft bombed and strafed their columns and convoys on road and rail. On 27 February 1939, 'a day of disgrace and folly' as Ivan Maisky called it in his diary, London and Paris recognised the government of General Franco. The Soviet ambassador in London drily noted that it had taken Britain and France seven years to recognise the Soviet Union, but barely seven days to recognise General Franco. In London, Azcárate was forced to hand over the Spanish Embassy to the Francoist Duke of Alba. Nationalist troops entered Madrid. 'The war is over,' Count Ciano wrote in his diary on 28 March. 'It is a new, formidable victory for Fascism, perhaps the greatest one so far.' Spain joined Italy and Germany in the Anti-Comintern Pact. General Franco declared the civil war at an end on 1 April 1939.

Claude Bowers, the US ambassador to Spain for the previous six years, saw the democratic failure to arm and help the Spanish Republic as an act of fatal appeasement, and when he met President Roosevelt at the White House, Roosevelt admitted: 'We have made a mistake; you have been right all along.' Nevertheless, the pragmatic USA also recognised Franco's regime on 3 April.

In May 1939 there were huge victory parades at Barajas airport, in Madrid and in León for the Italian and German armed forces who were now leaving Spain for home after their triumphant intervention on Franco's side. On 15 June, Italian airmen returned to Genoa, accompanied by the Spanish air force general Alfredo Kindelán, who had used Gibraltar's telephone system at the beginning of the uprising. In an interview, Kindelán claimed, 'The union of the Spanish and Italian air forces has made the Mediterranean into a lake which cannot be traversed by the enemy.'

General Edmund Ironside left Gibraltar on Monday 26 June 1939, to be replaced as governor by a rugger-bugger from 'the Tigers', the Royal Leicestershire Regiment, General Sir Clive Gerald Liddell, a former adjutant general of the British army. As Ironside drove through the gate at Four Corners, heading north for Burgos and Paris, the band of the 1st Battalion Welsh Guards played 'Auld Lang Syne', the same tune the band of the King's Regiment had played for Harington when he left by sea, lashed by wind and rain. Ironside had ridden (awkwardly) to hounds with the Royal Calpe Hunt and, like Harington and Godley before him, had learned to sail in Gibraltar. His worst crisis on the Rock was not, like Harington, seeing his dentures trapped in an egg while wrestling with a tiller, but the grief that overcame him when his beloved dog, a scarred and savage Staffordshire bull terrier called Caesar, chased a goat off Europa Point and was drowned in the battering surf.

Ironside arrived in London on 1 July and went straight to see Lord Gort, the Chief of the Imperial General Staff. Ironside's new job and title was Inspector-General Overseas Forces, but his understanding was that he was to be the Commander-in-Chief of the British Expeditionary Force supporting the French on the European mainland when war came, under a French general but with the 'right of appeal' to London. When Ironside asked the Secretary of State for War to whom he should appeal – the Cabinet? the prime minister? the War Office? – Leslie Hore-Belisha said he did not know. Although Hore-Belisha had managed to double the Territorial Army since 1937, bring in conscription, get the cavalry into tanks, improve anti-aircraft defences and modernise the army in many ways, the British armed forces were still not really prepared for the gigantic onslaught approaching. The three services did not work together effectively – the navy was going to blockade Germany, the air force was going to bomb it and the army was going to commit its very few divisions to Flanders.

Ironside knew Neville Chamberlain was not a prime minister for wartime. 'He is a pacifist at heart. He has a firm belief that God has chosen him as an instrument to prevent this threatened war.' Winston Churchill should be the war-lord, he reckoned; Churchill in return admired Ironside's energy and ability. Ironside went to Chartwell, Churchill's home in Kent, for dinner in late July and they talked through the night until 5 a.m., with Churchill striding in front of the map and explaining his ideas – how the Germans would smash into Poland, how Italy would attack Egypt and how Hitler might well make a pact with Stalin. When this cynical volte-face did indeed, as Churchill predicted, happen in late August, any dreams of an Anglo-Franco-Soviet 'Eastern Front' against Nazi Germany disappeared. On 1 September, Churchill telephoned Ironside at 10 a.m. to tell him that Warsaw and Krakow had been bombed at dawn and German forces were invading Poland. Winston Churchill outside government clearly had better sources than the War Office.

The Royal Navy was first of the services off the mark on Sunday 3 September 1939. At 11.17, the Admiralty signalled all its ships and units 'TOTAL GERMANY'. The Gibraltar government received a telephone message from General Forces Headquarters at 1 p.m.: 'WE ARE NOW AT WAR WITH GERMANY'. An hour later came the first of many telegrams dated 3.9.39 from London: 'See preface defence scheme. War has broken out with Germany'; then a series of single code-words – 'BISTO', 'VIXEN', 'SNAIL', 'TIT-BIT', etc. – indicating specific things to be done. All enemy merchant ships and enemy civil aircraft were to be seized 'in prize', their radio gear carefully dismantled. As the news spread in Gibraltar, melancholy hooters sounded from the dockyard. People were calm, however; the police incident book for all Gibraltar that day only records a man in City Mill Lane accusing a neighbour of damaging his spectacles.

War was declared in London by Neville Chamberlain announcing it on the wireless, but in Gibraltar it was royally proclaimed on a parchment with a large red seal:

I, SIR CLIVE GERALD LIDDELL, Governor and Vice-Admiral of Gibraltar, being satisfied thereof by information received by me, DO HEREBY PROCLAIM that War has broken out between His Majesty and Germany.

Given at Gibraltar this 3rd day of September, 1939.

By His Excellency's Command.

Alexander Beattie

Colonial Secretary.

The final approval to form a Gibraltar Defence Force came through on the day war was declared. By year's end Gibraltar's Anti-Aircraft Section had one officer (the Gibraltarian Second Lieutenant Freddie Gache RA) and forty-seven other ranks, who manned two quick-firing three-inch 20 cwt guns of First World War vintage. Two dozen men made up the signal section, and another twelve were medics. Because they were Gibraltarian colonials the British army only paid them three quarters the rate of British soldiers.

When the war broke out, Governor Liddell later admitted, 'Gibraltar was practically undefended.' The coastal defence batteries could deal with some ship bombardment, but 'the possibility of an attack from the mainland was ignored altogether.' Anti-aircraft defences were almost 'non-existent' and the harbour and beaches were defenceless against landings. 'The garrison was insufficient to man even the armament which had been installed, inadequate though it was.'

In London that Sunday, 3 September 1939, General Ironside was summoned from an evening drink at his club to the War Office. Expecting to be appointed commander-in-chief of the four divisions of the British Expeditionary Force (BEF) being sent to France, Ironside was astonished to be asked instead by Leslie Hore-Belisha to become the Chief of the Imperial General Staff – in effect the army's brainbox; Winston Churchill, newly returned to the Admiralty, had backed Hore-Belisha's choice. Ironside was bitterly disappointed not to command an army in the field but, as ever, said he would do his duty. (He said he never asked for nor refused a job; his whole life was based on doing what he was told.)

'And here is the Commander-in-Chief of the BEF,' said Hore-Belisha, ushering in fifty-three-year-old Lord Gort from another office. The top job in the field had gone to another fighting soldier, the Irish Viscount Gort, who had been mentioned in dispatches eight times in the Great War, when he also won the Military Cross, three Distinguished Service Orders and the Victoria Cross for conspicuous bravery. John Gort, delighted with his field command after being shut up in the War Office as Chief of the Imperial General Staff under Hore-Belisha (whom he had come to loathe), set off for France with the 152,000 men of the BEF, leaving Edmund Ironside in charge, and in the lurch.

Ironside was 'flabbergasted' to discover how unprepared Britain was for war – no men, no munitions, no armour, no stocks – and appalled by how red tape strangled every initiative. Hore-Belisha told him it would be like ordering a car: you asked the Ministry of Supply for the equipment for a division and they delivered it. Ironside said it was somewhat like ordering a car, except the vehicle arrived all in bits and you had to assemble it yourself. The war would last three years, Ironside thought, and Britain would need to raise fifty divisions, each of around twenty thousand men, to add to the existing two complete infantry divisions and one partially armoured division.

On the Home Front, the nation was not yet sure it was at war. Fascists and communists were vying with each other to become the British people's 'peace party'; there were panics and alarums, hysteria and spy fever. MI5, the Security Service, were unhappy with Ironside's appointment as Chief of the Imperial General Staff because rumour led them to believe he was a secret sympathiser with the British Union of Fascists. These suspicions seemed to be confirmed when Ironside asked for Major General J. F. C. Fuller to be his deputy. (MI5 was tapping Fuller's telephone because he was an extreme right-winger.) In fact, Ironside wanted Fuller not because he was pro-fascist but because he was an expert on the tanks which Britain so badly needed for armoured warfare.

Fuller never got the position, but his anti-Semitic lobbying probably helped bring down Leslie Hore-Belisha, the Jewish Secretary of State for War, on 5 January 1940. Chamberlain offered Hore-Belisha the Board of Trade; Hore-Belisha resigned instead, and Oliver Stanley, a lesser man, took his place as Secretary of State for War.

Meanwhile, across the North Sea, in the seven months from January to July 1940, Nazi Germany's armaments production doubled.

10

The Disrupters

A devastating medical diagnosis skewed Vice Admiral James Somerville's naval career in 1939. He had just been appointed Commander-in-Chief, East Indies, head of the Royal Navy forces who would confront Imperial Japan in case of war, when his check-up detected pulmonary tuberculosis. The bacilli of the 'white plague' gradually destroy the victim's lungs while the body loses strength and wastes away, hence the common name 'consumption'. The cough-borne contagious disease is dreaded aboard ships, where men live at close quarters. At sea, any patient with TB must be taken off duty and isolated in a well-ventilated cabin, and his clothing, bed-linen, crockery and cutlery boiled and washed separately. So Somerville was sent home and compulsorily retired from the RN active list.

However, the fifty-seven-year-old sailor completely rejected the diagnosis, found a Harley Street doctor to support him and forced a Navy Medical Board to regrade him for employment without command at sea. Wisely, the Admiralty did not waste his talents. Somerville, former Director of the Signal Division, had specialised in radio communications, and his twenty years' experience made him the right man to develop applications of the new invention, RDF (radio direction finding), also known by its American name: RaDAR (radio detection and ranging).

RDF work had been going on since February 1935 when Robert Watson-Watt first demonstrated that passing aircraft interrupted and bounced back pulses from the BBC radio transmitter at Daventry. Watson-Watt continued developing it in secret at the experimental station of Bawdsey Manor in Suffolk, where tall towers were built for transmitting and receiving signals. On 13 March 1936, an

aircraft flying fifteen hundred feet above the North Sea was successfully detected seventy-five miles away. RAF officers were trained to
use the apparatus and by May 1937 could locate the bearing and
range of all hostile aircraft. This changed the nature of the game: in
modern parlance, RDF was a 'disruptive technology'. Enemy bombers could no longer suddenly appear out of the blue without being
tracked, giving RAF Fighter Command time to marshal its defensive forces. Eventually, a network of twenty RDF or radar stations,
'Chain Home', was constructed, covering the airspace from Scotland
to the Solent at a cost of £2,000,000.

In October 1937, six months after the Condor Legion bombing
of Gernika, three very senior German air force officers including
General Erhard Milch, the creator of Lufthansa, and heavy-drink-
ing Ernst Udet, a former First World War air ace now promot-
ing the dive-bomber, were on a friendly visit to the RAF Fighter
Command HQ at Bentley Priory, Stanmore, northwest London.
The Germans were proud and cocky. Earlier that month, Udet
had shown the famous US aviator Charles Lindbergh round the
secret German air-testing base at Rechlin in Pomerania, where he
examined the new Messerschmitt Bf 109 fighter and the Dornier
Do 17 light bomber-reconnaissance plane. Udet also took him up
in a folding-wing Fieseler Fi 156 *Storch*. At pre-lunch drinks in the
RAF HQ, General Milch, the man who had built up and rearmed
the Luftwaffe, caused consternation among the British VIPs by
saying: 'Now gentlemen, let us all be frank! How are you getting on
with your experiments in the radio detection of aircraft approaching your shores?'

At least one glass crashed to the floor and the head of Fighter
Command, Air Chief Marshal Sir Hugh Dowding, tried to laugh it
off in embarrassment.

'Come, gentlemen!' said Milch. 'There is no need to be cagey
about it. We've known for some time that you were developing a
system of radiolocation. So are we, and we think we are a jump
ahead of you.'

RDF/radar's main function at the time was detecting aircraft so the Air Ministry monopolised the research on behalf of the Royal Air Force. James Somerville, however, wanted radar for the Royal Navy. Back at the Signal Division with a cover title, Inspector of Anti-Aircraft Weapons and Devices (IAAWD), he went to work in unofficial liaison with Fighter Command, helped by Winston Churchill, a member of a sub-committee on Air Defence Research.

Churchill had gone to Bawdsey Manor one day in June 1939 to inspect a new coastal radar that would help guns and searchlights aim accurately at low-flying aircraft and ships at sea. This was more difficult than spotting objects high in the sky, and required a high-power 'split beam', created by a brilliant New Zealand scientist called Alan Butement (who also went on to develop the proximity fuse that revolutionised anti-aircraft fire).* Churchill pronounced the split beam 'Marvellous', and said, 'We must have this for His Majesty's ships. I will see to it.' The very next day, 21 June 1939, Admiral Somerville arrived to view and test the equipment.

Somerville's travels on behalf of RDF for the Royal Navy took him from Portsmouth in the south of England to Fair Isle in the far north of Scotland, installing early warning Coast Defence (CD) stations. He was also encouraging new research and development for the Admiralty: the Inspector of Anti-Aircraft Weapons and Devices was nicknamed the 'Instigator of Anti-Aircraft Wheezes and Dodges'. From his innovations sprang DMWD, the Department of Miscellaneous Weapons Development. Staffed by people such as N. S. Norway (who later became the successful novelist Nevil Shute), the DMWD helped to foil German magnetic mines with so-called 'degaussing coils', created the Hedgehog and Squid mortars to tackle German submarines, produced the Bouncing Bomb for the dam-busters, and made concrete Churchill's sketchy idea of the floating Mulberry Harbour in time for D-Day in 1944.

---

* The Wikipedia entry on W. A. S. Butement notes that he was one of the very first to conceive a radio apparatus for detecting ships, as recorded in the *Inventions Book of the Royal Engineers Board*, January 1931.

War disrupted the cloisters of academe too. On 14 January 1940, on his twenty-sixth birthday, Hugh Trevor-Roper, a bespectacled junior research fellow at Merton College, Oxford, about to publish his first book about seventeenth-century history, *Archbishop Laud*, found himself in jail. However, he was not banged up with old lags in Wormwood Scrubs prison in West London, but was surrounded by MI5 officers including Guy Liddell, 'Tar' Robertson and Dick White because the Victorian gaol was now one of MI5's wartime offices.

Trevor-Roper was actually working for the Radio Security Section (RSS), part of MI8, the signals intelligence department of the War Office. The young don had been recruited by his college bursar, Walter Gill, formerly a Royal Engineer wireless intelligence officer who used the Great Pyramid of Giza as an intercept mast in the First World War. Radio Security Section were monitoring enemy wireless signals inside the UK, particularly seeking any transmissions from spies who might be guiding bombers to their targets. RSS were also making use of a network of 'voluntary interceptors', members of the Radio Society of Great Britain, listening out on their 'ham wireless' and crystal sets for any illicit broadcasts. After Post Office detection vans located them, MI5 and Special Branch could then swoop in and bag the offender.

Trevor-Roper was as bright and sharp as a new sabre. Child of a loveless home, he threw his body into field sports and his mind into intense intellectual work. As an undergraduate Classical Scholar at Christ Church, Oxford, he taught himself German in order to read German classicists, breaking 'the code' of the language, as he said, by devouring Ferdinand Gregorovius's eight-volume *Geschichte der Stadt Rom im Mittelalter* (*History of Rome in the Middle Ages*) in the original.

Early in 1940, hardly any German spies were in England, but since 1938 MI5 had had its first double agent, a Welsh electrical engineer called Arthur Owens, code-named Snow, now installed in another prison at Wandsworth. His British case officer had alerted RSS to

Owens's messages, mysterious radio signals originating from outside the UK, and these enciphered messages were dutifully sent on to the SIS-run Government Code and Cipher School at its war station, Bletchley Park. For some reason, these early RSS intercepts had been dismissed as unimportant Russian messages from Shanghai. But Walter Gill, who knew some cryptography, and Hugh Trevor-Roper, who knew German, decided to have a go at breaking them themselves. These two amateurs, living in a flat in Ealing, were the first to crack a simple Abwehr hand-cipher in January 1940, and were thus able to eavesdrop on Abwehr Hamburg talking to its agents who were trying to get into Britain.

In March 1940, Bletchley Park formed a separate section to handle what Gill and Trevor-Roper had found. All Abwehr hand-cipher traffic was sent to the cryptanalyst Oliver Strachey, the piano-playing younger brother of the Bloomsbury writer Lytton Strachey, and the decrypts thereafter circulated under the name ISOS (Intelligence Service, Oliver Strachey). In December 1941, the legendary Dilly Knox's team at Bletchley broke the Enigma key that Abwehr headquarters used to communicate with its controlling stations in neutral countries like Spain. This decrypt material was then sourced as ISK (Intelligence Service, Knox). Because recipients did not need to know the difference, ISOS became the generic term for all decrypts of German secret intelligence service radio traffic. During the war, nearly a hundred thousand ISOS messages were distributed from GC&CS.

In time, the Radio Security Section became the Radio Security Service and was taken over by MI6 Section VIII, where it formed the Abwehr interception station at Hanslope Park in Buckinghamshire. Trevor-Roper's own Traffic Analysis section was hived off to MI6 Section V (counter-intelligence outside the United Kingdom.) They moved to a large country house in North Barnet called Arkley View and became known as V(w), that is to say the wireless part of SIS counter-intelligence. Section V itself was based in St Albans, and the head of its Iberian desk was Kim Philby. He had been a *Times* correspondent in the Spanish Civil War and had been decorated by Franco, which was good cover for his secret activities as a Soviet agent. Philby's job was to keep an eye on the enemy in the Iberian Peninsula, particularly Spain, eavesdropping on the Abwehr in Madrid communicating with its substations in Spain and Spanish Morocco, all of which could pose a threat to the Strait of Gibraltar.

Abwehr ISOS/ISK messages – a goldmine of information – were classified MOST SECRET and were not to be disclosed to anyone unauthorised. Their contents could not be summarised, extracted or even referred to without the approval of the Director of the Government Code and Cipher School at Bletchley Park. They had to be protected and kept secret so that the Abwehr would never get any hint that their ciphers were broken and that their secret service, together with its agents, instructions and reports, was open to British scrutiny and analysis. The distribution list of ISOS material in Britain was limited to three named individuals working in navy, army and air force intelligence, one man in B Division of MI5 and four men in MI6 counter-espionage, Section V of SIS, including Colonel Vivian, Major Cowgill and Captain Hugh Trevor-Roper.

Often the material was opaque, and had to be confirmed from other sources. Here, for example, is ISOS message 20247 as it appeared at St Albans, decrypted and translated into English, among a string of others from Bletchley Park.

GROUP 11/126
MADRID TO SAN SEBASTIAN
RSS 906/14/2/42
LF 5200 kcs. 1217 GMT 14/2/42
186/90
[No. 469] Sunday morning, the 15th, fetch RICHARD SCHUBERT from HENDAYE and arrange for a sleeper to MEDIA.

This is an instruction from Abwehr Madrid to its *Stelle* (station) in San Sebastián in the Basque country to move an individual by car and train from the French border to Madrid, code-named Media. 'Richard Schubert' would now have a file opened on him or have his existing one amended with travel details. Good files are crucial to intelligence work, much of which is keeping tabs on suspect individuals. Kenneth Benton of SIS, who ran the key Section V office in the British Embassy in Madrid from 1941 to 1943, handling ISOS material from St Albans, ended up with a fourteen-foot row of sixteen card cabinets over which five women worked every day just checking and adding names. If 'Schubert' was an alias then Benton, with a network of contacts across Spain, would know from whom to obtain the passenger lists of sleeper cars or aeroplanes as well as copies of hotel registers, guests' bills and ships' manifests to cross-check the real name. Twenty-two British consular posts in the key ports and junctions of Spain, each with its own networks of friends and helpers, also supplied information. So any German agent or *V-mann* travelling anywhere via Spain or Portugal was identified and tracked early. When such an agent was arrested, say, at Bermuda on his way to the USA, a search of his cabin would reveal the invisible ink, the secret instructions in the microdot, the miniature radio, etc., and everyone would think the discovery of this paraphernalia of espionage was responsible for his capture and downfall, and have no idea of the covert listening and decrypting and card-indexing done so far away.

Yet when young then Lieutenant Trevor-Roper wrote and circulated a paper on the activity of the German secret service in Morocco he was not congratulated by his employers but condemned. Felix Cowgill, the deputy head of Section V, an ex-Indian policeman obsessed with safeguarding secrecy, said Trevor-Roper should be court-martialled for his effrontery.

In his later writings, Trevor-Roper identified the great rift in the wartime intelligence community between the 'dons' and the 'cops'. 'Dons' were intellectuals who wanted to critique ideas and techniques and to share information, even between rival services, in a collegiate way; 'cops' were subversion-fighters like Cowgill and his boss Valentine Vivian who wanted everybody always to shut up for fear of breaching security. Trevor-Roper thought secrecy often cloaked stupidity.

At Arkley View, Trevor-Roper put together a brilliant team of Oxford professors and lecturers, including the philosophers Stuart Hampshire and Gilbert Ryle and the historian Charles Stuart, who used ISOS material to monitor and analyse the global networks of German intelligence revealed via their radio communications. These clever, sarcastic men helped provide the feedback loop for the successful Double-Cross system. They collated and connected what was eavesdropped from the Abwehr either side of the Strait of Gibraltar and across the world, filing and cross-referencing and footnoting with scholarly precision. They wrote reports of admirable clarity and cogency as they rose to the new challenges of the war, exemplifying intelligence in action. But in their elitist Oxford way they also scathingly derided the secret world, inhabited by 'timid and corrupt incompetents, without ideals or standards' whose labours consisted largely of 'bum-sucking under the backstairs of bureaucracy'.

The Chamberlain government thought the Hitler regime was fragile and would soon crumble under popular discontent if the material economy was hit hard enough. Blockade had been a British weapon of war since the eighteenth century. Against Napoleon, against the Kaiser and now against Hitler, Royal Navy ships endeavoured to cut off supplies to enemy territory and to sever their communications. In the Great War, the British and the French had taken eighteen months to set up their Ministries of Blockade or *du Blocus*, and three years to start a system of escorted convoys, although their efforts eventually had a real impact on the Central Powers, where *die Blockade* was alleged to have starved over half a million people to death by 1918.

Of course Germany also attempted its own blockade of Britain by waging unrestricted submarine warfare on merchant shipping from 1916. An island nation was vulnerable to attacks on its supplies of food and raw materials. In 1939, Great Britain had fifty million mouths to feed. Meanwhile, its industry and commerce relied on sixty million tons of maritime imports every year, much of it carried by the British Empire and Commonwealth's merchant navy, the world's largest, with some 6700 vessels of all kinds.

This time there was no dawdling. Immediately after the German torpedoing of the transatlantic passenger liner *Athenia* on 3 September 1939, the Admiralty took control of a renewed system of escorted convoys, grouping merchant ships and warships together as protection against U-boats, setting their course and speed and appointing a senior naval officer called a convoy commodore to each group. The civilian Ministry of Shipping, working with the Ministry of Supply, requisitioned the ships and authorised their cargoes, although the operation of individual vessels remained with their owners or agents.

At the same time, in September 1939, a new ministry, the Ministry of Economic Warfare (MEW), took over the buildings of the London School of Economics and Political Science in the Aldwych, London WC2. MEW used the Royal Navy as its executive instrument to enforce the blockade of Germany in a system called Naval Contraband Control. Neutral ships were stopped and searched at five maritime choke points.

Here Gibraltar was key because it handled Iberian traffic to South America as well as all eastbound shipping into the Mediterranean. Haifa, Port Said and Malta dealt with westbound traffic, while Aden checked the Gulf and Indian Ocean. Kirkwall in Orkney dealt with Scandinavian and North Sea shipping, while Ramsgate and Dover controlled the English Channel. The French had *blocus* bases at Le Havre and Dunkirk, Oran and Marseilles, Dakar and Casablanca.

Boarding parties going aboard neutral ships were looking for two kinds of goods to seize. 'Absolute contraband' was obvious war matériel: arms, ammunition, explosives, precursor chemicals and minerals, fuel, means of transport and communication, machine tools, dies, components, bullion, coins, currency, evidences of debt. 'Conditional contraband' was all foodstuffs, hides and skins, textiles and clothing: all materials potentially helpful to the enemy war effort.

Much contraband cargo was carried in ships heading to neutral countries, particularly 'adjacent neutrals'. This was a ploy the British had spotted in the First World War, when food imports to Germany's neighbours in Denmark and Holland shot up dramatically. The first Ministry of Blockade was set up after Basil Clarke of the *Daily Mail* reported that neutral Denmark's 1915 imports of cocoa, coffee, lard, pork and rice had increased grotesquely since 1913. 'WE ARE FEEDING THE GERMANS', shouted his dramatic headline. Boarding parties had to keep their wits about them. At Gibraltar in the First World War, they found wolfram being smuggled in barrels of grapes and guns inside hollowed-out timber stacks.

Contraband control was also paralysingly slow in the Second World War. A neutral ship could be delayed for many days while manifests and bills of lading were posted to headquarters for verification and cargo holds were minutely examined. From December 1939, obtaining a 'navicert' (navigation certificate) from an official of a blockading power at the port of embarkation speeded the process. A navicert was a kind of commercial passport issued to neutral ships certifying that the cargo had been checked at point of egress. Gibraltar's boarding parties went aboard with crowbars and pincers, led by an uncanny petty officer nicknamed 'The Ferret' who had the gift of sniffing out any hidey-hole of contraband. A dozen large canisters marked on the Buenos Aires manifest as 'Tinned Soup' did indeed contain a beefy broth, but each also had a secret compartment welded inside, holding a slab of platinum and a bundle of letters for the German Foreign Office.

The Admiralty term for anything legally confiscated was 'condemned in prize'. In the first four months of the war, British Contraband Control seized nearly 530,000 tons of contraband heading for Germany, including 190,000 tons of base metals, 130,000 tons of petroleum products, 48,000 tons of oilseeds, 25,000 tons of textiles, and 22,000 tons of food and drink.

The Second World War disrupted women's lives in many different ways. One of those working in the Naval Contraband Control office in Gibraltar was twenty-three-year-old Mollie Spencer, who was not quite twenty when she was first evacuated from Spain on the destroyer HMS *Beagle* at the start of the civil war. She was English, but raised in Andalusia, one of the five daughters of Tom 'Don Tomás' Spencer, the British pro-consul in Jerez de la Frontera and manager of the Williams & Humbert sherry *bodega* there. He was the man who first introduced soccer to the city before the Great War. Mollie Spencer was bilingual, having grown up in the heart of Jerez, though she was mainly educated in England and was a devout Anglican. She hated the civil war because she knew people on both sides and it threatened the whole world she had known as a child.

Come the Second World War, however, Mollie Spencer was determined to join up and serve, just like her brother Tom. She was in Gibraltar on her way to England to join the women's branch of the British Army, the ATS, when someone offered her a job in Gibraltar Contraband Control office, where they held a copy of MEW's continually updated, loose-leaf *Black List* of firms and companies trading with the enemy, plus all the names of 'undesirable' seamen. (Anyone *persona non grata* could not sail on an ocean-going neutral ship because their presence would block the issuing of a navicert.) Mollie's photograph appeared in *The Times* on 8 February 1940, showing her in the Contraband Control office with a poster on the wall behind her which says 'DON'T HELP THE ENEMY! Careless Talk May Give Away Vital Secrets'. A naval cap with a white cotton cover hangs on the same nail as an aircraft identification chart, and there are eight RN and RNVR officers also visible. The only woman, Mollie, is sitting, pen in hand, bent over some papers at a wooden desk with a typewriter on it (she was a skilled shorthand typist). She is wearing a dark dress with a plain white collar and her dark hair is tied back in a roll which rests on her pale curved neck. She has the still beauty of a Madonna, and although she appears demure, she regularly rose to the challenge of boarding suspect vessels out in the bay, on duty with her new colleagues.

The RN Contraband Control patrols were on the lookout for letters. The right of 'visit and search' extended to post; a ship's navicert stated that all sacks of mail carried aboard would be submitted for British censorship. This was a vital function of wartime intelligence. People might be less shocked by Edward Snowden's twenty-first-century revelations if they knew the process of screening world communications has been going on for over a century. By the time of Hitler's War, the British authorities owned the major telegraph companies and had an effective 'Y' or listening service so that they could read most cables and eavesdrop on nearly all wireless messages. In those analogue days, most of the world (including its agents, spies and traitors) entrusted handwritten letters and brown-paper parcels to the universal postal service. Perhaps because the penny postage stamp had been a British invention of the 1840s, and because their national security was now at stake, the British arrogated to themselves the right to screen not only their own domestic post but much of the world's mail in transit through the British Empire or Allied countries.

The global censorship system was run first by the War Office and then, after April 1940, by the Ministry of Information. Its first headquarters was in Liverpool, using the offices of Littlewood's Football Pools, before it moved to London and the massive Prudential Assurance building in Holborn. Gibraltar was the first of six Imperial Censorship Stations to be set up round the Atlantic; later additions included Bermuda, Trinidad, Jamaica, and Bathurst (now called Banjul) in the Gambia.

In Gibraltar, the 230 Imperial Censorship staff took over the newly erected King George V Memorial Hospital as their office. Staff slept in bunks set up on the ground floor of the now evacuated Loreto Convent School in Europa Road. Germany redirected a lot of its post through neutral Italy for the first nine months of the war, so there were thousands of bags of mail to check at Gibraltar, and staff pleaded for even more office space on the South Mole where the ships docked. When the liner SS *Rex* tied up in February 1940, President Roosevelt's special envoy Sumner Welles, on his way to talk to Mussolini, Hitler, Daladier and Chamberlain, had to wait for several hours while 334 US mailbags were hauled off for inspection.

Contraband Control at Gibraltar also looked for letters that were not in mailbags. They regularly cleared out ship's lavatories blocked by the epistles stuffed down there by panicking couriers. Ratings rowed dinghies round many a ship's hull scooping up correspondence ditched through portholes. On large passenger ships, they sometimes searched all the cabins on one side, port or starboard, duly chalking each door. The next day, they would search exactly the same cabins and find loads of booty stowed there by the occupants of the unchalked cabins.

Imperial Censorship employed intelligent linguists and boasted that it never opened a letter it could not read. Indiscreet sentences in letters, perhaps revealing the names or whereabouts of military units, were physically snipped out of the letter with scissors, and the envelope was stamped 'PASSED CENSOR' or 'EXAMINED BY CENSOR'. The artist and SAS soldier John Verney noted how the 'savage, irrational depredations' of the censor's scissors turned his descriptive letters to his wife Lucinda into Surrealist poems. He likened them to the trick of some Cubist painters, sticking random strips of paper on the blank canvas, which, when pulled off the completed painting of jugs, fruit, guitars or whatever, left the picture suggestively incomplete.

Much of the surveillance was secret. Though some letters were destroyed entirely, others were sent on to their destination having been photographed and logged for the attention of the Secret Intelligence and Security Services in London. Envelopes could be gently steamed and their letters extracted, read, returned and resealed without obvious evidence of tampering. They could be tested for invisible ink by two diagonal chemical slashes, back and front; microdots could be immensely magnified. The diplomatic and consular bags of allied, friendly, neutral and hostile nations were regularly perused by 'Special Examiners' in an unmentionable, highly classified (and illicit) operation known as XXX or TRIPLEX.

★

Belfast-born Harford Montgomery Hyde was no longer a working barrister, and was not yet the Ulster Unionist MP who would campaign so vigorously for homosexual law reform that it would cost him his parliamentary seat in bigoted Northern Ireland. H. Montgomery Hyde arrived in Gibraltar at the end of January 1940 to carry on the secret service work that the war had pitched him into. Colonel Lawrence Grand in D Section of the Secret Service first employed him in the Adelphi Hotel in Liverpool inserting anti-Nazi black propaganda leaflets into letters inside sealed US mailbags destined for Germany. He would do the same sort of thing in Gibraltar, though he could not tamper with everything because he said he lacked the facility to reproduce wax seals.

Montgomery Hyde shared a house with the man who ran Gibraltar Censorship, Captain Humphrey Cotton-Minchin. They lived in Secretary's Lane, at the back of the Convent, in between the Colonial Secretary's residence and Fortress Headquarters on Line Wall Road. Montgomery Hyde thought garrison Gibraltar 'unattractive' and 'no great credit to our colonial administration'. He deplored the lack of a good bookshop in a place with a population larger than Oxford, finding the Garrison Library contained little 'beyond military manuals, *Leaves from a Staff Officer's Diary* and so forth'. He was amazed that after 240 years of British occupation, so 'few of the natives can speak English. I am quite certain that were the French to take over for five years everyone would be able to speak French . . .'

Gibraltar's Postal Censorship kept busy. In the porter's lodge of the hospital, renamed Room 99 after the secret site in Liverpool, Montgomery Hyde was soon removing pro-Nazi propaganda leaflets in English, Spanish and Portuguese from the German postbags heading towards the republics of North and South America. Once they were extracted, he substituted anti-Nazi propaganda leaflets in the same languages, delighted that the Nazis were paying for the postage. The 'Special Examiners' interfered with personal mail too. One *Fraülein*, writing passionately to her lover in Argentina, enclosed a sample of her pubic hair, which accidentally got lost when the letter was opened. So Montgomery Hyde plucked some coarse bristles from a floor-broom and substituted them instead.

Many of his two hundred-plus censors, termed 'examiners', were formidably intelligent women. Myrtle Winter had been brought up in India and could read and speak Dutch, French, German, Italian, Persian and Spanish, as well as excelling at photography, swimming and horse-riding. Another was the thirty-year-old, Egyptian-born Alethea Hayter, a thin, elegant beauty who had been the fashion editor of *Country Life* before war disrupted her life. She would go on to become a distinguished independent scholar, author of the classic *Opium and the Romantic Imagination*. Perhaps her years in postal censorship in Gibraltar, Bermuda and London helped Hayter later to become such a brilliant close reader, alert to layers of meaning within a text, able to synthesise and distil from many sources. (The exigencies of war may have shaped other women writers too. Did Muriel Spark's work in the Political Warfare Executive's black propaganda unit in London prompt the interest in fakery and double-dealing shown in her fictions? Did Christine Brooke-Rose's work at Bletchley Park perhaps lead her to write the kind of novels that need decrypting?)

Alethea Hayter drew on her Gibraltar experience as well as her imaginative sympathies in her early 1970s book *A Voyage in Vain*, the story of the poet Coleridge's journey by naval convoy to Malta in 1804, during the Napoleonic Wars. 'England was fighting for her life against a power that had dominated the Continent and threatened her with invasion, and the war at sea, of which this convoy was part, was the most vital and active sector of the war at this time.' Hayter explained Coleridge's apparent indifference to history and the wider world of England's war against Napoleon by referring to her own experience of returning from Gibraltar with 175 other colleagues from Postal Censorship when they were evacuated in mid-June 1940, yielding their sleeping quarters in the Loreto Convent School to scores of 'listeners' from the radio interception 'Y' service working at Middle Hill.

It had been decided that now Italy had formally entered the war as a belligerent and the Mediterranean was a war zone, Western Hemisphere postal censorship must be moved 3500 miles west to Bermuda and that all the censors should go with it. The Gibraltar 'examiners' left aboard a 3900-ton steamship with a chequered imperial past. The ship had taken Indian indentured labourers to the sugar-cane fields of Trinidad, Surinam, British Guiana and Fiji, and had carried Muslim pilgrims to Jeddah on the *haj*. Now renamed SS *Al Rawdah* and war-requisitioned, it became a troopship.

Twenty-one ships in naval convoy HG 34F left Gibraltar on 13 June 1940, heading for Liverpool. It was dangerous. Their convoy – only protected by a single sloop, HMS *Scarborough* – was attacked by German submarines northwest of Portugal and three of its vessels were torpedoed and sunk by *U-48*. And yet, Alethea Hayter says, her own diary of the perilous voyage reflected 'the timeless irresponsible life of a passenger on board ship', with minor observations and shipboard gossip, just as Coleridge in 1804 had written nothing of Nelson and Napoleon but merely sketched sails and scribbled his complaints about fat Mrs Ireland's endless gorging and gourmandising. 'One cannot be afraid twenty-four hours in twenty-four,' wrote Hayter, 'or even consciously resolute and aware . . .' In the face of danger, 'one's mind persists in trivial routines and enjoyments.'

Having survived their voyage home, the censors soon set sail again across the North Atlantic to Bermuda, which became the busiest station, growing to employ some fifteen hundred so-called 'censorettes' in the requisitioned waterfront Princess Hotel in Hamilton. They could process a hundred bags of mail a day – around two hundred thousand letters – and test fifteen thousand of them for microdots and secret ink messages, before putting the bags on the next flight or ship. Bermuda, the place where all the transatlantic passenger liners and the Lisbon–New York Pan American Airways clippers called, was the ideal spot for scooping up spies and contraband. The Americans, having initially grumbled, soon saw the advantages of this useful infringement of freedom. The Office of Censorship USA became part of the intelligence-gathering machinery, sharing the information gleaned with its allies.

The blockade of Germany leaked like a sieve. One curiosity was that Germany's exports were not targeted like her imports. For example, 'neutral' Fascist Italy produced only a sixth of its own coal and was completely dependent on the nine million tons of coal imported from Germany. Most of this passed through the Strait of Gibraltar, having been shipped down the English Channel. When Contraband Control finally stopped thirteen ships carrying German coal for Italy in early March 1940, the Italians kicked up such a storm of indignation about breaches of international law that Neville Chamberlain let the vessels go.

The Labour MP Hugh Dalton pointed out other gaping holes in the blockade in the House of Commons on 19 March 1940. 'We are much too gentlemanly, too slow-witted and too traditional in the conduct of this war,' he declared, robustly.

Philip Noel-Baker described Dalton as 'a man of violent passions, uncertain temper, great ambition and real ability . . . flamboyantly a Socialist and a social rebel'. This had begun early. The four-year-old son of the Dean of Windsor had said to Queen Victoria when she came to tea, 'Go away, Queen, I don't like you.'

Dalton's criticism of the blockade in parliament was the more pointed because he was using information secretly acquired from inside the Ministry of Economic Warfare itself, where his young economist protégé Hugh Gaitskell (later leader of the Labour Party) was the Head of Intelligence for Enemy Countries. Dalton pointed out exactly how the Germans were using adjacent neutral countries to obtain oil from Romania, iron ore from Sweden, cotton from America. Dalton also indicated the blockade's great hole in the Pacific Ocean, where the British and the French could not stop and search the ships of Japan, the USA and the USSR. As a result rubber, tin, copper, nickel, chromium and other resources were pouring in through Vladivostok, the main port of Soviet Russia's Far East, and being transported to Nazi Germany via the Trans-Siberian railway. 'I suggest that in certain directions we have been outwitted and outdistanced by Hitler.'

Hugh Dalton was also making a naked political play. Focusing on economic warfare's offensive possibilities meant that he was very well placed when Chamberlain fell and Churchill had to set up a new wartime coalition government that included Labour and the Liberals. On 15 May 1940, Dalton replaced Ronald Cross as the Minister for Economic Warfare and quickly established his own team, including his 'mole', Gaitskell. Dalton was the kind of politician who lets his civil servants know who is boss. He once sent an underling to summon a senior official 'immediately' from the lavatory. 'Tell him to wait,' said the man with his pinstripes round his ankles, 'I can only deal with one shit at a time.'

Dalton's antennae were ever alert for more sources of power. When he heard in late June that the military were looking to coordinate 'covert' and 'irregular' activities abroad, he immediately began lobbying to run the new organisation. 'Dalton ringing up hourly to try and get a large finger in the Sabotage pie,' the head of the Foreign Office, Sir Alexander Cadogan, wrote in his diary on Friday 28 June.

Dalton thought that subversive economic warfare had to be 'ungentlemanly' and told the Foreign Secretary Lord Halifax so.

We have got to organise movements in enemy-occupied territory comparable to the Sinn Fein movement in Ireland, to the Chinese Guerrillas now operating against Japan, to the Spanish Irregulars who played such a notable part in Wellington's campaign . . . This 'democratic international' must use many different methods, including industrial and military sabotage, labour agitation and strikes, continuous propaganda, terrorist acts against traitors and German leaders, boycotts and riots.

Dalton the intellectual socialist thought this stirring up of revolutionary insurgency had to be done from the left. As George Orwell

observed: 'Patriotism has nothing to do with conservatism.'* On 19
July 1940, Neville Chamberlain, the dying but still game Lord President of the Council, drafted a memorandum setting up the Special
Operations Executive (SOE) 'to co-ordinate all action, by way of subversion and sabotage, against the enemy overseas', and announced
that the organisation would be 'under the chairmanship of Mr Dalton, the Minister of Economic Warfare . . . Mr Dalton will also have
the cooperation of the Directors of Intelligence of the three Service
Departments and of the Secret Intelligence Service (M.I.6) for the
purpose of the work entrusted to him.'

With the Special Operations Executive, Hugh Dalton was soon
'poaching on C's preserves', annoying the Secret Intelligence Service. With the Ministry of Economic Warfare, Dalton also bullied
his way into the china shop of diplomacy with Iberia. David Eccles
wrote a perceptive letter about him from Lisbon later that summer:

Hugh Dalton, that renegade Etonian, has laid hold of MEW and aspires
shortly to be Foreign Secretary. He hates dictatorship on principle; Franco
in public and in particular, and Salazar in private and half-heartedly. Therefore seeing that the [Iberian] Peninsula now has open communications with
Germany, and must be regarded as an adjacent neutral, he would like to
teach the dictators a lesson by starving them out with a ferocious system of
rationing. Nothing could make the entry of Spain into the war on Germany's side more certain.

'You don't marry a girl by throwing stones at her window,' Eccles
wrote in a later letter: 'out with the guitar and a bunch of roses.' Eccles
was proved right and Dalton wrong: offering to trade with Spain, loos-
ening the economic chokehold of navicerts and contraband control,
was ultimately more effective than outright starvation of the country
by blockade. The promise of carrots rather than the threat of the big
stick helped preserve Spanish neutrality and thus Gibraltar's freedom.

---

* Orwell also distinguished 'patriotism', love of one's own country, from 'nationalism',
which was often hatred of someone else's.

II

Fight and Flight

Adolf Hitler unleashed his attack on western Europe at 5.35 a.m. on 10 May 1940. In some ways, the armoured assault of *Fall Gelb* (Operation *Yellow*) looked similar to the Schlieffen Plan of 1914, a right hook to punch through Belgium and then curve round behind Paris. But this analogy was deceptive. When the British and French armies left their defensive positions and moved forward into neutral Belgium, they were charging into what Liddell Hart called 'the matador's cloak'. The real attack was coming from the German left, a scythe-sweep by three German armies through the wooded hills of the Ardennes to slice round the Allied troops and trap them against the sea. Eighteen hundred tanks spearheaded the charge of a vast column of German vehicles that stretched back a hundred miles to the Rhine, making a fantastic target for the Allied air forces. But nobody did anything.

RAF Bomber Command was in its own solipsistic world. The French air force was under-equipped, short-staffed, lacking in ground crews, air transport and anti-aircraft defences. They plainly failed at reconnaissance. The war correspondent Noel Monks claimed he never saw a French fighter plane in his seven months in France. Things were not good among the ground troops, either. Staying in fixed positions, many French soldiers were bored and listless. Officers didn't button their jackets and their men couldn't be bothered to salute. The US diplomat Robert Murphy described the national mood as 'sullen apathy'. One theory is that France, scarred by the First World War, which killed 1.7 million soldiers and left over two million *mutilés*, no longer believed in aggressive warfare, instead slumping into a posture of defensive passivity behind the bunkers of the Maginot Line.

Assiduous German propaganda helped *l'écroulement moral*, the crumbling of morale. Goebbels's line was that England had confected the war and was shoving unwilling French soldiers into the front line as cannon fodder. (Not that German propaganda always worked. When they put up a huge sign facing the trenches, warning the Armée du Nord or Army of the North that behind their backs English squaddies were ravishing their womenfolk, a French regiment put up its answer: *On s'en fout, on est du Midi* – We don't give a bugger, we're from the south.)

The German *Blitzkrieg* in May 1940 employed air power, armour and radio communications in devastating new ways. One of the surprises of their decoy attack was the brilliant use of special forces dropped from the air. An elite volunteer unit of German *Fallschirmjäger* or paratroops had been set up in 1936 and had been led since July 1938 by *Generalmajor* Kurt Student. A handpicked group of 440 trained for six months prior to May 1940 for a special mission in Belgium, north of Liège. One of four assault groups, code-named 'Granite', was to seize Fort Eben Emael, a massive triangular artillery citadel at the junction of the Maas River and the Albert Canal. Moated, armoured, reinforced, structured on three twenty-metre-high levels and incorporating its own heating, lighting and air filtration systems, with twelve hundred soldiers serving thirty big guns that dominated the entire local area, Eben Emael was in theory designed to be absolutely impregnable. Unfortunately, the German sub-contractors used in its construction had supplied complete internal plans to German military intelligence. Moreover, when the fort was built in 1932–5 they put a meadow on the roof, in between the gun cupolas. At the time, nobody was thinking of airborne assault. Did it have obstacles or barbed wire on it? No, it was being used as the garrison football pitch.

At about 5.25 a.m. on 10 May 1940, nine German DFS230 combat gliders hissed down onto its grass. Heavily armed men in brimless helmets spilled out shooting, eliminating the infantry posts, the anti-aircraft positions and the guns pointing north. This was the first glider-borne assault in military history; in ten minutes, fifty-five men managed to blind and silence 'the world's strongest fort', like a scattering of ants nipping at an elephant's eyes and scuttling in through its ears.

Each glider held a squad of up to half a dozen men. They were all combat sappers from the *Fallschirm-Pioniere Kompanie*, the parachute engineer company, and every glider was packed with a ton of kit for achieving their tasks. Among these weapons were flame-throwers, Bangalore torpedoes and the revolutionary new *Hohlladungwaffen* or 'cavity charge weapons' developed at the Luftwaffe Weapons Institute in Braunschweig. These were explosives fitted inside a heavy metal hemisphere, weighing 50, 12.5 or 3 kg, which could be attached to a wall or an armoured cupola. On detonation, the hydrodynamic energy of a 'shaped charge' explosion was focused into a jet whose directive force penetrated the concrete or metal, sending shattered fragments and splinters flying the other side. Once again, this was the first use of a brand-new weapon in war.

Another striking aspect of the raid on Fort Eben Emael was the fact that the temporary absence of the commanding officer did not stop the mission. *Oberleutnant* Rudolf Witzig was in a glider whose tow-rope snapped in flight. Instantly, Witzig told its pilot to wheel around and go back as close as possible to Cologne Ostheim airport from where they had taken off. He got the glider down in a suitable field and directed his men to move it to a good take-off position, and cut down willow hedges ahead of it to make a rough runway. Witzig himself set off on foot, commandeering first a civilian's bike and then a medic's car to get to Luftwaffe HQ at the airfield, where he requisitioned another Junkers Ju 52 aircraft and pilot, landed in the field with a new tow-rope, took off again with his squad in the glider and finally got to his battlefield, only three hours late.

The Eben Emael operation went smoothly because Sergeant Helmut Wenzel had stepped up and carried on, an outstanding example of battlefield *Auftragstaktik* or 'mission command'. The German sappers paralysed the fortress and the 750 men trapped inside it by dropping bombs down the ventilation and ascent shafts, losing only six dead and fifteen wounded in their brilliant raid. Every man in 'Granite' was awarded the Iron Cross and promotion by one rank; officers got the *Ritterkreuz*, the Knight's Cross, from Adolf Hitler himself, with lots of publicity photos, and Rudolf Witzig was assigned as an adjutant to *Reichsmarschall* Göring, head of the Luftwaffe.

Meanwhile, Operation *Yellow*'s great German tank attack crossed the River Meuse on 13 May 1940 and raced for the sea, which they reached in a week. 'Success lies in speed,' said Panzer Group von Kleist's attack order. 'The important thing is to keep surprising the defender.' Drivers drove for three days and three nights pepped on German methamphetamine pills brand-named 'Pervitin'. Special chocolate bars called *Panzerschokolade* also contained 'uppers'. According to Norman Ohler, some thirty-five million tabs of 'speed' were issued to the Wehrmacht and Luftwaffe for this campaign.

Hitler's *Blitzkrieg* was three-dimensional. Fast armoured vehicles dominated the land, while death stooped from above. For sheer bowel-loosening terror nothing beat the gull-winged Stuka dive-bomber which screamed down like a pterodactyl from the air. In actual fact, it was quite a slow plane, vulnerable to faster fighter aircraft, but with its shrieking siren and sickening swoops to bomb and strafe it seemed satanic to soldiers and civilians on the ground. The historian Marc Bloch, analysing the *Strange Defeat* of France in 1940 from personal experience, said that the sound was what did it: he felt cold fear being shelled, but genuine terror being dive-bombed.

All the lessons learned in Spain were now used to devastate Allied forces and clear a way towards the sea. The thousand Stukas of the VIIIth *Fliegerkorps* were commanded by Major General Wolfram von Richthofen, the man who firebombed Gernika in April 1937. His boss was General Hugo Sperrle, the first commander of the Condor Legion. The Stukas could fly as many as six sorties a day because the Luftwaffe were practised at moving their airfields forwards with the front line. German military engineers could repair or expand an airfield in twenty-four hours, protected by mobile flak teams who had also honed their skills in Spain. Then the workhorse Junkers Ju 52s brought up fuel, supplies and ammunition to replenish the fighters and dive-bombers, to keep them airborne, hurrying, harrying.

Richthofen's Stuka dive-bombers, working as mobile artillery in close support of the tanks, were all connected by wireless. They operated in three packs of about forty planes, protected by the faster Messerschmitt Bf 109s and 110s. The first group of Stukas attacked in successive clutches of three or four, diving down from about five thousand feet, while the second circled above at twelve thousand feet, spotting prey for later, and the third group picked off individual moving targets. French defenders reeled backwards from the violence. The British general Alan Brooke saw the French army lose discipline and become a rabble, 'panicking every time a Boche plane came over'.

Down on the ground too, aggressive firepower against the demoralised French paid off. Lying hidden in a field of rye, Captain Philippe de Hauteclocque listened to the ceaseless firing of German machine guns. The French relied more on telephone lines and dispatch riders than wireless, so their communications were soon cut. The Germans gained control of time through their mastery of radio. As Erhard Milch confided to William Stephenson before the war: 'the real secret is speed – speed of attack through speed of communications.' According to French politician Pierre Cot, the average age of French generals was seventy, and that of German generals forty. The old and the slow were bowled over by youth, speed and violence. In 1916, the Germans took ten months trying to take Verdun and lost 162,000 men; in 1940, they took it in a day, and lost only two hundred.

The fast-moving attack induced paralysis and then terrified flight in the French. Without strong leadership or clear information, rumour metastasised, feeding on the memories of German atrocities in 1914. Two million Belgians left home in fear to pour into France, and up to fourteen million French citizens also took to the highway, heading south and west on roads made dusty by a hot, dry summer.

Pierre Mendès France saw the refugees pass through his town like different species of migrant bird. First the chauffeur-driven, sumptuous American cars of the rich, with the wife clutching her jewel box and the husband studying the map (which almost sounds like the Duke and Duchess of Windsor, who at that moment were fleeing from Paris towards Blois with trusty George Ladbrook at the wheel of their Buick), then the middling sort with older, not so fancy cars, then vintage bangers, and cyclists, many of them young, behaving like picnickers, and people on foot and peasants in their creaking carts piled high with all their goods and chattels. Mendès France watched the collective move of French villages, with the mayor, the schoolmaster, the priest and the policeman, 'a colossal uprooting, the avalanche of one entire region onto another'.

The writer Denis Freeman and the art collector Douglas Cooper, long-time French residents of France, joined up as ambulance men in June 1940 and related their experiences in *The Road to Bordeaux*. Its last four sections are headed 'Retreat', 'Panic', 'Chaos', 'Escape'. The enterprising young American Helen Hiett had abandoned a PhD at LSE to become the Paris correspondent of NBC radio in May 1940, and she also worked as a volunteer with some of the refugees reaching the capital, including silent, shell-shocked children and orphans. 'Some of them had walked too many miles. When we pulled off the pieces of their socks and shoes, skin came too. I mentioned the fact, describing my night at the refugee center in the next morning's broadcast, and almost got fired.'

'That was bad judgement,' a chiding voice from NBC told her. 'Don't forget, some Americans will be at the breakfast table when they are listening to you. We don't want any more of that kind of stuff. And you are never to mention the word "blood".'

The collapse of France galvanised Gibraltar's treatment of its own twenty thousand civilians. In the Great War, when Spain was neutral and the fighting was far away, life had carried on normally on the Rock, with a few problems over food but no great movements of people. In September 1939, with Spain and Italy neutral and the prospect of fighting far away, there at first seemed no need to do very much. When General Ironside was still governor, early in 1939, he had tentatively discussed with General Noguès, Commander-in-Chief of French Morocco, the possibility of evacuating Gibraltarian women, children and old people there, but little groundwork had been done. On 8 May 1940, Governor Clive Liddell sent Lieutenant Colonel R. A. Hay of the Royal Engineers and Mr Charles Gaggero of Bland's shipping company to explore the possibilities, 'in certain eventualities', of accommodating thirteen thousand Gibraltarian refugees in Casablanca, on French Morocco's western coast. Liddell wanted to avoid premature evacuation because he thought it might send the message to Franco that Britain was running away from the Rock.

The Hay report took a cavalier approach: lodging would be partly in hotels, partly in empty houses and billets. Hay suggested the Gibraltarians were quite used to overcrowding and would fit six or eight to a room. Food might be a problem but he reckoned that with a ration allowance in cash they could fend for themselves, though a supply of army biscuits might be useful. Evacuees would have to take their own blankets and cutlery, but the ships would have no room for bulky mattresses. The French would provide medical services – probably. The sanitary arrangements were not ideal. Perhaps a camp would have to be built.

The War Cabinet met in London at 11 a.m. on Thursday 16 May 1940. (Later that day, Churchill, prime minister for less than a week, flew to France to try and rally the French, offering them back-up with ten squadrons of RAF fighter planes.) The Cabinet decided that the evacuation of Gibraltarian civilians to French Morocco should go ahead and all British service families should return to the UK. When this was transmitted, official Gibraltar was not sure if this meant merely that the evacuation scheme was approved, or if it was an executive order with immediate effect. Two days later the Secretary of State confirmed that it was an order, a precautionary measure 'in view of the disturbed situation in the Mediterranean'.

On Tuesday 21 May, the day that German Panzers reached the English Channel and the British counter-attacked at Arras, the

Governor of Gibraltar issued a notice saying that all families with children under fourteen were to be evacuated from the Rock. (It was three years to the day since four thousand Basque children were evacuated from Bilbao to Southampton.) Under the wartime Defence Regulations, this order was compulsory. 'His Excellency fully realises that these steps will cause a great deal of anxiety and inconvenience ... He feels sure that all citizens will abide loyally by his instructions, and cheerfully endure such sacrifices as they are called upon to make.'

'So it began', wrote novelist Warren Tute in his 1957 novel *The Rock*:

All over the Rock, in every home from the Battery Major's married quarters up by Ince's Farm to the meanest hovel down by the small ship-repairing yards at the North End, from Europa Flats to Catalan Bay, wives were preparing to say good-bye to the familiar things, to separate from home and husband, neither of which they might ever see again. Young children cried, not understanding the rupture that was taking place, older children were fobbed off with vague stories of the need to run away from the wicked Germans with their bombs ...

The Bland Line steamer *Gibel Dersa II*, the car ferry that had been bombed by Franco's planes on its regular run to Tangier at the start of the civil war, took the first shipload of 'independent' or 'voluntary' evacuees to Casablanca. This first contingent of 328 adults and 166 children, who had passports and visas from the French consulate at Scud Hill, were wealthier people who could pay their way and find accommodation in hotels and flats in Morocco. Charles Gaggero of Bland's was leading them and with a medical officer, some policemen and control staff on board, it was a pleasant six-hour trip.

The next day, 22 May, the first government-sponsored compulsory contingent of 950 women, children and old men left on the specially chartered seven-thousand-ton Egyptian ship SS *Mohamed Ali el-Kebir*. This was not half so agreeable. There was muddle and misery, horrible packing and frayed tempers, loss and parting, all swirling up into what Warren Tute called 'a funnel of distress and despair'. After a three-hour wait on the quay, the evacuees – many of whom had never left the Rock before – were confused and fearful. The British servicemen charged with enforcing the evacuation did their clumsy best to be kind: 'The rough good nature of the British fighting man . . . came to the rescue', but there was still hysteria in the air. When they went on board ship, some Gibraltarians refused to go below decks and others began wailing and shrieking, calling out to the family and menfolk they were leaving behind.

The thirteen-hour trip was a nightmare. The ship hit heavy seas and everyone was sick, including the two midwife nurses, who became unable to help others. The toilets were soon overflowing; sobbing children fouled themselves. Three special constables were overworked to exhaustion. When people fainted below decks, often for lack of food, they had to be carried up to fresh air, and when people on the promenade decks became chilled they had to be moved inside to thaw, assisted through scuppers swashing with vomit as the ship wallowed southwards. Nor was Casablanca their final destination: they went on for an hour by train to Rabat to be settled in three hotels and five dozen properties scattered round the periphery of the Moroccan city. Many of the houses were dirty and their water and electricity disconnected. Back and forth the *Mohamed Ali el-Kebir* went, making another eleven voyages from Gibraltar to Casablanca, carrying a further 11,094 people to Morocco between 24 May and 24 June.

Hundreds of women and children were distributed among Casablanca's dance and entertainment halls, Ocean Plage, Luna Park, Park Beaulieu and Guinguette Fleurie. The lavatories were not adequate and movable huts with buckets were promised. There were an awful lot of flies in Morocco. People had no mattresses and had to sleep on straw. Two more dance halls, the Robinson and L'Hermitage, were pressed into service as more evacuees arrived and then the overflow of people were sent to a barracks camp at Ain Chuk. The medical staff pleaded for the process to slow down, but still they kept coming, hundreds shovelled in boatloads away from the Fortress, including inmates of the mental hospital and very frail old people.

Later evacuees were moved to Mazagan, Saffi and Ouadzen in the interior. Some occupied the workmen's houses of an abandoned phosphate mine at Andrea Del-pit. These new cottages, under shady trees, with a tiled kitchen, a living room and two bedrooms, a verandah, a bare garden and an outside washhouse and WC, represented better accommodation than many had enjoyed in Gibraltar. The Moroccans were hospitable; food was cheap, chicken plentiful. But inevitably some of the new occupants complained that they were not in big cities like Casablanca or Rabat. Mr A. M. Dryburgh, the Controller of the Evacuation Scheme, sharply deplored these malcontents: 'I recognise some of the Shorthorn Farm squatters, others were from La Linea.' He thought it a shame that 'these beautiful trim little houses have fallen in too many cases into the hands of people who do not appreciate them and would rather be "pigging" it ten or twelve in a room in a Casablanca slum'.

Things were deteriorating further in France. Like its 1914 predecessor, the British Expeditionary Force of 1940 had to manage a fighting 'withdrawal' from the invading Germans, this time back to the beaches of Dunkirk. Three of Gibraltar's governors, one past, Edmund Ironside, and two future, John Gort and Noel Mason-MacFarlane, were in the thick of it.

Fifty-three-year-old General Lord Gort was Commander-in-Chief of the BEF, but he acted more like an army commander when, on 10 May, he left his GHQ at Arras to move forward to new field command posts, first near Lille, then near Brussels, taking with him his Director of Military Intelligence, Major General Noel Mason-MacFarlane.

When things got sticky, then chaotic, communications broke down. Like the French, the British depended on telephones more than the Germans, and when they had to abandon land lines and go to wireless, the radio traffic overwhelmed the cipher personnel. Information at GHQ was not always relayed to the field command post and vice versa, and the divisions at the front who actually needed the intelligence did not get it. The situation did not improve when Mason-MacFarlane was sent off on 17 May to lead a scratch unit called 'Macforce', hurriedly improvised to protect the right rear of the BEF.

Gort realised that the overcomplicated French command structure was ineffectual and the Belgians were soon going to collapse (they capitulated on 28 May). On 19 May he warned London that the BEF might have to evacuate. The War Cabinet in London, relying on optimistic French assessments, thought that all nine divisions of the BEF should instead strike southwards to meet the French striking northwards, thus severing the German advance. Burly and forceful Edmund Ironside, Chief of the Imperial General Staff, travelled out to France on 20 May to give Gort 'what was practically an order': attack south in the direction of Amiens. The two bull elephants met in the same room once again, each knowing that either could have had the other's role. 'After some thought, Lord Gort did not agree,' wrote Ironside later. 'I asked him to try, but the C-in-C said no . . .'

On 21 May, two British divisions counter-attacked successfully at Arras, but two days later Gort withdrew them. On 25 May he decided to cut his losses. Squeezed by the Germans, the remains of the BEF and the French First Army pulled back northwards towards the coast, making for the long sandy beaches east of Dunkirk.

Queen Victoria's birthday – 24 May – was Empire Day, and over the BBC wireless King George VI broadcast a message to the people of the British Empire, slowly and deliberately, negotiating the stammer we know about from *The King's Speech* and the same kind of inability to pronounce the letter 'r' as Graham Greene. People in Gibraltar heard the king say, 'It is no mere territorial conquest that our enemies are seeking. It is the overthrow, complete and final, of this Empire, and everything for which it stands. And, after that, the conquest of the world . . .'

At this moment of dire national emergency, British tolerance snapped. A new law passed through all its stages in the House of Commons on 22 May 1940 and went through the House of Lords in a few minutes on the following day. The Treachery Act 1940 (United Kingdom) prescribed the death penalty:

If, with intent to help the enemy, any person does, or attempts or conspires with any other person to do, any act which is designed or likely to give assistance to the naval, military or air operations of the enemy, to impede such operations of His Majesty's forces, or to endanger life, he shall be guilty of felony and shall on conviction suffer death.

Also on 24 May, after long surveillance by the security services, Sir Oswald Mosley, leader of the British Union of Fascists, together with thirty-three of his prominent members, was arrested and locked up under paragraph 1A of Defence Regulation 18B of the 1939 Emergency Powers Act ('a danger of the organisation being used for purposes prejudicial to public safety').

Gibraltar soon followed suit. On 29 May, the police arrested Luis Bertuchi and nearly a dozen blue-shirted Gibraltarian fascists. The prominent barrister Albert Isola wrote to vouch that 'Mr Lewis E. Bertuchi' was 'a true Britisher' who, during the Spanish Civil War, merely 'identified himself rather too openly on the side of General Franco'. However, his police docket described him as a 'very keen Fascist and great friend of members of Falange Española in La Linea'. The Defence Security Officer reported the internment had 'a most sobering effect on the Gibraltarian population'.

On 22 May there had been a major breakthrough in Hut 6 at Bletchley Park, when the cryptographers once more broke the 'Red' key for the German air force's general-purpose Enigma messages, which had been changed on 15 May. Now they started breaking a thousand Luftwaffe messages a day.

More progress on communications followed. With the invasion of England apparently looming, the wireless intercept (WI or 'Y') listening station that the Air Ministry had set up early in 1940 in a cottage at Hawkinge in Kent began picking up non-Morse, plain language German speech on the VHF (very high frequency) band. When these wireless conversations from German aircraft over the battlefield were plotted, they provided further valuable intelligence about German positions and intentions. Not having enough linguists among their male ranks, the RAF found German-speaking WAAFs (from the Women's Auxiliary Air Force) to staff these Home Defence Units.

Aileen Clayton (*née* Morris), later the first WAAF to be commissioned as an intelligence officer, was among them. In her invaluable memoir of the 'Y' service, *The Enemy Is Listening*, she describes how the female listeners got to recognise and know the voices of individual Luftwaffe pilots as they moved closer to the Battle of Britain. One cheerful young man, call-sign *Amsel Eins*, used to joke with them in English: 'I know, you English listening station, can you hear me? Would you like me to drop a bomb on you? Listen – whee – boomp!' The day came when the WAAF listeners had to let 11 Fighter Group know where *Amsel Eins* was operating and a group of Spitfires shot him down in flames. The happy-go-lucky young German was trapped in the cockpit of his burning plane and the listeners who had enjoyed his light-hearted banter now heard him screaming desperately for his mother and cursing the *Führer* all the way down until the reception crackled out. Aileen, who had pinpointed this friendly enemy but prayed for him to escape, left the building to be sick.

At 6 a.m. on Sunday 26 May, deep under Dover Castle, the old front-line fortress built on England's White Cliffs, James Somerville relieved his friend Bertram Ramsay, so that the Flag Officer Commanding Dover could get some sleep in his spartan cabin curtained off from his busy command post. Ramsay's headquarters were historic, sited in three casemate tunnels quarried out of the chalk in Napoleonic times by Royal Engineers in imitation of the tunnels inside the Rock of Gibraltar.

Vice Admiral Ramsay – one of the great British admirals of the Second World War, and an organisational genius – had been creating this command centre since 1938, turning the easternmost tunnel (the

First World War 'dynamo room') into the Admiralty Casemate, partitioned into a series of offices, meeting and operations rooms, with better lighting, ventilation and signalling facilities. He placed the coastal artillery and anti-aircraft operations in the next tunnel and the telephone exchange and repeater station in the third. Ramsay made sure that Dover got the proper wireless telegraphy equipment because, like Somerville and Mountbatten, he had specialised in signals and knew the vital importance of good radio work. The RN Codes and Cipher Office, staffed by the Women's Royal Naval Service, WRNS, or 'Wrens', was next door to the Communications Room. Rosemary Keyes, who worked there, remembered:

. . . a rabbit warren of dark, dreary, damp and airless passages and rooms. We worked all day in electric light and the only time we saw daylight was when we went to the 'heads'. This was a small room with a noisome 'thunderbox', but a beautiful view of Dover Harbour, seen through a window cut out of the cliff face. It was a wonderful place for watching the air raids.

Somerville took over the reins while Ramsay slept, dealing with the warships engaging the enemy off Calais and the Admiralty and politicians in London. Evacuations were not new to the British army: there had been nineteen during the Napoleonic Wars, including Sir John Moore's army from Corunna, and the Gallipoli evacuation in the Great War had been an amazing vanishing act. But this one from Dunkirk, Operation *Dynamo*, looked like a potential disaster. In the event, 'the Nine-Day Wonder', the rescue of an army of 338,000 exhausted British and French soldiers by a fleet of 'little ships', was extraordinarily well handled by Admiral Ramsay's team. And when the evacuated soldiers did set foot again in England, many of them to Ramsgate in Kent, the civilians pitched in to help 'our boys'. Hundreds of Thanet housewives set to baking with commandeered flour for the exhausted men; Ramsgate ARP and WVS combined to provide canteens:

They carried huge trays of cake and rolls and sandwiches, enormous cans of tea. Children carried stacks of postcards and pencils, and collected them as the men scribbled a brief message upon each. There were nurses from voluntary and official organisations that met each party to dress minor wounds or to move men more seriously hurt to improvised dressing stations in the fun fair that was called, with a strange irony, 'Merrie England'.

Fleets of buses took men from harbour to railway station. The Railway Executive Committee had gathered 186 ten-coach trains from five different railway companies to help Southern Railway reroute up to sixty thousand men a day to camps at Aldershot, Blandford, Dorchester, Oxford, Tetbury and Tidworth. At stations along the way, more women in summer dresses pressed 'wads and char', sandwiches and tea, 'fags and chocs', cigarettes and sweets, on the blokes who had made it back.

Somerville acted as Ramsay's right arm, hustling and energising, organising and commanding, racing between Kent and the Admiralty and War Office in London. He dealt with Winston Churchill early every morning, often when the prime minister had not yet put his teeth in and his chumbling speech was not easy to understand. He also pushed forward the evolution of signals intelligence. At Hawkinge, Women's Auxiliary Air Force linguists had been picking up the chatter of German E-boats, the fast torpedo and minelaying craft deployed in the English Channel. Somerville now made sure that the Admiralty's Naval Intelligence Division Section 9 set up its own wireless intercept stations on the White Cliffs to listen to all German naval VHF radio traffic on their horizon, so if there ever came a cross-Channel invasion, they would be the first to hear of it. Like the RAF's, these NID 9 stations employed young women who could speak German, some picked out so swiftly for 'Special Duties' from the WRNS that they did not yet have their uniforms. They worked in six-hour shifts, listening to the German navy, but also picking up the speech of the victorious German army and air force just across the English Channel.

The intense but tedious work of the 'Y' Service was vital to the triumphs of Bletchley Park, and some of the four hundred young

'Wrens' on 'Special Duties' paid the highest price. The first twenty-two WRNS to be sent abroad in the Second World War were destined for Gibraltar. Twelve women cipher officers and ten women wireless operators were in a large naval party in Convoy OG 71 when the German submarine wolf-pack attacked off the Azores. Seven ships were sunk, including the civilian passenger liner SS *Aguila*, torpedoed by *U-201* on 19 August 1941. None of the women survived.

The 'colossal military disaster' of Dunkirk – Churchill's frank description of the evacuation of the British Expeditionary Force without any of its tanks, artillery, vehicles, stores and ammunition – was soon followed by another body blow. Just a week later, on Monday 10 June 1940, Fascist Italy entered the war on the side of Nazi Germany. Italy's declaration of war had few direct effects in England, except that Italian aircraft would support the Luftwaffe in the Battle of Britain, though many hundreds of innocent Italians working in the catering trade found themselves interned in the indiscriminate sweep for supposed 'fifth columnists'.

In the Mediterranean, however, the naval balance of power was now completely overturned. It had relied on the French navy protecting the western basin while the British Mediterranean Fleet, based at Malta and Alexandria in Egypt, looked after the eastern end. With France collapsing and Italy on the side of the Nazis, the enemy was right at the gates. Malta was soon under attack by the Italian air force and Gibraltar, a thousand nautical miles from British territory in any direction, felt acutely isolated.

The Italian merchant marine struck at Gibraltar on the first day of war by attempting to scuttle half a dozen cargo ships in Algeciras Bay to try and block the mouth of Gibraltar's harbour. Only one ship was successfully scuttled; the tanker *Olterra* beached herself in Spanish waters and the Royal Navy salvaged two others.

Nevertheless, the Italian navy now threatened the whole Mediterranean. It had four battleships afloat and two newly built thirty-five-thousand-ton super-dreadnoughts, capable of thirty knots and carrying nine fifteen-inch guns. In addition, Italy had seven heavy cruisers, twelve light cruisers, ninety destroyers, fleets of fast motor-torpedo boats and more than one hundred submarines. Churchill wrote on 10 June to President Roosevelt that Italy's submarines were a real threat:

To this the only counter is destroyers. Nothing is so important as for us to have the thirty or forty old destroyers you have already had reconditioned. We can fit them very rapidly with our Asdics [an early form of sonar] and they will bridge the gap of 6 months before our wartime new construction comes into play . . .

On the same day, President Roosevelt spoke in Charlottesville, Virginia. Cautious diplomats in his State Department were appalled by his reference to Italy – 'the hand that held the dagger has plunged it into the back of its neighbour' – but the US President went further in ignoring an isolationist Congress, pledging:

In our American unity, we will pursue two obvious and simultaneous courses; we will extend to the opponents of force the material resources of this nation; and, at the same time, we will harness and speed up the use of those resources in order that we ourselves in the Americas may have equipment and training equal to the task of any emergency and every defence.

That day, Reynaud's French government began to quit Paris. There was chaos at the Quai d'Orsay, the French Ministry of Foreign Affairs, with thousands of files thumping and fluttering down into the courtyard to be crammed chaotically into requisitioned Renault buses. A smudging pall of smoke rose as the French General Staff ordered the burning of Standard Oil's petroleum stocks to keep them out of German tanks and trucks. Up to three million Parisian civilians began swelling the ranks of the refugees. After Luftwaffe bombs destroyed her NBC Paris office at 15 rue Poussin, journalist Helen Hiett was among them, pursuing the government to Tours and then Bordeaux. 'Touraine had never been lovelier. June roses trailed on every fence,' she wrote. For years she had planned to drive through the 'garden of France', but she had not planned for

> . . . weary travelers, or the screech of German dive-bombers, or the dusty, tear-stained faces of a motorcycle corps of young Frenchmen, hurrying to meet the enemy in the direction in which we had come, or the anguished face of an exhausted peasant woman who dragged heavy buckets to the roadside and stood handing cups of cold water for the soldiers to gulp as they passed.

The French army was clearly in a state of collapse, and the solidity of the French navy had become a worry to the British. It was the fourth largest fleet in the world after those of the USA, Britain and Japan. What would happen to all its ships if France was completely overwhelmed? Could they be put out of action? In a meeting at his room in the Admiralty on 7 June, the First Sea Lord, Admiral Sir Dudley Pound, had said that the only way to stop their vessels falling into German hands was 'to sink the French fleet'. That conclusion was presented to Churchill the next day, followed up by a memo suggesting that the French gold reserves should be moved to the USA and the French should be asked to scuttle their ships.

Winston Churchill flew to France on 11 June to attend two meetings of the French Supreme War Council at General Weygand's HQ in a château near Briare. The French prime minister, Paul Reynaud, and the tall Under-Secretary for Defence, General Charles de Gaulle, were the only French delegates who seemed to have any spirit. Elderly Marshal Pétain, recently summoned from Madrid where he had been French ambassador to the Franco regime, looked 'woebegone', and General Weygand himself had the depressed air of a commander without military hope. 'I am helpless. I cannot intervene, for I have no reserves . . . *C'est la dislocation* – the break-up.' The British visitors tried to rally their hosts, but the French recoiled from the barbaric suggestion of fighting on for months in a Paris ruined by combat. Weygand said the French army needed more British air support: 'Here is the decisive point. The British ought not to keep a single fighter in England. They should all be sent to France.'

'This is not the decisive point,' replied Churchill. 'The decisive moment will come when Hitler hurls his Luftwaffe against Britain. If we can keep command of the air over our own island – that is all I ask – we will win it all back for you.'

The British PM paused. 'Of course if it is best for France in her agony that her army should capitulate, let there be no hesitation on our account. Whatever happens here, we are resolved to fight on and on for ever and ever and ever.'

'If we capitulate,' said Reynaud, 'all the great might of Germany will be concentrated upon invading England. And then what will you do?'

'I have not thought it out very carefully, but broadly speaking I propose to drown as many as possible of them on the way over, and then to *frapper sur la tête* anyone who manages to crawl ashore.'

At the War Council meeting the next day, Churchill had a private word with Admiral François Darlan, the head of the French navy, who had revived its fortunes over the last seven years. Churchill, at the beginning of the war, when he was First Lord of the Admiralty, had met Darlan and worked with him. Now he said solemnly to the *amiral*: 'I hope you will never surrender the fleet.' Darlan replied: 'There is no question of doing so; it would be contrary to our naval tradition and honour.' Churchill reported to the War Cabinet and to Roosevelt that Darlan had said that the French fleet would be sent away 'to Canada'. However, we know that Churchill mangled the French language. The historian David Brown suggests that the prime minister may actually have misheard; perhaps Darlan said that the French fleet would be sent away '*en cas de danger*'.

Only two days later, Churchill met his French counterparts again at Tours. By then only de Gaulle was still staunch, with the others all infected by defeatism. 'Don't give in, don't go over to the enemy. Fight on!' Churchill urged the French premier. But it was becoming clear the French would instead make a separate peace with Nazi Germany.

★

Early on 14 June, the first German motorcycle outriders in leather coats roared through the echoing empty streets of Paris, eerily deserted for the last two days. The first German troops who marched in to occupy Paris were *sehr korrekt* and unopposed. The US ambassador, Anthony Biddle, had arranged that the French capital, as an 'open city', offer no defence, to avoid further bombing and shelling of its architecture and inhabitants. Quartermasters started requisitioning the best hotels. The Germans made *les pompiers*, the French firemen, go through the streets with their long ladders, replacing every Republican tricolour with a Nazi swastika, and clocks were moved forward an hour to Greater Reich time. It was on this shocking day of acute Allied discomfiture that opportunistic General Franco sent his troops from Spanish Morocco to occupy the international zone of Tangier, calculating, quite rightly, that the British, French and Belgians were too busy to do anything about it.

General Alan Brooke still commanded 150,000 British troops in France, south of the Seine. Over the telephone that evening, the general told a truculent Churchill that the French army was, 'to all intents and purposes, dead'. Brooke thought that all Allied fighting troops – Belgian, British, Czech, French, Polish – should now be withdrawn from the Atlantic ports of France or they would be lost forever. After Churchill agreed, Operation *Ariel* evacuated a further 215,000 soldiers.

On Saturday 15 June, Churchill sent another personal appeal to Reynaud, asking him to send all French warships to British ports. The British ambassador, Sir Ronald Campbell, went to Reynaud's lodgings in Bordeaux near midnight to find the French premier in bed with his mistress, the poisonous Comtesse Hélène de Portes. On hearing Churchill's message, Reynaud picked up the telephone to give Admiral Darlan the order, but the comtesse snatched the receiver from him and refused to let him speak. Reynaud shrugged and lay back on the pillows.

The next day, the formal message arrived from HMG in Cipher Telegram 368, giving its consent for France to enter negotiations with

Germany for a separate peace, 'provided, but only provided, that the French fleet is sailed forthwith for British harbours'. The message annoyed Reynaud, rather than persuading him. Then General de Gaulle telephoned from London with the astonishing proposal of an Act of Union to join Britain and France forever. An excited Reynaud took down the text of the Declaration of Union that de Gaulle dictated, using a gold propelling pencil with a long lead on sheets of foolscap sliding about on a table:

At this most fateful moment in the history of the modern world the Governments of the United Kingdom and the French Republic . . . declare that France and Great Britain shall no longer be two nations, but one Franco-British Union . . .

Every citizen of France will enjoy immediately citizenship of Great Britain; every British subject will become a citizen of France . . .

. . . The Union will concentrate its whole energy against the power of the enemy, no matter where the battle may be.

And thus we shall conquer.

But it was too late for this implausible utopia. At Bordeaux, defeatism won the day. The proposed Act of Union was seen as a cynical ploy to make France a British Dominion, whereas they hoped to get gentlemanly terms from the Germans. Reynaud was forced to resign, and Marshal Philippe Pétain was asked to form the new government. On Sunday night Pétain sent a message via Franco's Spain to ask the Germans for an armistice. On Monday 17 June 1940, Pétain said, '*Il faut cesser le combat*' – 'we must stop fighting'.

Britain now stood alone. The prospect was awesome but not appalling. 'We are even exhilarated by being on our own,' Sybil Eccles wrote to her husband in Lisbon. 'No one left to desert us – no more failing friends to support.' Britain was not really alone, of course; the British Empire stood behind her. But all the resources of the empire were overseas, and who would command those waters was now the pressing problem – nowhere more pressing than in Gibraltar.

12

Operation *Boomerang*

Fear that the Germans would add the warships from defeated France to their own navy concentrated Churchill's mind wonderfully. He sent a flattering message to the new French government, hoping that 'the illustrious Marshal Pétain and the famous General Weygand, our comrades in two great wars, will not injure their ally by delivering over to the enemy the fine French fleet' and urged them to waste no time in sending their ships away to British or US ports.

On 18 June, A. V. Alexander, the British government minister in charge of the navy, and Admiral Sir Dudley Pound, the First Sea Lord, flew to Bordeaux to talk to Admiral François Darlan. The British politician accompanied the First Sea Lord because Darlan was now Minister of Marine in Pétain's government as well as commander-in chief of the French navy. Political office changed him. The Radical French politician (and three times former prime minister) Édouard Herriot records Darlan saying on Saturday 15 June that if 'those bastards Pétain and Weygand' conclude an armistice, 'I am leaving with the Fleet.' But the very next day, after Reynaud's government fell, Herriot went up to Darlan and said, 'Admiral, you are doubtless taking steps for the departure of the government to North Africa,' and Darlan, by now thinking like a politician, replied, 'No. A government that leaves never returns.' Herriot commented: 'This admiral knows how to swim.'

Alexander and Pound's meeting with Darlan seemed cordial and lasted one and a half hours. 'If the [German] armistice terms are dishonourable,' Darlan told them, 'the Fleet will fight to the end and anything that escapes will go to a friendly country or be destroyed.' Darlan wondered aloud how Britain would be able to fight on, and said he was sure that Franco would let Hitler's armies through Spain to take Gibraltar and so block off the Mediterranean. What then? Pound bluffly said that imperial convoys could be routed round the Cape of Good Hope to the West Indies, Canada and over the North Atlantic, but that a new squadron would soon be based at Gibraltar to protect the opening to the Med and prevent any blockage.

Back in England, Churchill upset the wooing of the French by rashly declaring that French radio broadcasting stations were now under enemy control so any instructions from them should be disregarded. He also asked merchant shipping of all nationalities not to proceed to French ports.

That same day, 18 June 1940, forty-nine-year-old Charles de Gaulle hoisted his colours in London. As he said in his war memoirs, he felt he was in an impossible position. 'In France, no following and no reputation. Abroad, neither credit nor standing.' He responded by being intransigent. He spoke on the BBC, saying '*Non*' to hopelessness and defeat, appealing to French officers and men, French engineers and armament workers to get in touch with him, and to keep the flame of French resistance alive. The next day he declared, in the name of France, that it was 'the bounden duty of all Frenchmen who still bear arms to continue the struggle', especially in French North Africa.

On the following day, General Władysław Sikorski of Poland met Churchill and pledged that the Poles would fight on, thus becoming, for the next eighteen months, the British Empire's most significant foreign ally. Although forty thousand Poles had been killed, wounded or captured in the Battle of France, twenty thousand soldiers were evacuated to UK to form the 1st Polish Corps. The Polish air force also re-formed in Britain under the RAF, and Nos 302 and 303 Polish fighter squadrons would play a key role in the Battle of Britain. Two submarines, three destroyers and forty Polish ships also joined the Allied cause.

Across the Channel, after Pétain's new government started negotiating an armistice with Germany and Italy, Darlan gathered ships to take government officials overseas. Many parliamentarians opposed to Pétain sailed aboard the liner *Massilia*, which finally left for Morocco on 21 June. How different the war might have been had the French government managed to rally and reconstitute itself in its African empire, like the Belgians, Dutch, Norwegians or Poles, whose governments-in-exile resisted the Nazis from London. Admiral Somerville commented: 'What damned fools the French were not to go on fighting from North Africa.' There the French military establishment under General Noguès still had 125,000 men on active service and 200,000 in reserve.

The French navy, meanwhile, had scattered. Some warships were in British-controlled ports, some smaller vessels at Toulon, but the cream of the French fleet was in French North Africa. There were cruisers at Algiers, submarines at Bizerte, the new battleships in Senegal and Casablanca, and the most powerful fleet, the Force de Raid, was in the French naval base at Mers-el-Kébir, just west of the port of Oran in Algeria. Berthed there were two powerful battle cruisers, *Dunkerque* and *Strasbourg*, which were superior to the German *Scharnhorst* and *Gneisenau*, as well as two other battleships, an aviation transport called the *Commandant Teste*, three light cruisers, ten destroyers and four submarines.

German naval intelligence had already tried to deceive the French on 19 June. A fake French naval cipher signal ordered all French warships to cease hostilities and make for the nearest French port, adding '*pas, je dis pas, suivre ordres anglais*' ('not, repeat not, to follow English orders'). '*Vive la France. DARLAN.*' Authentic Darlan messages were signed 'XAVIER 377'. In fact Darlan had signalled that while there was no armistice in force the French navy's duty was 'to pursue maximum resistance'. Any warship or aircraft unable to reach North Africa 'or at risk of falling into enemy [German] hands without a fight should be destroyed or scuttled following orders from a senior authority'. Another genuine draft XAVIER 377 signal ended: 'whatever orders are received, do not let the enemy take possession of any intact warships'.

But the armistice signed between France and Germany on 22 June in a railway carriage in the forest at Compiègne said in Article 8 that those elements of the French fleet not required for colonial policing were to be 'collected in ports to be specified, demilitarised and disarmed under German or Italian control'. The original phrase was *'sous le contrôle de l'Allemagne ou respectivement de l'Italie'*. The French word *contrôle* can mean 'supervision', as in the British usage of, say, 'Passport Control'. But Churchill understood *contrôle* in the sense of 'command and control', and thought that this placed the French navy directly at the disposal of the German and Italian dictators, even though in the next paragraph of the armistice text, 'the German government solemnly declares to the French government that it does not intend to use for its own purposes in the war the French fleet in ports under German control.' Churchill did not believe it. 'Ask half a dozen countries what is the value of such a solemn assurance,' he told the House of Commons.

On 23 June, the BBC broadcast a statement from the British government stating that the armistice terms 'reduce the Bordeaux Government to a state of complete subjection to the enemy', and therefore they could no longer regard 'the Bordeaux Government as a Government of an independent country'.

After Pétain's government signed the armistice with Italy, all hostilities ceased at 1.35 a.m. on 25 June 1940. Adolf Hitler, billeted in a French village near Sedan, ordered the lights to be turned out and the windows opened onto a hot summer night flickering with sheet lightning, so that he could savour the sound of the bugler blowing *Das Ganze halt* – Parade, halt! – at his historic moment.

The American journalist Helen Hiett, in Bordeaux, woke trembling from an intensely vivid dream. She was Joan of Arc, in the main square of Bordeaux, exhorting the people to act, and they were beginning to follow her when the tone changed: hearing her English accent, the crowd sensed betrayal and turned on her. The vision still haunted the young American by daylight. She thought the French populace would act 'if only there was someone to lead them'. There was someone – but he was over the sea in Britain. 'This capitulation', Charles de Gaulle declared angrily on the radio, 'delivers into the hands of the enemy our arms, our aeroplanes, our warships, our gold.' On 28 June 1940, the British government recognised 'General de Gaulle as leader of all free Frenchmen, wherever they may be, who rally to him in support of the Allied cause'.

Also on 28 June Vice Admiral Émile Muselier arrived in Gibraltar harbour, bringing with him from the French fleet two warships and three merchantmen. A flying boat took him to London, where de Gaulle made him the head of the Free French navy.* Not all those who opposed the Vichy regime followed de Gaulle, however. Bold Corsican Claude André Péri, captain of another cargo ship, *Le Rhin*, chose instead to join the Royal Navy under an assumed name, 'Lieutenant Commander Jack Langlois RN'. His first lieutenant, a Belgian doctor called Albert Guérisse, was renamed 'Lieutenant Commander Patrick O'Leary RN'. They became part of the Secret Intelligence Service's 'private navy'; *Le Rhin* would be converted into the Q-ship *Fidelity*. (A 'Q-ship' or 'query-ship' is a merchant ship with concealed guns, or one that alters its identity through camouflage.)

Some of the first to die for *France libre*, 'Free France', perished in Gibraltar. A group of eight French aviators took three Glenn Martin 167F bombers from an airfield south of Casablanca on Sunday 30 June and headed for British territory, hoping to join the Allied cause. The first two monoplanes landed successfully on the racecourse emergency airstrip, but their arrival alerted Spanish anti-aircraft gunners who shot the last plane down. It crashed into Gibraltar Bay and burst into flames, killing *sous-lieutenant* Robert Weill,

---

* Muselier, a life member of the awkward squad, was imprisoned in Pentonville and Brixton early in 1941, accused, among other treacheries, of having betrayed the Dakar expedition (see Chapter 18). Guy Liddell of MI5 found the 'proofs' were forgeries, produced by another faction among the feuding Free French. In December 1941, Muselier caused huge diplomatic ructions in Canada, the UK and the USA by 'liberating' St Pierre and Miquelon from Vichy.

sous-lieutenant Bertrand Jochaud du Plessix, *lieutenant* Jean-Pierre Berger and *capitaine* Jacques de Vendeuvre.

Some Frenchmen served two masters. The 'Claire case' in 1941 involved a French naval officer called Pierre Lablache-Combier who was sent by SIS or MI6 to Spain as a secret agent under the name 'Paul Lewis Claire'. This 'trustworthy' man was actually a Pétainist, who started revealing SIS secrets to the Vichy embassy in Madrid. Lured back to the British Embassy to pick up his passport with a Spanish exit visa, he was seized, injected with morphia and bundled into the military attaché's Chevrolet which was supposed to drive him to Gibraltar. In Andalusia, the drug wore off and 'Claire' started yelling from the back seat that he was being kidnapped. His escorts explained to the villagers that he was a member of the chancery who had gone mad – he was only being taken to a sanatorium. Finally, to keep him quiet, a man from the embassy called Langley hit him on the head with a revolver. Rather too hard; by the time they reached the Rock, 'Claire' was dead. His body was buried at sea, discreetly, from a steam drifter.

Lieutenant Commander Ian Fleming RNVR of Naval Intelligence (later the creator of James Bond and already a master of fiction) informed the British Red Cross that Lablache-Combier had gone down with twenty-six others on SS *Empire Hurst* after a Focke-Wulf 200 bombed the ship in August, four hundred miles west of Gibraltar. Lablache-Combier's widow was paid a lifelong pension by the British and everyone stayed tight-lipped. Langley was shipped home and the Chevrolet in which the Frenchman had died was quietly disposed of, sold in Gibraltar, perhaps with incriminating stains in the boot, for £111 13s 2d. A new car had to be purchased for the military attaché from Imossi Motors for £450 – a dark blue five-seater Nash Lafayette sedan – but the Chief Clerk's department in London refused to pay for the new vehicle and chauffeur until the disappearance of the old vehicle was accounted for. The motor caused far more bureaucratic bother than the dead man.

★

'The defection of France', Churchill wrote to Australian Prime Minister Robert Menzies, 'has thrown the whole Middle East into jeopardy and severed our communications through the Mediterranean.' The British needed something to fill the French vacuum, to help keep the sea lane to Suez open, and to operate when needed in the Atlantic. Therefore on 27 June 1940 a heavyweight 'detached squadron', under the command of Vice Admiral Sir James Somerville, was formed.

Force H, as it was called, was to be based at Gibraltar, and under the direct command of the Admiralty for all purposes other than the direct defence of the Rock. Force H comprised the modern aircraft carrier HMS *Ark Royal*, carrying sixty aircraft – three squadrons of Fairey Swordfish torpedo biplanes and two of Blackburn Skua fighter/bombers – which could take off from her eight-hundred-foot-long flight deck; the enormous battle cruisers HMS *Hood* and HMS *Renown*; the battleships *Resolution* and *Valiant*; the light cruisers *Arethusa* and *Enterprise*; the cruiser *Sheffield* (the only ship with air-warning radar in the summer of 1940) and two flotillas of destroyers. Force H's first task was 'to secure the transfer, surrender or destruction of the French warships at Oran and Mers-el-Kébir so as to ensure that [they] do not fall into German and Italian hands'.

Three days before Somerville left England at high speed to get to the Rock, Rear Admiral Sir Dudley North, the Flag Officer Commanding North Atlantic Squadron (FOCNA), went by destroyer from Gibraltar to Algeria to visit the Commander-in-Chief of French Naval Forces in North Africa, to try and persuade him that his ships should join the British. Admiral Estéva was away, but North saw Admiral Marcel Gensoul, Commander-in-Chief of the Atlantic Fleet, and Admiral Jarry, Admiral Commanding Oran and Mers-el-Kébir. Both Frenchmen were in a state of 'stupefied misery'; tears actually trickled down into Jarry's long grey beard. Although Gensoul promised never to yield his ships to the Germans, he was not prepared to do anything that would 'rupture the armistice agreement' and bring down unpleasant consequences from the Germans on French sailors' families at home. He also said he was awaiting orders from his superior officer, Admiral of the Fleet François Darlan.

The French attitude to the British was a complex mix of shame and pride, enmity and friendship, and the nation was divided against itself. Admiral Gensoul, although '*nettement anglophil*', a complete Anglophile, was convinced that Britain too would soon be under the Nazi jackboot. It was the standard Vichy view; General Weygand, Pétain's defeatist Minister of Defence, reckoned that Britain's neck would be wrung like a chicken. ('Some chicken. Some neck,' grunted Churchill.)

France was splitting apart in what Robert Murphy called 'a curious kind of civil war'. The majority, like the civil servants, gave their patriotic loyalty to the new conservative government led by the eighty-four-year-old Marshal Pétain, now establishing its machinery at the spa town of Vichy. The minority were the 'Free French', the ones who rejected the surrender, the armistice and any form of collaboration with the Nazi victors. Forming around General Charles de Gaulle, these 'Fighting French' wanted to battle on for what they saw as the freedom and honour of France. Under Article 10 of the June 1940 armistice, however, all Frenchmen and Frenchwomen were forbidden to fight against Germany 'in the service of other Powers'. If captured, they would be shot. De Gaulle, considered by Vichy as a rebel and a traitor, was stripped of his French army rank and ordered to be court-martialled on 23 June, though he was out of reach. Muselier was condemned to death *in absentia* on 26 October.

Georges Mandel, the valiant former Minister for the Colonies, had not left on the plane with de Gaulle because he did not want people to think that he, as a Jew, had run away. Instead Mandel had gone aboard the *Massilia* to North Africa with the other veteran ministers of the Third Republic, including Daladier and Mendès France, arriving in Casablanca on 24 June, where they hoped to raise the flag and rally the French Empire against the Nazis. Churchill sent Lord Gort and Duff Cooper by flying boat to Rabat to talk to *les résistants* in exile, but the Vichy French authorities in Morocco forbade them to meet. Mandel and the others were confined to the ship, watched by the police. The *Massilia* voyage had just been a Vichy trick to get radicals, socialists and Jews out of the way and brand them as traitors and deserters. Duff Cooper described flying to Gibraltar and landing soon after 8 a.m.:

It was pleasant to feel we were under the British flag again and to be welcomed by ADCs, by butlers and footmen, by hot baths and eggs and bacon. All this was in Government House, very English in its dowdy dignity and Victorian comfort. We spent a pleasant day there – a real holiday – reading and sleeping in a beautiful garden. I finished *Fanny by Gaslight* and enjoyed it to the end.

Things were not so agreeable for Georges Mandel in Morocco. He was arrested and tried at Meknes, acquitted, rearrested on the orders of Pierre Laval and handed over to the Gestapo. After imprisonment in Oranienburg and Buchenwald for two years, he was handed back to the French. Pétain's Vichy militia – *la milice* – murdered him in July 1944.

When Admiral James Somerville arrived at Gibraltar on 30 June he transferred his flag from *Arethusa* to the battle cruiser HMS *Hood* and then went up to Admiral Sir Dudley North's house, the Mount. He told North that if negotiations with French officers failed his instructions were to sink the French fleet in Operation *Catapult*.

'Operation *Catapult*?' said North. 'Operation *Boomerang* would be more like it. This puts us all at risk.'

Later that evening, after seeing Governor Liddell, Somerville summoned his flag officers and captains to the admiral's day cabin aboard HMS *Hood* to discuss the impending action against the French. He had listened to Admiral North; now he listened to Admiral Wells, paying particular attention to two lieutenant commanders who had been liaison officers with the French navy and to Captain 'Hooky' Holland, commander of *Ark Royal*, naval attaché in Paris until very recently. These men spoke fluent French, knew Admiral

Darlan and other French navy commanders and understood their way of thinking. All the officers were convinced that using force on such a recent ally would only convert them into enemies. Backed by this consensus of opinion, Somerville then appealed in writing to the Admiralty to reconsider or moderate their decision to sink the French fleet.

In Alexandria, Admiral Cunningham felt the same way. Kicking a man when he was down, turning on a friend and ally, was 'utterly repugnant', he wrote later in his autobiography, 'an act of sheer treachery which was as injudicious as it was unnecessary'. But there was to be no compromise. Churchill's Cabinet determined to immobilise the French fleet on 3 July. The French navy at Oran received an appeal from the British government:

It is impossible for us, your comrades till now, to allow your fine ships to fall into the power of the German or Italian enemy. We are determined to fight on until the end, and if we win, as we think we will, we shall never forget that France was our ally . . . and that our common enemy is Germany.

Should we conquer we solemnly declare that we shall restore the greatness and territory of France. For this purpose we must be sure that the best ships of the French Navy will also not be used against us by the common foe.

Then they offered the French navy four alternatives:

1) To sail to British harbours and continue to fight with us;
2) To sail with reduced crews to British ports from which the crews would be repatriated whenever desired;
3) To sail with reduced crews to some French port in the West Indies such as Martinique. After arrival they would be demilitarised to British satisfaction or be entrusted to United States jurisdiction for the rest of the war, the crews to be repatriated;
4) To sink their ships.

If either of the first two choices was accepted, the ships would be restored to France at the end of the war and full compensation paid for damage. Should the French refuse all the above alternatives but make an offer to demilitarise their own vessels, Somerville was authorised to agree, but only if the sabotage was carried out under his supervision within six hours, causing damage that would take at least a year to repair.

Everyone hoped the French would see sense. In the end, though, if the proposals were rejected and the negotiations failed, Somerville had formal orders from His Majesty's Government to use whatever force was necessary to prevent the French capital warships falling into German or Italian hands.

Operation *Catapult* proceeded.

Force H sailed from Gibraltar on the afternoon of 2 July 1940, heading eastwards into the Mediterranean. At 10.55 p.m., Winston Churchill and Dudley Pound sent Somerville a wireless message: 'You are charged with one of the most disagreeable and difficult tasks that a British Admiral has ever been faced with, but we have complete confidence in you and rely on you to carry it out relentlessly.'

At least, this is the text as written in *Their Finest Hour*, volume 2 of Churchill's memoir *The Second World War*, published in 1949. But Somerville does not record receipt of the signal in his diary or in his after action report, and no researcher has ever located it in official Admiralty archives. Could this be a literary flourish Churchill added afterwards, an emotion recollected in tranquillity? It was a time of turmoil for Churchill, facing 'a hateful decision, the most unnatural and painful in which I have ever been concerned'. He loved France, but knew he was going to hurt France deeply. The strain told on his character and behaviour. It was around this time that Clementine Churchill wrote her husband the only letter she sent him in 1940, telling him he was becoming unkind, and that his 'rough sarcastic & overbearing manner' and his 'irascibility & rudeness' were not getting the best out of the people around him.

As so often when he had a difficult decision to make, Churchill sent for his old Canadian friend, the maverick Max Aitken, Lord Beaverbrook, who was now directing his ferocious energies into driving forward the Ministry of Aircraft Production. Many people did not like 'the Beaver'. The waspish General Alan Brooke, for one, disgusted by the press baron's 'monkey-like hands' stretching out to grab more ice cubes for his copious whiskies, called him 'an evil genius who exercised the very worst of influences on Winston'. But Churchill needed his old friend now. Beaverbrook says that he found Churchill on 2 July in the Cabinet Room of 10 Downing Street, together with A. V. Alexander and Dudley Pound, and was asked his opinion. His response was gung-ho. The French must be attacked because: 'The Germans will force the French fleet to join the Italians, thus taking command of the Mediterranean. The Germans will force this by threatening to burn Bordeaux the first day the French refuse, the next day Marseilles, and the third day Paris.'

Churchill seized Beaverbook's arm and rushed him out into No. 10's garden. 'There was a high wind blowing,' Beaverbrook recorded. The prime minister 'raced along. I had trouble keeping up with him. And I began to have an attack of asthma. Churchill declared there was no other decision possible. Then he wept.'

13

'An Absolutely Bloody Business'

In the early hours of the morning of 3 July 1940, British and Canadian sailors seized French warships and submarines in thirteen ports in Britain and Canada, and interned their crews. In the western Mediterranean at 4 a.m., the destroyer HMS *Foxhound* sped on ahead of Force H, taking Captain Cedric Holland of *Ark Royal* to meet the French Admiral Gensoul for a final parley. At 6.20 a.m., *Foxhound*'s motorboat was given permission to enter the Algerian harbour, and Holland radioed a personal message to Gensoul on the battle cruiser *Dunkerque* hoping that his proposals – if acceptable – would put the two navies on the same side.

If the Bay of Oran is seen as a great bowl with the city of Oran at the bottom to the south, then the naval base of Mers-el-Kébir is a few miles away from the city, tucked under the western lip of the bowl, with a fort and a lighthouse on the headland. From this headland, a long mole runs southeast across the bay, and there the French battleships were moored stern first. Nearest the fort, and most northerly, was *Dunkerque*, then *Provence*, then *Strasbourg*, then *Bretagne* and the *Commandant Teste*.

Admiral Gensoul refused to see Captain Holland, although the British officer insisted his proposals were 'Eyes Only Admiral'. Perhaps Holland's inferior rank posed a problem for Gensoul's *amour propre*. The French flag lieutenant Bernard Dufay took the message and there was a slow to-and-fro of written replies from Gensoul stating that his assurances to Admiral North remained exactly the same: French ships would never fall intact into German or Italian hands. Admiral Gensoul added a warning, however, that force would be met by force, and that the first British shot would turn the entire French navy against them.

What Holland did not know was that Gensoul had hurriedly sig-nalled to the French Admiralty only a point-blank British ultimatum – scuttle your ships in six hours, or else – and had relayed none of the more reasonable alternatives. On the British side, nobody took into account that the French Admiralty was in the chaos of relocating itself, with its staff in two different places. Admiral Darlan was at his birthplace, Nérac, 150 miles away from his team, and reliant on the provincial Post Office for communications.

Meanwhile, Force H was hovering ten miles to the northwest of the French ships at Mers-el-Kébir. This gunnery position was calcu-lated so that any British overshoots would not land on Oran, while the French ships would have to fire back over the fort on Mers-el-Kébir's hundred-foot-high headland. On the crown of HMS *Hood*, the thirty-foot range-finder for the guns was already turning. The British crews were ready in anti-flash gear – white leather gaunt-lets, stockinette balaclavas and asbestos hoods. When British spotter planes reported that the French ships were making steam and pre-paring for sea, Somerville ordered magnetic mines to be dropped by aeroplane at the harbour mouth to stop them escaping.

News arrived that French Admiral René-Émile Godfroy had been persuaded to disarm the French warships at Alexandria, but Admi-ral Gensoul did not respond. Somerville kept postponing H-Hour in the hope of a French change of heart. The 3 p.m. deadline he had given passed. Finally, at 4.15 p.m., Gensoul received Holland in his hot cabin on *Dunkerque*. Piped aboard, the British captain wear-ing his *Légion d'honneur* ribbon saw with foreboding that the decks were cleared and the tompions removed from the mouths of the bat-tle cruiser's big guns.

Gensoul was indignant at the British demands. He reiterated that he would scuttle his ships before the Axis ever got them. Holland, sweating in the heat, explained that the British government feared that mere verbal assurances could be undermined by German or Italian treachery; Somerville was deadly serious about opening fire, and very soon. Gensoul stolidly refused to change his position in the absence of a new direct message from Admiral Darlan. He did not consult his officers and men, nor offer them possibility of sailing to somewhere like Martinique and disarming without loss of honour.

Meanwhile, the British Admiralty put more pressure on Somerville by telling him that signals intercepts indicated more French warships and perhaps submarines were coming from Algiers, and he must act before nightfall. Somerville signalled Gensoul visually and by wireless that he would open fire at 5.30 p.m. Gensoul got this message at 5.15 while still conferring with Holland. A brief signal was sent back saying the ships would sail to the West Indies 'if threatened by the enemy'. But this option was not among the terms offered, and Gensoul did not raise a large square flag to signal assent to the British proposals. Time ran out. As Captain Cedric Holland and Lieutenant Bernard Dufay said their hurried farewells on the French ship, both men were crying.

The tragedy commenced at 5.54 p.m. Having given Holland's motorboat time to get clear, *Hood*, *Valiant* and *Resolution* opened fire from the northwest with their fifteen-inch guns, thirty-six four-gun salvoes in something over ten minutes, at a range of 17,500 yards. A fifteen-inch gun fires a one-ton explosive shell from its twenty-yard-long barrel; their multiple effect on the French ships struggling to slip cables and hawsers and unmoor from the jetty was devastating, frightful. *Bretagne* was hit in the first few minutes and was soon completely ablaze. When her ammunition store blew up, she rolled over and sank, killing 977 French sailors by blasting, burning or drowning. Many had been ashore at Gibraltar recently, perhaps carousing at the Right Shoulder Forward or in the bars of Irish Town with the very British matelots who killed them.

Dunkerque was hit by four projectiles, which crippled her steering, electrics and hydraulics. Stokers were boiled alive as scalding high-pressure steam escaped shrieking from ruptured pipes. Before she ran aground off St André, in the lee of Fort Santon, *Dunkerque* banged off over 150 anti-aircraft rounds at the British spotter planes up above and forty big shells at *Hood*. The French used different coloured dyes in their rounds to help each turret distinguish where its own shots fell and *Hood*'s crew were astonished to see great spouts of red, blue, yellow and green erupting from the sea as French shell fire straddled them. There was little damage: splinters wounded a couple of hands.

Hidden by the huge thick column of black smoke from *Bretagne*, the French battle cruiser *Strasbourg* and five destroyers slipped their berths, avoided the mines and escaped eastwards, unscathed. Somerville sent Swordfish bombers from *Ark Royal* after them but they made no hits and the ships escaped to Toulon in Vichy France.

Force H returned to Gibraltar in sombre mood on 4 July. 'How I loathe it all,' Somerville wrote in his pocket diary. He poured out his feelings in a letter to his wife on the same day. 'We all feel thoroughly dirty and ashamed that the first time we should have been in action was an affair like this.' He thought he might be relieved of command 'forthwith' for letting the battle cruiser *Strasbourg* escape. 'I don't mind because it was an absolutely bloody business to shoot up these Frenchmen who showed the greatest gallantry. The truth is my heart wasn't in it and you're not allowed a heart in war . . .' Somerville, who was 'damned angry at being called on to do such a lousy job', thought that Mers-el-Kébir was 'the biggest political blunder of modern times and I imagine will rouse the world against us'.

It was indeed a propaganda gift to Goebbels. Immediately he broadcast the line that Britain had cynically dragged France into the war, let it be fought on French soil with the sacrifice of French soldiers, then set up a pseudo-French government on British soil before attacking French ships and pretending that it was 'in the French interest'. A Berlin newspaper called Churchill 'the greatest criminal in the world'. Vichy France broke off diplomatic relations, but did not actually declare war.

Some neutrals, however, were awed by this demonstration of British ruthlessness. The news reached the USA on the Fourth of

July 1940 and impressed the Americans on their Independence Day. Never mind the defeatist poison the US ambassador in London, Joseph Kennedy, was whispering, the British were clearly still bloody, bold and resolute. Roosevelt's chief adviser Harry Hopkins later told Churchill that Oran was the action that convinced a doubtful president that Britain would fight on. From India, the viceroy said that Indian public opinion approved 'vigour and decision on our part'.

In the House of Commons, Churchill gave a masterly exposition of the tragic necessity of the deed and the inflexible resolve now required as the home country faced invasion. He read out the exhortation he was sending to every servant of the Crown, urging steadiness and resolution: 'We shall not fail in our duty, however painful . . . No negotiation with the German and Italian governments . . . We shall prosecute the war with the utmost vigour by all the means that are open to us until the righteous purposes for which we entered upon it have been fulfilled.' Even the Tories in the House cheered Churchill to the rafters, and once again he burst into tears.

The Algerian bloodshed was not yet over. On 6 July, a dozen torpedo bombers flew from *Ark Royal* to finish off the lightly damaged *Dunkerque*. One torpedo hit a trawler laden with depth charges moored near the battle cruiser; the blast killed scores more Frenchmen and crippled the ship for a year.

James Somerville was in Gibraltar when he received a parcel with a message:

The Captain and Officers of the *Dunkerque* inform you of the deaths, for the honour of their flag, on 3 and 6 July, of nine officers and 200 men of their ship.

They return to you herewith the mementoes which they had from their comrades in arms of the British Royal Navy in whom they had put all their trust.

And they express to you on this occasion all their bitter sadness and disgust that these comrades did not hesitate to soil the glorious flag of St George with an indelible stain, that of murder.

Robert Murphy, a US diplomat in France for the past ten years, reckoned the sinking of the French fleet 'the most serious British mistake of the war' because it undermined the Free French and wiped out any moderate, pro-British sentiments in Vichy. In *Le Figaro*, François Mauriac wrote: 'Monsieur Winston Churchill has arrayed against England – for how many years? – a unanimous France.' The consummately crooked politician Pierre Laval rode that wave of anger into absolute power in Vichy: within a week of Mers-el-Kébir, he had got the French parliament to commit political suicide by dissolving itself and voting in a totalitarian dictatorship headed by the venerable Marshal Pétain, a state 'with only one road to follow . . . a loyal collaboration with Germany and Italy'.*

The naval bombardment at Mers-el-Kébir also caused blowback on the Rock. The raging grief of French citizens at the death of their sailors was turned on the hapless Gibraltarian refugees now living in French North Africa, AFN, *l'Afrique Française du Nord*.

Lourdes Pitaluga was nearly thirteen years old, an evacuee in Casablanca with her mother and two teenage sisters, Carmen and Angeles. Her two elder sisters had stayed behind in Gibraltar as nurses at St Bernard's Hospital, as had their father, an accountant and Special Constable. The first sign of animosity was that no one in AFN would serve the Gibraltarians in the local shops: no food for the hated *anglais*. Then came a knock at the door and the message that they all had twenty-four hours to leave Morocco. They had just rented a flat, bought four beds, a table and chairs, pots and pans, and now they had to leave everything behind.

On Wednesday 10 July, they had to make their own way to the port with only what they could carry. No taxis would take them; no horse gharries were available; no French citizen would give them a

---

* 'The French grew tired of the Republic as if she were an old wife. For them, the dictatorship was a brief affair, adultery. But they intended to cheat on their wife, not to kill her. Now they realise she is dead, their Republic, their freedom. They're mourning her.' Irène Némirovsky's notebook, 1942.

lift: people pushed them aside on the street and spat at them. The hot sun was rising in a blue sky. Angeles Pitaluga found a Moroccan boy with a decrepit cart and a broken-down old donkey and persuaded him to take some old people and a few pieces of luggage. The others set off on foot, dragging their suitcases past hostile, angry faces. Thousands of Gibraltarians slowly converged on the port, women and children, young and old, the frail and the sick. Senegalese *tirailleurs*, French colonial black soldiers with rifles and fixed bayonets, pushed them up against the fence and gates in the hot sun, where there was no shade and no water. All day they waited, and wilted.

Meanwhile, a kind of rescue was on its way, from an unexpected quarter. As we have seen, the collapse of France had led to a split in its armed forces and among its people. Many French soldiers had been evacuated to Britain in Operations *Dynamo* and *Ariel*. A few joined de Gaulle's Free French to carry on the fight, but a rather larger number just gave up and wanted to go home. Nearly fifteen thousand of these disillusioned and unruly Frenchmen were gathered in camps near Liverpool, and gained an unfortunate reputation for thieving and for molesting women. They had to be got out of the country, but as all of France's coast from Belgium to the Bay of Biscay was now enemy occupied territory, their nearest possible destination was Casablanca in French North Africa.

Fifteen British cargo ships were readied to transport 8100 French soldiers and 5100 French sailors. The Royal Army Service Corps provided rations and fitted field kitchens in the empty holds where around nine hundred men in each ship could live and cook their meals. Their convoy commodore, Rear Admiral Sir Kenelm Creighton, was not impressed with his new charges: 'They made a sorry sight; unshaven, dirty and, though a good many still had rifles, ammunition and equipment, they had made no attempt during their weeks of idleness in England to clean them. This was no doubt due to the poor leadership of their officers . . .'

Convoy OG 36 formed at sea on 3 July. OG stood for Outward-bound Gibraltar, but some ships were heading for Bilbao, Oporto,

Lisbon, Seville and Cádiz. It was the same day as the seizing or sinking of the French fleet and as soon as Creighton heard about the
actions being taken he signalled all the masters of his fifteen Casa-
blanca-bound ships to keep Frenchmen away from the radio room
and ensure there were no private wireless sets on board, fearing that
news of the Oran events would enrage them, and that with the arms
and ammunition they held, they could overwhelm the two dozen
merchant navy crew on each ship. Thus the French officers who
wandered up to see Creighton on the bridge of SS *Balfe* remained in
the dark, and demoralised. When Creighton urged them to carry on
the fight and never surrender, they only shook their heads, pityingly:
'*La France est vaincue; la guerre est finie*', 'France is beaten; the war
is over.'

The British convoy of cargo ships, *Bactria, Balfe, Beckenham,
Belgravian, Brittany, Calumet, City of Evansville, City of Windsor, Clan Macbean, David Livingstone, Dromore Castle, Euryades,
Fidra, Strategist* and *Swinburne*, got a harsh welcome off Casablanca on 8 July. Two French submarines surfaced, a squadron of
light bombers passed low overhead, almost at mast height, and the
destroyer which had signalled them to stop sent over a motorboat
with three submachine-gun-toting sailors and a blue-chinned officer,
who scrambled up the jumping-ladder and made for the bridge of
the *Balfe*. The *capitaine de frégate* leading the boarding party was
brusque and rude. He ordered the ship's wireless room to be closed,
elbowing Captain Woods, *Balfe*'s master, out of the way.

Admiral Creighton's fierce temper flared; he was not the sort of
Irishman to treat lightly. (Once, when the Egyptian Minister of Communications for the third time did not deign to arrive for the arranged
appointment, Creighton picked up the chair he had been made to
wait in and smashed it, shatteringly, straight through the glass door
of the secretary's office. They paid attention promptly thereafter, and
King Farouk made him a pasha.) On the bridge of the *Balfe*, Admiral
Creighton grabbed the French commander by the lapels and snarled
that he objected to his insult to the ship's master; British ships were

risking their lives to bring Frenchmen to Casablanca. But when the French officer started to talk about the criminal murder of French sailors, Creighton let the man get it all off his chest before telling the *capitaine* he needed to disembark the troops and get on his way. The French destroyer lamp-signalled permission to enter and at the breakwater a pilot came aboard who was equally disagreeable and handled the *Balfe* with deliberate carelessness, bumping her against the jetty and damaging the hull.

On the quayside, lines of black African French colonial soldiers were standing to attention with their rifles butt-down at order arms. The French soldiers and sailors from Liverpool disembarked, were fallen in and marched off. There were jeers and catcalls, not cheers; the atmosphere was tense. Creighton wrote:

No sooner had the repatriated [French] troops disappeared from view than a mass of civilians poured through the dock gates and spilled across the road leading to the jetty. Black troops forced them forwards with rifle butts. I saw as they came closer that they were Europeans; men, women and children of all ages, they stumbled along the baking dusty quayside. Old men and women were collapsing in the heat, young mothers were trying to shield their babies from the sun. Clutching battered suitcases and parcels roughly tied with string these people – there were thousands of them – were a pathetic sight.

Then another French officer handed Creighton a note from the Vichy admiral in charge of Casablanca. It said his ships were under arrest until each one embarked a thousand of the people squatting miserably on the quayside. Creighton realised: 'They were the women and children, the old and infirm, of the population of Gibraltar.'

The ships in Creighton's convoy were in no condition to take these pathetic civilians. They were not passenger ships with cabins and stairs, but cargo ships. Fit young men might be able to climb up and down iron ladders in order to get in and out of the holds, but frail old people, children and pregnant women could not be expected to. And besides, the holds were in a disgusting state because the lazier

Frenchmen had preferred to foul their living quarters than find the heads. The smell was appalling.

Creighton was between a rock and a hard place. The French wanted to be rid of the Gibraltarians; the Fortress authorities didn't want them back in. 'For Heaven's sake don't,' cabled Admiral Dudley North, 'we had enough trouble getting them out.' Creighton decided that he must ignore this message and get the hungry, thirsty and sunburned Gibraltarians on board, crammed into all the space available on his cargo ships. The French troops started enthusiastically pushing the women and children up the gangways with their rifle butts. Lourdes Pitaluga was bruised on the buttocks, Mariola Benavente fell and hurt her left knee. British merchant navy officers and sailors went down among the Gibraltarians and started pushing back, yelling and shouting, making such a scene that the French captain was forced to restrain his soldiers from overcrowding the ships. As twelve-year-old Lourdes reached the top of the gangplank of the *Swinburne*, clutching her mother's hand, a sailor motioned her towards a stairway but, recoiling from the faecal stench, she pulled her mother around onto the deck where they crouched by a stack of sandbags.

The strung-out convoy of re-evacuated refugees set sail on Wednesday 10 July. It was a six-hour trip from Casablanca to Gibraltar. As night fell, it grew horribly cold for the girls in their flimsy summer dresses, but the merchant navy sailors moved among them with sweaters, scarves, blankets and greatcoats, handing out mugs of hot bitter cocoa that warmed their icy hands. 'I pray for them every night,' Lourdes told me, seventy-five years later. As the children slept, the elders watched and prayed. At 3 a.m., on board the *Clan Macbean*, Mrs Pizzarello gave birth. They named the boy Alex after the naval officer who wrapped and rocked him.

Things were moving in Gibraltar. Governor Sir Clive Liddell issued a press communiqué on Wednesday 10 July which appeared in the *Gibraltar Chronicle* on the Thursday. But the Rock is a small place where word of mouth travels fast. Everybody knew the facts by Wednesday night: the Gibraltar families were leaving Morocco, and were being transferred 'to another destination, calling at Gibraltar only for replenishment of the ships'. The governor further stated: 'It will not be possible to allow any landing, but lists of passengers will be published for information as early as possible.' He unimaginatively requested the public 'not to make personal enquiries which can only hamper and delay the organisation'.

It was a bad mistake to think that Gibraltarian workers would allow their exiled families to pass through the Rock without seeing them. The Gibraltarians were seen as colonial subjects completely at the disposal of the fortress, garrison and naval base; treated with cheerful racist contempt by generations of swaddies and matelots, they were expected to do what they were told. But this latest order touched family, the heart of Mediterranean civilisation. The day when the first cargo ships of refugees started arriving, Thursday 11 July 1940, is the day when the Gibraltarian people stood up for themselves, the day that the people dismissively termed 'Rock Scorpions' or 'Scorps' struck back.

Early in the morning, shops stayed closed, and workmen did not go to their places of employment in the shipyard, in the docks, and even in the police station, for the policemen had wives and children too. The Gibraltarians began gathering in the old Jewish marketplace, El Martillo, Commercial Square, which is the Rock's political equivalent of Trafalgar Square. (It had recently been renamed John Mackintosh Square after a wealthy local philanthropist's death. Today it is often called Piazza.) Emotions ran high; there was angry talk of *la huelga*, strikes; the mood was ugly. The young lawyer Joshua Hassan, then manning a gun in the Gibraltar Defence Force, vividly remembered the Gibraltarian men standing right up against the lines of British troops with fixed bayonets, soldiers sent out to control the civilian crowds. He wondered what would happen if push came to shove – bloody noses and broken heads? Anthony Baldorino, one of the two Gibraltarian elected members of the City Council, woke the other, his colleague Samuel Benady, and told him he thought there was going to be a riot and serious fighting with the soldiers, if they did not do something quickly.

The two councillors spoke to the crowd from the balcony of City Hall. Benady said it was monstrous that their families were being shipped like cattle, and not being allowed to see them was adding insult to injury. He said he and Baldorino were going immediately to confront Governor Liddell at Government House, but he asked the crowd not to follow them down Main Street as it might cause trouble with the soldiers. Abraham Serfaty, head of the Exchange and Commercial Library, was still talking to the crowd when the two men hurried off to their impromptu meeting.

General Sir Clive Liddell was reluctant to change his mind because of British fears that if the civilians were allowed off the ships they would refuse to be re-evacuated. But Benady and Baldorino said they were more in touch with the Gibraltarian people than his British advisers, and warned Liddell he would have an ugly riot on his hands if he did not let the families come ashore. At one point the governor left the room, probably to communicate with London. When he came back, Liddell conceded. He said he would allow the evacuees ashore, but only for a few days, until the ships could be put in a proper state for their transport elsewhere, and asked the councillors for an undertaking that they would co-operate. They agreed and requested, 'May we tell the people in John Mackintosh Square?' Liddell nodded.

Back on the balcony of City Hall, the two councillors announced what had transpired. The crowd was jubilant. Victory! They could meet their families later! In the meantime the councillors asked everyone to go back to work. After three cheers for His Majesty the King and His Excellency the Governor, they all dispersed.

There had been some trouble on the ships too when people were told they could not go ashore to their homes and their menfolk. On the ships tied up at the South Mole, some of the evacuees, including Mariola Benavente's mother, started throwing their luggage over the side onto the wharf. But food and water were sent out to the ships and, in the afternoon, the first tenders started bringing families ashore to anxious relatives waiting at the Waterport Wharf entrance and in Casemates Square. Buses, taxis, army lorries, private cars and horse-drawn gharries carried folk home. The Pitalugas got into an army lorry with a sign saying Governor's Parade, nearest to Gavino's Court. By Thursday night, half the refugees were back on the Rock.

While negotiations began to bribe neutral countries like Spain and Portugal to accept some civilian evacuees, Creighton reckoned it would take ten days to clean and fit out the cargo ships properly to carry the rest of the Gibraltarian women and children to Britain. He took a room at the Rock Hotel, where officers of the three services and senior WAAFs and WRNS were billeted, and found it very pleasant.

In the early hours of 18 July he was woken by the wailing of air-raid sirens and the loud sounds of a bombing raid, the Vichy revenge attack on Gibraltar for the sinking of the French fleet. While Gibraltarian civilians, like the Pitaluga family under Governor's Parade, huddled on benches in the City Council's 'Ironside' ARP shelters, Creighton merely buried his head under the pillow and went back to sleep. In the morning he found a metal splinter embedded in the plaster a few inches above the bed-head, and the carpet salted and peppered with broken glass and grits of stone.

On Friday 19 July, the richer evacuees were once again the first to go. Four hundred and fifty people from families who could pay their own passage were evacuated to Portuguese Madeira aboard the RNR ex-passenger liner HMS *Royal Ulsterman*. Also on board was the governor's wife, Lady Liddell, with their son. Another fifteen hundred would follow them to Madeira in the days to come.

Over the weekend, the first ships destined for the UK with civilian evacuees left in Convoy HG (Homeward Gibraltar) 39. The *Bactria* was carrying a hundred mental hospital patients and the paupers from the City Poor House (the only people who had not been allowed to disembark after their return from Casablanca), with their nurses and family carers. The *Clan Macbean* was transporting 213 evacuees to Cardiff, and the *Avoceta* took 146 Gibraltarians together with the hundred-odd Polish, Czech and French refugees who had arrived from Lisbon.

Even A. M. Dryburgh, Controller of the Evacuation Scheme, found his sixteen-day voyage to Swansea on the *Avoceta* dismal. He had to bunk in a cubby-hole with a sapper lance corporal, the food was deplorable because there was no fruit or vegetables, the only drink was stewed tea, and everyone ended up crawling with lice.

The pressure to get the civilians out of Gibraltar increased as bombing raids began. Following the air raid of 18 July which killed four people, in the early hours of Friday 26 July another fleet of Vichy bombers attacked from the north, dropping a chain of bombs between Four Corners and Europa Point. Two civilians were killed, one a thirty-year-old woman, the other a little boy of two, and forty people were wounded. That evening, the Union-Castle line troop-ship *Athlone Castle* (which had brought out the 4th Battalion of the Black Watch to defend the Rock) carried some sixteen hundred Gibraltarians away to the UK, mainly elderly and disabled, families with toddlers and expectant mothers. Mrs Lopes's baby girl, born *en voyage*, was christened Athlone Angeles Lopes. The next day, three more troopships evacuated another nineteen hundred people.

By the time Admiral Creighton's original cargo ships were ready, the five thousand-plus Gibraltarian evacuees had all been listed and labelled. Everyone had to bring soap and towel, knife, fork, spoon, plate, and cup or mug in their hand luggage, and each family brought simple cooking utensils, as well as enough food for the first meal. Mattresses and blankets had to be rolled and kept separate from the other baggage, which was collected by lorry. No private cars, only official buses or medical ambulances ferried everyone down to Waterport, and only naval and military personnel were allowed to help people aboard the ships – the Fortress did not want families' emotional farewells cluttering up an orderly departure.

After two days in the bay, Convoy HG 40 finally left on Tuesday 30 July 1940. There were twenty-four ships, including a dozen of the vessels that Creighton had come out with, and a bunch of Swedish ships carrying iron ore. Their escort for the first four days out into the Atlantic was the destroyer HMS *Wishart*, together with the anti-submarine trawler HMS *Leyland*. A lone corvette, HMS *Wellington*, stayed with them the whole long route west of Ireland, and round into the Irish Sea via the North Channel, arriving at Liverpool on 14 August.

One of the ships of convoy HG 40, SS *Calumet* out of Avonmouth, held a special group of eleven prisoners among its 259 evacuees. Formerly kept in prison at Moorish Castle, these were the Gibraltarian Fascists arrested under Regulation 18B – Bertuchi, Bonifacio, Bonitch, Byrne, Canilla, Facio, Figueras, Frendo, Garcia, Gonzalez and Scicluna. They were being escorted to the UK by three police officers led by Chief Inspector Santos. One of the police escorts, fifty-year-old Constable Joseph Baglietto, had just retired injured with an annual pension awarded for his 'diligence and fidelity'. Baglietto was the police officer badly wounded by shrapnel while helping civilians at Catalan Bay during the *José Luis Diez* firefight in the Spanish Civil War. Taking retirement now meant he could accompany his wife Mary and children Francis and Concepcion to England. Young Frank noticed that one of the Fascists was bawling like a baby as he boarded the ship in handcuffs.

As the Gibraltarians watched their dear Rock slide away, changing its shape over the water, there was sorrow and dread among the more cautious, but hope and excitement among the more adventurous. They were leaving homes that were being bombed by the French and going to another country that was under attack by the Germans, but who on earth could know what would happen to them?

Lourdes Pitaluga was on the *City of Evansville* with both her parents and her four sisters, and nearly five hundred others. Although the Gibraltar dockyard carpenters had tried to make the ship's holds habitable, she found them airless and appalling. In the centre of each hold was a long trestle table with a dozen holes for metal washbasins. Families picked a spot in the remaining floor space and unrolled their mattresses. Large cockroaches came scuttling across the floor, making the girls scream, and sometimes there were rats. Up the wooden stairway from the hot hold were the lavatories, rough sheds with a coarse sacking curtain for a door, fitted on the side of the lower deck. Inside, up a wooden step, was a long shelf overhanging the ship's rail, with bottom-shaped holes cut in it through which you could see the sea below. For those too weak to climb the stairway or too inhibited to use these long-drops, there were night-soil buckets which a friend or family member would have to empty. Luggage was buried too deep in the hold for anyone to get a change of clothes for a fortnight and water was so strictly rationed that it was hard to wash properly. Lourdes was grateful that her darkening suntan hid the dirt on her skin.

The shipyard carpenters had also rigged up a stove or two by the funnels for volunteers and families to cook hot meals. After a few days of summer heat, the Gibraltarians on the *City of Evansville* found all the fresh foodstuffs they had brought with them had gone mouldy and had to go overboard to feed the seagulls. Instead they subsisted on boiled rice. On the first day, Lourdes refused to eat it, and then she did, squeamishly pushing the weevils to the side of her plate. By the end of the trip they had boils and mouth ulcers and felt faint with hunger. Lourdes's two elder sisters, Carlota and Victoria, were volunteer nurses with very little experience, and one of their charges was a three-year-old girl called Elena Bagna who had a terrible wound on the left side of her forehead from the last bombing attack – her father was also wounded and her mother heavily pregnant. Every day the girls had to change the dressing on the big hole in Elena's skull. An officer gripped her between his knees and held her arms as she wriggled. The wound stank of sepsis; the little girl screamed with so much pain and distress that everyone ended up in tears. Carlota and Victoria were excused duty when Mrs Bagna had her baby: a woman from the next hold acted as midwife to the newborn, later christened Marina. James Balfe Gomez was another baby born during the voyage – the *Balfe* was another of the convoy ships – but four people also died and were buried at sea.

The trip was a worry for the convoy commodore and the ship's masters, concerned for their merchant navy crews as well as the wretched flock they were shepherding. Approaching Ireland, submarine scares sent the ships into their pre-arranged zig-zags: ten degrees to starboard for ten minutes, then twenty degrees to starboard for another ten minutes, then thirty degrees back to port for fifteen minutes, another thirty to port for ten minutes before a thirty-degree turn to starboard brought the convoy onto its original mean track. Then repeat, until the order 'Cease Zig-zag'.

Six convoys earlier, HG 34F (Homeward-bound from Gibraltar, Number 34, Fast) had lost four of its twenty-one ships to U-boat torpedoes, and sixty-six men had died. On Creighton's twelve cargo ships, each carrying anywhere between 250 and seven hundred passengers, there were nowhere near enough lifeboats for everyone on board. Though they had scrounged every extra raft and lifebelt they could lay their hands on in Gibraltar, if any ship had sunk, most people on board would have certainly drowned or frozen to death in the Atlantic. If HG 40 had been attacked and any of its ships abandoned, the officers and men would have been forced to do their duty and give up their places in the lifeboats to save the women and children. The merchant seamen were knowingly facing the prospect of almost certain extinction if there were enemy action, but still they were kind to the children, giving them treats like bread and butter from their own ration, Lourdes Pitaluga recalled, and once, magically, a plate of egg and chips to share. Seven of them in turn, each solemnly dipping a chip in the yolk. The matelots enjoyed seeing so many women and girls on board. One sailor surprised his mother by returning home with a kitbag full of clothes beautifully folded and ironed by Gibraltarian women's hands.

Some of Convoy HG 40 went to Liverpool and others to Cardiff. The *City of Evansville* docked at Swansea. A tender came out and asked them if there was anything they wanted. 'Bread! Bread! We are hungry!' the girls chanted. 'We want bread! We want bread!' More boats came out and Lourdes got her own loaf, which she crammed into her mouth in fistfuls of crust and crumb, with a single sweet and delicious tomato. She was also given a hen's egg, which her mother pierced with a pin from her brooch so she could swallow it raw from the shell.

The Gibraltarians disembarked on 14 August and, after a high tea of bread and butter, buns and cakes, were put on a night train to London. There were no lights because of the blackout so they sat back and watched mysterious dark shapes and silhouettes rushing past the window. Distant searchlights, like long probing fingers, caught a tiny plane in the sky and puffs of smoke appeared around it. Then it burst into flames and fell out of the sky. When they reached Paddington Station it was two thirty in the morning. The dazed foreigners got out of the train to see lines of red buses waiting. Suddenly, scores of people poured out of the buses and filled up the empty train. These were British women and children being evacuated from London. Though they did not know it, the Gibraltarians were replacing them just in time for the Blitz, which would begin in three weeks.

But first they were processed. Like all foreign refugees, they had not properly 'landed' in England until they had been through Empress Hall. This was a huge building at Earl's Court, originally constructed for spectacular entertainments, where Queen Victoria had seen real Sioux Indians re-enacting the battle of the Little Big Horn for Buffalo Bill's Wild West Show. In 1915, Empress Hall had housed thousands of Belgian refugees; then it had become an ice-skating rink. Now it was a principal London County Council holding centre where refugees were registered, housed, fed, bathed and given a medical while papers and credentials were checked. They were not allowed out until they had been 'cleared', although they could receive visitors. The control was strict but the supervisors were friendly and courteous, reported a Basque priest who was there from 28 June to 4 July 1940.

The canteen workers, the 'Pentecost Brigade' of interpreters, the carers and caretakers and distributors of clean second-hand clothes were all from the Women's Voluntary Services, WVS, the remarkable organisation founded by Sir Samuel Hoare and Lady Reading, initially to assist ARP, Air Raid Precautions, in 1938.

However nice the British personnel may have been, Lourdes Pitaluga was not impressed with the physical conditions for 750 Gibraltarians. There were long queues for the ablutions and the communal soap was seething with lice. As she lay in her camp bed, jammed between tiers of bucket seats, she looked up at the Victorian cast-iron dome with its hundreds of panes of glass and thought it no protection against German bombs. When the air-raid siren wailed they went down into a deep shelter, and at the 'all clear' came back to find their folding camp beds crazed with glinting shards. Soon the Gibraltarians were moved into big hotels in Kensington.

London was full of foreign refugees in 1940 – displaced people of scores of nationalities including Belgians, Czechs, Danes, Dutch, Finns, French, Norwegians, Poles, Romanians, Slovaks, Yugoslavs. Amongst them was the Basque priest mentioned above, Canon Alberto Onaindia, who had witnessed the bombing of Gernika in 1937, gone into exile in France and eventually arrived in Plymouth on a Canadian destroyer. In August 1940, Onaindia, by then living in a community of refugees at Redhill in Surrey, was summoned by an English friend to Empress Hall to meet two elderly, frail and sick Gibraltarians who spoke no English and wanted to give their confession in Spanish. It is not that easy to administer the sacrament of penance. Under Catholic canon law, an ordained priest must also be granted the faculty of exercising absolution by the competent authority. In other words, Onaindia needed the permission of a bishop or higher. So the Basque wrote to His Eminence the Roman Catholic Cardinal Archbishop of Westminster, offering to serve the exiled Gibraltarians as their priest.

The secretary of seventy-five-year-old Cardinal Arthur Hinsley wrote back to say he regretted very much that His Eminence could find no place for the Basque priest in his diocese. This was because Cardinal Hinsley remembered Canon Onaindia from their political disagreements at a Eucharistic Congress in Budapest in May 1938, in the middle of the Spanish Civil War.

Hinsley, a no-nonsense Yorkshireman who kept a picture of *Generalísimo* Franco on his desk and saw the Spanish Civil War as a battle between Christ and Antichrist, had been very keen to send back all the Basque children who had been evacuated to England a year earlier, 'especially as I learn that many of them . . . are already imbued with Communist doctrines'. Onaindia, a Christian democrat and a Basque patriot, knew dozens of Basque Catholic priests were among Franco's six hundred thousand prisoners and disbelieved Franco's claims to the Christian moral high ground. Onaindia felt the Basque children were far better off in 'a free country which is fighting for the liberty of the oppressed'.

Some see Cardinal Hinsley (who died in 1943) as a benign figure in English Roman Catholicism, whose 'Sword of the Spirit' campaign against totalitarianism was useful propaganda in the Second World War. But Canon Onaindia only saw his unquestioning support for Franco, and his denigration of decent Basque Christians as communists. He wrote an impassioned follow-up letter to Cardinal Hinsley on 22 August, which a Basque friend finally persuaded him not to send. The draft ended:

In exile, we Basques have been working for France and England who defend the principles of Christianity among the nations. Hundreds of Basques have fought on the French fronts, thousands of specialist workers have worked in the war factories, the whole of the Basque propaganda has been put at the service of the Democratic Powers, and today they co-operate closely in all fields of their activity for the triumph of the cause which the British Empire is defending. On the contrary, Spain is living under German Nazi dictatorship; Spanish propaganda is a branch of that of Goebbels . . . Today, Gibraltar is a prize which Franco wants to grasp . . .

Once more I pray for the triumph of England and of all of the oppressed nations . . .

You will, I hope, pardon this intimate expression of feelings from a humble priest who is enduring exile for his ideals, which are those of England and are the ideals of Christianity.

Princess Elizabeth, the daughter of King George VI, was not much older than Lourdes Pitaluga when she made her first broadcast on the wireless, on 13 October 1940. She spoke on the BBC's *Children's Hour* to all the Commonwealth children who had been evacuated. 'My sister Margaret Rose and I feel so much for you as we know from experience what it means to be away from those we love most of all.'

Before I finish I can truthfully say to you all that we children at home are full of cheerfulness and courage. We are trying to do all we can to help our gallant sailors, soldiers and airmen, and we are trying, too, to bear our own share of the danger and sadness of war.

We know, every one of us, that in the end all will be well; for God will care for us and give us victory and peace. And when peace comes, remember it will be for us, the children of today, to make the world of tomorrow a better and happier place.

My sister is by my side and we are both going to say goodnight to you.

Come on, Margaret.

Goodnight, children.

Goodnight, and good luck to you all.

14

The Indian Boy and His Cook

Krishna Khubchand Daswani started life as someone special: officially recorded on 2 July 1932 as the first Indian child ever to be born in Gibraltar. His handsome father, Khubchand Bulchand Daswani, had come from Hyderabad in Sind where he was a newspaper editor. In 1893 he formed a business partnership with two other merchants to explore commercial prospects in the wider world. They sent a scout ahead, carrying his own bedding, cooking on deck, lugging a couple of bags of Indian goods – sandalwood elephants, kukri knives, necklaces, knick-knacks – bought for a shilling and sold for a pound. His stock was snapped up in Gibraltar and he reported that it was a promising spot. There were only three Indian firms there – they could be the fourth.

In time, Khubchand Bulchand Daswani himself followed and by the mid-1920s he was firmly established with a shop called Bulchand & Sons at 160 Main Street (now the health food store Holland & Barrett). He brought over his wife, Bulibai Khubchand Tikamdas, his son and two daughters. Their fourth child, Krishna, was born in Gibraltar's Irish Town.

When the family came over, his wife's sister, Mathuribai, gave them the gift of a *chota* boy, twelve years old, to be a servant and a cook for the vegetarian family. He was small and dark with a mole and a birthmark some thought disfiguring on the right side of his face, and he had only one testicle. His name was Barsati Karya.

The family lived in a flat in a handsome house at 32 Irish Town, and close by in Parliament Lane was a pub then called the Bull and Bush. During the Spanish Civil War, Barsati Karya used to drink with the Republican supporters there and join in their songs.

One was sung to the the tune of the socialist anthem, the 'Internationale':

> *Arriba los pobres del mundo,*
> *¡Viva la International!*
> *¡Que mueran todos los fascistas*
> *Del Peñon de Gibraltar!*

> Up with the poor of the world
> Up with the internationale!
> May all the fascists die
> On the Rock of Gibraltar!

Like many others in Gibraltar, Krishna's father accommodated a Spanish refugee family, who lived in the flat above the shop in Main Street. (Many years later, one of them returned from Madrid to say thank you.)

Little Krishna was a privileged middle-class boy, woken, washed and dressed by Spanish maidservants from La Línea. He knew no Hindi, spoke Spanish and some English, and went to various schools: Miss Silva's in Bomb House Lane, the Hebrew School and the Lourdes School. During the Munich crisis in 1938, young 'Kisha', as he was often called, carried a gas mask every day to school.

When the Gibraltarian civilians had to be evacuated, his father did not want to go. Business was busy – Mr Bulchand was now Gibraltar agent for Parker ballpoint pens and Van Raalte lingerie. Bulibai, his pregnant wife, would not leave without him, so the whole family waited until the very last possible ship before they finally all got away from Gibraltar on 8 June 1940. A party of twenty-eight Indians of three merchant families plus their employees boarded the Henderson line passenger and cargo vessel SS *Kemmendine*, which ran back and forth from Scotland to Burma, carrying the families of planters, settlers and colonial officials.

As the Indians crossed the Mediterranean en route for the Suez Canal, news came that Fascist Italy had entered the war, and the

Kemmendine had to turn back smartly from what were now enemy waters. The ship traversed the Strait of Gibraltar and then made its slow, fourteen-knot way towards Rangoon via the South Atlantic, going round the Cape of Good Hope. Krishna remembered that every Thursday they had lifeboat drill with lifejackets at about 10 a.m. He had his eighth birthday on the ship. From Cape Town, *Kemmendine* continued eastward across the Indian Ocean. They were seven hundred miles south of Ceylon on Saturday 13 July 1940 when, just after breakfast, they met with the German raider *Hilfskreuzer* (auxiliary cruiser) *Atlantis*.

Originally called *Goldenfels*, known to the German Kriegsmarine as *Schiff 16* and to the British Admiralty as *Raider C*, the *Atlantis* was the first of ten German 'Q-ships', a 7860-ton freighter converted in fourteen weeks into an armed merchant cruiser at the DeSchiMAG shipyard in Bremen. Six six-inch guns, a three-inch warning gun, two twin 3.7 cm anti-aircraft guns and four 2 cm automatics were all hidden beneath tarpaulins, deck crates and ingeniously hinged bulwarks, but could be exposed in two seconds when the ship went into action. *Atlantis* carried enough flags, paint, costumes, fake running-lights and dummy funnels to assume the identity of either an innocent British, Dutch, Norwegian, Japanese or Russian cargo ship.

A raider's job was to remain at sea for as long as possible, stealing fuel and supplies, laying mines and ambushes, dispersing enemy naval forces and disrupting their trade and communications.* HK *Atlantis* left Germany in March 1940 and stayed out for a remarkable 602 days, managing to sink or capture twenty-two ships. Admiral Raeder reported to Hitler on 7 September 1940 that 'the successes of all the auxiliary cruisers have exceeded expectations. *Schiff 16* has sunk 41,000 tons.'

---

* *Atlantis*'s greatest coup was capturing the Singapore-bound SS *Automedon* on 11 November 1940. A wealth of secret intelligence material, including War Cabinet minutes, revealed all Britain's military weaknesses in the Far East. *Kapitän* Rogge was rewarded with an ornate samurai sword for supplying information that would help Imperial Japan to plan and launch its December 1941 attacks.

When it encountered *Kemmendine*, *Atlantis* had already attacked four ships. It had sunk three of them, but not the Norwegian vessel MV *Tirranna*, en route from Melbourne to Suez with treats for Australian and British troops in the Middle East. *Tirranna* was kept afloat with a German 'prize-crew' aboard so its cargo could be enjoyed in Germany: six thousand bales of merino wool, three thousand tons of Australian wheat, twenty-seven thousand sacks of flour, thousands of cases of beer, tobacco, jam and canned peaches, as well as 178 trucks and cars. The Germans also found bags of mail destined for the 1st Australian Corps in Egypt, loving letters and gift parcels packed with cigarettes and sweets and thousands of pairs of soft knitted socks. The ship's doctor scooped a new book on war surgery and a fine drill that would do excellently for skull-trepanning.

Raiders relied on radio, not only for instructions from home, but to find new prey and to avoid enemy predators. They monitored all wireless traffic for news of themselves. They had to stop victims signalling for help, thus giving away their location and current identity. When the *Kemmendine*'s transmitters started up, ready to signal QQQ – 'have sighted a suspicious ship' – or RRR – 'raider' – the radio operator on *Atlantis* picked it up and alerted the bridge. Captain Rogge ordered salvoes. Several shells hit the mark: one shot holed the *Kemmendine*'s waterline, another exploded in the port boiler room and two more wrecked the bridge and the radio cabin. *Kemmendine* ran up the flag K – 'I am stopping' – and the Germans ceased fire. As the crew of the *Kemmendine* lowered their lifeboats to abandon ship, *Atlantis* moved in closer. To save on ammunition and torpedoes, its normal practice was to send over boarding parties in cutters, first to search for code-books, documents and useful things, then to take everybody prisoner and finally to place two hundred pounds of explosives in key spots of the hull, to scuttle the ship and leave no trace.

This time things did not go according to plan. The *Kemmendine* had surrendered and her passengers were all in their lifeboats as per the 'Abandon Ship' drill, when a lone figure on the stern – a former

London window-cleaner – pulled the lanyard on the three-inch gun, firing a shot at *Atlantis*. 'Salvoes!' ordered Rogge, furious, and a return volley of shells and tracer set the *Kemmendine*'s stern ablaze. Krishna remembered his brother Balu being sick, and then being carried up the Jacob's ladder to *Atlantis* under a German sailor's arm. He watched the matelots rigging a stretcher to lift his heavily pregnant mother out of the boat and safely onto the deck. Then there were big tins of orange and lemon squash which they drank, thirsty from the salt water, smoke and excitement. The Germans were very polite, apologising for interrupting their journey, but there was a war on.

The people from *Kemmendine* crowded on board the *Atlantis* before their burning vessel was finally torpedoed. White-haired Captain R. B. Reid led twenty-six white officers and men, eighty-six Lascars, twenty-eight Indian passengers and seven white passengers – five women and two children. One *memsahib* bound for Burma execrated the Germans in the vilest of language.* The German Surgeon-Commander Reil diagnosed shock, apologised copiously and offered the sharp-tongued woman a large drink – part of his job was to befriend and soothe the civilian prisoners. One of the small white boys was weeping because he had not been able to rescue the small wooden chair that *Kemmendine*'s carpenter had hand-made for him. A mother was anxious for the safety of her convent-educated fourteen-year-old daughter among all these rough sailors. The high-caste Gibraltarian Indian merchants were philosophical about the loss of all their jewellery and ornaments and wealth that had gone down. 'Life is the main thing,' said one. 'We'll get our money back somehow.' Captain Rogge berthed all these Indians together, and gave them their own cooking facilities.

Eight-year-old Krishna Khubchand had a family of seven. There was his father and pregnant mother, his elder sister Sati, then

---

* In February 1946, this woman, Mrs Dorothy Hilton, once editor of a British Union of Fascists' newspaper, pleaded guilty to eight charges of assisting the enemy by broadcasting for Germany and preparing scripts for German propaganda, and got eighteen months in prison.

Krishna and three younger siblings, his seven-year-old sister Gopi, six-year-old brother Balu and four-year-old sister Savitri. The presence of children had a softening effect on those German sailors who were family men, much as the Gibraltarian evacuees had touched the hearts of their British matelots. The Germans sang and played with *die Kinder.* Captured Chinese and Indian crewmen were put to work. Tastier meals came from the galley, and the Indians improved the oiling and cleaning; some Chinese became stewards, others labourers, shifting cargoes of loot. One Indian even became the ship's accountant and cash paymaster. But when they caught another Norwegian ship, the *Talleyrand*, the *Atlantis* definitely became overcrowded with 327 prisoners, and so it was decided to send the prize-ship *Tirranna* home. Fourteen Germans had to guard 274 passengers (ninety-five European, 179 Asian and Indian) including all the women and children and the men over fifty taken off the captured ships. One hundred tons of diesel oil and other useful items were offloaded and on 4 August, the privateer *Atlantis* and the merchant vessel *Tirranna* parted.

Bletchley Park's breaking of German naval Enigma finally trapped the elusive *Atlantis* – not by reading the commerce raider's own signals, which were never cracked, but by decrypting the wireless traffic of the U-boats sent to refuel from her. The British cruiser HMS *Devonshire* finally sank HK *Atlantis* in the South Atlantic on 22 November 1941. The raider was not forgotten, however. In 1960, Dino De Laurentiis produced an Italian-American movie about her – 'The Killer-Ship with a Thousand Disguises!' – *Sotto Dieci Bandiere* or *Under Ten Flags*, starring Van Heflin as *Kapitän* Bernhard Rogge.

After a ten-thousand-mile voyage from the Indian Ocean, the *Tirranna* crossed the Bay of Biscay and finally reached the mouth of the Gironde estuary in German-occupied France on 21 September 1940. *Atlantis* had signalled Berlin she was a prize-ship, so no U-boat would sink her valuable cargo. Since 10 September they had an extra passenger, because Krishna's mother had given birth to a baby called

Bhagwan *en voyage*. A Burmese carpenter on board hand-carved a cradle for the infant boy.

The prize-crew captain, Lieutenant Mundt, went ashore to telephone German naval headquarters and was told he would have to wait twelve hours for minesweepers to escort him to Bordeaux.

'What about enemy submarines?'

'Don't worry, Lieutenant, there aren't any submarines in this area.'

After lunch on Sunday 22 September 1940, Krishna Khubchand was on deck, playing alone with a red wooden train that an English boy had given him that morning. The rest of his family were below in their cabins having a siesta. In rapid succession, three British torpedoes, fired by the British submarine HMS *Tuna*, hit the MV *Tirranna*, which immediately listed and began sinking.

The ship tilted sharply and everything started sliding downwards. Krishna, a small boy in blue shorts and a white shirt, clung to the deck-rail. He had no idea what else to do. As the *Tirranna* settled – she took seven minutes to sink – he saw below him on the water one of the ship's home-made life-rafts, a vessel of four rusty oildrums lashed together with green-painted planks. Among the people on it was the dark figure of Barsati Karya. The cook called up to him: 'Kisha! What are you doing? *Ven, ven*. Come, come.' Krishna walked down a gangway; the little cook caught him and put him on the raft. The boy lost one of his sandals but did not get wet at all.

Then the rough raft went to help other people in the water. Tarachand's wife was there, with her infant Rupi in her arms and her four-year-old daughter Sarsati clinging to her shoulder. Barsati grabbed the infant and handed her to Krishna to hold and then pulled the little girl out. But the girls' mother was too heavy. She slid away, to be picked up by another boat. By now the *Tirranna* had turned turtle and sunk.

Some German seaplanes with floats touched down on the water to help survivors. Other rescue boats arrived. Krishna asked:

'Where are my family?'

How do you tell a child that his mother, his father and five brothers and sisters, including the newborn baby, have all gone down with the ship? How was Barsati Karya to let the boy know his whole family were drowned? The cook found the answer in an imaginative lie. He pointed:

'Look! They are all on that aeroplane, and they are flying straight to India.'

The eight-year-old believed what he was told and simply began to worry about his missing sandal. It was dangerous to walk in bare feet on wooden planks because you might get splinters. As he bobbed in a raft on the water with the little servant who had saved his life, he began making himself a kind of sock out of paper.

15

Diplomatic Dandies

As we saw in Chapter 1, by the summer of 1940 Gibraltar was facing four enemies. Nazi Germany controlled western Europe from the Arctic to the Basque country, with its submarines ranging the Atlantic; Fascist Italy straddled the central Mediterranean; Vichy France dominated the Maghreb. And Falangist Spain, to which Gibraltar was soldered by geography, threatened the peninsula from north, west and south.

On 13 June 1940, three days after Italy joined the war on Germany's side, Spain changed its status from 'Neutrality' to 'Non-Belligerency'. The term did not exist in international law but, ominously, it was the same one that Italy had used at the start of the war. Did it mean 'Pre-Belligerency'? David Eccles of the Ministry of Economic Warfare, sent to Portugal by the Bank of England to help prop up the escudo, obtained a private clarification from Franco's older brother, Nicolás, the Spanish ambassador in Lisbon, to the effect that 'they meant nothing more by non-belligerent than they had previously meant by neutral, the new phrase was used to please the Axis and the extreme *Falangistas* who were looking for an excuse to throw over the government. General Franco was as firmly determined as ever not to have a shot fired on Spanish soil.'

In Eccles's discussion with Nicolás Franco there was 'some skating round the Rock of Gibraltar'. The Rock was clearly a site of key strategic interest to the British and the Axis, and Spain's leaning towards Nazi Germany was worrying for the Fortress. The Falangist newspaper *Arriba España* for some time had been baying for Gibraltar's return to Spain, and saying that the democracies should not be surprised 'by the ardent sympathy with which Spain follows today the victories of the Axis Powers'.

On 14 June 1940, twelve hundred Spanish Moroccan troops, led by Spanish marines, occupied the international zone of Tangier, just across the Strait of Gibraltar; 'provisionally', it was said, 'to maintain neutrality'. Spain might have been tempted to seize some of French Morocco as well, but on 17 June the French cunningly checked that move by asking Spain (rather than Switzerland, as expected) to mediate the Franco-German armistice. Any Spanish land grab in French Morocco now would only dishonour Franco: holding the coats disbarred him from picking their pockets.

As the pieces moved on the international chessboard, the new British Ambassador Plenipotentiary to Spain was trying to find his feet. Sixty-year-old Sir Samuel Hoare arrived in Spain on 1 June 1940 with his wife, Maud, and was now staying at the Ritz Hotel next to the Prado Museum in central Madrid. The Spanish capital was swarming with police, soldiers, Falangists and German agents; the atmosphere was strongly anti-British; all the telephones were tapped. The new ambassador felt genuinely frightened, although he had a Scotland Yard detective as bodyguard and carried an automatic pistol with him day and night.

Hoare had lost his job as Secretary of State for Air with the fall of the Chamberlain government on 10 May, and had not been re-appointed to Cabinet rank by the new prime minister. But on 17 May, Winston Churchill picked Hoare as ambassador to Madrid, sending the man nicknamed 'Slimy Sam' to soft-soap the dictator. Sir Alec Cadogan, the head of the Foreign Office bureaucracy, loathed Samuel Hoare for a 'dirty little dog [who] has got the wind up' and likened him to a rat 'leaving the ship'. In his diary for 20 May 1940 Cadogan saw only one bright spot in Hoare's appointment – 'there were lots of Germans and Italians in Madrid and therefore a good chance of S.H. being murdered'.

In June 1940, three Beaverbrook journalists, Michael Foot, Frank Owen and Peter Howard, under the pseudonym 'Cato', wrote a best-selling polemic called *Guilty Men*, which set out to name and shame a dozen key appeasers of the 1930s. (This pamphlet, though influential, distorted history by not acknowledging Labour's pacifism and solely blaming the Conservatives of the 'National' Government for the failure to rearm.) Among the 'guilty men' was Sir Samuel Hoare, still tarnished by the 1935 Hoare–Laval Pact.

Hoare (later Viscount Templewood) had to vindicate himself in print. He called his 1946 memoir of his four and a half years in Spain *Ambassador on Special Mission*. That mission – 'the most difficult task of my whole career', he said – was, essentially, to keep Spain neutral and out of the war. As Hoare said to Eden a year later, the job was 'buying time – local time for the fortification of Gibraltar and world time for British recovery after the French collapse'.

In his introduction to *Ambassador on Special Mission*, Hoare sketches his banking family as 'English', 'traditional', 'respectable' and 'reputable'. He describes himself as 'alert both in body and mind', 'very sensitive, perhaps over sensitive to his environment', 'cautious and unaggressive' and 'usually ready to accept a compromise'. These comments point towards the flaws others saw in this fussy Anglo-Catholic monarchist. David Eccles of MEW, for example, himself a smoothly confident man educated at Winchester and Oxford, described Sir Samuel on first meeting as the sort of 'well-connected and superbly intelligent man' who 'had a duty to tell inferior mortals what to do. His contempt for the lower classes was matched by his admiration for authority.' Eccles deplored 'his vanity, his jealousy, his fits of nerves', and considered Sir Samuel's 'bouts of physical and moral cowardice' pitiable in 'a potentially great man'. Later, as Eccles got to know and admire Hoare's subtle gamesmanship in dealing with the Spanish regime, he saw that Hoare's attacks of panic were just tics, like his habit of saying things three times, 'Yes, yes, yes', or the way he kept pulling his handkerchief out of his sleeve and stuffing it back in again. There may have been other layers to the ambassador's personality. In his 2015 book *Closet Queens*, Michael Bloch suggests that Hoare was a celibate homosexual.

Educated at Harrow and Oxford, an elegant ice-skater and tango dancer as well as a good shot, Sir Samuel Hoare had been in politics for thirty years as the MP for Chelsea, with a sheaf of major posts in different British governments: Foreign Secretary, Home Secretary, First Lord of the Admiralty, Minister for Air (four times), Secretary of State for India, and Lord Privy Seal ('maid-of-all-works for the PM') in the Neville Chamberlain War Cabinet. Hoare also understood the secret world. In the First World War, he had been an officer in the Secret Intelligence Service in Russia and Italy and was therefore not overly respectful of 'spooks'.

The SIS man in Madrid, a former RN lieutenant commander called Leonard Hamilton-Stokes, now posing as one of the embassy's first secretaries, had been based in Gibraltar during the Spanish Civil War. In truth he was fairly useless, providing scant information on what the Germans and Italians had been up to. The head of the secret intelligence service, 'C', Admiral Sinclair, was appalled to hear from the Air Ministry in November 1938 that SIS had supplied no technical and tactical information about the new guns, bombs, fuses, shells, etc. being used in Spain. Hamilton-Stokes was now secretly plotting with the left-wing opposition to Franco; Hoare put a stop to it because it contradicted his policy of constructive engagement with Franco's regime.

More congenial to Hoare, and far better informed, was the naval attaché in Madrid, forty-one-year-old Captain Alan Hillgarth RN. Born Hugh Evans, in the 1920s he had changed his name to give himself a *nom de plume* for the adventure books and thrillers he longed to write. A Spanish-speaker who had quested for treasure in Bolivia and who actually liked Spaniards, Alan Hillgarth had been vice consul and consul in Majorca during the Spanish Civil War. There he came to the attention of Rear Admiral John Godfrey of HMS *Repulse*, who rose to become the Director of Naval Intelligence in January 1939. Godfrey handpicked Hillgarth to be the naval attaché in Madrid.

Hillgarth shrewdly chose to live in Spain rather than in Paris like his predecessors. If British Naval Intelligence merely relied on the Flag Officer Gibraltar or on visits by RN ships to acquire information, then they were looking at Spain through the wrong end of the telescope. 'Contacts through Gibraltar are purely local,' Hillgarth wrote in an excellent memo on his role, 'and naval visits, besides being infrequent, are usually not to the chief naval bases. There is neither intimacy, nor continuity.'

Though Alan Hillgarth visited Gibraltar regularly, he never stationed himself there. But Gibraltar was a lifeline to the outside world from Franco's Madrid. At least once a week, a British Embassy car with diplomatic plates shuttled between the Rock and the Spanish capital, bringing food and drink as well as files and correspondence in the 'diplomatic bag'. And Hillgarth owed much of his success in Spain to a native Gibraltarian. His 'invaluable' right-hand man, the assistant naval attaché, was forty-eight-year-old Lieutenant Commander Salvador Gomez-Beare.

Born in Gibraltar and a member of the Calpe Rowing Club presided over by the Marqués de Marzales, 'Don' Gomez was a veteran of the First World War. Like a true Gibraltarian, he joined the Dorsetshire Regiment because its cap-badge incorporated the Gibraltar Castle and Key symbol, and after two years' service, he signed up as an airman in the Royal Flying Corps. In 1926 Salvador Gomez married Yvonne O'Sullivan-Beare and thereafter changed his surname to Gomez-Beare. He worked for Franco's intelligence service during the Spanish Civil War, like the Marquesa de Povar, thus gaining contacts right through Franco's Spanish armed forces. In August 1939, Alan Hillgarth got him an emergency commission in the Special Branch of the Royal Naval Volunteer Reserve and said he would hire him as his assistant naval attaché, so long as he shaved off his Royal Flying Corps handlebar moustache.

Don Gomez-Beare turned out to be the perfect Gibraltarian for the job of *agregado naval adjunto*. Impeccable in uniform, courteous and humorous, he was English to the English, Spanish to the Spanish, resourceful and energetic in finding information, chatting people up, running agents and carrying out clandestine missions. 'His loyalty and discretion are unequalled,' wrote Hillgarth, 'and the Spaniards, especially the Spanish Navy, love him.'

Hillgarth was pleased when Hoare arrived in Spain: 'Now we had a chance,' he wrote. The previous ambassador was Sir Maurice Peterson, a bad-tempered man who had rubbed Franco up the wrong way and kept everything in sealed compartments, but 'dapper Sir Samuel Hoare . . . treated his staff as a team.' Himself an excellent collaborator, Hillgarth was soon on top of security and secret intelligence in the Madrid embassy. It helped that he had a direct line to Winston Churchill, whom he had known personally before the war. Crucially, he was also a friend of the millionaire Mallorcan Juan March, who had helped bankroll Franco's rebellion.

Barely had Sir Samuel Hoare arrived in Madrid than Hillgarth had him involved in the scheme with Juan March to try and ensure that Spain stayed neutral by bribing key figures in the Franco regime with British money. Hillgarth later told an American officer that this idea had originally come from 'C', the head of SIS, Sir Stewart Menzies, who also knew March. At Churchill's insistence, Hillgarth was also reporting to 'C', under the code-name 'Armada'.

Hoare's first enciphered secret message on the 'Spanish Neutrality Scheme', dated 4 June 1940, requested that 'up to £500,000' should be sent to a bank in Lisbon. Three weeks later, the sum required had risen to US$10 million, placed in a New York bank for the credit of Banque Suisse in Geneva. This money was to be used to organise a counter-force to those Spaniards like General Yagüe and Ramón Serrano Suñer who wanted to push Franco's Spain into the war on the Axis side. None of the influential Spaniards 'sweetened' by Juan March's secret bank accounts knew that the money they were given came indirectly from the Bank of England, who transferred it to March. Top of the list of recipients was the Caudillo's brother Nicolás Franco ($2 million), then the Minister of War, General José Enrique Varela ($2 million), General Antonio Aranda ($2 million), Colonel Valentín Galarza of the Falange ($1 million) and General Alfredo Kindelán in Majorca ($500,000). Money also went to Generals Queipo de Llano in Sevilla, Orgaz in Catalonia and Asensio in Morocco. By May 1941, the amount expended by the British government in the first instalments had risen to an eye-watering £3,478,000 or US$14 million, leaving Anthony Eden 'rather aghast'.

Baron Eberhard von Stohrer, the German ambassador to Spain, was the foreign diplomat Franco most regularly saw. Stohrer was far from a Nazi in his private beliefs, having helped Jewish people when he was in Cairo (although in late 1941, he also wrote a memorandum proposing that the German Reich woo Islam). He despised his boss, Joachim von Ribbentrop, and was being spied on by *Kriminalcommissar* Paul Winzer, the Gestapo man in Madrid, who was working for Heinrich Himmler.

Joseph Goebbels also had his agent inside the German Embassy. The man who was actually orchestrating Nazi propaganda through the Spanish newspapers was Hans Lazar, a smoothly sinister Turkish Jew who claimed to be an Armenian from Vienna. 'The Germans pay heavy weekly subsidies to the Spanish press for lying in their favour,' wrote David Eccles. 'Taking it all round,' remarked Adolf Hitler on 5 September 1942, 'the Spanish press is the best in the world!'

Spain was the most pro-Axis of all the neutral countries: German submarines were provisioned and U-boat crews changed in Spanish ports, German reconnaissance planes flew in Spanish markings and were repaired by Spanish mechanics, and a radio station beam transmitter at La Coruña was at the service of the Luftwaffe. The Spanish Foreign Ministry – headed from August 1939 to October 1940 by the German-speaking Colonel Juan Beigbeder Atienza – passed most of the intelligence gleaned from its missions abroad straight to the German Embassy in Madrid. Information from José Félix de Lequerica, the 'neutral' Spanish ambassador to France, was particularly valuable to German political and military intelligence during the negotiations for the Franco-German armistice in June 1940. Lequerica also ensured that Lluís Companys, the ex-president of autonomous Catalunya, was sent back from his French exile to be shot by the Francoists in Barcelona.

★

In June 1940, Franco sent the Chief of the Spanish General Staff, General Juan Vigón, to congratulate Hitler personally on his military victories, carrying a glozing letter from Franco which had a sting in its tail. Although the country was entirely in sympathy with Germany, it said, Spain was not at that moment able to join the war against France and Britain. Hitler treated the proud Vigón like a centurion from some distant satrapy, keeping him waiting six days before he accorded him a mere forty-five minutes on 16 June at the Chateau Lausprelle in Acoz, Belgium. Yet when they did finally meet, with Foreign Minister Ribbentrop in attendance, the conversation was friendly enough. Vigón said that Spain was worried by the United States coming into the war, and Hitler replied that 'if any attempts were made by enemy powers to land in Portugal or Morocco, all Germany's forces would be at Spain's side'.

After the *Führer* said he wished to destroy the dominance of France and England, their talk turned to the Strait of Gibraltar. Hitler said he was pleased by the Spanish occupation of Tangier and approved of the idea of reincorporating Gibraltar into Spain. When Vigón said that Spain also wanted all of Morocco under her protectorate, Ribbentrop stepped in to suggest that if only Hitler, Mussolini and Franco could get together then 'a solution satisfactory to all parties would certainly be found'.

Ambassador Plenipotentiary Sir Samuel Hoare had his first private meeting with *Generalísimo* Franco on 22 June 1940, the same day France signed its humiliating armistice at Compiègne. Going to see Franco was more like visiting an oriental despot than a western general, Hoare thought, as he travelled through the ruined suburbs of Madrid, the wrecked university city with its stumps of walls, past begging children, and across the dried-up Manzanares river, to reach a squalid village where Moorish guards let him into the Pardo Palace, the hunting-box of kings since Carlos III.

Franco received him in a spacious library, seated by a writing desk that held signed photographs of Hitler and Mussolini, with only an interpreter present. Hoare thought Franco a cold fish, but what struck him most about the *Generalísimo* was the impossibility of penetrating 'the cotton-wool entanglements of his amazing complacency'. In General Franco's mind, Spain was neither half-starving nor war-wrecked, and needed absolutely nothing from the British Empire. 'Why don't you end the war now?' Franco asked the British ambassador. 'You can never win it. All that will happen if the war is allowed to continue, will be the destruction of European civilisation.'

The following day, Sir Samuel Hoare received some awkward guests. The exiled Duke and Duchess of Windsor, who had fled their home in the south of France to escape Axis troops, arrived at the Ritz Hotel in Madrid. At first, the plan was to sweep them off to Lisbon and a flying boat straight back to England, but that had to be postponed because the ex-king's younger brother, Prince George, the Duke of Kent, was on an official visit to neutral Portugal to celebrate the eight hundred years of Portugal's existence and the three hundred years of its independence from Spain. In this crucial visit to Britain's oldest ally (the first Anglo-Portuguese treaties date from 1373 and 1386), the Duke of Kent's more glamorous sibling could not be allowed to overshadow him.

The Windsors stayed nine days in Madrid and Hoare reported to London that the German Embassy rumour mill was in overdrive, claiming the duke 'had come to make a British peace negotiation . . . [and] make trouble against the British'. Samuel Hoare thought 'the only possible course was to take [the Duke of Windsor] as much as I could under my wing and to make it as clear as I could to the whole world that he was in friendly relations with all of us and merely stopping in Madrid on his way to England.' Hoare kept the duke away from journalists, and Hoare's wife, Lady Maud, organised the largest cocktail party in many a year for *le tout Madrid* at which the duke uttered patriotic banalities. In private, however, the aggrieved ex-king was treacherously indiscreet. 'He is pretty fifth column,' the MEW official David Eccles confided to his wife. Stohrer reported to Ribbentrop: 'Windsor has expressed himself . . . in strong terms against Churchill and against this war.'

When he was Prince of Wales, the trenches in France had horrified the young royal; he wanted no more 'Great Wars'. The Duke and Duchess of Windsor had visited Germany and met Hitler in October 1937; the Nazis thought of him as politically pro-German (ancestrally, of course, he *was* German, from Haus Sachsen-Coburg und Gotha, and he was a fluent German-speaker, top of his class at Dartmouth). In the Nazis' slightly outdated view of how the British establishment worked, with monarchy and aristocracy still ruling supreme, the duke was seen as a powerful trump card to play in the future when Britain would be conquered and 'the Churchill clique' removed: the Third Reich would then restore the Duke of Windsor as King Edward VIII, possibly with that other Hitler enthusiast, David Lloyd George, as the British Pétain. From this notion sprang a bizarre plan by Ribbentrop and Hitler to kidnap the duke and duchess or otherwise induce them to remain in neutral Spain so they would be to hand if and when required. The vain and petulant duke himself, busy squabbling with Churchill about the latter's insufficiently attractive job offer of the governorship of the Bahamas, constantly fussing about his clothes, servants and possessions left behind in France, may have been semi-oblivious to all these Nazi plottings.

One of the Duke's Spanish aristocrat cronies, Javier 'Tiger' Bermejillo, who had known him in England as the Prince of Wales, reported on the royal guest to the Spanish Foreign Minister Juan Beigbeder on 25 June 1940, intelligence duly passed on to Franco and, one may safely assume, also to the Germans.

Explaining his current situation, the Duke of Windsor says 'I am nothing more than a portrait. I don't know where they want to put me, nor what I have to do. All these disasters have happened in the four years since I retired from politics.'

He said it was all the fault of the Jews and the Reds and Eden's gang at the Foreign office and a lot of other politicians whom he would put up against a wall . . .

Internationally, he does not put England ahead of other countries (this was a train of his thought I heard many times in 1932–4.) He completely lacks any kind of nationalist sentiment, which is why he wants peace at all costs and a fair and equal settlement that will benefit all Humanity rather than this or that state . . .

More damningly, Bermejillo reported the Duke of Windsor as saying 'that if England were bombed effectively that could bring peace. He seemed to want this to happen . . .'

The Luftwaffe's first daylight bombing raids on Britain began in early July.

The irresponsible ex-king was still in Madrid on 30 June 1940 when the small, white-haired German intelligence chief, Wilhelm Canaris, also slipped into the city. Admiral Canaris was a great admirer of General Franco, whom he had known since October 1936, and kept his personally dedicated photograph on the wall of his office in the Abwehr HQ in Berlin. First, the little admiral talked to his old friend Colonel Juan Beigbeder and his acolyte General Juan Vigón. Beigbeder later reported to Franco that Canaris was not at all optimistic about the German attack on England: a sea landing would not be easy. The Abwehr chief thought Spain should stay neutral and do nothing to extend the conflict, and he said that Germany had not actually been pleased by Italy's entrance into the war. Vigón and Canaris wondered if the presence of German troops on the Spanish frontier might prompt the British to invade Portugal.

The Wehrmacht, storming through southwest France, had reached their finishing line, the river Bidasoa between France and Spain, on Thursday 27 June. Baron von Stohrer, the German ambassador, and General José López Pinto, Captain-General of Spain's VI Military Region, Burgos, with all his staff and a Spanish military band, were there to greet the German soldiers at the Franco-Spanish border. At the formal lunch in Biarritz, López Pinto toasted, '¡Viva Hitler!' 'As to gossip here,' Sir Samuel Hoare wrote to Winston Churchill, 'you can imagine the state of nerves in which Spain and Madrid find themselves after the German arrival on the Pyrenees.'

When Spanish newspapers proudly announced a Wehrmacht parade through San Sebastián, the capital of Guipuzcoa, on the following Sunday, 30 June, plus visits by German military detachments to Spain's northern garrisons, Hoare acted. Fearing Hitler's old techniques of fraternisation and infiltration would lead to the occupation of the whole country, he went to see Juan Beigbeder, the Spanish Minister of Foreign Affairs, to try and quash the move.

Colonel Beigbeder (whose surname was originally Breton) is an attractive and quixotic character in Hoare's book, a dark, thin Arabist with a pencil moustache who slept in a velvet-backed royal four-poster covered in purple damask shot with silver. He and Hoare were both dandies. Beigbeder lived in three rooms on the ground floor of the Palacio Viana where his study was lined from floor to ceiling with glass-fronted bookcases holding a fine collection of eighteenth-century bindings. Beigbeder adored Morocco and had piles of Arab clothes in amazing stuffs and colours that he made his guests try on before admiring themselves in the long glass in his bedroom. He kept an illuminated Koran on his desk and would occasionally chant from it in Arabic. '*Somos todos moros*,' 'We are all Moors,' he once confessed to Sir Samuel.

You can see Morocco from Gibraltar and southern Spain. Arabic-speaking Moors had occupied Spain for eight hundred years (almost twice as long as the Romans were in Britain). Iberians had been in Morocco for centuries too, since the Portuguese conquered Ceuta in 1415 and the Spanish took Melilla in 1497. Beigbeder and Franco were both *africanistas*; the colonel had successfully recruited seventy thousand Moroccan soldiers for the *Generalísimo*'s cause. Hoare learned from Beigbeder how deeply Morocco mattered to military nationalists in Spain. The great Spanish empire that once girdled the world had shrunk to a strip of North Africa conceded by the French in 1912, and they were determined to expand again. 'Morocco is Spanish earth,' said Franco once, 'because it has been

acquired at the highest price and paid for with the dearest coin –
Spanish blood.'

Hoare was pleased to discover that Beigbeder was not like the
Falangist minister Ramón Serrano Suñer, who considered 'the
democracies were decadent, corrupt and vicious and that totalitarianism was the new dispensation revealed to save the world'.
Although Beigbeder spoke German, had been an attaché in Berlin,
admired the German army, and was regularly talking to the German
ambassador and flirting with his wife, he was not enamoured of German brutality. The violent fall of France and the Dunkirk evacuation had given him some pause for thought. Beigbeder did not know
much about the UK, but he had read enough history to know about
the inhabitants' bloody-minded stubbornness. 'The British bull has
not yet come into the arena,' Beigbeder said to Hoare. 'Will it fight?
And if so, how will it fight? No one can say that it is dead until the
corrida is over.'

Sir Samuel pointed out the grave dangers of allowing Hitler's
'invincible' troops across the Spanish frontier. People everywhere
would think that Spain was no longer neutral. Should the official
German military parade in San Sebastián go ahead, Hoare's diplomatic mission would end and he would return to England forthwith.

Beigbeder passed on this warning to '*mi Caudillo*' Franco with
his usual signing-off – 'Respect and Loyalty' – and Franco acted.
The parades did not happen; fraternising General López Pinto was
relieved of his post, and General Juan Yagüe Blanco, 'the Butcher of
Badajoz', Göring's acolyte who had authorised the Luftwaffe use of
the La Coruña radio station, was dismissed as head of the air force.

'An Allied success had been achieved,' wrote Hoare in his memoirs. But he added that 'no Allied success in Spain was ever complete
. . . Whilst the organised parades were forbidden, the fullest latitude
was given to smaller parties of Germans to cross the frontier in uniform and to travel to and fro at their will in northern Spain.'

Some of these incursions may have been even larger than Hoare
knew. Since 1938, the Spanish Foreign Minister Juan Beigbeder had

supported an English mistress, Mrs Rosalinda Powell Fox, who was then living in a rented villa on Mount Igeldo in San Sebastián, over-looking the curving sandy bay known as La Concha. In her intriguing if not wholly accurate memoir, the patriotic Mrs Fox claims that during her siesta one sunny afternoon in late June 1940, her son Jonny, picking wild strawberries up the hill, spotted a long motorised column of German troops. The Foxes warned Beigbeder in Madrid by telephone: German 'guns, tanks and heavily armed personnel with fixed bayonets' were heading southwest past San Sebastián towards Vitoria. 'No bands were playing. No flags were flying. It was certainly no parade.' She says her lover Beigbeder later told her what he did after her call:

I immediately telephoned the local Army Commander and asked what the hell was going on . . . He thought the order had been given in Madrid to let them in! By whom? I didn't give any such order. I have made it plain that as Foreign Minister I will not permit any warring soldiers of either side to set foot in Spain. We are neutral!

Further confirmation of the incursions came from a British spy. Major Hugh Pollard of SIS, working behind Sir Samuel Hoare's back with the Madrid military attaché, Brigadier Wyndham Torr, sent a British officer from Portugal into northern Spain, posing as a summer tourist recuperating on the Basque coast. He was Captain Peter Kemp, an English adventurer who had served with the Carlist *requetés* on Franco's side in the Spanish Civil War, and later been recruited into MI(R), a War Office cell which, together with the Electra House propaganda unit and Section D (for 'Destruction') of SIS, later morphed into SOE, the Special Operations Executive. Wearing a Francoist medal as proof of his bona fides, Peter Kemp arrived in San Sebastián on or around 8 July 1940, his brief to keep an eye on any German cross-border activity.

Shortly before my arrival the Germans staged a great demonstration in San Sebastian, in which numbers of their troops took part, marching through the streets in uniform and fully armed; the surrounding country as far as Bilbao had been full of these troops. Most of them were withdrawn before my arrival but the population was most indignant and anti-German feelings strong.

The appearance of the Panzers on the northern border alarmed Franco as much as it frightened Beigbeder – 'we have a monster on our frontier.' The German *Blitzkrieg* through France had made a deep impression on Franco and he knew that if those tanks were to roll on south, supported by Stukas, the Spanish armed forces were in no state to resist.

How could the Spanish deal with the hulking bully at the door? Coquettishly. They flattered and appeased, they squirmed and flirted, and they made promises they never intended to keep.

In early July 1940, Admiral Canaris of the Abwehr met General Franco again. Gibraltar loomed over their talks. The German suggested that if Portugal joined the war on the British side, or if Britain invaded Portugal, German troops should be allowed to cross Spanish territory in order to attack them. Of course, he added, they could also be helpful in retaking Gibraltar.

Franco said that the honour of recapturing Gibraltar must be reserved for the Spanish army. What he needed from Nazi Germany was heavy artillery, naval big guns which could be mounted on railways, and aircraft, especially dive-bombers. Canaris took note of Franco's large shopping list for operations against the Rock.

On 17 July, in a grandiose speech to the Falange on the fourth anniversary of the foundation of his 'national movement', Franco laid public claim to Gibraltar. He boasted that 'two million warriors' were ready to revive Spain's glorious imperial past. 'It is necessary to make a nation, to forge an empire,' he shouted. 'To do that, our first task must be to strengthen the unity of Spain.' He said his duty and mission was 'command of Gibraltar and African expansion'.

The next day's huge Francoist victory parade along Madrid's Via Castellana required the attendance of the entire diplomatic corps, waiting in the hot sun for the tubby dictator to arrive. An anti-British claque in the crowd shouting '¡*Gibraltar español!*' drove Sir Samuel and Lady Hoare to leave the ceremony ostentatiously.

But the victory parade was the open-air theatre of politics. Other things were going on quietly behind the scenes. While declaiming publicly, Franco was under intense private pressure. His regime was economically vulnerable, ruling a ravaged country full of hungry people.

The subhead of a story in the *New York Times* on 20 July 1940 about increased US exports of oil to Spain – 'Fear Expressed in Washington Diplomatic Circles That It May Be Going to Hitler' – disturbed the Franco regime. The British press picked up the story and some UK newspapers began shouting for a more stringent blockade of this new back door into Germany. Only oil tankers flying the Spanish flag were now allowed to obtain navicerts from the British, and it was a struggle for Beigbeder to find cargo ships to deliver enough oil and petrol for CAMPSA, the state oil company, to keep the economy going. In *San Demetrio London*, a propaganda film about the British merchant navy set in late 1940, a character remarks that 'a cargo of petrol is worth all the tea in China'. Fuel was so scarce in Spain that some of the Spanish fishing fleet could make more money by selling their petrol quota to private motorists than by using it to help feed their compatriots.

Nevertheless, on 24 July 1940, only six days after his blustered threats against Gibraltar, Franco shamelessly signed a three-way commercial War Trade Agreement with Britain and Portugal that gained him one hundred thousand tons of wheat for his starving country, access to Portuguese colonial products (castor oil seeds, coffee, copra, groundnut oil, maize and sisal) paid for out of the sterling proceeds of Spain's exports to the UK, and up to £750,000 credit facilities if required. Naturally, this deal was not bruited in Franco's propaganda press. His *hábil prudencia* (crafty caution) was serving him well.

16

Digging In

Isolated Gibraltar was a key link in what *The Times* called 'the steel chain of sea-power'. When Winston Churchill pored over his maps in 1940, the 'Former Naval Person' (as he described himself to President Roosevelt) grasped immediately that the British Isles had never been more dependent on long sea lanes to build up their strength. Across the North Atlantic came ships from Canada, the USA and the West Indies, bringing vital food and fuel, weapons, raw materials and finished goods, in convoys protected by the Royal Navy and RAF Coastal Command. The rest of the faraway British Empire and Commonwealth, in Africa, India, Asia, Australia and New Zealand, was connected via long voyages through the South Atlantic, Indian and Pacific Oceans. Sea power to supply the nation and air power to erode and harass the enemy would help the British to survive.

Central in Churchill's 1940 world map was the Mediterranean Sea. Britain still held its choke points, the two key ocean entrances and exits, at Gibraltar and Suez, even though the old 'all-red route' of the British Empire – Gibraltar, Malta, Suez – was imperilled by Italy's entry into the war. The British army had been drubbed out of northwest Europe by the Germans, evacuated from Norway as well as France, so the fight now had moved to the Mediterranean. From July 1940 onwards, the major land battles of the British Empire would be along the shores of North Africa and in the greater Mediterranean basin.

The first Axis enemy they had to try to eliminate was the last one in and the weaker of the two: Fascist Italy. This job would be undertaken by the Allied 'Army of Egypt', made up of troops from India, Australia, New Zealand, southern Africa and the UK, led by the

Commander-in-Chief, Middle East, General Sir Archibald Wavell, and supported by the Royal Navy's Mediterranean Fleet at Alexandria, headed by Vice Admiral Andrew Browne Cunningham. At the western end Admiral James Somerville's Force H guarded the Pillars of Hercules at Gibraltar.

The Mediterranean is a much larger body of water than it may at first seem from the map. It is two thousand nautical miles or 2200 standard miles from Gibraltar to Suez, and midway between them, eleven hundred miles east of Gibraltar, lies the rocky island of Malta. Looking at his map in July 1940, Winston Churchill could see the strategic importance of Malta as a stronghold from which British aircraft, ships and submarines could harry and interdict enemy ships supplying Axis forces in North Africa. Because Malta was so perilously close to Italy, being only sixty miles south of Sicily, the British army and the Royal Air Force had been quite prepared to yield the island in 1940, but Winston Churchill and Admiral Cunningham agreed that Malta must stay British. This would take a tremendous effort of supply and reinforcement, often via Gibraltar.

First, Admiral Cunningham evacuated all 'useless mouths' (including his own family) from Malta and, as the British fleet protected the slow convoy evacuating hundreds of women and children from Valletta to Alexandria, engaged the Italian fleet off Cape Calabria. Cunningham's flagship, the thirty-five-thousand-ton Queen Elizabeth-class battleship *Warspite*, was attacked by the Italian air force thirty-four times in four days, with over four hundred bombs dropped around her. On 9 July, *Warspite* took on the leading Italian battleship *Giulio Cesare*, firing seventeen salvoes from her huge guns at a range of almost fifteen miles. One of *Warspite*'s fifteen-inch shells, weighing nearly a ton, hit the aft deck of the *Giulio Cesare*, killing and wounding scores of Italian sailors. Admiral Campioni promptly withdrew the *Regia Marina* to Messina. Then the Italian aircraft attacked again, in their hundreds.

Those who stayed behind in Malta got used to a troglodyte existence, regularly taking shelter in tunnels dug out of the island's limestone. On the first day of war, there were eight Italian air raids with Savoias dropping bombs from on high. In the days, weeks and months to come the numbers of air raids would rise from dozens to scores and finally to well over three thousand. If you strung all the hours of Maltese wartime air raids together it would amount to ninety-eight days of continuous bombardment, that is to say over three months without respite, and with bombing around the clock, twenty-four hours a day, seven days a week. No wonder the entire population of the island was awarded the George Cross, the highest civilian award for bravery, for its 'heroism and devotion' in April 1942.

At first, the island could only be defended from the attacks of the Regia Aeronautica Italiana by a handful of RAF Gloster Gladiator biplanes, only three of which could be in the air at the same time. The pious Maltese christened them Faith, Hope and Charity, but a wing and a prayer were not quite enough. On 15 July 1940, Churchill minuted the First Sea Lord, Dudley Pound:

It becomes of high and immediate importance to build up a very strong anti-aircraft defence at Malta and to base several squadrons of our best fighter aircraft there . . . I understand that a small consignment of A.A. guns and Hurricanes is now being procured . . . The urgent first consignment should reach Malta at the earliest moment.

On 23 July, a bunch of RAF Fighter Command pilots embarked on the elderly aircraft carrier *Argus*, bound for Gibraltar. Ranged below deck were a dozen Hawker Hurricane monoplanes and a pair of Fleet Air Arm two-seater Blackburn Skuas which would carry the spare pilots as passengers. At Gibraltar, the fighter planes were reassembled on *Argus*'s deck, while two Short Sunderland flying boats (capable of carrying two thousand pounds of bombs) were loaded with Hurricane spare parts and some two dozen mechanics who were also going along to service the aircraft. If any of the fighter planes had to ditch in the sea, the theory was that one of the flying boats would swoop down to rescue the pilot.

On 31 July, escorted by the big guns of Force H – the aircraft carrier *Ark Royal* and the battleships *Hood*, *Valiant* and *Resolution*, as well as two cruisers and ten destroyers – *Argus* set off eastwards into enemy waters on the first of what would be termed 'Club Runs' from Gibraltar to Malta. It was too dangerous to go the whole way so *Argus* intended to take the aircraft within range, from where they would fly to Malta on their own. There was a heated discussion about what 'within range' was. The ship's captain proposed to let them go four hundred nautical miles from Malta, but the RAF officer in charge of 418 Flight said that 330 nautical miles with a 20 per cent safety margin was the Hurricane's accepted endurance. They split the difference at 360 nautical miles.

The aircraft got away early on 2 August 1940. A Skua, flown by a Hurricane pilot because the others did not have carrier take-off experience, led each flight of six. Because the Hurricanes were crammed on deck, the first Skua had a very short run and immediately vanished below *Argus*'s bow. The following pilot thought it had ditched. In fact, pilot Harry Ayres managed to nurse his aircraft over the waves until he could climb. Then all the Hurricanes leapt off.

It was a fine clear day and Africa was a haze to starboard. The whole flight of fourteen planes made Malta in two hours and twenty minutes, a distance of 380 miles. All landed safely except Sergeant Robertson, who wasted the last of his Hurricane's fuel 'beating up' the airfield at Luqa in a cocky low-level pass and then crashed when his engine cut out. Malta-based Pilot Officer Jock Barber remembered it clearly:

The aircraft flicked over to the right onto its back and ploughed into the ground upside down. I think it went through three stone walls. We were shattered to say the least – this was our first reinforcement of pilots and aircraft and we had really been looking forward to this. We wrote him off but, fantastic as it may seem, he only sustained minor concussion and was flying again within a few days.

Gibraltar, like Malta, also had to dig in and hold on. Because there needed to be landward defences against possible attack from Spain,

Britain sent men who had fought in France to reinforce the peninsula. Prominent among them was General Noel Mason-MacFarlane,
the head of Military Intelligence who had commanded the scratch
'Macforce' for eight hectic days in France and been evacuated at the
end of May. When Gibraltar officially announced on 1 July 1940: 'His
Excellency the Governor hereby appoints Major-General the Hon
F. N. Mason-MacFarlane to be second-in-command of the City and
Garrison of Gibraltar' there was some confusion. 'Mason-Mac' (as
he was universally known to superiors and subordinates) thought he
was going to be deputy governor to Sir Clive Liddell, but this was not
the case; his appointment came from the War Office, not the Foreign
and Colonial Office. Mason-MacFarlane was sent as an aggressive
gunner with an intelligence background who could get the defences
up to scratch, something which Liddell's administrative experience in
Q branch at the War Office had not really fitted him for.

Mason-MacFarlane brought with him other soldiers blooded in
France, the 4th Battalion of the Black Watch (Royal Highland Regiment). This was a Territorial unit that recruited from the Scottish
county of Angus and so drew men from places like Arbroath, Bre-
chin, Broughty Ferry, Dundee and Montrose. Led by Colonel Rory
Macpherson, it had gone to France in January 1940 as part of the
51st Highland Division. After hard fighting in the retreat, its survivors were lucky enough to be evacuated from Cherbourg to Southampton on 15 June. (Many of the other Highlanders were captured
and spent the rest of the war as 'kriegies' or PoWs.)

In early July, the 4th Battalion were issued with khaki tropical
kit and embarked on the Union-Castle liner SS *Athlone Castle*, now
requisitioned as a troopship. Bombed by German aeroplanes on their
first night at sea, they arrived in Gibraltar just in time to be bombed
by Vichy aircraft in their first night on the Rock, early on Thursday
18 July 1940. The Black Watch would stay on the peninsula as part
of the garrison for the next two and a half years, doing (as their post-
war memorial cairn says) 'unrelenting work on the defences of the
north and east sides of the Rock from July 1940 to April 1943'. The

monument's fading bas-relief shows a kilted Jock in a tam o'shanter bonnet standing guard with a fixed-bayonet Lee Enfield .303 rifle, and, at his feet, a pick and a shovel laid St Andrew's cross-wise.

The 4th Black Watch helped build the infantry defences, beginning at Forbes Quarry at the North Front (the place where the first Neanderthal skull was found in 1848) round east and south through the barbed-wire beach of Catalan Bay down to Sandy Bay, where the Admiralty Tunnel emerges. The soldiers gave Scottish place-names to their works, so the steep-sided moat or anti-tank ditch already dug across Devil's Tower Road from the cliff to the beach was christened 'the Caledonian Canal'; pillbox 25 by the old slaughterhouse was 'Fort William'; pillbox 23, camouflaged to look like a fisherman's beachside cottage hung with nets, was 'Fort George'; and the pillbox by the Vacuum Oil Company, defended by a Vickers machine gun and a spigot mortar, became 'Fort Augustus'.

In early July 1940, the whole of the North Front, north of Bland's Foundry and north of Devil's Tower Road along to Eastern Beach, was declared a Protected Area for the purpose of the Defence Regulations 1939. Trees were cut down and buildings demolished to give a clear field of fire, including the old 'Devil's Tower' itself, an indistinct structure by the eastern beach variously supposed to have been Phoenician or Genoese or Spanish. In his final report, Governor Liddell raged against the clutter of structures and accumulated rubbish the Gibraltarians had created at the North Front and were so tardy in removing. The Cross of Sacrifice at the war memorial was dismantled, but the cemetery, with its catafalques and stone crosses, remained as a kind of tank barrier. 'Dragon's teeth' and concrete baffles cut up the road to Spain, and at night they parked a heavy steamroller across the gate at Four Corners to block any tanks. Front-line Forbes Quarry was armed with a six-pounder Hotchkiss gun, with another six-pounder and a 75mm field gun mounted in a tunnel higher up. They dug a sixty-foot shaft with sallyports to let infantry withdrawing from the frontier back into the fortress.

Building defences could be dangerous work. 'A' Company, 4th

Black Watch, busy on the Caledonian Canal, had a bad experience on 29 July 1940. As they lifted or relaid some of the three hundred anti-tank mines, one exploded, triggering a chain reaction. Three NCOs were killed, six Other Ranks injured and the old Admiralty Wireless Telegraphy Station by Eastern Beach was damaged. Captain G. L. Galloway of the Royal Engineers was awarded the George Medal, the second highest decoration for non-combatant gallantry, for entering two stores with unsafe roofs in order to remove explosives, including a box of detonators into which a brick had already fallen. Then he helped disarm the anti-tank mines nearest the explosion site. Four NCOs and two private soldiers from the Royal Army Ordnance Corps also won the GM for bravery that day.

The Black Watch's defence responsibility was not just horizontally along the shore road, but vertically up the Rock too, extending from the pair of 3.7-inch anti-aircraft guns down by the oil tanks at Sandy Bay up to the 9.2-inch Mark X gun at O'Hara's Battery on the Upper Ridge, and then covering the whole of the water catchment area on towards the Holy Land and as far as Farringdon's Battery, with its magnificent view north to La Línea and the coast and mountains curving round eastward to Málaga. They dug in four mortars up there, in ideal positions for dropping explosive rounds down onto attackers.

The defences were not only external. Because space was at such a premium in Gibraltar, men had to start living and working *inside* the Rock, and room needed to be found for stores, food, kit, accommodation. A two-storey barracks was constructed inside Water Reservoir No. 10, a huge empty tank, to accommodate the 4th Black Watch. A few days after arrival, Major Robin Thomson was told to take B Company high up into the Upper Galleries which had been carved out inside the north face of Gibraltar by Sergeant Major Ince long ago. B Company was to live there for a month and improve the defences just as the redcoats had in the Great Siege 160 years earlier.

This is where the Second World War tunnelling in Gibraltar began. Horizontal shafts known as 'adits', seven foot high and seven foot wide, were driven off from the Upper and Middle Galleries and Royal Engineer tunnelling companies carved new chambers out of the limestone, big enough to take a standard twenty-four-foot semi-cylindrical Nissen hut made of wood and corrugated iron with a two-foot clearance all round. The name 'Thomson's Chamber' records Major Thomson's presence, as 'Macpherson's Chamber' does that of his CO. It was not a cushy billet: choking dust alternated with mouldy damp, and there were bats. On 25 July, a petrol cooker exploded ferociously inside the Rock: Second Lieutenant Napier and Lance-Sergeant Robertson were badly burned and Private J. Hand was injured so severely that he died two days later.

The tipping place for tunnel spoil which eventually became known as 'Jock's Balcony' yawned 574 feet above a vertiginously sheer drop down to a jumble of boulders that had smashed into the ground behind Devil's Tower Road. Major Thomson had no head for heights and found his new post alarming. His instinct was to cling on and grope his way anywhere near the windy gaps looking towards Spain, but he couldn't because General Mason-MacFarlane was showing him round at terrific speed, suggesting where best to place guns for maximum effect against a land attack from across the isthmus. Leaning out and looking down from one of the gaps in the rocky wall to try and get the precise fields of fire for an effective killing ground below induced terrible vertigo in the major. There was good reason to be cautious. When Private Nicholas Mulligan fell down the drop in November 1940, he died instantly of his multiple injuries.

Another young British soldier in Gibraltar was the twenty-six-year-old actor Anthony Quayle, now a second lieutenant in the Royal Artillery. He had been defending the Rock since May 1940 and was now in charge of two six-pounder guns on the Detached Mole, the long middle stretch of Gibraltar's harbour wall only accessible by boat. His Scottish sergeant major, 'an oak-tree of a man', maintained discipline among his half section of gunners by punching them in the face if they came back drunk from shore leave.

'Believe me, sir,' he told Quayle, 'the men don't mind at all. They'd far sooner take justice from my fist than be put on a charge. If they're on a charge then their pay is docked. They would rather be hit in the mouth than in the pocket.'

A few days later, on a rare expedition into town to change his book at the Garrison Library, Quayle ran into his commanding officer, who congratulated him. 'First-class discipline you're keeping. I never have any of your men before me on a charge.'

But Anthony Quayle described Gibraltar as 'impregnable as a poached egg':

The big 9.2 guns pointed the wrong way, they had been mounted and sunk in concrete so that they controlled the Strait, but they could not deal with an attack from the north; in the whole fortress we had only six anti-aircraft guns and two 4.5 Howitzers to cope with the heavy Spanish artillery with which Gibraltar was ringed. There were no pill-boxes, no bomb-proof hospital accommodation for troops or stores, and only two battalions of infantry. The Spanish could have walked in with a troop of Boy Scouts.

Quayle's section had moved to the North Mole near the destroyer pens when, one hot day in July 1940, a small open car pulled up nearby and a big man climbed out and walked purposefully towards their gun position. Quayle had no idea who he was, though the officer had the crossed baton and sword and single-pip epaulettes of a major general on his open-necked shirt. It was not so much his rank that impressed Quayle, but his face and demeanour. In a world of dogs, here was a tiger: 'Experience of life had engrained the face; the tawny eyes held a threat of danger.'

The stranger confirmed that Quayle was in charge, then asked politely if he could 'take a squint at things' from there.

'Of course, sir. Please. Here's the gun position.'

What sort of general asked if you minded? Quayle was puzzled by the man in khaki shorts sitting on the concrete emplacement with his binoculars, maps and chinagraph pencils. The gunners lived an isolated life out on the Moles, ignorant of what went on even in

Gibraltar itself, though Quayle had heard that some major general had been flown out in a hurry after Dunkirk to take over military command and to get the defences into shape. Perhaps this was him.

It was indeed General Sir Noel Mason-MacFarlane. As he was leaving, he asked Quayle: 'You're not a Regular, are you?'

'No, sir.'

'What did you do in civilian life?'

'I was an actor.'

'An actor? Well – that's wonderful. I love the theatre – and theatre people. D'you know Noël Coward? He's a great friend of mine . . . I'm very glad to know we have an actor on the Rock. You'll have to get busy and organise some entertainment for the troops. God knows they need it. Could you put something together?'

'Yes, sir. I'm sure I could.'

'Good. I'll send my ADC down and arrange a time when you can come and have lunch.'

Anthony Quayle later cooked up a couple of revues and a pantomime, drawing on talent among the troops: a comedian in the Black Watch, a virtuoso on the spoons in the King's, an entire orchestra from the Devons, plus a brilliant pantomime dame in Captain Sir Robert Ricketts, late of the Cambridge Footlights. This became the basis of the Garrison Variety Company, whose full-time job was to provide entertainment for the troops. One of its members was a young conscript gunner called Jimmy Jacques who had worked as a projectionist in a cinema in Hounslow and now started showing films at different sites all over Gibraltar, from the tunnels to Government House. Once, when Vivien Leigh came out with an ENSA (Entertainments National Service Association) concert party that included John Gielgud and Beatrice Lillie, she wanted to see Katharine Hepburn in the 1942 film *Keeper of the Flame* and Jimmy went up to the Rock Hotel to give her a special showing. Quayle found a niche too. Because he was big, handsome and personable, Governor Sir Clive Liddell picked him out as an aide-de-camp.

★

On Monday 12 August 1940, the first of several thousand explosive shells slammed into Folkestone, killing and injuring English civilians. The Germans had brought eleven-inch railway guns up to Cap Gris Nez on the French coast to fire right over the English Channel and bombard seaside Kent. The Krupp-made K5 guns had a range of twenty-four miles. From the white cliffs of Dover you could see the flash of the big gun in France and then you had to wait seventy-five seconds – a minute and a quarter – for the projectile with its 150 pounds of high explosive to arrive.

Far away in Gibraltar, news of this development spurred further excavations and burrowings into the Rock. Gibraltar was far closer than Dover to hostile artillery: only five miles away across the Bay of Algeciras or a mile from La Línea, heavy howitzers like the 21 cm Mörser and even field guns like the '88' could easily bombard the east and northern side of the Rock 'over open sights' or looking directly at the target. In the Sierra Carbonera, the semi-circle of hills from Punta Carnero to San Roque, even more artillery could be hidden. The Spanish Civil War fears about 'guns over Gibraltar' were back with a vengeance.

Mason-MacFarlane was not the only new commander in the vicinity of the Rock in July 1940. His opposite number in Algeciras had just been named. Replacing General Francisco Martin Moreno, in post since August 1939, was a tough new military governor, General Agustín Muñoz Grandes. Described by David Eccles as 'very dark and hatchety, with great character and no nonsense about him', Muñoz Grandes was a hardened veteran of the Moroccan wars who founded the urban riot police, *los guardias de asalto*, in 1931. Once a loyal servant of the Republic, he had refused to allow his Moroccan troops to join the 1936 Francoist conspiracy, but then resigned his command at the request of old comrades. His subsequent imprisonment by Republicans embittered him and drove him to join the Nationalists.

Muñoz Grandes led the Legion at the fall of Málaga, commanded a brigade taking Santander, headed a division into Catalonia. In August

1939, Franco made him Secretary-General of the rag-bag 'Movement', *Falange Español Tradicionalista y de las Juntas de Ofensiva Nacional Sindicalista*, and chief of the Falangist militia, but Muñoz Grandes resigned in March 1940 – soldiering was his forte.

This was the man who now determined to crack the nut of Gibraltar. His troops began actively training in the *sierra* for the assault. According to Mason-MacFarlane's biographer, Muñoz Grandes reckoned that, with adequate air and artillery support, the forces under his command could capture the Rock within twenty minutes. Mason-MacFarlane conceded in private that they might be able to do it in twenty hours. Especially with enemy help. In July 1940, Zeiss binoculars in most unfriendly hands were closely scanning the Rock.

In his history of the Gibraltar Defence Security Office during the war, Major David Scherr pointed out how the Rock was under constant enemy surveillance:

From Spain one can see every ship in the Admiralty harbour. The commercial anchorage in the Bay of Gibraltar is inside Spanish territorial waters . . . From innumerable vantage-points overlooking the Rock, one may plot at leisure the position of Gibraltar's powerful batteries, radar-sites, ammunition-dumps, wireless transmitting and receiving stations, and the adits and exits to the network of underground tunnels.

With no more powerful weapon than a small telescope the enemy agent may penetrate into the recesses of the most famous fortress in the world, watch the unloading of cargoes and the progress of repairs in the dry docks, calculate the amount of coal with which ships are being refuelled, see the convoys assemble and sail away, and follow their progress through the narrow Straits . . . Safe in 'neutral' Spain, he may study the equipment, armour, manoeuvres and disposition of British troops . . .

Scherr saw the fortress as 'the chief show-piece in an immense military tattoo, set down, flood-lit, in the very centre of an open arena . . .'

17

Operation *Felix*

In early 1945, a month or two before he shot himself, Adolf Hitler tried to work out where it had all gone wrong. His thoughts turned back to the peak of his career, five years earlier.

On 23 June 1940, having conquered Poland in twenty-one days, Norway in a month and France in six weeks, the *Führer* was able to take a three-hour early morning 'art-tour' through the streets of Paris, accompanied by his favourite architect, Albert Speer, the sculptor Arno Breker and his official photographer, Heinrich Hoffmann, the civilians all wearing grey *feldgrau* uniforms to blend in with the greatcoated military entourage. They travelled from the Paris Opera House, down the Champs-Elysées to the Arc de Triomphe, pausing for a long meditative moment at the tomb of Napoleon at Les Invalides, then on past the Panthéon, Notre Dame, the Tuileries and finally up the steps of Sacré Coeur in Montmartre, where the *Führer* could look out, for the first and only time, over the beautiful grey and silver city that the artist *manqué* in him had long dreamed of seeing. 'I cannot say how happy I am to have that dream fulfilled today,' he said to Albert Speer. But Hitler was 'not in the mood' for a victory parade in Paris, because 'We aren't at the end yet.'

In fact, Hitler did not know what move to make next. The summer of 1940 became what General Warlimont called a 'morass of uncertainty', and headquarters planning became 'woolly, aimless and paralytic'. The German Field Marshal Erich von Manstein put his finger on Hitler's problem in his well-titled memoirs, *Verlorene Siege* (*Lost Victories*): 'When the head of a State or a war machine has to ask himself "What next?" after his military operations have far exceeded his expectations . . . one cannot help wondering whether such a thing as a "war plan" ever existed on the German side.'

In June 1940 the German Supreme Command had to contend with an unbeaten Britain and the threat from the Soviet Union. We know, of course, that in 1941 Hitler repeated Napoleon's fatal mistake of invading Russia. But the real error had happened a year earlier, when Germany's prime task was, in Field Marshal von Manstein's words, 'to rid herself of her last opponent, England, by force of arms'. There were three ways to do this – a quick invasion of Great Britain (Operation *Sealion*), a slow strangulation by naval and submarine blockade, or a geostrategic move on Britain's periphery, cutting out the Mediterranean links of Gibraltar, Malta and Suez, starting with Gibraltar (Operation *Felix*). Instead, Hitler havered between these choices, never quite committing his forces.

The Royal Navy's devastating attack on the French fleet at Mersel-Kébir on 3 July 1940 drew Hitler's attention back to the strategic importance of the mouth of the Mediterranean. On 7 July, in talks with the Italian Foreign Minister, Count Ciano, Hitler said that Spain was indispensable, 'should one wish to make an attempt on Gibraltar'. A conquered Rock would open the gates of the Mediterranean and liberate Italy from its captive sea. Over lunch, Hitler's chief of staff, General Keitel, too, 'insisted at length on the necessity of striking at Gibraltar as a means of dislocating the British imperial system'.

12 July 1940 was the day when General Jodl presented Hitler with a preliminary study for invading England, but it was also the day when the German Naval Staff recommended a reconnaissance mission to Gibraltar, working through the German naval attaché in Madrid. On 13 July, General Franz Halder, the Chief of the German General Staff, reported to the *Führer* on the invasion of Britain, but Halder's war diary also had the first mention of Hitler wanting 'to draw Spain into the game'.

On 14 July, Winston Churchill gave a defiant speech: 'And now it has come to us to stand alone in the breach . . . But be the ordeal sharp or long . . . we shall seek no terms, we shall tolerate no parley; we may show mercy – we shall ask for none.' Two days later, Adolf Hitler issued his War Directive No. 16, 'On preparations for a landing operation against England' with the cover name *Seelöwe* or Sealion. Invasion was to be a last resort; Hitler expected England to seek peace terms, so the order was more of a threat than a plan. Directive No. 16 begins: 'Since England, in spite of her hopeless military situation, shows no signs of being ready to come to an understanding, I have decided to prepare a landing operation against England, and, if necessary, to carry it out.' (Both Peter Fleming and Ian Kershaw have pointed out how half-hearted this sounds.)

In a speech to the Reichstag on Friday 19 July, where he rewarded all kinds of officers with promotions and elevated Göring to *Reichsmarschall des Grossdeutschen Reiches*, Hitler made what Erich von Manstein called 'his far-too-vague peace offer' to England: 'I feel it my duty before my own conscience to appeal once more to reason and common sense. I can see no reason why this war must go on. I am grieved to think of the sacrifices which must claim millions. I should like to avert them, also for my own people.' *A Last Appeal to Reason* became a German propaganda leaflet to be dropped over English fields at the start of August.

To Germans, the *Führer* seemed magnanimous in victory, but the speech fell flat across the Channel. Within an hour, a completely unauthorised reply came from the BBC's German Service (German citizens were forbidden to listen to it, but many did). It happened to be the first performance at the BBC microphone by the thirty-six-year-old *Daily Express* reporter Sefton Delmer, a robust hack who was fluent in both high and vulgar German, and had known Adolf Hitler personally since February 1929, long before he was famous.

'Herr Hitler,' said Delmer politely in his most deferential formal German *Hochdeutsch*, 'you have on occasion in the past consulted me as to the mood of the British public. So permit me to render your excellency this little service once again tonight. Let me tell you what we here in Britain think of this appeal of yours to what you are pleased to call our reason and common sense. *Herr Führer und Reichskanzler*, we hurl it right back at you, right in your evil-smelling teeth . . .'

On 22 July, Wilhelm Canaris reappeared in Spain. The Abwehr KO (*Kriegesorganisation* or war station) in Madrid was alerted that Canaris, code-named 'Uncle', was in town. Always sly and secretive, the great spymaster was now disguised as an Argentine called Señor Juan Guillermo (Guillermo is the Spanish equivalent of Wilhelm) and was relishing the leadership of a small high-level staff group exploring the possibilities of assaulting the Rock of Gibraltar. For a time, Canaris had wondered whether his own special forces, the Abwehr Section II commandos in the 3rd Battalion of the Brandenburg Regiment, might carry out the task unaided. His commandos were foreign language-speakers who put on enemy uniforms to infiltrate Poland, Norway, Denmark, Belgium, Holland and France ahead of the main German infantry assaults, seizing bridges and crossroads, eliminating sentries and sabotaging installations. But Canaris decided the Rock was too tough a nut for them to crack. He needed the advice of gunners, engineers and parachutists.

Canaris's team had all travelled to Madrid by different routes in civilian clothes. Colonel Hans Piekenbrock, the competent and humorous deputy chief of the Abwehr, was posing as his chauffeur and factotum. Also in the mission were a paratroop captain called Osterecht, a gunner called Langkau, and two men who were crucial in taking the key Belgian Fort Eben Emael on 10/11 May, and who had been awarded the Knight's Cross by Hitler himself. They were forty-two-year-old Colonel Hans Mikosch, leader of the 51st Engineer Battalion, and twenty-three-year-old Captain Rudolf Witzig, the resourceful assault leader who had commandeered a replacement aircraft to tow his glider into battle. Soon after getting his medal from Hitler, Witzig had been assigned for three months as an adjutant to the head of the Luftwaffe, *Reichsmarschall* Hermann Göring. Men like Göring often choose to surround themselves with handsome war heroes and to reward them with perks: Witzig was given a BMW two-seater sports car. As the victor of Fort Eben Emael, Witzig was exactly the right man to judge whether airborne forces could pull off the same success at Gibraltar.

The German reconnaissance group met with General Juan Vigón, the new Minister for Air, and Colonel Martínez Campos, the head of Spanish military intelligence. Canaris told them the Germans were planning to attack Gibraltar. 'The already famous parachutists' led by Mikosch and Witzig would spearhead the assault, but first they wanted permission to make a detailed recce of the area. Canaris asked for Spanish help in mapping the British defences on Gibraltar and estimating the military requirements for an assault.

Then Canaris went to see Franco, who moaned about Spain's economic woes and the meagre oil supplies from the USA. He said that of course he wanted *el Peñon*, the peninsula of Gibraltar, back, but was this the best time to do it? Gibraltar had just been reinforced by the British army and the Royal Navy still packed a mighty punch. Franco said he was worried that a provocation in Gibraltar might lead the British to seize *las islas Canarias*, the Canary Islands.

What Franco did not tell his German visitor was that the British, for their part, were also offering blandishments. A fortnight earlier, R. A. Butler, deputy head of the Foreign Office, had suggested to the Spanish ambassador, the Duke of Alba, that were Spain to stay neutral, at the end of the war all Spanish aspirations could be discussed, including the restoration of Gibraltar.*

The German team arrived at Algeciras on the Spanish coast on Wednesday 24 July 1940, accompanied by Spanish Minister of Air Juan Vigón, taking rooms at the Reina Cristina Hotel with its spectacular views across the bay to the Rock of Gibraltar. Canaris liked Algeciras, where his Madrid head of station Wilhelm Leissner (alias Gustav Lenz) had set up an early Abwehr war station or KO during

---

* This was a Foreign Office kite that Prime Minister Winston Churchill soon shot down: 'If we win, discussions would not be fruitful; and if we lose, they would not be necessary.'

the Spanish Civil War, before moving on to San Sebastián. A man called Albert Carbe now ran this *Kriegesorganisation* from the Villa León. He was a former Siemens manager in Málaga who had also been a German consul in Algiers. He was now pretending to be a German and Italian consular official, while actually running agents among the Spanish workmen who crossed the frontier every day into Gibraltar, as well as keeping paid informants inside the Guardia Civil and the *carabineros* who guarded the border. He was assisted by Major Fritz Kautschke, who had been ejected from the German artillery because he had Jewish ancestry and given an Abwehr foreign posting by Canaris out of pity. The Abwehr's relations were also very tight with Spanish military intelligence in Spain's Campo de Gibraltar, where Lieutenant Colonel Eleuterio Sánchez Rubio Dávila recruited agents for them and passed on information, assisted by Comandante Ignacio Molina Pérez.

Sánchez Rubio had form in Gibraltar. He first came to the Rock before the civil war as a right-wing refugee from the Spanish left. He bought an oil-shop at 29 Irish Town and had many friends and acquaintances in Gibraltar. In August 1937, SIS in Spain had alerted MI5 and the Defence Security Office that Major Sánchez Rubio, described as 'a member of General Franco's military delegation attached to the command of General Queipo de Llano', was showing too keen an interest in the Upper Rock fortifications and guns, and was offering bribes for the names of British intelligence officers and anti-Nationalist 'Reds' on the Rock.

The British put up the iron border fence between Spain and Gibraltar in 1908, and the Spanish had recently reinforced the neutral ground that lay between that fence and the town. In May 1939, the 20th Company of Engineers of the 112th Division of the Spanish army had arrived in La Línea to begin fortifications. From August 1939 the Spanish army were also using Republican prisoners to help install a chain of concrete bunkers, tank-traps, pill-boxes and barbed-wire fences between *la verja*, the British fence, and the Spanish border town. During the digging, the Spanish chief military engineer, Pedro Jevenois Labernade, a man of Belgian ancestry, was delighted to discover archaeological remains of the original chain of fortifications across the isthmus, *la línea de contravalación* (from which the town took its name), constructed from 1730 onwards by another Belgian, the Marquis of Verboom. Jevenois was proud to redraw the old battle line.

The Canaris team drove to La Línea de la Concepción and scanned the North Front of Gibraltar with binoculars from the top of the military headquarters. Looking south over Spanish pill-boxes they could see where the few shade trees had been felled and the British 'dragon's teeth' laid across the road, concrete pyramids to impede tanks. Beyond the sunburned grass of the emergency landing strip lay the cemetery where the *Deutschland* sailors had been buried and exhumed, then barbed wire and minefields and ant-like men labouring on new British defences along Devil's Tower Road and in the galleries of the sheer cliff face. The isthmus would be the battlefield for any German assault force. They would have to cross the narrow neck of land from Spain to Gibraltar, in the aftermath of a heavy artillery bombardment.

From the Algeciras observation posts at the Villa Saladillo, and from the lighthouse at Punto Carnero, Captains Witzig and Osterecht concentrated on spotting the positions of the British defences against aerial attack, and studying the vagaries of Gibraltar's winds. The geography of the Rock made surprise from the air impossible. Any aeroplanes slowly towing gliders would be vulnerable to concentrated anti-aircraft fire. The steepness of its slopes gave the Rock a natural defence against air landings. The only places where gliders or parachutists might possibly land on Gibraltar were on the two plateaux at the southern end of the peninsula. The upper one is called Windmill Hill Flats or Buffadero, and the lower one, where the lighthouse stands, is Europa Flats. But once again, Gibraltar's geography was its saviour, because the very bulk of the high Rock played havoc with the air currents. Witzig could see that the violently erratic winds at *Windmühlenhügel*, as he called Windmill Hill, would scatter parachutists or blow them into the sea.

Meanwhile, Hans Mikosch's new Spanish friends had arranged for the regular Seville–Ceuta passenger plane to fly closer to the Rock than usual so Mikosch could make aerial observations, and the gunner Wolfgang Langkau was working out what artillery would be needed to shell Gibraltar's harbour and batter its defences. It may have been at German suggestion that the Spanish at this time shifted four twelve-inch mobile howitzers from Mount Bujeo to the Sierra Carbonera.

The German reconnaissance team went to bed for their second night at the Reina Cristina Hotel. At around 1.30 a.m. on Friday 26 July there was a series of explosions. From their balconies the Germans could watch the Rock across the bay being bombed at night. Spiky searchlights probed the sky. Witzig said later it was just like watching a spectacular film in the cinema. The hostile aircraft, which were almost certainly Italian, were bombing from north to south, and so the reconnaissance party could track all the British anti-aircraft guns in turn from left to right as they put up a moving curtain of fire in a co-ordinated 'box'. The muzzle flashes of the guns, reflected off the low cloud, gave away their positions while the size of the flash indicated their calibre.

Was it just an accident that the air raid coincided with the visit of the German reconnaissance party? Or was it co-ordinated with the Italians? The greatest expert on the German plans for Gibraltar, Spanish local historian Alfonso Escuadra, says it was pure chance ('*totalmente fortuita*'). It is true there is no hard evidence of co-operation. But what a stroke of luck for the experts to observe the dispositions!

The night's events confirmed young Rudolf Witzig in his judgement that trying to take Gibraltar by glider or parachute assault alone would be suicidal. That was his main contribution to the discussions in Madrid on 27 July when the group pooled their ideas, and it was the conclusion of his three-page report in the dossier that Canaris delivered to army headquarters in Berlin on 2 August 1940.*

The day that the Canaris–Mikosch group arrived in the Campo de Gibraltar, 24 July, Hitler had sent for Wolfram Freiherr von Richthofen, the former head of the Condor Legion who had just been promoted to *General der Flieger*. They talked not about the current European operation, the Luftwaffe clearing the skies for the invasion of Britain, but about Spain. Hitler wanted Richthofen to use his old relationship with Franco and the top Spanish generals to try and persuade them to forge an alliance with Germany. Hitler ordered Richthofen to tell the Spanish he would help them to get back Gibraltar, following which there could be further territorial compensations for the Spanish in North Africa. Hitler said this attack on Gibraltar could be a joint effort if the Spanish wanted to take part. Once again, Germany would be offering to provide heavy artillery, anti-aircraft guns, fuel and ammunition.

Wolfram von Richthofen flew to Biarritz and met his old friend General Juan Vigón, who, acting on Franco's instructions, gave the usual story: Spain was still unable to commit to entering the war. They admired Germany and her astonishing victories, and wanted her to win even more, but current circumstances . . . the civil war . . . not enough food or fuel or equipment . . . They needed enormous German support. Vigón laid on the flattery, claiming that Franco had already sent a message to Hitler asking for Richthofen himself to be assigned as commander of the German troops if the operation went ahead.

On 8 August 1940, Baron von Stohrer, the German ambassador in Madrid, sent a 'Strictly Secret' memorandum to Berlin about the conditions under which Spain would enter the war. It included the Canaris shopping list of military supplies as well as the economic

---

* *Hauptmann* Rudolf Witzig left Göring's staff in August to take command of a company of parachute engineers. He fought in Crete, North Africa, Russia and western Europe, and died in 2001, a retired colonel of the post-war *Bundeswehr*. He had never trusted Admiral Canaris, who he claimed had leaked details of *Fall Gelb* to the Dutch.

and territorial demands of the Spanish government. Basically, they needed petrol and bread: Spain only had enough oil for six weeks of war, and wheat for maybe eight months, with strict rationing. In land terms, they wanted Gibraltar, all of French Morocco, Oran in Algeria and the enlargement of the Spanish colonies in Río de Oro and the Gulf of Guinea.

In his memorandum, Ambassador von Stohrer weighed up the pros and cons of Spain joining the Axis and taking Gibraltar. The plus side would be a great blow to British prestige, the cutting off of Spanish supplies of iron, copper, pyrites and other minerals to the UK, and Spanish control of the Strait of Gibraltar. The disadvantages to Spain were that if the British got wind of the plan they might well jump the gun and attack Spanish territory first. They might occupy the Campo de Gibraltar, or the Canary Islands, perhaps even the Balearics. Spain did not trust the French General Noguès in Morocco; Anglo-French operations against Tangier and the Spanish colonies in Africa might follow. There could be consequences in Portugal, too: the British could occupy Lisbon or Lagos and then attack Spain from the west. Above all, since Spain did not have sufficient food and fuel to keep people happy, military setbacks could trigger domestic riots.

Continuing in this negative vein, Baron von Stohrer laid out the transport difficulties for the German military. The only way to get the tanks and heavy artillery into Spain from German-occupied France over the Pyrenees was via the rail and road links that ran from Bordeaux to Hendaye on the border. But the trains would have to be unloaded and then reloaded, because the gauge of track was different in France and Spain. The rail lines ran from Irún on the frontier to San Sebastián and then via Burgos and Madrid down to the south; all major lines passed through Madrid, so there were no secret back-country tracks along which you could run tanks and guns covertly. The road route through the middle of the mountains from Saint-Jean-Pied-de-Port to Roncesvalles was too narrow and twisting, only suitable for light trucks and passenger cars, so all the heavy equipment would have to go from Bayonne to San Sebastián where, for long stretches, both road and railway were visible from the Bay of Biscay and thus open to bombardment by warships of the Royal Navy. The ambassador suggested camouflaging the movement of gasoline and ammunition and only bringing the big guns south at the very last minute.

His ultimate conclusion was that bringing a weak and vulnerable Spain into the war too early was dangerous. They must wait and see how the campaign against England developed.

In Berlin, Warlimont's planners worked up the Canaris–Mikosch survey into an outline plan of devastating attack. If Gibraltar could not be taken by secret commandos or by parachutists dropping from the air, then it would have to be done the hard way, by infantry fighting over the land bridge of the isthmus and through the northwest corner of the peninsula below Moorish Castle. Leaving aside what the Spanish armed forces might or might not contribute,[*] the planners reckoned a German assault would require two infantry regiments, including a mountain regiment, three battalions of combat and construction engineers with special vehicles, and a company of men to deal with land mines. Up to a dozen artillery regiments with howitzers and heavy AA guns would be needed to take out the deeply embedded British casemates and embrasures. Around 170 guns would be used to give the Germans a three-to-one advantage. Heavy artillery fire, combined with the German air force, flying at first from Bordeaux and then from nearer Spanish airfields, would drive away the British fleet. That would allow more Stukas and other dive-bombers to destroy anti-aircraft gun sites, sink all surviving ships, smash up the town, block known tunnel entrances, wreck

---

[*] 'Spain can without foreign help wage a war of only very short duration,' said a secret German report on the Spanish army, dated 10 August 1940. Poor-calibre officers, worn-out artillery, tanks without spare parts and lack of ammunition were the reasons given. 'Installations built around Gibraltar are of little value and essentially represent a waste of material.'

all communications. Once the aeroplanes had done their work, the artillery would start again, this time with a hail of four or five thousand rockets bringing down even more destruction. Then, with the defenders reeling in shock, the German assault force and combat engineers would move across the open ground to the North Front. Assault boats would also cross the Bay of Gibraltar from La Línea to attack the Old Mole. The objective of the first day would be to take the Rock's northwest shoulder with Moorish Castle. In three days of hard fighting, Warlimont's men assessed, the whole Rock would be theirs.

Warlimont handed the plan for what would become *Unternehmen* (Undertaking or Operation) *Felix* to General Jodl on 20 August 1940. Two days later Captain Anton Staubwasser of the military intelligence staff appended his accurate estimation of the British enemy land forces holding Gibraltar Fortress: a garrison of ten thousand men, comprising five infantry battalions with artillery, engineers and service troops, enough food for eighteen months and a system of tunnels, galleries, firing-points and shelters dug deep inside the Rock.

The Royal Navy's Force H arrived back in Gibraltar on the evening of 20 August, escorting Admiral James Somerville, returning from a trip to the UK, aboard his new flagship, the fifteen-inch-gun battle cruiser HMS *Renown*. That night, there were three air-raid alerts. In the first attack, bombs were dropped in the harbour 'about a cable and a half' (three hundred yards) from HMS *Cormorant*, the Gibraltar naval base. The aircraft was picked up and held by the searchlights just before bomb release but the shore batteries and ship's anti-aircraft guns were slow to fire. When they did engage, a salvo from the twin 4.5-inch quick-firing AA guns of *Renown* winged the bomber, which crashed a mile or so west of Europa Point. From a salvaged chunk it was identified as most likely an Italian Savoia-Marchetti SM.79 Sparviero ('Sparrowhawk').

Somerville took a piece of the crashed aeroplane to Government House at 11.30 a.m. on 21 August for the reception that His Excellency was holding for the new Spanish military governor of the Campo de Gibraltar, General Agustín Muñoz Grandes, making his first official call since his appointment. Muñoz Grandes was a VIP guest and the Fortress was keen to establish good relations. At the personal request of both Admiral North and Governor Liddell, Somerville invited the Spanish military governor to pay a visit to *Ark Royal* on some future occasion, explaining that: 'This was, in a sense a *quid pro quo* for [Muñoz's] concurrence in the use of the Racecourse by British fighter aircraft.' The 'neutral ground' between Gibraltar and Spain was contentious. It mattered to keep on side with a man who would not make a fuss over British aircraft landing and taking off.

But not only the perfidious English could play a double game. While the Spanish general was hobnobbing with the British like a good neighbour, his subordinates were escorting the German officers in mufti who were preparing their military attack on Gibraltar. Muñoz Grandes was supremely pragmatic. During the civil war, while he was being held by the Republicans in the Modelo Prison at a time when extreme leftists were murdering prisoners, he realised it would be fatal to act the rigid, polished officer, so he went shirt-less, unshaven, in *alpargatas*, rope-soled sandals. He duly survived. In August 1940, England had not surrendered, but Germany had not yet won the war. It was prudent to get on with both sides.

Admiral Wilhelm Canaris returned to Spain from Germany for another week, following up Richthofen's talk with Vigón and tell-ing him that Hitler wanted to go ahead with the attack on Gibral-tar, but that Spanish roads and airfields first needed to be improved and maintained. Vigón asked for two hundred large-calibre artillery pieces, one hundred anti-aircraft guns and three squadrons of sea-planes. Canaris then went down to Algeciras again in plain clothes to make sure the Abwehr kept its surveillance low-key so as not to alert the British to what was afoot.

Canaris's report to Halder on 27 August made pessimistic reading: Franco would not come in until Britain was defeated, because he was afraid of what the Royal Navy's battleships and aircraft carriers could do to his ports and supplies. Spain's internal situation was bad, with many in the army and the church opposed to Franco. Canaris said Franco's only real support was the Interior Minister Serrano Suñer and even he was really more pro-Italian than pro-German. Canaris concluded that Franco would be 'an ally who will cost us dearly'.

The German foreign intelligence service, army and air force were not the only people reconnoitring the Rock. On 6 September 1940, in his fortnightly meeting with the *Führer*, Grand Admiral Erich Raeder, head of the German navy, presented the Kriegsmarine's ideas for waging war against Britain if Operation *Sealion*, the invasion of England, were to be called off. First on Grand Admiral Raeder's list was action against Gibraltar and the Suez Canal, in order to exclude Britain from the Mediterranean. 'The loss of Gibraltar would mean crucial difficulties for British important traffic from the South Atlantic.' Preparations for this operation should be made at once, Raeder urged, reporting later that 'The Führer gave orders to this effect.' General Wolfram von Richthofen was once again sent back to Spain to see General Franco in person.

The two men met in the Basque country that the Condor Legion had helped Franco to conquer, at *Generalísimo* Franco's residence in San Sebastián, the Palace of Aiete, where King Alfonso XII and Queen Maria Cristina used to summer. In early September 1940, as the Luftwaffe launched flight after flight into the Battle of Britain, Franco flattered Richthofen by saying he thought Germany would beat Britain in about three weeks. But he told Richthofen that he was still reluctant to join the war, because Spain was so desperately short of food, fuel and other materials.

18

The Price of Dakar

One aim of the Nazi conquest of Europe was a simple grab for gold. After the Germans won the war, the city of Berlin (grandiosely rebuilt as 'Germania' by Albert Speer) was to replace London as the financial centre of Europe, with the Reichsmark as the currency, pegged to a new gold standard. The Nazis lusted after gold like Wagnerian dwarves. The *Anschluss* or incorporation of Austria in 1938 netted around ninety tons of gold and the occupation of Czechoslovakia the following year another forty-five tons, raising the German gold reserves to almost US$750 million (around US$12.6 billion today). But by the time the Second World War broke out, much of this had been spent and the Reichsbank was almost bankrupt. Hence the urgent need for more gold, to be converted into Swiss francs to purchase what the German war machine required from abroad: tungsten/wolfram from Portugal, oil from Romania, iron from Sweden, chrome from Turkey. In spring 1940, only very fast footwork by people in Denmark, Norway and Holland got their gold away before the Third Reich laid hands on it.

France promised the Nazis the richest pickings, because so many other countries had moved their bullion there. The Banque de France, by clinging to the gold standard, had increased its share of world gold reserves from 7 per cent to 27 per cent between 1927 and 1932, accumulating an astonishing total 2430 tons of gold ingots and coins in its Paris vaults. As a precautionary measure after the Munich crisis, however, this had all been moved out of the capital and cached nearer key ports. Then, during the May 1940 *Blitzkrieg*, the order was given to ship it all out of the country, which duly went ahead. The last thousand tons of French gold was hidden from the

Germans in Brittany. Shuttling this precious hoard to Brest harbour on 17 and 18 June, using too few (and too small) vehicles that had to struggle through roads clogged with refugees, was a nightmare. The Wehrmacht was pressing nearer; sporadic air attacks interrupted the loading that went on night and day. Imprisoned convicts were promised freedom if they helped lug and stow boxes. Only three hours after the last bullion ship sailed, German troops were on the quayside.

The five French warships carrying twelve hundred tons of gold bars arrived at Casablanca on 21 June 1940, the day Hitler handed over the terms of armistice to France. The Bank of France's representative in Morocco ordered the shipment to move on south to the port of Dakar in Senegal, one of the federation of nine colonies that made up French West Africa. There, the French gold joined that of other nations: an unknown quantity from Latvia and Lithuania, ninety cases from Luxembourg containing a total of 319 gold bars, perhaps two hundred tons of Belgian gold in 4944 packing cases, and seventy-five tons of Polish gold which had been diverted from Martinique in late May. The entire hoard was buried seventeen miles inland from Dakar, near Thies air base.

'*Nervos belli pecuniam*,' said Cicero two thousand years ago: 'the sinews of war are money.' War is ruinously expensive, and this one was costing Britain over £10 million a day (perhaps around £160 million today). The debts accumulated in the Second World War almost bankrupted Britain in the 1940s and early 1950s, and were not finally paid off until 2006.

Money was a perpetual problem for Winston Churchill, but it was a far more vexing one for General de Gaulle, starting from scratch in raising his French force of volunteers to fight the common enemy. Recruitment was an uphill struggle for de Gaulle. When French sailors interned in Britain were asked to choose, only nine hundred opted to join de Gaulle, while more than nineteen thousand wanted to go back to Vichy territory. Many other potential volunteers for the Free French turned away in disgust after the British sank the fleet at

Mers-el-Kébir. By the end of July, de Gaulle claimed to have seven thousand 'effectives' wearing their new badge of the Cross of Lorraine, although British Cabinet figures suggest half that. Nevertheless, Churchill wanted to support de Gaulle, and on 7 August 1940 the two men signed an agreement at Chartwell (backdated to 1 July) in which the British government agreed to fund the Free French.

Churchill also backed a plan, put up by the liaison officer Edward Spears and the secret fixer Desmond Morton, to install de Gaulle in Dakar on the Atlantic coast of West Africa. This operation, initially called *Scipio*, the first wholly seaborne invasion of the Second World War, was at first going to employ three battalions of Free French. But with Churchill, in Correlli Barnett's phrase, 'truly bulldozing the project through', it evolved into the Anglo-French Operation *Menace*, including the warships *Resolution*, *Barham* and *Ark Royal* and eight destroyers diverted from Force H at Gibraltar. Four battalions of Royal Marines would make up the spearhead, among them an acerbic Captain Evelyn Waugh (who would later portray the whole thing as a fiasco in his *Sword of Honour* novel trilogy).

Churchill told President Roosevelt that the Dakar expedition was a strategic move to foil any German attempt to set up a naval base there which would threaten Atlantic shipping routes. But at the back of Churchill's mind must have been the hope of gold. On 7 July, General Władysław Sikorski, prime minister of the Polish government in exile and commander of its armed forces, had asked Churchill for help in retrieving the Polish gold that was stored there. When Churchill spoke about Dakar to the chiefs of staff on 8 August, among the reasons he gave for the operation was: 'The Poles and the Belgians would also have their gold recovered for them.'

If Churchill knew that there was an even greater amount of French gold stored at Dakar, that would have made the operation yet more pressing. In six weeks between July and August 1940, the British gold reserves had dropped from £380 million to £290 million. French gold could help restore the balance, and Operation *Menace* thrilled the *Treasure Island* side of the prime minister's imagination. Planting the flag of the Free French in West Africa to rally their colonial empire was a splendid gesture, but scooping the gold into the bargain would have been a swashbuckling coup.

Other greedy eyes were looking for the loot. When King Leopold III of Belgium, who had surrendered his country on 27 May, asked his German captors to restore the Belgian gold (in order to buy wheat for bread), the Reich economic envoy, Dr Johannes Hemmen, went looking for it, aggressively questioning the chairman of the French armistice commission, General Charles Huntzinger, the man who had actually signed the document at Compiègne for France. Citing its Article 17 – 'The French government to prevent the transfers of valuables and stocks from occupied to non-occupied territory or abroad' – Hemmen demanded to know how much gold bullion and coin the Bank of France possessed and exactly where it was. On 20 August, Huntzinger informed Hemmen that, regrettably, the French gold – worth 844.6 billion francs – was now dispersed in London, New York, Martinique, Casablanca and Dakar. Hemmen warned the Vichy French that they would be liable for any loss, and advised them to move the Dakar gold away from the coast.

The Free French were making inroads in Africa. Most of French Equatorial Africa declared for de Gaulle: Chad on 26 August, Cameroon on 27 August and Ubangi-Shari (now the Central African Republic) on the 30th. This helped the Allies by offering a land and air route through friendly territory from British Nigeria to the British Sudan via Fort Lamy. This was the way many people subsequently went from the UK to Egypt, not through the Mediterranean but travelling via West Africa.

Operation *Menace* was as leaky as a sieve. When Charles de Gaulle went shopping at Simpson's in Piccadilly for tropical kit (perhaps including what Evelyn Waugh put into his character William Boot's mountain of gear for Ishmaelia, 'a cane for whacking snakes'), he openly revealed his destination as West Africa. 'Many got to know,' wrote Churchill in his memoirs later. 'Dakar became common talk among French troops. At dinner in a Liverpool restaurant French officers toasted "Dakar!"' Churchill continued, 'We were all in our war-time infancy' with secrecy. A naval lieutenant wrote to the First Lord of the Admiralty, A. V. Alexander, about the gross breaches of security: 'I was told of our destination by a man on the Liverpool docks.' He thought the Germans must know too.

Vichy France had indeed learned what was afoot. Six of their warships – three super-destroyers and three heavy cruisers – left Toulon on 9 September, passing unchallenged through the Strait of Gibraltar on the morning of 11 September, something that would cause ructions later. Captain Alan Hillgarth, the British naval attaché in Madrid, said he had the first news of ships heading westward from a French naval officer and alerted the Admiralty in London as well as Gibraltar, with his message arriving around midnight on 10 September. The naval officer on duty in London did not choose to wake Admiral Dudley Pound, so the First Sea Lord only got the message on the morning of the 11th, when the six Vichy ships had already passed through the strait. Three of the French ships stopped at Casablanca but the three cruisers arrived at Dakar on 15 September to reinforce the Vichy presence there. The whole stash of gold bullion was moved 450 miles east towards the desert, to Kayes on the Senegal River, a fiercely hot town that today lies in Mali.

At this point Churchill wanted to cancel Operation *Menace*, but de Gaulle wished to go ahead. However, the Free French were not welcomed at Dakar. De Gaulle's emissaries were all arrested or shot at by Vichy colonial forces. Fog blinded the military operations that started on Monday 23 September; ships without radar fumbled and groped; planes were shot down. The Vichy batteries at Dakar fired back at the Anglo-French force, joined, alarmingly, by the fifteen-inch guns of *Richelieu*, not as badly damaged in the July attack as everyone hoped. The dye from one close-landing, huge-splashing shell turned the ensign at HMS *Forester*'s foremast head yellow. Three Intelligence Corps NCOs who had infiltrated Dakar's Vichy naval base disguised as Swedish and Spanish sailors discovered that two submarines were lurking. But the NCOs' warning was ignored, and so one of the submarines, the *Bévéziers*, managed to torpedo the battleship HMS *Resolution*. The Anglo-French force at first withdrew, and then abandoned the mission entirely. The British press and Parliament were scathing about the debacle: 'blunder' and 'muddle' were the words bandied about; Ambassador Kennedy reported to the USA that Churchill's popularity was dented.

But there was a sort of happy ending to de Gaulle's first, failed, adventure in West Africa. A small Free French force under Colonel Philippe de Hautecloque – now known as 'Colonel Leclerc', a pseudonym to protect his family in occupied France – had successfully wrested French Cameroon from Vichy control in late August, and in early October General de Gaulle himself arrived in the Cameroonian port of Douala. 'Beautiful reception, simple but perfect,' wrote Lieutenant Christian Girard in his diary. 'Troops impeccable, crowds enthusiastic, *Marseillaise* ... The general [de Gaulle] jumped from the boat onto the quay to be welcomed by Leclerc in dazzling whites and dress sword. Once again we were in France.'

En route home from West Africa by ship from Freetown in Sierra Leone to Gourock in Scotland, Captain Evelyn Waugh RM spent three days at Gibraltar, 15–18 October 1940, and caught some of its flavour in his diary:

Gibraltar has a garrison of 10,000 men and a local defence corps. The women have been evacuated, all but six or seven; there was no beer in the town. When the last Englishwoman has left, a corps of harlots will come from Tangier to amuse the troops. At the moment they have little recreation. I spent two pleasant afternoons ashore. The garrison library, soon, presumably, to be demolished, was delicious – a large collection of nondescript leather-bound books in a series of clubrooms with leather and mahogany furniture and a subtropical garden through the windows. One modern room full of novels, smelling of scent. I bought a silver velocipede, ridden by a bearded man in a tall hat, with a trailer for carrying toothpicks: £2.10s ... The battalion did some ceremonial exercises in the Alameda gardens and got uncommonly drunk: Baxter, brigade intelligence officer, paralytic before tea in the Rock Hotel . . . All letters from home were about air-raids . . . We were like wives reading letters from the trenches.

Winston Churchill was bitterly disappointed by the failure to get the port of Dakar and the gold, and the losses brought out the vindictive side of his character that must be acknowledged along with his virtues. In August 1940, for example, the prime minister had hectored General Wavell for retreating from British Somaliland with only light casualties. Wavell's stinging reply, 'Heavy butcher's bill not necessarily indication of good tactics', marked him for the sack, which came in June 1941.

Now Churchill wanted a scapegoat for the West African fiasco. In his speech to the House of Commons on 9 October, he alleged that the situation at Dakar

. . . was transformed in a most unfavourable manner by the arrival there of three French cruisers and three destroyers which carried with them a number of Vichy partisans of the most bitter type . . . By a series of accidents and some errors which have been made the subject of disciplinary action or are now subject to formal enquiry, neither the First Sea Lord nor the Cabinet were informed of the approach of these ships to the Straits of Gibraltar until it was too late to stop them passing through.

The relevant signals were traced. Admiral Dudley North in Gibraltar had seen Alan Hillgarth's message but merely followed standing Admiralty instructions: 'If French warships are seen passing through Straits identity is to be reported immediately but no action taken.' The British mania for secrecy was also partly to blame. Because Admiral North was not in the picture about the Dakar expedition and, like Admiral Somerville, only learned about it later from the BBC, he naturally did not realise the threat that the Vichy warships posed to it. By contrast, Sir Samuel Hoare in Madrid, who had been informed in confidence about the Dakar raid, was told about the six Vichy warships by Juan Beigbeder 'as a friend' on 11 September and immediately telegraphed the information to London. Hoare wrote later, 'From the Madrid angle it seemed as if the London reaction was disappointingly slow.'

But Admiral North was the senior flag officer at Gibraltar and was now in the line of fire. North had already blotted his copybook with the prime minister two months earlier on 4 July, when he wrote a letter explaining why most naval officers in Gibraltar opposed the use of force on the fleet at Mers-el-Kébir. This affronted Churchill, who minuted A. V. Alexander on 20 July: 'It is evident that Admiral Dudley North has not got the root of the matter in him, and I should be very glad to see you replace him by a more resolute and clear-sighted officer.'

Someone's head had to go on the block for Dakar, so on 25 October 1940, after forty-four years of service in the Royal Navy, Sir Dudley North, Admiral Commanding North Atlantic, received a formal letter from the Board of Admiralty concerning his reaction to the naval attaché's signal. Their communication ended: 'Their Lordships cannot retain full confidence in an officer who fails in an emergency to take all prudent precautions without waiting for Admiralty instructions. They have accordingly decided that you should be relieved of your command at the first convenient opportunity.'

Until the day he died in 1961, Admiral North tried to get an inquiry or a court martial so he could clear his name. After the *Daily Mail* journalist Noel Monks wrote an impassioned book about North's dismissal, *That Day at Gibraltar*, published in April 1957, the prime minister, Harold Macmillan, finally met with a group of senior admirals and made a placatory statement to the House of Commons on 23 May, which declared that Admiral Dudley North was not guilty of negligence or dereliction of duty, and his integrity was not impugned. Nevertheless, it was always up to the authorities to decide to whom command should be entrusted, Macmillan added, and ultimately this was a matter of judgement of character. Therefore he saw no point in holding any further inquiry.

It was Admiral Dudley North's misfortune that Sir Winston Churchill outlived him by three years. Only when both men were long dead did Admiral Lord Mountbatten feel free to tell Charlotte and Denis Plimmer, the authors of *A Matter of Expediency*, their book about the Admiral North case, what he really thought:

If you pursue this matter it comes back to Winston.

The great magic formula was, 'We mustn't offend the great old man. After all, he saved England and he saved the world. He may have made a few mistakes but it's a terrible thing during his lifetime that he should be accused of vindictiveness and so forth.'

And so there was a conspiracy of silence.

19

Helen among the Trojans

On the morning of 18 May 1940, Randolph Churchill found his father shaving with his old-fashioned Valet razor in his bedroom at Admiralty House in London.

'I think I see my way through,' said the new wartime prime minister.

'Do you mean that we can avoid defeat?' said his son. 'Or beat the bastards?'

'Of course I mean we can beat them.'

'Well, I'm all for it, but I don't see how you can do it.'

'I shall drag the United States in.'

Wooing the isolationist United States of America became a prime objective. Britain had to persuade American diplomats, emissaries, celebrities, politicians and journalists, leaders and leader writers, that it was fighting the good fight for democracy against totalitarianism, and was not going to give in ('We shall never surrender'). The encouraging voice of Ed Murrow of CBS, for example, broadcasting resilience from London, the city where he had lived since 1937, became a vital antidote to the defeatist messages the US government was getting from its own diplomats, like William C. Bullitt in Paris and especially the US ambassador to the Court of St James, that ex-bootlegger from Boston, Joseph P. Kennedy.

Thus the wind was in her favour when, in September 1940, another enterprising American broadcaster, resourceful young Helen Hiett, told the British Embassy in Madrid that she wanted to visit the heavily restricted Fortress of Gibraltar. Hiett managed to scoop a trip to the Rock, where no American journalist had yet gone. Tom Burns at the embassy passed the word to the Ministry of Information in London, who checked Hiett out with Fred Bate of NBC and gave

the thumbs up. Then Mason-MacFarlane, down in Gibraltar, said
yes because he remembered her name from his time as Director of
Military Intelligence in France: one of his officers had talked to Hiett
at a party about her Xmas 1939 visit to Nazi Germany, and reported
what she said about morale and conditions. Finally, the Spanish
director of propaganda extruded his official permission.

She had only been in Spain for two months but, as we have seen,
Helen Hiett was intelligent, curious and capable. A week short of her
twenty-seventh birthday, she had seen a lot more of life than most
women from Pekin, Illinois expected to see in a lifetime. Resident in
Europe since 1934, she'd worked at the League of Nations in Geneva,
visited Fascist Italy, and spent three weeks in a Nazi Girls' Labour
Camp at Königshorst in the summer of 1937 as part of her PhD thesis
on indoctrination at the London School of Economics. Hiett was in
Paris when the war broke out, spent Christmas 1939 inside Nazi Germany again with a girl-friend from the Labour Camp, and started the
'Paris Letter' to tell neutral Americans what the French were fighting
for. In April 1940 she revisited New York City and Abe Schechter of
NBC Radio hired her to go back to Paris as a correspondent, right in
the middle of the crucial month of May 1940.

On 3 June, the Luftwaffe started bombing Paris: one explosion
destroyed NBC's Paris office and Hiett followed the retreating French
government south, travelling chaotic roads by day and sleeping nights
unwashed in fields. She was bombed in Tours and again in Bordeaux.
On 27 June she and three other young women left the city in a Chrys-
ler Plymouth with Hiett driving, and got caught up in a huge column
of German vehicles heading south through Les Landes to the Spanish border: motorcycles, armoured trucks, staff cars, supply lorries,
gun carriages bristling with machine guns. She eventually made it
to Switzerland, where she told that story to NBC before getting a
visa for Spain. In ten days in Madrid she wangled permission to
broadcast to the USA, and slowly adapted to Spanish habits: rationing, siestas, the procrastinations of *mañana*. This deadline-conscious
modern American woman was rather relieved when her importunate

Swiss watch was stolen while she was busy swimming in the Manzanares, allowing her to embrace a more relaxed attitude to time.

Helen Hiett flew from Madrid to Málaga on Monday 16 September 1940, and the next day the British consul and his wife drove her the eighty miles to Gibraltar. 'The scenery is perfectly grand, following the sea all the way,' she wrote to her parents, 'and then suddenly the gigantic Rock looms up, dominating all the land and sea around.' On arrival, she lunched with the American consul, Mr Hawley, and declined his invitation to stay. At the Rock Hotel she was astonished to get a phone call from the reception desk saying that 'the general' was downstairs. Major General Noel Mason-MacFarlane himself, handsome, tanned, fit, turned up for tea, invited her to dinner and, like the consul, also asked her to stay at his house. She turned him down too, staying on at the Rock Hotel.

The next morning, however, the general appeared again with a typewriter to lend the reporter. She would write her own copy, but on his machine. This is part of the trade-off between the military and the media: in return for access, the media get the military's 'angle'. Mason-MacFarlane came out of military intelligence and understood the impact of propaganda. He had selected Helen Hiett to be one of the very few journalists to visit the Rock because he calculated that a human interest piece by a woman reporter from the neutral USA on the indomitable resilience of Gibraltar could be invaluable in the war of morale.

Hiett spent a couple of hours at the American consul's, reading up on Gibraltar, and then, at one o'clock sharp, was at Government House for lunch with His Excellency the Governor, Sir Clive Liddell. Despite feeling that she wasn't looking her best – the salty sea air made her pageboy cut 'stringy' – the young American wowed everybody. The men liked the girl and the girl liked the men:

The other ADC, Freddie Inglis, Gordon Highlanders, was simply grand – the sort of man one falls for at first glance. He brought in 'H.E.' (as he is most frequently called here). Dispensing with any 'Your Excellencies' we shook hands and I liked him immediately. With all of them in bare knees, and me innocently unschooled about the exact meaning of the crowns and bars on their shoulders, I was neither frightened into a formalism that ill becomes me, or bored into the same.

The suntanned officers in khaki shorts, so hungry for female company, were unlike the limp and long-haired intellectual Englishmen she had met before, but more like the chaps in Rudyard Kipling's 'In Partibus':

> It's Oh to meet an army man
> Set up, and trimmed and taut . . .
> [Who] walks as though he owned himself
> And hogs his bristles short.

At lunch they discussed English public schools and the foppish 'Eton-and-Oxford' breed. Hiett said she preferred Scotsmen to Englishmen and Paris to London. The soldiers happily agreed the Englishmen she had known were insufferable professorial types whom the army scorned.

As I sat looking at them – H.E. with his tattooing on his forearms, his legs crossed negligently so that his bare knees stuck up over the table top, his fine head and sunbrowned face that a thick shock of grey hair only made seem all the younger, I liked them instinctively, liked their naturalness. They are real people, so different from the affected kind of Englishmen I have known, always seeming to be so self-conscious about what is done and 'not done'.

His Excellency Sir Clive Liddell had only just met Helen Hiett when he, too, invited her to stay at Government House. This offer she accepted, bringing her things down from the Rock Hotel and then going out for the afternoon with Noel Mason-MacFarlane to inspect the defences. The month before, Sir Samuel Hoare had visited Gibraltar from Madrid and pronounced himself 'horrified' by their unreadiness and the general peacetime sense of security. Now things were getting gingered up: 'First we inspected some of the tunnelling in the North face where they are putting in new gun positions, blasting about six feet a day in the limestone. He showed me, too, some spacious new living quarters that are just being completed in that part of the Rock.'

Today the Rock of Gibraltar conceals within itself some thirty-four miles of tunnels, which is almost twice the length of the roads visible on the outside of the peninsula. Much of that expansion happened during the Second World War, when the existing seven miles of tunnels were more than tripled to twenty-five miles. It is a huge amount of tunnelling in a Rock that is barely three miles long. From June 1940, just as the infantry were reinforced from two to four battalions, so the Royal Engineer Fortress Companies were brought up to 'war establishment' status under the Chief Engineer, Colonel H. M. Fordham OBE, MC, and the first Tunnelling Company, consisting of former coal miners, was brought out by sea from Britain. Eventually teams of men like these would work around the clock, in eight-hour shifts, all through 1941, 1942 and 1943, joined by hard-rock miners from the Canadian army with their diamond-tipped drills.

The immediate need in 1940 was to create accommodation for men and stores of food and ammunition inside the humid limestone rock. Existing stalactite caves like St Michael's already had brick and concrete magazines built inside them, with corrugated-iron roofs to keep out the wet. The embrasures in Willis's and Queen's and the Upper Union Galleries were now fitted with bunks; their new denizens pinned up pictures of sweethearts and Hollywood movie stars on their whitewashed walls. Old eighteenth-century tunnels sprouted new extensions and connections that grew more spacious as the troglodytic network spread through the Rock. The tunnellers doggedly worked away, widening and deepening the tunnels from seven feet to eight feet and beyond to twelve feet. In the end, lorries would be able to pass each other as they drove along 'the Great North Road', a new King's Highway fifteen feet wide and fourteen feet high, quarried out deep inside the Rock.

Helen Hiett found the North Face of the Rock of Gibraltar a formidable sight:

I stood there feeling small, looking up at a quarter mile rise of sheer limestone, trying to imagine how an invading army would feel approaching that forbidding wall. But it is not only the rock wall that fills you with awe, what is inside is more awful still, as I soon found out. For the rest of that afternoon we climbed and slipped and clambered and crawled and slid in and out, along, around and on top of the maze of tunnels and caves and galleries that honeycomb the Rock, sheltering a myth-like underground city of warriors. There seems to be more tunnels in the North Face than anywhere else – because it guards the single land approach.

Hiett had only brought one evening dress with her, so that became her uniform in Government House whenever the men appeared in their tartans and scarlet-and-blue mess dress. But Lieutenant Colonel Inglis had lent her his Spanish maid (senior officers did not stint on servants) and the pair tried out different hairstyles to ring the changes. This unnamed maidservant was not a bad match for Hiett, having swum the five miles from Algeciras to Gibraltar to escape the Spanish Civil War – she had been a fixture in the household ever since.

On Thursday 19 September, the assiduous reporter saw inside the dramatic Cathedral Cavern of St Michael's Cave, the Rock's largest, which had cases of bully beef and baked beans piled high among the stalagmites. She sat through forty-six explosions as more tunnels and caves were blasted out, and shivered in a giant refrigeration room full of beef, butter and eggs. Helen Hiett loved Europe's mountains, and down at Catalan Bay she stood on the beach inside the barbed wire looking up – 'my Alpinist eye picked out several routes a good climber could probably deal with. But the Rock is treacherous. The limestone holds aren't as sure as granite . . .' Then she clambered over the water catchment area's wide flat structure of wood and corrugated iron above Sandy Bay and saw the huge freshwater reservoirs inside the Rock, all spare space round them packed tight and high with more stores. She got a great surprise at Reservoir No. 10, where she expected to see one more lake like the others:

No water in this one – instead a fantastic, well-lighted cavern that rang with the sound of hammers. Swarming workmen were just completing a modern, three-storey barracks as living quarters for hundreds of soldiers, down there deep below the Rock's surface. It seemed so much like the control room of Gulliver's Island of Laputa, that I half expected to feel the whole Rock rise up and gently float away.

As Mason-MacFarlane showed Helen Hiett around the camouflaged cliff-face defences of the North Front, she saw crates of beer by the embrasures and thought the Scottish soldiers were well provided for. Then she saw this was not India pale ale. Each bottle was topped with a cloth wick: they were actually Molotov cocktails made from soap and petroleum. A red-handed Scot explained that they had been throwing some bottles of red paint to mark where the missiles would hit down below. She also noticed they kept their boxes of 'pineapple' hand grenades close.

On Thursday night, Helen Hiett went to the theatre in Gibraltar with the governor, the admiral, the general and all their staffs, the only woman in the box for the opening night of an amateur show that the staff of the British Embassy in Madrid had brought down to Gibraltar. Hiett had actually tried to get into the show in Madrid as a way of wangling a visit to Gibraltar (doing an 'Apache' dance with a press officer at the tryouts) but was very glad she had not succeeded.

[T]heir show is so rotten it is absolutely painful. We just sat in our boxes and groaned, almost ashamed to look up, and scared to death that the troops would give them a raspberry and walk out at any moment . . . It was rather funny, too, to see the surprise of one or two of [the embassy staff] who had snubbed me, at finding me here installed and very much in favour.

She was meant to go back and broadcast from Madrid on Saturday, but after agonising, she sent a cable to New York saying 'IMPOS-

SIBLE'. Instead, on Friday she took a boat over to Morocco for a weekend at Tangier's El Minzah Hotel, eager to experience the new continent's sight and sounds. On the boat back on Monday 23 September she held the captain's sleeping pet monkey in her arms and made the spectacle of the leaping, darting dolphin accompanying them across the strait an excuse to get five silent Frenchmen to talk.

The five turned out to be escaping pilots. After the fall of France, they had volunteered to take the exams to become primary school teachers in Morocco, but this was all a ploy. Once in receipt of their first month's pay, they shed the deception, skipped to Tangier and were now heading to Gibraltar, seeking the chance to fly for de Gaulle. The general had claimed in August that Vichy was transferring hundreds of planes from North Africa to Marseilles, so other Free Frenchmen thought it was a good idea to pinch the aeroplanes before they ever fell into German hands. Hiett had already seen a brand new Douglas aircraft parked at the emergency airstrip at the North Front in Gibraltar – a quick-witted Free Frenchman at a Moroccan airstrip had hijacked it from a Vichy-led party of Italian Armistice Commission officers when they left the plane to go for lunch.

As they approached Gibraltar, anti-aircraft shells were bursting in the sky. Hiett thought the British were shooting at 'Persistent Percy', the regular Italian spotter plane, but her five new friends made a definite identification of Vichy French war planes on hostile reconnaissance. She did not know it, but Dakar had been attacked that day and Vichy was looking for revenge. There was a late party at Government House that evening because it was her twenty-seventh birthday, and Raven, the governor's imperturbable butler, served sandwiches in his red silk pyjamas and dressing gown.

Late on Tuesday morning, 24 September, Helen Hiett was tapping out her NBC radio piece on the typewriter borrowed from Mason-MacFarlane when the air-raid siren sounded outside. The familiar 'crump' of a bomb told her this was no practice. She went downstairs to find shelter in the governor's ground-floor office with its partially sandbagged window. An ADC brought in three girls from the British Embassy theatrical revue party who were due to go back to Madrid that afternoon. Dragged protesting from bed, they hated appearing in public wearing curlers and no make-up, so they slumped into corners, clutching their war-paint.

By that time the bombs were falling pretty fast. We heard windows breaking in the room above us, another bomb hit on the ramparts just behind, a paint store was flaming up at the end of the garden, an ammunition store next it seemed doomed to blow up, and us with it; the Bofors guns started going off overhead, more planes zoomed in and down, the Rock guns barked and the fleet guns boomed and the whole Rock fairly shook. But the three girls, quite oblivious to it all, sat calmly looking into their mirrors, taking their hair-curlers out, streaking on lipstick, stretching their mouths to wipe away the smears and patting their curls into place. I was amazed at their sang-froid, particularly since it was the first raid for all of them. Yet they showed no fear, and their concentration on the faces in their mirrors was complete.

Only when their make-up session was over did her female companions begin to turn green and tremble. Had the air raid gone on much longer, Hiett was sure they would have panicked. But the job of making themselves presentable had kept fear at bay. There was the moral, she thought: if you are caught in an air raid, keep your mind occupied with something else, even if it is just taking off hair-curlers. 'Fear comes first to the idle, who have nothing else to think about but fear.'

Hiett later looked at research into British reactions to air raids. Women stood up to them better than men (who lost control of their nerves when they couldn't *do* anything) because women thought of their children's welfare and their loved ones first, and so forgot about their own fear. The working classes, more used to suffering and physical danger, were not in fact any more resilient than the liberal and intellectual professions who distracted themselves by turning their minds to the aesthetics of searchlights and explosions, the technical identification of aircraft and ordnance, the mathematics of range and trajectory, plus relevant historical perspectives and future prognostications.

As to fear itself, it doesn't upset your nervous system so much, as soon as you learn not to be afraid of fear. But this may take a long time to learn. I still didn't know that fear can be a good thing when I learned from a Spaniard that a man who is afraid is also courageous, just as long as he doesn't run or let the fear take mastery. I thought that at best fear was an undesirable thing to be accepted. But the more you see of this war the more you think about fear.

The 'all-clear' sounded at 4 p.m. and they all dashed to the dining room for a lobster lunch. Nobody talked about the air raid till the crustacean was demolished and Raven came in with coffee and a cigar-lighter fashioned to look like an anti-aircraft gun, which he had been saving for just such an occasion. That broke the voluntary silence. Governor Liddell explained what they had been through: it was a Vichy revenge air raid by several score Potez and Glenn Martin aircraft. The Anglo-French attack on Dakar had brought the war to Gibraltar. Liddell said he thought a couple of the Vichy planes had been shot down over La Línea for violating Spain's neutral airspace. 'It did seem like a queer kind of war when American-built planes, piloted by Frenchmen, should bomb the British at Gibraltar on German orders and be brought down by Spaniards. We laughed over that for a while, and then H.E. let me come with him on his official tour to inspect the damage.'

Cormorant Wharf, the Dutch Shell stores, the south generating station, the married quarters in Naval Hospital Road, King George V Memorial Hospital and Scud Hill were all damaged by Vichy bombs. One projectile had exploded in the middle of South Barracks parade ground and a coal shed on the South Mole caught fire. There were six dead and seventeen injured. The AA batteries had fired 750 rounds.

The chorus girls left for Madrid on the morning of Wednesday 25 September, but something kept Helen Hiett from going with them, so she had the journalist's luck of being in a bad place at the right time.

The sirens went off again just after noon, announcing the fifth air raid on Gibraltar, the longest and heaviest so far. Wave after wave of Glenn Martin bombers from Casablanca dropped ordnance south to north along the Rock, then flew back to reload and refuel and attack again. Government House had lunched early and now Hiett sat in the shelter with her typewriter, the only woman among a group of men:

It does you no harm to sit for three hours listening to the terrible crump overhead, knowing every minute that death may pick you for a partner. It helps you settle down generally thereafter, for your body refuses to stay in a perpetual state of panic. You sense a new serenity in seeing how much you can take . . . As to being alone with a group of soldiers, facing danger and doing it as well as they, it's like the thrill of learning a new language, or of practicing a new profession with success. Then, too, in such a case, men are always grateful to a woman who doesn't panic, and their gratitude is pleasant to receive, the more so if disproportionate to your own merits.

She kept asking for more whiskey and handed the glasses under the tablecloth to a young man called Paddy who, although an ADC to Mason-MacFarlane, was not yet inured to bombardment. She was glad to have the typewriter so she could write her script. It proved the truth of what she had learned the day before about keeping busy, and the sound effects outside inspired some descriptive copy for NBC's listeners in North America, people who had never been bombed, and whose country had not been invaded in living memory. But Hiett was sensitive enough, too, to know when to stop typing during the bombing, and she saw that the others in the room were glad of that: 'For the moment before a near one strikes and you think, "Well, this is it" – that moment must be spent in silence.'

You quickly learn that the bombs are far away which you thought were ringers at first. That gives you new confidence. And because of it, you soon find that you are calmer in your daily living in face of lesser troubles. So don't dread the first enemy raid that is bound to come to us. Look forward to it, rather. It will give you a chance to discover how courageous people can be, and how bravely they can pretend to be brave if they aren't, both of which will make you admire your fellow beings probably more than you ever did before.

The air raid killed seven British people. The two three-inch ack-ack guns on Signal Hill, firing four rounds a minute, exhausted all their ammunition, and several French bombers were shot down. The Gibraltar Defence Force gunners had tin hats but no ear-protectors; the gun-layer on John Porral's gun was deaf for several weeks. A litter of unexploded ordnance blocked some of Gibraltar's streets. One bomb hit the British anti-submarine trawler *Stella Sirius*, moored on the South Mole, killing two seamen named Thomas and Griffin and setting the ship ablaze. Four Gibraltarian men – Peter Buttigieg, Antonio De La Paz, Joseph Stagno and Second Officer W. H. Jones – went aboard and bravely hacked their way into the fo'c'sle to rescue the trapped and injured. They managed to scuttle the ship before the flames reached the magazine and the depth charges. The number of bombs dropped harmlessly in the sea made some wonder if every French pilot had his heart in the Vichy cause. Their explosions killed a lot of fish. A dockie speared a big one with a pitchfork and many a Spanish workman walked home to La Línea dangling a fish dinner.

That day, Fortress HQ put out an upbeat press communiqué: 'After an afternoon of intense air bombardment Gibraltar's high morale remains entirely unaffected and the traditional Ceremony of the Keys was carried out in the presence of His Excellency the Governor with full ceremonial.'

The Key is part of the Rock's symbology. The coat of arms of Gibraltar, first granted in Toledo in 1502, is an escutcheon (shield) with a three-towered red castle under which hangs a golden key ('pendent therefrom a key Or'). This signified in heraldic terms that Gibraltar was the key to the strait, as for the Moors it had been the key to Spain. The Ceremony of the Keys at Fortress Gibraltar dates from the Great Siege, when Governor Eliott held the keys to the three gates in the North Wall, and only handed them to the Port Sergeant to lock the gates at sunset, and then to open them again in the morning. (Eliott carried the keys at his belt by day, it was said, and slept with them under his pillow.)

After peace was restored in 1783, drums and fifes accompanied the Port Sergeant, warning aliens to leave Gibraltar before the gates were locked. This happened every night until the end of the First World War, like the nightly ceremony at the Tower of London. Governor Harington revived the tradition in 1933, with a ceremonial parade in Casemates Square where the senior NCO requested and was given the keys by the governor. The ritual is still performed annually by the Gibraltar Regiment, and every Saturday at midday the Gibraltar Re-Enactment Association Society dress up to do a tourist version.

Helen Hiett wrote in September 1940:

I had seen the ceremony before and I've seen it since – the marching, the stirring music, the drummers in full dress of crimson and white, the age-old query, 'Whose keys?' and the answer 'King George's keys', before the gate in the ramparts is locked for the night, but never has it been so impressive as it was that day, a few moments after the last bomb fell, when searchers were still hunting unknown dead.

20

Dealing with Dictators

Because the fate of Gibraltar hung on the actions of Spain, it mattered greatly to the Rock when, in September 1940, General Franco sent Ramón Serrano Suñer at the head of a top-level mission to Berlin. Ten senior Falangists, including Miguel Primo de Rivera, the orator Dionisio Ridruejo and Demetrio Carceller (once a Catalan associate of Juan March), were among the flock of bureaucrats who accompanied the envoy on his important diplomatic task, shepherded by the German ambassador himself, Baron Eberhard von Stohrer.

Ramón Serrano Suñer was then head of the Falangist political junta and *el Ministro de Gobernación* (Interior Minister), which is to say the man who controlled Spain's prisons, police and press. He was, according to Admiral Canaris, 'the most hated man in Spain', but his star was rising because he was also the brother-in-law, *el cuñado*, of General Franco's wife, Carmen Polo. If Franco was *el Generalísimo*, the joke went, Serrano was *el Cuñadísimo*. To Sir Samuel Hoare, however, the Falangist hard-liner Serrano was no laughing matter but one of the chief villains, 'a pinchbeck Robespierre', a fanatic 'in the grip of the Axis'. Serrano had very limited experience of foreign affairs, but he had been to Italy and met Mussolini and his Foreign Minister Galeazzo Ciano in June 1939. The Italian foreign minister described him as 'a slender and sickly man – one of those characters given to study and reflection . . . But it is always *feeling* that dominates him: he hates and loves impetuously. His *bête noire* is France. He . . . considers France the eternal enemy of Greater Spain.'

On 13 September, the day after his thirty-ninth birthday, Ramón Serrano Suñer led the Spanish diplomatic party across the bridge at Irún into German-occupied France. Quiet, shuttered Hendaye was now hung with giant swastikas; the beret-wearing locals seemed cowed. The Germans laid on a luxurious train that bore the Spaniards to occupied Paris where the new German ambassador, Otto Abetz, greeted them at the Gare d'Austerlitz. They spent a day in the French capital, enjoying the lack of traffic around the famous sights; buses, taxis and private cars were now prohibited, so Parisians rode thousands of bicycles. German army signposts – black on white – pointed at key junctions and crossings, and more swastikas hung over the arcaded rue de Rivoli, where the W. H. Smith bookshop at No. 248 was now *Frontbuchhandlung*. Uniformed but unarmed Wehrmacht personnel shopped with Reichsmarks that bought twice as much as before.

The Spaniards travelled on to Germany by rail. At the Anhalt Bahnhof in Berlin, Joachim von Ribbentrop, the Reich Foreign Minister, met them with an entourage including the immensely tall chief of protocol, Minister Dr Freiherr von Dörnberg. The Nazis laid on a smart guard to inspect, and a crowd with children waving little Spanish flags. A convoy of Mercedes-Benz motor cars drove them to the Adlon Hotel. Serrano Suñer did not like Ribbentrop, finding him vain, affected and stupidly robotic. Their three hours of talks were tedious. Ribbentrop pressed the question of when Spain was going to join the war; Serrano talked the usual high emotions and low economics, and Ribbentrop found his plea of poverty annoying. When they discussed Spanish ambitions for North Africa, Serrano soon realised that the fall of France would yield no easy pickings, no ripe colonial fruit. The Germans were not going to give away the French Empire, as some Spanish Falangists hoped and believed. Nazi Germany still wanted to keep Vichy France sweet in North Africa. Spain would have to insist on its claims to Morocco.

At what Serrano in his memoirs called a 'brilliantly boring' reception where the Spaniards mingled with leading Nazis like Frick and Ley and Himmler, Ribbentrop declared that Spain's equivocal foreign policy 'looked like ingratitude' and had upset Hitler. And why was one Spanish minister working for England? Serrano says he bridled at this clear reference to Beigbeder. 'Spanish ministers might be right or wrong in their thoughts and actions,' he replied stiffly, 'but we only serve the national interest.' Ribbentrop blundered on, saying that Hitler might have to occupy Spain for security reasons, given the country's strategic location. And what about Portugal? Hitler's troops might have to come and invade there, like Wellington's in the Napoleonic Wars. There were good business reasons to stick with Germany, the crass *Reichsaussenminister* suggested.

Serrano Suñer left the party early to prepare for his meeting with Adolf Hitler the next day. He felt daunted: a poor provincial was about to encounter the sovereign of Europe. On 17 September 1940, in his black-shirted Falangist uniform and flattish peaked cap that made him look like a senior railway-ticket inspector, Serrano entered the huge Reich Chancellery, designed by Albert Speer to overawe visitors and impress them with the Third Reich's grandeur. An eagle with a twenty-five-foot wingspan on a laurel-wreathed swastika hovered over the neo-classical portico. Inside were huge carved doors, kitsch statues of naked athletes, and long rooms that he had to proceed through in turn. The Marmorgalerie or Marble Gallery – at 146 metres exactly twice the length of the Galerie des Glaces at Versailles – led to the imposing entrance of Hitler's vast study. Speer wanted to lay a carpet along it, but Hitler insisted that the red marble floor stayed highly polished so that visitors were made uneasy by its slippery surface before they reached the dictator's sanctum. After being made to wait for hours, President Emil Hácha of Czechoslovakia walked this walk in the early hours of 15 March 1939. When he got there, Hitler's harangue was so ferocious that he fainted. Dr Theo Morell, Hitler's tubby drug-dispenser, revived him with a stimulant injection, and Hácha promptly signed his country away.

Serrano had only seen Hitler once, from afar, an idol in a car with his arm outstretched, among the torches and banners and searchlights of the 1937 Nuremberg rally, which he had attended with Nicolás Franco, the general's brother. Hitler close up in person was both impressive and vulgar, he thought. The *Führer* had a powerful

gaze, and was self-controlled. He ranged like a cat from the armchair
to the table covered with maps and charts, but when he hooked on
his clerical spectacles and fussed with compasses to measure Stuka
bombing ranges he looked a German petty bourgeois again. Hitler
seemed to take a childish pleasure in tracing lines and jabbing at
points on the map with his big fleshy hands. He was assertive in his
opinions and boastful about Germany's military prowess.

There were six people present at the hour-long meeting. Joachim
von Ribbentrop and the veteran civil servant Otto Meissner supported Hitler, while Serrano's back-up was the committed Falangist
and philologist Antonio Tovar. The interpreter was Hitler's usual
multilinguist from the Foreign Ministry, Minister Dr Paul Otto
Schmidt, a decent-seeming man who nevertheless badly irritated Serrano. When the Germanophile Tovar translated back what Schmidt
was saying in German to Hitler, Serrano realised that the mellifluous
subtleties of his eloquence were not getting through to the *Führer* at
all – Dr Schmidt spoke Spanish like a *gringo* travelling salesman in
South America. But Schmidt claimed to have photographic recall,
and his notes summarising the conversation have survived.*

According to Schmidt's account, Serrano opened the meeting with
a glozing message from *Generalísimo* Franco, which 'expressed to
the *Führer* his gratitude, sympathy and high esteem, and emphasised
to him his loyalty of yesterday, of today and for always'. Serrano
said that the Spanish attitude to Germany had not changed in the
least; it was only a question of clarifying the conditions under which
Spain would be ready to fight alongside Germany. And once again
he played the economic squeezebox: 'Whenever Spain's supply of
foodstuffs and war material was secure she could immediately enter
the war.' He mentioned the shopping list given to Admiral Canaris

---

* Interpreter Schmidt had opinions too. He said that Ribbentrop ('a dangerous fool')
reminded him of the terrier in the famous gramophone advertisement: yapping at the
sound of His Master's Voice. Galeazzo Ciano also records Hermann Göring calling
Ribbentrop 'Germany's no. 1 parrot'. US interrogators later dubbed the minister 'von
Rippenshit'.

and stated that ten 38 cm (fifteen-inch) guns would be 'necessary for Gibraltar'.

Hitler said the German people had never forgotten Spain's help for German prisoners of war in 1914–18. It was that appreciation which had led to German involvement in the Spanish Civil War. But now Germany was in the decisive fight against England. The continent of Europe, from Norway to Iberia, was secure; the British could not mount any kind of cross-Channel landing, but they might try to alienate the Vichy French colonies in North Africa and wage war from there. Serrano said that Spain was concerned that the British might land on the Cantabrian coast, where the communists of Asturias might support them. Hitler told him not to worry: the whole population of Norway had been on Britain's side and that had not helped the British landing there to succeed.

'Air supremacy is the main thing. That is the principle of this war,' Hitler announced. Were a group of Stukas and other dive-bombers made available for the conquest of Gibraltar, within a week there would be no British ships for 350 kilometres because heavy bombs would cripple them. 'In Norway, we forced the English to retreat using Stukas alone.' (Serrano noted that Hitler never called the Junkers Ju 87 dive-bombers 'Stukas' like everyone else but always used their full name: *Sturzkampfflugzeuge*, literally 'fall-fight-aircraft'.)

Hitler, who was a military 'nerd', stuffed with specs and stats, launched one of his pedantic disquisitions on the effectiveness of aerial bombing versus artillery in tackling a stronghold like Gibraltar. The huge bombs dropped on the Maginot Line had destroyed structures built to withstand artillery in ten minutes. 'Even when there is no direct hit, the concussive effect of a thousand-kilo bomb was in itself tremendous. Therefore, the decisive factor for the conquest and later defence of Gibraltar is the guarantee of absolute air supremacy.' Hitler continued to argue against supplying big guns to Spain. It was true, the *Führer* went on, that 38 cm heavy artillery had been set up on the French side of the English Channel, shooting across at England, but that had taken several months and was only for use in bad weather when air attacks were out of the question. Hitler compared the limited amount of explosive a long-barrelled gun could deliver in two hundred shots to the amount a Stuka squadron of thirty-six planes flying thrice daily could drop. He thought 38 cm guns would not be possible for Gibraltar: the transport would be too difficult and installation would take three or four months. (Ian Colvin interpreted this stress on aircraft versus artillery as a matter of power and control: Hitler could loan the German air force, but he would have to give away the guns.) Germany would do everything in her power to help Spain, Hitler said, because once she entered the war, Germany would have every interest in her success – any Spanish victory would also be a German victory. 'In the Gibraltar undertaking, it would be primarily a matter of taking the fortress itself with extraordinary speed and protecting the Strait.'

Serrano Suñer thanked the *Führer*. In the previous discussions that General von Richthofen and Admiral Canaris had had with General Franco, German intentions had not been quite clear. His request to the *Führer* to put this all down in writing for the benefit of General Franco was granted.

Hitler then referred to the reconnaissance mission that Admiral Canaris and the paratroop heroes of Fort Eben Emael had made to Algeciras and La Línea, and said they had concluded that Gibraltar could be taken by a modern but relatively modest attack that would silence the big guns. Germany was offering Spain aircraft to clear enemy ships from the strait and selected assault engineers with special armour-destroying weapons called *Scharten* or 'pillbox-crackers'.

Now Serrano talked about Morocco. Surely it was Spain's *Lebensraum*? Hitler replied that Germany had economic and strategic interests in Africa too. England and Free France had their eyes on Madeira and the Canary Islands and they were trying to entice the USA to the Azores. The meeting concluded with Hitler saying he wanted to meet Franco on the Spanish frontier. He also invited Serrano to visit the battlefields of his great victory in the west and to see the big guns now being set up along the English Channel, before returning to Berlin.

Serrano had another meeting with Ribbentrop in his office, overlooking the old park behind the Wilhelmstrasse. There are two contradictory accounts of this. Both involve a large wall-map. Paul Schmidt the interpreter recalled Serrano and Ribbentrop standing before a map of the French colonial empire in Africa and the German Foreign Minister in effect saying 'Help yourself'. Serrano then started with the port of Oran in Algeria and traced an arc south past the Strait of Gibraltar to include all Morocco and a big chunk of Mauritania in French West Africa to 'round off' the Spanish colony of Río de Oro, the southern half of Spanish Sahara. 'Ribbentrop eagerly sold the goods which did not belong to him,' wrote Schmidt; 'apparently no price was too high for Spanish collaboration.' In return, Ribbentrop asked for the concession of one U-boat base at Villa Cisneros in Río de Oro and another at Santa Isabel in the island of Fernando Póo, part of Spanish Guinea in the Bight of Biafra (nowadays Malabo on the island of Bioko, part of Equatorial Guinea). Serrano was, according to Schmidt, 'niggardly': Río de Oro might be possible, but Fernando Póo was out 'for historical reasons' and 'on account of Spanish public opinion'.

Serrano, on the other hand, recalls Ribbentrop doing all the talking, standing before the map of *Afrika*, indicating a huge band across the middle of the continent, south of Lake Chad, north of Angola and Mozambique, an area taking in the Cameroons, both French and Belgian Congos, and British East Africa – Kenya, Uganda and Tanganyika. In Serrano's account, Ribbentrop said this was the German zone of interest, an economic empire in the very heart of Africa, which the German people needed and deserved. Looking at the Atlantic coast of French Morocco, Ribbentrop said Germany needed air and military bases at Mogador (now Essaouira) and at Agadir, the port where the Kaiser had caused the 'crisis' in 1911. Then something more worrying: Ribbentrop asked for one of the seven main Canary Islands as a German military base. Serrano Suñer had been quite happy for Nazi Germany to take over other people's territory all across Africa, but he was not prepared for this, and he bridled.

'Bear in mind, Minister,' Serrano said stiffly, 'that the islands you are talking about are part of our national territory, a province of our country.'

'The common needs of Euroafrican defence against American imperialism demand it. I trust the *Generalísimo* will understand.'

'I cannot even transmit this request. Don't you understand that while the youth of Spain, who have shed their blood for the greatness of their *Patria*, are crying out for Gibraltar, it would be monstrous, even criminal, for us to entertain any thoughts of amputating, ceding or limiting our territory or our sovereignty? The Canary Islands are as much a part of Spain as Madrid or Burgos. You can establish your bases in Senegal at Saint Louis or at Dakar, without encroaching on Morocco, let alone our national territory.'

All memoirs are self-serving. Ramón Serrano Suñer wrote his *Entre Hendaya y Gibraltar* in 1947 partly to defend himself from the charges in Sir Samuel Hoare's 1946 book *Ambassador on Special Mission*, in which he was painted as the villain. The modern Spanish historian Ángel Viñas has described Serrano's memoirs as 'untrustworthy' ('*no fiables*') and says that 'at key points, he lied like a trooper' ('*mintió como un bellaco*'). By the time he wrote them, Joachim von Ribbentrop was dead, the first Nazi to be hanged after the war crimes trial at Nuremberg, so could not contradict Serrano's account. Whether their Berlin encounter was like that or not, the Spaniard was keen to present himself as a man defending the integrity and independence of Spain, rather than, in his own words, 'a Nazi serf'.

Serrano sent a courier back to Spain by air with Hitler's letter and an urgent note to Franco warning him of the German threat to the Canary Islands, a Spanish possession for nearly five hundred years. They did not know, though might have surmised, that in June 1940 Winston Churchill had also asked the British Admiralty to draw up plans to seize the Canary Islands (code-name 'Bugle'), as well as the

Portuguese Cape Verdes ('Shrapnel') and the Azores ('Alloy'), as fall-back positions should Gibraltar ever be lost.

Then Serrano went on a week-long Nazi battlefield car trip, nursing a streaming cold which he picked up in a damp Berlin air-raid shelter. (The RAF had started bombing the German capital with scores of aircraft on 25 August 1940.) He found totalitarianism 'a mixture of puerility and grandiosity', like the ostentatious palaces of its leaders. Food rationing gripped even the elite: they ate a lot of roast duck because game was the only meat not on points. Once they had a stew made of deer so well hung it was barely edible. The Nazi 'new order' was both impressive and boring. Serrano recalled a ghastly day being driven around in big cars, inspecting Heinrich Himmler's SS empire. They saw barracks, sports halls and a criminology museum, then wasted an hour inspecting an automatic card index. By the time they came to the fourth explanation of its functioning he felt like screaming.*

In Belgium, Serrano took the obligatory tour of Fort Eben Emael, already becoming a legendary German victory. He saw desolate Dunkirk's beaches with overturned ambulances and carts in the sands, the wreckage of downed aeroplanes and the funnels of sunken ships sticking up from the sea. The gung-ho German admiral cheerfully showed them how the Organisation Todt (OT), the construction enterprise headed by engineer Fritz Todt, were building the Atlantic Wall of *Festung Europa* (Fortress Europe), ramparts and ditches of reinforced concrete, immense casemates for artillery draped in camouflage netting, long-barrelled guns that could reach the English coast clearly visible over the Dover Strait from Cap Gris Nez. In Calais and Boulogne he saw shoals of motor torpedo boats and barges ready for an invasion which he suspected was not going to happen.

Ribbentrop, meanwhile, had flown to Rome on 19 September, and was childishly pleased with the 'applauding squad' that greeted him.

---

* These were Hollerith punch-card machines, purchased from the USA, useful for identifying and targeting Jews and computerising the concentration camp system. See Edwin Black, *IBM and the Holocaust* (Dialog Press, 2012).

In the car, he told Count Ciano, the Italian Foreign Minister, that he had a surprise in his briefcase: a military alliance with Japan, to be signed soon in Berlin. Ribbentrop saw this personal diplomatic triumph as a double winner, because both the USSR and the USA would feel threatened. Ribbentrop wanted to meet lots of people and got busy socialising. 'Everyone disliked him,' Count Ciano wrote in his diary, also recording the German Foreign Minister's bullish account of his talk with Serrano:

Spain is ready to enter the war and has informed the German Government of her requirements ... grain and war materials ... certain specialised weapons as well as a guarantee that at the end of the war the coastal strip of Morocco from Oran to Cap Blanc will be transferred to Spanish sovereignty. The Führer is in principle in favour of making these concessions for the sake of ensuring Spain's entry into the war, which would have as its immediate object the occupation of Gibraltar ... If the Duce agrees, Ribbentrop hopes to draw up a protocol with Serrano Suñer on his return to Berlin in order to lay down the conditions for Spain's entry into the war.

Meanwhile, Franco had read Hitler's letter and replied on 22 September in his usual opaque prose. 'My dear *Führer*!' it began. After the familiar flurry of 'cordial thanks' and 'complete agreement' with 'your esteemed ideas', Franco's anxieties about Morocco emerged. He was bothered in particular by 'the establishment of an enclave for German military bases by occupying both harbours of the southern zone'. Franco said that these (unspecified) enclaves would be 'unnecessary in peacetime and superfluous in wartime' because Hitler could count on the use of every single one of Spain's harbours 'since our friendship is to be sealed firmly for the future as well'.

Franco agreed that 'the first act in our attack must consist in the occupation of Gibraltar ... within a few days by the use of modern equipment and trained troops'. Franco said there had been a misunderstanding about his request for big guns. He did not want large-calibre static artillery, but movable ones of about twenty centimetres or eight inches. It would be hard to build new airfields because the terrain was so rugged and the weather so bad, but air power would be indispensable.

Franco went on with his fears about a British surprise attack on the Canary Islands. Spain was moving men and food, arms and ammunition, artillery and shells, planes and pilots from less threatened regions to the islands. The letter ended in more verbiage:

I would like to thank you, dear Führer, once again for the offer of solidarity. I reply with the unchangeable and sincere adherence to you personally, to the German people, and to the cause for which you fight. I hope, in defence of this cause, to be able to renew the old bonds of comradeship between our armies. In the expectation of being able to express this to you personally, I assure you of my most sincere feelings of friendship and I greet you.

Your

F. FRANCO

On 26 September 1940, Adolf Hitler and Grand Admiral Erich Raeder had one of their regular conferences on naval affairs. Hitler disliked the sea, because he got seasick easily, and he feared the ocean. 'On land I am a hero,' he once told Raeder, 'but at sea I am a coward.' Unlike Churchill, the *Führer* had never read Mahan's *Influence of Sea Power*. Instead he had consumed Friedrich Ratzel and Karl Haushofer and so believed in *Lebensraum* on land, expanding territories to the east across Eurasia. The seaman Admiral Raeder, like the airman Marshal Göring, was not at all keen on invading Russia. He had read enough history to know how Napoleon began to lose his empire.

Now the *Führer* listened to Raeder expounding a maritime strategy. The admiral argued cogently that the Mediterranean should be tackled in the winter of 1940–1. Raeder said the British considered the Mediterranean the pivot of their world empire. British armies in Egypt and the eastern Mediterranean were being reinforced from Australia and India. Italy and its African empire was going to be the main point of attack because the British always picked off the weakest enemy first. However, added the admiral, were Germany to seize Gibraltar, then this would completely alter the balance of power in the Atlantic. German U-boats could throttle British supply lines and force *die Engländer* to surrender without the Germans having to undertake a difficult amphibious invasion of the British Isles.

Hitler was already getting bored with the *Sealion* plan for invasion, so this argument appealed to him. Following his southern strategy, Raeder said Germany should then strike at the Suez Canal, which the Italians would never be able to take without German help. Then the German armies could advance through Palestine towards the oilfields of Iraq and Persia, which would threaten the USSR from the south. Some actions at Dakar and Casablanca to keep the British and French out of Africa would secure the whole of the west and south. Then Germany could turn all its military might eastwards against the Soviet Union.

The *Führer* enjoyed this conversation and the new possibilities it opened up. The OKW (Oberkommando der Wehrmacht) headquarters planners had done more work on the Canaris–Mikosch assessment of how Gibraltar might be taken, and had assigned mountain troops and artillery for training and rehearsals. Things could soon get moving.

On Friday 27 September 1940, in a big media event with photographers and newsreel cameramen and Serrano Suñer watching, Chancellor Adolf Hitler, Italian Foreign Minister Galeazzo Ciano and Japanese ambassador Saburo Kurusu signed the Tripartite Pact in Berlin. The old 'Pact of Steel' now embraced its third member, the Axis became a Triangle, and Nazi Germany, Fascist Italy and Imperial Japan were joined in a mutually defensive military alliance for the next ten years, with the right to establish 'New Orders' in their respective continents.

The following day, Saturday 28 September 1940, Hitler had a long talk with Count Ciano about Spain. Hitler wanted the war finished, decisively, and he was sarcastic about Spain's contribution to that end. The Spanish wanted Germany to supply seven hundred thousand tons of wheat per year, all the oil and petrol they required, all the equipment the Spanish army lacked, all the artillery, aeroplanes, special weapons and troops needed for the conquest of Gibraltar, plus all of Morocco and Oran in Algeria. And what was Spain offering in return? *Her friendship* . . .

Hitler wondered what would happen if Vichy France ever got wind of Spanish ambitions for French Morocco. Pétain might well do a deal with the English in order to save French North Africa. It might be better for Germany if Vichy France held on to Morocco and defended themselves against the English – after all, Vichy had managed to beat off the Anglo-French attack at Dakar – whereas if Franco's Spanish troops occupied French North African territory they would probably yell for German and Italian help as soon as the English came at them. The *Führer* needed to talk it all over coolly with Mussolini. Helping Spain would mean heavy sacrifices and tiresome military obligations for both Germany and Italy. And even then, the Spanish might still scuttle back into neutrality. Spain was all take and no give. Germany had assisted Franco in the Spanish Civil War and although Hitler did not want to calculate the blood sacrifice in economic terms, the fact was that Spain owed Germany four hundred million Reichsmarks in war debts;* but whenever reparation was brought up, the Spanish talked about their noble ideals, making the Germans seem like Jews, screwing cash out of something sacred.

Hitler told Ciano that Franco had invited him to a meeting at the border between France and Spain and he was not sure whether or not to accept. He would talk to Mussolini first.

Ciano said that Italy had not forgotten burning its fingers in the Spanish Civil War either, when Franco had claimed that if only he could get a dozen transport planes or bombers from Italy he would win the war in a few days. 'A few days' became three years, and those twelve planes turned into more than a thousand aircraft, six

* According to the modern economist E. Martínez Ruiz, Francoist Spain's total civil war debt to Nazi Germany was 732.6 million Reichsmarks, equivalent to US$295.4 million then.

thousand Italian dead and costs of fourteen billion lire. Would the same thing happen again? Caution was needed, and a good long talk. Ciano said that *il Duce* was eager to meet *der Führer*, too. Would Herr Hitler like to meet Mussolini at the Brenner Pass on Friday 4 October, when Serrano would be in Rome?

Back in Rome on Monday 30 September, Ciano went to see Mussolini, who was very happy that his Italian troops in Libya were slowly rolling eastward against British Egypt, whose patrols were falling back. *Il Duce* yearned for the military glory that Italy 'has sought in vain for three centuries'.

The next day, the Spanish Foreign Minister Ramón Serrano Suñer arrived in Rome on the train from Munich. Among the Spanish Embassy welcoming party at the railway station was General Gonzalo Queipo de Llano, but he refused to greet Serrano or shake his hand or to attend the lunch that was laid on. Murderous Queipo de Llano – the man Arthur Koestler described as a sexual psychopath – had been exiled to Rome since August 1939 and was living at the Hotel Excelsior with his attractive thirty-two-year-old daughter Mercedes, known as Maruja, whom Queipo's own wife Genoveva suspected he had incestuously molested. Ostensibly the head of the Spanish Military Mission to Fascist Italy, Queipo de Llano was being spied on by his aide-de-camp and was in disgrace because he had insulted Franco in his Tourette's-like outbursts. Serrano Suñer, Franco's brother-in-law, told Ciano that he thought Queipo de Llano was 'a bandit and a beast'.

Mussolini had Serrano installed in the Italian Foreign Service's charming Renaissance palace, Villa Madama, set in terraced gardens on Monte Maria, and they met that afternoon, Tuesday 1 October. Serrano began by saying that Spain had always given the Axis moral support, but it was now preparing to take up arms 'to settle its centuries-old account with Great Britain'. Spain had a host of internal problems, but he thought that war would be a unifying factor: people would rally to the cause of regaining Gibraltar and Morocco, especially young people.

Serrano was much more at home in Fascist Italy than he had been in Nazi Germany. Because Mussolini seemed friendly, intelligent and loyal – *muy simpático* – the Spaniard poured out his heart to him and Ciano. He could not hide the worry and anguish that had been caused him by Ribbentrop's unfriendly, sometimes threatening and always difficult attitude, which undermined the good impression he got from his talks with Hitler. He railed against the tactlessness of the Germans and their complete ignorance of the Spanish moral universe. He strongly disliked their attitude to the Catholic Church and said they were not the right people to create the new order of European civilisation.* Mussolini, who understood far better than the Germans what Spain had suffered in the civil war, calmed his fellow Latin down. Ciano recorded him saying to Serrano that although Spain should accelerate her military preparations, they should only come into the war on the basis of a collective decision and when the time was right.

When Ciano sent a copy of the conversation to the Germans, he naturally left out Serrano's 'colourful invectives against the Germans', only adding in his personal diary: 'The Germans are not models of courtesy, and Ribbentrop less so than the others, even though this time there is something to be said for him. For years the Spaniards have been asking for lots and giving nothing in return.'

On Friday 4 October, Adolf Hitler and Benito Mussolini met in the Alps. Each Axis dictator arrived in his own special armoured train at the Brenner Pass between Austria and Italy. They had met here two and a half years earlier to celebrate the so-called 'Pact of Steel' that was now being corroded by their own bad faith; both men lied about the present and concealed their plans for the future.

Hitler said the attack on England was going well, although he had postponed the actual invasion; Mussolini boasted about his advance

---

* Serrano Suñer from Catholic Spain made a major blunder on this trip to Rome by failing to pay his respects to the Pope at the Vatican.

into Egypt, next stop Mersa Matruh and then forward to Alexandria and the Suez Canal, although this was not going to happen. Hitler did not say he was going to take over Romania, and Mussolini did not say he was going to attack Greece. They talked about Spain's intervention in the war. Hitler summarised his conversations with Serrano – 'the crafty Jesuit' – and spoke of the Spanish demand for large supplies of wheat, at a time when there was not enough grain in Germany and potato flour was already being added to bread. The Spanish wanted the whole Moroccan coast, but Germany herself needed a base at either Casablanca or Agadir. The *Führer* was prepared to cede Gibraltar to the Spanish but he was not minded to give them everything they wanted in Morocco: if Spain got a strip of French Morocco as requested, the English might invade the Canaries and Vichy North Africa could swing to de Gaulle. Finally, Hitler stated that he considered the war as good as won.*

On the same day, far away in Tokyo, Prince Konoye, the Japanese premier, declared that if the USA recognised the leadership of Japan, Germany and Italy in eastern Asia and Europe, then those three Powers would logically recognise the leadership of the USA in the western hemisphere. If, however, 'the USA . . . challenges the three Powers, we are ready for a fight to the finish'.

In the USA, the America First Committee, recently founded by Yale University students, was getting organised in Chicago as the foremost non-interventionist pressure group to keep the USA out of foreign entanglements.

In the British parliament, at the end of his wide-ranging 'War Situation' speech of 8 October, Winston Churchill was placatory towards Spain, which he described as a country 'much nearer home which has for some months past seemed to hang in the balance between peace and war'.

---

* When Ribbentrop parroted 'The war is already won' on 2 November 1940, a German army major turned to Count Ciano and said in his laboured French: 'This phrase was given to us in 1914, in 1915, in 1916, and in 1917. I believed it. In 1918 I wished I were dead.'

We have always wished well to the Spanish people . . . There is no country in Europe that has more need of peace and food and the opportunities of prosperous trade than Spain . . . Far be it from us to lap Spain and her own economic needs in the wide compass of our blockade. All we seek is that Spain will not become a channel of supply to our mortal foes . . . British interests and policy are based on the independence and unity of Spain, and we look forward to seeing her take her rightful place both as a great Mediterranean Power and as a leading and famous member of the family of Europe and of Christendom . . .

On the Spanish side, things looked rather different. Serrano Suñer had flown back to Madrid from Italy, and conferred with his brother-in-law Franco. On 10 October, he wrote to Ribbentrop in Berlin asking for Spain's proposal to join the Axis alliance for the next ten years to be treated with the utmost secrecy. Serrano could not afford to jeopardise the shipments of Canadian and Argentine wheat that Beigbeder and his Spanish diplomats were then struggling to get through the British economic blockade's navicert system. It was vital that the food be seen as Red Cross humanitarian aid for hungry people in Spain, not as extra rations for a nation about to join the Axis. Serrano ended his missive with his 'respects to the Führer, with best wishes for the collaboration of our two peoples for the common good'.

German military planning for the taking of Gibraltar continued. On 12 October, General Franz Halder, chief of the OKH, the Army General Staff, picked Mountain Troop General Ludwig Kübler to lead the attack. Kübler, who was later hanged for war crimes in Yugoslavia, only liked to be photographed from the right because the left side of his mouth and cheek was hideously scarred by a wound from the First World War. He was sent to train with his soldiers at Valdahon camp in eastern France, in the foothills of the Jura Mountains. General Halder reckoned that the 98th Mountain Infantry Regiment, mainly Bavarians and Austrians, together with a regular infantry regiment like the Grossdeutschland, could do the job, backed up by twenty-six medium and heavy artillery batteries with 165 guns, plus three engineer battalions, three observation battalions, two smoke battalions and appropriate logistics. The preparations would take six to eight weeks, and the 3rd SS Panzer Division *Totenkopf* plus extra artillery would be needed for flank protection when they were on the move through Spain.

The German planners talked to the Luftwaffe about their requirements for Gibraltar: reconnaissance and observation planes as well as attack aircraft like dive-bombers and fighters, and sufficient anti-aircraft batteries. The logisticians were also working out the 1200-kilometre route for a land march through Spain: Irún–Burgos–Valladolid–Salamanca–Caceres–Mérida–Seville–Algeciras, and the right places for supply bases that would meet the requirements of 65,383 men and 1094 horses for 136 tons of food a day, as well as shifting 13,179 tons of ammunition and 9000 tons of oil and petrol without damage or loss over inadequate roads and railways. Halder talked with Lieutenant Colonel Mikosch and Major Staubwasser, both just back from their reconnaissance trips to Spain. Staubwasser estimated that there were ten thousand British troops on the Rock; Halder thought Mikosch 'over-optimistic' about how long it would take to beat them.

The 'New Order' in Nazified Europe ground on mercilessly. On 15 October, Lluís Companys, the extradited former president of autonomous Catalunya, was executed by firing squad in Barcelona. The next day, 16 October, General Franco changed his cabinet. He made himself Minister of the Interior and promoted Demetrio Carceller, the Falangist leader in Catalonia, to Minister of Industry and Commerce. There was an additional bombshell for the British. Their friend in the regime, Colonel Juan Beigbeder, was sacked as Foreign Minister, without notice. When they heard that his replacement was Ramón Serrano Suñer, there was consternation at the British Embassy: the arch-enemy was now inside the gates. Hoare's staff were convinced that Spain would soon join the Axis, declare war, and attack Gibraltar.

★

The signs from Spain were as ominous as the gloomy autumn skies. Early on Saturday 19 October 1940, the German *SS-Reichsführer* Heinrich Himmler set off for Spain via Bordeaux with his chief of staff *SS-Gruppenführer* Karl Wolff and a large entourage of Gestapo and SS officers in their long greatcoats and high-peaked, eagle-badged caps. Further south at Hendaye, they crossed the bridge-border into Irún, where they were greeted on Spanish soil by the German ambassador, Eberhard von Stohrer, accompanying José Maria de la Blanca Finat y Escrivá de Romaní, the Count of May-alde, who was Spain's dreaded Director General of Security.

José Finat, the man who had had Lluís Companys extradited from France and shot at Montjuic Castle in Barcelona, was keen to achieve even closer links with the Gestapo. The German and Spanish police had already signed a collaborative agreement on 31 July 1938 which meant they could swap communist, anarchist or other 'usual suspect' prisoners without any diplomatic niceties. Germans who had fought for the International Brigades could be handed over to the German police, and Spanish Republicans sent back to Spain. Or either country could punish them as they saw fit. Some 4800 Spaniards died in Mauthausen concentration camp.

In 1941, just before he left to become the Spanish ambassador in Berlin, Finat asked the governors of every province in Spain to compile registers of all Jews and people of Sephardi Jewish ancestry, including those *conversos* or converts who were now 'passing' as Spanish Christians. Finat's idea was that this racial information would be ready for the SS Hollerith punch-cards, to ease 'ethnic cleansing' when Spain joined the war on Germany's side and to enforce what Churchill had called 'the odious apparatus of Nazi rule'.

That Saturday, Himmler's party drove to San Sebastián in a holiday mood. It was not all police business. They had brought their shotguns, hoping for a spot of game in the Basque hills, but it was too rainy. In the wet streets of the city that the Basques call Donostia they were met by Falangists in blue shirts and red berets who demonstrated marching and flag-waving and elevating of right arms. Then they drove on to Burgos, the former headquarters of the Francoist uprising. General López Pinto, who was said to have been dismissed as head of the VI Military Region after his '*¡Viva Hitler!*' gaffe in June, was prominent among those who escorted the uniformed Germans. Shops were shut so that the Burgaleses could turn out with their umbrellas in the rain to cheer the *Reichsführer*. The city's dignitaries greeted him on the steps of the Cathedral, where Himmler was eager to see the red marble tomb of Rodrigo Díaz de Vivar, El Cid *Campeador*, a Visigoth whom his racial theories conceived as an ancestral Germanic warrior hero. (Perhaps he was also shown there the battered old iron-bound chest that El Cid had employed to hoodwink some Jewish money-lenders, filling it with sand rather than gold as security for a cash loan.) At dinner that night, Himmler sat next to *SS-Sturmbannführer* Paul Winzer, his Gestapo attaché at the German Embassy in Madrid since 1936, who filled him in on everything he needed to know. At 11 p.m., cars took them to the railway station for the night sleeper train across the *meseta* to Madrid.

Serrano Suñer, the new Foreign Minister, was among the military and civil chiefs waiting on the platform at Madrid's Atocha station to greet the distinguished Nazi visitor at 9 a.m. sharp on Sunday. Hundreds of swastika banners hung along their route up the Paseo del Prado, past the Botanical Gardens and the Prado art gallery to the Ritz Hotel. At midday, Himmler went to meet Franco at the Pardo Palace. They had lunch at the German Embassy, then went to the Plaza de Toros de Las Ventas to see 'six magnificent bulls' meet their ends in a muddy rain-lashed arena. Bespectacled Heinrich Himmler was not averse to organising the extermination of millions, but he was personally squeamish and did not enjoy the spectacle of ritual slaughter: the gouging picador, the stumbling blood-slicked beast, *la estocada*, the glittering toreador strutting with a severed black ear held triumphantly aloft. There was a small disturbance afterwards in the cheap seats when two young men from the British Embassy refused to stand when they played the *Deutschlandlied*, the

German national anthem, and plain-clothes Gestapo men roughly jostled them out.

Among other tourist highlights, Heinrich Himmler visited the National Archaeological Museum. The *SS-Reichsführer* was delighted to have as his guide a German-speaking Spanish archaeologist whose Visigothic excavations in Segovia seemed to confirm the crackpot racial theories of *das Ahnenerbe*, the Ancestral Heritage department of the SS Race and Settlement Office, which carried out pseudoscientific research into Aryan, Germanic and Nordic origins while deftly looting antiquities. Near Barcelona in Catalonia, the occult-minded Himmler also visited the Benedictine monastery of Santa María de Montserrat, in the belief that it was the Montsalvat of Wagner's *Parsifal*, the sacred place that was guarding the Holy Grail. Solaced by wishful thinking, Himmler flew home to Germany.

21

'Every Inch Must Be Pulverised'

As Adolf Hitler's armoured train moved westward across France, the *Führer* was fretting. Amid all the problems of a multinational conqueror running an overstretched dictatorship, he now had the impossibility of squaring the triangle of Italy, Spain and France. Mussolini and Franco wanted to carve off chunks of the Vichy French empire in Africa, but at the same time Hitler needed to keep Pétain as an ally. So he had to move pieces on the geostrategic board. Ideally, Italy would be happy to gain Nice, Corsica and Tunisia, and Vichy France and Spain might be bribed with the promise of fragments from the British Empire: Nigeria for the French, and Gibraltar, with a slice of French Morocco, for the Spanish.

Hitler needed yet more meetings with the French and Spanish leaders to help him decide what course to take. This time, the *Führer* broke with routine. Instead of summoning these lesser Latins up to the Berghof, his eyrie in the Bavarian Alps, as he usually did, he sallied out to find them. The historians Elizabeth Wiskemann and Norman Goda both think this 'unprecedented' move indicates the importance of the strategic aim.

A busy few days stretched ahead. On Tuesday 22 October 1940, Hitler met Pierre Laval on a siding at Montoire-sur-le-Loir, near Tours. Laval, desperate to retain France's African possessions and ease the heavy burden of armistice reparations, was ingratiatingly eager to collaborate with Nazi Germany. Hitler and Laval arranged for a second meeting, this time with Marshal Pétain, at Montoire, two days later. In between, Adolf Hitler met Francisco Franco for the first and only time.

Hitler's powerful seventeen-car German train, *Führersonderzug 'Amerika'*, was the first to arrive at the railway station of Hendaye, half a kilometre north of the Franco-Spanish frontier, in good time for the Wednesday 3 p.m. encounter. Ian Kershaw says Hitler saw this meeting as 'purely exploratory': he wanted nothing to upset the active collaboration he aimed to get the next day from Pétain and Vichy France. Hitler had little to offer Franco. He and Ribbentrop paced the platform beside the red carpet that had been rolled out, talking about how to handle the agenda.

Franco's train, coming from San Sebastián through Irún, was eight minutes late, probably not the psychological gamesmanship that was later claimed but mere inefficiency. What was Franco bringing to the table? Access to the strategic fortress and Strait of Gibraltar, yes, but at the price of his insatiable appetite for aircraft, artillery, food, fuel, transport, training, weapons and ammunition of every size and calibre, and, of course, the longed-for French territory in North Africa.

Black-and-white German newsreel footage shows Franco's elderly train (once Alfonso XIII's) pulling into the station. *España* is painted on one carriage and there is a solemn man giving the fascist salute out of the window. The train stops just where the camera can catch the *Generalísimo* stepping down from the right and moving to greet the waiting *Führer* on the left. Franco is wearing a Spanish Legionario's *chapiri*, a greenish side-hat with a bobbing red tassel. He is sleek and tubby, grinning and gabbling as he eagerly shakes Hitler's hand. Between the two dictators, facing the camera, is Paul Schmidt, yet again the interpreter, with the glazed look of a man who does not quite understand what Franco is so effusively babbling. As we have seen, Spanish is not one of his principal languages and a Foreign Ministry official called Gross will do the actual interpreting in the meeting proper while Schmidt hovers in the background. There are ceremonial salutes and introductions, then the two booted and uniformed dictators walk down the platform past a line of German soldiers presenting arms, Hitler flapping his lazy wave and Franco straight-right-arming vigorously. Franco is shorter than Hitler, but much stouter, amply bulging his cummerbund. Spain may be starving, but the *Generalísimo* is certainly not. They climb up into the conference car of Hitler's train and hand hats to servants. The last shot is of slick, balding Franco as a blanket-like window blind is lowered.

The nine-hour dance of the dictators that ensued was 'nothing short of a fiasco' according to Elizabeth Wiskemann, and 'torture for both Franco and Hitler' according to Wayne H. Bowen. The British Hispanicist Paul Preston sees the idea that Franco outwitted Hitler at Hendaye as a central myth of post-war Francoist propaganda, also used by the Western Powers to justify their acceptance of Franco's regime as part of their Cold War anti-Communist front.

No exact account of what happened on 23 October 1940 exists. The English version of the German Foreign Office record in the US government's 1946 book *The Spanish Government and the Axis* ends abruptly: 'The record of this conversation is incomplete.' Serrano Suñer said nothing about the meeting in his 1947 book *Entre Hendaya y Gibraltar*. The Spanish interpreter's account only appeared in the 1980s.

What follows is put together from the fragmentary accounts that exist. There were seven people present: Hitler and Ribbentrop, with Gross the interpreter plus Schmidt in the background, and Franco and Serrano with their interpreter, a Spanish aristocrat, Luis Alvarez de Estrada y Luque, Baron de las Torres.* Hitler and Franco spoke only their own languages although Ribbentrop and Serrano could both talk in French. The translation method used was 'full consecutive interpretation', in which an entire speech is given by one side without interruption and then the other side's interpreter translates it all from his notes taken during the speech.

Hitler began with a glowing account of German victories. 'England is already decisively beaten,' Schmidt recalled him saying, 'only she is not yet prepared to admit the fact.' Then came the key word – Gibraltar. If the English lost it they could be excluded from the

---

* Jimmy Burns suggests that the Baron de las Torres might have been 'Agent T', the prominent member of the Falangist 'old guard' whom Alan Hillgarth was paying five thousand pesetas a month for intelligence, including the very earliest report of what went on at Hendaye. Ángel Viñas considers him an unlikely candidate for the role.

Vulnerable fortress in wartime. Every day, Gibraltar allowed up to ten thousand Spanish workers over the frontier and across the airfield into the British colony. Among them were enemy agents bent on mischief, and good security foiled dozens of sabotage attempts.

The Rock of Gibraltar, a distinctive massif of Jurassic limestone, seen from the western beach at La Línea in Spain.

Exiled emperor among the journalists at the Rock Hotel, Gibraltar, 30 May 1936. From left to right, the Ethiopians visible are Lij Asfaw Kebede, Crown Prince Asfa Wossen, H.I.M. Haile Selassie I and Ras Kassa Hailu.

Fascist dictators (1). Spanish *Caudillo* Francisco Franco meets German *Führer* Adolf Hitler at Hendaye railway station, 23 October 1940. The interpreter is Paul Schmidt; the other man is the Spanish ambassador to Berlin, Eugenio Espinosa de los Monteros.

Fascist dictators (2). *Generalísimo* Franco encountering Italian *Duce* Benito Mussolini at Bordighera, 12 February 1941. On the left is the Spanish Foreign Minister, Ramón Serrano Suñer.

Democratic warlord. British Prime Minister Winston Churchill greeting well-wishers with a V-for-Victory sign. With him is his loyal wife Clementine.

Bloody war at sea. On 3 July 1940, a Royal Navy squadron from Gibraltar bombarded the French fleet at Mers-el-Kébir in Algeria to stop their warships falling into enemy hands, killing thousands of *matelots* who had been allies days earlier.

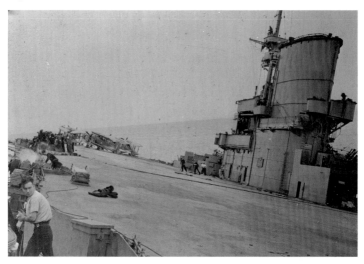

The British aircraft-carrier HMS *Ark Royal* listing heavily to port after being torpedoed by a German U-boat on 13 November 1941. The Ark finally sank twenty-five miles from Gibraltar.

New broom at Government House. Viscount John Gort VC takes over from Sir Clive Liddell as Governor of Gibraltar, 14 May 1941. Between them is Admiral James Somerville RN, commander of Force H.

LEFT Helen Hiett, the enterprising young US journalist who won a prize for reporting two bombing attacks on Gibraltar in July 1940.

RIGHT General Noel Mason-Macfarlane, second-in-command of British forces in Gibraltar July 1940–May 1941 and Governor of Gibraltar from May 1942–February 1944.

LEFT Evacuated to London during the Blitz, the fifteen-year-old Gibraltarian Lourdes Pitaluga, later Galliano, served as a St John Ambulance Brigade cadet.

RIGHT Lionel Crabb led the counter-sabotage submarine divers in wartime Gibraltar. In April 1956, he disappeared in Portsmouth harbour on an underwater mission for MI6, examining a new Russian warship.

The USA's first major combat experience of WW2 was Operation *Torch*, the invasion of Northwest Africa in November 1942. General Dwight D. Eisenhower's HQ was in Gibraltar, while General George S. Patton led the attack on Casablanca.

LEFT Talia Larios, the Marquesa de Povar, talking to Spanish military engineer General Pedro Jevenois. MI5 kept an keen eye on her activities.

RIGHT Krishna Khubchand Daswani, the first Indian child born in Gibraltar, with Barsati Karya, the family cook who saved his life at sea.

LEFT John Burgess Wilson, better known as Anthony Burgess, married Lynne Jones on 22 January 1942. Burgess served three years in wartime Gibraltar.

RIGHT David Scherr married Mollie Spencer in Gibraltar on 25 August 1945. The DSO, Philip Kirby-Green, gave the bride away; Billy Bulman was best man.

Mediterranean and Africa. According to Schmidt, Hitler proposed an immediate treaty under which Franco would come into the war in January 1941. The attack on Gibraltar would begin then, spearheaded by the special forces who took Fort Eben Emael. 'Hitler, there and then, offered Gibraltar to Spain and, somewhat more vaguely, colonial territories in Africa also.'

Talking to Leon Goldensohn during the Nuremberg trials of 1945–6, Schmidt added:

'It was our idea to conquer Gibraltar. Special troops were being trained in fortress warfare . . . with a view to an assault on Gibraltar. Of course, it was necessary to get Franco's consent . . . The meeting didn't go well at all. In the first place, Franco was hesitating, uncertain; he is of weak character. He obviously played for time. We wanted to precipitate matters as usual. We thought that getting Franco's consent for the attack on Gibraltar would be a matter of one afternoon . . . but it wasn't. Hitler and Franco separated without achieving anything.'

Schmidt described Franco sitting huddled up in his chair, saying nothing until it was his turn, then wriggling down the usual channels. Spain needed thousands of tons of wheat. Could Germany deliver? Spain needed modern armaments. How could Spain ensure the Canary Islands would not be lost? As a matter of national pride, Franco insisted that only Spanish soldiers could take Gibraltar. Great Britain was not defeated yet but would carry on the fight from Canada, with US support. All this familiar complaint and negativity, uttered in a 'monotonous sing-song reminiscent of the muezzin calling the faithful to prayer', infuriated Hitler, who at one point got up saying there was no point in continuing, but then sat down again to try and win Franco over. Finally Franco said he was ready to conclude a treaty, but the content was so hedged about with reservations and demands that it really did not amount to anything at all.

The meeting was adjourned. Ribbentrop and Serrano Suñer (who did not like each other at all and whose relationship now worsened) continued the quarrel in another coach. Then there was a dinner in

Hitler's banqueting coach and the two dictators spent another couple of hours disagreeing and misunderstanding each other before parting in the early hours. Franco had promised to come into the war – at a time of his own choosing. Hitler had promised to satisfy Spain's demands – if he could square it with Vichy. Hitler muttered as he left, '*Mit diesem Kerle ist nichts zu machen*' ('There's nothing to be done with this chap'), and Franco whispered to Serrano, 'These people are intolerable.'

As his rain-slicked old train jerked out of its inertia, Franco nearly fell heavily off the step onto the platform. Back at the Aiete Palace, he and Serrano haggled over the details of the draft Secret Protocol which von Stohrer had prepared, with Ribbentrop sending it straight back to his Spanish counterpart for revision like an angry schoolmaster. Schmidt and Ribbentrop then had to drive furiously to make a plane from Bordeaux to Tours to catch up with Hitler's train, Ribbentrop cursing the 'Jesuit' Serrano and the 'ungrateful coward' Franco 'who owes us everything', as they raced through the French countryside.

The final document, the Secret Protocol of Hendaye, completed later but backdated to 23 October 1940, contained six articles agreed not just by the German and Spanish governments but also by the Italian. When Hitler met Mussolini in Florence on 28 October, Hitler remarked that he 'would prefer to have three or four teeth taken out' rather than go through a nine-hour conversation with Franco again.

The main points of the Secret Protocol were that Spain declared her accession to the Treaty of Friendship and Alliance between Italy and Germany ('the Pact of Steel') of 22 May 1939. Spain also declared her readiness to accede to the Tripartite Pact of Germany, Italy and Japan at a later date agreed by all four powers. Spain would intervene in the war against Britain, once the Axis Powers had provided military support and economic aid.

5. In addition to the reincorporation of Gibraltar into Spain, the Axis Powers state that in principle they are ready to see . . . that Spain receives territories

in Africa to the same extent that France can be compensated, by assigning to the latter other territories of equal value in Africa ...

6. The present Protocol shall be strictly secret, and those present undertake to preserve its strict secrecy, unless by common agreement they decide to publish it.

After the bad-tempered wrangling with Franco, Hitler was curiously passive in his meeting with Marshal Pétain the following day, Thursday 24 October, at Montoire-sur-le-Loir. Pétain said he had always thought the war was a tragic folly. Sitting erect and smart in his uniform, the white-haired old soldier said he wished, in general, to collaborate with Germany, but he would have to consult his government as to the details. Legally, the National Assembly would have to meet and vote before Vichy could commit to any military action against Britain. France wanted 'the least onerous peace'. Pétain hoped the nearly two million French prisoners of war could soon return to their families. Nothing of substance was achieved.

German military planning to take Gibraltar continued to be refined at several conferences held by General Halder in early November. Admiral Canaris attended one on 2 November, bringing the latest reports from Algeciras. New photos, maps and sketches of the Rock (obtained with Spanish help) were given to the Operations Section. On 4 November, Walther von Brauchitsch confirmed that Walter von Reichenau of the 6th Army would be in charge, with XXXIX Corps protecting the flank of General Kübler's attack on Gibraltar, and 16th Motorised Infantry Division, 16th Armoured Division and SS *Totenkopf* moving into positions across Spain to thwart any British thrust from Portugal. On 6 November General Wagner and Colonel Weinknecht issued the logistical orders – all troops to carry four or five days of fuel and supplies. The next day, Göring and Richthofen discussed the contribution of the Luftwaffe's VIII Air Corps to the attack. They would provide some eight hundred aircraft including two dive-bomber wings, one fighter wing, various reconnaissance and artillery spotter planes, and three thousand Luftwaffe vehicles transporting three heavy and three light anti-aircraft batteries.

On 9 November 1940, the code-name Operation *Felix* was issued for the attack on Gibraltar. Three days later, Hitler issued *Führer* Directive No. 18 about German intervention in Iberia. Gibraltar was to be captured, the strait closed, and the English driven out of the western Mediterranean.

Führerweisung 18 laid out a four-phase assault on Gibraltar. Reconnaissance, intelligence, planning, training, supplies and other preparations were already busily under way; Phase II would be a well-timed air attack by two Ju 88 bomber wings, carried out on the British forces in Gibraltar harbour, at the same time as operational units crossed the frontier from France into Spain. In Phase III, two German infantry regiments would attack and seize Gibraltar while other armed forces stood ready to block any British counter-attack from Portugal. In Phase IV, the Spaniards would be assisted to close the Strait of Gibraltar, if necessary with German support in Morocco.

Hitler stressed that German land and air forces had to be strong enough to capture the Rock without any Spanish contribution, and have the spare capacity to help the Spanish if the British attempted landings elsewhere along the coast. Dive-bombers would be used and there had to be enough 88 mm anti-aircraft artillery 'to allow them to engage targets on the ground also'. Submarines were to attack the British Gibraltar naval squadron, particularly when it left harbour after the attack. Admiral Raeder and Field Marshal Göring would work out the best ways of helping the Spanish defend the Canary Islands and of occupying Portugal's Cape Verde Islands. The pros and cons of seizing Madeira and the Azores had also to be considered and submitted as soon as possible.

Even though the Mediterranean was 'their' sea, there was no suggestion of any Italian involvement in the attack on the Rock. The Axis members were not fighting together, but pursuing parallel wars. Mussolini's armies were now bogged down in Egypt, failing to reach the Suez Canal, and were also being thrashed in Albania and Greece. During the night of 11/12 November 1940, a daring attack by Fleet Air Arm Swordfish torpedo bombers flying from the British aircraft carrier HMS *Illustrious* crippled three Italian battleships at anchor in Taranto. Admiral Cunningham wrote: 'In a total flying time of about six and a half hours – carrier to carrier – twenty aircraft inflicted more damage on the Italian fleet than was inflicted on the German High Sea Fleet in the daylight action at the Battle of Jutland.' From fifty feet above the water the biplane *Stringbags* dropped torpedoes that had been fitted with newly designed Duplex magnetic firing pistols. These allowed the torpedoes (often called 'kippers') to pass right under the Italians' shallow torpedo nets and then explode beneath the battleships, triggered by the strong magnetic signal of their steel hulls.

The coup at Taranto was made possible by US help. An American-supplied Glenn Martin 167 photo-reconnaissance plane, flying from Malta, first located the battleships for British Naval Intelligence. But Taranto eventually blew back on the Americans. Imperial Japanese naval and military attachés came to Italy to study the damage inflicted by this new technique of war. Told in detail about the action, Lieutenant Commander Minoru Genda went home from London to build a torpedo-dropping range in a Japanese inland sea, and started practising. When it came, on 'a day that will live in infamy', Sunday 7 December 1941, the Japanese surprise attack on Pearl Harbor would be a copy of the British raid on Taranto.

On the morning of Friday 14 November 1940, two days after Führer Directive 18 was issued, Baron von Stohrer brought a letter from Ribbentrop to Serrano Suñer in Madrid, inviting him to meet Hitler at Berchtesgaden on Monday for important talks.

'May I say yes?' Stohrer pressed him.

'No, not just yet,' said Serrano. 'Maybe this afternoon.'

As soon as the German ambassador left, Serrano hurried to the Pardo Palace.

'What do they want?' asked Franco, nervously.

Both men knew what the Germans wanted. At first they thought about inventing excuses for not going to the meeting. Then they changed tack, thinking if the Germans really were determined to take Gibraltar, they would just drive through Spain without permission. Only by going to the meeting could they possibly be headed off. Serrano asked General Juan Vigón, the Minister of Air, General José Varela, the Minister of the Army, and Admiral Salvador Moreno, the Minister of Marine, to a brief meeting with him and Franco. All agreed that a weakened Spain could not and should not take part in the war. (Varela was the only one who was actually being bribed by the British to adopt that view.) The difficulty ahead was how to finesse neutrality without bringing down German wrath on their heads. 'Might it be better not to go to the meeting?' someone suggested. 'If we don't face him in Bavaria,' said the Foreign Minister, 'we might find him at Vitoria.'

Late on Tuesday afternoon, 18 November, Serrano arrived at Berchtesgaden railway station, accompanied by the interpreter Baron de las Torres and the Falangist classical philologist Antonio Tovar. After a night in the hotel, they had to get up early the next morning because Ribbentrop wanted to show off his hunting lodge near Fuschl. In autumnal Salzburg they met Ciano's team from Italy. Ribbentrop served a poor lunch of spaghetti and crêpes, which severely disappointed the Italians, and then they drove another seventy kilometres to Hitler's retreat in the Bavarian Alps.

The Berghof was built on a hillside. A long esplanade led up to the large chalet, on whose steps Hitler had often been photographed meeting the likes of David Lloyd George, the late Neville Chamberlain (he had died on 9 November), and other famous fraternisers including the Windsors. The three Spaniards went up the steep stairs. Almost before they could get their breath back the conference started in a large room on the second floor. There was no small talk. Hitler said the current situation demanded rapid action in order to end the war and to stop more bloodshed.

'It is vital to close off the Mediterranean completely. In the west, the strait of Gibraltar must be closed swiftly, and we shall attack Suez in the east. Sealing the western strait is Spain's honour and duty, as is the defence of the Canary Islands . . .' Hitler added: 'I have decided to attack Gibraltar. The operation is planned in detail. We are ready to start and we must begin. All we have to fix now is the date.'

In his *Memorias*, Serrano Suñer pauses at this moment on 19 November 1940 to ask the reader to sympathise with what he and his two compatriots were experiencing. Adolf Hitler, the tyrant of Europe, was telling them the die was cast. Serrano now had to argue the toss. He pointed out that the Hendaye protocol did not say that Spain would enter the war when Germany decided, but only when Spain was capable of doing so. The harvest had failed, the country was starving, an attack on Gibraltar now would mean that no wheat would cross the Atlantic, just as the Spanish were negotiating for four hundred thousand tons from Canada and Argentina. Spain really needed a million tons of wheat to be safe: that was the bald truth. Serrano urged Hitler to send economic experts to Spain to see how bad things were. At the moment, he added, Germany was not helping Spain with foodstuffs, or other supplies. Indeed, Franco had recently told him about the German Heinkel aircraft factory promised for Seville, contracted and paid for by Spain, but not yet delivered.

Hitler replied that Germany could not weaken herself for a non-belligerent. Once they were in the war, help would come. Look how Germany was now helping Italy, supplying a million tons of coal per year, five times more than in peacetime!

Serrano said that even though he had informed the British and American ambassadors in Madrid that the Franco–Hitler meeting at Hendaye had merely been an affirmation of friendship, they had still reacted by holding up the shipment of thirty thousand tons of wheat promised by the Red Cross. This was why Spain had to be so careful. Most Spaniards would prefer to get their bread in peacetime than at the cost of another war, so they had to stay neutral to get food and fuel from abroad. But the Spanish were not faltering in the cause. Serrano said: 'Man does not live by bread alone, I know. We put ideals first, we feel the call of destiny and the justice of our claims.'

According to Serrano, Hitler now became middle-class and fatherly: 'Let me speak to you as Spain's best friend, which I think I am. I don't want to insist. I can't say I share your point of view, but I do understand the difficulties you are going through. Let's say that Spain can have another month to get ready and decide. But believe me, the sooner the better.' Summer would be too hot for German soldiers in Gibraltar and Morocco.

But Spain had just come through a ruinous civil war, Serrano pointed out, and people were still suffering and starving. It was not right to ask them to sacrifice even more without some national prospect to sustain them.

'That dream is Gibraltar,' said Hitler.

Serrano stayed quiet.

As soon as Spain came into the war, Hitler continued, Gibraltar would be taken. The sooner Franco intervened, the less likely it was that the United States would enter the war.

Serrano said that when he went home, the American and British ambassadors in Madrid would question him about what had transpired in these talks at Berchtesgaden. He proposed to tell them that it was the Anglo-Americans' grudging attitude that was driving him into the arms of the Axis and forcing him to go to Hitler to beg for grain. This might help speed up transatlantic food deliveries.

This deception amused Hitler, but he came back to the main point. Would Spain allow German troops to pass through her territory to attack Gibraltar? Serrano now insisted, 'pathetically', as he realised in retrospect, on the friendship of their two countries, but said that speaking sincerely, as a true friend should, he did not think the idea could be entertained.

Curiously, Hitler did not insist. There was no bullying harangue or spittle-flecked rage. Hitler merely nodded, as though he understood. Serrano wondered if the *Führer* had grasped that Spanish pride would not allow it, that the people who had waged guerrilla warfare against Napoleon would do so once again.

In Serrano's account in *Memorias*, Hitler then ushered them into the large room next door which had a large table covered in charts and plans and other maps on the wall stuck with little flags indicating the positions of armies. General Jodl gave a brilliant military exposition on how the Rock would be retaken for Spain. Serrano, the representative of a supposedly grateful country, sat through it all. Finally, face to face with Hitler and Ribbentrop and their general staffs, he stood up to speak. He praised Nazi Germany's genius in the arts of war, but said he refused to go along with their plans. He regretted that Spain was in no condition to take part in the operation against Gibraltar, and would not accept the passage of foreign troops through its national territory.

This last scene is not described in his earlier autobiography, *Entre Hendaya y Gibraltar*, and smells strongly of *l'esprit de l'escalier* – polishing on the stairs, after leaving the party, what he wished he had said inside. As an old man, Serrano clung to this account, wondering if anyone else could have stood up to Hitler like that. Probably not, but it is impossible to know if it really did happen that way.

Hitler moved on to a meeting with the Italian Foreign Minister Ciano (where he urged that Mussolini put pressure on Franco) and the Spanish envoys slept in a Berchtesgaden hotel. Before they took the train the next day, there was another meeting with Joachim von Ribbentrop. This time Ribbentrop bent over backwards to try to be charming and to get the Spaniards on side, but Serrano only let him talk grandiose geostrategy, then ground him down with interminable talk of wheat, wheat and more wheat.

Serrano Suñer and Franco were appalled and frightened by the threat of what Hitler might be hiding from them: the possibility that German forces would march straight through Spain and take Gibraltar with no Spanish help at all. The planning, logistics and training were already far advanced in November 1940. The Abwehr, the army and the navy all had officers on detailed reconnaissance in Spain. Major Tzschöckl and Colonel Lamey of the engineers had closely examined the railway bridge at Irún, which was too weak in the middle to bear the enormous load of freight required for the advancing army, and they were exploring alternatives: the coast road, the other rail line through the Pyrenees from Pau to Canfranc, and, *in extremis*, laying new track and building another bridge across the Bidasoa near Behobie. Other engineers had gone over the entire route south through Spain checking roads and bridges.

In the French Jura mountains near Besançon, realistic all-arms military training was cracking on. The artillery were working with 'brisance' ammunition that could shatter caves and casemates. Limestone cliff faces like those in Gibraltar were located and prepared by engineers so the artillery could practise pin-pointing tiny targets like lookout posts and sally-ports at elevation. Troops rehearsed moving in close behind drumfire artillery barrages that cleared lanes for them amid clouds of dust, which necessitated hand radios for communication.

The details were impressive. The smokescreen battalions used wind machines to try and recreate the Rock's peculiar turbulence. Others fitted smoke-makers into the small assault boats that would cross the bay from La Línea and Algeciras. Chalky-fingered and edelweiss-badged mountain troops, festooned with ropes, carabiners and grappling hooks, bricked up the ground-floor doors and windows of their barracks to make every entrance and exit an athletic scramble. There was endless rehearsal of co-ordination and co-operation: artillery with aircraft, artillery with infantry, engineers with signals and riflemen, all preparing to fight squashed together over the no-man's-land of the peninsula's narrow sandy neck. By 27 November 1940, the assault forces were ready, but the order did not come.

On 5 December, Hitler, who had just written to Mussolini saying, 'If we encompass the fall of Gibraltar, we shall bolt the western door of the Mediterranean,' held a final briefing with his top generals – von Brauchitsch, Halder, Keitel and Jodl. There were two ways to launch the march on Gibraltar. If the troops assembled openly at the French frontier, there would be no element of surprise, but the operation would be over in twenty-five days. If stealth were employed and conspicuous movements avoided, it would take thirty-eight days. Hitler wanted Franco to agree to the shorter time-frame: begin the air attack on 10 January 1941, with the final infantry assault on 4 or 5 February.

The plan was that Richthofen's Ju 88 bombers would drive away the British fleet. A few days later Ju 87 dive-bombers would pick off remaining targets as the Abwehr commandos seized the gates and cleared the fence at Gibraltar's Four Corners. Then the artillery would start: over two hundred guns would fire twenty thousand rounds at the defences. Eighteen batteries would clear six lanes twenty-five metres wide along the neck of the peninsula and fire one hundred rounds at every one of the twenty-seven British casemates in the North Front rock face.

Halder jotted some notes: 'Every inch of English territory must be pulverised . . . Unlimited expenditure of ammunition . . .'

22

The Greatest Mistake

On 7 December 1940, Adolf Hitler, Brauchitsch, Jodl, Keitel, Warlimont, Richthofen, Reichenau and General Kübler gathered round a large table for the final presentation of Operation *Felix*. The 1st Mountain Division's intelligence *Oberst* Hans Roschmann had spent a week building a giant photogrammetric model of the Rock of Gibraltar at a scale of 1:1000, a thirteen-foot-long sculpture which showed every aspect of the defences: each barbette and bastion, every building, casemate, embrasure, gun emplacement, machine-gun nest, minefield, mortar point, platform, redoubt and tunnel mouth.

Meanwhile, on the same day, Admiral Wilhelm Canaris arrived in the Spanish capital, flying in from Bordeaux, where he had been briefing German military reconnaissance teams who were about to go into Spain in plain clothes. Hitler had sent him to Madrid because he thought at the moment of maximum pressure the white-haired old Spanish hand was the very best man to persuade General Franco to join the war. Spain seemed to be moving towards the Germans: the regime had just allowed German oil tankers to moor discreetly by night in out-of-the-way bays on the north Spanish coast in order to refuel German destroyers from the Atlantic, but this was not yet open alliance.

Admiral Canaris, who had been deeply involved in Operation *Felix*'s intelligence and planning, would have loved to take Gibraltar from the British. How often, on espionage missions to Algeciras, had he stared across at the Rock, eating paella in the dining-room of the Reina Cristina Hotel, so accommodatingly run by the Austrian Hans Lieb? In his heart of hearts, however, the Hispanophile German spymaster knew that Spain's best interest did not lie in joining the war that had engulfed Europe. Some of Canaris's biographers believe that the wily admiral worked hard to keep Spain out of the conflict, partly so he had a neutral bolt-hole to escape to. The Spain he loved was already war-wrecked and wretched: in Madrid, he had seen children and cripples begging in the street, queues at the Auxilio Social soup kitchens and people rootling through the embassy dustbins to gobble scraps from the diplomats' garbage. Another war would not make this better.

At 7.30 p.m. on 7 December 1940, Canaris, accompanied by his two Abwehr aides and with General Juan Vigón, went to see *Generalísimo* Franco. To protect his own position with Hitler, Canaris made absolutely sure that Vigón took careful official notes, which were then sent to the German Embassy. On 12 December, Ambassador von Stohrer cabled the translation of General Vigón's notes to Berlin.

Admiral Canaris told Franco that the *Führer* wanted his troops to march into Spain on 10 January 1941 and finish the Gibraltar business in early February. As soon as the march started, the doors of the German granaries would swing open.

Franco told Canaris point-blank that 10 January was impossible, and then rolled out the old arguments. Certainly Gibraltar would be taken quickly, but then Spanish Guinea or one of the Canary Islands would be taken in return. Britain's Royal Navy was still a threat. The loss of Gibraltar could be a pretext for Britain or the USA to seize the Portuguese islands in the Atlantic. Spain was indeed trying to improve defences in its own islands and artillery positions in the Strait of Gibraltar, but everything was as yet unfinished. However, that was not his main reason for delaying, which was, of course, that Spain was still short of that million tons of grain. If Spain joined the war and sea transport was cut off, life in many provinces would become unbearable and 'The islands would simply starve to death.' The *Generalísimo* and his government were doing their best to remedy the situation: buying grain from Canada and South America, purchasing locomotives and railway cars to improve their transport network, fitting gas generators to trucks to make up for petrol shortages, but a weak Spain would really only be a burden to Germany.

Admiral Canaris asked Franco to set another date and, unsurprisingly, he did not, but he did say that the admiral was very welcome to see the progress being made in the Strait of Gibraltar. The *Generalísimo* proudly showed Canaris pictures of the 1940 model 240 mm Placencia heavy trench mortar that Spanish engineers had built and were testing. He wanted all Hispano-German joint military studies to continue, discreetly. His most cordial greetings to the *Führer*. Canaris immediately cabled this prevarication to Berlin; Generals Jodl and Keitel had the task of passing on the message to Hitler, who was furious.

Admiral Canaris went back down to Algeciras to join his local Abwehr team – Carbe, Kautschke, Keller and Kühne. Their Spanish contact man, Lieutenant Colonel Eleuterio Sánchez Rubio, had rented a waterfront house in Algeciras, Villa Isabel, telling the Gibraltarian owner, Lionel Imossi, that General Muñoz Grandes wanted it for an officers' mess. It became a key German observation post for the next three years.

Canaris briefed the leader of the 1st Mountain Division who was going to spearhead the infantry assault. General Hubert Lanz, though a fine soldier, was appalled at what faced him once he was in La Línea and studying the Rock in solid reality – not a sketch or a map or a model, but the monstrous bluff of the North Front itself, with all the signs of vigorous tunnelling within it and defensive works going on night and day. Lanz thought a head-on attack from the north would be almost impossible. 'What about the eastern side?' he asked. 'Can we look at it from the sea?'

At least one of three Spanish army officers accompanied the German reconnaissance team at all times. Staff officer Lieutenant Colonel Ramón Pardo Suárez had come down with them from Irún, and in the Campo de Gibraltar they met up with Lieutenant Colonel Eleuterio Sánchez Rubio and Lieutenant Colonel Fernando Cárcer Disdier. Sánchez Rubio was the soldier who arrested the Republican mayor of Seville during an abortive military coup in 1932. SIS had clocked him as a member of the very right-wing Unión Militar Española in April

1936. Sánchez Rubio had hunted down 'Red' miners early in the civil war and then established good relations with the Germans stationed at San Roque. Cárcer was a regular who would go on to serve with the División Azul Española that Franco sent to help Hitler on the Eastern Front. To answer Lanz's question and survey the Rock from the sea, Pardo and Canaris arranged to go aboard a Spanish warship along with General Lanz and his chief gunner, General Walther Lucht, former Artillery Commander of the Condor Legion.

Early on 16 December the Spanish mine-layer *Júpiter* left Málaga and sailed south. Between 9 and 10 a.m. she was stationed less than two miles off the eastern side of the peninsula of Gibraltar. A small British spotter aircraft was circling overhead. It was like the old days for everyone: *Júpiter* had been in these waters before, having helped block the escape of the Republican destroyer *José Luis Diez* at the end of 1938, and Canaris had peered through a periscope here in his First World War U-boat. As the sun rose over the Mediterranean, it shone directly on the beaches of Sandy Bay and Catalan Bay and illuminated the slopes and cliffs above and behind them, enabling the Germans to study the landscape carefully through high-powered binoculars and scissor telescopes.

General Lanz thought that *La Caleta*, Catalan Bay, was the weak spot. There were new embrasures above the oil tanks at Sandy Bay, others covering the road from the northeast, but the few batteries overlooking the water catchment area on the eastern slopes could never survive the bombardments Lanz and Lucht intended to direct on them. Using 'dead' ground where they could not be spotted, Lanz reckoned that his experienced mountain troops could make the ascent in two hours. The Spanish officer Pardo reported:

The German general worked out a way to the top via a route starting in some sandy bits north of the village at Catalan Bay, beginning with a 60° slope, continuing with one of 70° for a few metres, then going up a level 10 cliff (easy to climb with grapnels) before going through a stretch of scrub in order to reach the pass south of Middle Hill Battery.

Canaris travelled back to Germany via Lisbon, where he told the Abwehr *Nest* (station) in the Portuguese capital about his abortive meeting with Franco on 7 December in which the latter had refused to co-operate with a German attack on Gibraltar. This was overheard by a lighthearted young Yugoslav playboy whom the Abwehr thought they were sending to England as a spy, code-named 'Ivan'. His real name was Dusan Popov and the news of the postponement of the German attack on Gibraltar was in fact a useful piece of information he intended to give his new masters in British Intelligence.

Popov, under his other, English code-name, 'Tricycle', was actually starting his career as a British double agent, under the new system supervised by the XX, 'Double-Cross' or Twenty Committee, which had its first formal weekly meeting on Thursday 2 January 1941. The committee was run by the Security Service and chaired by MI5's man, the *'capo* of the Christ Church Mafia', Oxford Professor J. C. Masterman. After Popov arrived in England, William Cavendish-Bentinck, Chairman of the Joint Intelligence Committee, closely questioned him about Canaris's visit to Madrid, concluding that Spain would not at that moment 'willingly enter the war on the Axis side'.

London's understanding of the Spanish position was enhanced by the arrival of Captain Alan Hillgarth in early January 1941. The naval attaché from Madrid, already appreciated by Churchill, mounted a formidable charm offensive on the intelligence community. His excellent ten-page memo to Hugh Dalton persuaded the political head of SOE not only to back off from looking for 'Reds' to support in Spain, but also to allow Hillgarth himself to supervise all activities by SOE's Iberia or H Section there.

At the start of 1941, Hillgarth thought, the game was moving beyond neutrality and the Spanish had to consider actual resistance if German invasion came. Their military contingency plans were already prepared: a series of delaying actions, coupled with sabotage, and a big stand if necessary on the Sierra Morena north of the Guadalquivir, with a final defensive position even further south covering Cádiz, Gibraltar and Málaga. Morocco would be the Spanish army's supply base for men and materials; there would be both regular army tactics to delay the invader and guerrilla sabotage behind the lines, 'cutting German communications and murdering Germans'.

Hillgarth had talked to the millionaire Juan March about the danger of a possible German thrust through Spain. 'If that happened (and Juan March was very firm about this) the Spanish government would resist, and British aid in guerrilla and denial operations would be acceptable.' But there could be no question of forestalling the Germans. 'If we come in five minutes before the German, we turn the Spaniards against us.' For now everything had to be covert and discreet.

Hillgarth discouraged any employment of Spaniards for special operations in Spain. 'There are very few Spaniards who do not talk, and even fewer who will not talk when beaten up . . . When Spaniards, of all kinds, get hold of money and arms or explosives they are at once tempted to think of their private feuds.' Hillgarth thought it better to have 'a cadre of useful personnel waiting in Portugal', to assist the expeditionary force that would be sent to help Spain if the Germans invaded. Hillgarth recommended that the military in Gibraltar should get in touch with the Spanish military HQ as soon as any Germans crossed the frontier.

The deceptions on both sides were always in danger of exposure. In late December 1940, three weeks after the Spanish government gave permission for German tankers to refuel German navy warships with 'utmost discretion' in remote Spanish bays, the German Embassy in Madrid somehow obtained the contents of a coded telegram from US Secretary of State Cordell Hull to the American ambassador in Madrid on 18 December which revealed that US President Roosevelt was authorising the American Red Cross shipment of grain and flour to Spain, 'in consideration of the political assurances given by the Spanish Chief of State to the US Embassy on 28 November'. When Stohrer challenged the Spanish Foreign Minister, demanding to know if Franco had promised the USA neutrality in return for bread, Serrano shrugged his shoulders and said they had only made 'vague, non-binding' statements about not changing current policies.

★

By now, Hitler had lost patience with Spain. On 11 December 1940, *der Führer* said that although reconnaissances already under way should continue, actual preparations for Operation *Felix* should cease. At the end of the month Hitler wrote a long letter to Benito Mussolini, saying that by refusing to co-operate with the Axis, Franco was making 'the greatest mistake of his life'. Hitler did not yet see that by not pressing onwards past Franco's hesitations he too was making one of his greatest mistakes. By the time he wrote to Mussolini, the action was already in the past tense.

I regret [Franco's hesitation], for we had made all the preparations for crossing the Spanish border on January 10 and attacking Gibraltar at the beginning of February. In my opinion the attack would have led to success in a relatively short time. The troops for this were excellently selected and trained, and the weapons were especially designated and readied for the purpose . . . I am very sad about this decision of Franco's which does not take account of the help which we – you, Duce, and I – once gave him in his hour of need. I have only a faint hope left that possibly at the last minute he will become aware of the catastrophic nature of his own actions . . .

Yet on 9 January 1941, Hitler once again told a conference of German military leaders that 'Although it seems scarcely promising, we shall try again to induce Spain to enter the war.' Time was now pressing: just before Christmas 1940, Hitler had issued his War Directive No. 21, Operation *Barbarossa*, 'to crush Soviet Russia in a quick campaign'. The troops currently committed to Spain would need to be deployed east in the summer of 1941, so this was their last chance to get the seizure of Gibraltar out of the way. After the meeting, Ribbentrop summoned Stohrer from Madrid to Salzburg and gave him detailed, strict instructions on what to say to Franco. On 20 January 1941, the German ambassador delivered 'with ruthless candour' his sternest *démarche* yet to the *Generalísimo*. There was a forty-eight-hour deadline to commit to entering the war, or he faced the end of Nationalist Spain.

But at the same time, the German and Italian leadership were gathering at the Berghof. The war was altering course again. In the longer term Nazi Germany was going to attack Soviet Russia, but right now it was about to commit its tougher troops and leaders – von Rundstedt in the Balkans, Rommel in North Africa – to help Fascist Italy win the battles it was so signally losing in those theatres.

In return, Hitler urged Mussolini to appeal once again, in person, to the exasperating Franco, someone he considered 'not a sovereign but a subaltern in temperament', a man malignly influenced by Serrano and the sinister Catholic Church.

Mussolini said, 'I will speak, but I will not apply pressure.'

Hitler declared, 'I only ask that the German troops should be enabled to take Gibraltar.' Did he still really believe it was possible?

Count Ciano arranged for Franco and Mussolini to meet at Bordighera in Italy. Now it was Mussolini's turn to try and persuade the Spaniards. On 11 February 1941, Serrano and Franco crossed from Spain into France at Le Perthus, where Spanish Ambassador Lequerica was waiting to meet them. They travelled eastward through France in a seventeen-car convoy, escorted by Vichy's motorcycle outriders. A pleasant journey through towns like Arles where respectful crowds watched their passing was only marred by a group of Spanish exiles who shouted and raised clenched left fists. They reached the Ligurian Riviera at nightfall and met Mussolini the next day.

Ciano was away, so *Il Duce* held two conversations with Franco and Serrano on his own. Mussolini was looking a lot older. The Italian dictator emphasised Hitler's great personal sympathy for the Caudillo, great sympathy for Spain, but also his very great desire that Spain should join their military plans and allow German troops to pass through Gibraltar into Morocco and French North Africa.

Franco said the most important question was Gibraltar itself, an age-old problem that had to be solved, and began another disquisition on how well the Spanish were doing, siting big guns and heavy mortars around the peninsula. The Germans were wrong to think the stronghold could be taken by air attack from above: what was needed against the caves of the Rock was continuous mortar bombardment.

All these preparations Spain is making because she is absolutely convinced of the necessity of taking Gibraltar with her own resources . . . A few months ago, Admiral Canaris came to Spain to persuade the Spanish to allow German troops to pass through as far as Algeciras . . . Now, the Gibraltar operation is a *Spanish* operation, and we Spaniards will never allow other troops to replace us.

Then it was time to recite the usual shopping list. People were starving – the hundred thousand tons of grain on offer would only last twenty days. Coal and oil; ships and trains; seeds, manure, mules and tractors for the next harvest. And also, by the way, they wanted all their colonial aspirations in Africa met. *Il Duce* politely promised to inform *der Führer*.

On 13 February 1941, on the route home, Francisco Franco and Ramón Serrano Suñer met Marshal Philippe Pétain and his new heir apparent, Admiral Darlan, over a banquet in Montpellier. Pétain had known Franco from the Moroccan wars in 1925 and recommended the Spaniard for the highest French order, the *Légion d'honneur*; from March 1939 to May 1940, he had been the French ambassador in Madrid. Serrano says that Franco and Pétain talked about how not to irritate the Germans and how to keep the war away from the west. Pétain later told his *chef de cabinet* that Franco 'wanted me to support him with Hitler to prevent the passage of German troops through Spain . . . something which I cannot decently undertake'.

The US ambassador to Vichy, Admiral William Leahy, reported to President Roosevelt some time later that Marshal Pétain 'expects an early advance of German troops through Spain with the purpose of either taking Gibraltar or occupying some place on the coast from which the Straits can be controlled by gunfire . . .'

'But would the Germans have captured Gibraltar? The answer must surely be "Yes".'

In their magisterial 1995 study of the military fortress, *Strong as the Rock of Gibraltar*, Quentin Hughes and Athananassios Migos reckon that Hitler could have won the day. Had Reichenau, Kübler and Richthofen managed to assemble their military and aviation forces in the Campo at the end of 1940, 'it is difficult to see how the Germans could have failed to swamp the defences.'

At the end of his life, Adolf Hitler himself also decided that this was the moment when he had taken the wrong path and lost the war. His conclusion? 'We ought to have attacked Gibraltar in the summer of 1940, immediately after the defeat of France.'

Field Marshal Hermann Göring agreed. In June 1945, by then a prisoner lying on his iron bedstead in a flowered dressing gown, Göring told the British diplomat Ivone Kirkpatrick that Hitler's gravest mistake was the failure 'to march through Spain, with or without Franco's assent, [to] capture Gibraltar and spill into Africa. This could have very easily been done and it would have altered the whole course of the war.' A month later, on 25 July 1945, interviewed by Major Kenneth Hechler, a US army historian, Göring repeated the charge: 'The loss of Gibraltar might have induced England to sue for peace. Failure to carry out the plan was one of the major mistakes of the war.' He said the same again on 9 August 1945, to Lieutenant Commander R. W. B. Izzard of British Naval Intelligence, who reported that 'from Gibraltar the Germans would have occupied the Azores, the Cape Verde Islands and the Canary Islands by airborne invasion and would have established additional U-boat bases down the coast of Portugal and North Africa, particularly at Dakar . . . In [Göring's] opinion, the establishment of these bases would have led to the downfall of England.'

The historian Hugh Trevor-Roper (1914–2003) backs their conclusion. Like Hermann Göring, Ulrich von Manstein and others, he thought that the failure to take Gibraltar in 1940 was one of Hitler's greatest mistakes in the Second World War. As we have seen, Trevor-Roper was a wartime intelligence officer in the Radio Security Service and in SIS who studied the Abwehr traffic from Spain and Spanish

Morocco and was an expert on the whole German intelligence set-up. It is worth looking again at his May 1980 valedictory lecture as Regius Professor of History at Oxford, 'History and Imagination'.

History, said Trevor-Roper, was not just a march-past of the victorious, written by historians who were 'in general, great toadies of power'. Nor was history inevitable, predictable and logically deducible. It was alive at every moment, contingent on chance and human character. History is read backwards, with hindsight, but it is lived forwards, in ignorance. The good historian imagines and portrays what people were thinking at a time when the future was unknown and events were still surprising and accidental. Trevor-Roper looked at the crucial summer of 1940 when Hitler had already won the war in western Europe: 'Britain's refusal to accept defeat was illogical, unrealistic, absurd. If only Britain had recognised this, and given up the struggle, Hitler would have been . . . free to concentrate his forces against the last enemy and, by its defeat in a third Blitzkrieg, to establish his new empire.' He believed Hitler would have defeated Russia in 1941 if he had clinched the west by taking Gibraltar in 1940.

And how easily, in that year, the German victory in the West might . . . have been made final! . . . Had Franco agreed to allow an assault on Gibraltar, that assault – as the experiences of Crete and Singapore were to show – would probably have been successful. Then the Mediterranean sea would have been closed to Britain and a whole potential theatre of future war and victory would have been shut off.

This 'counter-factual' thought fascinated Trevor-Roper:

I cannot but think that if General Franco, at Hendaye on 23 October 1940, had effectively substituted one monosyllable for another – if instead of *No* he had said *Yes* – our world would have been quite different: the present, the future and the past would all have been changed. But once they had been changed, no one would have dwelt on that little episode. The German victory would then have been ascribed not to such trivial causes but to historical necessity.

23

Nosey Parker

An interesting observer of wartime Gibraltar was David James Scherr, who enlisted in the British army on 16 May 1940, three months short of his twenty-fifth birthday. He found himself square-bashing in a chemical warfare battalion of the Royal Engineers in Hampshire, but was too bright to stay long as gas-attack fodder.

David Scherr was a grammar-school boy from Walthamstow who had won scholarships and sailed through his Higher Certificates, before earning two university degrees in three years. Later he became a vigorous schoolmaster who spoke three languages and organised plays, debates and sports. He was an articulate, engagingly decent young man who taught Sunday school for the Congregationalists, had been one of Baden-Powell's scouts since he was thirteen and was now an assistant scoutmaster.

Somebody removed this cheerful paragon from the Sappers and pushed him towards the new corps established on 19 July 1940 by Army Order 112. The Intelligence Corps was re-founded because military intelligence in the Second World War could no longer remain informal and *ad hoc* as it had been from 1914 to 1929; it was now granted its own administration and depot, its own badges and insignia: a double Tudor rose framed by green leaves, soon mockingly described as 'a pansy resting on its laurels'.

The writer Norman Lewis served in the Intelligence Corps and later said its members were identifiable by their 'fierce and vague eyes' and 'the faint aroma of lunacy'. In his fantastical autobiography *Jackdaw Cake*, Lewis wrote: 'For centuries the meaning of the word "intelligence" had been changing, slowly assuming overtones of intellectuality it never originally possessed. Even the Army had fallen into the error of upgrading the mundane task of gathering information . . .'

David Scherr arrived in Winchester on 24 July, reporting to the teacher-training college that now housed the Field Security Other Ranks Wing. Exactly one month later, Private D. J. Scherr was transferred from the Sappers to the Intelligence Corps and, on passing the NCOs' course and surviving the alarming motorcycle tests, became a temporary unpaid lance corporal in No. 54 Field Security Section, which was soon to be sent to Gibraltar.

Field Security was a good billet for the quick-witted and worldly wise in the Second World War. Geoffrey Household and Norman Lewis, who served separately in different Field Security posts across the Levant, North Africa, Greece and Italy, both describe in their autobiographies how enterprising Field Security NCOs could take advantage of their curious status, somewhere between military police and intelligence officers. Most people were simply not sure what Field Security was, or what exactly its people were supposed to be doing.

'A Field Security Section', wrote Geoffrey Household, 'consisted of an officer, a sergeant-major and twelve NCOs. Its transport was a truck and thirteen motor-cycles; its armament fourteen pistols and a typewriter; its other lethal weapons, its comforts, its blankets and its furniture, when it had any, were whatever it could more or less legally acquire . . .' The primary duty of an FS section, Household further explained in *Against the Wind*, was to take precautions for the security of the division or corps to which it was attached – which meant discreetly supervising all civilians the formation dealt with. They also had to investigate leaks of information and guard against the curiosity of enemy intelligence. Household thought this was interesting work, because 'the section became the eyes, ears, languages and mobile reserve of I(b) . . .'*

---

* 'And here . . . is I or Intelligence. I is subdivided into I(a), which obtains information about the enemy, and I(b), which prevents the enemy obtaining information about us.' Compton Mackenzie, *Gallipoli Memories* (Cassell, 1929), pp. 46–7.

People in Field Security came from 'commerce, teaching, journalism, the law, the stock exchange: men of education with languages or experience which specially fitted them for the work. In those early days promotion from lance-corporal to lieutenant and then to captain could be very rapid . . .'

Norman Lewis thought that Field Security NCOs were regarded with suspicion, 'seen as knowing more than was good for them, of being too clever by half, potentially dangerous, and therefore to be kept under constant supervision' by a sporty officer and a reliable company sergeant major. In his biography of Lewis, *Semi-invisible Man*, Julian Evans describes Field Security Sections as 'half envied, half distrusted, virtually autonomous', and lists their duties as guarding wartime ports against looting and sabotage, inspecting vessels and aircraft, securing buildings, searching houses, rounding up suspects, arresting people, interrogating prisoners, escapers and refugees, vetting war brides, watching brothels and prostitutes, and trying to intercept Axis agents.

Mobilised on 18 September 1940, Scherr's No. 54 Field Security Section left Liverpool the next day in convoy OG 43, Outward to Gibraltar No. 43. A recent tragedy meant the section was a reconstituted one. The first 54 FSS party had embarked with hundreds of sappers, gunners and pioneers on a Rock-bound ship, *Mohamed Ali el-Kebir*, but they had been torpedoed by the German submarine *U-38* in the Western Approaches on 7 August, 230 miles west of Ireland's Bloody Foreland. The doomed transport ship was the same vessel that had evacuated the thousands of Gibraltarian civilians to Casablanca in May and June of that year. *Mohamed Ali el-Kebir*'s master, John Thomson, died with his ship, as did the ship's doctor, eight other merchant navy crewmen, four Royal Navy sailors and eighty-two British army soldiers, including two members of 54 FSS, Lance-Corporal William Young Brown and Lance-Corporal John Jack Antoine Sidney. Dozens of bodies from the ship eventually washed ashore in County Donegal.

Convoy OG 43, however, reached the Rock safely. Lieutenant P. S. Gubbins and Company Sergeant Major Allan led David Scherr and the rest of 54 FSS ashore in Gibraltar, where they were installed in College Lane with the Defence Security Officer, Major H. C. 'Tito' Medlam. A photograph of the thirteen of them in thick khaki battledress, blinking in the bright Gibraltar sunshine, shows Scherr at top left in the back row, 'looking dopey', as he wrote on the back of a copy of the picture. Everyone but Gubbins is clean-shaven, but the latter sports a little moustache and is wearing a tie. Sitting cross-legged in the front row, either side of Sims, are a pair of black-haired identical twins, Nelson and Bernard Fisher. Almost immediately, two of the best Spanish-speakers were peeled off from the unit to work in HM Dockyard, keeping their eyes and ears open for any suspicion of sabotage, subversion and espionage.

When David Scherr got to Gibraltar in October 1940 with the Field Security Section he became a foot-soldier of MI5. The Security Service, along with the representatives of GCCS, the signals intelligence organisation, were the only two of the nine wartime British secret services then active on the Rock. The DSO, Major Medlam, communicated regularly with B Division of MI5 in London and so represented the Imperial Security Service. The Field Security Section also had three score Gibraltar Security Police at their disposal. The DSO's office was next to the Gibraltar police station in Irish Town where they liaised with Inspector Gilbert, head of the CID, and had weekly meetings with the Staff Officer (Intelligence) RN and the GSO2 intelligence officers of the four infantry battalions.

The Defence Security Officer had the right of instant access to the governor. In Warren Tute's knowledgeable novel *The Rock*, the fictional wartime DSO, Atcheson Hobart, is almost his own master. 'He was responsible to the Governor as Defence Security Officer for certain parts of his duty, but in the main it was his headquarters in London with whom he dealt. He could come and go as he pleased. He had links in Tangier, Algeciras and Madrid . . .'

David Scherr would himself rise to become the DSO in Gibraltar, but that was in the future. In his first five-year posting on the

Rock, which lasted from October 1940 to October 1945, D. J. Scherr was transformed. He went from a lonely lance-corporal to a married major of thirty whom everyone knew and all but his enemies liked. He was just the man for Gibraltar – he had Jewish ancestry, a good sense of humour, leaned more to the left than the right, and was fluent in Spanish. In his first five-year stint in Gibraltar, he flourished as a writer. The long report he completed for MI5 in 1949, flatly entitled *The History of the Security Intelligence Department of the Defence Security Office Gibraltar 1939–1945*, is actually one of the liveliest and most informative pieces of Rock reportage to come out of the war. No one knew the place better.

Scherr's *History*, well illustrated with photographs, was more than a war diary. His commanding officer called it 'a factual and interesting survey of Gibraltar and its environs', and the first three chapters – 'Gibraltar and the Campo', 'The People of Gibraltar' and 'Franco's Spain' – are travel writing of zest and depth.

From the streets of La Linea, the Spaniard can look up at the North Front and see the Union Jack fluttering dark against the steady bright blue of the sky, more than thirteen hundred feet above the sea. With a sense of dramatic purpose and effect most unusual to the English temperament, the conquerors of Gibraltar have kept their flag flying up there at Rock Gun, the summit of the northern face of the Rock, since 25 July 1704. The Spaniard can also see the row of those dark blotches splattered across the grey limestone face of the Rock which reveal the embrasures opening out from Gibraltar's earliest tunnels, the Galleries designed in the seventeen-eighties by Sergeant Ince as a means of bringing flanking fire to bear on the besieging Spanish armies down below in the Neutral Ground. Against the skyline, and breaking the sharp downward plunge of the north-west angle of the Rock, he can see, too, the ponderous bulk of the Moorish Castle's Tower of Homage, built one thousand years before Ince's sappers started to hack their way through the limestone.

Scherr's travelogue surveyed the peninsula from the heights of the Upper Rock, panned over the Spanish hinterland and then zoomed in on one of the 'obvious bases for subversive activity against

Gibraltar', the frontier town that fastidious Sir Samuel Hoare had found 'sordid':

La Linea de la Concepción, though of recent growth, has a population (c. 70,000) more than three times that of Gibraltar . . . Some eight thousand people leave it daily to work on the Rock, returning at night. It is a depressing town built on sandy wastes, and degenerating in its outskirts into primitive huddles of one-roomed huts made of flattened-out petrol tins obtained by stealth from Gibraltar. [But] alongside these miserable huts are ornate and expensive villas built from the proceeds of tobacco-smuggling or ships' chandling or some other local industry . . .

La Linea is chiefly remarkable for its flies, its beggars, its pimps and touts galore, its large bullring, its football team (the Real Balompedica Linense, if you please), and an extraordinary number of bars and cafes. It is hardly an exaggeration to say that its chief industry is the organisation of teams of petty smugglers or *estraperlistas* to bring out of Gibraltar and into Spain quantities of foodstuffs, tobacco, medicines, wool, tyres and petrol, and in fact anything portable that can be bought more cheaply on the Rock than off it . . . Thus, during the war, enemy agents in Algeciras and La Linea were drinking English whisky, washing with English soap, smoking English cigarettes, and buying English tyres for their cars on the black market.

One of the advantages of being in Field Security was the pass that freed a man to go anywhere, in any dress, because authorised 'to wear plain clothes' or *'vestir de paisano'*. David Scherr went regularly to and fro across the Spanish frontier, enabled by his cream-coloured, bilingual military identity card – *cedula personal militar* – stamped '54 F.S.S. Gibraltar', and bearing his photograph, right index fingerprint, name, rank, number, signature and authorising officer's signature. Armed with his card, Scherr saw the seamy side of Spanish La Línea, whose brothel quarter was based on the straggling cobbled street known as Calle Gibraltar:

This district is a strident, garish hotch-potch of bars with flamboyant titles and cunning, unshaven barmen; sawdust, spittoons and music; cabarets crammed with dancing couples; heavily painted ladies croaking 'Come in

Johnny' from the other side of the iron *rejas* that cover the windows where they wait for customers; bedrooms littered with ramshackle furniture, aspidistras in pots, and religious pictures on the walls; ancient hags hobbling out of dark doorways, purveyors of vice and of lice; and a busy stream of barefoot children, blind beggars, wall-eyed guitarists, mules, Spanish soldiers, and sellers of lottery-tickets, prawns, sweetmeats, roast sparrows, tobacco, typewritten messages from the Holy Ghost (in English), and a variety of other curious commodities.

What about the natives of Gibraltar? Scherr wondered. Who were they? A Gibraltarian was any British subject born in Gibraltar, regardless of ethnic ancestry, and the population was therefore of mixed origins. To illustrate this, Scherr printed the programme of a Dockyard Police Institute concert containing twenty-six Gibraltarian surnames. Nine are Spanish, four Maltese, four Italian (probably Genoese), four English, two Scots, and one each Catalan, Portuguese and Moroccan Jewish.

Scherr noted that the Gibraltarian male was 'the butt of contemptuous humour'; today, the terms would be called racist. To the Englishman, he was a 'Rock Scorpion' or merely a 'Scorp'. To the Spaniard, he was a *chingongo*, from some African tribe, or more commonly a *llanito*. Scherr did not know the origin of this term but believed it to be a diminutive of 'Johnny', which Andaluces and Maltese thought every Englishman was called. In *The Yanito Dictionary*, the Gibraltarian historian Tito Vallejo Smith says there could be three spellings of the name – *llanito* (Spanish), *giannito* (Italian) or *johnnito* (English); he prefers 'Yanito', which has the virtue of distinctiveness and is easier for foreigners to pronounce correctly. He suggests that *llanito* derives from the days of the Barbary pirate attacks, when *gente alta*, high-class people, were afraid to settle on the Rock, but *gente llana*, common people, weren't. Hence the diminutive *llanito*, 'little commoner'.

'The ordinary Gibraltarian speaks English, if at all, only as a foreign language, and rarely uses it at home,' Scherr opined. He printed a letter of denunciation written by a Gibraltarian to the 'Cheafe of Polise' in June 1940: 'I have heard some conbercachion on wish they are dangers for the Scetuachion'. Scherr also warned that even though the Gibraltarians spoke an anglicised corruption of Andalusian Spanish, woe betide anyone who ever confused one of them with a Spaniard. The Gibraltarian would then insist, vociferously, on his British status: 'When talking with an Englishman, he will insist on talking what he thinks is English. Being more emotional and high-strung than the average Englishman, he is apt to overdo the flagwagging. At the same time, he has developed the Colonial's traditional dislike of the Englishman's traditional assumption of superiority.' This is perceptive. A modern Gibraltarian writer, novelist and historian, M. G. Sanchez, has commented on the experience of encountering English soldiers and sailors, 'nearly all of whom were aloof and high-handed when sober, and aggressively, shockingly insulting when drunk'. Just as George Orwell saw that patriotism had nothing to do with conservatism, so David Scherr was learning that Britishness was not at all the same thing as Englishness. As someone working in security, the paramount question for him was whether the British Fortress could trust the Gibraltarians. From the wartime evidence, Scherr estimated that there had been an absolute maximum of twenty-five rotten apples out of a barrel of seventeen thousand Gibraltarians. This meant only 0.15 per cent were unsound: 99.85 per cent were completely loyal. This remarkably high figure is consistent with Gibraltar's post-war referendums. Asked in 1967 if they wanted British or Spanish sovereignty, 99.64 per cent voted British. Asked in 2002 if they wanted Britain to share sovereignty with Spain, 98.48 per cent of the Gibraltarian electorate said 'No'. They saw themselves as British *and* European, however. In the 'Brexit' referendum of June 2016, 96 per cent of Gibraltarians voted for Remain.

Chapter 4 of Scherr's *History* is called 'The Spanish Invasion'. Every day, from 5.30 a.m., the wartime fortress opened its gates to between eight thousand and ten thousand Spanish workers. Hundreds came on the morning ferry from Algeciras to Waterport, and thousands from La Línea to the gate at Four Corners.

There was a tension here. The Rock's need for manpower – Spanish muscle for docks and tunnels – conflicted with the Rock's requirement for security. Actually, most of those entering Gibraltar wanted to smuggle luxuries *out*, but security worried about what dangers they might be bringing *in*.

Of course, not just anybody could enter in wartime. All Spanish workers had to have an identity carnet with their photograph and registration number, personal data and employment record, plus the special passes or permits needed for more restricted areas. Having shown their papers to the Gibraltar Security Police on entry, they could be searched by customs officers or soldiers detailed for the task who were looking for explosives, fuses and time pencils, possibly hidden in boxes, bottles, cases, cans, lunch-pails, lanterns, almost anything. Searches were a deterrent, keeping folk on their toes, but intelligence from informers helped most.

The compulsory ID card, with its duplicate held in an efficient filing system, was the best way of keeping tabs on the great shoal that flowed in and out of the Fortress. As Scherr observed, this was largely a negative process, recording black marks against a few offenders, but you could not know about the motives or loyalties of the vast majority, nor could you effectively police everything that these visitors saw or heard inside Gibraltar, all those bits of information that might be useful to an enemy, supplementing their continuous hostile visual observation from Spain. Where did you draw the line with people? The deeper frontiers of insular Gibraltar – frontiers of ancestry and history, the frontiers of heart and mind – were harder to chart than the line of the rusting border fence.

In wartime, the names of ships, their cargoes, their crews, their destinations, the identities and movements of soldiers being carried on board, were all supposed to be kept secret. When the writer Muriel Spark escaped from Rhodesia to England, the black-bearded 'black' propagandist Sefton Delmer interviewed her in the Political Warfare Executive offices on the eighth floor of Bush House, Aldwych WC2.

'Did you come in a convoy?' asked Delmer.

'I don't know,' I said, smiling a little.

It was an elementary test: we had all been warned 'not to know' about the movement of ships and troops, past and present. Great signs were plastered over the walls of public buildings: 'Careless Talk Costs Lives'.

Vigilant security was not easy. Donald Darling of SIS said that 'Gibraltar was the most loquacious place I had ever known and the manner in which the grape vine hummed was uncanny.' Sometimes only a deliberate provocation could sharpen people's awareness of the potential dangers.

Nick van der Bijl tells how two Field Security NCOs dressed up in Spanish workmen's overalls and, carrying fake ID cards made out to 'A. Hitler' and 'B. Mussolini' as well as their coils of wire and pliers, managed to get through the building's outer security right into the Gibraltar Fortress HQ in Line Wall Road, where, while shouting at each other in guttural Andaluz, they filched various documents from officers' desks. That was one lesson well learned.

David Scherr relates how three other Field Security NCOs got onto the Gibraltar airfield on April Fool's Day 1942 for a joke with a serious point.

Two were disguised as Spanish workmen. They were equipped with home-made identity cards, obviously false ... They were carrying a box of dummy bombs, a 100 foot tape measure, some tent-pegs and a couple of mallets. They acted a pantomime of measuring out a strip of grassland to be covered in tarmac, stretching from the administrative buildings out to the planes.

They spent an hour among the aircraft without being challenged or questioned, and left a dummy time-bomb under a tailplane.

In his early days in Field Security, Scherr got to know the Rock by mixing and mingling with soldiers and sailors, listening, observing, sometimes eavesdropping, keeping his eyes and ears open for any loose talk or breaches of security. 'I like to get around and see things for myself' is the first line of the very first article that Sergeant D. J. Scherr wrote in August 1941 for the sixth issue of the Gibraltar magazine *The Rock*. The twenty-page magazine, 'By the Troops, For the Troops', price threepence, had been started in March by a gunner from Cardiff called Reg Cudlipp, a sub-editor on the *News of the World* before the war. (The Cudlipp brothers had a genius for journalism: by 1953, Reg, Hugh and Percy Cudlipp were all editors of British national newspapers.)

'Roaming Round the Town' headlined the first of Scherr's regular columns, written under the appropriate byline 'N. Parker', soon to be revealed as 'Nosey Parker'. There is a rather rose-tinted visit to Gibraltar's Little Bay Rest Camp, where men could take three days' leave. Scherr describes 'men reading or playing table-tennis in the Recreation Hut; others throwing darts and drinking beer in the Canteen. They all thought the Camp grand. The Camp staff does all the work so there are no fatigues . . . The Camp meals are excellent. There are swimming-sports, films, concerts, dance-bands, sea-trips etc.'

Mason-MacFarlane later turned Governor's Cottage into another rest-camp, where Jimmy Jacques ran the cinema. Jacques told the pioneering historian of sexuality Emma Vickers:

We had 200 Army, 200 Air Force and 200 Navy come for a week where they needn't wash or needn't shave or needn't do anything and they had their food provided and they had films and entertainment from the Garrison Variety Company . . . The Rock was a terrible place to be on. There were so many people there and of course there was no outlet. They used to let the soldiers go out to La Linea to have a break but they mostly all went to the brothels there and they got diseases. Got syphilis or whatever. And that was stopped eventually. So it meant everybody was stuck on that place with very little to do except drink, basically quite a boring life really. That's why the entertainment was set up, for them to be a bit more happy and that.

Scherr's September 'Roaming Round the Town' column wrote up Mr William Edwards's forty-strong Gibraltar Symphony Orchestra, now looking for double basses, French horns, clarinets, tubas and bassoons – both instruments and players. His piece began in his favourite little bar on Main Street where he could get a *café con leche* for two pence or an *almendrita* (brandy and hot milk) for three pence.

The house begins to fill. In Main Street, beyond the barred window, I can see the heads of a hopeful group of soldiers waiting for the Emporium to close [and for the girls who worked there to come out]. The old dockyard worker at my table shows me the six latest photos of his daughter in London and promises me an introduction; the Navy and the Black Watch begin to sing, sometimes the same tune but more often in a spirit, I think, of friendly rivalry.

The future author of *The Cruel Sea*, then Lieutenant Commander Nicholas Monsarrat RNVR, ashore from his corvette, saw similar scenes at the Rock:

Gibraltar becomes a sort of Boom Town at night, the narrow streets crammed with Forces in white or khaki shorts. Standing, as I did, at a balcony window with a tallish glass of Tío Pepe sherry, one looks down on Main Street chockful of people, a parading stream eddying out at the corners and overflowing into shops and bars. The latter, luring customers with music and chorus-singing, do a roaring trade; and in the oddly-named shops everyone buys silk stockings and cosmetics and perfumes of considerable fame and rarity and suspicious abundance.

· The naval coder Charles Causley arrived in Gibraltar in autumn 1940. 'October (when it doesn't rain) is I think the best month in Gib: clear, crisp & a view for miles over the hills in Spain.' He found Main Street 'always a bedlam: a frieze of drunks and the competing bands of the bars, the taxi-men banging their car-doors (no horns were allowed in Gibraltar), and the clop-clop of the weary gharry horses.' Causley the young Cornishman, whose first poems were published in *The Rock* and who took part in plays and concerts, kept observant diaries.

By the time David Scherr started writing his monthly column for *The Rock*, Garrison Variety Entertainments was working hard to keep up morale. Listlessness and depression had to be fought against hard. 'Nosey Parker' reviewed the shows, reporting on the development of Ince's Hall, half the year a cinema with a one-hour programme shown continuously from 4 to 10 p.m., and the other half a repertory theatre for variety acts and straight plays. An amateur dramatic society was being formed, as well as a full-time concert party with a twelve-man dance band to tour different venues on the Rock. Keeping the men lively and active was the thing, not slumping into torpor, drink and depression.

In a solidly male garrison, Spanish-speaking Scherr made a point of talking to the dancing girls who came across the frontier to entertain the soldiers and sailors in theatre shows, and he also reported the arrival of the first dozen WRNS or 'Wrens', led by Second Officer Langmaid, whose husband was a naval officer in Alexandria.

None of the others is married and their average age is just under twenty-three . . . About half are blondes and half brunettes, though one of the prettiest has auburn hair . . . Their first reaction on arrival here was to note that there was no black-out and that the shops were chock-full of silk stockings and cosmetics! They work hard, for long watches, and are allowed out only with an approved escort. (Still, there's no harm in your trying, Sgt Snooks!)

The reality of the womanless Rock was that a lot of men turned to other men for emotional comfort and sometimes for sexual release. Charles Causley, who was sensitive and artistic, but not gay, noted 'shocking homo-displays' among other sailors and was bothered by the behaviour of his 'hyper-sensuous' friend Frank, who

. . . likes to lie naked on the beach & imply in a Boy-Scoutish way, let's all be manly and do likewise which drives me from the complete emancipation from nakedness-fear of my destroyer days – where, bathing in a bucket, we were completely disinterestedly naked & unashamed – to a horror stricken Puritanism, trying to be 'decent' and 'manly' and it makes me sick with disgust . . . This is difficult to write about properly . . . What we all need is a pretty girl to talk to & take out to tea.

As Gore Vidal used to point out, in those days homosexual acts did not always equate with homosexual identity. Doing was not being. For a straight sailor, a friendly 'flip' or a 'wet-dream with a hand-start' did not necessarily make a man a 'poof'. Of course, homosexual acts were illegal then and punishable. En route from Dakar to Gibraltar, for example, Captain Evelyn Waugh RM had to defend in a court martial one of two marines accused of buggery. His man got eight months, his 'oppo' eleven. Yet Gibraltar had a certain reputation, even toleration. One of the Rock's nicknames was 'Brown Hatter's Castle', a queering of the title of A. J. Cronin's first novel and 1942 film, *Hatter's Castle*. Twenty-year-old Jimmy Jacques, who already knew he was gay, had only been in Gibraltar for a few hours when he was seduced by a physical training instructor in the showers.

I had regular sex with him. He done special favours and put me on special jobs and things like that and of course it was very much against the law and if you were caught you were court-martialled and sent home. Well I had an affair with him until I was moved up to work with an entertainment group. They had a newspaper called The Rock magazine. Reg Cudlipp, one of the newspaper group executives came out there and they wanted to know whether anybody knew anything about films and projectors and so on and to cut a long story short, I was made to be in charge of seven or eight people, they sent projectors out to Gibraltar, and I used to go round the Rock every night showing films and to the navy and the air force . . .

Like many gay people, Jimmy Jacques had learned when young the art of the bluff, unconsciously developing techniques of dissimulation and concealment, so leading the double life that kept him safe until he could reveal himself to another he could trust. He told Emma

Vickers about the importance of discretion in those days when it was criminal to be 'out':

I mean there were lots of people who were gay in the army, and in the navy and in the air force as you can imagine and you just kept everything hushed up. You weren't able to, you know. Anything you did was illegal, sexually I'm talking about. No, all these things were clandestine. In Gibraltar, just off the town, there's Trafalgar cemetery and also a garden called the Alameda Gardens which is a kind of tropical garden in Gibraltar and that was the cruising place which was very, very dangerous because the Red Caps came round you know. You could cruise in the Alameda Gardens and meet sailors and soldiers . . . big long toilets there, Victorian toilets that ran right, very much like the ones that used to be in Hyde Park here and you could meet people in there you know, a lot of people in there.

Gibraltar was a small place where it was easy to feel trapped: 'cabined, cribbed, confined'. A lot of men felt lonely and bored, a mood made worse by the oppressive Levanters, when the easterly wind forms a muggy cloud over the Rock. One of Scherr's pieces in *The Rock* caught the melancholy.

When I feel moody and depressed, I like to climb up out of the steep crooked alleys till I am high above the town and there sit on a wall in the sunshine for an hour.

The Rock towers over my right shoulder and beneath me the flat roofs go cascading down to the sea. Past the harbour and the bay, sprinkled with shipping, lie the glittering towns of Spain, white and tantalising in the clear air, and beyond the towns rise the gaunt, grey-green hills.

There I squat, scowling at it all.

The thin wail of *flamenco* oozing up from a far away radio is interrupted by a harsh voice, the whimper of a dog, and the slapdash of bare feet in loose sandals on a stone roof.

He described a slatternly washerwoman called Mariana, scrubbing clothes in a tin bath and moaning about her hard life:

'My sister is a widow with six children, but they do not allow her into Gibraltar. They have put my young brother in prison for twelve years and my other brother for thirty years. Thirty years!'

There follows an unprintable Spanish oath. Suddenly, with fear in her tiny eyes, she looks round; then, reassured, spits freely into the suds and goes on scrubbing.

Seeing someone else's sadder life, David Scherr thought, was 'a grand cure for the blues'. It helped him to remember that although the Rock could feel like a prison to those confined on it, it was also a *zaguán*, a portal to freedom, an escape valve from the oppressions of Spain, and of all Europe under the jackboot.

24

On the Run

Sir Samuel Hoare estimated that some thirty thousand people of many nations were helped by British embassy and consular staff in Spain to escape from Nazified Europe in the Second World War. Many of them finally got out through Gibraltar. Between a quarter and a fifth of the thirty thousand were Allied servicemen, either escapers or evaders. An 'escaper' was someone who had been held prisoner, however briefly; an 'evader' was someone who had managed to avoid capture. Under international law, an 'evader' could be interned in a neutral country, but an 'escaper' was entitled to be repatriated.

Just before Christmas 1939, the War Office had founded the secret organisation called MI9 to assist all such British escapers and evaders. MI9 was, like SOE, a secret service that had emerged from a small section in the War Office called MI(R), Military Intelligence (Research), where ingenious officers like Jo Holland, Colin Gubbins and Gerald Templer worked. First MI9 consulted a lot of men who got away in the First World War. Penguin had just republished *The Escaping Club*, a 1921 classic by A. J. Evans, a pilot who had been captured by both the Germans and the Turks in the Great War. Its author was signed up to lecture for the new escape and evasion organisation and record the experiences of those who made it back from captivity or life on the run from the Germans. You could prepare well, be confident and motivated, Evans said, but luck was always paramount.

Major Norman Crockatt commanded MI9. It began in Room 424 of the Metropole Hotel in Northumberland Avenue, but ended up with two separate departments: MI19 for enemy prisoners and MI9 for British prisoners, escapers or evaders. Crockatt ran both, with the title DDMI (P/W) – Deputy Director Military Intelligence (Prisoners of War). The organisation grew to have a British headquarters at Beaconsfield in Buckinghamshire, and an interrogation centre for returnees on the second floor of the Great Central Hotel at Marylebone, as well as 'Room 900, War Office', which was actually inside Broadway Buildings, the HQ of SIS/MI6.

The Secret Intelligence Service/MI6 had been wary of getting involved with escapers and evaders after it got its fingers burned in the First World War over Edith Cavell. Miss Cavell was supposed to be running an intelligence-gathering service in Brussels under cover of her work as a nurse, but after she helped two hundred Allied servicemen to escape through the lines on her own initiative, she was arrested by the Germans and shot at dawn on 12 October 1915. For brutish Colonel Claude Dansey, Assistant Chief of the Secret Service, Cavell's noble sentiments merely imperilled her intelligence work.

The fall of France made MI6 change its attitude to MI9. With networks blown and links down, they needed fresh pathways to neutral Spain and Portugal. SIS wanted an overview of all covert and underground activities, so on 6 August 1940, 'C', Sir Stewart Menzies, Chief of the Secret Service, had a meeting with Norman Crockatt and 'offered to set up an escape line to run from Marseilles into Spain'.

The SIS officer Donald Darling was sent out to do the job. Darling was not a stereotypical pink, fair Englishman but burly and dark-haired, fluent in French and Spanish, and able to pass as a native of either country. In Madrid, Sir Samuel Hoare was rude and panicky, and forbade Darling to work in Spain or to deal with any 'enemies of the regime', so the SIS man returned to make his base in the Portuguese capital, Lisbon, where the ambassador Sir Walford Selby had greeted him warmly and said he would ask no questions. (Later, Hoare was effusively over-friendly when passing through Lisbon, but Darling disliked his insincerity and did not enjoy having his thigh touched by the smiling ambassador's grey cotton-gloved hands.)

Soon based in Portugal, Darling had a contact in Marseilles, a Scottish escaper called Captain Ian Garrow, as well as a boss in London who was another escaper, Captain James Langley. Now he had to create networks between Britain, Portugal and France and routes for escapers. He began using citizens of neutral countries who could move more easily as couriers. One of the most helpful was the pro-British Armenian millionaire Nubar Gulbenkian, who travelled on an Iranian passport.

As mentioned earlier, in June 1940 some Free Frenchmen brought a 270-foot French cargo vessel called *Le Rhin* into Gibraltar. This was later sailed to the UK where Commander Frank Slocum, who ran SIS's 'private navy', had it refitted as a 'Q-ship' or camouflaged merchantman named HMS *Fidelity*. The ship was able to change its identity and flags so it could appear either Spanish or Portuguese, and was used for clandestine sea transport in the western Mediterranean. On 20 April 1941, *Fidelity* returned to Gibraltar, quietly dropping the *Relator* party, nineteen officers and seven signallers specially recruited for SOE, before sailing up to the French Catalan coast to insert two agents near Perpignan, to link up with Spanish smugglers who regularly traversed the eastern Pyrenees. Then she was to pick up some Polish evaders at the port of Cerbère on 26 April 1941. The Vichy French police became suspicious, and a crewman who called himself Pat O'Leary and claimed to be French Canadian (in reality the Belgian doctor Albert Guérisse; see p. 200) was arrested and imprisoned. But he boldly escaped and managed to join Ian Garrow in Marseilles.

Garrow could not speak much French and badly needed Guérisse's help. The doctor said that, as he was an officer in the Royal Navy, he had to report back home for duty, but Garrow said he would ask the Admiralty to let him stay. It was an elaborate process. Garrow had to send a written message by hand of cross-border courier from Marseilles to the British Consulate at Barcelona, from where it went on to Madrid and Gibraltar, before reaching London. The answer to the question came back three weeks later, via the BBC French

Service, listened to quietly on a wireless set behind locked doors and closed windows. One evening, after the 9 p.m. news, a deep voice pronounced the agreed code-phrase: '*Adolphe doit rester*' ('Adolphe should stay').

And so Albert Guérisse began setting up a famous escape network under his pseudonym, the 'Pat O'Leary Line' or 'Pat Line', which ran escapers and evaders down from Belgium and northern France across to Catalan Spain and eventually to Gibraltar. Spanish anarchists and guerrillas, especially a group led by Francisco Ponzan Vidal, acted as guides and escorts. The going rate MI9 paid for smuggling a man over the Pyrenees was £40 for an officer, £20 for other ranks. But the price was well worth it because returned servicemen were valuable: a flier cost £10,000 to train, and a man's appearance back in the mess after having been shot down did wonders for squadron morale. Some men took months; the record for fastest 'home run' was eleven days from Belgium to Britain, travelling via Gibraltar.

British military personnel had first started reaching Spain in August 1940, mostly soldiers who had missed the boat at Dunkirk and had headed south out of German-occupied France into Vichy France to avoid capture. There were extraordinary stories. Three Highlanders from the 51st Division tramped all through France to Spain, speaking only Gaelic. When puzzled Germans gave them a world map to indicate where they had come from, the Scots pointed at Russia, then Germany's ally, and were allowed to go free. Anthony Quayle met two Yorkshiremen who spoke no foreign languages at all and yet had managed to walk through Europe: 'Folk were very kind. They hid us and they passed us on.'

Luck often ran out in Spain. While some were interned in Marseilles, Franco's police arrested many of those who crossed the Spanish border. A scrap of paper smuggled out from Figueras prison in northeast Spain saying there were British prisoners there, crammed thirty to a cell with one latrine-bucket and a six-inch window, alerted British diplomats and consular officers. Then a tug-of-war began with the Spanish authorities, behind whom lurked the Germans, Samuel Hoare thought, eager to seize more PoWs. Spanish treatment was brutal: Sergeant Jack Horsman of the Durham Light Infantry was almost blinded by the beatings he got. At Burgos, men were struck with rifle butts for not giving the Fascist salute.

Fifty British soldiers ended up in Miranda de Ebro, Franco's vile concentration camp for Republican prisoners of war, now containing, in addition, Polish, Belgian, French and Yugoslav inmates, as well as twenty German deserters. When British diplomats managed to negotiate the release of their citizens, they found them skinny, scabby, itching with lice, suffering from dysentery. They were taken to the chapel of the embassy in Madrid and then travelled down to Gibraltar, some hidden in the back of the regular food lorry, others escorted by Spanish detectives. After so much privation, Gib was paradise. 'Tinned sausages in real grease!' exclaimed Driver W. B. A. Gaze of the RAOC, who had run an ambulance helping the wounded left behind at Dunkirk. 'Bread, margarine and jam unlimited, and tea so strong with sugar and condensed milk the spoon would nearly stand alone.' Twenty-three-year-old Private Gordon Instone, an endlessly daring and resourceful escaper who had lost fifty pounds in weight behind the wire at Miranda de Ebro, ate fourteen sausages and six eggs to celebrate his arrival as a free man on British soil.

In the summer of 1941, another courageous Belgian, a twenty-four-year-old nurse known as Dédée, turned up in the British Consulate in Bilbao with a Scottish soldier and two Belgian officers in tow, men whom she said she had escorted from Brussels through Paris and occupied France to Bayonne, and then over the Basque end of the Pyrenees into Spain. SIS cynics like Claude Dansey thought this was utterly incredible: she had to be a German stooge. But Andrée de Jongh was nothing of the kind. She was the ever-reliable 'Postman' who personally escorted 118 people to safety through enemy territory along her escape route, *le Réseau Comète*, the Comet Line. This staunch young woman was brought up by her schoolmaster father Frédéric to revere Edith Cavell, and both father and daughter joined the Belgian resistance, determined to rid their beloved homeland of the invaders and occupiers. 'Don't thank us,' she once wrote; 'we had the joy of fighting, without striking a blow.'

These two Belgians forged secret pathways to freedom, but thousands of other ordinary people – men, women and children – helped along the road to Gibraltar, at risk of their own lives. There was constant danger of discovery by the police. Idle gossip was as dangerous as malicious tale-telling. A few traitors within the system, like the thieving British sergeant Harry Cole, men who befriended escapers and evaders and then betrayed them to the Germans for money, damaged but did not break the networks. One hundred and fifty-six members of the Comet Line were executed or died in German concentration camps for helping Allied servicemen get away. Among them was Dédée's father, shot by firing squad in March 1944. Dédée de Jongh herself was betrayed and captured in the French Basque country on her thirty-third trip. Although tortured, she stayed defiant, and survived Fresnes, Ravensbrück and Mauthausen concentration camps. After the war, she became a nurse in African leper colonies.

Poland had been violently dismembered between the totalitarian powers Nazi Germany and Soviet Russia, but the Polish resistance kept a secret state going underground at home, supporting the Polish government in exile, headed by the liberal, democratic-minded General Sikorski. The Poles had three intelligence services operating in neutral Portugal. There were nearly half a million Poles in France and their intelligence networks flourished in Marseilles, Toulouse, Clermont-Ferrand, Lyons, Limoges and Vichy itself. With the assistance of Jack Beevor of SOE (who called the Poles 'the most vivid and valiant of all our allies'), the Polish general Juliusz Kleeberg sent a small naval mission from Lisbon to Gibraltar in the spring of 1941 to help link up the international networks. Commander Trzaska-

Durski headed it, together with his best sailor, Lieutenant Marian Kadulski, operating under the name Mischa Krajewski.

With the help of SOE, Krajewski acquired a small, nine-ton fishing vessel, and in August 1941 rescued two dozen Polish servicemen who had been detained by the Vichy authorities at Casablanca, 190 nautical miles away in Morocco. This was the first of his many covert voyages from Gibraltar. People and weapons for resistance in enemy territory were being clandestinely moved around in tramp-ships and feluccas that could change their identity from Portuguese to Moroccan overnight.

On Krajewski's fourth trip, bad weather forced him into the Spanish port of Tarifa. The Pole pretended that he was a Gibraltarian fisherman and that the fifty-odd passengers on board his fishing smack *Dogfish* were all survivors of the torpedoed ship SS *Kirken*. He managed to get away with it and returned to Gibraltar in quiet triumph. Commendations and decorations followed. Krajewski made the Duke of Gloucester laugh at a Government House garden party in October 1941 by telling him that the Vichy camp commandant in Morocco boasted that hair would grow on his palms before any of his Polish prisoners managed to escape. In fact, Krajewski had got seventy-eight of his Poles away and back into Allied service, so the commandant must have had curls sprouting from his hands.

The Rock's traditional occupation of tobacco smuggling into Spain was taken over by SOE in 1941, on the initiative of an enterprising Anglo-Argentine called Peter Musson, one of the original officers sent out for Operation *Relator*, who had grown bored of waiting for the Germans to invade. This was how the scheme worked. The chief Gibraltarian smuggler, Jose Herrera Saavedra, and the legitimate Gibraltarian trader he bought his tobacco from, L. M. Serruya, were squared and protected. All other contraband tobacco seized by Customs or the Admiralty was added to their pot, free of charge, which made the smuggling business very profitable in pesetas for SOE. Herrera's fishing boats continued their night-time black-market trade, not only transporting the regular 112-pound canvas bales of the *picadura* tobacco leaf from Brazil and the Dominican Republic that Spaniards were gasping for, but also carrying to and from Spanish territory people that the secret services wanted infiltrated or exfiltrated discreetly. They included agents like 'Hollowshoes', real name Emilio Varas Canal, resisters, couriers and wireless operators, but never sundry escapers and evaders, in case they talked. A Spanish-speaking British SOE officer – often an Anglo-Argentine – always went along on the 'body line' trip with a couple of tough soldiers, ready to bluff or bribe their way out of trouble if the unexpected happened.

Tuesday 5 January 1942 was a red-letter day for MI9. First, Donald Darling, cover-named 'Sunday', arrived in Gibraltar from Lisbon to set up shop for escapers. Secondly, Lieutenant Airey Neave, who would soon become his MI9 colleague 'Saturday', walked out of imprisonment at Colditz Castle. The Old Etonian Neave was disguised as a German officer, *Oberleutnant* Schwartz, wearing a costume made by ingenious fellow prisoners. His *feldgrau* greatcoat was a slightly altered Dutch Home Army bluey-green issue that would pass at night, and his black peaked cap his own British service dress uniform cap carefully reshaped, re-covered, restitched and decorated by Squadron Leader Brian Paddon. His cap-badge and braided epaulettes were made of painted linoleum and his belt, revolver holster and leggings of cardboard. The authentic-looking metallic insignia – eagles, swastikas, stars and buttons, a 'Gott Mit Uns' belt buckle – were formed of painted wood or from lead taken from a prison lavatory pipe and poured into moulds carved by a Dutch craftsman. Neave managed to get to Switzerland and then made his way down to Gibraltar, where Darling debriefed him and put him on a ship to the UK. Neave was the first British officer in the Second World War to escape and make a 'home run'. In London, over lunch at Rules restaurant in Covent Garden, Jimmy Langley and Norman Crockatt recruited him for MI9, where Airey Neave duly took the cover name 'Saturday'.

Two days after he had arrived in Gibraltar, Donald Darling had his first customers, among them Sergeant Jack Newton, a 'tail-end Charlie' (rear gunner) in a Wellington bomber shot down over Aachen. Newton was the first RAF evader successfully brought down the Comet Line by Andrée de Jongh. He and his two companions were kept isolated at the end of the airstrip because Darling wanted no word of who had helped them, where they had been, the forged papers they carried, or any other secrets of the Comet Line to reach anyone who might tell the Abwehr agents in Algeciras. After five months on the run, Jack Newton worked his passage home from Gibraltar by manning the four Browning .303s at the stern of a Short Sunderland flying boat – after they had hosed the previous occupant's blood out of the turret.

Donald Darling sent a scrap of paper from hand to hand into France, with a message for 'Pat', alias Dr Albert Guérisse: 'Want to see you as soon as possible. Speak to no one. Cheri.' So 'Pat O'Leary' came back to Gibraltar, overland from France this time, going through the pass-the-parcel routine, handed on, moving through, finally being transported past the La Línea border guards in the boot of a Sunbeam Talbot motor car with its British Corps Diplomatique plates. The vehicle was driven by Michael Creswell (MI9 cover name 'Monday'), who worked closely with the Madrid Embassy's second secretary, Harry Hankey, getting refugees and escapers down to Gibraltar. Darling welcomed them at Fountain Ramp, behind the police station, and introduced them to his SIS boss, Lieutenant Colonel J. A. Codrington, commonly known as 'Fish Paste'. Three weeks later, one-armed Jimmy Langley from MI9 HQ flew in from London to join them. Gibraltar was being firmly established as the gateway to freedom.

Donald Darling later estimated that some three thousand escaping or evading aircrew came through Gibraltar. One of them was the Sumatran-born Dutch air ace Bram van der Stok, who had escaped from Holland and joined the RAF, where he was known as 'Bob'. Shot down over France in 1942, he was imprisoned in the German

PoW camp Stalag Luft III at Sagan and was one of the seventy-six Allied airmen who got out in the fabled 'Great Escape' of March 1944 (later turned into a famous Hollywood movie). After travelling through Holland, Belgium, France and Spain, Bob van der Stok reached Gibraltar on 8 July 1944, one of only three of 'the great escapers' to make a home run, safely out of enemy territory. (Two Norwegians managed to get to Sweden.) On the personal orders of Adolf Hitler, Himmler's Gestapo executed fifty recaptured escapers, including 'Big X', Squadron Leader Roger Bushell. The men they murdered were Australian, British, Canadian, French, Greek, New Zealander, Norwegian, Polish and South African.

Darling interrogated every escaper about who they had met and built up a card-indexed family tree of the helpers who made up the escape networks. He reckoned that two thousand people were actively aiding escape and evasion in Belgium and at least five thousand were regularly doing so in France, as well as unknown hundreds who gave food or shelter or clothing in spontaneous acts of altruism. As M. R. D. Foot and J. M. Langley, the historians of MI9, noted: 'They were of many nationalities, of all ages; of both sexes, of all classes; rich and poor, learned and plain, Christian and Jew, Marxist and mystic.' Ordinary people doing the extraordinary, risking their lives for strangers.

25

From the New World

Churchill wished to 'drag the Americans in', but netting and landing the big fish was not easy. Although President Roosevelt wanted to help 'the opponents of force', he was constrained from intervening by legislation: the Neutrality Act and the Johnson Debt-Default Act (permitting no loans to any country that had not paid back its First World War debts, which meant pretty much everywhere except Finland). Domestic politics also thwarted him. The US Congress was largely isolationist, embodying a tradition going back to Thomas Jefferson's desire 'not to intermeddle in word or deed' abroad and especially 'never to entangle ourselves in the broils of Europe'. When Roosevelt sent US marines to help occupy Iceland in July 1940 (to stop the Germans doing so first), he only got away with it on the grounds that Iceland and Greenland were part of 'the Western Hemisphere' – west of longitude 25 degrees – that the USA had pledged to defend under the long-standing Monroe Doctrine.

Standing for an unprecedented third term as US president in November 1940, Roosevelt could not afford to alarm the nation's parents, so he pledged: 'Your boys are not going to be sent into any foreign wars.' Once re-elected, however, his genius summoned up a homely metaphor for the kind of help that he wanted to provide. 'The best immediate defence of the United States is the success of Britain in defending itself, ' Roosevelt said in one of his folksy press conferences on 17 December 1940. But Uncle Sam would not be doling out US currency to the old imperialist power: 'Now, what I am trying to do is eliminate the dollar sign. That is something brand new in the thoughts of everyone in this room, I think – get rid of the silly, foolish old dollar sign.' Roosevelt was thinking of other kinds of practical help: 'Suppose my neighbour's house catches fire, and I have a length of garden hose . . .' Neighbourliness was as American as apple pie. An exchange of useful goods rather than cash on the barrel-head was made the basis of the USA's Lend-Lease deal with the UK, which only got on stream three months later when it had passed through the suspicious Congress and the Senate. It began with the swapping of fifty old US destroyers for nine forward US bases in British Empire territories in the Atlantic and Caribbean. Eventually the USA would provide sixty billion dollars' worth of arms and oil and goods from farm and factory, before President Truman stopped the whole thing on the day Japan surrendered, 15 August 1945.

Once safely elected president in the November 1940 poll, Roosevelt sent out three emissaries to report back to him personally on what was happening across the Atlantic. They were all on their travels around Christmas 1940 and New Year 1941. The soldier and lawyer Major General William J. Donovan undertook a sixteen-week trip around the Mediterranean; Roosevelt's special aide Harry L. Hopkins went to the UK for a month to see how the British people were coping, as well as meeting the king and queen, Winston Churchill, and other members of the British establishment; and the diplomat Robert Murphy was sent to French Africa for three weeks.

Bob Murphy was summoned back from Vichy by the US State Department in October 1940, and soon found himself in the White House, alone with President Roosevelt and some large maps of the French empire in North and West Africa. The president wanted Murphy to go and inspect the region and find out if the French colonies in Africa could be wooed into the war against the Nazis.

The month before, on 5 September 1940, Pétain had appointed seventy-two-year-old General Maxime Weygand as the top man in that empire, *le Délégué géneral du Gouvernement français en Afrique française à Alger*, and a month later made him commander-in-chief of all French forces in Africa. Weygand's power in a semi-independent North Africa intrigued the US president. It was true Weygand had been defeatist in the recent fall of France, but in the Great War he had been right-hand man to the great Ferdinand Foch, the commander-in-chief of the Allied armies, so he knew about coalition and co-operation. Surely a patriot like Weygand would not endure French subservience to Germany? Could he possibly be brought over to the Allied side? Murphy was urged to get close to him, maybe go to church with him (Murphy was Catholic) and study French imperialism. Roosevelt barely mentioned de Gaulle, except to say that his Dakar fiasco showed poor judgement.

'If you learn anything in Africa of special interest,' the president ended, 'send it to me. Don't bother going through State Department channels.'

Five days after the fall of Laval from power, Murphy finally got permission to fly to Algiers. Weygand's aide told him Churchill was wooing the general too, and that Weygand was away inspecting the West African port of Dakar. Murphy travelled for two more days to Dakar, arriving on 20 December 1940. He paid his respects to Weygand and their talks led to the Murphy–Weygand Agreement, in which the USA agreed to provide fuel and non-military goods to the civilian populations of French Africa, to be distributed by a dozen US vice consuls (who would also be covertly gathering useful information).

French officials held little back from the charming Murphy, fluent French-speaking representative of the neutral USA. He learned that the Belgian and Polish gold was going to be shipped back from Kayes to the Germans in Europe, but not the French ingots. He discovered that many Vichy French officers were pro-British because anti-German. He found General Weygand had been irritated and annoyed by British propaganda claims that he, the Vichy commander-in-chief, was going to take independent action against the Germans in Africa. Weygand believed that de Gaulle was behind all these stories in the newspapers, trying to alarm the Germans so they would force Vichy to push him out. De Gaulle was not a popular man among those who were running French Africa.

★

President Roosevelt's closest confidant, the frail, untidy, brilliant Harry Hopkins, flew by Pan Am Clipper to Lisbon in Portugal then BOAC to Poole Harbour in Dorset, where he landed on 9 January 1941. England was indubitably a war zone: his train reached Waterloo Station amid wailing sirens while behind it a blaze of incendiary bombs disrupted the lines to Clapham Junction. Searchlights swashed over barrage balloons tethered in the night sky above blacked-out London; from his room in Claridge's Hotel, Hopkins could hear the banging of the anti-aircraft guns in Hyde Park.

In his time in the UK, Hopkins gave people hope that the New World would indeed come to the rescue of the Old. In Glasgow, having seen Lord Halifax off to the USA as the new British ambassador, Hopkins quoted the wonderful line in the Bible's Book of Ruth: 'Whither thou goest, I will go . . . even to the end.' And Hopkins was making lists of some of the hardware the British needed: destroyers; cargo ships; Catalina patrol bombers; B-17 bombers; engines for Lockheed planes; propellers for Curtiss Tomahawks; twenty million rounds of .50 calibre ammunition and hundreds more .50 calibre machine-gun barrels; 250,000 Enfield rifles with fifty million rounds of ammunition; tools for manufacturing .303 bullets, and so on.

As a sign of 'bipartisanship' with the Republican Party, the Democrat Roosevelt also sent Wendell Wilkie, his defeated Republican rival for the presidency, to London with a handwritten letter of introduction to Churchill, quoting Longfellow:

> Sail on, O Ship of State
> Sail on, O Union, strong and great!
> Humanity with all its fears,
> With all the hope of future years,
> Is hanging breathless on thy fate!

What answer should Churchill give Roosevelt, 'this great man, the thrice-chosen head of a nation of a hundred and thirty million?' the prime minister asked in a broadcast to the USA on 9 February. It was the day after Hopkins bade him farewell, but it was also the day when the US Congress passed the Lend-Lease Bill, by a vote of 260 to 165. Churchill's answer was a doughty piece of rhetoric:

Put your confidence in us; give us your faith and your blessing, and under Providence all will be well. We shall not fail or falter. We shall not weaken or tire. Neither the sudden shock of battle nor the long-drawn trials of vigilance and exertion will wear us down. Give us the tools, and we will finish the job.

The USA gave Britain the tools, but Lend-Lease came at a high price. The isolationists in Congress claimed Britain was stinking rich, with a billion dollars invested in the USA. The largest British-owned asset was the American Viscose Company, a subsidiary of the Courtaulds textile empire, which had seven plants, employing eighteen thousand people to make rayon. To show that Britain had exhausted all options before pleading for aid (and to throw a bone to isolationist 'America First' critics like Charles Lindbergh), in early March 1941 US Treasury Secretary Henry Morgenthau proposed that the British sacrifice their American Viscose Company. Washington gave Whitehall a seventy-two-hour deadline to sell the business. Britain had its back against the wall: when Samuel Courtauld was told the sale was 'essential in the national interest', he agreed.

Morgan Stanley and Dillon Read headed the syndicate that acquired American Viscose for the knock-down price of US$54.4 million; Courtaulds' tangible assets alone were worth US$128 million. What made the pill even more bitter to swallow was that Morgan Stanley then sold on the company for US$62 million, and pocketed the $7.6 million difference themselves.

William J. Donovan was an ambitious Republican, like his good friend Frank Knox, whom the Democrat Roosevelt had appointed Secretary of the Navy. He was an Irish Catholic like Murphy and he was a war hero. Lieutenant Colonel Donovan had picked up the Distinguished Service Cross and the Congressional Medal of Honor for courage under fire 'above and beyond the call of duty' in the

First World War. He had recently been portrayed by George Brent in the James Cagney movie about New York's 'Irish' regiment, *The Fighting 69th*, where he had the nickname 'Wild Bill' Donovan. Ever since serving in Mexico in 1915, Donovan had had an interest in unorthodox warfare. He had been in Siberia with anti-Bolsheviks after the First World War, visited General Badoglio in the Abyssinian War and General Franco on the Ebro front in the Spanish Civil War, where he was among the first to take note of the new German 88 mm gun.

Donovan, in peacetime a charismatic but unsuccessful politician, had found a new cause in the Second World War, becoming a 'determined interventionist' who did not believe America should be isolated from the world. Donovan's first trip to London in July 1940 was a fortnight's propaganda mission on behalf of Frank Knox, who owned the *Chicago Daily News*, when Donovan met everyone, made particular friends with Admiral Godfrey, Director of Naval Intelligence, and reported back to Roosevelt that 'Britain under Churchill would not surrender either to ruthless air-raids or to an invasion.'

Colonel Donovan's second trip, starting on 6 December 1940, was much more ambitious in scope, taking in Bermuda, London, Gibraltar, Malta, Egypt, Greece, Bulgaria, Turkey, Cyprus, Palestine, Iraq, Spain and Portugal. This odyssey was paid for, and under the aegis of ,'C' or CSS,* the Chief of the Secret Service, Sir Stewart Menzies. Donovan was accompanied on the first leg of the trip, from Baltimore to London, by C's man in the Americas, 'the quiet Canadian' William Stephenson, who had been the so-called Passport Control Officer in New York City since June 1940. Part of Stephenson's mission in the USA had been to establish a good relationship with J. Edgar Hoover's Federal Bureau of Investigation. President

---

* 'Is C a Naval man?' 'Yes, but he's apparently attached to the War Office, though he gets his money from the Foreign Office.' 'What's he like?' 'Funny old boy with a wooden leg.' (Compton Mackenzie, *Greek Memories*, 1932 first edition, p. 27.) The book was suppressed and the author prosecuted under the Official Secrets Act for first revealing, amongst other facts, that the head of MI6, one-legged Sir Mansfield Cumming, was known as C, first for Cumming, then for Chief.

Roosevelt recommended 'the closest possible marriage between the FBI and British Intelligence', and Hoover saw that by working with the British he could expand his counter-espionage empire through the Caribbean, Central and South America. Stephenson's organisation in New York, British Security Co-ordination, was trying to get the Americans into the secret intelligence game, and then, if possible, into the war. Colonel Donovan, half hero, half huckster, and a 'can-do' character, was, Stephenson thought, just the right man to help charm tens of thousands of outdated spare rifles and ammo, scores of useful aircraft and, eventually, fifty old destroyers from the USA to help the UK. This new trip would take Donovan deeper into a clandestine world of intelligence and covert warfare that intrigued his Fenian cast of mind. Among the generals, kings, prime ministers, propagandists and spies that Donovan met on this trip were leaders of the British sabotage and subversion organisation, the Special Operations Executive, and the men who founded the Commandos and the Long Range Desert Group.

Bad weather for flying detained the American and the Canadian for a week in Hamilton, Bermuda, but this was not uninteresting because, as we have seen, the island was now a main hub for transatlantic Postal Censorship and Contraband Control, feeding the ever-hungry intelligence agencies. There was a lot to learn about the screening of sea and air passengers for enemy agents, and the many intricate ways that mail and parcels were scanned for codes, invisible writing, microdots, and material extracted for 'Box 500' (the Security Service) and 'The Firm' (the SIS) in London. Bermuda was also to be one of the new Lend-Lease bases where the British Empire and the USA would learn to co-exist.

They reached London on 16 December. Two days later Donovan lunched with Churchill. The prime minister commanded that 'every facility' be afforded the American he believed had 'great influence with the President', and gave him as a travelling companion 'the best man in the Cabinet Secretariat', Lieutenant Colonel Vivian Dykes of the Royal Engineers, who, luckily, kept a partial diary of what the CIA historian Thomas F. Troy called 'one of the most extended, varied, and important trips taken to scenes of World War II action by any American, certainly up to that time'.

First they flew to Gibraltar, where bad weather again detained them, from 31 December 1940 until early on 5 January 1941. Dykes records their arriving at Gibraltar at 11 a.m. and being driven straight to Government House to meet Governor Liddell. After lunch, Major General Noel Mason-MacFarlane gave them his energetic tour of the defences. Canadian engineers with diamond-tipped drills were now inside the Rock; noisy work was progressing on all the tunnels behind their blast-traps. Donovan was shown the galleries and the guns, the stores and the barracks, and went to the top of the Rock to see the spectacular view of Spain and North Africa. The harbour below was full of vessels: three battleships, two aircraft carriers, cruisers, destroyers, cargo ships packed with munitions – a wonderful target for air attack.

The defence tour was much like the one Mason-MacFarlane had given the American journalist Helen Hiett three months earlier. The British general, somewhat smitten, was now corresponding with her in Madrid. She had done a brilliant job of praising the Rock's resilience in her journalism, including a quote from US Major General John N. Greely that encapsulated Mason-MacFarlane's own message to the enemy: 'I'd rather defend Gibraltar with ten thousand men than have to attack it with one hundred thousand.' Mason-MacFarlane wanted to invite her back. In one letter in early January 1941, he wrote: 'Incidentally I had the great privilege and pleasure of seeing a good deal of your President's Colonel Donovan here the other day. He's a man and a most intelligent and clear headed one at that. Also I think 100% sincere. I liked him a lot and it was a treat to talk to him.'

On New Year's Eve in Government House, Brigadier Bill Torr, the British military attaché in Madrid, joined Donovan and the others for dinner. Dykes recorded that Torr 'was confident that Spain would resist a German invasion directed against Gibraltar'. Note the choice of words: 'would resist' is a much stronger claim than 'would not permit'. It was the same message, with the same words, that the naval attaché Alan Hillgarth was delivering simultaneously in London.

The British ambassador in Madrid was putting his naval and military attachés to work. When Juan Beigbeder was sacked without warning as Spain's Foreign Minister on 17 October 1940, Sir Samuel Hoare says in his book that he merely wrote the 'haggard and distraught' Beigbeder a letter, hoping that 'our personal friendship will long continue', and that was that. In fact the two men met the very next day, and stayed in surreptitious contact. Colonel Beigbeder was convinced that Germany would demand a right of passage through Spain within a few months, that Franco would wobble, and that the chances were fifty–fifty that he would accede. Beigbeder thought it essential that the British make plans to block them. The best, if not the only, hope for effective resistance to a German invasion, he said, was the Spanish army. If the army resisted then even the Basques and Catalans would join a national movement to fight the invaders. The British should be ready to provide munitions and support to Gibraltar and to the regional commander in the south, *el Gobernador militar del Campo de Gibraltar*, General Agustín Muñoz Grandes, whom Beigbeder knew well from Moroccan days. He was going to Algeciras soon and would talk to him.

Hoare had actually spoken to Muñoz Grandes the day before Beigbeder was sacked, and found the hatchety soldier in a 'plague-on-both-your-houses' mood. According to Muñoz Grandes, Spain had been 'the instrument and dupe of foreign powers' in the civil war, and he had no wish for that to happen again. Muñoz Grandes was a patriotic Nationalist who had told Hillgarth he would resist any invasion from any country, but he now thought that of the belligerent nations, England was the least likely to interfere with Spain's autonomy. Hoare sent a Most Secret Telegram to Whitehall, and the War Cabinet asked the chiefs of staff to draw up a plan for operations in Spain, which they delivered on 6 November 1940. The directors of plans (Charles Daniel for the navy, Ian Playfair for the army and

Charles Medhurst for the RAF) saw clearly that the object of any operation should be 'to enable us to maintain our present degree of control of the Straits of Gibraltar'. They planned to occupy a line from Cádiz to Málaga, falling back to secure the Tarifa Peninsula and Gibraltar. They required a force of four divisions, two army tank brigades, two anti-aircraft brigades, six fighter and two medium bomber squadrons, whose transport would require 1.25 million tons of shipping. Gibraltar would need an extra 5500 RAF and army personnel, plus a thousand vehicles and 4500 tons of stores. This contingency plan became known as Operation *Blackthorn*, with its naval side called Operation *Goldeneye*. The Special Operations Executive had a small dog in the fight too: there was Operation *Relator* in Gibraltar and, if the Spanish army resisted German invasion, the British would help them (Operation *Sprinkler*), but if the Franco regime chose to aid the enemy, the British would start guerrilla and sabotage activities with former Republicans (Operation *Sconce*). SOE trained 140 tough and sometimes unruly Spaniards for this eventuality.

Meanwhile, the problem of Tangier was worsening. On 3 November 1940, Colonel Antonio Yuste, the Spanish military commander, had abolished the Enclave and its International Administration established in 1928, sacking all its bureaucrats without compensation; on 1 December he effectively annexed the entire 'InterZone' of Tangier, making it part of Spanish Morocco with Yuste himself as the governor general. At his Gibraltar dinner with Donovan on New Year's Eve, Brigadier Torr said that he thought the British should be fostering the new spirit of resistance to Germany in Spain by not making too much fuss over this Spanish occupation of Tangier and by using the weapon of blockade against Spain with discretion. But an Italian-led anti-British riot in Tangier soon after the annexation had inflamed Fleet Street and led to aggressive questioning in parliament of British government policy; Labour and Liberal MPs who thought the wrong side had won the Spanish Civil War said Britain should not be supplying any food and fuel to the Franco regime.

In Madrid, David Eccles of MEW and the diplomats Arthur Yencken and Sir Samuel Hoare defended the British corner, threatening Franco's regime with a tightening of the blockade unless Britain retained some rights in Tangier and the sacked civil servants were paid three years' salary. At the same time the Madrid contingent had to ensure that the Ministry of Economic Warfare in London did not actually tighten the blockade too much or too soon. In this delicate use of the choke-chain they succeeded.

Winston Churchill worried about whether the Spanish annexation of Tangier was the thin end of the Nazi wedge. Was Franco now going in with Hitler? David Eccles read it more as an assertion of Spanish pride, after the Hitler–Franco meeting at Hendaye. 'When bread is lacking, men desire, more than ever, to prove to themselves that they do not live by bread alone. A little glory, and they can put up with hunger.' The annexation was popular in mainland Spain.

Spanish Morocco was, in fact, showing little subservience to German designs. Although Hitler told Serrano that he wanted a presence in Morocco, and Germans took control of the Armistice Commission in Casablanca (previously run by the Italians),[*] the Spanish disliked any expansion of *Kontrollinspektion Afrika* into what they considered their territory. At the end of the year, the German consul at Tetuán, Herbert Georg Richter, noted Spain's resentment at any German activities on Moroccan soil. German films, propaganda and personnel were being blocked, their agents watched, and the long-standing grievance over the German Legation building in Tangier, confiscated by the Spanish in the Kaiser's War, was still unresolved. (When Spain handed it back in March 1941, it soon became the centre of German Abwehr espionage under *Sonderführer* Hans Paul Krüger.) Although ignorant of actual American plans and of what Robert Murphy was up to, Consul Richter's warning to the German government was prescient: 'Should Spain attack French Morocco anew,

---

[*] For fans of *Casablanca* (Michael Curtiz, 1942), this is when Major Heinrich Strasser (Conrad Veidt) arrives to put pressure on Vichy Captain Louis Renault (Claude Rains).

a dangerous front will develop in North Africa and the whole area will be driven into the arms of de Gaulle. The consequences would be still more serious if the United States should enter the war. French Morocco would then become the base for American operations in Europe.'

During his stay on the Rock, Colonel Donovan touched base with everyone important, including Admiral James Somerville, who was in charge of H Force. On 2 January 1941, Somerville recorded:

Colonel Donovan, US representative, accompanied by Colonel Dykes, lunched with me on board *Renown*. In compliance with Colonel Donovan's request I informed him as fully as lay in my power of the general situation in the Western Mediterranean and the functions of Force H . . . We also discussed the manner in which the American Navy could best be employed to assist the British Navy should the occasion arrive . . . in dealing with raiders, convoy protection, and anti-submarine activities.

Donovan rightly considered Somerville 'really a high class man', but their lordships who ran the Royal Navy from London did not always seem to think so. They sent an Admiral of the Fleet, the Earl of Cork and Orrery, to Gibraltar to conduct an Admiralty Board of Inquiry into why, during Operation *Collar* in late November 1940, Somerville had discontinued the chase of a large Italian warship near Cape Spartivento. The Board said that 'the ultimate object of the Royal Navy is the destruction of the main enemy forces when and wherever encountered'; this seemed to suggest that Somerville's inaction was a dereliction of duty or, lurking unsaid, cowardice.

Nothing could be further from the truth. Somerville had always been a fighting sailor, out at sea in all weathers for weeks at a time, at home in a world of rough humour and foul language. At sea he was not the kind of senior officer who stayed in his spacious cabin – he led by example, from the front. When his flag was on the aircraft carrier *Ark Royal* he went around the engine room, all decks, through the hangars and even up in the air with the three-man Swordfish biplanes; as an old signaller he helped the telegraphist air gunners or TAGs to improve their wireless technique. And the men loved him for it. Once, when a lone British destroyer was damaged and limping behind the rest, Somerville made the big ships of Force H slow down to shepherd the vessel, despite the real danger to them of air attack. If 'Dad' was not there, Somerville said, 'the boys' would lose confidence.

The Board of Inquiry into the Spartivento incident was ordered even before Somerville had made his report on it and, needless to say, the animating force behind it was Winston Churchill, continuing 'to pester, nag and bite' as he characterised himself in another context, and perhaps still resentful of Somerville's reluctance at Mers-el-Kébir and his staunch support of Dudley North. Somerville's defence was that he was escorting ships carrying a vital armoured brigade and 1400 soldiers and airmen for the Middle East, and having successfully driven the enemy away, pursuing them further to destruction would have conflicted with his specific Fighting Instructions, namely 'the safe and timely arrival of the convoy at its destination'. The Board concurred with his judgement in the end, but the process wasted time and was demoralising.

Having visited Malta (where Dykes said the General Officer Commanding 'was not so vigorous as Mason-Mac at Gib'), Donovan and Dykes flew on to Cairo. On their second day, 8 January 1941, General Archibald Wavell, Commander-in-Chief, Middle East, gave them a long briefing. In December, Wavell had attacked westward from Egypt into Italian Libya in Operation *Compass*. British forces had captured Sidi Barrani, Sollum and Bardia,* and were heading for Tobruk and then Benghazi, taking thousands of prisoners. However, Wavell told Dykes there was a rumour that Germany had sent three hundred aircraft to Italy.

---

* This last capture, by the Australians on 3 January, occasioned a new *ITMA*-style joke for the Gibraltar Christmas pantomime. 'Are there any Italians?' asks Aladdin fearfully in the cave, to which Abanazer replies: 'No. They're barred 'ere!'

The rumour was true. Five days earlier, on 3 January 1941, pilots and planes of Luftwaffe *Fliegerkorps X* led by Hans-Ferdinand Geisler had arrived in Sicily from Norway. They trained to attack shipping and then on 10 January they struck, hard, at the 'Excess' convoy which was heading from Gibraltar through the Sicilian Narrows towards Malta.

Five British cargo ships were protected by two battleships, three cruisers and the aircraft carrier HMS *Illustrious*. The cargo ships were not the main target. Two months earlier the Fleet Air Arm Fairey Swordfish had taken off from the deck of *Illustrious* to deliver a devastating torpedo attack on the Italian fleet at Taranto, and now twenty German Ju 87 dive-bombers flying from Italian bases were seeking revenge on the aircraft-carrying mother ship.

The Stukas came at the bow in clover clusters of three, diving down through the barrage of anti-aircraft fire put up by the quick-firing 4.5-inch guns and the eight-barrelled 'pom-pom' auto-cannons. HMS *Illustrious*, nicknamed *Lusty*, was hit six times, mostly with armour-piercing thousand-pound bombs which caused horrendous internal damage, killing 126 and wounding ninety-one all ranks. Among the dead was Lieutenant Neil Kemp DSC, Peter Kemp's older brother and hero, whose Swordfish aircraft L4K had scored one of the three torpedo hits on the battleship *Littorio* at Taranto. He was decapitated when the fire screens in the aircraft carrier's hangar exploded into flying splinters. *Illustrious* limped into Malta, tied up at Parlatario Wharf crippled and still burning, and was out of action for a year under repair in the USA. The next day, more Stukas dive-bombed HMS *Gloucester* and damaged the other cruiser, HMS *Southampton*, so badly she had to be sunk by British torpedoes.

Positioning Luftwaffe aircraft in Sicily and southern Italy created a serious threat to the Mediterranean convoys from Gibraltar to Malta. By the end of January 1941, Admiral Somerville was looking at an intelligence report on *Fliegerkorps X* saying that a long-range bomber group of forty aircraft, practised in mine-laying, was reinforcing the German squadrons in Sicily, already estimated at 160 long-range bombers, twenty bomber-reconnaissance, 150 dive-bombers, forty twin-engined fighters and forty to sixty transports. Should their air bases ever move nearer the Rock, Gibraltar's sometimes deplorable anti-aircraft defences could not cope.

On 31 January 1941, the Paramount Newsreel carried a story from Baltimore. 'FIRST MERCY SHIP SAILS', read the screen caption, and then the narration began:

The American ship *Cold Harbor* sails for Spain and Unoccupied France with a million-dollar cargo of mercy. The American Red Cross provides six thousand tons of foodstuffs, medical supplies and clothing. Flour for Spain whose 26 million people face actual famine, and 28 light trucks go along to supplement Spain's crippled transportation system. Under the Red Cross flag, Germany and Britain have pledged safety for Captain Moore's ship, the first American ship granted permission to carry relief through the British blockade. Cadiz, Barcelona and Marseille are the ports of call at the end of the mercy ship's long voyage.

James Somerville carried a weight of responsibility for the lives of others. He had to cope with the stupid small brutalities of war, like when a Vichy French convoy was being stopped and searched by Contraband Control and in a sudden explosion of gunfire a harmless French passenger and small girl were killed and four people wounded. This kind of enforcement was just bullying, Somerville wrote to his wife: 'It seems to me that we are just as much a dictator country as either Germany or Italy and one day the Great British public will wake up to ask what are we fighting for.' Writing letters to Mollie helped to ease the loneliness of command and 'this ruddy load of responsibility on my shoulders. At times it seems very light and at others particularly heavy . . . Wherever one is war is a bloody senseless business and the sooner mankind realises it the better.'

Helen Hiett only dined once with Admiral Somerville, on HMS *Renown*.

I got from him (through my persistent questioning for never would he have volunteered it) a new appreciation of how big a single man's responsibility can be. Responsibility is a thing so many people shirk, and even fear. I wonder how many promising careers the fear of responsibility has ruined, and what, exactly, is the process by which one learns not to fear it? Here was a man who could calmly do battle, knowing that the prestige of a whole nation, perhaps its very future, depended not only on him alone, but on the value of the instantaneous judgment he would make at the crucial point of beginning an engagement. How much of the vital force of a country a fleet can represent!

With Dudley North gone, sacked by Churchill after the Dakar failure, it was hard for troubled Admiral Somerville to find someone he could open his heart to. North's replacement as VACNA, Vice Admiral Commanding North Atlantic, from 1 January 1941, was Vice Admiral Sir George Frederick Basset Edward-Collins KCB, KCVO. Somerville did not like him and always referred to his portly colleague as 'Fat Fred Collins'. Somerville's own Force H battleship captains were all 'good chaps' whom he could talk to quite freely in a way, 'but not so freely in another sense because it wouldn't do for them to know how I feel about war. The leader must be out for blood all the time (which I am of course) but he must not show how filthy it all is.'

Somerville wrote that particular letter to Mollie aboard HMS *Renown* en route with Force H to attack the Italian mainland on 10 February 1941. Fourteen Swordfish from *Ark Royal* were to bomb the Azienda oil refinery at Leghorn (Livorno) and lay mines off Spezia, while *Renown*, *Malaya* and *Sheffield* were to bombard Genoa, the ancestral city of Christopher Columbus and many Gibraltarians, from ten miles away. Somerville's broadsides were aimed at the Ansaldo shipyards:

Our guns were laid by gyro and our aircraft over the town spotted us on to the various targets. The first salvoes fell almost exactly where we wanted them and *then* I felt content. The curtain was up and the tragedy was on.

For half an hour we blazed away and I had to think of Senglea, Valletta, London and Bristol, etc., to harden my heart. But I was watching the map and the reports of the aircraft and I do believe that practically all our salvoes fell on works, warehouses, shipping, docks, etc. Still it is no use pretending that some innocent people were not killed. War is lousy.

The civilian casualties in Genoa were given as 144 dead and 272 wounded, more than when the German battleship *Admiral Scheer* shelled Almería in 1937.

Anthony Eden, the British Foreign Secretary, and John Dill, the Chief of the Imperial General Staff, had flown out to Cairo via Gibraltar and Malta to coincide with Donovan and confer with Wavell about the threat to the Balkans and to Greece, the fear that Germany would move down through Bulgaria to take Salonika. Donovan's situation report, cabled to Washington DC on 20 February 1941, included the following paragraph:

As part of offensive Germany will probably try to seal up Mediterranean by: (i) mining Suez Canal, (ii) possibly advancing into Spain and denying Gibraltar. Counter measures to (i) are being taken by British. Germany is already taking over from Italy task of air attack on shipping in Mediterranean. Nevertheless Malta is still used as repair base and Commander in Chief, Mediterranean, is confident he will still be able to take Fleet through the narrows with air support from carriers. Possible that Germany may seize Balearic Islands as a step to French North Africa as a base for attack on Gibraltar; but this would be hazardous operation for her. Despatch of German armoured formations to Libya is reported. If Germany could obtain French bases in North Africa, British task of clearing Mediterranean would be most difficult.

On Monday 24 February 1941, Donovan and Dykes landed back in Gibraltar after their momentous trip to the Middle East and the Balkans. At Government House, Donovan had an eye cyst excised and so missed dinner with the governor that night, which was a pity because there were some interesting guests. Captain Alan Hillgarth, the naval attaché from Madrid, was there with his wife, Mary, plus Brigadier Reggie Parminter, Gibraltar's chief administrative officer, handsome Freddie Inglis of the Gordon Highlanders, Major Anthony Quayle and Lieutenant Peter Forbes. The last guest came from the Admiralty in London: thirty-one-year-old Acting Commander Ian Lancaster Fleming RNVR, personal assistant to the Director of Naval Intelligence (DNI), Admiral John Godfrey.

Ian Fleming had been handling Iberia for his boss for six months. He had driven down to the Rock from Madrid with the Hillgarths a week before, with a small White Ensign flying on their car's radio aerial, and had seen Admiral Somerville, which gave them 'an excellent opportunity of discussing Spanish affairs'. Fleming and Hillgarth's main concern was Operation *Goldeneye*, the naval side of Operation *Blackthorn*, the contingency plans for when the Germans invaded Spain in order to attack Gibraltar, which allowed for Franco's forces either helping or hindering them. Fleming and Hillgarth's responsibity was the movement of all shipping and the maintenance of secure and efficient enciphered communications. This was an area where Fleming had the full confidence of his boss, John Godfrey.

As early as 8 April 1940 'Lieutenant Fleming RNVR' had been one of six on the nominal list of those 'having access to Huts 1 and 6 at G.C.C.S. [Bletchley Park], or to whom the source of the reports is known', meaning that he was 'indoctrinated' into the ULTRA secret very early indeed.[*] The other naval names on the select list are the DNI himself, Admiral James Somerville, Admiral John Clayton, Lieutenant Commander Clive Loehnis (a future director of GCHQ) and Commander Humphrey Sandwith, the head of NID9, the Naval Intelligence signals section. The Admiralty Tower at Gibraltar had a Special Liaison Unit (SLU) handling Most Secret messages earlier than most commands.

---

[*] 'ULTRA was the British security classification chosen in 1940 to denote the new and highly secret intelligence produced by the decryption of intercepted German (and some Italian) radio messages enciphered in the Enigma machine cipher or transmitted on the Geheimschreiber.' *The Oxford Companion to the Second World War* (1995), p. 1165.

The very first idea for Gibraltar's extraordinary 'Stay-Behind-Cave' may well have come to the minds of these two Naval Intelligence officers in February 1941, since they were tasked with thinking about what to do should the Rock be overrun by the Germans and have to be abandoned. There were military 'scorched earth' plans for the Royal Engineers to blow a lot of things up, but it would also make sense to leave behind some hidden observers in Gibraltar who could report what shipping was in the bay or on the Mediterranean side. Starting in the summer of 1941 and extending through 1942, Admiral John Godfrey evolved a detailed plan, called Operation *Tracer*, to leave behind a small naval team (two doctors, three signallers and an executive officer) walled up in a sealed chamber, forty-five by sixteen by eight feet, high up at the top of the Rock near Lord Airey's Battery. They would have at least a year's food and water and access to two observation windows, a larger one looking east where a man could crawl out to get some sunshine and still be concealed, and the other a narrow slit looking west towards Algeciras. Thus they could report on all enemy ship movements via an SIS Mark 3 radio transmitter, whose three twelve-volt, 120-amp batteries would be charged by hand crank or the exercise bike that also helped the ventilation system. The ingenious hideaway was secretly plumbed, constructed and concealed in 1942, with the builders swiftly shipped home lest they talk. The floors were tiled with cork to minimise noise and one passage had loose earth and bags of cement and sand in it: anyone who died in the cave would have to be embalmed, buried and sealed up, deep inside the hiding place.

Early on 25 February 1941, Donovan and Dykes drove up to Madrid with the Hillgarth party. Dykes gossiped with Fleming in one of the two cars. He heard Fleming's yarns from his days with Reuter's before the war and thought he had not lost the journalist's habit of drinking too much. SIS were at serious loggerheads with SOE; once again SIS (espionage) wanted silent discretion, while SOE (sabotage) yearned for noisy action. Fleming and Dykes had both noticed that General Noel Mason-MacFarlane was busily intriguing against Governor Sir Clive Liddell, whom he considered 'a useless poop'.

In Madrid, Colonel Donovan stayed with the ineffectual US Ambassador Weddell, and the following morning had a full briefing from Sir Samuel Hoare. The British ambassador's first suggestion was that President Roosevelt should take Iberia, the whole Spanish Peninsula, and northwest Africa under his special protection. Could not this area be subsumed within the Monroe Doctrine? The hope that Spain would stay out of the war was being strengthened by growing xenophobia in the country, and the Spanish army's hostility to the Falange party, 'the chief centre of German activities'. Hoare wanted President Roosevelt and the South American republics to put pressure on Franco, replacing his mesmerised belief in the invincibility of the German military machine with the idea that Britain and her allies were going to win in the end. Hoare's third point was that there was 'a will to resist' in Spain that only needed strengthening. 'At present it is hesitating and disjointed. It was hesitating and disjointed in 1808. But in 1814 with British help it destroyed Napoleon.' The help needed was military and economic. 'If we can keep the Peninsula out of the Axis, we frustrate Hitler's effort to conquer all Europe and we keep Spain and Portugal in the orbit of the oceanic powers, the United States and the British Empire, and prevent them being absorbed into Hitler's bloc.'

Franco was 'too busy' to see Donovan, but on the Friday the American met Serrano Suñer, who told him 'we hope for and believe in the victory of Germany in the present conflict', but that Spain would continue to stay aloof until her 'honour or interests or dignity' were at stake.

26

Helen's Return

On 28 February 1941, Admiral Somerville had General Agustín Muñoz Grandes, the Spanish Military Governor of the Campo de Gibraltar, piped aboard HMS *Renown*. Accompanied by his diplomatic adviser, the Marqués del Vallecerrato (another member of the Larios family), and two other aides, Muñoz Grandes was invited to lunch with all the senior naval officers present on Gibraltar. Such events were stage-managed to flatter and impress. As they were steered past carefully choreographed displays, official visitors were meant to get glimpses of power that their imaginations would amplify later – a pair of submarines, a flight of aircraft or a squad all carrying Thompson sub-machine guns, though these were actually in very short supply. Even the food in the galleys played its part.

Captain Holland of *Ark Royal* related that one Spanish official visitor was taken all over his ship, seeing everything. What awed the Spaniard most on the mighty aircraft carrier was not the arms or the armour or the enormous aeroplane hangars, but hundreds of loaves of fresh white bread racked by the ovens. The ship's baker had made this visitor a special large loaf, which incorporated the Falange symbol of the yoke and arrows. Half embarrassed, the Spaniard asked if the man would bake a tiny one for him to keep, so he could take the big one home and eat it.

In Spain, hard yellowish rolls were all you could get. One great advantage of regular work in Gibraltar was that you could register with a baker and take the daily bread – perhaps a large fresh loaf of white bread – back home to La Línea. In Gibraltar you could also find 'Tinned loaves/*Pan de lata*, English loaves/*Restas*, Coburg loaves/*Coronas* or Moorish loaves/*Molletas*'. A twenty-eight-ounce loaf cost sixpence, a fourteen-ounce one threepence.

Three days later, at 1 p.m. on 4 March, General Muñoz Grandes was in Gibraltar again for another official visit, lunch with Governor Liddell and fourteen others at Government House, followed by a drive to the theatre. As well as the Marqués de Vallecerrato, Muñoz Grandes brought Lieutenant Colonel Fernando Cárcer, one of the Spanish officers who had escorted Admiral Canaris and the German soldiers when they were busily scoping out the Rock with hostile intent in December 1940.

'There was much mutual visiting between officials of Gibraltar and of Algeciras,' wrote the NBC correspondent Helen Hiett, back on the Rock and a guest at that particular lunch. She was alert to the ironies: 'And the big British guns trained on the Spanish shore, and the German spies and manoeuvrings based on Algeciras, were all treated like the backdrop to some other unrelated story.' Governor Liddell had a parrot, which spoke more Spanish than he did. Someone gave the bird some absinthe at coffee time and the parrot sat swearing coarsely on its perch: '*¡Carajo! ¡Carajo! ¡Carajo!*'

Hiett's second visit to the Rock inadvertently lasted a fortnight. She had arrived from Portugal, the only woman on a two-thousand-ton armed tramp steamer that sailed from Lisbon on Sunday 2 March with a cargo of wine and whisky and 128 'distressed seamen', merchant sailors who had all been torpedoed by German submarines off the Azores, now en route back to England via Gibraltar. Their trip from Portugal took thirty-six hours. In the darkness of Sunday night, high above in the opposite direction, the flying boat carrying Donovan and Dykes was on its way back to England.

At sea level, Helen Hiett found that total blackout on a rolling ship disturbed proprioception and motion sensing. Out on deck, 'rhythmic flashes from a far-away lighthouse sent weird shadows creeping over the deck, too fleeting to be believed in, but you fixed on a point in the blackness and held your breath till the light came on again. An uncanny night, that held no promise of morning.'

The torpedoed seamen kept all their possessions in ridiculous wicker baskets bought in Madeira. They had a long discussion about the pros and cons of being sunk, and whether it was worth being a good swimmer when the ship went down. Would striking away from the sinking ship mean you might be lost? Would those who clung to debris near the ship have a better chance of being picked up? One lad, a non-swimmer, had caught a line thrown down by his rescuers. As the ship rolled in a high sea it had dislocated his shoulder. Everyone agreed the sailor's first priority was knowing how to stay out of the water.

They're a pretty sturdy lot, these merchant seamen, in more constant peril, and getting less glory for the risks they run, than almost any other branch of the services . . . Yet these are the ships that are feeding England today, and the men are duly proud of the role they play. The thing that surprised me most was how young they were, many still in their teens, and yet, as I talked with them, I sensed a straightforward simplicity, a refreshing frankness and calm achieved rarely enough by men twice their age. I suppose that comes from a daily, unfearing familiarity with death.

Their boat couldn't berth straight away when they reached Gibraltar because a submarine was somewhere down below on a practice dive, so they sat with their legs dangling over one of the hatches, sampling the captain's special port wine while tipsy stevedores threw huge cases of it about down below, masters of the art of dropping a case so that just one or two bottles broke. The straw packing held the shards of glass at bay while the wine trickled out into their improvised containers. Hiett and the seamen saw *Ark Royal*'s huge flat hulk slipping out to sea with a screen of destroyers.

The movement of merchant shipping was a drama vital to everyone's survival. Hiett liked to go up to a favourite vantage spot on the Rock at sunset and watch as 'big cruisers slowed their speed and mothered their flock of helpless ships out of the harbour's shelter into the sea. Sixty ships, in even pattern, growing smaller, and slipping out of sight into danger, while behind me, the beautiful but unfriendly Spanish shore disappeared in dusky shades of rose and bluish grey.'

In 1941, the year of Hiett's second visit to Gibraltar, German submarines, mines and aircraft sank 992 vessels, nearly four million tons of shipping. The Gibraltar convoys were not immune. In 1941, the three worst-hit convoys outward to Gibraltar (OG 69, 71 and 74) lost seventeen ships with 311 dead, and the three worst-hit convoys homeward (HG 53, 73 and 75) lost twenty-one ships with 378 dead. Seafarers faced a horrible variety of deaths – by burning or drowning, blood loss and shock, exposure, raging thirst, madness. In the Second World War, over thirty thousand British merchant seamen gave their lives. As John Masefield wrote:

> Unrecognised, you put us in your debt;
> Unthanked you enter, or escape, the grave;
> Whether your land remember or forget
> You saved the land, or died to try to save.

Helen Hiett had a busy two days, all that regulation allotted, but then found herself barred at the Spanish frontier post at La Línea. Her name was 'blacklisted in the frontier police card files as an undesirable un-allowed to re-enter Spain'. She had to return to Gibraltar for ten more days until she finally got permission to ride a sardine boat bound for Faro in Portugal as the sole passenger.

Mason-MacFarlane won the fight with Liddell over who would host the pretty American. She moved into the big house where 'the Wicked Uncles' lived: Mason-MacFarlane, with his Labrador bitch picked up in the retreat to Dunkirk ('She's black, she's vibrant, she wiggles her behind, her name must be Josephine!' said Mason-MacFarlane), and the men who were in charge of the tunnelling: Colonel H. M. Fordham, the Chief Engineer (the rows of Nissen huts installed in underground chambers where hundreds of soldiers slept each night were called 'Fordham's Accommodation'), Colonel E. X.

Clifton, the garrison engineer, and Colonel D. M. Thomson, who wrote the official account of the tunnels in 1946.

On this visit, Hiett first encountered Gibraltar's macaque monkeys (miscalled 'Barbary apes') as well as the legend that they came originally from Morocco via a secret tunnel under the strait. She was woken one morning by the sound of typing, and found a monkey pounding away on the machine on the general's desk while its mate sat with a precious tin of Craven A cigarettes, chucking them one by one over the verandah railing. The monkeys fled empty-handed and she went back to bed. She awoke again to find one monkey by her bed picking the sugar lumps off her morning tea tray and the other trying to eat her lipstick. She shooed them out and went to shower, to find they had been swinging in the bathroom, leaving paw-prints, turning on the hot water tap and exiting via the window, trailing the lavatory paper to festoon over the front door. They stole the breakfast bananas and a loaf of bread.

It is said that when the ravens quit the Tower of London, the British monarchy will fall, and that when the macaques die out on Gibraltar, the British will leave the Rock. Churchill's genuine concern for this rumour in September 1944 prompted two fictional works after the war, Paul Gallico's novel *Scruffy* and the Terry-Thomas film *Operation Snatch*. Both 1962 comedies are about the efforts of the wartime Officer in Charge of Apes to try and keep the numbers up to two dozen as Churchill commanded.

Helen Hiett benefited from the scarcity of women on Gibraltar. She basked in flattering attention and, being so well connected, she could get her way and open doors. She noticed another absence to add to gender imbalance. Although there were a few WRNS and WAAFs as well as the Spanish women who came every day from La Línea to work, there were no children on the Rock, no high voices laughing, no games chalked in the street. Just lots and lots of men in uniform. Starved of femininity, some longed for women, not just for sex, but for a gentle touch, a sweet look, or simply talk. John Porral saw awkward English squaddies offering to carry Spanish maids' or laundresses' shopping to the frontier ('*Keery takey bolso?*') just so they could walk with a woman for a while. British soldiers could not cross the frontier to La Línea, only those with a pass, in plain clothes. If they wanted, the lucky Spanish-speaking Gibraltarians in the Gibraltar Defence Force got six hours' leave once a month to slip over to 'Gib Street' in La Línea where the prostitutes were. Sex cost about five shillings.

Hiett was wooed, of course. When she tried to hook a ride on the American Red Cross ship *Cold Harbor*, the good-looking British naval commander (whom she never names) was brisk and gruff in processing her request only because he was protecting his acute self-consciousness. They later had dinner at the Rock Hotel on 15 March (Consommé, Hot or Cold; Red Mullet Meunière; Roast Turkey, Chip Potatoes, French Beans; Cold Meat; Ice Cream) and she wrote down on the back of the menu some of the naval slang he taught her: names for bases – Pompey, Guz, Chats and Sheernasty (Portsmouth, Plymouth, Chatham and Sheerness); names for officers – The Old Man, Number One or Jimmy, Chief (Captain, First Officer, Chief Engineer); names for Royal Marines – Bootneck, Leatherneck, Grabbie. Torpedoes were Mouldy or Fish; mines were Warts. In the parked car afterwards he made a long speech about how he loved his wife and two children, whom he hadn't seen for two years, and then asked permission to kiss her on the grounds that he had never kissed an American before. 'I refused his permission,' she wrote, '(what fools men are ever to ask it) and an approaching sentry facilitated quick leave-taking, for it was curfew time.'

The next morning, the handsome commander knocked on her door.

'Oh, I'm *so* glad you've come,' she said.

'I've been to church,' he said. 'Here, I've brought you some buttons.'

(Two gold Royal Navy buttons.)

'Oh, thank you. I wanted to see you again.'

'I'm sorry about last night. I knew it was a mistake.'

Follows a very quiet quick kiss, the kind that generates electricity.

'Actually I came to see Allen.'

'Oh? I hope to see you again, in London or the South Seas, and we'll soon be fighting on your side.'

'Goodbye, and, uh, you won't write, will you?'

'No.'

That night, she had more evidence of the strange rigidities of British behaviour. She was woken by the groans of an officer's heart attack in the next room, and alerted the general, who was still awake downstairs. There was no fuss, everyone was calm looking after him, getting a doctor, an ambulance. By the time those who had been with him to hospital got back, it was 3.30 a.m. and everyone was shattered.

'Let's raid the ice-box,' Hiett said.

No response from officers limp in armchairs. 'I'm famished,' said one.

'Let's raid the ice-box,' Hiett repeated directly to General Mason-MacFarlane, who did not understand what she was saying, thinking it a new dance or game.

'Not just now,' the general said.

'Perhaps it might be a very good thing if we had some food.'

'I . . . I hardly think that I should wake the servants.'

'Why on earth should you do that?'

'They do the cooking you know.'

'C'mon!'

Hiett led the way to the kitchen, where Mason-MacFarlane had never been. He worried what his relations with the staff would be if they found out he had violated their domain. Through a succession of pantries, bakeries and sculleries she traipsed in search of last night's joint of roast beef, located it in triumph and handed it to the general, together with a carving knife. Then she rustled up bread and butter and milk and tomatoes and lettuce for one of her most successful meals ever. The general was holding a huge sandwich when he said: 'All those nights we worked late and got hungry – strange we never thought of this before.'

British master–servant relations, Hiett thought, so rigid in their class-consciousness, were something the war was beginning – at last – to break down.

Other reserves were melting too. Before she left, Hiett received a white envelope with a crown on the flap, and 'Helen' written on the front in Noel Mason-MacFarlane's hand. Inside was a single sheet of paper.

> Helen,
> To me my Dear you'll ever represent
> The incarnation of a lifelong dream –
> A girl that I've designed and God has sent
> To cross my path. And yet, my child, you seem
> To lack one quality that may appear to you
> A non-essential trait and yet I'll bet
> That what I'm going to say is true,
> And truth from me is always what you'll get.
> You're lovely. For at any rate to me
> Sheer beauty is a gift that I assess
> Without recourse to those who don't agree
> With my ideals of joy and loveliness.
> Your quickness, your vitality, your guts,
> Your energy, your frankness and your fun,
> Your loathing of those awful grooves and ruts
> And rails on which our hidebound leaders run –
> All these are qualities I love, my Dear,
> But just because they make me love you so
> There's one thing Helen Darling that I fear
> I must impress upon you ere you go.
> Life seems to you something that only you
> Can really savour and appreciate
> And yet my Dear I'm one of quite a few
> Who think that's rather inconsiderate.
> And if you go through life without much thought
> For those whose path your radiant self has crossed
> The joy of winning every fight you've fought
> Won't compensate for something that you've lost.
> I would not have you different. I adore
> Your way of life, your beauty and the light
> Of your blue eyes. But you want something more

To win a battle than the wish to fight.
So when you charge upon your carefree way
Remember that you've got at least one friend
And when you're charging – be it night or day
He's by your side, and will be to the end.

N.M.
Gib. 15/3/41

27

Bloody War

Change came to Gibraltar in 1941 with a new governor. After supervising the evacuation from the beaches of Dunkirk, Viscount General John Gort seemed 'a lost soul' in the months following his return from France. Although 'Dunkirk' is now seen as something heroic, at the time it felt like a great defeat. The government delayed publishing Gort's dispatch about the British Expeditionary Force in the *London Gazette*, and one of Dennis Wheatley's ridiculous but best-selling Gregory Sallust novels, *The Black Baroness*, implied that Gort was a coward, which hurt him badly. Churchill called him 'gallant', but the authorities put Gort, a soldier with a VC, in the non-fighting job of Inspector of Training and the Home Guard. 'Gort was such a splendid and upright character,' wrote Sir John Kennedy, the Director of Military Operations, 'with such magnificent qualities of leadership and courage, that everyone sympathized with his sense of frustration when he failed to get another command in the field after Dunkirk.'

The war-horse was not yet being put out to pasture, however. They had another job in mind for him that would take him to the Mediterranean as things were hotting up. On 25 April 1941, Viscount General Gort was appointed Governor and Commander-in-Chief of Gibraltar. The Foreign Secretary, Anthony Eden, and the Chief of the Imperial General Staff, Sir John Dill, had picked up that there was 'bad blood' between General Mason-MacFarlane and Governor Liddell, so they purged both leaders and replaced them with Gort. Liddell went back to the UK to take over Gort's old job as Inspector of Training until he retired from the army in 1943. (Anthony Quayle went with him as his ADC.) Mason-MacFarlane was given command of the 44th (Home Counties) Division based at Canterbury, in charge of the front lines if southeast England were ever invaded.

Gort arrived in Gibraltar on 7 May 1941. He was photographed officially with Somerville and Liddell in the garden of Government House, where he and Duff Cooper had relaxed. Two days earlier, Haile Selassie, who also once stood in that garden, had been restored as Negus in Addis Ababa. With the Italian occupation of his country defeated by a multiracial force of Africans, Asians and Europeans, Ethiopia now became the first country to be freed from Axis rule.

There would be fewer lobster lunches at Government House under the frugal new governor. Food was fuel, not fun. Gort was a Spartan soldier, a fitness fanatic who liked to winkle sedentary staff officers from out behind their desks and get them marching up the Rock. Gort's aides did not loll in armchairs. Life was leaner, though the preamble to official ordinances became weightier:

By His Excellency General the Viscount Gort, upon whom has been conferred the decoration of the Victoria Cross, Knight Grand Cross of the most honourable Order of the Bath, commander of the most excellent Order of the British Empire, companion of the Distinguished Service order, member of the Royal Victorian order, upon whom has been conferred the decoration of the Military Cross, Governor and Commander-in-Chief of the city and garrison of Gibraltar, &c., &c.

One of Gort's early duties, on 19 May 1941, was to pay a formal visit, in uniforms and medals, to his opposite number in Algeciras, the ambiguous General Agustín Muñoz Grandes. The motor launch *Roberts* took the party of eight across the bay to Algeciras from Ragged Staff wharf, arriving at 11.30 a.m. sharp. Five senior officers from the three services accompanied Gort, together with the two fluent Spanish-speaking Gibraltarians, Assistant Colonial Secretary H. J. S. Norton and Gort's ADC, Major R. M. Sheppard-Capurro, whom Anthony Quayle once described as 'a bear of little brain, but great loyalty'.

The Spanish 9th Infantry Regiment honour guard, in khaki and helmets, with flags, drums and trumpets, presented arms and the band played 'God Save the King', *el himno nacional inglés*, to a seventeen-gun salute. After inspecting the guard to the sound of a march, a convoy of cars drove them along Calle de la Miel and Calle Queipo de Llano to the front door of the Spanish military headquarters, a former cavalry barracks facing the plaza, where the 7th Infantry Regiment honour guard presented arms and their band thumped and squeezed out 'God Save the King' once more.

Their Excellencies Gort and Muñoz Grandes met inside the *Gobierno Militar* building. The Spaniard and the Irishman were both warriors who had been wounded in combat. Gort won his Victoria Cross at Prémy Ridge in 1918 soaked in his own arterial blood, and nineteen-year-old Muñoz Grandes had been shot in the chest at the Alhucemas landing in Morocco in 1925. They got on well, with Harry Norton and Bobby Capurro as the fluent translators and interlocutors. After more salutes and flags and national anthems, the launch returned them to the Rock. Despite his puritanism, Gort understood it was important to socialise with the Spanish gentry of *el Campo de Gibraltar*. Soon Talia Larios, the Marquesa de Povar, would be back, Venus fluttering around Mars, and Gort would fall for her charms.

On Tuesday 20 May 1941, the day after Gort met Muñoz Grandes, war at its bloodiest came to the eastern end of the Mediterranean, when German airborne forces attacked the Greek island of Crete. The ten thousand *Fallschirmjäger* or paratroopers of General Student's *Fliegerkorps* were decimated, many shot dead in the sky as they floated down towards Maleme and Heraklion airfields. Some who reached the ground were bludgeoned or stabbed to death by Cretan civilians. The battle honour *Creta* which the surviving German paratroops later put on their arm-cuffs was a black brassard of mourning.

A bad wound in the left thigh immobilised Captain Rudolf Witzig, the hero of Eben Emael who had reconnoitred Gibraltar with Admiral Canaris. He was lucky not to encounter Lieutenant Charles Upham, an extraordinary New Zealand sheep-farmer soldier who won the first of his two VCs on Crete, throwing grenades and knocking out machine-gun posts despite being wounded by bullet and shrapnel and suffering from dysentery. Trapped and cut off in an olive grove, the skeletal figure feigned dead until two German soldiers were close enough for him to deal with using his one good arm. With the crook of a tree as a prop he shot one, then worked the bolt one-handed and killed the other so close up that the man fell dead on Upham's rifle.

But more Germans were poured in. Bloody massacre was duly visited on the islanders in return. After twelve days of ferocious fighting the Germans won, and mountainous Crete was occupied. German casualties were heavy: over nine thousand men killed or wounded, as opposed to 7200 Australian, British and New Zealand dead and wounded, and more than twelve thousand captured.

The Royal Navy had to evacuate over ten thousand British Empire soldiers (including Captain Evelyn Waugh RM) to Egypt to fight again another day. The cost was high: three cruisers and six destroyers were sunk, with the loss of two thousand sailors, and seventeen other ships were damaged. But the toll was necessary. As Admiral Cunningham said: 'It takes the Navy three years to build a ship, but three centuries to build a tradition: we must not let the Army down.'

Dive-bombers sank HMS *Kelly*, the destroyer of the leader of the Fifth Flotilla, Lord Louis Mountbatten, and the story of the ship became the basis for Noël Coward's *In Which We Serve* (1942). The film, co-directed by David Lean, was structured around a group of oil-stained survivors clinging to a raft after their ship, fictionalised as the *Torrin*, has been bombed off Crete. Coward not only wore Mountbatten's naval cap in the film, and had 'Captain (D)' – for Destroyers, Mountbatten's title – painted on his character's tin hat, but copied many details of Mountbatten's experience, including holding his nose and mouth shut while struggling underwater, later pencilling messages from wounded and dying men, and the captain's farewell to his shipmates in Alexandria.

★

As war raged in the eastern Mediterranean, the battle of the Atlantic continued its grim course in the west. Also on 20 May 1941, British Naval Intelligence became aware that the German battleship *Bismarck* and the heavy cruiser *Prinz Eugen* were breaking out into the Atlantic to attack the vital shipping convoys. On 24 May – Empire Day – the battle cruiser HMS *Hood* and battleship HMS *Prince of Wales* closed in to prevent them by force. As the German ships turned their fifteen- and eight-inch guns on 'the Mighty *Hood*', Leading Sick Berth Attendant Sam Wood was three hundred yards away, watching from the starboard side of *Prince of Wales*.

The leading seaman with me said, 'Christ, look how close the firing is getting to the *Hood*.' As I looked out, suddenly the *Hood* exploded. She was just one pall of black smoke. Then she disappeared into a big orange flash and a huge pall of smoke which blacked us out. Time seemed to stand still. I just watched in horror. The bows pointed out of this smoke, just the bows, tilted up, and then this whole apparition slid out of sight, all in slow motion, just slid slowly away. I couldn't believe it. The *Hood* was gone.

HMS *Hood* sank in four minutes. Of her crew of 1418, only three men survived: seaman Ted Briggs, midshipman William Dundas and seaman Bob Tilburn.* *Prince of Wales*, so new she still had dockyard workers on board, fought on even though she was hit and one of her quadruple turrets jammed. She scored two or three hits on *Bismarck*, causing her to lose a thousand tons of fuel and suffer an explosion in her auxiliary boiler machinery room, but the great German battleship escaped in smoke, squalls and night. This prompted alarm and lurid rumour in the USA: the monster might now pop up to bombard Halifax, or New York, or Norfolk. *Bismarck* would assault Martinique, or amaze the Brazilians at Rio. Would she go round Cape Horn, and over the Pacific to Japan?

British signals intelligence managed to track what the ship was

* One of Ted Briggs's last wishes was that HMS *Hood*'s bell be recovered as a memorial to his shipmates. A robot submersible salvaged it from a depth of 2848 metres in August 2015 and affixed a White Ensign on the war grave. *Navy News*, September 2015, p. 9.

really doing. The GCCS Naval Section spotted that *Bismarck* changed radio frequency from Wilhelmshaven control to Paris control at midday on the 24th. Then the Luftwaffe chief of staff in Athens enquired after the ship (anxious about a young cadet on board), and the German air force, using its Enigma, which Bletchley Park could read, told him *Bismarck* was making for the west coast of France. Only one dry dock could accommodate the ship there: Chantiers Penhoët at St Nazaire. British ships and planes refocused their search. Finally, an American-supplied (and American piloted) RAF Coastal Command PBY Catalina flying boat spotted the *Bismarck* seven hundred miles west of Brest.

Force H at Gibraltar was alerted, and HMS *Renown* (with Admiral Somerville on board), the cruiser HMS *Sheffield* and the aircraft carrier HMS *Ark Royal* steamed north from Gibraltar to intercept the great German warship. The *Ark*'s Fairey Swordfish biplanes lined up on the deck. The weather was foul. Their engines started with flashes and sparks and spurts of smoke. They took off, one after another, and flew away to find *Bismarck*, maintain reconnaissance and finally to try and slow her down. Visibility was so bad that the lead aircraft, the only one so equipped, relied on its radar rather than eyesight, and so led an attack on HMS *Sheffield* by mistake; very luckily, all eleven torpedoes missed.

When the aeroplanes flew back to *Ark Royal*, the great carrier had to turn straight into the eye of the wind to allow them to land, or rather very slightly to the port bow so the smoke from the ship's funnel was blown clear of the aircraft coming in from astern. Pilots could see exactly which way the wind was blowing by the white line of steam pluming along the flat top of the flight deck from a nozzle set in the centre line at the forward end. Approaching to 'land on' was a difficult job because the pilot was bringing the plane in over the rounded-down stern of a moving ship whose surface might be pitching and rolling, rising and falling by over fifty feet in each direction, landing on a deck which he could not see clearly because of the position of the aeroplane's engine, but which he still flew onto, trusting and adjusting his trim according to the 'bats' of the yellow-jacketed Control Officer farther along the deck, manually signalling if his approach was level. If the enemy had attacked the *Ark* at that time, the captain would not have been able to manoeuvre the ship for fear that the aeroplanes would crash or go over the side.

The Swordfish biplane looks ridiculously antiquated in the age of the monoplane, but its old-fashioned double wings (whose intercon-necting struts and wires led to the aeroplane's nickname: 'String-bag') did help in its handling. A Swordfish could fly at fifty-five knots (63 mph) without stalling, so flying into a stiff headwind could make its ground speed (relative to a deck moving in the same direction) slow right down, with the aircraft seeming momentarily to hover in its approach to touchdown. Across the deck there were 'arrester wires' to catch a hook lowered from the fuselage; then the pilot throt-tled back the engine and the wires would bring the biplane to a halt. Finally, the 'pin party' on deck would fold back the plane's wings and a hydraulic lift lower the fat thorax to its hangar.

But in the dismal weather that day, three of the planes crashed on landing on the rain-slicked deck. It was only good luck that nobody was badly injured, and the Swordfish could refuel and rearm.

The second striking force of fifteen biplanes tried again, taking off from the slippery rearing deck up into the storm. Radar-equipped *Sheffield* gave them a bearing and at last the Fleet Air Arm Swordfish dived in to attack the *Bismarck* through a blizzard of anti-aircraft fire. An eighteen-inch torpedo dropped by Lieutenant Commander John Moffat's Swordfish struck on the starboard side right aft, jam-ming *Bismarck*'s rudders and flooding the steering gear compart-ment. The German battleship circled drunkenly, then steered into the rising gale, heading back towards the British Home Fleet and her doom.

The final act took place on 27 May 1941. It took forty-five min-utes to avenge the *Hood*. HMS *Rodney*'s nine sixteen-inch guns and HMS *King George V*'s fourteen-inch guns flamed orange as their rushing one-ton explosive shells pounded the great *Bismarck* into a blazing hulk. On board, there was carnage, but still the battleship would not die; HMS *Dorsetshire* administered the *coup de grâce*, three torpedoes that finally sank the *Bismarck*. Only 114 men from her 2200 crew survived. A character in Warren Tute's novel *The Rock* was sickened by the 'grim and filthy' business, feeling 'the same disgust as at a botched bullfight where the bull has not been properly killed and the memory of the mauled horses returns to sour the taste'.

Force H turned for home. As *Ark Royal* entered Gibraltar harbour on 29 May, the crew saw to their wonderment that the garrison had hired every seaworthy boat available to come out on the water and cheer her in. 'Every rating, soldier and airman who could find a foothold afloat stood shouting and waving up at the carrier's decks to welcome her return.'

Admiral Somerville had found a new ally in Gibraltar. He wrote to Admiral Cunningham in Alexandria on 11 June:

Gort – the new Governor here – is giving this place a proper shake up and high time too. He's established a new priority:
(1) Aerodrome to facilitate passage of aircraft east.
(2) Fixed and A/A defences to protect the naval base.
(3) Fortress defence against assault.
. . . The Pongos are very angry with me for laying bare their deficiencies and lack of drive but Gort welcomes every criticism and suggestion.*

The new ordering of priorities whereby the airport came first was helped by the relationship that Gort had struck up with Muñoz Grandes, because the Spanish military governor was the man who

---

* 'Pongo: Any member of the British Army, more completely known as *Percy Pongo* or (also) as *Perce*. A *pongo* is a hairy African sand-ape native to the deserts south of the Med; Royal [Marines] will have you believe (incorrectly) that the word is derived from Perce's occasional failure to wash on a daily basis, so where the Army goes, the pong goes as well.' Rick Jolly, *Jackspeak: a guide to British naval slang and usage* (Palamanando, 2nd edn, 2007), p. 337.

could, if he chose, have made the most difficulties about a British air base being sited so close to Spain. The Italian air force also helped, by mistake, dropping a stick of bombs from a Savoia-Marchetti SM.82 Marsupiale across La Línea de la Concepción on the night of 11/12 July 1941. Three houses were destroyed, five people killed and many wounded, and the town's electricity was knocked out. The bomber plane returned for the next three nights, and Gibraltar's practical help and medical support for the injured and damaged across the frontier in Spain helped make the idea of British fighter aircraft nearby seem more palatable.

The British government was tiptoeing cautiously into a diplomatic minefield. As we have seen, the isthmus between Gibraltar and Spain was not really covered by the Treaty of Utrecht. What was 'emergency use' of the airfield at Gibraltar, which the Spanish had ageed to? 'In one sense the war itself constitutes an emergency,' Churchill wrote to Hoare. 'In a narrower sense an emergency is created by the fact that aeroplanes cannot safely fly direct to the Middle East. In a third sense landings of these aircraft will not be regular but intermittent.' In his own mind, this satisfied all the assurances already given to the Spanish. However, 'I do not think it is necessary or desirable to consult the Spanish authorities or to inform them of what is proposed.'

The decision had been taken to widen and lengthen the airfield. Despite what Mason-MacFarlane's biographer claims, this happened on Gort's watch and was enthusiastically encouraged by the new governor. For the landing surface, tunnellers' broken stone could be steamrollered and then cold-sprayed with bitumen. But lengthening the entire landing strip over five hundred yards into the western bay was a major engineering challenge. Raising it six foot six inches above high water would take four hundred thousand cubic yards of filling, dumping thousands of tons of limestone spoil into the sea. Work went on twenty-four hours a day, seven days a week, with Gort chivvying the men to see it as a kind of team competition. This meant blasting and quarrying day and night with lorry-load after lorry-load of broken rock hurtling through what James Joyce called 'the queer little streets' of Gibraltar and lorry drivers banging their hands furiously on the outside of their cab doors to make people get out of the way, since they were forbidden to use their horns. It meant dust and disruption, but the final goal, achieved in January 1943, was the creation of a mile-long landing strip – 1800 yards, to be exact – so that every conceivable type and weight of aircraft could land and take off in Gibraltar. For Britain in the western Mediterranean, it was a vital strategic step.

Hitler's attack on the Soviet Union began on 22 June 1941. The largest force ever assembled in European military history, some 3.6 million men drawn from Axis countries, organised in three army groups and three tactical air forces, started crossing the German–Soviet frontier. Churchill called it 'the fourth climacteric' of the war, after the fall of France, the Battle of Britain and the passing of Lend-Lease.

The British prime minister had warned disbelieving Stalin of Hitler's attack. After two meetings with Anthony Eden in early June, Ivan Maisky, the Soviet ambassador in London, passed on (Enigma-based) information to the Soviet General Staff, including a list of all German troops and units massed on the border. The Eastern Front now became the pitiless arena where the hammer and sickle bashed and slashed at the scything swastika. Millions would die.

There was a curious little link to the Rock. Late on 23 June, Noel Mason-MacFarlane received a telephone call in his Canterbury HQ from Sir John Dill, the Chief of the Imperial General Staff. Mason-MacFarlane was to come to London, immediately, with all his kit. At one in the morning Dill asked him to head the British military mission to Russia. Mason-MacFarlane said yes. First he went to see the exiled Polish commander-in-chief General Władysław Sikorski at his London headquarters. The Russian secret police had murdered about half the Polish officer corps, over eight thousand men, in the Katyn massacres, but thousands more Polish soldiers were being held captive in the Soviet Union, and it would be helpful to try and get them out. Later that day Mason-MacFarlane travelled with the British ambassador Sir Stafford Cripps by Catalina flying boat to Archangel, from where Marshal Timoshenko's own Dakota took them on to Moscow.

Mason-MacFarlane spent a busy year in Russia. He became the intelligence conduit passing on all the ULTRA-derived information that Churchill wanted the Soviets to have, always disguising its real origin (British decrypted signals intelligence) by suggesting it came from a secret agent inside German headquarters. The first time he met Joseph Stalin, Mason-MacFarlane said how glad he was to find himself co-operating with the great Red Army against a common foe. Stalin's answer was typically disconcerting: 'How splendid if I thought that you meant what you said.'

In his year in Russia, Mason-MacFarlane helped negotiate the release of over forty thousand Polish soldiers, 'the Anders Army', who, together with seventy thousand civilians (and their mascot brown bear called Wojtek), then made their way out of Soviet Central Asia, via Iran, Iraq and Palestine to fight as the Polish II Corps under British command in places like Tobruk and Monte Cassino.

The Spanish right wing were thrilled by the Nazi invasion of the Soviet Union. At a huge Falangist rally in Madrid on 24 June, Ramón Serrano Suñer blamed the Soviets for the Spanish Civil War and called for 'the extermination of Russia'. The anti-Bolshevik struggle was 'an extension of the Spanish crusade', he said; Spain was now 'a moral belligerent'.

Mason-MacFarlane's Spanish counterpart, General Agustín Muñoz Grandes, obeyed a summons to the capital by his superiors. Like Mason-MacFarlane, Muñoz Grandes would lead a military mission to the Soviet Union, but for the other side: he became the commanding officer of *la División Azul Española* (the Spanish Blue Division, named for the blue shirts that Falangists wore). It was Franco's delayed fulfilment of his oft-cited commitment to the *Führer*.*

Some 18,400 initial volunteers, mostly Falangists, formed Wehrmacht Division 250: Spanish 'Blues' to fight Soviet 'Reds'. They wore German uniforms, used German equipment and received German rations (and hated the fatty sausage). They had few trucks: their transport was horse-drawn, using spavined nags from Serbia that died in their hundreds. They took with them from Spain their Enigma machines, still wired the same way, which meant the Knox group at Bletchley Park could eavesdrop on communications between their Berlin HQ and the Eastern Front.

Muñoz Grandes would soon find himself in the Russian steppes, in coal-scuttle helmet and *feldgrau* greatcoat, swearing allegiance to Adolf Hitler on an officer's sword. Against regulations, however, he wore a yellow scarf at the neck so his men – *los guripas*, the swaddies – could recognise him. He was often at the front, courageous but quite ruthless, ordering all cowards – deserters or men with self-inflicted wounds – to be shot. From 1941 to 1944, around forty-seven thousand Spanish volunteers served on the Eastern Front. Nearly five thousand were killed and seventeen thousand were wounded, ill, missing or captured. Where they had no winter clothes or boots, they stole them; pets and livestock were fair game for their cooking pots. 'Terrible thieves, but not cruel, and with a certain compassion for the locals' was how a teacher from Novgorod remembered the Spanish soldiers to the researcher Boris Kovalev.

Just as Mason-MacFarlane met Stalin, so Muñoz Grandes several times encountered Hitler. The *Führer* admired the Spanish:

One of the best things we ever did was to permit a Spanish Legion to fight at our side. On the first opportunity I shall decorate Muñoz Grandes with the Iron Cross with Oak Leaves and Diamonds . . . When the time comes for the Legion to return to Spain, we must re-equip it on a regal scale, give it a

---

* On 10 July 1941, SOE propaganda started spreading the rumour (S for Sib/1028) around Spain that it was because Franco had refused to send workers to the Third Reich that Serrano Suñer had started his anti-Soviet legion. This 'whisper' alleged that no Spanish volunteers would ever reach the Russian front: these men would all be diverted to factories in the Ruhr.

heap of booty and a handful of Russian Generals as trophies. Then they will have a triumphal entry into Madrid, and their prestige will be unassailable.

Vital convoys kept isolated places like Gibraltar and Malta alive. In the Mediterranean, there were increasing clashes at points where the Axis and the Allied convoy routes crossed. In February 1941, Rommel's Afrika Korps had arrived in Libya to stiffen the Italian backbone, which meant the Italian and German supply lines now ran north–south between Italy and North Africa, protected by the Luftwaffe and the Regia Aeronautica Italiana. The British Empire supply lines ran east–west through the Mediterranean, a thousand miles from Gibraltar to Malta and eight hundred miles from Malta to Egypt.

When the Germans finally captured Crete they stationed swarms of aircraft at Maleme and Heraklion, which imperilled all convoys from Alexandria to Malta. This meant more provisions for the beleaguered island would now have to come from the west, via Gibraltar. But after decryption of German air force signals at Bletchley Park revealed that many Luftwaffe squadrons had been withdrawn from Sardinia, Sicily and southern Italy in order to support the invasion of Russia, a window of opportunity opened, and in July 1941 a major British convoy was sent to reinforce and resupply Malta.

The aim of Operation *Substance* was to ship two infantry battalions, two anti-aircraft units and a battery of thirty field guns, plus masses of ammunition, fuel, food, stores and spares to depleted Malta. If ever the Germans tried an airborne invasion of Malta like the one that took Crete, these forces would stop it.

The heavily laden store ships *City of Pretoria, Deucalion, Durham, Melbourne Star, Port Chalmers* and *Sydney Star*, together with two troopships, *Leinster* and *Louis Pasteur*, made up the 'Winston Special' convoy WSC9, escorted from the UK to Gibraltar by Force X from the Home Fleet. Force X comprised the battleship HMS *Nelson*, the cruisers *Edinburgh, Manchester* and *Arethusa*, eight destroyers and the fast mine-layer HMS *Manxman*. From Gibraltar onwards, the convoy became GM1 (1st convoy Gibraltar–Malta) with additional protection from Force H: the battle cruiser HMS *Renown*, the aircraft carrier HMS *Ark Royal*, carrying twenty-four Fulmars and thirty Swordfish, the light cruiser *Hermione* and eight destroyers. Submarines, six from Gibraltar, two from Malta, were stationed to intercept any moves by the Italian fleet. In addition, Cunningham's ships were staging an elaborate diversion in the eastern Mediterranean. Three days into GM1's journey from Gibraltar to Malta, convoy MG1 (1st from Malta to Gibraltar) would set off in the opposite direction, westward, 'bringing back the empties', the fleet supply ship *Breconshire*, a destroyer and six unloaded cargo ships.

Among the hundreds of soldiers being transported in Operation *Substance* to join the Central Infantry Brigade on Malta was my own maternal grandfather. In the spring of 1941, at Duns in Scotland, Lieutenant Colonel G. F. Page DSO had taken command of the thirty-two officers and 742 other ranks of 11th Battalion, the Lancashire Fusiliers, an enthusiastic but very new battalion raised in Rochdale in October 1940. They arrived in Gibraltar from Gourock aboard HM Troopship *Louis Pasteur*, a new French liner which had carried two hundred tons of gold from Brest to Nova Scotia and then been commandeered by the British government to carry troops.

The soldiers had not been informed they were to transship in Gibraltar and most of their kit was locked behind watertight doors that could not be opened *en voyage*. They saw nothing of the Rock, but did set foot on its detached mole. In three and a half hours, using two lighters, the battalion moved itself and all its baggage, plus twenty tons of ammunition, along the mole and into the cruiser HMS *Edinburgh*. 'Some 5 tons of phosphorus bombs for mortars were carried as deck cargo and did not conduce to the safety of the ship,' Lieutenant Colonel Page wrote in his report. 'Once aboard, I cannot speak too highly of the arrangements made for the accommodation of the troops. I doubt if another man could have been carried but every man had somewhere to sleep and meals were regular and ample.'

Convoy GM1 sailed on 20 July 1941, at night, in fog. The smaller troopship *Leinster*, carrying a thousand men including RAF personnel from Gibraltar, ran aground in the strait and took no further part in Operation *Substance*. Spain had the right to intern all the uniformed passengers stranded on its territory, but chose to turn a blind eye to the *Leinster*. British destroyers took the shipwrecked soldiers and airmen back to the Rock after their bizarrely brief excursion. At the hospital, the stranded medic Reg Gill met a monocled British RAMC colonel who was wearing his German medal given by Hitler for helping the *Deutschland* wounded in 1937 and who was now only too eager to demonstrate an enormous fly-trap he had invented.

Substance proceeded eastward. On board the fast cruiser HMS *Edinburgh*, flying the flag of Rear Admiral Neville Syfret, 18th Cruiser Squadron, the captain's day cabin became the Lancashire Fusiliers' orderly room and the battalion was organised into working parties to keep the men busy on their way to Malta. Soldiers and sailors would fight side by side. The keenest-eyed soldiers were assigned to the pom-pom guns and the bridge as extra lookouts for enemy aircraft and submarines. From first light to last light, under the direction of the ship's gunnery officer, the Lancashire Fusiliers deployed sixteen Bren light machine guns, each with a team of six (two men per gun and one NCO per team on duty at a time, working two hours on and four hours off), to supplement *Edinburgh*'s already formidable anti-aircraft defences: a dozen four-inch AA guns, two eight-barrelled two-pounder pom-poms and sixteen Vickers .50 machine guns. The Mortar Bomb Disposal Party was tasked with throwing overboard any phosphorus smoke bombs ignited by enemy action before they caused excessive damage. The Gun Crew Action Ration Party was to keep ship's gun crews supplied with food and drink when they were unable to leave their posts during 'action stations'. The Shell Supply Magazine Parties were to help naval personnel get the cordite charges and semi-armour-piercing shells to the turrets of the twelve six-inch guns, and to shift the 55 lb fixed rounds from the four-inch magazine.

All ranks detailed for ship duties were told they were under the command of the navy (or their own officers liaising with the navy) in order to achieve their objective of disembarking at Malta. Admiral Somerville had sent out a mission statement to all ships, ending: 'THE CONVOY MUST GO THROUGH.' As for the German and Italian enemy, the Lancashire Fusiliers were told there were 'the normal routine hazards of submarines and mines' but 'attacks by aircraft from high level and torpedo- or dive-bombing are almost certain'. Everyone was ordered to keep their field dressing in the front pocket of their KD (khaki drill) shorts and carry a gas mask. Those above deck during action were to wear steel helmets.

Lieutenant Colonel Geoffrey Page was a regular soldier with a neat moustache, a good regimental officer now in charge of a green if keen battalion. He was a firm disciplinarian, not unkind to young soldiers, but they did have to 'keep steady' and follow orders. There were few bad soldiers, he thought, just poor officers. His own mode was studied imperturbability; his 1916 DSO in Macedonia was for calmness and good leadership under heavy fire. He was an impatient man, so that required some will-power. Now he took up his position on the bridge with the captain.

At 9.20 a.m. on the third day, Wednesday 23 July, hands went to action stations. The convoy was in the gap between Sardinia and Algeria when the Regia Aeronautica Italiana flying from Cagliari pounced. Firing began at 9.45. The attack was well synchronised: while the nine CANT Z.1007 high-level bombers drew eyes upwards, the seven Savoia-Marchetti SM.79s flew in low, carrying deadly torpedoes. The Force H destroyer HMS *Fearless* was hit by one such 'kipper' or torpedo at 9.54 and caught fire. Thirty-five men were killed and the rest of the crew abandoned ship, rescued by the Dakar veteran HMS *Forester*, which then sank the burning *Fearless* by gunfire.

The cruiser HMS *Manchester* managed to dodge three torpedoes, but in avoiding a collision with *Port Chalmers* was caught port aft by another 45 cm torpedo, whose explosion killed and wounded another forty-four men. The damaged cruiser, carrying 750 soldiers from the

8th Battalion, King's Own Royal Regiment, could still make nine knots, but because that would slow everyone else down, Admiral Somerville ordered *Manchester* with its soldiers back to Gibraltar, escorted by the destroyer HMS *Avon Vale*. Convoys could not afford to dawdle. *Manchester* herself had signalled the day before: 'S stands for Straggler and Sunk.'

Meanwhile, battle raged in the air. The barrage of anti-aircraft gunfire from the ships brought down three of the SM.79 Sparviero torpedo bombers, and the Fairey Fulmars from the *Ark Royal* shot down two more, plus a brace of high-level bombers, for a loss of three of their own. When a soldier from the Cheshire Regiment aimed his rifle purposefully at some downed Italian fliers in their rubber dinghy, his officer tapped him on the shoulder: 'We don't do that in the British army.'

Now the convoy was reaching an even more dangerous stretch, the Sicilian Narrows between Cape Bon in Tunisia and Sicily, the passage known to the sailors as 'Bomb Alley'. At around 5.30 p.m., the big ships of Force H turned back to cover the damaged *Manchester*, leaving *Hermione* and two destroyers with the convoy, as well as the *Ark*'s fighters, flying top cover until Beaufighters from Malta could take over. Rear Admiral Syfret in *Edinburgh* was now in command of *Substance*. They endured two more bombing attacks on the 23rd, at 7.00 and 7.45 p.m. People under hatches on *Edinburgh* knew what was happening because the ship's Air Defence Officer on the bridge, Lieutenant Commander Talbot, 'piped' information over the ship's broadcasting system. 'Torpedo bomber attacking starboard' would be followed by the din of the guns: the booms of the four-inch, the bang-bang-bang-bang of the pom-poms, the hammering chatter of the machine guns, the squirts of Bren, then 'Cease firing' and 'Friendly fighter coming down portside', followed by 'Lancashire Fusiliers four-inch guns emergency supply party fall in on flight deck' and so on. The running commentary 'was much appreciated and greatly assisted morale', Lieutenant Colonel Page wrote. The convoy was running in two lines, each led by a destroyer with its minesweeping paravanes out and streaming. *Firedrake*, the destroyer heading the port column, was holed in the second bombing attack and had to be towed back to Gibraltar by *Eridge*.

Admiral Syfret took the convoy northeast to avoid mines and an air attack at dusk. Enemy aircraft were searching for them along the original line of advance and around midnight the sailors on watch could see parachute flares being dropped by planes twenty miles to the south. Syfret ordered the convoy to change course south again to pass close by the island of Pantellaria.

In the darkest hour of the night, just before 3 a.m. on Thursday 24 July, there was a roar of engines over the sea and the convoy was attacked three times by Regia Marina speedboats. The Italian torpedo-armed motor boat – *motoscafo armato silurante* or MAS – carried two torpedoes and a machine gun and was the fastest thing afloat, capable of forty-five knots. The British warships, rapidly at action stations, turned on their searchlights and soon red tracer was stitching the blackness.

When *Edinburgh* illuminated a fast Italian craft eight hundred yards away, a splashing broadside from the four-inchers, the multiple pom-poms and the machine guns seemed to blow the thing to pieces. However, another Italian speedboat – *MAS 532* – got through and put a torpedo into the largest cargo ship, the eleven-thousand-ton MV *Sydney Star*. Soon the *Sydney Star* had thirty foot of water in the hold and although Captain T. S. Horn stayed on board to nurse the ship home, HM Australian Ship *Nestor* came alongside to take off all the soldiers from a light anti-aircraft unit.

This operation took fifty minutes, in the darkness, three miles off enemy-held Pantellaria. *Hermione* stood by to help with cover and, sure enough, as the sun came up, a flight of Ju 87 Stukas attacked the three ships from the east. It was the first of four air attacks that day. The action log of the Fusiliers on HMS *Edinburgh* recorded:

0734 Enemy aircraft approaching. Range 10 miles.
0740 Firing commenced.

0743 Friendly Beaufighters passing down port side.

0747 'This is the Captain speaking. We are now on the last part of our journey. Have opened up speed to 26 knots. Making straight for Malta. Expect to arrive 1130 hrs.'

At 11.30 a.m. on 24 July, the first three ships of convoy GM1, HMS *Arethusa*, *Edinburgh* and *Manxman*, steamed into the Grand Harbour of Valletta, four hours ahead of the transports. The old walls were black with Maltese people: what looked like the whole populace had turned out to welcome them in, and the Royal Navy intended to make a show of it. The ship's company and the Lancashire Fusiliers were all standing to attention, lining the port and starboard guardrails of HMS *Edinburgh*, while on the turret of the aft six-inch gun the band of the Royal Marines was pumping out 'The British Grenadiers' and other patriotic marches. Lieutenant Colin Kitching RNVR, one of the *Edinburgh* boarding party who had 'pinched' Enigma papers off the German weather-ship *München*, was on deck when they arrived in Valletta with all the people cheering them in. 'The emotion of the moment was so great that I found tears were rolling down my cheeks, a reaction which seemed to apply to everyone around me.'

An order went out over the ship's tannoy: 'Lancashire Fusiliers. Adjutant calling. The Navy is returning the way we came. Clean the mess decks. Leave lifebelts on board. Don't forget your haversack rations.'

At 12.25 p.m., the Lancashire Fusiliers started disembarking on Malta, where they would stay for the next three lean years. Personnel and baggage were all unloaded in two hours, and at 3.30 HMS *Edinburgh* departed, heading back to Gibraltar.

Their troubles were not over. The arrival of the *Substance* convoy in Malta prompted the Italian navy to order its small craft and submarine assault unit, Decima Flottiglia MAS, the 10th Light Flotilla, to attack Valletta Harbour.

The British made many jokes about 'the Eyeties', 'the Macaronis', 'the Ice-creamers', like the one about more reverse than forward gears on their tanks, but no one could doubt the bravery of the Italian sailors who made this assault. There was a narrow channel under the three-pillared steel bridge between the Sant'Elmo mole and the Maltese mainland that in peacetime used to allow small vessels into the main harbour. A wartime anti-torpedo net of interlocking steel rings now blocked this gap, but the Italians planned to blow the net open with a two-man piloted torpedo, known as a *maiale* or 'hog', letting eight fast speedboats into the harbour to attack the cargo ships. Another two-man *maiale* would enter the western bay nearby, Marsamxett, the wintering harbour where British submarines were moored side by side, and attach its explosive charge to a hull to try and sink one or two of the 'boats'.

The night of 25 July was moonless, and the sea calm. British radar spotted the raiders. All the guns and searchlights waited. Both the Italian torpedo 'hogs' got engine trouble and missed their deadline, so it was the explosive speedboats that set out to breach the steel net. The MT (*Motoscafo Turismo*) was essentially a torpedo embedded in the shell of a carvel-built, mahogany-hulled seacraft, powered by a six-cylinder, ninety-five-horsepower Alfa Romeo engine. The single operator sat at the back in a wooden seat that was ejected from the boat at the pull of a lever. He aimed his craft at the target and, about a hundred metres away, he was supposed to lock the steering and throw himself off. When the craft hit the target at speed, the hull would split open and the fuse (set for impact) would trigger the 330 kg explosive torpedo.

The two leading MT speedboats aimed for the net at around 4.45 a.m. Sub-lieutenant Roberto Frassetto threw himself off about fifty metres from the net but his boat was not going fast enough to split open and detonate. Sub-lieutenant Aristide Carabelli saw what had happened, set his own fuse to 'impact' and drove straight at the net at full speed, heroically, suicidally. His detonation set off Frassetto's boat too and the double explosion not only shredded Carabelli but brought down the bridge overhead, completely blocking the way in.

None of the other MT speedboats would have made it anyway. Valletta's searchlights blazed on and a two-minute hail of gunfire from six-pounders, Bofors guns and machine guns annihilated the Regia Marina flotilla. As the sun rose, British Hurricane fighter planes attacked their support ships. Only eleven Italian sailors made it back home. Twenty of their unit were killed, including some of the leading commanders, and eighteen others were captured. Two *maiali*, eight MT boats and three other vessels were lost. But Decima Flottiglia MAS would keep trying, and their next attack would be on Gibraltar.

The German submarine was a frightening weapon to people on land, but Admiral Karl Dönitz pointed out that the landlubber's view of it as a primarily *under*-water vessel was wrong. In both world wars, U-boats spent most of their time on the surface, where they travelled much faster and could see more. They were 'diving vessels' only for their own protection or for daylight attack. But being on the surface made them vulnerable to aircraft. (Swordfish biplanes alone sank twenty-one U-boats.)

In September 1941, Hitler ordered more U-boats away from the battle of the Atlantic and into the Mediterranean to operate against the Gibraltar convoys, which the Italians alone were failing to stop. Admiral Dönitz, however, thought that stationing up to fifteen U-boats in the vicinity of Gibraltar was a distraction from the main task of blocking American supplies to Britain, and a strategic error. The Mediterranean might have looked like a happy hunting ground, but it was also a death trap. The stronger Atlantic current carried the U-boats in fast, but getting back out, when submerged and slow, was almost impossible. None of the five dozen German submarines that entered the Mediterranean after 1 January 1940 ever came out again.

On 30 October 1941, *Kapitänleutnant* Fritz Guggenberger's submarine *U-81* was heading for the Strait of Gibraltar when it was attacked southwest of Brest by an RAF flying boat piloted by the

Anglo-Argentine Flight Lieutenant Denis E. Ryan. The US-built Consolidated Catalina patrol bomber with a ten-man crew, carrying depth charges, three heavy machine guns (and later radar), was a brand-new weapon in anti-submarine (A/S) warfare, sinking its first enemy submarine on 25 August 1941. This particular attack damaged *Unterseeboot 81* badly enough to send her back to Brest for repairs before she could return to sea.

But *U-81* crept back into the Mediterranean and waited east of Gibraltar for Force H to return from escorting Operation *Perpetual*, the delivery of more aircraft to Malta. On 13 November 1941, at long range, *U-81* torpedoed the great workhorse of the British Fleet, HMS *Ark Royal*, dead amidships. British destroyers, following sonar echoes from ASDIC, dropped 160 depth charges, but *U-81* jinked away to safety. What Goebbels had claimed so many times was now true. The *Ark*, the great aircraft carrier which had sailed over two hundred thousand miles and been engaged in thirty-two war operations in her four years, was at last done for.

Severed communications meant Captain Maund could not stop the huge vessel quickly enough, and water drag fatally widened the *Ark*'s wound; they could not staunch the flooding. Remembering how the torpedoed aircraft-carrier HMS *Courageous* turned turtle in September 1939, Maund evacuated all surplus men.

The crippled, listing ship was being towed back to Gibraltar by the tug *Thames* and was only twenty-five miles from port when she finally turned over and sank, at 6.30 a.m. on 14 November. Only one man died, Able Seaman Edward Mitchell RN, but the passing of 'the old *Ark*' was grievous. In Madrid, Sir Samuel and Lady Hoare, who had launched the *Ark Royal* four and a half years earlier, 'felt that we had suffered not only a national calamity, but also a very poignant personal loss'. Men in Gibraltar who had cheered her in after she helped sink the *Bismarck* looked sadly at her long and empty berth at the South Mole. Charles Causley wrote in his diary, '*Ark Royal* down today & feel depressed.'

28

Hands across the Sea

The fates of big ships always affected morale. News of the successful sinking of the *Bismarck* had added extra fizz to Ian Fleming's thirty-second birthday celebrations on 28 May 1941. The RNVR commander was in New York City with his boss, the Director of Naval Intelligence, Admiral John Godfrey, on a mission from the British chiefs of staff and the Joint Intelligence Committee to help the Americans 'set up a combined intelligence organisation on a 100 per cent co-operative basis'. The two men travelled south by train to Washington DC.

Before the Second World War, the United States of America had left foreign intelligence variously to the diplomats of the State Department, the Military Intelligence Division (or G-2) of the War Department and the Office of Naval Intelligence. (The FBI was purely domestic, though J. Edgar Hoover had bigger ambitions.) No one below the White House was collating intelligence and thus seeing the big strategic picture. Godfrey believed that what the Americans needed now was a unified secret intelligence service combining the functions of the four different bodies which in the UK all had different masters: sabotage and resistance in occupied countries (SOE), political warfare (PWE), economic warfare (MEW) and covert intelligence-gathering (SIS). Although Godfrey found the US army, navy and State Department all polite and friendly towards him, he was surprised to discover how much the army and navy loathed and detested each other, and what a snakepit bureaucratic Washington could be, like Whitehall at its very worst.

The only man who could knock heads together and make them co-operate was the Commander-in-Chief, the President of the United

States. Admiral Godfrey was invited to dine at the White House on 10 June 1941, and given an hour with President Roosevelt afterwards in the Oval Office. According to Godfrey, after watching what he called 'a rather creepy crawly film of snake worship',* FDR drawlingly recounted his reminiscences of British Admiral Reginald 'Blinker' Hall's brilliance as Director of Naval Intelligence in the Great War, while Godfrey himself reiterated three times the crucial need for the Americans to have 'one intelligence security boss, not three or four'.

By arrangement, on that very same day, 10 June, Colonel William J. Donovan submitted a memorandum to the president recommending the establishment of 'a central enemy intelligence organization' to analyse and appraise all information on enemy intentions and resources, both military and economic, and to determine the best methods of waging economic and psychological warfare. A week later, on 18 June, President Roosevelt accepted this proposal and appointed Donovan himself as his head of intelligence, under the camouflage title of 'Coordinator of Information' (COI). His job was to 'collect and analyze all information and data which may bear upon national security: to correlate such information and data, and to make such information and data available to the President'. Roosevelt scrawled a note on the memo's coversheet, 'Please set this up *confidentially* . . . Military – not O.E.M. [Office of Emergency Management].' The CIA historian Thomas F. Troy glosses '*confidentially*' to mean there would be access to the president's secret funds and 'Military' to denote 'by virtue of the president's authority as commander in chief'. William Stephenson, running British Security Co-ordination in New York, was jubilant. He cabled his boss, the Chief of the Secret Service, Sir Stewart Menzies, in London: '[Donovan] will be co-ordinator all forms intelligence . . . He will hold rank of Major General and will be responsible only to the President . . . You can imagine how relieved I am after three months of battle and

---

* Eleanor Roosevelt's 'My Day' column suggests this was footage shot in Burma by Armand and Michaela Denis of a priestess ritually dancing with a dangerously spitting king cobra.

jockeying for position in Washington that our man is in a position of such importance to our efforts.'

On Saturday 9 August 1941, Franklin Roosevelt and Winston Churchill met in a circle of warships at Placentia Bay off the little town of Argentia in Newfoundland, Canada. Churchill had crossed the Atlantic aboard the battleship HMS *Prince of Wales*, a trip organised in secrecy and later announced with a fanfare of publicity. The night before the two leaders met, Churchill watched once again the Alexander Korda romantic propaganda film *Lady Hamilton*,* which had premiered in Britain a week earlier. Laurence Olivier as Admiral Nelson defying Napoleon Bonaparte was speaking Churchillian words against Hitler. 'Believe me, gentlemen, he means to be master of the world. You cannot make peace with dictators. You have to destroy them. Wipe them out!'

The President of the United States of America – 'thrice-chosen head of the most powerful State and community in the world' – encountered the British prime minister – 'the servant of King and Parliament at present charged with the principal direction of of our affairs . . . approved and sustained by the whole British Commonwealth of Nations' – and together the two leaders issued a joint declaration, the eight-point Atlantic Charter, with 'certain common principles . . . on which they base their hopes for a better future'.

Churchill saw the meeting as symbolic of the unity of English-speaking peoples on 'the broad high road of freedom and justice', but also of 'something even more majestic, namely the marshalling of the good forces of the world against the evil forces which are now so formidable and triumphant'. For this reason the agnostic premier stage-managed the Church Parade of Sunday 10 August on

* Alexander Korda was subpoenaed by a US Senate Committee to answer the charge that his Nelson film was 'inciting the American public to war'. He did not have to testify on 12 December 1941 because the Pearl Harbor attack proved a more effective incitement. The fiercely non-interventionist America First Committee also had to disband itself after the event in Hawaii.

the quarter-deck of the *Prince of Wales*, facing the four guns of the fourteen-inch turret. The sun shone bright and warm. Hundreds of British and American sailors mingled in a congregation around the two leaders with their chiefs of staff, by a lectern draped with both flags. An American and a British chaplain alternated the prayers; the lesson was from Joshua: 'I will not fail thee, nor forsake thee. Be strong and of good courage . . .' They sang the old hymns: 'O God our help in ages past', 'Onward Christian soldiers', 'Eternal Father, strong to save'.

Some today dismiss the Atlantic Charter as empty rhetoric, but it came like cool fresh water to some of the hot and thirsty people caught up in a nightmarish world war. Take the passengers on the Swedish ship MV *Vasaholm*, all of whom were on the high seas because they were escaping from Nazi-occupied Europe to the freedom of the Americas. On 14 August 1941, the ship's radio broadcast the news that Roosevelt and Churchill had met and agreed the Atlantic Charter, a statement of aims, the purposes for which the war was being fought. The Basques and Polish Jews on the ship, persecuted people going even further into exile from beloved homelands now occupied and oppressed, were moved by a vision for a better world, achieved on the very ocean they were now crossing. It seemed that the English and the Americans together were giving them a special message of hope:

They do not seek territorial aggrandisement.

They do not wish to make any territorial changes that do not respond to the wishes of the people.

They respect the rights of all countries to choose freely their form of government, and wish to see restored the sovereignties and self-government taken away by force . . .

Big and little countries will have access to the raw material of the world.

All countries should collaborate economically to better the standard of work, the economic progress and the social security of all.

When the Nazi tyranny has disappeared, a peace will be established so that people can live without fear and without want.

The peace will give the right to sail freely on all the seas and oceans of the world.

A system of collective security will abolish force and arrange for disarmament.

The exiled Basque president José Antonio de Aguirre was one of those passengers on the Swedish ship heading for Brazil. A good friend of the Basque priest Father Onaindia, the man who tried to become the pastor of the Gibraltarian exiles in England, Aguirre himself was ending nearly a year and a half of clandestine life, hiding in Europe, a hunted man disguised as a Panamanian doctor. As a true Christian democrat, passionately opposed to what he called the 'Christian dictatorships' of Franco, Mussolini, Pétain and Salazar, Aguirre thought that the Atlantic Charter was 'magnificent': 'It has a universality which could only be given by men of such moral stature as Roosevelt and Churchill, who understand perfectly that they are guardians not only of their own country, but also of the entire world.'

Every nation fighting for liberty soon put its name to the Atlantic Charter. It was accepted and endorsed by Belgium, Czechoslovakia, Free France, Greece, Luxembourg, the Netherlands, Norway, Poland and the USSR at the Inter-Allied council on 27 September 1941. The message went out loud and clear to imperial subjects and colonised peoples in every continent, including Gibraltar: a promise that one day they could freely choose their own form of government.

The US navy now put itself in harm's way by escorting convoys half the distance across the North Atlantic. On 4 September, a German U-boat's torpedo narrowly missed the USS *Greer*, while she was on Neutrality Patrol. President Roosevelt took this as an act of piracy and warned in a fireside chat on 11 September that 'in waters which we deem necessary for our defence', US warships would now shoot on sight any hostile Italian or German vessels. He added: 'When you see a rattlesnake that is poised to strike, you do not wait until he has struck before you crush him. These Nazi submarines and raiders are the rattlesnakes of the Atlantic.'

On 17 October, the destroyer USS *Kearny* tried to depth-charge the predatory German submarine *U-568*, but was itself torpedoed, and eleven American sailors died. Roosevelt made a rousing speech ten days later on Navy Day, 27 October, declaring, 'America has been attacked.' The president painted a lurid picture of Nazi plans to take over South America and abolish all religions in favour of a Nazi church offering blood and iron instead of love and mercy. A fortnight later, *U-552* sank the destroyer USS *Reuben James*, killing 115 American sailors. The USA's 'state of unlimited emergency' was fast slipping towards war.

World war engulfed the Pacific and the Far East. Eight aircraft carriers of the Imperial Japanese Navy carried 350 aeroplanes to attack Honolulu's Pearl Harbor in Hawaii early on Sunday 7 December 1941, 'the day that will live in infamy' in US history, sinking battleships, destroying aircraft, killing 2400 people and wounding another 1100. 'What a holocaust!' said Churchill.

Imperial Japanese forces also invaded Thailand and Malaya and attacked the British colony of Hong Kong, which surrendered on Christmas Day 1941. They also attacked Guam, the Philippine Islands, Wake Island and Midway Island. The Pacific had turned martial.

On 10 December 1941, Japanese aircraft caught the Royal Navy's Force Z north of Singapore. At five foot four, Admiral Tom Phillips was even smaller than Nelson, but had fewer of his other qualities. An 'armchair admiral' with no practical war experience and little sea sense, a man who had flattered Churchill and annoyed Somerville, he had been rash enough to sail without air cover, which was exactly what the Japanese wanted. Admiral Phillips's flag was on HMS *Prince of Wales*, the battleship that had wounded the *Bismarck* and carried Churchill to Placentia Bay. Also with him in Force Z were the battle cruiser HMS *Repulse*, John Godfrey's old ship, now captained by Bill Tennant who had done such sterling work at Dunkirk, and four destroyers, *Electra*, *Express*, *Tenedos* and *Vampire*. But, without air cover, as James Somerville observed, '[b]attleships by themselves are quite useless.'

Eighty-five Japanese Mitsubishi G3M and G4M bombers and torpedo bombers, flying southwest from Saigon in Japanese-occupied Vietnam, tracked the *Repulse* and the *Prince of Wales*, then attacked and sank the vulnerable ships with four hits each from 800 kg torpedoes. British destroyers rescued nearly 1300 survivors from *Prince of Wales* and *Repulse*, but 763 men were lost. Admiral Tom Phillips had the courage to go down with his ship.

The news came as a bombshell in London. Churchill was in bed working on official papers when Dudley Pound rang with the news that both ships were sunk.

'Tom Phillips is drowned.'

'Are you sure it's true?'

'There is no doubt at all.'

Churchill put the telephone down. He was thankful to be alone. 'In all the war I never received a more direct shock.' Actually he was not wholly alone. His secretary Kathleen Hill was in the room, sitting unobtrusively in the corner, waiting to take dictation if the PM ordered. 'When he was upset I used to try to be invisible. When the two ships went down, I was there. That was a terrible moment. "Poor Tom Phillips," he said.'

General Sir Alan Brooke had just taken over from Sir John Dill as Chief of the Imperial General Staff at the beginning of the month. His diary for 10 December records:

Arrived at WO [War Office] to be informed that both the *Prince of Wales* and *Repulse* had been sunk by the Japs! This on top of the tragedy of Honolulu puts us in a very serious position for the prosecution of the war. It means that from Africa eastward to America through the Indian Ocean and the Pacific, we have lost command of the sea. This affects reinforcements to Middle East, India, Burma, Far East, Australia and New Zealand!

Now Admiral James Somerville was sent east to sort things out, leaving Force H behind in Gibraltar. In the Mediterranean too, things were going badly. On 25 November 1941, *U-331* had torpedoed the battleship *Barham*, which blew up. On 14 December, *U-557* sank the cruiser *Galatea*. Five days later, the cruiser *Neptune* hit a mine; only one man survived. Worst of all, the next day, Italian divers from Decima Flottiglia MAS crept into Alexandria harbour in Egypt and planted limpet mines underneath the dreadnought *Queen Elizabeth* and the battleship *Valiant* whose explosions crippled both vessels. Seven of His Majesty's big ships lost in four weeks emasculated the Mediterranean fleet.

But, Westward, look, the land is bright . . .

America seemed the best hope. The US Congress had declared war on Japan; Germany and Italy had duly declared war on the USA. But where would the USA range its armed forces? Across the Atlantic, as agreed in the earlier American–British conversations, or over the Pacific, to avenge Pearl Harbor?

Right at this moment of historic decision, the Spanish millionaire Juan March erupted as a hideous embarrassment. American banking laws had blocked the 'Spanish Neutrality Scheme' (i.e. secret bribery) dollar funds in New York from getting to Geneva, from where Juan March usually distributed them. Lord Halifax, the British ambassador in Washington, had consequently appealed to Henry Morgenthau, US Secretary of the Treasury, to get them released as a 'personal favour' to Winston Churchill. This was quietly achieved. Then the British learned that March was actually using the US dollars for his own private transactions: buying more shares in the Barcelona Traction, Light and Power Company;* buying tobacco in Central and South America for shipment to the Spanish govern-

---

* Juan March finally gained control of BTLP Co. Ltd in 1948; the complicated 1970 court case (*Belgium v. Spain*) is well-known in international law for asserting that states have an obligation *erga omnes* (towards everyone) concerning the treatment of foreign investments, once they admit such investments or foreign nationals into their territory.

ment's tobacco monopoly in Spanish Morocco; purchasing Argentine pesos. If this were to become apparent to the American banking authorities it 'would put Halifax and Morgenthau in a most difficult position'.

On 15 December 1941, US Treasury agents stormed aboard the Juan March-owned, Spanish-flagged ship *Isla Tenerife* just as it was about to leave New York harbour. Detaining her master and wireless operator, they found war contraband in the ship's stores: numerous parts of radio transmitters, rolls of armoured cable, two hundred drums of lubricating oil and $36,000 worth of silk. March's local shipping agents, García and Díaz, were denounced as 'fascists'; there was talk of a 'spy ring'; a US radio station attacked March as a piratical, two-timing crook. The British authorities sent Juan March frantic messages to stop rocking the boat.

The Arcadia conference, from 22 December 1941 to 14 January 1942, was intended to decide the joint effort and grand strategy of the war. Winston Churchill seized the moment, flying to Washington DC to spend Christmas 1941 with Franklin Roosevelt at the White House. On 22 December, the two leaders agreed that the war would be waged first against Germany, the predominant member of the Triple Axis. This meant the Atlantic and European area was 'the decisive theatre', not the Pacific. The US chiefs of staff, General Marshall and Admiral Stark, confirmed Germany was the prime enemy. 'Once Germany is defeated, the collapse of Italy and the defeat of Japan must follow.'

There were many meetings of the two Allies. In the fourteen days Churchill was in the White House, he and Roosevelt had lunch and dinner together every day but one. There were eight major White House meetings of president and prime minister, secretaries of war and navy, British and American chiefs of staff, plus Beaverbrook and Hopkins, and eight meetings of the British and American chiefs of staff alone. They still had not yet agreed on where precisely to hit at Germany. Churchill and Roosevelt favoured *Gymnast*, the plan to land in northwest Africa, but the American chiefs of staff wanted *Bolero*, a big build-up of Allied troops in the UK, prior to *Roundup*, a landing at Calais in France to strike for the heart of Germany. Not until 24 July 1942 would the decision be made to invade Morocco and Algeria before northwest Europe.

First things first. One of many complex political tasks was to create a coalition of all the countries fighting the Axis, a grand alliance of peoples to get them to co-ordinate their efforts and resources, and agree that no one should make an individual peace with the 'savage, brutal forces seeking to subjugate the world'. On New Year's Day 1942, representatives of the twenty-six 'Associated Powers' signed a joint declaration at the White House. President Roosevelt himself had made the final change to the draft that was circulated. He struck out the words 'Associated Powers' and inserted a name which he had thought up and was proud of: '*the United Nations*'.

And so, on 1 January 1942, Australia, Belgium, Canada, China, Costa Rica, Cuba, Czechoslovakia, the Dominican Republic, El Salvador, Greece, Guatemala, Haiti, Honduras, India, Luxembourg, the Netherlands, New Zealand, Nicaragua, Norway, Panama, Poland, South Africa, the UK, the USA, the USSR and Yugoslavia all pledged, as 'the United Nations', 'to defend life, liberty, independence and religious freedom, and to preserve human rights and justice . . . in the struggle for victory over Hitlerism'.

29

The Clandestine Struggle

Allied special forces were settling down in Gibraltar after a dynamic visit by Commander Frank Slocum. Slocum wore two hats. In the Admiralty, he was Deputy Director Operations (Irregular); in SIS, he ran the secret service sea lanes for Claude Dansey's 'O' or Operations section, getting officers and agents in and out of enemy-occupied territory.

At a time when cross-Channel activities were becoming more dangerous, both SOE and MI9 needed vessels to move people to and from southern France. (Peter Musson's smuggling fleet did not range beyond eighty miles from Gibraltar.) At the same time, the 'private navies' of Czechs and Poles, such as Lieutenant Marian Kadulski aka 'Krajewski', who worked for SIS and SOE, needed a solid base with engineers, stores, spares, etc. Slocum's sensible solution was to put the undercover Poles in with the 'underwaters'. The Poles' two small feluccas, *Dogfish* and *Seawolf*, got a new home in Gibraltar with the 8th Submarine Flotilla and their depot ship, HMS *Maidstone*. *Maidstone* had been commissioned in 1938 and looked after nine operational 'boats', as submariners referred to their submersible vessels. There were forges and foundries on board, repair works and machine shops, as well as a baker's, a barber's, two canteens, a chapel, a cinema, a dentist's, a hospital with full operating theatre and two laundries. In addition to normal duties, the 8th Flotilla submarines ran supplies, including vital aviation fuel, to Malta and would sometimes land people in out-of-the-way places, too. Bill Jewell's boat, P.219, HMS *Seraph*, came to specialise in this 'silent service'.

The clandestine fleet, now called the Coast Watching Flotilla, was soon joined by HMS *Tarana*. A modern 347-ton trawler, 150 feet long, with a twenty-four-foot beam and a cruiser stern, *Tarana* had been refitted in Portsmouth as a Q-ship, with a concealed twelve-pound gun fitted where the winch used to be and a pair of hidden two-pounders either side of the fo'c'sle. HMS *Tarana* became the workhorse of escape and evasion, winning the Croix de Guerre for rescuing upwards of six hundred 'parcels'. Rough voyages were horrendous: two score seasick people might be hidden below decks with three small toilets, or the weather was so hot that kapok-filled life-jackets actually combusted.

Tarana would slip out of Gibraltar at night, an ordinary RN vessel flying the White Ensign, with a black hull and 'crabfat'-grey upperworks. By morning the ship would be a brown Portuguese trawler with a differently shaped funnel and a crew wearing berets and scruffy French clothes. In three or four days she would be in the Gulf of Lions, anchored off shore while her twelve-foot clinker-built rowing-boat picked up various people from Canet Plage near Perpignan. At places further east – Cassis, St Tropez, St Raphaël, La Napoule, Juan-les-Pins – the larger ship would sometimes collect people picked up by the Poles in their smaller vessels. Krajewski and Buchowski's outward journey from Gibraltar would have carried arms, explosives and agents for the French Resistance, to be left on shore. To bring people back to Gibraltar it was more efficient to ferry them out to the *Tarana*. In the night before returning to the Rock, *Tarana* would be repainted and reflagged, appearing once again as a British ship to the eagle-eyed watchers of Algeciras, reporting to the Abwehr.

Ron Stephens from Poole, an ordinary junior rating on *Tarana*, had concealed his excellent seamanship skills because it wasn't worth the effort to use them for the two shillings and sixpence a day he was paid. But when Captain Clark asked him to row over and pick up some stores from the Admiralty Tower his sculling prowess was revealed. He was then promoted to Able Seaman and put to teaching two deck officers how to handle oars and the small boat.

On *Tarana*'s first round trip from Gibraltar to France in April 1942, the ship was standing off the coast of southern France when Captain

Edward Clark asked Seaman Stephens and Sub-lieutenant Whiting to row their first two passengers ashore. 'You will wear nothing that could connect you with the Royal Navy and take no guns.' Clark showed Stephens the small, flat, shiny tin he would be issued with. Inside were emergency raisins and chocolate, an amphetamine tablet and a quick-acting suicide pill. 'If you manage to evade capture, try to find the Hotel du Tennis at Perpignan to get help.'

The well-oiled sheaves in the blocks gave not a squeak as the matelots lowered the rowing boat from the deck of *Tarana* to the dark swell. The engine was still and everyone quiet because sounds ring out far over water at night. Two well-muffled passengers climbed down with small suitcases to join them, then the sailors, Stephens and Whiting, pulled away from the ship and bent for the French shore, backing through blackness. It seemed ages before they heard waves washing on a long sandy beach. They laid oars and skimmed ashore; Stephens jumped out and pulled the bow up the beach. He was in enemy territory, his only weapon a sharp marlinspike stuck in his belt. A chill wind soughed in the dune-grass. Then a voice with the password question:

'*Have you got a bottle of whisky?*'

'*No, we have a bottle of gin.*'

With the right answer, the 'parcels' were passed on to their greeters. The elder of the two passengers thanked the sailors and wished them luck. It was 'Pat O'Leary' himself, Albert Guérisse, going back to work helping escapers and evaders in France. But his thin companion turned towards the boat, crying out in panic, 'I want to go back! I don't want to go in!' This man was a new radio operator who had only volunteered because he was sick with longing to see his wife again, but in the event, his nerves could not take the danger, the fear. Frantic splashing back into the surf was of no avail. The matelots were already 'beetling' for the ship and did not stop.

When the businessman and former Tory MP Frank Nelson took over as 'CD' or Chief of the Special Operations Executive from

Colonel Lawrence Grand in autumn 1940, he became a managing director urgently in need of executives, and looked for them in the City of London. Half a dozen prominent men in SOE were drawn from Slaughter and May, a well-known firm of City solicitors who eschewed divorce and crime to make their money from commercial law. The most recently appointed partner, J. G. 'Jack' Beevor (father of the historian Antony Beevor), was picked to be head of the SOE mission in Lisbon, where he arrived on 3 January 1941 in the guise of assistant military attaché. If the Germans invaded Portugal, he was told, it would be his job to blow up all the Shell oil installations on the Tagus. Nelson selected another Slaughter and May partner, thirty-eight-year-old Hugh Quennell, to run the whole of 'H', the Iberia section, which covered Portugal and the Azores, Spain, northwest Africa and the western Mediterranean. According to the firm's centenary history, Hugh Quennell was 'a prickly personality, and prone to adopt a dictatorial manner with his subordinates that was highly resented'.

Hugh Quennell was plucked from his post as a lowly second lieutenant in the 1st battalion Welsh Guards to join SOE on 2 December 1940. Just over a fortnight later, travelling on a courier's passport as a King's Messenger, portering the Foreign Office diplomatic bags to their destinations, he flew to Lisbon and then on to Madrid. Quennell did not receive the warmest welcome in the British Embassy there, because Sir Samuel Hoare clearly remembered Quennell's brutal, voluptuary face from an incident when the latter heckled him abusively at a political meeting in Chelsea.

Their talks at Christmas 1940 mattered more than old grievances though. If the Germans invaded Iberia, what role could and should SO2, the armed side of SOE, play? From the start of his mission, the diplomat Sir Samuel Hoare had insisted that all thugs and spooks be kept on a tight leash within Spain in case their bombs or plots threatened his patient policy of constructive engagement with the Franco regime. But clearly Gibraltar, run by the naval and military, was another sphere of influence. The negotiations and discussions were led by the naval attaché, Captain Alan Hillgarth, who flew back to London with Quennell on 30 December to help present a case to the Joint Chiefs of Staff and the War Cabinet that some special forces were needed in the field to help block any thrust by Hitler into Spain. When outline plans were approved, Quennell went out with a delegation in February 1941 to see what was needed in Gibraltar. SOE acquired the Villa Lourdes, and room to accumulate weapons and explosives (10,000 lbs of gelignite and 700 lbs of plastic explosive, initially) to supply the French Resistance or Spanish and Moroccan *guerrilleros*, should the Germans ever invade Spain or Spanish Morocco.

On Sunday 9 March 1941 Quennell signed his name (just below that of H. A. R. Philby, the notorious 'Kim' Philby) in the guest-book of the Lochailort Inn. This highland hostelry was near the Special Training Centre 25 for commandos and SOE at Inverailort Castle in the west of Scotland. Philby had come up from the Iberia desk of SIS counter-espionage to give a lecture on the political situation in Spain to a group of men who were on a four-week intensive field course in guerrilla warfare, learning the basics of explosives, firearms, silent killing, outdoor survival and wireless. They were nineteen officers with backgrounds in Iberia and South America, including Austin Baillon, John Burton, Arthur Fletcher, Peter Musson and George Quiney, men who had been seconded to SOE to play the T. E. Lawrence role, blowing things up while liaising with and directing 'native' guerrillas, if ever the Germans invaded Spain. They were all promoted to captain and would wear Royal Engineer uniforms and badges so as not to arouse suspicion on the Rock. There were also seven sergeants from the Royal Signals who arrived in Scotland for the course with two Packard radio cars and three Vibrator suitcase wireless sets.

These men formed the *Relator* party, which had received a somewhat frosty reception from the Chief of the Imperial General Staff and the Foreign Office when SOE first put it forward in February 1941 as their sideshow contribution to Operation *Blackthorn*, with the jokey nickname 'Ali Baba and the Forty Thieves'. Their commanding officer, 'Ali Baba', was Lieutenant Colonel A. E. Hutcheon, and one of the 'thieves' was the anti-communist adventurer Peter Kemp, who had fought for Franco's side in the Spanish Civil War, and, as we saw in chapter 15, had been sent to northern Spain by MI(R) in July 1940. In one of his autobiographies, Kemp records meeting his new boss, Hugh Quennell, at Lochailort in March 1941:

He proved to be a large, plump lawyer with an oily smile and an ingratiating manner, who wore the badges of a lieutenant-colonel but tried to impress on us that he was just an ordinary jovial fellow like ourselves. Beginning with one of the oldest dirty jokes in the legal profession he went on to explain that it seemed likely the Germans would soon invade Spain to try and take Gibraltar. If so, there would be a surprise waiting for them: ourselves . . .

We would leave for Gibraltar shortly, to await the German invasion. We would divide into parties of two officers and a wireless operator NCO, each with its wireless set and store of arms, ammunition and explosives, to be carried in a one-ton Army truck. Each party was allotted its operational area, to which it would drive with all speed when the balloon went up . . .

After a few days at the SOE training camp Wanborough Manor, the *Relator* group sailed from Liverpool for Gibraltar in early April. It was a nightmarishly rough voyage on board the ill-fated Special Operations freighter HMS *Fidelity*, skippered by the black-bearded and foul-tempered Corsican buccaneer Claude André Péri, whose pseudonym was 'Lieutenant Commander Jack Langlois RN' because he was going to pretend to be French Canadian if ever caught by Vichy.

Quennell himself travelled out more comfortably, by air to Lisbon and Madrid, and then by car to Gibraltar. Sir Samuel Hoare effectively vetoed *Relator* from setting foot in Spain, saying that if the plan ever came to the attention of the Spanish authorities it might well precipitate the invasion it was designed to prevent.

While the SOE men in Gibraltar waited for their lorries and stores and missed their tommy-guns, buried under naval shells on board SS *Adjutant*, they ran up and down the Rock and played seven-a-side hockey to get fit, got used to driving American vehicles on the right, brushed up their Spanish and signalling and practised planting explosives. They were taken to see the miners drilling and blasting their way through the Rock, and were also shown the complete layout of the Royal Engineer demolition charges which would be set off if the Germans were ever on the brink of taking Gibraltar. Quennell was eager to use explosives. In May 1941, for example, he was hoping to cause 'a very satisfactory accident' to the ferry from Algeciras that was bringing Germans, disguised as Poles, Czechs, etc., across to Tangier and North Africa. The SOE attitude towards 'bangs' was cheerful. The American OSS agent Carleton S. Coon recorded spending 'extremely happy' days with 'the Villa Lourdes crowd (the British S.O.E outfit)'. He found them 'full of fun and among the finest of human beings. At the Villa Lourdes one could expect to have a piece of detonating cord go off under one's chair while drinking a glass of beer.'

Carleton Coon says he assisted Captain Charlie MacIntosh, the *Relator* officer whose job would be to blow up Spanish guns from Tarifa to Málaga if ever they threatened the Strait, in experiments with shaped charges for demolitions. This led to the astonishing idea of using exploding animal-droppings as tyre-bursters. On one of his North African road trips, Coon collected samples of Moroccan muledung, carefully packing them for shipment to London where SOE technicians copied their sepia-coloured small bun shape in painted plaster of Paris, embedding some plastic explosive and a detonator inside. When run over on a North African road, these *crottes* or turds would blow the tyre or track off an Axis vehicle. It was doubly effective because word of mouth made enemy drivers waste time and energy avoiding all animal excrement in their way, whether it was explosive or not.

Barred from Spain by Sir Samuel Hoare and increasingly realising that the Germans were not going to invade Iberia, especially after launching their massive attack on the Soviet Union, Hugh Quennell turned his attention more to North Africa. In the summer of 1941, two of the *Relator* party were captured in Algeria, making their way back to Gibraltar, and were interned in the Vichy prison camp for British and Commonwealth prisoners at Laghouat in the Sahara. Exactly what Captain E. E. Montgomery of the Royal West Kents and Captain J. A. Robert of the Intelligence Corps had been up to we do not know, but they may have been scoping out Tunisian railways to blow up.

In June 1941, Quennell recruited another young man, Edward Wharton-Tigar, a twenty-seven-year-old junior mine manager on his way home after being expelled from German-occupied Yugoslavia, and placed him across the strait in Tangier in Spanish Morocco, in an office next to the SIS representative, Colonel Toby Ellis. Wharton-Tigar was given access to a bank account full of money and instructions to make contacts high and low, prior to acts of sabotage. Quennell told Wharton-Tigar that SIS might be 'cloak' but SOE was definitely 'dagger', and that when Quennell set out to poke German intelligence in the eye, Wharton-Tigar would be the one to wield the burnt stick.

According to Edward Wharton-Tigar's account in his 1987 autobiography *Burning Bright*, in the middle of Saturday night, 10 January 1942, an SOE bomb, built in Gibraltar, exploded in Tangier. The device was made of two slabs of green, plasticine-like Nobel 808 explosive, weighing 36 lb or 16.32 kg, formed into a shape that could slip through the narrow bars of an iron grille. The bomb blew up under the supporting pillars of a cliff-top house at 4 rue de la Falaise in the Marshan district of Tangier, which then collapsed down the slope, killing eight people and destroying important German technical equipment.

Looked at more closely, however, the details of what happened and why become fuzzier. Contemporaneous news agency and newspaper reports indicate that 'a violent explosion' woke the whole city at 2.30 a.m. on a different date: Monday 12 January, with only one man killed and two injured. The newspaper *España* said the dead householder was a Greek sailor called Kiriacos and that his black Cuban wife, Carmen Ortiz, was rescued, wounded, from the debris of the building, described variously as a 'Nazi spy post' or 'Axis spy nest', overlooking the Strait of Gibraltar and 'used for spotting shipping passing in and out of the Mediterranean'. The Portuguese spy Manoel Marques Pacheco later confirmed that the German consulate had paid twenty-two thousand francs 'for the construction of a gallery on the terrace' of the house.

Quennell was eager for praise for the operation. 'Authorities here seem pleased', he cabled London. 'VACNA' (Vice Admiral Commanding North Atlantic, Vice Admiral Sir Frederick Edward-Collins aka 'Fat Fred Collins') 'shook with laughter like a jelly.' In a telegram on 14 January, Quennell wrote, 'While regretting death of Greek and wife they were given opportunity of working for British which they declined and it is better so as I understand that a dead Greek cannot talk.'

In his book *SOE: Recollections and Reflections 1940–1945*, J. G. 'Jack' Beevor of H Section SOE says the house was 'a special German-designed infra-red station set up to guide U-boats through the Straits of Gibraltar' that was destroyed 'in late 1942'. In the *Historical Dictionary of World War II Intelligence*, Nigel West says it was an infra-red device 'to monitor Allied shipping transits through the Strait of Gibraltar', blown up successfully 'in January 1943'.

Wharton-Tigar alleges that his destroying 'their valuable infra-red station' 'must have saved incalculable tons of Allied shipping in the Mediterranean and many hundreds of lives as well as depriving the Germans of a vital observation post for major troop movements such as the Anglo-American landings in North Africa in November 1942'. He also claims that the destruction of the building forced three German U-boats, 'waiting for signals from the spy-station', to use their radios instead, thus giving themselves away to the Royal Navy: 'all three were attacked and sunk. Survivors included the whole crew of one of the U-boats, who were interrogated in Gibraltar by a German-speaking Polish team who had highly effective methods of getting information out of German prisoners.'

Unfortunately, much of this is fantasy. The authoritative Ralph Erskine calls Wharton-Tigar's claims 'completely fallacious'. Yes, a lookout post was destroyed, but infra-red searchlights were not detected until the middle of February 1942 and so have nothing to do with the explosion in early January. The sinking of three U-boats is invented, as is the Polish interrogator/torturer team, although the destroyer HMS *Hesperus* did ram and sink *U-93* near Gibraltar on 15 January, picking up thirty-six prisoners. Exaggerated claims by members of SOE may be a retrospective smokescreen for their failure to achieve much of significance at the time.

Two could play at the sabotage game. The Germans struck back at Gibraltar on 18 January 1942. Correa and Mateos, two Spaniards working indirectly for the German Abteilung II sabotage section, managed to stick a bomb among the depth charges on the deck of HMT *Erin*, a trawler moored at the Detached Mole next to several other minesweepers and mine-layers. Charles Causley's diary records: 'Suddenly there is the most appalling explosion, the whole quarters rattle and shake, windows fly open. Then outside (I notice the blackout blown away & hanging): a cloud of brown smoke, the "E" sunk, the "I" burning, the "H" a big gaping hole torn in her side.' HMT *Erin* was blown in two, HMT *Imperialist* required heavy repairs and HMT *Honjo* was fatally damaged. Five British sailors were killed, including the sub-lieutenant on watch aboard the aircraft carrier HMS *Argus* moored nearby.

In late January 1942, Hugh Quennell, dissatisfied with the failure of French sabotage agents in Casablanca to set fire to nine thousand tons of Vietnamese rubber destined for the Axis, went down to Casablanca from Tangier on the SOE Q-ship *Vega* in order to ginger up Operation *Impinge*. Stupidly, he managed to get himself and his crew arrested by the Spanish on their return for not having the right papers.

Rather more damaging for SOE's reputation was the 'Tangier bomb incident' of Friday 6 February 1942. Wharton-Tigar had smuggled the plastic explosive for the January explosion under the house in the rue de la Falaise, he freely admitted, 'in the diplomatic bag, mixed up with the official documents' coming from Gibraltar to the British Consulate in Tangier. Pleased at this successful stratagem, and wanting another spectacular, Hugh Quennell used the same method to smuggle fresh ordnance from Gibraltar to Tangier. On Friday afternoon, an official courier brought the diplomatic bags, addressed on the outside to the British Consul General in Tangier, from the Colonial Secretariat in Gibraltar, down to the Bland Line mail packet SS *Rescue* at the docks. The ten bags, including a luggage trunk, were piled on the Tangier quayside in between two taxis. The mail boat was about to leave at 5.35 p.m. when a shattering explosion among the sacks walloped the cabs over, cratered the quay and mushroomed a huge cloud of black smoke and dust, out of which fluttered down sheets of British propaganda in Arabic. Fifteen people were killed, ten of them Moroccan, and a score more Moroccans wounded. Five of the dead were British subjects, including the diplomatic messenger, Eduardo Pitto, and four Gibraltar Security Police officers who guarded the consulate, on their shift change. These policemen wore plain clothes and were each armed with a pistol. They were PC Abraham Attias, aged twenty-six, PC Charles Curtis, aged thirty-nine, Sergeant Terence Henning, aged thirty-one, and PC Stephen McKillop. A very Gibraltarian group of policemen: two Catholics, a Jew and an Anglican.

The rumour that this was a British bomb spread rapidly, and the next day, Saturday 7 February, after the burial of the ten Moroccans, violent anti-British rioting began. Moroccan youth rampaged for three hours while the Spanish police and army did nothing to stop them. The mob broke all the windows of the British Post Office, pelted the British Consulate General's annexe and overturned all cars with Corps Diplomatique plates, then charged into the Hotel Minzah, ransacking the library. After trashing the Valor Stores next door, they broke into the British printing establishment, Éditions Internationales, wrecked machinery, threw papers about and started a fire. The Bland Line offices had their windows broken, the Bristol Hotel was looted and smashed and Café Central and Bar Consulat were pillaged, with much broken glass and crockery. A 'State of Siege' was declared; military order restored.

The British establishment in Tangier led by Alvary Gascoigne mounted a blustering storm of indignation: Axis agitators were behind both the bomb and the anti-British riots, events they referred to as 'the Tangier outrage'. The British claimed that German and Italian agents had been all around the quay, watching with binoculars for the bomb that they had planted to go off. The subsequent riot was prearranged with criminals and malcontents from the souk paid to take part.

Hugh Quennell, who was in Tangier at the time, loudly alleged it was all a German plot to kill him in revenge for blowing up the house in rue de la Falaise, and that he was jolly lucky not to have been on the quay himself. This version of events was recorded by David Scherr of Defence Security, who wrote later: 'The Abwehr scored a savage tit-for-tat by blowing up a British diplomatic bag and killing 29 people.' The SOE Iberia section history has had the entire 'unfortunate incident' redacted. All that remains is the sidebar heading: 'Retaliation'. Lord Gort, the governor of Gibraltar, denied British responsibility in telegram No. 61, cabled to Tangier and the Colonial Secretary in London on 7 February:

All baggage and passengers examined and double checked before leaving Gibraltar for reasons of currency restrictions and censorship control.

Rescue thoroughly searched by police before sailing. No question of any explosive emanating from Gibraltar.

Endorse strongest possible protest.

But the awkward truth started to dribble out after the weekend. Telegram No. 123 of Monday 9 February from Alvary Gascoigne in Tangier to the Foreign Office in London seems to have admitted the presence of 'certain toys' in the diplomatic bags, because the Foreign Office responded sharply in Telegram No. 78 to Tangier, repeated to Gibraltar, sent at 1.45 p.m. on Tuesday 10 February:

1. What are these toys?
2. From whom did you learn of their existence?
3. Why was their existence not disclosed to you earlier?
4. This disclosure is difficult to reconcile with Gibraltar telegram No 61 to you.

In the HS series of SOE files, 'weeded' and released to public view in the National Archives at Kew, the next six telegrams between Tangier, Madrid, Gibraltar and London are either missing or so heavily redacted, 'retained in department under section 3(4) of the Public Records Act 1958', as to make the events incomprehensible. The real story only emerges in other, uncensored files from the Colonial Office and the War Office. On the afternoon of 10 February, Lord Gort sent an admirably honest response to telegrams 78 and 123. It was labelled '**IMMEDIATE**, Most Secret and Personal', was enciphered, and made it clear that in SOE code, 'toys' were explosive devices:

The true facts are that 6 bombs (LIMPETS), 12 railway DETONATORS and 1 special explosive containing 7lbs of GUNCOTTON and 4 detonators were in my bags.

I accept full responsibility for misleading information contained in my telegram no. 61 to Tangier and I wish to express my personal regrets to H.M. Consul General for the lack of candour. I fear that I cannot subscribe to the view that there could be no risk of explosion when limpets, detonators etc are put into a bag without special precautions for careful HANDLING en route.

The British limpet mine, invented early in the war by Stuart Macrae and Cecil 'Nobby' Clarke, using an aluminium washing-up bowl with a grooved rim to which a sealing plate was screwed, was so called because it contained a ring of small horseshoe magnets that made it clamp to the iron side of a ship's hull just as a limpet or aquatic snail clings with its tiny teeth to a rock. Each 'limpet' bowl was packed with up to four pounds of high explosive gelignite. An August 1941 memo on the explosives that SOE in London was obtaining for Gibraltar had warned Quennell that the hundred limpet mines 'are still not regarded by the technical people as satisfactory in their operation . . . and these are the only fuses we can produce at present.'

The next day, Lord Gort wrote to the Colonial Secretary of State, Walter Guinness, Lord Moyne, adding more details about the twelve detonators and fifteen kilos of explosive that had blown up in a luggage trunk on the Tangier quayside:

Material was despatched from here packed by SOE staff at the request of the Senior SOE Gibraltar representative [Hugh Quennell], who was then in Tangier. I understand that this material was required for possible operations in Tunisia, and for other unspecified operations of which nothing is known in Gibraltar. The six bombs (limpets) were packed in separate wooden boxes, the twelve railway detonators in separate brown paper parcels, and the special explosive in a tin biscuit box with no markings.

From London, Hugh Dalton, in his last weeks as Minister for Economic Warfare before handing over to Lord Selborne, asked Gort to set up an immediate inquiry. The board convened in Government House at 10 a.m. on Saturday 14 February 1942. It was chaired by Gort's naval liaison officer, later his chief of staff, Captain the Hon. Guy Russell, with an infantry lieutenant colonel and an Ordnance Corps captain as its members. The first witness to be called and cautioned was A. M. Dryburgh, the Acting Colonial Secretary. He explained that eight closed bags had come from the JIC (Joint Intelligence Committee), which SOE used as its cover address, and that a clerk called Pons had put the official seal on them, marking them as Diplomatic Bags, without opening them. Then a Colonial Office messenger called Montado had taken all ten bags to Mr Willey, the Chief Officer of MV *Rescue*.

Major Harry Morris from SOE Gibraltar explained that on Thursday 5 February he had received an instruction from Hugh Quennell in Tangier to send across by the next bag six limpets and twelve railway detonators and also some special 'toys' to 'enable them to destroy the Terhessa Bridge in Tunisia'. Captain Fox and Captain Eckhart (both *Relator* officers) prepared the explosives on Thursday night and Friday morning and they were packed under the supervision of Captain Constance, together with some bundles of propaganda. The inner wrapping was addressed to E. E. Wharton-Tigar and the outer wrapping to HE Consul General, Tangier, and the bags went to the Colonial Office at about one o'clock. Morris's clerk, A. G. Dunnell, added that the packing was done 'in a rush'.

Captain Stephen Constance detailed the wrapping. The dozen railway detonators, each containing one pound of gun-cotton and an instantaneous fuse, were each packed separately in brown paper parcels, measuring about five by three by two inches. The six limpets were each in wooden boxes with the only vulnerable parts, the two time pencils, sticking out, safeguarded by paper and packing. The special explosive, seven pounds of gun-cotton with four detonators attached on a length of fuse, was packed in a square biscuit tin wrapped in brown paper. He felt 'confident there was no possibility of accident. No special handling was necessary on this occasion.'

Captain L. G. F. Fox of the Royal Engineers Independent Section told the Board what explosives he had prepared: six limpet mines, each with three and a half pounds of gelignite, packed individually in wooden boxes padded with felt, plus extra layers of felt, paper and rubber. He had replaced each limpet's two time delayers because the originals sent from London were useless. The time delayer was officially known as a time pencil and consisted of a steel tube containing a striker pin retained by a spring. The spring itself was held back by a metal wire, and alongside the wire was a glass ampoule containing sulphuric acid. To get the thing into action you pressed the detonator to crush the glass ampoule, thus releasing the acid. When the acid ate through the wire (and the thicker the wire the longer it would take) the spring would release the striker pin, to trigger the detonation of the gelignite. Fox was questioned about safety and the possibility of accidents through breakage. He said he had carried out many tests and had never seen a flaw in two or three hundred glass ampoules.

Fox said the 'special explosive' packed in the biscuit tin was intended to destroy a moving train by blowing up forty yards of track. Seven one-pound slabs of gun-cotton, each with a primer inserted, were interconnected by forty yards of Bickford express fuse. At five-yard intervals along the fuse, junctions were made for No. 27 detonators, and there were also four railway fog signals consisting of gunpowder which could only be set off by the weight of a train. Fox admitted that one accidental explosion might set off all the others in the bags. He considered that his one-month course in Scotland had been adequate training for this dangerous pursuit.[*]

The Board of Inquiry was unable to state if the fatal explosion was due to faulty packing or preparation, rough handling in transit, failure of the material or outside agency. But their findings were critical of SOE's organisation, procedures and training. No permission had been sought from authority to convey explosives in the diplomatic bags and no warning given about any careful handling, and these were 'serious collective responsibilities of the SOE representatives'. It seems remarkable that the SOE local boss Hugh Quennell was never questioned by the inquiry, nor shown a copy of its findings. But he had successfully schmoozed Gort, Gascoigne and Collins and even persuaded Brian Clarke, the Kiwi colonel from the Coldstream Guards whom SOE sent out to report and take over, that he was too well connected and integral to operations to be got rid of. Five dead Gibraltarians and ten dead Moroccans did not count as much as a ruthless lawyer from Slaughter and May.

The Colonial Secretary would have learned more about the Tangier explosion days earlier had he been able to read the German foreign intelligence service telegrams emanating from North Africa, sent by a fattish official with red-blond hair from the German Consulate in Tangier. 'Vice Consul Kruse' was actually Hans Paul Krüger,

[*] Captain Fox was lost overboard from the cruiser HMS *Aurora* in rough seas on 27 November 1942 while accompanying a consignment of SOE stores from Gibraltar to Algiers.

a thirty-seven-year-old Wehrmacht officer who had been with the Armistice Commission in Tetuán before taking over the Abwehr *Stelle* early in 1941, after the rue de la Falaise explosion. Krüger's many contacts with Muslim groups in North Africa were noted in his MI5 file, as was the fact that another German spy called Max Brandli had once denounced him as homosexual and been interrogated by the Gestapo for it. On 6 February 1942, 'Kruse' broke off his usual recording of all the ships and planes in the Strait of Gibraltar to report the fatal explosion on the mole, just over two hours after it happened, as a British accident. Krüger/Kruse also saw the propaganda possibilities of the event. In further messages, he urged the German Embassy in Madrid to donate generously to the subscription fund set up for those Moroccans wounded by the bombing, and suggested that the Grand Mufti should do the same to 'strengthen his influence' in Morocco.* He said that German radio broadcasts to the Maghreb should stress that the explosives were in English diplomatic luggage and they should 'express Germany's disgust at such methods' which had killed ten Moroccans and wounded almost twenty. He wanted the German Embassy in Madrid to put pressure on the Spanish government 'to demand the withdrawal of the English consul general in Tangier with all his staff including IS agents . . . as the whole English espionage and propaganda organisation for all Morocco might thereby be smashed up.'

And what was this about an 'infra-red signal station'? In late February 1942, the Knox group at Bletchley Park 'broke' a new Abwehr machine, known as 'GGG', (which was the call-sign of Algeciras), a 'K'-type Enigma rewired from the model used by Italy and Spain in the Spanish Civil War, and now employed by a clandestine German outstation signalling across the Strait of Gibraltar. In his 1968 book,

---

* Mohamed Amin al-Husseini (1897–1974), appointed Grand Mufti of Jerusalem (chief Sunni Muslim cleric) by the British High Commissioner of Mandatory Palestine, had turned strongly anti-British, and pro-Axis, in the Arab Revolt of 1936–9. In Nazi Germany he recruited Bosnian Muslims for the Waffen-SS and conversed with Hitler in November 1941.

My Silent War, H. A. R. 'Kim' Philby, who ran V(d), the wartime Iberia desk of SIS counter-espionage at 'Glenalmond' in St Albans, wrote about cryptic ISOS messages from Algeciras:

The Abwehr code-name for the operation was Bodden. The Bodden is the name of the narrow strip of water separating the island of Rügen from the German mainland, not far from the wartime scientific research station at Peenemünde. Taken together with additional evidence that the Bodden experts, with their instruments, seemed to be closing in on Algeciras, this seemed a clear enough indication that something affecting the Strait of Gibraltar was brewing. We therefore consulted the formidable Dr Jones, head of the scientific centre of SIS.

Tim Milne, a school friend of Philby's recruited by him to work in SIS V(d), explained the link to infra-red equipment in his own post-humously published book:

This enterprise appeared primarily to involve infrared searchlights, cameras and heat-sensing apparatus beamed across the Strait of Gibraltar between two German-manned posts on either side of the water; but radar equipment was also mentioned, and a *Lichtsprechgerät* or 'light speech apparatus' . . . After ten or twenty ISOS messages had accumulated, bristling with German electronic terms, it was clear that first-class technical advice was needed. Felix [Cowgill] suggested I should take the whole problem to R.V. Jones in Broadway.

Reginald Victor Jones was the remarkable physicist who explained clearly to Winston Churchill in 1940 the principle of the 'beams' that German bombers were using to find their targets, and how to counter them. When Milne went to see him at 24 Broadway Buildings, the SIS HQ in London, Jones was sitting happily with the Würzburg coastal radar set recently 'pinched' in the daring Bruneval raid, Operation *Biting*, when British paratroopers dropped from the sky, stole some new German technology and were evacuated by sea. Looking at the ISOS messages that Milne brought with him, it seemed to Jones that 'the Germans were trying to set up a great infra-red burglar alarm across the Strait of Gibraltar to count our ships in and out of the Mediterranean. There were to be three parallel barrages, with infra-red searchlights mounted on the southern coast of the strait, just west of Perejil Island.'

What the Germans called 'Bodden', the British code-named 'Blake'. The increasing sophistication of German ship surveillance in collaboration with the Italians alarmed the Admiralty. Other wireless intercepts showed that reports on all HM ships, troopers and convoys passing the Strait of Gibraltar were being sent to Paris (for the U-boat Command and *Fliegerführer Atlantik*), to Bordeaux, to the Luftwaffe command in Sicily and to Rome, where news of ship movements was received sometimes within an hour of sighting. On 7 March 1942, the Director of Naval Intelligence, Admiral John Godfrey, circulated a minute on the new apparatus being installed: 'what appears to be a combination of R/D.F. and infra-red ray'. He said the chiefs of staff and the Joint Intelligence Committee were considering the matter; Gibraltar, Malta and Alexandria had all been made aware.

The Director of Signals sent a scientific officer called D. J. Garrard out to Gibraltar to investigate techniques for jamming the 'Blake' devices. Photographic Reconnaissance based at Medmenham in Buckinghamshire had already photographed the sites the year before, and now distributed new 'vertical' pictures. In April, the Admiralty asked Coastal Command to take fresh photographs of three sites. Over the next six weeks, there was vigorous discussion about the merits and demerits of direct action against 'Blake'. Royal Navy officers wanted to strike hard, but the Intelligence people, like 'C' and Cavendish-Bentinck, the Chair of the Joint Intelligence Committee, urged caution because of the politico-military consequences. In April and May 1942, both Captain Alan Hillgarth in Madrid and Lord Mountbatten, the Chief of Combined Operations, were formu-lating plans to 'take out' the sites in lightning raids.

Then, on 19 May, the chiefs of staff turned down all ideas of direct action, preferring the diplomatic option. A long telegram from Sir Anthony Eden at the Foreign Office, emended in draft by 'C' and the DNI, was sent to Sir Samuel Hoare. It is worth noting how all information actually derived from 'most secret sources' (i.e. Signals Intelligence or ISOS) has to be presented as having been physically seen by an alert observer:

1. The Germans are establishing scientific spotting stations on Spanish territory on both sides of the Strait of Gibraltar . . . to observe and identify ships passing through the Strait at any time of day or night. Two of these stations, one on each side, are in advanced stage, others are in process of construction.

2. . . . For your information, Franco himself appears under pressure to have authorised the undertaking . . .

3. Recently the Spaniards appear to have been getting nervous and . . . have delayed the supply of Spanish uniforms for the German personnel concerned . . .

4. We obviously cannot tolerate this unfriendly action on the part of Spain, and the stations if allowed to operate will seriously interfere with the movements of our ships in the Strait . . . Violent action against the installations is under consideration, but . . . it is essential to stop the project at the source . . .

5. You should therefore make a strong intervention with Gen. Franco himself and let him see that we know what has been going on . . . About two months ago we began to receive indisputable eye-witness evidence of certain building operations that were being initiated on either side of the Strait at the narrowest point . . . and parts of the scientific apparatus were seen in Spanish government stores and being taken across into Morocco . . . [M]ore recently we have learnt that the German personnel operating these stations were to be put into Spanish uniforms . . .

6. You can say that Spanish connivance in this undertaking amounts to direct military assistance to our enemies and that unless it is stopped you cannot answer for the effect on the attitude of His Majesty's Government and the United States Government. Certainly the policy of letting Spain obtain essential supplies would be irretrievably compromised.

7. You must therefore ask for an assurance that the project will at once be abandoned . . .

8. You might also find an opportunity of letting Franco see . . . that every act of assistance, direct or indirect, by Spanish authorities to our enemies is noted, and that if the process continues it will have a most serious effect on Anglo-American policy.

Sir Samuel Hoare immediately and vigorously presented this diplomatic complaint or *démarche* to General Franco, with flanking protests from Hillgarth and Torr, the naval and military attachés in Madrid. The encounter between Franco and Hoare was tense: the Caudillo said that Germans were in the strait region only to help Spain improve its artillery batteries. On 29 May, ISK1 decoded a German message from Madrid to Berlin reporting that 'the Golfers [Abwehr code for the British*] have become aware of Bodden South and have lodged a note of protest with the Spanish government.' By early June, work on Bodden North and Bodden South had stopped. On 30 June, John Godfrey triumphantly reported:

Admiral Canaris (head of the German S.I.S.) was interviewed by Franco on 25th June, and as a result orders had been given by the Germans that the entire BODDEN undertaking must be abandoned and all German personnel recalled . . .

All the evidence to hand suggests the complete success of our démarche which has been undertaken by the Embassy at Madrid with unremitting zeal and persistence since the first telegram was despatched to Sir Samuel Hoare.

It is of course entirely due to 'C' that this German organisation was unmasked.

---

* *Golfspieler* for the British and *Golfplatz* for the UK were among the list of Abwehr cover-names that Trevor-Roper's unit compiled. Gibraltar was *Basta*, *Gatera* or *Heligoland*.

30

Lighting the Torch

The fourth volume of Winston Churchill's magnum opus *The Second World War* is called *The Hinge of Fate*, an apt title for a major turning point of the war, when President Roosevelt (with Churchill's support) made the decision in late July 1942 to go for landings in North Africa rather than western Europe. Gibraltar would be a key staging post for the Allied task forces. Despite opposition from George Marshall and other senior American soldiers, this choice laid out the path that Anglo-American ground operations would follow for the next two years of the war.

Things were not going well for the British Empire in 1942: Mandalay had fallen, Singapore had fallen, Tobruk had fallen, and Churchill needed a victory to brandish against those who would censure him. The fightback of Operation *Torch* in November 1942 was a large undertaking with only three months' notice, but Roosevelt was determined that US troops would get into action that year. It was also extremely risky. Ships of the Western Task Force would have to cross more than three thousand nautical miles of the U-boat-infested Atlantic Ocean before landing thirty-five thousand American GIs in Morocco, while two more task forces sailing from the UK would be carrying seventy-five thousand English-speaking men the fifteen hundred miles to French-and-Arabic-speaking Algeria, in order, as Churchill put it, 'to drive in against the back door of Rommel's armies'.

Although Gibraltar was a central springboard, and the planning mostly went on in London, Operation *Torch* was predominantly a US enterprise. It had to be presented as wholly American because, after the bitter conflicts at Mers-el-Kébir, Dakar and Syria, Vichy France, the occupying power in North Africa, loathed the British more than the Americans. George Marshall, Roosevelt's chief of staff, had already chosen the man to take charge, the efficient staff officer Lieutenant General Dwight D. Eisenhower. He had been made the CG of ETOUSA (Commanding General, European Theatre of Operations, United States Army) on 11 June, when the American landings were still intended to be on mainland Europe. 'See what needs to be done, then do it,' instructed Marshall. 'Tell me about it when you can.'

'Ike' Eisenhower and his team arrived in London on 24 June 1942. His headquarters was in a block of flats at 20 Grosvenor Square and after a brief stay at Claridge's and the Dorchester, he settled in Telegraph Cottage, Kingston-upon-Thames, Surrey, with two African American servants and Kay Summersby as his driver. When he heard that President Roosevelt had decided to postpone the attack on Europe and concentrate on northwest Africa, Eisenhower initially thought that 'Wednesday, July 22, 1942 could well go down as "the blackest day in history", particularly if Russia is defeated in the big Boche drive now so alarmingly under way.' But on Friday 7 August, Eisenhower was named Supreme Commander for Operation *Torch* and got a new Allied Force Headquarters at Norfolk House in St James's Square.

Alliances are never easy, and the Americans and the British were not natural allies, not only 'separated by a common language', as is often said, but with a host of cultural, economic and historical reasons to dislike or misunderstand each other. Dwight Eisenhower, born in Denison, Texas and raised in Abilene, Kansas, was wholly American in his addiction to Western cowboy stories and Camel cigarettes, of which he smoked four packs a day. Yet this honest, broad-grinning man from the Great Plains somehow made the alliance with the devious and snobbish British work. He became, in Carlo d'Este's phrase, 'the architect of co-operation'. The truth was that no single nation could have done it alone: the Second World War was won by alliance. In his interesting book *War by Land, Sea and Air* David Jablonsky argues convincingly that Eisenhower's whole life, from West Point to White House, can be read as a quest for unified command, doing whatever it took to overcome the parochialisms of inter-service rivalries and nationalistic squabbles in order to achieve a greater goal. Not a star, but simply the captain of a good team.

On 6 August 1942, Eisenhower's friend, the polo-playing cavalryman Major General George S. Patton Jr, arrived in London for two weeks' planning for *Torch*. 'I am not, repeat not, pro-British,' stated Patton. He thought all the pretty women in England must have died because the rest 'are hideous with fat ankles'. He was suspicious of Eisenhower 'going native' and beginning to use Limey words like 'petrol' instead of 'gasoline'. Patton was a stickler for discipline and correct dress, a macho tough guy in a shiny helmet who liked to wear two ivory-handled pistols (a .45 Single Action Army Colt and a .357 Smith & Wesson Magnum) on his belt. He turned the air blue with swearing, but always in a curiously high, falsetto voice. 'We won't just shoot the sonsabitches. We're going to cut out their living guts – and use them to grease the treads of our tanks. We're going to murder those lousy Hun bastards by the bushel.' Patton was, surprisingly, also an intellectual, who read the Koran out of curiosity when crossing the Atlantic to invade the Maghreb, finding it mostly boring. His religion was war. He told his ship's captain that he did not mind losing three quarters of his men as long as he was victorious. Eisenhower was shrewd enough to know that much of this was 'the shell of showmanship', the pose of the actor, and that Patton was actually more thin-skinned than hard-boiled.

Spies, diplomats and propagandists were now told to pave the way for the soldiers in North Africa, tackling enemy secret agents, doing deals with local French colonial troops, bribing auxiliaries, assuaging the neighbouring countries, and above all persuading the Vichy authorities that the American and British allies came in peace, that they were not against French interests in Morocco, Algeria and Tunisia, nor seeking to impose a new government on them. They were only in transit, they said: their true enemy, the Axis, was further east, the Italian and German armed forces in Libya and Egypt.

Roosevelt and Churchill agreed to keep de Gaulle's Free French right out of the planning and execution of any operations in North Africa. Dakar had been a fiasco, and it was vital to avoid a civil war between Vichy and Free French. The diplomat Robert Murphy found his work seeking co-operation with the French trying. Although tasked by the president with bringing local Vichy officials, both civil and military, on side, he found the American soldiers were not prepared to trust any of these potentially useful partners, so no one on the French side could be told what was going on until just before it happened. Naturally, this annoyed the Frenchmen, and made some unhelpful. Murphy had to tell the Vichy French that the task force was purely American, under American command, there to forestall a planned occupation by the Axis armed forces and to preserve French sovereignty. The Americans would welcome all French assistance, but any resistance would be put down by force of arms. The US would also guarantee the salaries, allowances, death benefits and pensions of all who joined in support of their expeditionary force.

President Roosevelt had his own penchant for secrecy. He told Murphy in September not to inform the State Department about what he was up to and arranged for him to be secretly flown to England, disguised in a lieutenant colonel's uniform – 'Nobody ever pays any attention to a lieutenant colonel' – to brief General Eisenhower and his staff on the political problems of French North Africa. Murphy remained a civilian, both as the 'personal representative of the US President' and as the 'Operating Executive Head of the Civil Affairs Section and Adviser for Civil Affairs under General Eisenhower'. He also had a foot in the intelligence camp, and when he arrived in Algiers in October 1942, ostensibly for diplomatic negotiations with key Vichy generals, he was also bearing five secret wireless transmitter/receivers for US agents.

The head of the American undercover warriors in North Africa was the newly promoted Lieutenant Colonel William A. Eddy, born to missionary parents in Syria, a decorated veteran of the US Marine Corps with a limp to testify to his war wounds, who also held a doctorate from Princeton University (his dissertation was on *Gulliver's Travels*). Officially, Eddy was the new US naval attaché at the American Legation in Tangier. But he was also '334', working for General 'Wild Bill' Donovan's new intelligence organisation, the Office of Strategic Services (OSS), established on 13 June 1942.

On that date, Donovan's previous Office of the Co-ordinator of Information, with its $10 million budget and six hundred staffers, had been split in two. The Foreign Information Service, which did the 'white' propaganda of overseas radio broadcasting, became the core of the new Office of War Information, which dealt with newsreels, newspapers, films and photographs, etc., and continued the radio service Voice of America, started in February 1942 and still broadcasting today. But all the 'black', clandestine, guerrilla and espionage work belonged to the Office of Strategic Services, OSS, which was the true forerunner of today's CIA, the Central Intelligence Agency. OSS was in charge of overseas operations worldwide outside the Americas and was an armed force, being under the military Joint Chiefs of Staff.

Donovan's earlier office, COI, had already been getting information from Murphy's dozen vice consuls in North African ports like Casablanca, Oran, Algiers and Tunis. These men now moved over, lock, stock and barrel to the Office of Strategic Services. What Murphy called his 'twelve apostles' in North Africa were just the type of upper-class Americans to fit right in to the OSS, dubbed 'Oh So Social'. They maintained good relations with the top Vichy naval and military: General Weygand in Algeria, Admiral Estéva in Tunisia and General Noguès in Morocco, all of whom needed the oil and petrol that the USA supplied. The apostles' brief widened from checking that gas and other US goods did not reach Axis hands to acquiring political, military and economic intelligence, suborning local officials, cultivating native chiefs, organising fifth columnists, setting up guerrilla networks, caching demolition materials. Subversive COI seeds sprouted and blossomed, watered by OSS.

Robert Murphy was the diplomatic head, but all the secret information went to the Arabic-speaking Colonel Eddy, who arrived in Tangier on 26 January 1942, only seven weeks after Pearl Harbor, and took up residence at the El Minzah Hotel. 'I was to do what Murphy, the policy man, ordered or approved, and nothing else,' Eddy said. The American 'consular' staff working for COI/OSS, linked by seven secret wirelesses, formed the tap roots of a spy system, but the fungal mycelium spreading wider into the soil of northwest Africa to draw up nutrients of information was mostly not American. Eddy used a disciplined group of exiled Spanish communists, who did not like the French, distrusted the British because they had let them down in the civil war, and who all detested Franco, as a 'human post office' for communications. Another helper was 'Agency Africa', a Polish intelligence network founded and run by Major General Rygor Słowikowski. Its legitimate cover was Floc-Av, North Africa's first porridge factory, and it had agents all the way from Dakar in the west through Río de Oro and Ifni, across Morocco and Algeria to Tunis in the east. The intelligence that these Polish agents gleaned went through Colonel Eddy in Tangier, and OSS reaped the credit. The Poles in exile were not just fine soldiers, sailors and fighter pilots, they led the way in Second World War decryption, secret flotillas and espionage too.

Britain's own sabotage and subversion organisation, the Special Operations Executive, had to play second fiddle to OSS in North Africa because the Americans were leading the invasion. On 26 July 1942, an accord between William Donovan of OSS and Charles Hambro of SOE split their responsibilities both by country and within countries. For example, in Tangier and Morocco, it was agreed that SOE handle the Christians and the Spanish, and OSS the Muslims. During *Torch*, however, SOE and OSS would share their radio networks.

The Harvard University physical anthropologist Carleton S. Coon (whose PhD had been on the tribes of the Rif mountains in Morocco) and his college friend Gordon H. Browne were allotted the Muslims.

Coon arrived in Tangier at the end of May 1942 and told the chargé d'affaires of the American Legation, J. Rives Childs, that he was merely doing research and propaganda work for COI, finding out what the Arabs were thinking. He promptly set out to acquire inform-ants, buy potential helpers and spy out the lie of the land. Moroccan Nationalists, he found, were men of theory rather than action. Pis-tol-packing Coon tried to persuade the powerful religious brother-hoods to help the Americans with intelligence, and to get remnants of Abd el-Krim's Rifian army to do the same and prepare to become guerrillas for the Allies if the Germans invaded or Spain entered the war.* Coon code-named the religious helpers 'Strings' and the warri-ors 'Tassels'.

On 7 May 1942, Lord Gort moved on from Gibraltar to replace exhausted Sir William Dobbie as the governor of embattled Malta. Noel Mason-MacFarlane returned from Russia and on 19 June 1942 was sworn in as the seventieth governor of Gibraltar, accompanied by, as his aide-de-camp, the actor Captain Anthony Quayle, who had re-encountered him at Brown's Hotel in London. Mason-MacFarlane was now lamer than before, with gradual paralysis attacking his spine. Pain made his temper shorter. The socialist-minded governor wanted no more flattering of the local Spanish aristocracy so invita-tions to the Marquesa de Povar and her ilk were sharply curtailed.

Mason-MacFarlane was very much the soldier. When the writer Eric Linklater came out to Gibraltar with the producer Vincent Korda and the actor Ralph Richardson to research a feature film about the Rock, they thought that if a governor character were to appear in their movie, General Mason-MacFarlane had to play him.

---

* After surrender in 1926, the Berber *guerrillero* had been confined to the Indian Ocean island of Réunion, guarded by twenty gendarmes. In August 1940, SOE considered snatching Abd el-Krim, freeing him to lead the Rif tribes again, against the Germans or the Spanish if they joined the war. In the *News Chronicle* in October 1940, Philip Jordan urged that Abd el-Krim be used to lead 'a new Arab Revolt'. In May 1942, the chiefs of staff instructed SOE 'to win over the Moorish population to the Allied cause', but that 'no promise of independence after the war should be made'.

He was a martinet, and looked it. His ponderously handsome, rather Roman head was carried slightly askew on his broad shoulders by reason of some misadventure, in a motor-car or on a horse, in which he had broken his neck. He had broken many bones, at one time or another, but refused to admit any disability from his fractures. The weather was cold, most bitingly cold in the early morning, but till evening came he wore nothing except khaki shorts and an open-necked drill shirt.

Vincent Korda noticed how, among soldiers, Mason-Mac just disappeared: 'When the Governor sat talking in a group of soldiers, easy and relaxed – his heavy body deep in a chair, a sergeant passing a pint of beer above his Roman head to another sergeant – he was like a foxhound in a pack of foxhounds: difficult to distinguish unless one knew his markings and his voice.'

The new governor had a most important secret visitor at the beginning of August 1942, on the first leg of a remarkable seventeen-thousand-mile journey. The Chief of the Imperial General Staff, passing through the week before, had warned that this guest would be arriving 'in disguise'.

An unheated Consolidated Liberator bomber called *Commando* touched down on the new Gibraltar airstrip early on 2 August 1942, carrying Prime Minister Winston Churchill. Flying under the pseudonym 'Colonel Warden', Churchill did not, in the event, wear the clip-on red beard he had brought, but stepped down in the blue uniform of an RAF air commodore, with a cigar in his mouth and carrying a cane. There was no reception committee for the prime minister, only Anthony Quayle, who opened the passenger door of 'a filthy little pick-up truck that was used for collecting stores'.

'Oh, yes, indeed. Is this part of the cover plan?' Churchill asked.

'Yes, sir, it is.'

'Good – good. But you know that I do have to take my detective with me. Do you mind if he comes too?'

'Not a bit, sir. He'll have to sit in the back though, and it's rather dirty.'

'Oh, that won't hurt Thompson. He can sit on those chains. He'll be all right.'

Churchill stared up at the white cliff of North Front and started asking questions. How many men were stationed there? He was surprised by the answer, thirty thousand. Did they get sufficient entertainment? Was the mail arriving regularly from home? Then there was a pause, and a sudden question:

'Young man – are you prepared to sell your life dearly?'

'I hope so, sir.'

'Because this old Fortress is soon to be the centre of historic events. I expect you know that.'

Quayle said he did, though he thought it odd that the prime minister should be confiding in a total stranger. They drove slowly over the tank traps and along the road that is now called Winston Churchill Avenue.

'We were told, sir, that you'd be arriving in disguise. But I hadn't expected to see you disguised as an air commodore.'

'Disguised as an air commodore? What do you mean? I am an air commodore!'

'Oh indeed, sir. I know that. I meant that I hadn't expected to see you wearing the uniform.'

'Oh yes. And what is more . . .' Turning in his bucket seat, Churchill tugged at the left breast of his tunic and patted it with his right hand. 'And what is more, I have my wings!' His eyes were full of tears, perhaps thinking of 'the Few', who lost so many in the Battle of Britain.

After a visit to Government House they had a quick tour of the Upper Rock. In one narrow street on their descent a vegetable seller's recalcitrant donkey halted their car. The Gibraltarians who peered in did not breathe a word to the Abwehr in La Línea about whom they had seen. At tea-time, the American pilot Bill Vanderkloot lifted the Liberator off the runway and, escorted by four Beaufighters, headed southeast over Melilla towards the Sahara.

Winston Churchill was in the aeroplane's cockpit at 4.25 a.m. on

3 August when the River Nile came into view and they turned north for Cairo. The prime minister was sixty-seven years old, flying in a modern aircraft along the railway line to Aswan, built by Lord Kitchener's engineers in the 1890s reconquest of the Sudan when they had taken the country back from the Islamist Dervishes who killed General Gordon in Khartoum. Churchill's mind went back to more than forty years before. On 2 September 1898, on horseback, the young Winston Churchill had charged with the 21st Lancers against the Khalifa's black flag at the battle of Omdurman. On another part of the battlefield British army Maxim guns mowed down hundreds of Sudanese warriors, but in *The River War*, Churchill saw horseback warfare as different: 'The other might have been a massacre, but here the fight was fair, for we too fought with sword and spear.'

In Egypt in early August 1942, Churchill replaced General Auchinleck with General Montgomery as head of the Eighth Army in Africa. Then the party flew on to Moscow to meet Joseph Stalin in the Kremlin. Winston Churchill, who detested communism, was in the tiger's lair, come to give Stalin the unwelcome news that there would not be a Second Front in Europe that year because the Allies did not have enough landing craft. But, said Churchill, there were other places for the British and the Americans to attack the Germans. The PM duly laid out their secret plan, Operation *Torch*, for the Russian leader.

'Stalin became intensely interested. His first question was what would happen in Spain and Vichy France.' Churchill drew a crude picture of a crocodile: while Stalin hit it on the hard snout, the Anglo-Americans would slit its 'soft belly'. Using a globe, he expounded the advantages of clearing the Mediterranean. Churchill said the astute and crafty Stalin soon grasped the four advantages of *Torch*: 'First, it would hit Rommel in the back; second, it would overawe Spain; third, it would produce fighting between Germans and Frenchmen in France; and, fourth, it would expose Italy to the whole brunt of the war.'

Aristocratic Churchill felt euphoric after that first meeting on 12 August: he thought he had won the 'peasant' over. The next night's meeting at 11 p.m. disabused him of that most unpleasantly. Stalin always liked to disconcert: first night, honey; second night, gall. Now he presented an *aide-mémoire* which dismissed *Torch* as irrelevant to the Soviet Union. He was scathing about the broken promises of a Second Front in Europe, and insultingly brutal about all the British failures and retreats – Norway, France, Crete, Singapore, Tobruk, etc. Stalin said all this, virtually accusing a man still haunted by the 1916 defeat in the Dardanelles of cowardice in the face of the German enemy.

Furious, sulky, the prime minister wanted to fly home the next morning, but Archibald Clark Kerr, the British ambassador, wisely advised him to swallow his pride. On the last night, Stalin did a volte-face, switching on the Georgian charm again, inviting Churchill for a private meal and drink, his daughter Svetlana Stalin in attendance, where he wooed the British premier for assurances of more military aid and a promise that Russia would smash Hitler's Prussian military machine and disarm Germany. At one in the morning, Alec Cadogan went to Stalin's room in the Kremlin and 'found Winston and Stalin, and Molotov who had joined them, sitting with a heavily laden board between them, food of all kinds crowned by a suckling pig, and innumerable bottles'. In a letter to Lord Halifax, Cadogan said that 'everything seemed to be as merry as a marriage-bell . . . I think the two great men really made contact and got on terms.'

Two planes now flew Churchill's enlarged party back the same route: two thousand miles from Moscow to Tehran, then thirteen hundred miles to Cairo, then another two and a half thousand miles, the fourteen-hour leg to Gibraltar, where they arrived on Monday 24 August and all repaired to Government House for a bath, shave and breakfast. (Mason-MacFarlane was away in London.) For security reasons Churchill was not allowed out into Main Street, but the high-spirited PM wondered if he might venture forth, swathed and swaddled, 'disguising himself as an Egyptian demi-mondaine, or an Armenian suffering from toothache'. They were about to have lunch at 1 p.m. when word came that London had approved a flight by daylight and they were to leave at 1.30, so they had to bolt their food and dash. The sixteen-hundred-mile flight to England took eight hours.

When Mason-MacFarlane was told in August that *Torch* was going ahead, he reported to London that Gibraltar was so closely watched that all unusual activity would be known in Berlin within twenty-four hours. If Spain came into the war against the Allies, the Rock's harbour and airfield would soon be knocked out.

This was a surprise to the Americans. Harry Butcher, Eisenhower's confidant and diary-keeper, wrote: 'Gibraltar, long the trademark symbolizing security* [was] actually extraordinarily vulnerable in the two particulars most important to us – i.e. airdrome and harbor.' Mason-MacFarlane advised complete security about *Torch*'s objective, and urged that the Spanish government be reassured 'convincingly and rapidly' if their suspicions and fears were aroused.

In late August and early September 1942, both Mason-MacFarlane and Samuel Hoare came to London. The Monday that Churchill was in Gibraltar, Mason-MacFarlane attended a long conference in Eisenhower's office, driving home the points made in his written report. Gibraltar's airstrip, he said, with up to two hundred Spitfires assembled on it for *Torch*, was a prime target for Italian or German bombing, and Spanish machine guns were positioned only twenty feet from the barbed wire by the airfield. There were a million gallons of petrol stored in flimsy four-gallon tins in every corner and crevice of the Rock, and he dreaded what a few incendiary bombs could do. He suggested a petrol tanker should be moored in the commercial harbour to lighter or hose fuel ashore as required. Mason-MacFarlane also pointed out that water would be a problem: Gibraltar's supply was insufficient for any unusual demand, so ships would need to bring their own water and oil. To confuse German surveillance of Gibraltar, all American officers should wear British or Canadian

---

* Since 1896, an image of the Rock had formed part of the logo of a major US insurance company, together with a slogan: 'The Prudential, with the strength of Gibraltar'. In 1965, 'The Rock' was registered as a trademark by the company.

uniforms. Because Gibraltar's airfield was so crowded, the land invasion had to succeed straight away to allow aeroplanes to move to
airfields in North Africa. But if *Torch* failed, Hitler would try to
bully Franco into war against the UK and the USA, though Mason-
MacFarlane thought that with the right reassurances, Spain would
stay neutral.

Reassuring Spain was Ambassador Samuel Hoare's job. He did
not meet with Eisenhower personally because that might well have
given the game away. The ambassador advised the Americans that
Franco's reaction would depend on events. If the *Torch* landings went
well and an Allied victory seemed likely, German pressure on Franco
would not work. However, if there were Allied failures and delays,
the Spanish government might be tempted to strike at Gibraltar, to
pre-empt a German onslaught. He agreed with Mason-MacFarlane
that establishing airfields in North Africa within range of Spanish
territory was vital. He recalled that the British attack on the French
navy at Mers-el-Kébir had frightened the Spaniards: 'The power of
retaliation against any hostile act on the part of the Spanish Government would be a powerful deterrent to Franco and Serrano Suñer.'
When authorised to do so, Hoare would reassure Franco that *Torch*
posed no threat to Spain or Spanish interests in North Africa. Meanwhile, because the preparations for *Torch* could not be concealed,
their purpose should be masked by a cover story: they would let it be
known that the true target was further east in the Mediterranean: an
attack on Italy, in defence of Malta.

Malta was on many minds in August 1942. The island's situation
was desperate, and a massive convoy – with four aircraft carriers –
was sent from Gibraltar to supply the beleaguered island with more
Spitfires, food, ammunition and above all the fuel needed to keep
Allied aircraft and ships moving to obstruct the Axis convoys supporting Rommel's Panzers in Africa.

Operation *Pedestal* (3–15 August 1942) was horrendously costly.
The Germans and Italians threw more than five hundred bombers

and fighters, a dozen submarines and a shoal of fast attack boats against the convoy. They managed to sink two light cruisers and a destroyer and torpedoed the aircraft carrier HMS *Eagle*, earmarked for Operation *Torch*, which went down carrying with it a quarter of the convoy's fighter planes. Hundreds of men died. Of the fourteen loaded merchant ships, just five reached Malta, and only two of them undamaged. The crippled tanker *Ohio* made it, hauled into the Grand Harbour of Valletta lashed to a destroyer and pulled by a set of tugs, and her vital fuel, 11,500 tons of kerosene and diesel oil, flowed safely out into two tankers before the broken vessel finally sank.

It was Saturday 15 August, the Feast of the Assumption, *Santa Marija* in Malta, when Roman Catholics celebrate the Virgin Mary being taken up into heaven, body and soul, at the end of her earthly life. The Maltese faithful gave thanks for this sacrifice and their salvation, and continue to do so on 15 August to this day.

At Bilbao in the Basque country on Saturday 15 August 1942, the Spanish right-wing Carlist *requetés* were also celebrating the Feast of the Assumption with a Requiem Mass at the basilica of Nuestra Señora de Begoña, remembering their comrades of the Tercio de Begoña who had died fighting for the Nationalist side in the Spanish Civil War. Among the congregation was the Traditionalist General Varela, the Minister of War in Franco's government, who was married to a wealthy Basque, Cecilia Ampuero. As some of the red-bereted Carlist veterans spilled out of the church, they shouted monarchist and anti-Franco slogans. A squad of pro-Franco Falangists objected and fierce scuffles broke out. Defending his one-legged friend Calleja as well as Franco's name, a young right-wing Francoist fanatic called Juan José Domínguez Muñoz threw a pair of hand grenades that another friend had brought back from service with *la División Azul* in Russia, wounding scores of people. General Varela came out of the church and claimed this was an attempt to assassinate him.

The incident exacerbated an ugly row between the army and the

Falange, which many soldiers saw as mired in the corruptions of the black market, and caused a crisis in Franco's cobbled-together coalition government. The Interior Minister, *Ministro de Gobernación* Colonel Valentin Galarza, poured petrol on the flames by sending out cables to all provincial governors saying that young Domínguez Muñoz was the agent of a foreign power.

If so, from which country? According to the British ambassador Samuel Hoare, he was 'a notorious criminal who had recently been employed in the German sabotage organisation at Algeciras'. But Spanish government sources said Domínguez Muñoz was actually an agent for the British or the North Americans.

Franco had to sort out the conflict. First, he had the young Falangist grenade-thrower shot by firing squad on 1 September. (He died singing the Falange anthem 'Cara al Sol'.) Then, to placate the Falange for this act, he sacked both General Varela and Minister Galarza. And finally, to counter-placate the army, Franco did something most dramatic: on 2 September he dismissed Serrano Suñer as Foreign Minister. (This may have been personal as well as political: Serrano was betraying his wife Zita, sister of Franco's wife, by having an extramarital love affair with María Sonsoles de Icaza y de León, the young wife of the old Marquis of Llanzol, and was sacked four days after she gave birth to their illegitimate daughter, Carmen Díez de Rivera.) A more compliant military man, little Count Jordana, took over the Spanish Foreign Ministry, which pleased Sir Samuel Hoare no end. 'How often I blessed my good fortune that I was dealing with a wise friend and not an excitable enemy!'

There remains a mystery around Juan José Domínguez Muñoz. Hoare had denounced him as a saboteur working for the Germans, a fact seemingly confirmed by Adolf Hitler awarding Domínguez Muñoz, on the eve of his execution, the Cross of the German Eagle, the principal Nazi medal for foreigners. But there is another level to these events. In his April 1942 diary, Guy Liddell of MI5 wrote of a British double agent in Algeciras called 'Sundae' who was arrested by the Spanish 'principally because the Germans thought he was working more for us than for them'. In his *History*, David Scherr also recounts the activities, from September to November 1941, of a double agent in the Algeciras area called Sundae. This 'young reserve lieutenant in the Spanish Army' was extremely useful, handing over to the British several German Abwehr high-tech sabotage devices that he was supposed to be employing against the Rock, including two large mines, an ingenious pen and pencil set that could be broken apart and rebuilt into a detonator, a high-explosive bomb disguised as a two-litre can of Atlantic Motor Oil, and another bomb hidden in a functioning thermos flask with a Mark II German clockwork delayed detonator concealed in the cap. Scherr added this note:

SUNDAE disappeared from the Gibraltar district and was not heard off [*sic*] again until on 25 July [*sic*] 1942 he took a prominent part in a Falange attempt at assassinating General Varela, then Minister of War, at a Carlist ceremony in Bilbao. The attempt failed, though there were a number of other people killed and wounded, and SUNDAE was arrested. In spite of the political issues involved, he was executed on 1 September 1942.

If it is true (and it would be rather astonishing) that the Spanish Falangist hero Domínguez Muñoz, so favoured by Hitler, and the anti-German, pro-British double agent Sundae were one and the same person, it might explain Franco's curiously gnomic utterance about the daring young man: 'I should have given him a medal, but I had to have him shot'.

On 18 August 1942, with Churchill out of the country, Lord Mountbatten launched Operation *Jubilee*, a ten-thousand-man Combined Operations attack on the French port of Dieppe, and it was a disaster: hundreds of Canadians were killed, thousands captured, tanks got stuck on the pebble beaches and many RAF planes were shot down. British propaganda puffed it as a palpable hit, but in reality the dream of a Second Front in Western Europe in 1942 or 1943 was finally over. All eyes turned back to North Africa.

Operation *Torch* would only work if Spain stayed neutral. The Allies feared that Spain could quench *Torch* by choking off the Strait of Gibraltar or letting the Germans do so. To be ready for any eventuality, Alan Brooke prepared special forces, 'in the event of Spain turning sour'. General Patton's Western Force, landing at Casablanca, well west of the strait, was ready to counter any Axis thrust south. So vital was it to know how much Spain knew, or whether she had hostile plans, that British Intelligence sanctioned regular burglaries of the Spanish Embassy in Washington DC, to photograph their diplomatic ciphers (which changed every month) so as to decrypt all messages to and from Madrid.

In the history of British Security Co-ordination, written at the end of the war, these provocative acts on US soil were attributed to 'helpful' Spanish Republicans and Basques, but after the McKellar Act was passed (requiring foreign agents to detail all their activities) British Intelligence turned to the OSS, who employed a gay American schoolmaster-turned-secret-agent called Donald Downes to do the job. In his lively autobiography *The Scarlet Thread: adventures in wartime espionage*, Downes describes breaking into the Washington embassy of a neutral country he calls 'Alphonia', having infiltrated a regular secretary into the building first. She was able to damage the safe so that Downes's locksmith would be called to repair it, and thus obtain a copy of the key and the right combination. Downes and his agents were actually inside the embassy on their fourth night-time burglary, in October 1942, when the FBI turned up outside in two squad cars with lights flashing and sirens wailing. The burglars were arrested, and James R. Murphy, the head of the OSS counter-intelligence branch, X-2, had to spring Downes from jail. This Watergate-style moment in Washington was part of the increasingly vicious turf fight between J. Edgar Hoover of the FBI and William J. Donovan of the OSS.

Security was a perpetual anxiety. The Dakar operation in 1940 had leaked like a sieve. What if *Torch* did? A Frenchman was indiscreet about it in Washington in August, and there were fears in Gibraltar too that someone might blab to enemy intelligence. SOE men there talked in theory about assassinating Albert Carbe, the Abwehr agent who ran German espionage from the Villa Leon in Algeciras, or blowing up the Italian spy base at the Villa Carmela in Campamento. Neither of these actions happened, but another alarum ended disastrously.

On the night of 14 September 1942, three Anglo-Argentine 'Thieves' from the *Relator* party, now the mainstays of the secret smuggling flotilla, SOE Captains Peter Musson, Austin Baillon and Arthur Fletcher, were in the Bar Tronio in 'Gib Street', La Línea, meeting Tison, the useful Spaniard who ran Venta El Cruce, when they noticed a blond man and his dark-haired accomplice taking an unnatural interest in their conversation. Alarmed that these two might be enemy agents who could connect the Spanish tobacco-smuggling network to British officers, the SOE men seized the dark-haired one (who carried papers in the name of Francisco Rodriguez and said he worked at Hassan's tailor shop) and bundled him violently over the Spanish frontier into British Gibraltar.

They took him first to the office of the DSO, Lieutenant Colonel 'Tito' Medlam, but their captive would not confess, so they moved on to interrogate him at the Villa Lourdes in South Barracks Road. Rodriguez was beaten up, but still refused to talk. He was either a hardened agent or an innocent man with nothing to confess, but because he might know too much, he was shot, dying instantly. His pockets were emptied and his body driven a bit further south-east to a spot on the Gibraltar peninsula called Dead Man's Hole near the Europa Point lighthouse. With 120 lbs of iron attached to his feet, Francisco Rodriguez slid off a 'corpse chute' and splashed into the sea. The SOE men returned to their billets at 2.30 a.m.

Governor Mason-MacFarlane thought the affair was characterised by 'stupidity and amateur impulsiveness' and was badly handled at Dead Man's Hole. The ordinary sentry stationed there now knew the identity of one of the SOE officers; more, he had found a pool of blood, which he duly reported to Fortress Headquarters, and talked about within his artillery unit. Mason-MacFarlane went on: 'Had I been informed of what was intended, and had I decided to agree to the elimination of this man, I could have laid on absolute security in the same way as already has been done successfully in a previous case of the same type . . .'

Until *Torch* was launched, Mason-MacFarlane ordered, no SOE officer was to leave the Rock unless his mission was personally approved by him as Gibraltar's Commander-in-Chief. However, Colin Gubbins, the head of SOE, 'commended the resource of the officers concerned', although officially they were to be 'censured'.

Other corpses caused worse security embarrassments. On 29 September 1942, General Alan Brooke recorded in his diary: '[A]larming information of loss of a Catalina between Lisbon and Gibraltar, and bodies washed up at Cadiz with letters in their pockets containing details of North African attack plans!'

Three days earlier, a Coastal Command Catalina flying boat heading for Gibraltar had crashed in the sea off Cádiz during a thunderstorm. All ten crew aboard were killed as well as their three passengers. One of them was Louis Daniélou Clamorgan, a Gaullist naval officer on his way to Tangier for SOE. Another was Paymaster-Lieutenant James Hadden Turner RN, who was carrying an official letter, dated 14 September, from US General Mark Clark to Mason-MacFarlane saying that his boss, General Dwight Eisenhower, would be arriving in Gibraltar just before the 'target date' of 4 November.

Wartime dead regularly washed ashore in Spain, so it was not unusual that a Spanish naval officer handed over Turner's body, still wearing blue overalls, to Mason-MacFarlane's Gibraltarian ADC Bobby Capurro, who brought it back to the Rock. The letter was in an inside pocket, and from the way the sand was still evenly packed in the fly of the overalls, which looked like the result of a body rolling, face down, in the surf while being washed up on the beach at La Barrosa, the Intelligence pundits reckoned the buttons had not been undone. Guy Liddell of MI5 recorded in his diary: 'The letter was sealed and did not appear to have been tampered with. The Inter-Services Security Board is now in a great flap as to whether Operation TORCH has been compromised.'

Then there was journalistic chatter in Fleet Street. Forty-year-old Philip Jordan of the *News Chronicle* was a well-known left-wing journalist who had covered the Spanish Civil War, then been in Russia for eleven months, and was now on the list of those who would become official War Correspondents when the 'Second Front' started. In early October, a colleague on the paper turned to him and said, 'I hear you are going off soon.' This other reporter, A. J. Cumming, had been talking to the Soviet ambassador, Ivan Maisky, who told him that General Eisenhower was going to command a large military operation in northwest Africa. Jordan got the distinct impression from Cumming that this information was being imparted as propaganda for the Soviet line that the campaign in North Africa was mistaken and that the Second Front should be in Europe. Maisky was telling American journalists like Fred Kuh of UPI the same thing.

Acting responsibly, Jordan tipped off Wing Commander Pedro de Casa Maury, the Chief Intelligence Officer of Combined Operations HQ, who in turn alerted the Security Service. On 8 October, Lieutenant Colonel Gilbert Lennox of MI5, under his usual pseudonym, 'Major Lester of the War Office', interviewed Jordan. The reporter knew perfectly well that Lennox was an MI5 officer: 'Fat, gay and obviously no fool at all.' Jordan told Lennox that he had lunched with the proprietor of the *Daily Mail*, Lord Rothermere, the day before, and Rothermere too seemed to know all about the North Africa campaign, though Jordan had not revealed that his own knowledge came via A. J. Cumming and the Soviet ambassador. Jordan – described by MI5 as 'frank and helpful' – said he thought it was quite wrong of the Russians to try and 'sway the British government by public clamour'. Knowing Moscow and the Soviets, he said: 'You don't have public clamour in Russia unless you want it. If you don't want it, you shoot the people who make it.' The two men agreed that Lennox should inform the Foreign Office.

The Foreign Office was not at all happy with the news from MI5. The 'incorrigible' Maisky was 'intriguing with the ignorant and the disgruntled', which Alec Cadogan found 'very disturbing'. The Russians were secretive; Maisky did not drink; therefore it was no accident. 'Can it possibly be that the Russians are deliberately trying to scupper TORCH and prevent its happening?' The Foreign Secretary, Anthony Eden, said it was 'inexcusable' and gave Maisky a stiff dressing-down on 15 October.

Across French North Africa, Vichy maintained five hundred aircraft and 125,000 regular army, navy and air force personnel as well as two hundred thousand reservists. It was vital that these armed forces not turn their firepower on the Americans when they landed. The US diplomat Robert Murphy had entered into indirect talks with General Henri Giraud in mainland France, and Giraud's designated representative in Algiers, General Charles Mast, said he would discuss possible co-operation with the Americans if they sent him a senior officer by submarine. Murphy found a discreet meeting place, a colonial villa on the coast about seventy-five miles west of Algiers.

US General Mark Wayne Clark, Eisenhower's deputy, volunteered to go on the important mission to North Africa to talk to General Mast. Clark was ambitious, 'seeking the bubble reputation, even in the cannon's mouth', and easily distracted. F. W. Winterbotham records going to Norfolk House in St James's Square in August 1942 with 'C', Sir Stewart Menzies, to 'indoctrinate' the senior American soldiers. This meant informing them about the British Signals Intelligence breakthroughs, which meant they would be receiving ULTRA intelligence derived from German ciphers broken at Bletchley Park. Clark was restless and incredulous and left after a quarter of an hour saying that 'he had something else to do'.

Clark finally set off for North Africa accompanied by a brigadier, two colonels and a naval captain. USAAF General Carl Spaatz laid on two Flying Fortresses to get them to Gibraltar, one piloted by Paul Tibbets, later to fly the B-29 that dropped the atomic bomb on Hiroshima. Meanwhile, the Admiralty alerted Captain Barney Fawkes of HMS *Maidstone* that His Majesty's Submarine *Seraph* was 'allocated to special political operations from this date. Utmost discretion in briefing of officers is necessary and all further orders are to be destroyed after committal to memory.'

The Americans met the British in conference at Government House in Gibraltar. Governor Mason-MacFarlane presided and Vice Admiral Commanding North Atlantic, Frederick Edward-Collins, represented the Royal Navy. Captain Fawkes was also there with Bill Jewell, *Seraph*'s cheerful young commander. Clark laid out the picture and asked if he could be got to the North African coast in a few days' time. 'Fat Fred Collins' aka 'The Giant Panda' expatiated on all the difficulties and risks. Clark said they were going regardless. He turned to Fawkes, who said they could but try, and introduced him to Jewell, who knew the Algerian coast from having recently landed Special Boat Section (SBS) commandos to reconnoitre the beaches.

'What do you think, son?' Murphy asked Jewell. 'Can you get us there and back, even during the full moon?'

'Of course, sir. No trouble at all, if the enemy stays blind and deaf.'

'When can you get me there?'

'If we leave tonight, we can make it by the 22nd.'

Mason-MacFarlane and Edward-Collins gave their approval and the Americans filtered discreetly onto the submarine. Three officers from the SBS, led by Captain Godfrey Courtney, were already aboard, equipped to paddle them ashore in folding kayaks or 'folbots'. During the night of 21 October, Trafalgar Day, they stopped to practise embarking and disembarking from the shaky boats.

Jewell got them to the right place on the coast and they paddled ashore at night to a wide beach that led to a bluff covered in scrub and olive trees. Bob Murphy said, 'Welcome to North Africa,' and led them to a scruffy farmhouse. The American officers were all in uniform. The British commandos discreetly hid their canvas boats and got themselves out of the way before Mast and five French staff officers arrived. Their discussions lasted all of 22 October, though General Mast left at lunchtime, having requested weapons for his underground resistance forces, including two thousand Bren guns. (Slocum's new Q-ship, the 347-ton *Minna*, would try to deliver ten tons of small arms, ammunition, hand grenades and mines to a beach near Algiers in early November, though the rendezvous failed.) Murphy and Clark could not tell the Frenchmen that the invasion was only sixteen days away, so the French mistakenly thought they had many weeks to get ready. The exact role of General Henri Giraud was not specified; his representative was led to believe he would have overall command 'as soon as possible', while his immediate task was to set up his HQ in Algiers and arrange for every garrison from Casablanca to Bône to accept and assist the invaders. The French said that General Giraud, who was in mainland France, had to be picked up by an American submarine and brought to North Africa. The status of Admiral Darlan in all this was left vague and unresolved.

The local police arrived in the early evening, causing a panic. The seven Americans and British commandos had to hide in a dusty wine cellar. Murphy stayed upstairs, declaring himself to be the American consul and acting slightly drunk; he asked the police not to embarrass him because there were some women upstairs and they were having a party. The police, tipped off by a sacked servant that something fishy was going on at the remote house, were looking not for subversives but for smugglers. Down in the cellar, under the trapdoor, Courtney the SBS commando started coughing and Clark gave him some chewing gum out of his own mouth to quieten him.

After two hours, the police went away, and the party set out to get back to the submarine. The sea was rising, the surf rough. A large wave capsized six-foot-two-inch General Clark and Captain Livingstone into the water and they had to give up the attempt. The party tried again before dawn next day and, after repeated swampings, eventually succeeded. In the struggle to get off General Clark lost his uniform trousers wrapped around his heavy money-belt. They also lost one complete folbot canoe, $2000 in gold, a weighted bag of secret papers, three .45 Thompson sub-machine guns with fifteen magazines of ammunition, one Luger automatic pistol with two magazines, a Colt automatic pistol and magazine, three hundred rounds of small arms ammunition, two torches, a fighting knife, a pair of binoculars, a compass and a 'walkie-talkie' radio set. But the Americans were jubilant; their diplomatic mission was accomplished.

A Catalina flying boat came out to pick them up in mid-Mediterranean. Encouraged to have seen the British army, navy and air force all co-operating, General Clark declared that 'this war is about to be won'. That same day in Egypt, on the other side of North Africa, Montgomery's Eighth Army was starting the twelve-day battle of El Alamein, and across the Atlantic in Norfolk, Virginia, USA, George Patton was about to sail with the US First Army. The great Allied pincer movement against the Axis was starting.

31

The North African Landings

The extraordinary task of naval planning for Operation *Torch* went to Vice Admiral Sir Bertram Ramsay, who had been knighted for achieving the Dunkirk evacuation, Operation *Dynamo*, in 1940. Appointed naval Commander-in-Chief, Expeditionary Force, and given an office in Norfolk House with no tables or chairs, no charts and books, just a solitary telephone in the middle of the dusty floor, Ramsay had only two months to get together a staff to organise and co-ordinate the location of many hundreds of different sea-going vessels (sailing anywhere between Scapa Flow and Sierra Leone), then their assignment, loading, distribution, fuelling and convoying so they could safely deliver the soldiers and their supplies from the UK to the right place, at the right time, inside the Mediterranean. Training exercises and rehearsals with landing craft had to be factored in. The Fleet Air Arm, flying off aircraft carriers, would need enough men and planes and ammunition to provide air cover for the troops that were landing. Apart from ships' crews, nearly nine thousand extra naval personnel would be needed to clear and run occupied ports and handle all the logistics of fuelling, repair and supply.

Ramsay – one of the most under-recognised heroes of the Second World War – had a genius for this kind of complex task, and after *Torch* would go on to plan and organise the even bigger 1943 invasion of Sicily (Operation *Husky*) and the enormous 1944 D-Day landings in Normandy (Operation *Neptune*). But in 1942, no one had ever undertaken an amphibious task of this complexity before. Ramsay created a dedicated and hard-working team that worked collegiately, not in silos. He held crisp daily meetings of up to forty officers and officials where problems could be raised, confusions cleared up. Minutes were circulated without delay so decisions could be acted on at once with everything done properly, ship-shape and Bristol-fashion.

As the giant jigsaw puzzle was assembled, Ramsay was conscious that he had never been at sea in command of such a fleet. After consultation with Admiral Dudley Pound, the First Sea Lord, naval command of the expeditionary force was offered to 'A.B.C.', Admiral Andrew Browne Cunningham, who flew back from Washington DC to head the team, with Ramsay becoming his deputy. Four officers and eight Wrens wrote the naval plan with operation and signal orders in eight interlocking parts, and it was printed secretly at night by Oxford University Press and proofread by Admiral John Godfrey's formidable wife Margaret. These plans covered the sailing, routing, exact timing and arrival at landing places at Oran and Algiers of two advance convoys of forty-five ships, which would be followed by a main body of more than two hundred vessels with a hundred escorts, transporting 38,500 British and American troops. 'Gibraltar would be the hinge-pin of the whole operation,' wrote Cunningham in his autobiography, *A Sailor's Odyssey*. Getting four hundred ships safely through a passage eight miles wide as quickly as possible meant sticking to the timetable. Cunningham himself sailed discreetly for Gibraltar on the cruiser *Scylla*, arriving on 1 November 1942 to set up his headquarters at the Admiralty Tower.

The Gibraltar airfield was crucial to the success of *Torch*. The decision to lengthen the nine-hundred-yard strip had been taken at the end of October 1941. The Airfield Construction Service and the Royal Engineers undertook the task of building an extension out into the western bay, using 750,000 cubic yards of rock and scree obtained by explosive blasting and hydraulic jets. Earth-and-rock movers, crushers, bulldozers, tractors, lorries, drillers, blasters, generators, pumps all laboured to make an airfield 1800 yards long and 250 yards wide, creating endless noise and dust.

RAF New Camp was a flying-boat base, so they set up RAF North

Front on land, a dismal collection of Nissen huts with no proper lavatories but overflowing buckets. The showers were salt-water and all the food was tinned. So much gritty dust permeated the biscuit-coloured blankets they slept on that men developed sores and rashes, which were duly painted with gentian violet. These blotchy, semi-human creatures could be observed stark naked, swimming and sunbathing at Eastern Beach. An unhappy conscript recalled:

We were in Gibraltar. Was it baking! They took us to this place which was the North Front Aerodrome. There was nothing there. They didn't expect us. There was nowhere for us to sleep. They had loads of petrol cans so they gave us six petrol cans, three biscuits and a couple of blankets. And that's how we had to sleep for nearly three months. You just wasn't used to it. You had to be very careful with water. There was so little of it. You had to wash in sea-water. And as you sat there – bleeding flies. As fast as you swatted them, they were on you again. Oh it was the most horrifying experience. Flies galore on every bleeding thing. The most unsanitary conditions. And as I say, you had to sleep out in the open. The officers? Where were they? Oh, they had quarters. Definitely. The Rock Hotel. Oh yes.

The airfield dispersal areas became packed with fighters and fighter-bombers which had arrived in crates and had to be assembled by the RAF Special Erection Parties. From October to December 1942, working in the open, in often dreadful weather, they assembled an astonishing 431 Spitfires and 134 Hurricanes at Gibraltar for use in Operation *Torch*.

Aeroplanes were continually landing and taking off on the airstrip. On 1 November 1942 two great British deceivers got out at Gibraltar to stretch their legs while their plane refuelled for their flight onwards to Cairo. One of the men was the ingenious Lieutenant Colonel Dudley Clarke, the head of 'A' Force, the deception organisation in Middle East Headquarters in Cairo, and the other was Major Peter Fleming, Ian Fleming's older brother, who ran deception against the Japanese for General Wavell in India. They had been in London, ensuring that all the false information to deceive enemy intelligence was co-ordinated before being propagated worldwide. Dudley Clarke's organisation in Egypt had just put together Operation *Bertram*, a huge scheme of camouflage and dummy vehicles, fake stores and railheads to mislead the Germans and Italians about the intentions of the British forces at El Alamein, the great battle now under way in the Western Desert.

Dudley Clarke had been in Gibraltar exactly a year earlier in somewhat embarrassing circumstances. He had been arrested by the Spanish police in Madrid, and formally photographed by them, while dressed in women's clothes. Alan Hillgarth got him out of custody and down to Gibraltar, but Clarke's ship back to England was torpedoed and after he was rescued he was returned to the Rock to be grilled by Lord Gort about what exactly he had been up to in Madrid. He explained away the transvestism as a gambit to help him pass false information to a German agent, and Gort allowed him to return to Cairo for General Auchinleck to deal with.

In late 1942, 'A' Force's job was spreading rumours to mask *Torch* with eight cover and deception operations, to keep enemy troops elsewhere, to conceal the convoys and to mislead the enemy about their destination. One deception, called *Solo*, was an attack on Norway. Another was that there was going to be a military move against Dakar from the Gambia, and that at the same time many ships were coming through the Strait of Gibraltar to reinforce Malta on a grand scale, prior to an attack on Sicily. Many maps of Malta arrived in Gibraltar; Mason-Mac flew to the besieged island to support the rumour. Or again, there was possibly going to be a landing in Tripolitania to support the Eighth Army in Libya. If these last stories were believed, the enemy would station U-boats too far south or too far east to interfere with *Torch* convoys. The Sicily deception, code-named *Kennecott*, seems to have worked. On 8 November, sixty German and Italian U-boats were lurking off the Azores and Madeira, and lots of German and Italian aircraft were massed in Sardinia and Sicily.

★

On 1 November, a panicky message came from Robert Murphy in Algiers. He had only recently been allowed to inform the local French commander, General Mast, that the invasion would be coming 'early in November'. The Frenchman was surprised and upset by the short notice, thinking it was political blackmail. Then General Henri Honoré Giraud, code-named Kingpin, said he could not leave mainland France until 20 November. Foreseeing catastrophe unless French forces agreed not to resist, Murphy, a diplomat who knew nothing of military affairs, naïvely asked Roosevelt to delay *Torch* by two weeks. With fleets at sea and forces committed, this was of course impossible; Cunningham called the idea 'lunatic'. So Murphy had to send Giraud 'assurances couched in ambiguous phrases'.

Giraud had demanded that an American submarine collect him, not a British one, because the hateful British had let his country down in the Battle of France and treacherously attacked at Mers-el-Kébir. So HMS *Seraph* in the gulf of Lyons became, for the moment, USS *Seraph*, under the temporary command of Captain Jerauld Wright, US Navy. In the official handover ceremony on the boat, Wright solemnly received a scroll bearing his duties and responsibilities upon this historic transfer of power. He unrolled it to find a saucy pin-up from a French magazine.

There is no doubt that General Giraud was a brave soldier. Captured in the fall of France, two years later he escaped from Schloss Königstein in Germany, sliding down a rope he had woven from parcel string and copper wire, before reaching Switzerland and then making his way home to Lyons. There, he had defied Otto Abetz, the German ambassador, as well as Vichy premier Pierre Laval, when they both urged him to return to captivity in Germany to avoid embarrassing their respective countries. Now, at one remove, Giraud was in touch with the Americans about French North Africa. The gallant general entertained elevated notions of what his own role would be, on the grounds that the Americans were amateurs and everyone knew that France produced the finest professional soldiers in the world.

At 1.15 a.m. on 6 November, Giraud and three aides were picked up from a rowing boat off La Fossette beach, half a mile east of Le Lavandou, on the Côte d'Azur between Hyères and Saint-Tropez. Everyone on the submarine pretended to be American until the general (who fell in the water) was safely aboard USS *Seraph* in his wet civilian clothes and they were under way. The radio was not working at first, but the next day they managed to rendezvous with a Catalina flying boat that took General Giraud, alias Kingpin, swiftly on to Gibraltar.

At 8.20 a.m. on 5 November 1942, five Flying Fortress bombers carrying General Eisenhower and his HQ staff finally took off from Bournemouth, bound for Gibraltar. During their twenty-four-hour weather delay, they had tried to distract themselves with a light-hearted new movie shot in Arizona, before it went on general release: Bob Hope and Bing Crosby in *Road to Morocco*. Finally General Eisenhower ordered Tibbets to take off in bad weather. At Gibraltar they circled the crowded airfield for an hour before landing at 5.20 p.m. Mason-MacFarlane welcomed them to Government House and Anthony Quayle showed Harry Butcher the air-raid shelter.

This was a curious moment in history. As Supreme Commander of the Allied Expedition, General Eisenhower outranked General Mason-MacFarlane. While remaining the civil governor, Mason-MacFarlane now yielded to the US general the military command of the Fortress and Garrison of Gibraltar.* To Eisenhower, the man from Abilene, this seemed like the symbolic handing over of imperial power from Great Britain to the United States:

In my service I've often thought or dreamed of commands, battle commands of various types that I might one day hold . . . [the one] I now have could never, under any conditions, have entered my mind even fleetingly. *I have*

---

* Churchill sent Eisenhower a cable saying that he felt 'the Rock of Gibraltar is safe in your hands'. In his jeep on the Upper Rock, Eisenhower patted a macaque monkey on the head for good luck, and was told that while these creatures were here, Gibraltar would stay British.

operational command of Gibraltar! The symbol of the solidity of the British Empire . . . An American is in charge, and I am he . . .

The reality was unromantic. 'At Gibraltar our headquarters was established in the most dismal setting we occupied during the war,' wrote Eisenhower. In the damp heart of the Rock, halfway through the dimly lit, mile-long east–west Admiralty Tunnel and three hundred feet below 'Maida Vale' on the north–south tunnel called 'The Great North Road', lay the set of stagnant rooms that acted as Allied Forces Headquarters (AFHQ). Clark and Eisenhower shared an office that was only about eight foot square and had two desks and a cot in it. 'Through the arched ceilings came a constant drip, drip, drip of surface water that faithfully but drearily ticked off the seconds of the interminable, almost unendurable wait which always occurs between the completion of a military plan and the moment action begins.'

Eisenhower had three days to wait. He smoked an awful lot of Camel cigarettes, chewed up with anxiety, and stood at Europa Point at the southern end of the peninsula watching the leading ships for *Torch* passing eastward into the Mediterranean through the strait, maintaining wireless silence. He was grateful for no news of air or submarine attack. But then, to add to the tension, just when he wanted information, the fragile radio communications set up by the regular US Army Signals Corps on the Rock broke down. Eisenhower had no idea what was happening at Casablanca. Would Patton's men, who had sailed directly across the Atlantic from the USA, be able to land through the Moroccan surf?

Second World War operations relied on radio. Although the Rock had reasonable wireless interception, with army, navy and air force Wireless Intelligence Unit personnel continually logging enemy radio communications in the Mediterranean and North West Africa, transmissions could be very erratic.

Now the work of a maverick signals officer from the secret world saved the day. 'Squadron Leader Hugh Mallory' had arrived in

Tangier a year earlier. His real name was Hugh Mallory Falconer and he had served in the French Foreign Legion before being recruited by SOE; the pseudonym was to protect his wife Susan, still in France, from reprisals. Mallory was described by the SOE historian William Mackenzie as 'a hustler, known in the service as the "human bombshell"'. When Hugh Quennell told him to set up a clandestine radio network linking Gibraltar with Tangier, French and Spanish Morocco, Algeria and Spain, Mallory outmanoeuvred the DSO, Tito Medlam, to gain possession of Embrasure V in the Upper Union Gallery, inside the western flank of the Rock, where he installed a two-room radio cabin. He scrounged enough kit to set up transmitters and receivers, including a mobile one in a Packard car, and a branch station high up at the eastern end of the Waterworks Tunnel. Working with the OSS man in Gibraltar, Joe Raichle, Mallory made sure that both American and British radio operators were well trained.

When the US army signal system dramatically failed, Mallory's network was ready, and came into its own. All the clandestine signals preceding *Torch* used it, as did the key operational messages during the early days of the invasion. William Mackenzie rightly called Mallory/Falconer's wireless station on the Rock, now boasting two generators, three transmitters and two receivers, 'SOE's most important contribution to history in North Africa.'

In the event, the Atlantic crossing was undisturbed by U-boats, but at 5.35 a.m. on 7 November, USS *Thomas Stone* was torpedoed in the Mediterranean, 150 miles short of its destination, Algiers. Still afloat, but unable to move his ship, Captain Bennehoff decided to send his escort and the 1450 troops in their landing craft on to Algiers. It was a gallant attempt, but they soon had to be picked up by destroyers and other escort vessels, and arrived twelve hours late. Submarines were sent ahead to place infra-red beacons to guide the ships, and to drop advance parties who paddled ashore in 'folbot' kayaks for inshore reconnaissance. Two SBS commandos were captured at A Beach, west of Algiers, but revealed nothing.

Everybody was gathering at the Rock. Eisenhower had ordered Eddy and Coon to move their OSS operation over from Tangier three days before the invasion. And in the afternoon of Saturday 7 November, General Giraud, who had been picked up by the submarine *Seraph*, arrived in Gibraltar by flying boat and was taken directly to Eisenhower and Clark's 'dungeon' in the hot and sweaty Admiralty Tunnel, where the chattering teleprinters were making a din. Giraud was thin, stiff, bedraggled, but proud. Anthony Quayle described him as 'a tall old beanpole [in] a long raincoat buttoned straight down from collar to knee'. Eisenhower switched on the red light outside the tiny office so no one else would enter, and explained their plans, adding that he had a message for the French people in North Africa that he wanted Giraud to sign. This stated that the United States was intervening to stop the Axis seizing North Africa and called on the officers and men of the French Army of Africa to do their duty in assisting them. Of Giraud's role it only said on his behalf: 'I resume my place of combat among you.'

'Now,' said General Giraud, 'let's get it clear as to my part. As I understand it, when I land in North Africa I am to assume command of all Allied forces and become the Supreme Allied Commander in North Africa.'

Clark gasped at this bombshell. Eisenhower managed to stay poker-faced. 'There must be some misunderstanding,' he said, cautiously.

The meeting that followed lasted three hours and was described by Eisenhower as 'one of my most distressing interviews of the war'. Giraud had got the wrong end of the stick completely. He had believed he was going to become Supreme Allied Commander of the Anglo-American forces, despite knowing nothing of their plans and capabilities, and then was going to lead an almost immediate invasion of mainland France. The Americans could not budge Giraud from what Eisenhower called his 'grave misapprehension', nor persuade him to agree to their wish that he only command French troops. General Giraud would not, could not, subordinate himself to anyone: 'his countrymen would not understand and his honour as a soldier would be tarnished'. The French general finally emerged, says Anthony Quayle, 'trumpeting with fury . . . mortally outraged'.

Admiral Cunningham, sweating in his usual submariner's thick rollneck sweater under his ancient uniform jacket and with his trousers tucked into rubber boots,* saw Eisenhower come out 'looking desperately tired and worried' from his office, and took him off for dinner at the Mount. Giraud, furious, went off to dine with Mason-MacFarlane at Government House. Quayle says the meal was 'a fiasco'.

Across the Mediterranean, things were not going well for the Italians. Mussolini was pale, drawn and tired. The rout of Axis forces at El Alamein and their headlong flight through Libya was cremating his African imperial dream. On Saturday 7 November, the Italian Foreign Minister Count Ciano wondered:

What will the various [Allied] convoys do that have left Gibraltar and are eastward bound? There are various conjectures. According to the Germans, they are for the provisioning of Malta or an attempt at landing in Tripolitania in order to fall upon Rommel's rear. According to our General Staff, they are for the occupation of French bases in North Africa. The Duce, too, is of this opinion: in fact he believes the landing will be accomplished by the Americans, who will meet almost no resistance from the French. I share the Duce's opinion; in fact, I believe that North Africa is ready to hoist the de Gaullist flag. All this is exceedingly serious for us.

NOVEMBER 8, 1942. At five-thirty in the morning von Ribbentrop telephoned to inform me of American landings in Algerian and Moroccan ports. He was rather nervous, and wanted to know what we intended to do. I must confess that, having been caught unawares, I was too sleepy to give a very satisfactory answer.

---

* 'This is what I always wear when I go into battle,' Cunningham told Quayle. 'I know damn well I'm not at sea, but I'm going into battle just the same – and I'm commanding the Fleet from under all this rock. If I don't dress right, then I can't think right.'

Sunday 8 November 1942 was indeed D-Day for Operation *Torch*. British and American aeroplanes dropped twenty-two million leaflets in French appealing for active co-operation and stating that their object was 'to destroy the German and Italian forces in North Africa'. The world's largest radio transmitter, 'Aspidistra', broadcast from near Crowborough in southern England a recorded message by President Roosevelt, spoken in French, an appeal which could be heard overriding the usual wavelengths of Morocco and Algeria. '*Mes amis,*' it began, 'my friends', and it ended: 'Do not, I beg of you, hinder this great purpose. Render your assistance where you can and we will see the return of the glorious day when freedom and peace will again reign in the world. *Vive la France éternelle!* Long live eternal France!'

On the ground, however, General Patton was annoyed that this blaring message shattered any hope of surprise. Eisenhower also broadcast radio messages saying 'We come as friends, not as enemies', asking Frenchmen not to resist, gun batteries not to fire, ships and planes not to move, searchlights to point straight upwards. Giraud broadcast; de Gaulle broadcast; all sorts of pro-Allied voices filled the airwaves.

US ambassadors delivered President Roosevelt's personal letters to Marshal Pétain, President Carmona of Portugal and General Franco in Spain, saying that Germany and Italy's intended occupation of French North Africa menaced all the American republics, and therefore had to be stopped. 'These moves are in no shape, manner or form directed against the Government or people of Spain or Spanish Morocco or Spanish territories – metropolitan or overseas. I believe the Spanish Government and the Spanish people wish to maintain neutrality and to remain outside the war. Spain has nothing to fear from the United Nations.' Sir Samuel Hoare (who almost never spoke of 'the United Nations' but habitually of 'Great Britain and its allies') also hastened to reassure Franco that 'the operations which have now begun in North Africa in no way threaten Spanish territory, metropolitan or overseas.'

*

The belief that the French would welcome the Americans with open arms was misguided. Two operations in Algiers and Oran set out to emulate the success of the British destroyer HMS *Anthony* in Operation *Ironclad* in May 1942, when the ship had dashed into Diego Suarez harbour with fifty Royal Marines on board and seized the Vichy HQ of northern Madagascar. But that sort of 'bow-and-arrow run' had not worked at Dieppe in August and neither did it work in Algeria in November 1942.

In Operation *Terminal*, two ageing British destroyers of the Eastern Task Force tried to take the port of Algiers, but they were fired on, with one later sinking, and the men who got ashore were all captured. In Operation *Reservist*, the Americans of the Central Task Force tried to seize the Algerian port of Oran, near the naval base of Mers-el-Kébir, to prevent it being sabotaged by Vichy. A pair of Lend-Lease cutters converted into HMS *Walney* and HMS *Hartland* ran the booms and tried to capture the moles of Oran at 3 a.m. on Sunday 8 November. When the Vichy searchlight caught them, the loudhailer under the large Stars and Stripes spoke: '*Ne tirez pas. Nous sommes vos amis. Ne tirez pas.*' 'Don't shoot. We are your friends. Don't shoot.' But the French navy ignored the plea and defended their harbour fiercely.

Reservist was a disastrous failure. The cutters were shelled, machine-gunned and set on fire, killing over three hundred British sailors, commandos and US Rangers, with another 250 wounded and captured. The skipper of the *Walney*, fifty-three-year-old Captain Frederick Peters, lost an eye in the action, and was awarded the British Victoria Cross and the American Distinguished Service Cross for his heroism – posthumously, because he was killed in a plane accident five days after the battle.

In Algiers on 8 November, there was a different kind of struggle on land. The BBC broadcast the message '*Allo Robert. Franklin arrive*', which was the signal for General Mast's resistance forces, supplied and armed by US Consul General Robert Murphy, to quietly take over key points in the city. The hope was that they could seize Algiers without firing a shot. Giraud had not yet arrived, but Murphy went to see General Alphonse Juin, the most senior officer in charge of Vichy ground forces in North Africa. He woke the tousle-haired, sleepy-eyed general in his pink-striped pyjamas at his villa and told him that half a million American soldiers were now landing across North Africa. (The true number was a little over one hundred thousand.)

'You mean the convoys are not going to Malta but will land here?'

Murphy nodded, and asked for Juin's support. The general said that normally he would be with him but the matter was out of his hands because Admiral Darlan himself was in town, visiting his sick son, Alain. Darlan, as commander-in-chief of all Vichy forces, out-ranked Juin, so any decision of his could be immediately overruled.

Murphy had to get Darlan on side in order to stop Vichy French troops shooting at the Anglo-American allied forces now landing; moreover, Darlan held the key to the French fleet at Toulon. Summoned by a telephone call from Juin, Darlan arrived at the villa twenty minutes later, a small man in stacked heels who went puce at the news. 'I have known for a long time that the British are stupid, but I always believed Americans were more intelligent. Apparently you have the same genius as the British for making massive blunders.'

Tall Murphy paced up and down with the short angry Frenchman, pouring on his emollient Irish American charm, trying to persuade him that this was the first stage of the liberation of France. Murphy reminded him that in 1941 Darlan had told US Ambassador Leahy he would co-operate if the Americans landed half a million men and several thousand tanks and planes at Marseilles. Now was the moment for him to give the order to stop shooting. No more French blood should be shed in resisting the Americans.

But Darlan said he had given his oath to Pétain and could not revoke it. Would he act if Pétain gave him permission? Murphy asked. Darlan said he would co-operate if Marshal Pétain approved. Together, Murphy and Darlan drafted a message and as they went to send it found the villa surrounded by General Mast's resistance forces, armed by Murphy. Effectively, Juin and Darlan were now under arrest. A US vice consul went to send the message to Pétain, but it never got through. Murphy, who had not slept properly for days, waited up for the American troops, who were expected at 2.30 a.m. but did not arrive. The exhausted consul confessed to Darlan what he had been up to, describing his contacts with Giraud. Darlan shook his head. 'Giraud is not your man. Politically, he is a child.'

Then matters took another turn. At 6.30 a.m., fifty Vichy Gardes Mobiles with sub-machine guns overwhelmed the pro-American resistance force outside Juin's villa. Now Murphy was under arrest and Juin and Darlan were free. The Frenchmen drove to military headquarters to confirm the truth of Murphy's story, and heard there had indeed been landings all along the coast. Juin's men started hunting down General Mast's resistance, whom they saw as Gaullists and traitors. At three in the afternoon, Darlan came back to the house and asked Murphy to get in touch with the Americans who were landing on a beach ten miles west of Algiers. Darlan laid on a chauffeured car with a French flag and a white flag to get Murphy through the American lines to meet US Major General Charles Ryder, who was leading the Eastern Task Force.

They were about to leave when gunfire outside the villa made Murphy look down the street. A patrol of American GIs was advancing, hugging the wall, occasionally shooting ahead of them. With the white flag prominent, Murphy stepped out into the road. This was brave because jumpy US soldiers tended to shoot first and ask questions afterwards. The diplomat kept a respectful distance from the troops with his hands well up, and explained who he was and what was happening. A young lieutenant asked him to repeat the story more slowly. Then he let Murphy approach.

'What is your name, son?' Murphy asked.

'Lieutenant Gieser.'

'You're the best-looking geezer I've seen in a long time.'

Gieser gave him a soldier escort and they drove down to the landing beach without incident. The first person Bob Murphy saw was the British prime minister's son, Randolph Churchill, wearing an American Ranger's uniform. Churchill took him to meet General Ryder, who seemed dazed. Murphy explained that Darlan was ready to negotiate a local ceasefire and that he had a car to drive Ryder to the Vichy French military headquarters at Fort L'Empereur straight away. Ryder said he first had to send a message to Gibraltar and change his uniform. He took ages to dictate a simple paragraph and kept on mumbling about his uniform. Then he said, 'You will have to forgive me. I haven't slept for a week.'

How many mistakes of war are because men are stupid with tiredness? Murphy took his arm and steered him into the car. About fifty French officers were waiting in a large room at Fort L'Empereur with General Juin and Admiral Darlan at a table covered in green baize. Not far away, an American aeroplane flew over and dropped some bombs. Ryder beamed idiotically at the bangs that shook the windows.

'How wonderful! This is the first time since World War I that I've been under fire!'

The French were not amused, but Murphy presented Ryder and talked fast. Soon a preliminary ceasefire in the Algiers area had been signed. Thus began 'the Darlan deal', in which the French admiral switched his allegiance from Vichy to the Anglo-American allies in order to stay in power. As Édouard Herriot remarked two years earlier: 'This admiral knows how to swim.'

Morocco was the hardest nut for the *Torch* invaders to crack. The Vichy army there had about forty-seven thousand men, plus sixteen thousand Sherifian riflemen and four thousand troops transferred from the Levant, following their defeat in Syria. The French air force in Morocco had around 175 aircraft, and at their best-defended anchorage, Casablanca, the battleship *Jean Bart* served as a fortress, with a cruiser, eight destroyers, eleven submarines and eight sloops as well. Although CIA Director William Casey's bullish book *The Secret War against Hitler* claims that all OSS's groundwork in Morocco paid off handsomely, Vichy forces still resisted. When the US fleet appeared over the Atlantic horizon near Morocco on 8 November, a naval battle ensued, and the Vichy French were punished by fearsome American firepower. Scores of Grumman Wildcats from the aircraft carrier USS *Ranger*, flying nearly five hundred combat sorties, bombed and strafed the French with their six .50 calibre machine guns. The battleship USS *Massachusetts* fired 786 rounds of sixteen-inch ammunition and the three heavy cruisers, *Augusta*, *Tuscaloosa* and *Wichita*, sent thousands of eight-inch shells against the French shore batteries, ships and submarines. The blast from these weapons was enormous.

Major General Patton was on board the headquarters ship USS *Augusta* when the shock-wave of three naval guns firing from the rear turret blew the bottom out of his Higgins landing craft in its davits, and he lost all his kit save his pistols. The concussion also fatally damaged his tactical radios, cutting Patton off from another way of talking to Eisenhower in Gibraltar. As at Mers-el-Kébir, the French shells had marker dye in them so the gunners could mark the fall of shot. When huge shells from *Jean Bart* straddled *Augusta*, Patton's leather jacket was splashed with yellow slime. An aide attempted to wipe it off, but Patton squeaked at him to leave it: 'This will stay on the fucking jacket as long as I am able to wear it.'

The battle for Casablanca lasted seventy-four hours. Landings were bungled and craft tipped over, drowning men. Frightened soldiers panicked or froze in the chaos; Patton kicked the squirming bottoms of some cowering in the sand: 'the men were poor, the officers worse'. The first American bazooka shot hit a tree, not a tank. American shells fell on American soldiers. A GI kept shouting '*Rendezvous!*' at black Senegalese, thinking it meant 'Surrender!' Ships had been wrongly loaded, which made muddle and delay in supplies and stores. Bewildered paratroopers who landed miles away in Spanish Morocco were all interned. One beat on the wall of his cell, crying, 'Fuck! Fuck! Fuck!'

★

General Mark Clark and General Henri Giraud flew separately from Gibraltar to Algiers on Monday 9 November. Giraud landed first and found that he was, in Eisenhower's later phrase, 'completely ignored'. Out of the equation, he went into hiding, while the eagle-beaked Clark, who had touched down during a noisy and dramatic German air raid, took over a large suite at the St George Hotel, now Allied Headquarters. Clark, an ambitious soldier, knew nothing and cared less about French politics and could not immediately grasp that Giraud was a busted flush: all the French officers and officials in North Africa had sworn their oath of loyalty to Marshal Pétain and they were not going to do anything without the authorisation of the marshal or his direct representative, Commander-in-Chief Admiral Darlan.

On the morning of Tuesday 10 November, Clark met Darlan and his senior officers in a room off the foyer of the St George Hotel, which Clark had had ringed with American troops to show that he meant business. Darlan the opportunist, 'a little man with watery blue eyes and petulant lips' as Clark described him, was nervous, uncertain, evasive, mopping his brow with a handkerchief.

The political situation was dire. Pétain had received Roosevelt's letter on 8 November with 'amazement and grief', and declared, 'France and her honour are at stake. We are attacked. We shall defend ourselves. This is the order which I give.' That evening, after a cabinet meeting presided over by Pétain, Vichy announced that by carrying the war into North Africa, the USA had *de facto* broken off relations with France, and the US ambassador was handed back his passports. This was obviously serious, though not actually a declaration of war.

But General Clark needed an immediate ceasefire across North Africa. Two days had been lost in fighting and foul-ups because of muddled talks. He decided to bang the table to get results. The whole strategic point of the North African landings was to get eastward fast and reach Tunis before the Germans: the Axis enemy had been taken completely by surprise, but were now reacting, and the first Germans flew from Sicily to Tunis on 9 November, starting a build-up of hostile forces.

Darlan played for time, saying he had sent a resumé of terms to Pierre Laval but there would not be a meeting of ministers in Vichy until the afternoon. 'I do not propose to wait for any word from Vichy,' said Clark. 'I can only obey the orders of Pétain,' said Darlan. 'Then I will end these negotiations and deal with someone who can act.' Darlan claimed that if he gave the ceasefire order to his men the Germans would immediately occupy southern France as retribution. Clark said Darlan must choose between obeying the Vichy government and grasping this opportunity to help the Americans.

An American captain told a French colonel that unless the armistice was signed, his barracks would be bombed, and Clark had to send Ryder to defuse aggressive commanders on both sides. Now Darlan wrote a weaselly letter to Pétain 'recommending the cessation of hostilities' but Clark insisted that Darlan produce instead a clear command to all French army, navy and air forces in North Africa to stop shooting. At long last, Darlan wrote out the order to the French forces in his own hand: to cease fire, to return to base, to observe neutrality. He said he was taking responsibility for North Africa 'in the name of Marshal Pétain', but the present military commanders and current political and administrative authorities would all remain unchanged.

That afternoon, before Clark could get Darlan to meet with Giraud, the news came that Pétain had rejected the armistice and had sacked Darlan as head of the armed forces, appointing General Noguès of Morocco (who was still fighting the Americans) in his stead. Darlan, depressed and upset, attempted to take back the order he had given that morning.

'You will do nothing of the kind,' said Clark. 'There will be no revocation of these orders; and, to make certain, I shall hold you in custody.'

Clark wanted Darlan to do two more things: to get the French fleet out of Toulon and over to Gibraltar, and to command Admiral Jean-Pierre Estéva to start resisting the Germans in Tunisia. Darlan was reluctant. But time was running out.

★

On 9 November, General Albert Kesselring, the German command-er-in-chief in Rome, had sent forty Luftwaffe bombers from Sicily to El Aouina airfield outside Tunis. After Pétain denounced Darlan, Vichy's Admiral Estéva in Tunisia, still loyal to Pétain and the idea of collaboration, offered the Germans a 'friendly reception', and by the next day, two hundred aeroplanes had arrived. The Axis had beaten the Allies to the jump into Tunisia.

Adolf Hitler summoned Mussolini and Laval to Munich on 9 November. *Il Duce* was not feeling well, so Foreign Minister Ciano went instead. He recorded in his diary:

I have my first conversation with Hitler this evening. He has not built up any illusions about the French desire to fight, and now among the rebels is General Giraud, who has brains and courage . . . He, Hitler, will listen to Laval. But whatever he says will not modify his already definite point of view: the total occupation of France, landing in Corsica, a bridgehead in Tunisia.

On 11 November 1942, the twenty-fourth anniversary of the end of the First World War, German and Italian armed forces crossed the delimitation line and proceeded to take over the previously Unoc-cupied Zone of France. Hitler apologised to Pétain but said it was a necessity to guard against further Anglo-American aggression. Pétain protested 'solemnly against a decision incompatible with the armistice agreements'.

In Algiers, Darlan thought the German move in France changed the complexion of things. He duly telephoned Estéva in Tunis and told him to resist the Germans. This pleased Clark, who in turn removed the guards from Admiral Darlan's villa in order to elevate the Frenchman's status.

General George Patton was preparing to destroy Casablanca early on 11 November when the Vichy forces capitulated. In a meet-ing with General Noguès and Admiral Michelier at the Hotel Mira-mar in Fedala, Patton realised that the draft surrender document they were about to sign meant that he, an American general, would have to run French Morocco and its million inhabitants with his tiny foreign force.

Thinking on his feet, Patton flamboyantly tore up the typescript of the treaty and appealed to them as French officers and gentlemen. Speaking in French, he said: 'If each of you . . . gives me his word of honour that there will be no further firing on American troops and ships, you may retain your arms and carry on as before – but under my orders. Agreed?'

'There is one more disagreeable formality we should go through,' said Patton after their word of honour was given. The doors opened and the champagne he had had prepared beforehand was ceremoniously served.

The short Moroccan war was over, with over three hundred Americans and twice as many Frenchmen killed.

But Clark woke up on the morning of 12 November to find that Darlan had rescinded the order to Estéva to resist the Germans in Tunisia. General Juin explained to the irate Clark that the order was only 'suspended until General Noguès arrives'. Juin added, 'I am willing to fight the Germans . . . but you must understand my difficulty. I am subject to the orders of Noguès and honour requires that I obey him.'

'And while you are delaying, the German troops are moving in! I want that order reissued now!'

The reissued order did no good. Estéva had gone over completely to the Axis. German pilots were getting fuel for their aircraft and access to more landing fields in Tunisia. German General Walter Nehring arrived to expand the Tunisian bridgehead with soldiers who would hold the area for the next six months. The Allies had missed the boat, and General Eisenhower was furious.

When Noguès arrived in Algiers, Clark threw Giraud into the mix. Then he left the hubbub of French officers to work out among themselves what arrangements they would make for running North Africa, with the proviso that they must not impede the Anglo-American allies. Clark reported to Eisenhower on 12 November that

Darlan was 'the only Frenchman who could achieve co-operation for us in North Africa'. When Eisenhower flew into Algiers for a meeting on the 14th, the French had decided that Giraud would head the armed forces and Darlan would lead the civil and political government. Eisenhower for his part agreed to acknowledge Darlan as High Commissioner of French North Africa, effectively the head of state.

The 'Darlan deal' was a pragmatic decision, an imperfect way of achieving some kind of equilibrium in North Africa. But while it made military sense there, it was very unpopular at home in the UK and the USA. The press saw Darlan as a Nazi collaborator in an anti-Semitic regime, 'America's first Quisling', a snake and a betrayer and so on. It galled people in SOE to see their French resistance, loyal to another France, being pushed around by a Nazi collaborator and turncoat.

War makes strange bed-fellows. After his volte-face, Darlan genuinely helped the Allies. He delivered Dakar into Allied hands and he tried hard to get French warships out of Toulon. Darlan had sworn that the French fleet would never fly the Nazi flag, and his naval officers kept their word. On 27 November 1942 at Toulon, the Vichy French navy scuttled seventy-seven vessels, including three battleships, seven cruisers, fifteen destroyers and twelve submarines, so the Germans, at that moment flooding unoccupied France with soldiers, could not seize them.

Also on 27 November 1942, US moviegoers at the premiere of a new Warner Brothers picture, *Casablanca*,* watched an American character called Rick Blaine abandoning neutrality up on the big screen with an act of violence at an airfield in North Africa. The cynical club owner who earlier in the picture claimed 'I stick my neck out for nobody' shoots dead a German officer in order to help a Czechoslovak freedom fighter escape. The French Prefect of Police,

---

* *Casablanca* (1942), written by twin brothers Philip and Julius Epstein and Howard Koch, directed by Michael Curtiz, produced by Hal Wallis, starring Humphrey Bogart, Ingrid Bergman, Claude Rains, Paul Henreid, Peter Lorre, Sidney Greenstreet, etc.

despite witnessing the assassination, orders his men away elsewhere to 'Round up the usual suspects.' This policeman, Captain Louis Renault, also changes sides and commits to the Allied cause: dropping an empty bottle of Vichy water into a waste-paper basket, he sets off to join the Free French, arm in arm with the American, who ends the movie with the line: 'I think this is the beginning of a beautiful friendship.'

By December 1942, Admiral Darlan was hoping to retire from the fray and join his wife and son in the USA. As we have seen, he had been in Algiers in November to visit his son Alain in hospital, where he lay stricken with polio – then called 'infantile paralysis'. Wheelchair-bound President Roosevelt, sympathetic to a boy in the same plight, and grateful to Darlan for his help, had arranged Alain's transfer to his own favoured spa at Warm Springs in Georgia.

But Admiral François Darlan never left Algiers. A young French royalist assassinated him by pistol on Christmas Eve, and was swiftly executed two days later. Giraud stepped up into Darlan's role, but by the end of the war he had been outmanoeuvred by Charles de Gaulle. In the end, the tall soldier who was left out of *Torch* became the dominant figure in post-war French history.

In November 1942, after the great British victory at El Alamein in the Western Desert, Churchill made his famous speech, saying: 'This is not the end. It is not even the beginning of the end. But it is, perhaps, the end of the beginning. Henceforth Hitler's Nazis will meet equally well armed, and perhaps better armed troops.'

In that month, three great hammer blows fell on the Nazis in the west and the east. Rommel's retreat from El Alamein became a rout. The *Torch* landings saw the USA's entry into the Mediterranean theatre. And Soviet forces encircled Stalingrad, trapping a quarter of a million men of the German 6th Army. Walter Warlimont at German OKW headquarters rightly called November 1942 'the month of doom'.

★

Eisenhower left his sweaty, troglodytic office under the Rock of Gibraltar for the last time on 28 November and moved to the white city of Algiers, where a vast staff headquarters of three thousand Allied officers was beginning to mushroom. The secret boys of SOE moved on to Algiers too, setting up the Massingham Mission to carry out clandestine operations against Italy. As the war moved east towards Tunisia, Gibraltar was once again becoming a shuttlestop, a supply base, almost a backwater.

Harold Macmillan, the future British premier, landed in Gibraltar with his private secretary and two typists on 7 January 1943, also on his way to Algiers to become the British Minister Resident in North Africa, responsible over the next two years for all British policy in the Mediterranean. The balance of world power was shifting. Macmillan would later tell the propagandist Richard Crossman, the deputy director of the Political Warfare Executive in Algiers, that the British were now subtle but secondary figures in the brash new American empire: 'You will find the Americans much as the Greeks found the Romans – great big, vulgar, bustling people, more vigorous than we are and also more idle, with more unspoiled virtues but also more corrupt. We must run [Allied Force Headquarters] as the Greek slaves ran the operations of the Emperor Claudius.'

The travellers slept at Government House, a little world of imperial privilege and plenty far from English blackout and rationing, as Macmillan's diary recorded:

We stayed the night at Gibraltar. Mason-MacFarlane (the Governor) very friendly. The best thing about Gibraltar is a *cask* (mark you, a cask) of sherry standing always in the drawing-room and available at any time.

Lord Gort was there on his way home for some leave. A very pleasant dinner in semi-viceregal surroundings – all the things we have forgotten in England – five or six courses, sherry, red and white wine, port, brandy, etc., etc.

There were still snakes in paradise, however.

The big battalions might have moved on, but the covert war against sabotage, subversion and espionage continued without cease.

32

Underwater Gibraltar

The Italian navy's 10th Light Flotilla had been waging its own clandestine small war on the peninsula, mounting nine operations in three years against Gibraltar. As we have seen in Malta, Decima Flottiglia MAS, the Italian navy's or Regia Marina's assault craft branch, had developed revolutionary new weapons and tactics: midget submarines, explosive motorboats, piloted torpedoes, swimmer-frogmen with 'leech' or 'limpet' mines, all of them technologies later copied by other navies in the Second World War.

At two o'clock in the morning of 30 October 1940, a curiously shaped submarine surfaced in the dark lapping waters at the north end of Algeciras Bay. This was the commercial anchorage, opposite La Línea, near Puente Mayorga and the mouth of the Rio Guadarranque, a couple of miles from the entrance to Gibraltar harbour where the British warships lay. *Scirè*, an Adua-class Italian submarine commanded by Junio Valerio Borghese, looked very odd. It seemed to have larval cases attached to its hull, three long ribbed cylinders, one for'ard in place of a deck-gun, two aft of the conning tower. The submarine also had 'distractive' camouflage painted on its grey hull, the dark shape of a trawler with its bow pointing towards the sub's stern.

Scirè had made its way through the Strait of Gibraltar the night before, then hovered seventy metres underwater all day, banging on rocks in the Bay of Tolmo halfway between Tarifa and Algeciras. Only when darkness fell did *Scirè* creep slowly and silently into the bay between Algeciras and Gibraltar, under the cover of a moonless night. The currents were tricky because of reefs and sandbanks, but Borghese was following the tidal flux that flows into the bay from the southwest.

Looking east, the periscope view had shown Gibraltar brightly lit up; sometimes searchlights played over the water. When submerged in the bay, the submariners tiptoed in rope-soled shoes, spoke in whispers or sign language, wrapped their tools in cloth so no 'clang' could alert enemy listeners above them. Deep under water, their hydrophones could pick up engine noises on the surface: motorboats, Spanish trawlers, a British destroyer.

When they surfaced, the hatch opened to the cool night air and six men, wearing tight-fitting black rubber frogman suits that left only their hands and faces exposed, made their way to the three cylinders on the submarine's deck. They opened the doors and rolled out the torpedoes or SLCs stowed inside. SLC stood for their official name, *Siluro a Lenta Corsa*, 'slow speed torpedo', but their Italian operators called them *maiali*, 'pigs' or 'hogs', because sometimes they were hard to steer properly. An operator cursed it, '*Maiale!*' and the epithet stuck. The British name for them was 'chariots'.

The *maiali* were manned torpedoes, 6.7 metres (nearly twenty-two feet) long, weighing 1.3 tons, with an electric motor and a propeller at the back. They were ridden underwater by two operators astride with their feet in stirrups, the officer in front steering and the NCO at the back ready to cut anti-torpedo nets and use tools. The whole rounded front of the 'hog' torpedo was a detachable warhead, containing three hundred kilos of explosive and a time fuse. On top of this warhead was a suspension ring through which a rope could be threaded. The mission consisted in getting close to a ship, then diving underneath it and attaching clamps to either side of the bilge keel, a ledge that runs round the bottom of a ship. The tricky task then was to hang the heavy warhead on a rope looped between the two clamps, so that the explosive was dangling directly below the keel when it blew up.

The operators put on goggled face masks with a single corrugated tube connected to the rubber breathing bag on their chests. This contained a canister of soda lime crystals which 'scrubbed' the carbon dioxide from their exhalations, while pure oxygen was delivered from pressurised bottles strapped horizontally across their bellies.

The six men mounted their 'hogs' and Borghese submerged the submarine, which crept southeast out of Gibraltar Bay and stayed underwater for the next forty hours, returning through the strait. When they finally surfaced, gasping for air, Borghese could see the sun setting behind Gibraltar on the western horizon, 'the great rock, crouching like a lion on the sea'.

Now the brave men astride their 'hogs' were left on their own to attack their assigned targets. The first pair, De La Penne and Bianchi, were depth-charged by a motorboat, which sank their torpedo. They abandoned their breathing gear, swam two miles to the Spanish shore and met their agent, retired naval officer and engineer Giulio Pistono, at the prearranged spot on the road at 7.30 a.m. An equipment failure in their breathing gear also scuppered the second pair, Tesei and Pedretti, although they got within sight of Gibraltar's North Mole. They too turned for Spain, detached the warhead after fifteen minutes, and headed north for the western lights of La Línea, the district known as La Colonia. They landed at 7.10 a.m. and Tesei opened the flooding tank of the torpedo and sent it off southwards. It did not sink, eventually coming ashore at Espigon Beach, La Línea, with its propeller still whirling, where the Spanish authorities took it away for examination. By then the operators had shed their diving suits and met up with their agent, Pistono, who arranged for all four men to get to Seville and fly back to base in Italy.

The last pair, Gino Birindelli and Damos Paccagnini, got into Gibraltar's harbour and within seventy metres of the battleship HMS *Barham* before their craft became immobilised on the bottom. Paccagnini's breathing apparatus had failed too, so he was sent to the surface. Birindelli set the time fuse on the warhead and tried to swim back to Spanish territory but, attacked by ferocious cramp, he had to crawl out of the water onto the North Mole. He managed to mingle with Spanish dock workers, got on board a ship called *Sant'Anna* and tried to hide.

When the crew found him they said they were under Contraband Control and that no one could leave without British permission.

Birindelli offered a bribe of two hundred pesetas; they were about to take it when a British sailor came on board and asked if Birindelli was one of the crew. When the men hesitated, the British sailor came back with two policemen, who arrested Birindelli and took him for questioning by a naval officer. He showed his Italian identity card and the astonished lieutenant immediately summoned a commander. Meanwhile, the sunken warhead exploded with a monstrous gout of water, lightly damaging *Barham* and setting the whole harbour in a flutter. Paccagnini had also been picked up and both frogmen became prisoners of war.

In a coded letter to 'his family', Birindelli urged his 'brother' to make another effort 'to get his university degree'. 'If at first you don't succeed, try, try again; if one makes the proper preparations, one finds the difficulties are not insuperable.' The 10th Light Flotilla got the coded message, and tried again in May 1941.

This time, to keep the operators fresh, not cramped in a stuffy submarine, it was decided to send the eight men overland to Cádiz, where a six-thousand-ton Italian tanker called *Fulgor* had been interned since June 1940. Pretending to be variously members of the crew or representatives of the owners, they got on board and waited for the *Scirè* to pick them up for the final run to Gibraltar. The submarine berthed nearby on 23 May; its crew got hot showers aboard the tanker, restocked with fresh fruit and vegetables and generally stretched themselves out, unbothered by the Spanish authorities. Someone from the Italian Consulate in Algeciras gave them all the latest intelligence from his recent reconnaissance of Gibraltar.

Just before midnight on 25 May 1941, the *Scirè* surfaced in Algeciras Bay and three 'hogs' were released. Gibraltar's harbour by now was more heavily guarded, so their targets this time were ships in the commercial anchorage. One of the 'hogs' failed straight away, so the riders detached the warhead and got another torpedo to tow it. Each 'hog' now had three crew. At the first ship they targeted, one of the operators lost consciousness, possibly through oxygen poisoning or hyperoxia which affects the eyes and the central nervous system, and in rescuing him the other two let go of the torpedo, which sank irrecoverably in deep water; the men swam for the Spanish shore. The crew of the third 'hog' were attaching a warhead when the rope snapped and that torpedo was lost too. But the six men all got ashore undetected, a car took them to Seville and LATI (Linee Aeree Transcontinentale Italiane) flew them home.

On 20 September 1941 they tried again. Operation *BG4* had the same routine: pick-up from *Fulgor* in Cádiz, ride in *Scirè* to Algeciras Bay, three two-man crews on their 'hogs', the escape team waiting in Spain. This time each of them scored. First the 2400-ton Shell oil storage hulk *Fiona Shell* was cracked in two and sank. Then at 8.43 a.m. the 15,800-ton naval tanker *Denby Dale* blew up, followed by the 10,800-ton freighter *Durham* at 9.16. The perpetrators all got away safely. Rumours reached Defence Security on the Rock that some of the divers had been arrested by the Spanish *carabineros* but had then been 'sprung' by the Italian naval officer Giulio Pistono, who had acquired diplomatic status as 'Chancellor' at the Italian Consulate.

Now Gibraltar had to wake up to the danger of underwater attack. The Royal Navy Extended Defence Officer started using his three harbour launches to drop light depth charges on their regular nighttime patrols of the anchorage, inspecting Spanish fishing vessels and sweeping the water and the sides of ships with their searchlights. Three months later, startling news reached the Rock from Egypt. In their greatest success, Italian frogmen from Decima Flottiglia MAS had managed to penetrate Alexandria harbour, plant mines and blow up the British battleships HMS *Queen Elizabeth* and HMS *Valiant*. Vigilance in Gibraltar was increased.

The Italians came up with an even more ingenious scheme. Why travel all the way by submarine from Italy to attack Gibraltar? Why not set up a base close by in Spain? The first step was purchasing properties. Pistono already lived at a house called Buen Retiro in Pelayo. The Italians acquired another house in the smart part of La

Línea, La Colonia, at 98 Avenida de Espana, which had an excellent view of Gibraltar's commercial anchorage, the North Mole and the Coaling Arm. Then they rented the Villa Carmela in Puente Mayorga from a Spanish estate agent acting for its Gibraltarian owner, J. L. B. Medina, who had been evacuated to Madeira. Antonio Ramognino and his new Spanish bride Conchita took up residence. Their honeymoon treats included adding a new window for telescope and binocular surveillance, screening activities behind the glass with a cage of screeching parakeets.

The actual secret base for the frogmen was the Italian cargo ship *Olterra* which, as we have seen on page 190, was scuttled unsuccessfully on 10 June 1940, the day Italy entered the war. A Spanish salvage company had refloated the ship and towed her into Algeciras harbour where she was now moored inside the breakwater, south of Isla Verde and more or less right under the windows of the British Consulate. A Spanish military guard consisting of a corporal and three privates, and occasionally visited by a junior officer, was stationed aboard with orders to let no boats near and allow no foreigners or civilians to enter the ship unless they were crew members with special passes. Since March 1941, the chief engineer and a scratch crew formed from other vessels interned in Spanish ports had been living on board, maintaining the vessel (and protecting property rights under international wreck and salvage law). The skipper, Domenico Amoretti, had married a local girl and lived ashore in Algeciras.

Early in 1942, Lieutenant Licio Visintini of the 10th Light Flotilla, the man who was on the *maiale* that sank the tanker *Denby Dale* in Gibraltar harbour on 10 September 1941 and brother of the dead fighter-pilot air ace Mario Visintini, was put in charge of the clandestine *Olterra* operation. The first thing Visintini did was purge the crew already on the ship and replace them with technicians and seamen from his own unit. They were sent to Livorno to live aboard a cargo ship and learn 'deck technique': how to walk, talk, smoke, spit and dress like Italian merchant seamen, scruffy, unshaved, in old patched clothes. With fake names, identity cards and log-books (but using their real passports) they made their way to Spain to join the ship and 'effect repairs'.

In fact, deep in the hold, they were building an entire submarine workshop, capable of charging the accumulator batteries and assembling the 'hogs' that would soon be arriving in bits. They prepared a compartment in the forepeak that was deep enough to trim the torpedoes and test them for water resistance. Then they started careening the ship, which had a list and was already down at the stern. One afternoon a large area of the port-side hull was raised above the water, and an awning was rigged to protect the workers from the sun (and any watchers from the British Consulate). There was lot of hammering and painting and scraping, but those workers were also there to mask and catch the sparks produced by another crew, inside the ship, who were using an oxyacetylene torch to cut a four-foot-square hinged hatch in the hull. By nightfall, with the ship's trim adjusted, there was an underwater exit and entrance from the flooded compartment, invisible, six feet below the waterline.

In the main base at La Spezia in Italy, the torpedoes were being broken down into sections and crated as the sort of spares required to repair a ship's engines and boilers – tubes, pistons, cylinders, valves, etc. The breathing sets were hidden in containers welded into the bottom two thirds of drums of diesel that carried enough fuel at the top to deceive any Spanish custom officer's probing dipstick.

In dribs and drabs, the torpedo pilots came on board ship, also disguised as seamen and workers. Leaning casually over the rail, they were actually studying the anchorage, the regularity of the patrols, the depth-charging, the movements of sentries, the procedures for entering and leaving harbour. Their doctor, Elvio Moscatelli, even went into Gibraltar with a donkey cart, selling fresh fruit in the dockyard, in order to look at the precautions that were being taken against divers. Through the porthole of an *Olterra* cabin he organised a twenty-four-hour watch of Gibraltar harbour, recording everything. They also spotted that on the balcony of the British Consulate behind them there was a superb set of binoculars, mounted on a tripod. One night the binoculars vanished, and *Olterra* gained sixty-four times magnification.

An elaborate pretence of normality on *Olterra* – systematic work routines, regular clockings in and out, standard deliveries – masked the project and kept it secret from the Spanish. The Spanish guards on board were lulled and gulled by a skilful new cook, generous with the *vino*, who kept them well fed aft, leaving the works down in the bowels of the bow undisturbed. And British intelligence across the water in Gibraltar were also fooled.

In June 1942, a new intelligence officer called Desmond Bristow arrived in Gibraltar. Bristow spoke fluent Spanish because he had grown up in Spain, where his father ran one of Rio Tinto's mines near Huelva, and he had been working on the Iberian desk of Section V, SIS Counter-intelligence, in St Albans, alongside Philby and Milne. Desmond Bristow's companion on the journey out to the Rock was another Spanish-speaking SIS man, the former priest Aelred O'Shagar.

The new men had to fit in with the Gibraltar intelligence community already crammed into a flat-roofed building in Cloister Ramp behind the police station in Irish Town. Here the Defence Security Officer, Lieutenant Colonel H. C. 'Tito' Medlam, with his four staff, worked assiduously to protect the Rock from espionage and sabotage. Here too beavered away Lieutenant Colonel John Codrington of MI6 and his assistant Brian Morrison, whose job was watching the Spanish armed forces for aggressive intentions. Over in another corner was Donald Darling of MI9, handling his evaders and escapers. Now Bristow and O'Shagar of Section V squeezed in.

Because their task – keeping track of German and Italian intelligence personnel and their agents working in the Campo de Gibraltar – overlapped with the work of both the DSO and MI6, the new men were not immediately popular. Medlam had to pass on his counterespionage files and some informants, including a pair of brothers in the Campo, F1 and F2, whom Bristow called 'the Josephs'. On grounds of Irish solidarity, O'Shagar tried to milk as much information as possible from the office clerk, Corporal Kevin Cavannah. Bristow soon moved into a shared third-floor flat in Plaza de la Verdura with Darling and Morrison, where they listened to jazz records and drank heavily. (Espionage and alcohol, as ever, walked hand in hand.)

Desmond Bristow cultivated whisky-drinking Biagio D'Amato, one of the brothers who ran the successful Café Universal and Embassy Club in Main Street. The Maltese Gibraltarian was a source of much interesting information as well as free drinks, and was valuable to the new members of the intelligence community when they were still scrabbling to get their own agents, contacts, 'cut outs' (mutually trusted intermediaries), informants and sources. But none of the intelligence officers knew what was going on aboard the *Olterra* across the bay.

In early July 1942, twelve strong assault swimmers from the Italian 10th Light Flotilla 'Gamma' group were smuggled into Spain from Italy. Six went via Bordeaux and crossed the Pyrenees either on foot or hidden in the false bottom of a lorry. Another six went as crew on a cargo ship to Barcelona, where they 'deserted' and were reported as such by the skipper, who was not in on the subterfuge. Helped by Italian agents, the swimmers were funnelled via a safe house in Madrid down to Cádiz and the *Fulgor*, before being smuggled to Algeciras by different routes. They reached the *Olterra* on 11 and 12 July. The ship was not yet fully prepared to be the base for an attack, so at dawn on the 13th they were taken to the Villa Carmela, where they had a good view of the ships in Gibraltar's commercial anchorage, and could rest on floor mattresses the Ramogninos had prepared.

Operation *GG1* was launched that night. The dozen swimmers in their black Belloni shallow-diving suits left the darkened villa, crossed the garden and, concealed by a low wall, made their way down the dry Mayorga watercourse to the beach of the bay between Algeciras and Gibraltar. They put on their fins and their breathing gear, topped by a camouflage head-net of trailing fronds that floated in the water like seaweed. Every man was carrying three Italian limpet mines, known as *cimici* or 'bugs', which each contained about three kilos of explosive. These mines did not rely on magnets to adhere to a ship's hull, but were set inside something like a child's swimming ring, a thin rubber tyre that could be inflated by a snap-off phial of compressed air. The physics of lighter air rising to the surface like bubbles through water would push the ring upwards, so it had to be put right under the bottom of a boat to stay *in situ*, not placed on the ship's flank where it might slide to the surface and give them away to the British.

The frogmen slipped into the dark water and swam out slowly and quietly, with no splashing, puffing or phosphorescence, into the anchorage. They had to freeze or duck just below the surface whenever the British patrol boats or searchlights went by. One frogman had his foot cut by a passing propeller and another was shocked by the explosion of a depth charge, but those who reached the ships dived down to place their 'bugs'. All made it back to shore. Seven were arrested by the Spanish *carabineros* and taken to Campamento, but then the Italian consul, Bordigioni, arranged for them to be only half-heartedly detained in a hotel in Seville. Some of the pneumatic limpet mines failed (and at least one floated to the surface), but early on 14 July, Bastille Day, a series of explosions damaged four British cargo ships in Gibraltar's waters – the *Shuna*, the *Empire Snipe*, the *Baron Douglas* and the *Baron Kinnaird*.

Two months later, five assault swimmers struck again. Two new-comers 'deserted' in Barcelona, and three others, among the detain-ees in the Sevilla hotel, traded places with three seamen from *Fulgor*, without the Spanish apparently noticing. Once again they went from the *Olterra* to Villa Carmela and then down to the beach. On this night, however, only three swimmers set out. The ships were moored further away from La Línea now, or were actually in the harbour, and the task was harder because they were more closely guarded, with more searchlights, five motor launches aggressively patrolling and even a couple of rowing boats keeping a close watch. Two Ital-ian frogmen nevertheless managed to plant pneumatic mines on the same ship, the 1787-ton steamer *Ravenspoint*, which sank.

★

This incident was a tiny part of a greater toll. 1942 was the worst year of the entire war for British ship losses. Over 350 Royal Navy ships were sunk and more than fifteen hundred merchant navy vessels went down – an appalling loss of 7.7 million gross tons of shipping, with thousands of men killed. In part this was because in February 1942 the German navy's U-boat command introduced 'Shark', the four-wheel Enigma key which British signals intelligence at Bletchley Park could not crack for the next nine months. On the other side, *B-Dienst*, German signals intelligence, had succeeded in cracking Naval Cipher No. 3, which was used by Britain, Canada and the USA in their Atlantic convoys, and so was receiving a flood of information.

As shipping built up for Operation *Torch* in late 1942, Gibraltar was determined to stop sabotage attacks in the harbour. Enter the rough diamond Lionel Crabb, whom all his friends called 'Crabby'. He did not like his nickname, 'Buster', because he was not at all like the super-fit American actor Buster Crabbe, who won a gold medal for swimming at the 1932 Olympic Games and went on to play Tarzan, Flash Gordon and Buck Rogers in the movies. (Nor, for that matter, was he much like the Lithuanian Jewish actor Laurence Harvey, who dyed his hair blond to portray Lionel Crabb posthumously in the 1958 British war film *The Silent Enemy*.) The real Crabb was red-haired, short and stocky. His friends insisted he was not homosexual, but a woman he was married to for a year in the 1950s said they never had sex and he liked to wear a rubber diving suit in bed. Crabb trained on cigarettes and alcohol, disliked physical exercise and was a poor swimmer. But he was a dogged gamecock who did not give up easily and he could endure discomforts that would put off weaker or less courageous people. According to Frank Goldsworthy, the *Daily Express* reporter who was then an RNVR officer in Gibraltar's Naval Intelligence Centre, Crabb was 'a bit of a character', but 'a great enthusiast for underwater work, and a great patriot'.

Crabb's route into the Royal Navy had been roundabout, drifting where the tides of life took him. Knocking about in odd jobs, he had sailed and sold, modelled trusses, pumped gas, been a Chinese calligrapher and a chaperon to an alcoholic. Roman-nosed and red-bearded, looking like a down-at-heel admiral, carrying a sword-stick, wearing a jade talisman and mixing with bohemians and gays in the art world, he lived a year in the top floor back of Rosa Lewis's Cavendish Hotel (paying for it by working as a porter), before sailing as a merchant seaman gunner on a tanker bound for Aruba. He was in the converted trawlers of the Royal Naval Patrol Service at Lowestoft until an eyesight defect – a so-called 'lazy eye' – debarred him from sea service.

Lieutenant Lionel Crabb had a shore job in Coastal Forces at Dover when a man he met in a pub got him into dealing with unexploded bombs. Not everybody has the kind of cool-nerved courage needed for this job. Crabb did. Although he could not be bothered with all the scientific theory and technical detail, Crabb eventually washed up in Gibraltar in November 1942 as a mine and bomb disposal officer. Commander Ralph Hancock at the Tower told him about the Italian attacks and said that they now had two divers checking ships' bottoms for limpet mines. It would be Crabb's job to dispose of whatever mines and ordnance they brought up. However, on his own initiative, Crabb went to see Lieutenant William Bailey, who with his assistant Leading Seaman Bell comprised the entire diving team, and asked them if they wanted a hand. He learned the divers did not have fancy rubber suits or fins but went down in swimming trunks and overalls with weights attached to their tennis shoes. For breathing they used the Davis Submerged Escape Apparatus, which was really an emergency oxygen rebreather device designed to help trapped submariners to get out of a watery tomb. Bailey and Bell had borrowed sixteen DSEA sets from Captain Fawkes of the submarine depot ship HMS *Maidstone* but they did not really know how to maintain them by regularly changing the granular crystals used for carbon dioxide 'scrubbing'.

Crabb did his first dive that November afternoon. He put on ill-fitting goggles, clipped his nose, clamped his teeth on the rubber mouthpiece and tried breathing in and out, inflating the rubberised bag on his chest. Then he climbed up and down a ladder that dropped from the dockside into the water, practising the unnatural process of breathing underwater. He did not want to go all twelve feet to the bottom because he had heard there might be small octopuses there and he hated the thought of their suckered tentacles snaking around his feet and ankles.

Then Lieutenant Bailey took him out in the diving launch to examine a ship. Crabb swam unhandily for the bottom line that depended from the ship and hauled himself down the red hull to cling to the ledge of bilge-keel. The current plucked at him as he worked around the ship, hand over hand, looking for anything alien clamped or attached. Above in the light were vanishing bell-shapes of greeny-blue but down below, where the waters deepened from navy into black, there was nothing but nameless primeval fear. He hauled himself around, examining propellers and rudder, and then checked along the other side. His muscles were exhausted in the cold water.

Onshore, Bailey accepted Crabb as a member of the clearance diving team. Bailey and Leading Seaman Bell had been the first responders to the thwarted twelve-strong Italian frogman attack back in July. Bailey had dived to find limpets, live and primed, underneath the ships' hulls. By knifing their pneumatic tubes he got the mines to drop to the sea bed where they could explode harmlessly later. Bailey won the George Medal for this, but soon after inducting Crabb into his trade, he tripped and broke his ankle. Now Lieutenant Crabb became the Diving Officer.

News came from a British agent at Huelva that a new kind of mine had washed ashore in Spain. It seemed to have a delayed-action fuse operated by a small propeller turned by motion through water. An enemy frogman could easily attach the mine below a ship's water-line in a neutral Spanish port, but it was not designed to go off there and then. Only after the ship had travelled a certain distance away, and the propeller had made a certain number of revolutions, would it suddenly explode, making people think it was a torpedo or a sea mine. Now British ships arriving in Gibraltar all had to be checked underneath. A week after his first dive, on 4 December 1942, Crabb found a device on the 1200-ton steamer *Willowdale*, which was carrying a valuable cargo of tungsten or wolfram.

The green torpedo, about a metre long, was attached to the bilge-keel near the ship's engine room by three clamps that Crabb had to undo. But did they turn clockwise or anti-clockwise? Was it 'righty-tighty, lefty-loosey' as normal, or the other way around? If you were wrong, would the attempt to unscrew it trigger a booby trap? Unexploded ordnance waiting to go off is frightening. It took Crabb forty-five minutes of effort underwater and three bottles of oxygen to loosen the clamps. He couldn't bring the mine up or let it drop in case it had a hydrostatic pressure gauge that would explode it at a certain depth, so he tied it at the same depth to a buoy, which was towed by rowing boat to Gibraltar's Rosia Bay. Crabb could not leave it there because it was a popular swimming spot. So, the next day, he rowed the buoy northwards and bravely carried the twenty-five-pound bomb ashore at the end of the airstrip, still packed with Spitfires after *Torch*. Without informing the RAF, he and Commander Hancock started dismantling it. The propeller mechanism was not the only way to explode the TNT, they found. Inside the casing were three time-clocks and three stubby detonators which Hancock went off to show to Admiral Edwards-Collins and General Mason-MacFarlane.

Crabb also inspected the improvised harbour defences against frogmen-swimmers and human torpedoes that ordinary nets and booms might not keep out. There were two entrances to the harbour, either north or south of the Detached Mole, and two crude mortars guarded each one. Necessity was still the mother of invention in Gibraltar, just as it had been in the Great Siege. These defensive mortars were essentially five-foot lengths of boiler pipe held upright in a wooden frame, with a Lee-Enfield .303 bolt-action rifle's mechanism, trigger and butt welded into the bottom of the pipe.

The mortar bombs were ordinary food tins, four and a half by three inches, filled with a pound and a half of TNT with a nitrocellulose fuse that would burn underwater.

The home-made mortar, or Modified Northover Projector as it was grandly called, was supposed to work in the following way, but didn't always. First you loaded it, by putting a blank .303 cartridge into the rifle's chamber, and then you slid a mortar bomb, made from a food tin full of TNT, fuse first down the barrel of the pipe so it sat snug above the cartridge. You fired the mortar by a sharp tug on the lanyard which pulled the trigger on the rifle. This drove the pin-striker into the cartridge's percussion cap, whose explosion ignited the gunpowder packed next to it in the cartridge tube. The result-ing jet of flame was supposed to light the fuse on the bomb and the expanding gases of the cartridge's gunpowder would blast the now sparking can of TNT out of the pipe and high up into the air before the projectile splashed into the sea, sank, and finally exploded under the water. If the fuse did not light, then the bomb was a dud. If the tin can did not come out of the barrel, you were advised to get down behind a concrete wall in case the whole contraption blew apart. This was why you pulled a lanyard from a distance and ducked until you saw the spark on the tin in the air.

When it worked, a bomb exploding underwater was more danger-ous than one exploding in the air. As those who fish with dynamite know, water transmits shockwaves horribly well. The radiating and bouncing pressure wave can pulverise soft tissue without breaking skin.

Across the bay in Algeciras, on board the *Olterra*, twenty-seven-year-old Lieutenant Licio Visintini was getting ready for his big coup. He had been studying the mortars through his British binoculars – the shots were irregular but at roughly three-minute intervals, and he reckoned he could slip in between them. 'Bursting bombs and dart-ing patrol boats only strengthen our will to defy the enemy offen-sive,' he wrote to his wife, Maria.

Visintini had three 'hogs' and six men ready and waiting for a good target – the return of Force H from *Torch* operations, led by the battleship *Nelson*, the aircraft carriers *Furious* and *Formidable* and the cruiser *Renown*. The fifth underwater attack on Gibraltar was to be his glorious moment. 'We are going to sea,' he pencilled on a sheet of paper to his wife for the last time, 'and, whatever happens, we are determined to sell our skins at a very high price.'

The six men set off for Gibraltar harbour early on 8 December 1942 in Operation *BG5*. Deep down inside the *Olterra*, the two-ton 'hogs' were lowered on slings into the flooded compartment. Licio Visintini and his 'oppo' Sergeant Giovanni Magro put on their breathing gear and pushed the first 'chariot' out of the hatch cut in the forepeak. Manisco and Varini followed, and Cella and Leone brought up the rear.

Only Vittorio Cella of the six-man team made it safely back to base in Algeciras. Operation *BG5* was a heroic but futile attack. What seems to have happened is that a rough and ready piece of kit, a tin of TNT lobbed from a bit of British drain-pipe, sank a fine piece of Italian engineering at the harbour mouth. Visintini and Magro were killed; Salvatore Leone drowned; Girolamo Manisco and Dino Varini scuttled their craft and were captured (they said they were off the submarine *Ambra*, to keep *Olterra*'s secret safe).

Crabb spent all night scouring ships' hulls for explosives, which could have potentially killed him if he had come within a half-mile of their explosion, but found no 300 kg warheads had been clamped in place. Then he searched deeper for the two-ton scuttled 'hogs', without success. Two corpses were recovered from the harbour, their names, Visintini and Magro, still on their overalls. In the mortuary, Crabb and Bailey saw what the TNT explosion had done to their bodies and their kit. This, then, was how divers came to grief, down in the depths. Crabb thought about dying underwater; this could be his own death. He was a Catholic, so he invited a priest to officiate on the tender as he and Bailey gave their enemies a respectful burial at sea, sliding them from under a couple of Italian flags, and then dropping a wreath on the waters. (Later, in 1945, while clearing German mines laid in the canals of Venice, Crabb would willingly give a secretarial job to Visintini's widow, Maria.)

New recruits joined Gibraltar's British Underwater Working Party, and they moved, together with the bomb-disposal men, into the strong-point of Jumper's Bastion. There was a catch-phrase in the wartime radio comedy show *ITMA* that everyone listened to, 'Don't forget the diver, sir!' and Admiral Edward-Collins did not, but raised their pay in Gibraltar. All ranks got an extra half-crown for every dive undertaken; both sides of a ship counted as two dives. Petty Officer Thorpe sorted out their oxygen booster pump and instituted regular changing of CO_2-scrubbing granules so that the Davis Submerged Escape Apparatus (DSEA) kits worked efficiently. A seventeen-foot-deep training-tank was built using an old ship's boiler, upended in Rosia Bay and warmed by salt water that had been cooling the distillery.

All ships had to be checked for mines, so they had plenty to do. A Spanish waterboat regularly brought fresh water for the garrison over from Algeciras, and the Italians thought it might be a good idea to tuck a manned torpedo underneath; but Crabb, alert to that possibility, checked the waterboat on every trip. Two British divers, Morgan and Knowles, went across to Algeciras on the waterboat disguised as crew and wandered over to where *Olterra* was moored. They strongly suspected that the ship was a frogman base, but because everything looked normal on the surface and they had no proof, higher authority forbade them from even making a secret inspection below the waterline in case it caused a diplomatic incident with Spain. According to Frank Goldsworthy, Crabb robustly suggested limpet-mining the *Olterra* at its mooring in Algeciras, but this was turned down at Cabinet level. Decima Flottiglia MAS was left with enough time in the summer of 1943 to achieve two more underwater attacks on Gibraltar and seriously damage six more ships.

33

Undercover and Underhand

Gibraltar's war was more insidious than Malta's because Gibraltar's enemies could stroll in across the land border from Spain. Saboteurs could mingle with the eight thousand Spanish workers who crossed the frontier daily to work in the dockyard or labour in the tunnels. More than isolated Malta, Gibraltar feared 'the enemy within'.

David Scherr of Defence Security calculated there were seventy attempts at acts of sabotage between October 1940 and April 1944, an average of five every three months, only eleven of which were successful. But from September 1942 the rate was stepped up, to equal one per fortnight. Fifty-eight sabotage attempts were German-inspired, nine were Italian and three Falange.

The great majority of Gibraltarians were loyal to the point of fanaticism, but not all. In any war there are vulnerable people who can be turned against their own side. Take José Estelle Key, born in Gibraltar on 1 July 1908 and thus a British citizen, but no great advertisement for his nation, being without scruples or a steady job. Estelle Key married a woman called Angeles Gómez de la Mata, whose brother was an agent of the Spanish secret police who worked on the side for the Abwehr in Algeciras. In 1940, when the feckless José was facing evacuation from Gibraltar as a 'useless mouth', his brother-in-law arranged for him to get a Spanish residence permit in La Línea. The return favour was called in when the Portuguese spy Manoel Marques Pacheco arrived in La Línea from Tangier to buy information from all and sundry with German-supplied money.

Marques Pacheco was acting for an Abwehr officer in Spanish Morocco often known as 'Juan Recke', or 'Müller' or 'Khalif', though his real name was Colonel Hans Joachim Rudolf. Rudolf spoke good

Spanish and had been with the Abwehr in Spain during the Spanish Civil War, before Canaris sent him to run the *Nest* at Tetuán. A 1945 Allied interrogation report describes Rudolf/Recke as 'the best operator in North Africa', running a string of agents among Arab and Moroccan traders as well as sub-agents like Marques Pacheco who concentrated on Gibraltar.

The easy money Marques Pacheco offered soon bought José Estelle Key. His job became trying to extract as much naval and military information as he could from the workers returning daily from the dockyard and underground tunnels. Meanwhile, Marques Pacheco was offering his own services as a spy to whoever would pay, belligerent or neutral. When David Scherr approached him, Marques Pacheco duly betrayed José Estelle Key to the British. Scherr says that this was his own 'first effort at the delicate art of treble-crossing a double-crosser'.

Estelle Key was persuaded 'to re-enter Gibraltar of his own free will', but the secret plan was to arrest him and try him in court. He crossed the frontier on 5 February 1942 and, having woven himself further into a tangled web of espionage, was arrested in Irish Town on 4 May under the Emergency Powers (Defence of the Realm) Act 1939. When he was searched, they found information that he was going to pass on to the Germans.

José Estelle Key was taken to the UK and charged under the Treachery Act 1940. He was tried *in camera* and condemned to death for treason by Mr Justice Humphreys at the Central Criminal Court in London on 18 May 1942. The Gibraltarian's appeal was dismissed by Mr Justice Tucker and Mr Justice Asquith on 22 June and he was hanged at Wandsworth Prison on 7 July 1942. As access to the papers relating to this case is denied, it is hard to see precisely what justified his death. But *Torch* was looming, secrecy was paramount, an example necessary.

The official hangman, Albert Pierrepoint, performed two executions on the morning of 7 July. The other condemned man, a very slight Belgian spy called Alphons Timmerman, had to be given a longer, nine-foot, drop so the rope would break his neck properly. The Gibraltarian José Estelle Key was one of only four British citizens among the sixteen spies whom the British executed in the Second World War. Forty-seven other spies were 'turned' and became double agents, continuing to spy for the Germans but in fact working for British Intelligence, sending back false information to Germany, co-ordinated by the Twenty, XX, Double Cross Committee.

Double agents played a crucial role in protecting Gibraltar. By the summer of 1942, Defence Security had realised they could not sit back passively and wait for sabotage attacks. They had to go over the frontier and penetrate the enemy organisations that were doing the damage on behalf of the German secret service in Madrid, Abteilung II of the Abwehr. Once again, the very best defence was attack.

The Defence Security Office's first requirement was informants. Police, security and intelligence organisations compete for such people and canny operators can increase their income by serving several masters at the same time. Although it was understood that informants were not always reliable, they did act as antennae for danger signals. By 1944, the Defence Security Office had two hundred informants, half of them regulars, and their information was all recorded and cross-indexed in an analogue database of file cards. The cards were key to keeping tabs on enemy agents and all their activities, contacts and connections, including the houses they used, the cars they drove, the bars and brothels they frequented.

Even more useful than people who just talked were actual agents who revealed enemy sabotage intentions or, even better, handed over the bombs they were supposed to be planting. In September 1942 there were no double agents on the DSO's books, but by the spring of 1943 there were nine. This refocusing of effort was David Scherr's idea and his vindication. It all came about with the arrival of a new Deputy Defence Security Officer, Philip Kirby-Green, in the summer of 1942.

Kirby-Green, the son of a colonial official, grandson of a diplomat, was born in Nyasaland, grew up in Tangier and achieved a double first in History at Cambridge.* He had joined the merchant navy and was one of the very first intake at Hendon Police College, set up by Lord Trenchard of the RAF in May 1934 to develop an officer class for the British police services. From the Metropolitan Police Kirby-Green was swiftly seconded to MI5 and sent to Tangier, then Gibraltar. He would go on to spend the rest of his career with SIME, Security Intelligence Middle East. Vigorous, swarthy Kirby-Green brought new thinking and dynamism to Lieutenant Colonel 'Tito' Medlam's realm. He realised that others could handle petty police work, but the brightest officers should focus on counter-sabotage.

Thus Company Sergeant Major David Scherr, who by then had nearly two years' experience as a non-commissioned officer and a warrant officer in Field Security at Gibraltar, now accepted a commission in the Intelligence Corps. On 1 September 1942, newly pipped Lieutenant David Scherr found himself in charge (and the sole occupant) of the new Security Intelligence Department of the Defence Security Office. He weeded out the rubbish from the old paperwork and set up a new filing and report system, all of which he typed himself. His job was to find out everything about sabotage directed against Gibraltar from across the border: who was doing it, who was behind them, and all their connections and networks.

No map of La Línea existed, so Field Security created their own on which to grid and log all enemy activity. Scherr communicated with hundreds of people, some directly, others through 'cut-outs', meeting the mad, the bad and the sad, idealists and zealots, secret policemen and smugglers, fascists and communists. Some worked only for money, others for nothing much at all. A bottle of whisky, a small permit, a bag of peppermints might be the only reward. It was a bizarre world of fantasists and fanatics he was grappling with. Scherr nicknamed the first group of Spanish saboteurs whom the

---

* His PoW brother, RAF Squadron Leader Tom Kirby-Green, got out of Stalag Luft III via the tunnel 'Harry' in the Great Escape of 1944, and was among the fifty executed in cold blood after recapture. Erich Zacharias, the Gestapo officer who murdered him, was hanged in 1948.

Germans employed 'the Crazy Gang' because of what he called their sheer 'incompetence, bravado, stupidity, mutual suspicion and internecine rivalry'. The gang was led by Emilio Plazas Tejera, and their controller and protector was Lieutenant Colonel Eleuterio Sánchez Rubio, notorious for helping the Germans.

It was Scherr who had lured the spy José Estelle Key over the frontier and trapped him. He had also helped 'turn' an old Falangist saboteur code-named Cock into a denouncer of his accomplices. Now he had to go one stage further, persuading saboteurs to become double agents. In November and December 1942, two Spanish brothers, code-named Frog and Bull, were the first to hand over bombs to the British, and then claim payment from the Germans for acts of sabotage which never happened. In January 1943, Scherr had to stage two fake 'explosions' in Gibraltar to back up this fiction. For one of them, he used the hulk of the trawler *Honjo*, crippled in the *Erin* explosion a year earlier, plus some SOE explosives that were long past their sell-by date.

By May 1943, Scherr had nine double agents on the go (Brie, Cock, Gon, Nag, Wig, Ogg, Pat, Eno and Joe) and could no longer manage the work on his own. He was deeply grateful when the unrufflable Lance-Corporal Louis Bush joined him, and with the arrival of Corporal William Bulman in June they had a crack team. Scherr recalled:

Our days and nights were long and very full. The inexorable mechanics of contacting secret agents soon studded the passing hours with urgent interviews with queer people and rendezvous in peculiar places. Before it was light enough to see in the mornings, there was someone to meet on his way to the dockyard, or a long wait at the frontier to receive a message; at all hours of the day and night, in fair weather and in foul, the series of successive and furtive encounters and whispered colloquies with one member of the 'Crazy Gang' after another had to go on: in deserted alleyways, in empty stables, ploughed fields, public lavatories, lorries, motor-cars, vacant houses, gardens, coal-stores, allotments, cabarets, inns, pine-woods, cane-breaks, tunnels, cemeteries and sand-dunes; in the Dockyard, on the Upper rock, in the town, at Waterport, and over in Spain – a tedious journey on foot there and

back; until the early hours of the morning came, and one went to bed rack-
ing one's brains for discreet places for the morrow's meetings, after reading,
translating, recording and commenting on the information received during
the day. Often one came away from these interviews loaded with bombs in
one pocket and detonators or igniters in another, and slipped away from one
XX agent just in time to keep an interview with another. And there was
always the nagging fear that one had forgotten something important – some
decision to be made, some sabotage material to be collected, some information that *had* to be be prepared for use as 'Chickenfeed',* some scheme
for a fake sabotage to be engineered without fail by a particular date, some
favour for an agent, some vital instructions to prepare and pass over.

Italian submariners used their own nationals to assault the Rock,
but the Germans preferred to use Spaniards as their saboteurs. They
employed young Spanish Falangists from the Diego de Salinas army
barracks at San Roque. A group of them were strongly influenced
by their medical officer, Dr Narciso Perales, a radical Falangist who
had struggled to save the life of Dominguez Muñoz after the Begoña
incident and as a consequence had had to leave his government post
in León. Stationed so near Gibraltar, Dr Perales determined to follow
Dominguez Muñoz by carrying out acts of sabotage for the Abwehr.
He planned a single great coup: to plant a bomb deep inside the Ragged Staff arsenal where the ammunition, bombs, mines and shells
were stored, and then blow the whole British Rock sky-high.

The Spanish army officers could not actually get into Gibraltar so
they leaned on civilians to do their dirty work of transporting and
placing a bomb. A man called Charles Danino was put under pressure to do the deed, but he secretly informed British Defence Security, who publicly arrested him as a cover story that helped protect
his family in La Línea. Finally, on 22 June 1943, a man called Luís
López Cordon Cuenca was arrested; a bomb was found among his
possessions at the Empire Fruit Shop, 114 Main Street, Gibraltar.

*

* Chickenfeed: deceiver's term for trifling information that looked appealing but was not
actually nutritious as intelligence.

Of all the Spanish XX double agents that British Intelligence employed in Gibraltar, the very best was the one code-named Nag, a man who perhaps deserves to be as well known as the famous Catalan double agent Juan Pujol (known as Garbo to the British and Arabel to the Germans). Pujol was an intellectual who sat at a desk in an MI5 safe house in North London, a scriptwriter dreaming up a completely fictional cast of useful spies in order to deceive the Abwehr. (His notional Agent No. 4, for example, was Fred, a disaffected Gibraltarian waiter in England.) Nag, on the other hand, a Basque, was an active double agent taking risks out in the field, on very unsafe ground in La Línea. It took great physical courage for the man whose German cover-name was Glorious to move among the gang of pro-German bombers and saboteurs who would have killed him if they had ever found out what he was doing. (The British government awarded both Garbo and Nag honours for their war work: Garbo the MBE and Nag the King's Medal for Freedom.)

David Scherr called Nag 'the most enterprising, courageous and trustworthy of our XX sabotage agents', who 'obtained extremely valuable information, penetrating the enemy organisation single-handed with remarkable skill, unflagging energy and unflinching courage'. He admired Nag as a man and was sympathetic to his people's plight: as a student Scherr had been one of those British volunteers who had assisted some of the four thousand Basque children shipped to the UK on the *Habana* in 1937 after the bombing of Gernika.

Nag's actual identity has never been revealed. As part of their duty of care, the secret services conceal the names of their officers and all agents who help them in order to protect them against acts of retribution. But if the medal-winning Nag is still alive today, he is over 107 years old and probably beyond caring. More than seventy-five years have passed since those wartime events, and it is time to tell the truth.

The Security Service 'weeds' or redacts agents' and officers' names from all documents released as public records to the National Archives and is allowed to do so under Section 23(1) of the Freedom of Information Act 2000. But someone slipped up when they were 'weeding' PF 666053/VI, the file on José Martin Muñoz, into its redacted form, KV2/1162, for public release. In the summer of 2015, scouring its pages, the Gibraltarian military historian Ian Reyes spotted that Nag's real name had not been whited out on one sheet, and so unmasked the double agent's true identity.

Nag was a Basque called Ángel Gauceda Sarasola, born in Bilbao on 12 April 1911. Like Garbo, he had fought for the Nationalists in the Spanish Civil War, but now was anxious to help the Allied cause. When he came to the attention of the Defence Security Office he was thirty-two years old, blond, tall and rather thin, a married man who lived in San Roque and crossed the border every day to work in Gibraltar as a lorry driver for the Naval Stores Office, moving supplies for ships. Early in 1943, he began a relationship as an informant with Detective Inspector Harold Smith. At this stage, he was simply an honest man who saw thieving and fiddling damaging the Allied war effort, and reported it.

In early May 1943, Gauceda told DI Smith that he had been approached and recruited by the Falangist Paciano González Perez and ex-Spanish army officer Carlos Calvo Chozas, known to the Defence Security Office as Boz and Brie respectively. Both were active members of the so-called 'Crazy Gang' of German-employed saboteurs led by the Falangist and former *requeté* Emilio Plazas Tejera and protected by Lieutenant Colonel Sánchez Rubio. This relationship with the Crazy Gang changed Gauceda's status from a police informant to a potential agent. Smith passed Gauceda on to the Defence Security Office agent-runner Captain Scherr, who, dressed in plain clothes, introduced himself as 'Mr Wood', and in return gave Ángel Gauceda Sarasola the code-name Nag.[*]

Gauceda/Nag entered into the double world with relish. On 14 May 1943 he handed over to David Scherr his first German-made *puro* or 'cigar' of plastic explosive together with a Mark I delayed

---

[*] Possible derivations of 'Nag': his mother's name Sarasola sounds like Saratoga, the famous US horse-racing track, and a 'nag' is a rude British term for a horse. Or more simply: the first three letters of 'Ángel' rearrange into 'Nag'.

fuse and detonator, and another time pencil explosive that he was supposed to employ inside Gibraltar. He was beginning to be trusted by the 'Crazy Gang', but was also reporting to Scherr every day after work. On 10 June, Nag was told by gang leader Paciano González that he had a sabotage agent code-named Manolo working on Coaling Island, the acre of reclaimed land in the Admiralty Harbour that was the depot for all HM Dockyard inflammable stores. With Nag's help, Scherr managed to identify Manolo as one Manuel Fontalba Carrasco, working in the NAAFI canteen on the naval depot ship HMS *Cormorant*, which was moored at Coaling Island. Carrasco was quietly moved to another workplace, then excluded from the garrison.

On Tuesday 22 June, Luís López Cordon Cuenca from the Perales/Castro gang was arrested, and his bomb discovered. Six days later, on Monday 28 June, Nag met Paciano González and Fermin Mateos (who had helped blow up the *Erin*) in the Bar Central in La Línea, the saboteurs' hangout. In the private room of another bar, González drew a sketch of Coaling Island and said they were thinking of acts of sabotage there, but their man Manolo had been moved to another place so they needed a new person to plant a bomb. 'We want to put the *galápago* under the middle tank,' he said, *galápago* being a 'clam', the Spanish term for a magnetically attached limpet; the Germans had captured some from SOE stores.

Nag reported the Crazy Gang's quest for a new saboteur to his controller David Scherr around 6 p.m. on Tuesday 29 June when they met quietly on Line Wall. He also said that he had been asked to find a good Falangist lorry driver who would be willing to do sabotage in the Dockyard. (Gauceda, while doing secret work for Scherr, had disobeyed Dockyard rules for lorry drivers, and so had been penalised by being taken off driving and put into a labouring gang.) Gauceda and Scherr managed to identify two anti-British, pro-Falangist lorry drivers as potential suspects but, unfortunately, Scherr did not think Gauceda/Nag's information about the quest for a new bomber constituted an immediate threat. 'This was a mistake,' Scherr admitted in a later report. Neither Scherr nor Nag had any idea that González and Mateos had actually already recruited a new agent, nor that he would strike the very next day.

At 1.45 p.m. on Wednesday 30 June 1943, there was a sharp explosion on Coaling Island, followed by a massive conflagration that took over an hour to bring under control. As the firefighters struggled, twenty-five thousand gallons of petrol, ten thousand gallons of lubricating oil and twenty thousand gallons of kerosene went up in flames. A huge column of smoke rose hundreds of feet into the air.

Three men were watching excitedly from the old Larios cork factory in La Línea. As the thick black plume smudged the sky above the Rock, Fermin Mateos pedalled off to the telegraph office to send a prearranged coded message to a German cover address in Madrid, informing Abteilung II that the sabotage had been successful and claiming his reward of one hundred thousand pesetas.

It was a most uncomfortable day for David Scherr. This was the first act of genuine sabotage since he had been put in charge of the security intelligence department eight months earlier, in September 1942. Nag told Inspector Smith that he had warned Scherr of an attack on Coaling Island the night before, implying by this that he had given rather more information than he actually had. Naval Intelligence thought the Dockyard authorities should have been warned. Lieutenant Colonel Medlam and Mr Kirby-Green, the Defence Security Officer and Deputy Defence Security Officer, were also asking penetrating questions.

When Captain Scherr was summoned to explain this breach of security, he handed Medlam a report ('DJS/93/43. Subject: Fire on Coaling Island, H.M. Dockyard') which summarised the information Nag had given at their meeting at 6 p.m. the day before.

'When did you type this, this morning, or this afternoon?'

'This afternoon.'

'What time? After the explosion?'

'Yes, sir.'

Scherr then had to write another report for Medlam ('DJS/96/43: Information regarding sabotage on Coaling Island') explaining the circumstances in which he received the information, the substance of the information and the action he took on receipt of the information. On that occasion, Scherr may have seemed incompetent to his superiors, but it was, in fact, a judgement call. There were daily threats of sabotage, often panicky reports that led to nothing, and it was not a good idea to cry wolf too often. Medlam knew that he and Kirby-Green and Scherr had spent much of the previous day and night receiving, sifting and passing on reports of an imminent Italian underwater attack in the bay which seemed more dangerous than a tale about a possible future Spanish attempt. Besides, what could the Royal Navy and His Majesty's Dockyard have done with Nag's information? Some unknown agent wanting to put a bomb under an oil tank somewhere in a one-acre site at an unspecified time in the future is not exactly 'hard' intelligence.

Nag knew he had got Scherr into trouble by talking too much and immediately offered to try and find the culprit for the explosion and bring him to book. That night he went boozing with the Spanish 'Crazy Gang' and discovered from their talk that the person who planted the bomb under the petrol tank was an agent of Calvo and González, assisted by Mateos: he was about twenty years old, worked somewhere in the Dockyard, though not Coaling Island, and had been wearing blue dungarees when he placed the bomb. This young man had carried the bomb through Four Corners on the 29th, the day before, under his crotch, held in place by a swimming costume and strapped to his thigh by Mateos's borrowed necktie. He seemed to have got into Coaling Island by showing a (purloined) photo of a man who worked there and pretending he needed to get him a message that his wife was seriously ill in La Línea. The young man said he placed the *galápago* bomb in a bracket holding a fuel tank, and when he bit the time pencil that would detonate it after a two-and-a-half-hour delay, some of its acid went into his mouth.

Nag promised to try and find the perpetrator; he knew he had to do it before the 'Crazy Gang' sent him back into Gibraltar to carry out more sabotage for their German paymasters. Meanwhile the gang was spreading the rumour that the British had arranged the fire at Coaling Island themselves to cover up the losses caused by their black-market scams with stolen fuel.

On 4 July, Nag learned some new details: the boy who did the Coaling Island job had a bad foot, and his foreman had told him he could get discharged if he wanted to. Dockyard police detective work soon revealed that the limping worker was a twenty-year-old called José Martin Muñoz.

After nightfall on Wednesday 7 July, there was a spurt of flames at the North Front airfield petrol dump. Another successful act of sabotage! Across the border in La Línea, the man who had organised it, Ángel Gaucera or Nag, went out to celebrate with the saboteur Juan Dodero Navarro, another of Sánchez Rubio's creatures. In fact, the fire at North Front was a fake. Nag had handed over the real bomb to the British authorities and Scherr had engineered some safe flames to give Nag credibility with the sabotage gang, and allow him to earn his German pay.

Nag got Dodero drunk and they went to the hut in Calle Nueva where José Martin Muñoz, the Coaling Island bomber, lived with a friend. The British double agent still did not know what the bomber looked like: both men were out on the razzle and neither could be located in the honky-tonk bars and brothels nearby.

Young José Martin Muñoz, because of the success of his bomb among the Coaling Island fuel tanks, had a German reward of twenty-five thousand pesetas to spend. He had never had so much money in his young life. He bought a little house and a fishing boat, went to the tailor's and bought identical outfits for himself and his boon companion Andres Santos Fernández to have their picture taken in. A self-conscious snap shows of a pair of Laurel-and-Hardy, cheeky-chappy *chulos*, with hats at the same cocky angle, sports jackets, short ties, belted baggy trousers, each man with one elbow up on the photographer's column, the other hand in the trouser pocket. Santos has a cigarette, and looks startled. Muñoz seems evasive or perhaps embarrassed.

The first glimpse Nag himself got of José Martin Muñoz, '*el de la isla*', was on 14 July, drunk in La Línea's Bar Tronio, carousing with Santos and Fermin Mateos and three prostitutes before they piled into two horse-drawn gharries with guitarists and flamenco singers to head off to another bar at the end of town.

Two nights later he saw Santos and Muñoz again in the Bar Tronio in Gib Street, and sent them over a couple of bottles of wine. Muñoz was aggressive: 'Who are you? How do you know me? I don't like being invited by strangers.'

'But I am one of the gang, *compañero*.'

'Are you the fellow who was here with Manolo the other night?'

'Yes.'

Nag also had his wad of money from the Germans for the 'fire' on 7 July, so they all partied together. They left the Tronio with some prostitutes and a flamenco *cantaor* called *El Chato* Mendez and repaired to the Lido bar in the brothel district. José Martin Muñoz told Gauceda his real name and boasted to his new pal about doing the Coaling Island job. He said he had brought the reinforced 'clam' bomb over first and hidden it in some empty boxes on the waste ground near the Naval Cinema, and then bought in a second plastique bomb of the *puro* or cigar-shaped type which was still hidden in a coal store in town. It had taken him three attempts to get into Coaling Island. First he had tried the ruse of the photo and the sick wife, then wearing his best clothes, and finally he had succeeded by putting on blue dungarees and mingling with the workers around midday on 30 June.

Nag had to tell some story in return, so he gave a grandiose version of his North Front act of sabotage. José Martin Muñoz got annoyed when he found nine pence in Gauceda's jacket and threw the British coins away, bouncing across the bar, saying he should be ashamed to have anything English on him. Muñoz then drunkenly tried to set fire to the jacket, saying it had come from a shitty Englishman, *un ingles de mierda*. By five in the morning, though, everybody was best pals again and they parted on good terms. Scherr found Gauceda crashed out on the Defence Security Office floor when he came in on the morning of 17 July.

Later that day police and security officers raided the Café Universal and Embassy at 153–155 Main Street, closed it down for twenty-four hours and arrested the owner of the bar, Biagio D'Amato, and his brother Angelo. They were held at the Detention Barracks to prevent them 'acting in any manner prejudicial to public safety' and accused of communicating and associating with eleven known enemy agents, including the Italian Renato Bernadi (who owned an ice-cream parlour), our old friend Lieutenant Colonel Eleuterio Sánchez Rubio, Pedro Domínguez, Manoel Marques Pacheco, Rogelio Ruíz, alias *El Mulo Blanco*, the newspaper reporter Ramón Fierro, and the German-speaking ex-army officer (cashiered for embezzlement) Mauro Rodríguez Aller.

One of the charges against Biagio D'Amato was that in April 1943 he had informed the enemy agent Rodríguez Aller about a proposed Allied landing in the South of France. Biagio's defence was the simple truth: he was told to spread this story by Desmond Bristow of SIS, then working with Dudley Clarke's 'A' Force deception team in Algiers. It was just a cover story for the real invasion of Sicily being prepared for July, a distraction the 'A' Force deceivers wanted spread far and wide.

April 1943 had indeed been a month of deceptions. It was the time of the famous Operation *Mincemeat*, when Bill Jewell, carrying out another secret mission on the submarine *Seraph*, dropped a real dead body, the fake Major Martin RM, off Huelva, carrying false papers and letters which suggested that the Allies were going to invade Sardinia and Greece. In chapter 10 of his 1993 book, *A Game of Moles*, Desmond Bristow said he flew back to Gibraltar expressly to spread deceptive rumours in La Línea, and that he used Biagio D'Amato for this purpose. D'Amato was certainly an agent/informant the SIS man had worked with before. Barmen like him are useful – they know everybody and they hear a lot, as well as providing free drinks. D'Amato also claimed that he had a paper or *laissez-passer* from Bristow, but that O'Shagar had taken it back for renewal and not returned it. The left hand of security did not know what the right hand was doing, and the poor agent was caught smack in the middle.

David Scherr admits, on page 99 of his report, that Section V of MI6 and the Security Service MI5 were sometimes 'working at definite cross purposes through insufficient liaison' and that this 'nonsensical lack of co-ordination worthy of inclusion in Compton Mackenzie's *Water on the Brain*' lasted until late 1943. Biagio D'Amato was a victim of that confusion.

José Martin Muñoz put off coming back to Gibraltar until he had spent all his money in the bars and brothels of La Línea. Finally, at 9.15 a.m. on 29 July 1943, he crossed the frontier at Four Corners for the last time, going to pick up the other bomb, the *puro*, which he had hidden in a coalshed. He had been lucky once too often. A Gibraltarian police sergeant recognised him from the work-file photo that Security Intelligence had circulated, and arrested him. Nag got a £100 reward.

Later that day, Mason-MacFarlane cabled the Secretary of State for the Colonies, asking 'with the utmost force, immediate permission to try this saboteur by military court martial at once'. Although no one had been killed, a decision was taken to make an example of the Spanish saboteurs. The Colonial Office was already havering over how to try Luís López Cordon Cuenca and the new case added some urgency. Victor Rothschild of MI5 wrote to Duff Cooper, then Chancellor of the Duchy of Lancaster, about the problem of 'trying a German agent'. Rothschild suggested that 'a Gibraltarian jury will almost certainly refuse to convict through their friendship with the Spaniards, apart from their being in many cases corrupt. This not only applies to the jury.' A trial in England would be inconvenient and 'the Security Service would prefer proceedings to take place at Gibraltar, as the deterrent effect of an execution there would be far greater than if it were to take place in England', where José Estelle Key had been hanged. Rothschild wondered if 'Dear Duff' could ask Oliver Stanley, the Secretary of State for the Colonies, to expedite the process so 'the latest saboteur could be executed quickly and in Gibraltar'.

The Colonial Office regretted that the men could not be tried by court martial because an Act of Parliament would be necessary. The only way to try them locally was to set up, 'by Ordinance', a court consisting of a judge alone with no jury, empowered to try any person charged with an offence against Regulation 23 of the Gibraltar Defence Regulations 1939. The accused would still have the right to solicitor and counsel and a right to petition for special leave to appeal to the Privy Council, though this was rarely granted in criminal cases.

Luís López Cordon Cuenca was tried in August and José Martin Muñoz in October 1943. Twenty witnesses gave evidence against Muñoz, who had confessed everything and led the police to his other bomb, hidden in the coal-hole of the Café Imperial in Main Street, the place where Spanish workers used to slip out of sight to hide in their underclothes whatever little goodies they were going to smuggle back across the frontier into La Línea. Both men were found guilty and sentenced to death. At the courthouse, John Porral saw López Cordon Cuenca condemned, the judge solemnly putting on a black cap to pass sentence, the accused in the dock 'hysterical'.

The Judicial Committee of the Privy Council heard López Cordon Cuenca's appeal in London on 13 December 1943. Five senior members of MI5, including the Director General, attended. López Cordon Cuenca's lawyer argued the sentence was invalid because the tribunal, with the Chief Justice sitting alone, was illegitimate. The Lord Chancellor, Viscount Simon, said the argument was confused. Simon pointed out the awesome powers of the man who ran the British Imperial Fortress: 'the Governor has two capacities: he is the executive and he is the legislature in Gibraltar.' Such a ruler – effectively a military dictator – could make the Defence Regulations and set up the tribunals that he thought he needed: 'the Letters Patent powers are clear and ample for the purpose.' The appeal was dismissed.

On 5 January 1944, the Colonial Office told MI5 that the Governor of Gibraltar had requested a hangman and his assistant to fly to Gibraltar on Saturday the 8th, and asked the Security Service to speed up approval for the passport and exit permits for Albert Pierrepoint of Manchester and Harry Kirk from Elton.

Albert Pierrepoint says nothing about Gibraltar in his intelligent and well-written autobiography, *Executioner: Pierrepoint*. It may have been just one among the more than four hundred executions he carried out for the Crown. On 11 January 1944, Pierrepoint and Kirk did the job they were contracted to do, hanging the two Spaniards on a gallows erected in the yard of Moorish Castle prison.

But something out of the ordinary and perhaps shocking seems to have happened, because, in a pivotal scene in his book, when they flew back to England, Albert Pierrepoint for the first time confessed the truth about his life to his wife, Anne: telling her where he had been, and what his grisly profession had been for the last twelve years, following in the footsteps of his father and his uncle.

'You knew it all along, didn't you?' I asked.

'I knew, but I didn't ask,' she said.

'Thank you for not asking.'

'I wanted it to be you who told me.'

'I didn't want to tell you. I wanted to keep you out of it. I wanted to save you from all that goes with it.'

'All that goes with it.' The Gibraltarian lawyer Joshua Hassan was the one who had to tell the two condemned men their appeal had failed. Cordon Cuenca and Muñoz took the news sadly and silently and he did not linger long with them. After the hanging, the British army Catholic priest who had accompanied the condemned men to their deaths in the yard at Moorish Castle brought the lawyer their pathetic few personal effects – a watch, a photograph, a wallet – to return to their families. Joshua 'Salvador' Hassan remembered many years later that 'the priest was in a most distressed state of mind and said he would never forget and could never overcome the suffering and stress he had gone through by having to attend them to the scaffold. He was never the same man again.'

34

'The End of Poland'

Important people passed through Gibraltar in wartime. General Wladyslaw Sikorski, the first prime minister of the Polish government in exile and now Commander-in-Chief of the Polish armed forces, landed in Gibraltar on Saturday 3 July 1943. Sikorski's plane, a four-engined bomber, was carrying him back to London from a five-week tour of his Polish troops serving under General Anders in the Middle East. His party was accommodated at Government House and wined and dined by Mason-MacFarlane, an old and good friend of General Sikorski and all the Poles, many of whom he had helped escape from Soviet clutches when he was head of the Military Mission to Moscow in 1941–2.

Late that night, the Governor of Gibraltar learned that a plane taking the Soviet ambassador Ivan Maisky back to Moscow from London would also be arriving early the next morning, and the Foreign Office requested that the Russian diplomat be offered hospitality.

This was tricky. Poland no longer had diplomatic relations with the USSR. There was bad blood between them not just because Russia had helped Germany tear Poland apart in the Nazi–Soviet invasions in 1939, but because earlier in 1943 it was revealed that the Russian secret police had murdered over twenty thousand Poles, including fourteen thousand army and police officers, in the Katyn Forest massacre. The Poles and the Russians had to be kept apart in Gibraltar, with some reason found to get Ivan Maisky's aeroplane away as soon as possible.

The governor directed the diplomatic theatricals that ensued. The Sikorski party were asked to have a lie-in on the morning of Sunday 4 July and stay quietly upstairs in their bedrooms till 11 a.m.

Mason-MacFarlane cleared out early from his own set of rooms at the far end of the Convent, installed Maisky there after his arrival at 7 a.m., and joined him for a good breakfast. The elaborate pantomime included an interruption by an urgent RAF message from Air Vice Marshal Sturley Simpson, the Air Officer Commanding Gibraltar, saying that bad weather was heading for Algiers, so the Soviet ambassador's refuelled plane would have to leave at 11 a.m. rather than 3 p.m. Mason-MacFarlane saw Maisky to the airport and returned to an amused household of grinning Poles.

The rest of General Sikorski's Sunday in Gibraltar was busy, with meetings, tours, inspections of British and Polish soldiers. After a boozy American Independence Day cocktail party in the Garrison Library garden and a good dinner at Government House, his B-24 Liberator aeroplane AL523 took off from Gibraltar just past 11 p.m. on Sunday. There were seventeen people on board, six crew and eleven passengers, distributed five in the bomb bay, six in the fuselage. They included General Sikorski, his daughter, Lieutenant Zofia Leśniowska, his British liaison officer, Colonel Victor Cazalet MP, the Polish chief of staff, Major General Tadeusz Klimecki, the Chief of Operations Staff, Colonel Marecki, his naval ADC, Lieutenant Ponikiewski, his personal secretary Adam Kułakowski, and a Polish courier called Gralewski, as well as the British brigadier John Percival Whiteley and two civilians, Walter Lock and Harry Pinder, believed by the conspiratorial to be British secret service officers, but actually the Ministry of Transport representative from the Persian Gulf and the chief of the Royal Navy's signal station at Alexandria.

The pilot was an experienced Czech called Edward Prchal. '[He took off easily with at least 500 yards in hand,' wrote Mason-MacFarlane a fortnight later. 'In fact, by the time he was over the eastern end of the runway he had reached an altitude of at least 2–300 feet.' Mason-MacFarlane and Simpson both knew that Prchal liked to put his plane's nose down first to gather speed before he climbed to cruising height, and they watched his navigation lights do that as usual.

We waited a moment expecting to see the lights start to rise again. But they never did! In fact, the aircraft flew on a level keel and apparently in perfect shape straight into the sea at an angle of about ten degrees and hit the water with a sickening crash about three-quarters-of-a-mile from the shore. A split second before she hit the water the pilot cut out his engines which had apparently been running perfectly.

Anthony Quayle was still standing there with Group Captain Bolland, the RAF Station Commander, and another ADC, John Perry. The actor did not remember an explosion or a sickening crash, just 'a sudden cessation of noise. Silence. Bolland, standing beside me, gave a shout, "Christ, she's gone in the drink!"'

They drove down to the end of the runway and turned their headlights out to sea: 'nothing but darkness and black waves. Then the searchlights came on from high up on the Rock, sweeping backwards and forwards till they lit up a horrifying sight: half a mile out to sea, one wing of the plane was sticking up out of the water. That was all; the rest of the fuselage had disappeared.'

Quayle helped someone push out a rubber dinghy. He saw a Polish pilot stomping up and down the beach sobbing and banging his head with his fists. 'You don't understand,' he kept saying, 'You don't understand. This means the end of Poland. The end of Poland.' There were no air/sea rescue fast launches on the eastern side of Gibraltar so it took nearly ten minutes for them to arrive from the docks in the west. By then the plane had sunk. The motor launch recovered only three bodies: Sikorski and Klimecki were dead from head injuries, the pilot Prchal unconscious but breathing.

Lionel Crabb spent the next twelve days diving from HMS *Moorhill*, the RN lifting vessel. His task was to help salvage the broken aircraft and all its scattered wreckage for a court of inquiry and air-crash investigation, and to retrieve the dead bodies, ghastly-green in the underwater light: one on Monday, two on Tuesday, a couple more on Wednesday, another one on Thursday. The body of Colonel Marecki washed ashore on Eastern Beach on the Friday. Lieutenant Zofia Leśniowska, who had looked lovely in her Polish Women's Auxiliary uniform, was among the seven whose corpses were never found.

Gibraltar is hot in summer and most dead bodies are buried within a day. Mason-MacFarlane recommended that the cadavers of Sikorski and Klimecki be flown to London immediately, but the Polish government in exile thought it would be more fitting to return them by sea for burial beside the Polish memorial at the Newark-on-Trent cemetery in Nottinghamshire, which Sikorski had much admired. They directed a Polish destroyer, ORP *Orkan* (G90), to carry out the task of collection and transport. Meanwhile, the two bodies would lie in state in the Roman Catholic Cathedral of St Mary the Crowned in Gibraltar's Main Street until the warship arrived on Thursday 8 July.

It looks easy enough on paper, but there was frantic activity backstage. Mason-MacFarlane handed over the grislier arrangements to his ADC Anthony Quayle, who tried to fob the job off on an armed forces medic. The navy said Sikorski was a soldier who had been in an RAF plane and it was absolutely nothing to do with them; the army said he had fallen in the sea, beyond their purview; the RAF said he was definitely a soldier so therefore not their responsibility. Quayle's next problem was that there were no coffins in Gibraltar, not even for ready money, because few people were buried at North Front cemetery any more. Most of those who died in Gibraltar during the war were slid into the sea with a weight in the foot of their sewn shroud. Quayle rang the British vice consul in Algeciras and asked for half a dozen Spanish coffins. All he could find were cheap ones made of zinc and plywood, which he put on a lorry to cross the frontier. With relish, the Spanish border officials charged £10 customs fee for each coffin.

Anthony Quayle and Ludwik Łubieński, the Polish liaison officer, met the coffins at the mortuary, a low whitewashed building by the Landport tunnel. Even in the early morning it was hot inside. The two Polish bodies lay on blankets on the floor. Łubieński identified Klimecki's body. Sikorski must have been preparing for rest in the plane, because he was wearing a pyjama jacket with his black-striped uniform trousers on below. Quayle noticed: 'He had various wounds about his face and a deep indentation in the corner of one eye.'

Dr Peter Sutton, the RAF medical officer who was the first man to examine Sikorski's body the night before, had also noticed 'this cut next to the nose, above the eye'. As he attempted to stitch it, his needle came up against something solid. Dr Sutton probed into the wound and pulled out a pencil-length wood splinter, which had gone through the whole of Sikorski's brain.

A Gibraltarian undertaker appeared in the mortuary and took off his cycle clips.

'Do you wish to have the bodies embalmed?' he asked.

'Can you do that?'

'No.'

'In that case, it's a silly question.'

'Do you want them wrapped in winding sheets?'

'Do you have a winding sheet, or a couple of them?'

'No.'

'Then that is another useless question.'

Quayle helped Łubieński fold the thin blankets over the bodies of his two compatriots and lifted them into the flimsy coffins.

'Do you wish the coffin sealed?'

'Yes. Please get on with it.'

The undertaker used a soldering iron to weld the thin zinc lid and screwed down the slender veneer. Quayle got out his penknife and scratched 'S' in the varnish of one coffin, 'K' on the other. The bearer party from the Somerset Light Infantry arrived with two open lorries and a pair of Polish flags to process the bodies solemnly to the Catholic Cathedral of St Mary the Crowned. The cortège crossed Casemates Square to Line Wall Road and then turned up into Main Street and marched south. The governor, the Flag Officer Gibraltar and other senior figures joined the procession. Polish soldiers mounted a vigil around the clock, through Monday, Tuesday and Wednesday. On Wednesday the 7th the British garrison spent hours rehearsing and timing every move of the next day's funeral ceremony, and high-ranking Poles arrived to stay at the Convent.

It was gone midnight when Brigadier Reggie Parminter, Royal Army Ordnance Corps, looking grave behind his monocle, shook Anthony Quayle to life in his bed.

'Are you awake?'

'Yes. This is me. I'm awake.'

'You're sure you're quite awake?'

'Of course. What is it?'

'General Sikorski has burst his coffin.'

Around midnight, Łubieński had been paying his last visit to his late commander-in-chief when he found the Honour Guard clustered outside the cathedral, chattering fearfully about 'ghosts'. He went in through the west door. There was a nauseating stench and strange noises emanating from the temporary catafalque. Beneath the flag he found that the chemical process of decomposition in almost African heat had bloated Sikorski's body enough to split open both solder and veneer. Vile gases escaping swollen orifices burbled and squealed and the weird farting groans from Klimecki's coffin indicated that he was bursting too.

Fresh coffins were found, the cathedral fumigated. Quayle searched for sheets of lead to lap the bodies. Perry drove Victor Cazalet's body to the ORP *Orkan* at Gun Wharf but *Orkan*'s superstitious captain refused to accept it. Engineers in shorts manhandled Quayle's lead sheets on board at the last minute. Nobody spoke much English or could understand why it was necessary.

It was 8.15 a.m. on 8 July. Hundreds of British soldiers stood with heads bowed and arms reversed, hands folded on the butts of their Lee-Enfield .303 rifles, barrels down on the right boot, the front sight resting in the crease between leather lace and gleaming toe-cap. The two coffins were carried aboard and laid on deck; the band played the Polish national anthem; the echoes of a seventeen-gun salute sent ORP *Orkan* off to Plymouth.

On 9/10 July Operation *Husky* began: the Allied invasion of Sicily. Meanwhile, Nazi radio propaganda was having a field day. Clearly, General Wladyslaw Sikorski had been murdered by the British secret service, just as the inconvenient Admiral François Darlan had been assassinated by them six months before. How could any foreigner trust the perfidious British? Gibraltar was a snake-pit of spies, Churchill a complete gangster.

For decades, controversy has surrounded the plane crash in which General Sikorski died. The official inquiry in 1943 concluded that the pilot had not been able to pull 'the stick', his control column, backwards to make the plane climb because something – perhaps a bottle which had rolled or a piece of luggage which had slipped – had jammed the system of chains and cables which were the elevator controls for the B-24's tail flaps. This banal explanation did not convince everyone. A clever mystery is better than a stupid accident, a conspiracy more exciting than a cock-up. People asked the old lawyer's forensic question, *Cui bono?* – 'Whose interest could this have served?' – and came up with various explanations for the death of Polish hopes in the cold sea off Gibraltar.

A controversial German play, *Soldiers: an Obituary for Geneva*, became notorious in 1967. Its main theme was supposed to be the wickedness of the Allied air campaign against German civilians in the Second World War. But a sub-theme of the play accused Winston Churchill of acquiescing in the murder of General Sikorski because the Polish soldier's indictment of the Katyn massacres carried out by the Soviets was alleged to be endangering Churchill's wartime alliance with Joseph Stalin. The author of the play, Rolf Hochhuth, who as a boy had been in the Hitler Youth, said that SOE men on board axed the general to death at the western end of the runway and then slipped out of the plane before it took off and crashed into the sea. Hochhuth claimed to have been told this by a former member of SIS and to have proof locked in a Swiss bank vault. A paranoid and nervous man, Hochhuth was convinced that he too was now the target of British Secret Service assassins.

At the urging of his literary manager, the fashionable Kenneth Tynan, Sir Laurence Olivier proposed to stage Hochhuth's play at

London's new National Theatre. It was a controversial choice. The then British prime minister, Harold Wilson, having ordered up and read the still secret RAF crash inquiry report, said Hochhuth's allegations against Winston Churchill should be brushed aside 'with the contempt they deserve'. A flurry of lawsuits erupted: both the Czech pilot of Sikorski's plane, Edward Prchal, and an SOE man alleged to be in on the plot, Bickham Sweet-Escott, sued Hochhuth for defamation. At the same time, the historian Hugh Trevor-Roper denied Tynan's claim that he believed in the murder conspiracy and remained unmoved by Tynan's subsequent threat to sue for libel.

What also emerged in 1967 was the source of Hochhuth's ideas about the death of the Polish general, the right-wing revisionist historian David Irving, who brought out his book *Accident: the Death of General Sikorski* to coincide with the intended London production of *Soldiers*. Irving, then a twenty-nine-year-old independent researcher and writer, was not yet the Holocaust denier and distorter of historical evidence that later law courts judged him to be. *Accident*, as published, is an investigation of Sikorski's air accident, not a murder mystery. David Irving clearly collaborated with Rolf Hochhuth, whom he first met in January 1965 (the day after Churchill died), and had begun the researches for the book at Hochhuth's insistence. In *Accident* Irving made insinuations but avoided the playwright's overtly conspiratorial conclusions. This is probably because the publisher William Kimber personally had the book 'lawyered' extensively for libel, and rewrote *Accident*'s final chapter, 'Open Verdict', which suggests that some of the mailbags loaded in the bomb-aimer's compartment at the front of the (slightly overloaded) plane may have come loose from their hatch and fallen into the nose-wheel compartment. (This suggestion also helps explain the mysterious single mailbag found on the runway afterwards.) The bags that did not fall out of the plane may have become entangled with the retracting nose-wheel, which, thus jammed, would have affected the elevator controls.

Another investigative book, by the Argentine actor and writer Carlos Thompson, called *The Assassination of Winston Churchill*, appeared in 1969. This devastating work, for which Thompson sought out every living witness or participant, demolishes the allegations by Rolf Hochhuth and David Irving, and vigorously defends Churchill against the charge of murdering an ally. The favourable review of Thompson's book in the London *Sunday Times*, ostensibly by 'Robert Blake' but actually written by Hugh Trevor-Roper, dismissed *Soldiers* as a 'drivelling farrago of lies'. Irving threatened to sue Carlos Thompson for defamation, but could not afford to because he was caught up in another major libel case resulting from what he had written in his 1968 book *The Destruction of Convoy PQ 17*.

Rolf Hochhuth's thesis, Churchill-as-murderer, was, unsurprisingly, the very same line put out by Joseph Goebbels's Nazi Propaganda Ministry soon after the fatal aeroplane crash at Gibraltar. According to Gdansk University Professor Jacek Tebinka, an expert on twentieth-century Polish–British relations, interviewed in the Polish daily *Gazeta Wyborcza* on 28 June 2013:

The assassination theory was made up by Germany to drive a wedge between the Poles and their Western Allies. Goebbels's propaganda proclaimed that the Soviets killed Sikorski with the approval of the British, because he dared denounce the Katyn massacre and turned to the Red Cross for help. [The Nazis] treated the general's death as an opportunity to extend the Katyn propaganda launched by them in April 1943 . . . It was widely believed in Arab countries. In the summer of 1943, Polish diplomats and the British were horrified by just how popular in Cairo was the theory that London was behind the death of Sikorski.

Other conspiracy theories about who might have murdered Sikorski involve right-wing renegade Poles, or Hitler and the Abwehr, or, and this is top of the list for many Poles, Joseph Stalin and the ruthless Russian secret service, the NKVD. The presence of the Russian ambassador Ivan Maisky's aeroplane for a few hours at the same airfield and on the same day as General Sikorski's aircraft has given rise to intense speculation that this was the perfect opportunity for the Russians to sabotage the Polish general's aircraft. The fact that

Kim Philby, the Soviet double agent, was on the SIS Section V Iberia desk at the time excites even more synaptic connections. Was the great British traitor implicated in a Soviet Communist plot to silence a Polish patriot? The spy-novelist and fabulist John le Carré thinks it possible; the historian Norman Davies even claims that Philby was actually working on the Rock of Gibraltar at the time, but there is absolutely no evidence at all for that.

General Mason-MacFarlane stated that Sikorski's 'machine had a Commando and RAF guard on her during the whole stay on Gibraltar aerodrome while Sikorski was on the Rock'. Carlos Thompson points out there was even a man stationed inside Sikorski's Liberator plane to make sure no one else got in.

In 2008, Ewa Koj, the head of the investigative division of the Katowice branch of the Polish Institute of National Remembrance (a Polish government-affiliated research institute, founded by the Polish parliament in 1998 to investigate and prosecute crimes against the Polish nation), started to look into the death of Sikorski as a possible 'Communist crime'. General Sikorski's poor body, which had already been moved from Newark in England to Poland in 1993, was duly exhumed from its resting place among the nation's kings and bards, St Leonard's Crypt beneath Wawel Cathedral in Krakow, to confirm the identity of the corpse and to try to establish whether he had been murdered in the aircraft (as Hochhuth claimed) before the plane crashed. DNA tests proved this was indeed the general's body, and the new autopsy showed no axe-cuts to the head, just death 'by trauma to internal organs caused by an accident'. The investigation petered out.

And then, on 10 April 2010, there was another disastrous accident when a Polish air force Tupolev Tu-154, carrying an official party to Russia to mark the seventieth anniversary of the Katyn massacre of twenty-two thousand Poles, crashed in thick fog near Smolensk North Airport. All ninety-six people on board were killed including the President of Poland, Lech Kaczyński, with his wife, and the Chief of the Polish General Staff, the top military and intelligence officers, plus senior government officials, civil dignitaries, parliamentarians and clergy, as well as relatives of victims of the massacre.

At first, the tragedy helped thaw Polish–Russian relations. State TV in Russia showed Andrey Wajda's film *Katyn*, the state archive released previously secret files, and the Russian Duma passed a resolution admitting that Stalin had authorised the Katyn massacre. Two investigations found the crash was an accident in thick fog. Nevertheless, paranoid conspiracy theories started to mushroom, once again. Was Poland under some malevolent curse? Hadn't there been a mysterious explosion on board? Wasn't the whole event a mass assassination, ordered by Russia's ex-KGB strongman, Vladimir Putin?

The seventieth anniversary of the Sikorski air crash in 2013 brought a large Polish delegation to Gibraltar, with representatives of the Polish government and military and Polish veterans of the Second World War coming to pay tribute to a great Pole.

The Governor of Gibraltar, Sir Adrian Johns, reminded people at one of the ceremonies that two hundred thousand Polish soldiers, sailors and airmen fought alongside the Allies, gaining victories in the Battle of Britain and at Monte Cassino. He praised the Polish intelligence networks and the Polish mathematicians who first broke the Enigma enciphering machines and so helped shorten the Second World War.

Bishop Józef Guzdek celebrated a High Mass in the Cathedral of Mary the Crowned in Main Street, Gibraltar, the place where Sikorski's body had lain, and said that his loss was a national tragedy and source of enduring grief for Poland.

General, sir, you fought for your Fatherland to your final breath. God spared you many disappointments and heartaches. You did not live to countenance the treacherous diktats of Teheran and Yalta. You did not hear the weeping soldiers of the 2nd Corps who had nowhere to return to because their homes, for the most part, were left beyond the borders of Poland. You were spared the sight of the despair of Polish soldiers who, at the end of the war, were not invited to participate in the victory parade. You did not come to know the fact of the reimposition of Soviet occupation . . .

The *danse macabre* continues. In November 2016, Poland's ruling Law and Justice Party, headed by Jarosław Kaczyński, ordered the body of the late president, his twin brother Lech, killed in the air crash, to be exhumed from the cathedral in Krakow for further post-mortem investigations, just as General Sikorski's body had been. In April 2017, on the seventh anniversary of the Smolensk crash, Reuters in Warsaw reported that a commission set up by the Law and Justice party was suggesting that a violent explosion had occurred on board the Tupolev aeroplane before it hit the ground, most likely caused by 'a thermobaric charge initiating a strong shock-wave'. The former head of Polish air crash investigations, Maciej Lasek, dismissed this assertion as 'propaganda aimed at strengthening the faith . . . in hypothetical causes of this accident'.

35

A Vision of Battlements

A young conscript from Manchester recorded some of Gibraltar's transition at the end of the war. He was Sergeant John Burgess Wilson, better known to us today as the polymathic author, critic and composer Anthony Burgess (1917–93). In October 1940, the twenty-three-year-old John Wilson, who had just gained his BA (Hons) from Manchester University with a mini-thesis on Marlowe's *Dr Faustus*, travelled by train up to a military depot in Scotland with another recruit, 'small, simian and silent', who turned out to be completely illiterate: 'I haven't learnt to write yet,' he said. Burgess Wilson, an ardent self-improver and lover of words, had not realised how much British illiteracy there was, or stupidity, and he was to encounter both as the Home Forces Territorial Army ingested and excreted him as 73888026 Private Wilson J. in the Royal Army Medical Corps (RAMC).

To judge from his own vivid and dyspeptic memoirs, *Little Wilson and Big God*, written forty years later, the young Mancunian entered an unclean, uncouth, unpleasant world of foul meals, filthy blankets, freezing cold, and effing and blinding NCOs who treated anyone well-spoken with contempt. This bred anger and resentment, the bloody-mindedness of the 'browned-off'. 'Sick and defiant' new recruits embraced idleness, theft and malingering as the only way of getting their own back on a system in which rank had nothing to do with merit. Officiousness thwarted talent: Burgess saw a pointless world of 'if-it-moves-salute-it-if-it-doesn't-move-whitewash-it', a moronic regime that wasted knowledge and intelligence.

Burgess, a man who wanted to compose music and who carried 'a copy of *Finnegans Wake*, generally supposed to be a code-book' in his kitbag, says he once found himself with a bank manager, a senior librarian and an anthropologist, in the pouring Scottish rain, tasked with shovelling a midden of human faeces into the back of a lorry. Having to give speech therapy in Winwick lunatic asylum seemed another metaphor for his life in the British army, at a place where the tertiary stage of syphilis – 'general paralysis of the insane' as it was then called – transformed some patients into genius *savants* and others into drooling idiots. Burgess, being musical, escaped by moving into the 'Entertainments' section of the RAMC and playing in a dance band called the Jaypees.

There were enlightened people in the British army in the Second World War. In Wellington's day and in Nelson's navy, 'the scum of the earth' could be flogged into discipline; in the Great War, the obedient had followed the educated 'over the top' like servants dutifully following their masters, but in Hitler's war a more humane approach was required to deal with the mostly civilian army that had to be conscripted after the destruction of the regular British Expeditionary Force in 1940. After the recommendations of the Haining Committee, the little-remembered Lieutenant General Sir Ronald Adam was the officer who tried to do something about the welfare and morale of ordinary soldiers when he became adjutant general (essentially head of personnel) of the British army in May 1941. Psychiatrists started to attend selection boards to weed out the psychotic and deranged from the officer class; training courses were instituted to help delinquent young soldiery on the one hand and to improve man-management among junior officers on the other; there was a reduction in meaningless 'spit and polish' and endless inspections. Radio programmes for the forces, army newspapers and legal aid for problems at home were all part of wider schemes to keep the essentially civilian wartime soldiery informed and educated.

The Army Bureau of Current Affairs organised weekly discussions among soldiers about the purpose and objectives of the war. Such debates, redolent of 'roundhead' radicalism, alarmed the 'cavaliers' – army traditionalists, Conservative MPs and even the prime minister, who tried to have them stopped as a menace to morale and discipline. But the war had blown open doors and windows. Things had to be talked about. 'What was the whole point of the bloody war?' men wondered. It had to be to make things right. To improve. To rebuild better. People did not want to go back to the bad old days of depression and poverty and slums and hunger marches: they wanted a fairer world, a better life for their children, an end to want and fear. There were plenty of 'progressive' people arguing for the ways and means to achieve it – initiatives like the Beveridge Report (which led to Britain's post-war welfare state), or the hopeful propaganda of the Crown Film Unit's documentary films. The same spirit was apparent among those who went out to teach soldiers and sailors and airmen about the best of the democracy they were supposed to be fighting for.

It was this new tide that carried bolshy, resentful, put-upon Anthony Burgess into the Army Educational Corps, whose badge was a book over crossed rifles. 'The weapon of political education', Burgess wrote later, 'was thoughtlessly put into the hands of educated sergeants. I left the Entertainments Section of the 54th Division to become one.' As in the First World War, the civilian intake in the Second World War leavened the regular armed forces by raising its intelligence quotient, bringing in new ideas and new approaches, and thus expanding its range of possibilities.

In November 1943, Burgess, still known as Sergeant John B. Wilson, lecturer in speech and drama, received the news he was to be posted abroad, by troopship, to Gibraltar. The men reported to a transit camp in west London and Burgess arrived late, drunk, maudlin, tearful. He had just come from a literary pub in Soho where, wretchedly, he had left his faithless and dipsomaniac Welsh wife, Lynne, enjoying being fondled by another man.

He sailed from Avonmouth aboard a converted banana-boat called *Highland Monarch* on 10 December 1943, zig-zagging from mid-Atlantic to the stormy Bay of Biscay. 'It was a long sick voyage . . . When we were not sick we were constipated.' A few years later, he would try to describe some of the experience in the characteristically Joycean language of his first novel:

The rehearsal was abandoned. The North Atlantic's black back cracked. Howling sea-ghosts scrabbled at the rigging. Soldiers lurched along the troop-decks, howling also, slopping tempestuous mess-tins of tea. Over the decks salty knouts of broken sea lunged and sloggered. Acres of frothing marble leered monstrously, as though Rome had melted. Riding the bitter uncertain ranges, the troopship soared and plunged in agony.

Wartime Gibraltar is the place where Sergeant John Wilson started to become the British writer whom we know today as Anthony Burgess. '*A Vision of Battlements* was, is, my first novel,' he wrote in the introduction when it was published in 1965 by Sidgwick and Jackson, illustrated by Edward Pagram. 'I wrote it in 1949,* three years after leaving the scene where it is set – Gibraltar. There, as a sergeant and subsequently a sergeant-major, I had spent the second half of my six years' war service.' At that time, Burgess wanted to be a composer of serious music, but he wrote this book 'to see if I could clear my head of the dead weight of Gibraltar. I had lived with it so long that it still lay in my skull, a chronic migraine: a work of fiction seemed the best way of breaking it up, pulverising it, sweeping it away . . . I have had to tame the Rock, an emblem of waste and loneliness, by other means.' It nagged him, the Rock, like a troublesome molar inflaming a tender jaw. 'I don't know whether I like Gibraltar or not,' he wrote on revisiting the peninsula in 1966, 'but it became an aspect of my private mythology.'

In the same way as his literary master James Joyce had turned Homer's *Odyssey* into *Ulysses* in 1922, so Anthony Burgess used Virgil's epic *Aeneid* as the backbone of his novel *A Vision of Battlements*. Exiled Aeneas has become enlisted Richard Ennis (R. Ennis

---

* In his not always reliable 1987 autobiography Burgess also says he wrote it in 1953, although his more reliable biographer Andrew Biswell suggests it was begun in December 1951 or January 1952 and probably rewritten twice before eventual publication.

is also 'sinner' backwards), a music-composing lapsed Catholic sergeant in the invented Army Vocational and Cultural Corps, 'who tries to blue-print a Utopia in his lectures and to create actual cities in his music'. The high-minded composer hero is also socially awkward ('he never knew what to do; he always chose the wrong time, never the right, knowing no mean between importunity and forwardness') and is of course a version of the author himself. Ennis is also, as Burgess liked to think, an early prototype of the anti-heroes depicted by the 'Angry Young Men' writers of the 1950s like John Osborne and Kingsley Amis: 'the Welfare State rebels were anticipated by the Army rebels, especially those who, stuck and frustrated, waited in vain for the siege of rocky and invincible Troy'.

Christmas Eve. They awoke with a shock to find their future was upon them. It had appeared suddenly in the night, the giant threatening rock, the vast crouching granite dragon, the towering sky-high Sphinx, its forehead bathed in the mild sun. It brooded, an incubus, but also their bride and mother . . . Like Andromeda, he thought, chained to this rock-face till time should send the deliverer,* they now had to learn the great gift of patience. No ill-wind Germans would dislodge them from here.

By Christmas 1943 the Allies had not yet won the war, but the Axis were losing it. Italy had surrendered on 8 September, save for a die-hard Fascist rump called the Italian Social Republic. Germany had lost the tank-battle at Kursk to the Soviets, relearning the bitter lessons of Napoleon's failed invasion of Russia. Japan, beaten at Midway, was losing islands in the Pacific. 'There is a tide in the affairs of men', wrote Shakespeare in *Julius Caesar*, 'which, taken at the flood, leads on to fortune'. Hitler had missed his moment in 1940 by not invading Spain and seizing Gibraltar, and now the tide was flowing the other way, carrying the Allies to victory.

None of this was clear to the draft of Army Educational Corps

---

* Andromeda's father chained her by the shore to placate the waters and a sea monster. Her rescuer, Perseus, used the Medusa's severed head to turn to stone all his rivals for her hand in marriage.

sergeants – Norman Parker, Harry Stevens, Ben Thomas, Jimmy Wilkinson, John Wilson – moving down the gangways to the quayside in Gibraltar on 24 December 1943. They 'minced clodhoppingly down to the unfamiliar feel of stone underfoot. The Rock was twinkling to life, lights in tier after tier.' Accustomed to British blackout, the blaze of the town and the lights of Algeciras across the bay surprised them. A sharp-featured WO1 (warrant officer, class one) arrived in a small truck. His name was Norman Crump and Wilson found him unfriendly, like their new commanding officer, Captain, soon to be Major, W. P. 'Bill' Meldrum, a professional soldier whose whole career had been in the Education Corps. Burgess conceived an intense irrational hatred for both men. The names Meldrum and Crump would feature frequently in his early fiction, and never favourably. In *A Vision of Battlements*, the real-life Meldrum is fictionalised as Major Muir, a man with delusions of grandeur who 'had invented many fantasies about himself – the many books he had written, the many universities he had attended. He spoke often ungrammatically, with a home-made accent in which Cockney diphthongs stuck out stiffly like bristles. His ignorance was a wonder. But he had power, pull, in high places, nobody knew how.'

Anthony Burgess described himself as 'essentially secretive and mendacious', a fantasist. Self-made, like Muir's accent, he suffered from status anxiety. He name-dropped compulsively to show off his wondrous knowledge and cleverness, and yet he felt an outsider, lacking in 'pull'. In the second volume of his autobiography, *You've Had Your Time*, he wrote truthfully, 'Like a colonial, I have a sense of exclusion, a chip on the shoulder.' This was the old deathly power of class in England, the wound that for Burgess never healed. Burgess despised ignorant philistines around him and resented those above him: 'the Rock Raj' is a phrase for these hated superiors in *A Vision of Battlements*. (Burgess never became an officer.) It galled him that Other Ranks were barred from the elite Rock Hotel, up on the slope above the town, which was for officers only, and where there were women he lusted after but could never touch. Watching a rare Wren officer crossing her black-stockinged legs, Burgess said that he ejaculated in his khaki shorts. (Yet when the published author finally achieved the Rock Hotel two decades later in 1966, he was disappointed. 'Even my English breakfast, Spanish-cooked, was a deliberate yolk-smashed, cold-fat-swimming lampoon of an English breakfast, like a desecration of the flag.')

All his life Burgess would feel unhonoured in his own country because he hadn't got into Oxford or Cambridge and was from the north, Catholic and working-class. In fact, the British media – press, TV, radio – loved him because he was good in front of a microphone and produced clean copy fast. The disdain he imagined from others was not really there, but it was what he felt inside, and perhaps what he needed to feel, to fuel his embattled, put-upon and rejected creative self. In *A Vision of Battlements*, Ennis laments his 'base stock' to the woman who taught him Spanish –'the real Castilian, not the Calpe mush' – his mistress Concepcion: 'It isn't a question of education. It's a question of family. You can have the best education in the world and all the money in the world, but if your ancestors have let you down by not being the right sort of people – It's hard to explain.'

'Silence, exile and cunning' was the watchword of his master James Joyce: in Gibraltar Anthony Burgess discovered exile from Protestant England and a new kind of home in Catholic Europe. Reading St John of the Cross in Spanish, a romantically ecstatic Ennis feels he knows where his home is: 'back in the Church . . . his home was here, the Mediterranean, the womb of history. No, not here on the Rock . . . but over there in the land of bullfights and religious processions.'

A Vision of Battlements is a key Anthony Burgess text. When in the 1980s he came to write of Gibraltar in his first book of confessional memoirs, *Little Wilson and Big God*, he did not quarry contemporaneous notebooks from the 1940s but reread his own novel and re-remembered the memories that it prompted, the stories he had shaped and chamfered.

Of course I was *in* Catholic Europe, despite the bobbies in British helmets and the insistence of the Gibraltarians that they were, though mostly Geno-ese with a Spanish admixture, really a kind of brown Englishmen. They were Catholic, when they were not Jews, and held baroque processions on feast days . . . But they were of my own kind . . . I was drawn to the women with crosses hanging from their delectable necks.

Anthony Burgess wrote about the real life he lived in Gibraltar in at least three ways afterwards: in fiction, in journalism and in con-fessional memoir. Each is as true and untrue as the other. Scenes are changed, events reordered, characters and parts invented or embel-lished, but the four books and occasional pieces make up a palimp-sest of the wartime Rock that still has the pungency and bite of raw garlic.

At Christmas in 1943, Burgess was quartered near Moorish Castle with a view across to Spain: 'the mess clung like an eyrie to the Rock, commanding a magnificent panorama – the border town, the dis-tant sierra, a bullring like a lost coin . . .' The barracks was plagued with fleas, lice and bed-bugs. Walking down the white, sun-beaten road to Casemates Square he was vunerable to attack by the snarl-ing chief macaque, Scruffy. The monkey was not the only inhabitant of Gibraltar who was suffering mental problems. When the educa-tion sergeants were gathered together on Christmas morning, Major Meldrum told them that the Gibraltar garrison had a problem with boredom and depression and low morale, a condition which he called 'Rockitis'. The sergeants' duty was to stimulate interest and enthu-siasm in study and vocational courses that would help men after the war when they went back to 'civvy street'. In his autobiography, Burgess says that Meldrum told him his job was 'to travel the height and width of the Rock, take boats to the Detached Mole and back, visit the lucky units at sea level, and deliver the British Way and Purpose according to a plan devised by Mr Crump there'.

The British Way and Purpose (Consolidated Edition) 1944 is an interesting book into which much thought has been put, bringing together all eighteen B.W.P. booklets prepared by the Directorate of

Army Education to help fill the three hours a week that every unit in the army had to give over to education, as part of their training quota. Essentially it was a worthy and structured discussion course about citizenship, in Britain, in the British Empire and in the world. With contributions from experts like Denis Brogan on the USA, Richard Coupland on India, Barbara Ward on citizenship and Hilary Marquand on people at work, it covered democracy, government, law, justice, education, health, social services, America, Russia, China, Europe, the United Nations. The authors looked at economics, sociology, responsibility, town and country planning, homes, jobs, neighbourhoods, populations. There were discussions about how the war started, what had happened in it, what should happen next, what ought to happen afterwards in the peace, when there should be freedom for nations, freedom from want and freedom from fear. Then there were chapters called 'You and the Empire', and 'You and the Colonies', which talked about 'the ladder of self-government', about development, welfare and education in the colonies, about 'haves' and 'have-nots'. Burgess wrote in his autobiography: 'My duty as a purveyor of the British Way and Purpose was to uphold an inveterate political system kindly being modified in the direction of a philosophy of state welfare. I had to make a negative war (defending the bad against the worse) appear positive.' But Burgess also picked up something essential: 'War itself was turning into a metaphor: we were enacting the charade of a struggle to turn Britain into a democracy. Equality of rights was one of the shibboleths.'

In chapter 2 of *A Vision of Battlements* Sergeant Ennis goes to lecture to fifty men of the Docks Operating Group, 'simian, distrustful, the hardest men on the whole Rock to handle. They would strike against route-marches, crown their N.C.O.s with half-bricks, steal lavishly from the cargoes they unloaded.' He calls them 'Gentlemen' and is met with derision. He attempts a lecture on the future of the British Empire and is overwhelmed by their complaints and rage against 'them bastards at the top' who will not let them go home and the 'bleeding Yank' who stole Jack's wife. As the meeting slips hopelessly out of his control, Ennis shouts, 'To hell with this lecture! To hell with these stripes I'm wearing! You don't want the lecture and you don't want me. What you want is a drink,' and the cheering uneducated mob carry him off to the boozer, the Universal Café in Main Street. The supposed educator has become an agent of insubordination.

If the dockers could not give a fig about the future of the empire and the colonies, those who really cared about the subject were the Gibraltarians, the people the British soldiers called 'Rock Scorpions'. Now they were developing their sting. It had started in September 1940 when a Gibraltarian foreman mechanic and City Council employee called Albert J. Risso got a group of clerks and fellow workers together to protest to Governor Liddell about the convincing rumour that their families, already evacuated to England, were going to be shipped across the U-boat-infested Atlantic to Jamaica, where fifteen hundred had already gone directly from Gibraltar. Beyond this protest, this group also began to think about how things ought to be in Gibraltar after the war. 'For the duration', which meant 'until the end of the war', they were definitely second-class citizens in their own home.

Albert Risso, the son of Gibraltar's vet, was an active trade unionist, but his new group could not agree on the rules and constitution of their workers' committee or even what name to choose for themselves, so they turned to the young Gibraltarian Joshua 'Salvador' Hassan to help them. As we have seen, Hassan was the civilian lawyer who represented the two Spaniards hanged in Moorish Castle. He had been about to be commissioned as an officer in the Royal Artillery when General Mason-MacFarlane cancelled the process and gave him leave of absence from the Gibraltar Defence Force so that he could continue his legal work in courts martial. Defendants felt they might get justice with a man in a suit helping them amid all the uniforms. What Hassan did was shrewdly come up with the clumsy-seeming title 'Association for the Advancement of Civil Rights in

Gibraltar' or AACR. This deliberately echoed the USA's National Association for the Advancement of Colored People, NAACP, which had been founded in February 1909 to fight for equality of rights for those whose skin pigment was different.

'Civil Rights' did not figure in the index of *British Way and Purpose*, but it fitted the political agenda of the Atlantic Charter and other expressions of the war's supposed aims and values. 'Civil Rights' was a crowbar of a term that could jemmy a chink in the constitutional armour of British hypocrisy. The right to have 'rights' was critical. Nor was the parallel between AACR and NAACP frivolous, because colonial systems are usually based on racial hierarchies. Kenya Colony in British East Africa had invented the tripartite racial layer cake of 'Europeans', 'Asians' and 'Africans' which is perhaps the nearest analogy to the Rock's colonial hierarchy, mirrored in the signs on the toilet doors in the Gibraltar dockyard: 'British', 'Gibraltarians', and 'Aliens' for the Spanish. As ever, the class in the middle chafed at the group above and looked down on the one below. But, writing in 1945, Major David Scherr observed the great shift in sensibility that was taking place in the British Empire as a result of the war:

The Gibraltarians have worked for the dockyard and garrison for nearly two and a half centuries as dockyard labourers, ships' chandlers, shopkeepers, fetchers and carriers, hirelings and underlings. They are now feeling more and more that as British subjects they are entitled to rights as well as responsibilities, and that as Europeans as well as Colonials they are capable of and worthy of a standard of living and a form of self-government different from that enjoyed under British rule by African natives.

John Burgess Wilson stayed on Gibraltar well into 1946, when he reviewed twenty-eight films in four months for the *Gibraltar Chronicle*, his first critical journalism. With the return of many of Gibraltar's evacuees he and his colleagues found themselves teaching more Gibraltarians than British soldiers. There is a telling scene in chapter 16 of Burgess's novel when his hero Richard Ennis bumps into 'a knot of brown dapper civilians, talking excitedly in the slack Spanish of the colony' near the steps of the Garrison Library. An educated Gibraltarian called Rioja stops him.

'You, Sergeant Ennis, are on our side. I know you are. In the Matriculation English you have talked much about freedom and democracy . . . Though you are English, you will admit that we are in the right. This is our Rock and it is we who should govern it.'

'Come along,' said Lavinia. 'We're going to be late.'

'It is only right,' said Mr Rioja, with gestures. 'India has self-government now. It is the professed and general aim of the British government to give self-government to all the colonies. We are an old colony. We are older, for instance, than Australia, and Australia has been for a long time a dominion.' He knew it all, by God.

'Come on.' Lavinia tugged Ennis's arm.

'But,' said Ennis, 'it's hardly a country, is it? It's only a rock, a strategic point in the Mediterranean. What good would it be if the British went?'

'No, no, no, no,' said a lined brown man with a twitch. 'We are British. We would still be British. We would be the British in charge of the Rock, you see.'

'It is small, but it is our home,' said one small fat man, not without dignity. 'As it is, we are not properly represented.'

The Governor and Commander-in Chief of Gibraltar, General Mason-MacFarlane, greatly helped the Association for the Advancement of Civil Rights in Gibraltar. It may seem curious that the head of the military structure should seek to yield fortress power in the name of civil rights, but then Mason-MacFarlane was a socialist. (He would stand as a Labour MP in the July 1945 general election and defeat Churchill's acolyte Brendan Bracken to win his North Paddington seat in Parliament.) The encouragement of His Excellency gave the new body political respectability. Mason-MacFarlane permitted Gibraltarian workers to visit their evacuated families abroad, allowing the AACR to organise the Special Leave scheme from July 1943.

The most immediate threat to Gibraltar and the Mediterranean had ended with the surrender of Italy in September 1943. The

Gibraltarians could see no military reason why their families should not be allowed back home again, and with repatriation as their rallying banner, AACR grew to become, as Dr Joseph Garcia says in *Gibraltar: the Making of a People*, 'the first mass movement in the history of Gibraltar, the product of circumstances created entirely by the war.'

In December 1943, the Resettlement Board was set up in Gibraltar. Mason-MacFarlane travelled to England to join his wife, who had been working with and visiting the Gibraltarian refugees making do in London. With Bishop Fitzgerald, the pair went around many of the centres where Gibraltarians were accommodated in London. They were apparently quite cheerful, with the children well looked after, but everyone was asking, 'When can we get back to Gibraltar?' In his New Year's Day broadcast on Forces radio, also reported in the *Gibraltar Chronicle*, Mason-MacFarlane said that was why he had gone to England:

It is my firm intention to commence repatriation as soon as the progress of the war and the shipping situation permits . . . First priorities will be the near relatives and dependants of all of you who have borne the heat and burden of the day out here for the past three and half years. Jamaica will get highest possible priority in the earlier categories . . . As I told you, I am promising absolutely nothing. But I hope and pray personally that it won't be long . . .

Not everyone was happy of course. Pettifogging restrictions by busybodies were beginning to irk some of the Gibraltarians in London. Why shouldn't they be allowed to take their food to their own rooms? Why did they have to eat in the communal dining room? The same sort of 'why' questions, challenging more political restrictions than domestic ones, were being asked in Gibraltar by the AACR. They lobbied for the Governor's Executive Council to be replaced by a Legislative Council that would bring democracy to the Rock. Albert Risso talked in stronger language of 'doing away with tyranny and the system of the privileged few'.

The trouble was that Mason-MacFarlane had moved on to Naples in the musical chairs following Eisenhower's return to London to prepare for D-Day. On 16 January 1944, the day he assumed duty as the Deputy President of the Allied Commission for Italy, Mason-MacFarlane relinquished his post on the Rock and was replaced as Governor and Commander-in-Chief of Gibraltar for the next three years by Lieutenant General Sir Ralph 'Rusty' Eastwood, a man markedly less sympathetic to Gibraltarian aspirations. Eastwood offered an 'Advisory Council' but the Gibraltarians rejected this. When the Town Council was re-established, AACR took all seven seats. They finally gained their Legislative Council in 1950, after the unpopular Eastwood had been replaced.

On 26 May 1944, General Eastwood had an important VIP stop off at the Convent, en route to Algiers and Cairo. People at the airfield and soldiers in the street were surprised to see whippet-thin General Bernard Montgomery, late of the victorious Eighth Army in North Africa, and wearing his characteristic two-badged black beret, descending from an aeroplane to inspect a guard of honour before being driven off to meet the governor.

Major Ignacio Molina Pérez of the Spanish *carabineros*, who, as a liaison officer between Spanish and British forces had a permanent pass to the fortress and a car with Gibraltar number plates, was particularly pleased to catch a glimpse of 'Monty' with Eastwood at the Convent when he went to a meeting with the Colonial Secretary. This was a really juicy titbit that Major Molina could swiftly report by telephone to his true masters, the Germans in Madrid. Molina had no idea that the DSO's six-page counter-espionage report on all his activities and meetings and conspiracies in the Campo since 1939 had just been sent to the Director General of MI5 in London, and certainly had no idea that he was being played like a fish, and witnessing a charade enacted largely for his benefit.

It was not, in fact, General Bernard Montgomery whom people had seen on his way to the Convent. It was his double, an actor from the Pay Corps called Meyrick Clifton James. This was all part of an elaborate deception, Operation *Copperhead*, part of a series of D-Day deceptions called Operation *Bodyguard*. The real 'Monty' was in England, preparing to lead the 12th Army Group across the English Channel for the landings on the beaches of Normandy on 6 June 1944. The deception was to distract the Germans' attention and make them think that Montgomery was up to something in the Mediterranean. It was 'a large performance', as Anthony Burgess wrote, 'apt for the theatricality of the British soul'.

But the reality of the war was now elsewhere: the bloody last acts of the real struggle had moved on. Gibraltar was becoming a diversionary stage-set, suitable for elaborate, well-acted falsehoods, like the *Olterra*, revealed as a sham after the Italian armistice in September 1943. In the tunnels, the unused hospitals were beginning to rust and the provisions were turning putrid. In the boarded-up shops on Main Street where more food was stored, the rats pullulated.

'We were out of the war,' Burgess wrote of his latter days in Gibraltar: 'It was something remote to be followed on maps, or seen, in a stench of oranges, at the cinema. On June 4, 1944, allied forces entered Rome . . . The Russians took Minsk. The Western allies took Caen. The Americans took Guam. Warsaw rose. Mytkina fell. Paris was liberated. Marseilles was taken. Rumania surrendered. Holland was entered . . .'

The Gibraltarian evacuees started returning on 6 April 1944, when the SS *Duchess of Richmond* and SS *Antenor* berthed at Gibraltar with 1367 people, mostly women and children, coming back from the UK. One of the first ashore, Miss Elena Chini, gave a sound-bite to the *Gibraltar Chronicle* reporter: 'We are very happy to be home. We thank God and England for our safe return.' Children's voices could once again be heard echoing in the ramps, playing the old street games: tin-kicking *taco la lata*, leap-frogging *una la mula*, *shishi la haba* (or high cockalorum). It was noticeable that some of the younger kids spoke better English than their parents. With women and children back, more domestic and civilian problems pressed upon the new governor: not guns and bullets and land-mines, but housing, schools, jobs.

The streets were not yet safe in the UK. When the German V-1 and V-2 rockets started raining down on London after D-Day, Gibraltarian families were moved from the West End to bleak camps in Northern Ireland that once been occupied by the first US soldiers to cross the Atlantic. Lourdes Pitaluga found herself stranded at Warbleshinny, Clondermot Parish, County Derry. The Nissen huts were freezing cold, the thick mud glutinous, the farm rats enormous.

On 6 January 1945, the Gibraltarians finally left Ulster on the SS *Cap Tourain*. In the middle of the night a great bang knocked them out of their bunks. It was not a torpedo but a convoy collision. Twenty-two mattresses had to be stuffed roly-poly style into the gash in the hull, wedged and 'fothered', before the ship could limp on.

On 15 January, Lourdes saw land on both sides. This could only be the Strait of Gibraltar! There at last, waiting for them, was their Rock, which the religiously minded returnee Mariola Benavente thought of ever after as 'the Mountain of the Lord'. The girls and young women jumped for joy, screaming and laughing.

The reality of return was grim. 'It was horrible,' Mariola remembered, after they disembarked in alphabetical order from the *Duchess of Richmond*, 'grey and dirty, barbed wire everywhere. It was very restricted, under the military, and we couldn't go out after nine because the streets were full of soldiers, sailors and airmen who had drunk too much. The drunkenness was very bad.'

Lourdes Pitaluga's family also came back early in 1945 to find rubbish piled up in street corners and dismal news at home. The sealed-up rooms in their house that had been requisitioned by the military had been broken into and all their things looted and pilfered. Lourdes saw drunken fights in Gibraltar's streets with servicemen thrown out bodily through the window of the Royal Bar, and she remembered the tall, tough, red-capped military police taking off their webbing belts, wrapping them once or twice round their fists and then wading into crowds, flailing left and right, laying men out like flies. There were plenty of scenes like that at the war's end: Gibraltarians today still speak with awe of a massive street fight between the Gibraltar police and a mob of jug-eared Australians.

David Scherr identified two co-existing systems in Gibraltar: the military fortress and the crown colony. In wartime, 'for the duration', the fortress came first. But all wars end, and the gulf between the soldiers and the civilians would have to be bridged. The running-down of the war in Gibraltar marks the beginning of that change. What started in 1944–5 was a slow but enormous shift in the balance of power (and of land-ownership), with the ratio on the Rock transforming over the next seven decades from 90 per cent military and 10 per cent civilian to its complete opposite today, more than 90 per cent civilian and far less than 10 per cent military.

The tide of empire was receding everywhere. Sir John Shuckburgh wrote a four-volume *Colonial History of the War*, which was never published by the Colonial Office. His 'General Conclusions and Comments' are striking. Shuckburgh identified what he called 'a complete change of heart on the part of the ruling race':

The cult of 'Imperialism' was almost entirely extinguished; what had once been a high-minded political doctrine passed into a term of vulgar abuse. Britain, to all appearances, had lost all sense of pride in her Imperial position. The 'White Man's Burden' no longer made any appeal to the public imagination. The task of empire had come to be regarded as an incubus rather than an obligation.

The effect of this change of attitude at home was felt in every part of the Colonial Empire, Shuckburgh thought. Local administrators could no longer represent a faraway country that wanted to enforce its will on others. The interests of discipline and good order carried no weight against the growing body of opinion to which all concepts of empire were anathema. This was the new movement in history that the Governor of Gibraltar, General Eastwood, a military man who had been at Sandhurst with Montgomery, was struggling against.

He was like the cut-and-dried Roman centurion in the Bible, 'a man under authority, having soldiers under me: and I say to this man, Go, and he goeth; and to another, Come, and he cometh; and to my servant, Do this, and he doeth it.' But Shuckburgh saw that giving orders was not enough, and that the rules were changing for every European administrator: 'His task is to collaborate with Colonial peoples, not, as in the past, merely to direct them. He must exercise the arts of persuasion rather than of authority.'

On the morning of 8 May 1945, Regimental Sergeant Major Ben Thomas found Warrant Officer Class Two John Burgess Wilson still asleep in his army bed in the barracks at Moorish Castle and shook him awake. Cigarette smoke aspirated from Thomas as he loudly announced in his Welsh accent: 'The whole of fucking Europe is liberated, except fucking you. Come and get fucking drunk.'

It was VE Day, Victory in Europe Day, but Burgess already felt ill and headachy from getting his celebration in a day early. They were too late for breakfast in the sergeants' mess so they marched down to Casemates Square for 'a cup of chah and a wad' in the Café Trianon, a dirty place, full of rough soldiers who were already drunk and who jeered at them because with the end of the war they no longer feared or respected their rank. 'We promised them immediate transportation to the mysterious East, there to fight the Nips. The war, as Ben Thomas said, was not yet fucking over.'

The two men went to get drunk in the garrison sergeants' mess. In *A Vision of Battlements* their fictional equivalents proceed from there in a drunken taxi-cab race to the engineers' mess where the Hogarthian bacchanal continues: 'the glassy-eyed C.P.O. swaying by the bar, the naked veteran capering round the billiard table, the tubby sergeant vomiting into the open piano . . .'

Burgess was twenty-eight, smoking eighty cigarettes a day and getting drunk whenever he could. Cheap booze and fags has long been a siren song of Gibraltar. In the mess everyone was comparing their Python numbers – which calculated the time of their discharge from the army using a points system based on age, decorations, total length of service, time spent overseas, marital and familial status. The Python calculations were meant to let servicemen achieve repatriation, or spend their accumulated leave if they were regulars, or be demobilised if they were 'Hostilities Only' or a non-regular. There was also LIAP (Leave In Addition to Python) or LILAP (Leave In Lieu Of Python) which meant you got leave instead of repatriation if you volunteered to be sent overseas again. And there was LOLLI-POP: Lots Of Local Leave In Place Of Python. Burgess got the number 30 and calculated that that must mean he had another year to serve in the army before he got out in May 1946. Boredom, frustration, repression. Better have another drink and a gasper.

The two men went to the Alameda Garden Bar where there were trestle tables outside, 'burning sun . . .unbuttoned soldiery . . . spilling pints, hops floating like wood-shavings, the end of the free barrels in sight'. Tennent's was two and six a pint here and the draught was normally two shillings or 'two bob', but the donated free barrels of Simmonds and Allsops were beginning to run out and the men who did not want to pay were snarling and getting rowdy. Ben Thomas had an alcoholic vision of all the dead in Europe marching towards a bonfire to the tune of 'Cwm Rhondda', and, being Welsh, started preaching hellfire to the assembled drinkers.

Burgess left before the punch-ups between soldiers and sailors started and staggered off to the 172 Tunnelling Company bar, where he was thrown out for climbing onto the billiard-table to give a funeral oration for a cirrhotic old sergeant who had died that day of heart failure following liver failure. Richard Ennis in the novel finds himself at the Detached Mole on VE Day. Coming back to Ragged Staff steps, he falls in the water, pissed. Crouched soaking wet in a car back to the barracks, 'he heard the smashing of windows, the insulting of shopkeepers, everybody happy.'

The British Way and Purpose was cancelled for the day. Or had perhaps revealed its true face, drinking and fighting and breaking things. 'I could stand VE Day in Gibraltar no longer. It was damnably depressing.' Burgess decided to visit Fascist Catholic Spain as a refuge. No one from the British garrison could cross over to La Línea in uniform, so he put on civilian clothes. Burgess says he had 'fairly free access to Spain. One of my jobs had been to dress up as a civilian and spy on the transfer of British money to enemy agents.' But he found he had no Spanish money, so he stole four counterfeit watches from the desk of a company quartermaster sergeant he loathed and sold them for a handful of pesetas to a barman in Main Street called Frank but nicknamed *El Burro* ('the donkey') because of the size of his penis. Then Burgess walked across the hot unshaded airfield to the frontier. The mandatory gift of two tins of 'Victory' cigarettes got him past the unshaven Spanish guards.

There was no VE Day in La Línea, where VD was more likely. 'I fought off the whores, mostly war widows or the wives of political detainees, and drank alone and sadly in bar after bar.' La Línea was depressing, its poverty Moroccan.

The streets were potholed and the drains stank and ragged urchins howled for *peniques*. The town was full of mantillaed prostitutes for the servicing of British troops, and not all were habituated to the trade: there were too many young women whose husbands had been killed or imprisoned or had taken to the hills and corkwoods in defiance of the regime: they needed the pesetas for which they hired themselves out . . .

Burgess says he regretted using prostitutes. 'I still feel shame at having carried an urgency over the border to discharge in a wretched room smelling of garlic and cheap scent. And yet I have learned to associate garlic with the erotic and to feel excited in retrospect at the sound of Andalusian Spanish in the mouth of a girl.'

La Línea functioned below Gibraltar's belt, as border towns in Mexico do for the United States. The Fortress, wrote Burgess,

. . . recognised the need for carnal relief. Not only did it issue condoms, it provided a little pocket inside the fly of the service trousers for storing them, the pocket FL. It issued tubes of prophylactic ointment and had built a kind of venerean bus shelter with running water for the laving of the penis, mid-way between the Spanish frontier and the North Shore airfield.

Burgess says the troops on the whole felt friendly towards Spain.

The girls there slept with them, though for money, while the Gibraltar girls were aloof and had money enough, thank you, of their own. The Spaniards were real Iberians and the Gibraltarians merely imitation ones . . . The Gibraltarians produced no art, yet they despised their cousins over the border as ignorant serfs who lacked the benefits of britannicisation . . .

In his fiction, Burgess made La Línea a place of death as well as love. In 1989 he published a novel called *Any Old Iron*, a mock-Arthurian saga of twentieth century wars, whose title reduced Evelyn Waugh's *Sword of Honour* (and Cardinal Hinsley's 'Sword of the Spirit') to the status of a music-hall song about scrap metal. In 1944, the book's Welsh know-it-all hero, Reginald Jones, is a sergeant in the Intelligence Corps in Gibraltar, a man whose 'ludicrous' duties include inspecting the food bags of Spanish workers and ensuring that British banknotes do not fall into enemy hands. One night, drinking in La Línea, Reg meets a German consular official, also in plain clothes. Two enemies, but on neutral territory. After Wolfgang Trautwein utters anti-Semitic obscenities, Reg Jones murders him in the squalid alley behind the bar, stabbing him in the back as he urinates against the wall. The ensuing comedy, such as it is, concerns the military, civil and legal shenanigans caused by an embarrassing act of war disrupting the elaborate pretences of neutrality at the frontier.

In his autobiography, Burgess is aggressively heteronormative about his wartime life in Gibraltar. But one of the striking things about the earlier novel, *A Vision of Battlements,* is its campness. Early in the prologue we meet Sergeant Julian Agate, 'ballet-dancer, one time Petrouchka praised by Stravinsky and patted by Diaghilev', a cut above the usual sergeants of the AVCC, busy with his embroidery: 'So hard, my dear, to get exactly the right silks, but it should be terribly gay when it's finished.' The slovenly Ennis, who has been pigging it in barracks at Moorish Castle, moves in with trim Agate at King's Bastion:

'My dear! The state of your underwear! . . . I must take you in hand.'

And indeed he did. He became a mother to Ennis, insisting . . . on his going early to bed, giving his soiled linen – 'it has a really *bitchy* smell' – to the Spanish daily help to scrub, to scour, to iron, watching over him while he washed in the morning. 'Behind the ears, now . . . Really, I shall have to tub you myself.'

The critic Christopher Ricks was the first to notice Anthony Burgess's interest in homosexuality in an April 1963 *New Statesman* piece called 'The Epicene'. It is there in gay Ibrahim in the Malayan trilogy, in *The Wanting Seed* ('It's Sapiens to be Homo'), in *Honey for the Bears*, in the bisexual Shakespeare of *Nothing like the Sun*, in 'that omnifutuant swine' Rawcliffe and assorted Tangier sodomites in *Enderby Outside*, in the famous opening sentence of *Earthly Powers*: 'It was the afternoon of my eighty-first birthday, and I was in bed with my catamite when Ali announced that the archbishop had come to see me.' And it is there from the very start in the cosy friendship that Richard Ennis shares with Julian Agate in *A Vision of Battlements*:

The little dinner-parties they held were gay with talk, foot-touching under the table, covert hand-holding. As they sat at the snowy table in the Winter Gardens Restaurant, digesting a meal that was as near civilised as one could hope for . . . smoking, chaffing, giggling over coffee, Ennis often felt almost happy. The world of women was far; the cool flutes of the epicene voices were soothing him to a strange peace.

Not everyone was going to get home peacefully. Biagio and Angelo D'Amato (see p. 533), the beefy Maltese-born brothers who ran the Café Universal and Embassy Club in Main Street, had been arrested on 17 July 1943 under Regulation 16(1) of the Gibraltar Defence Regulations 1939. Unsuccessfully defended by a London barrister,

Gerard Osborne Slade KC, in front of a tribunal or special 'Advisory Committee' that met over three days in late September, they were flown under guard on 7 October to Hendon Airport in England, then detained in Brixton Prison and on the Isle of Man under Defence Regulation 18B for the next nineteen months. In June 1945, they tried to come back to Gibraltar but were refused permission by the new Defence Security Officer, Colonel Philip Kirby-Green, on the grounds that they might start working for Falange Intelligence or even – implausibly – for the as yet undefeated Japanese.

The fairness of this is debatable. Biagio D'Amato certainly felt he had been treated unjustly. Exile and detention and the smear that he was a 'traitor' made him desperate to clear his name. Italian parentage did not make a man an enemy. He said that as a Maltese and a long-term resident of Gibraltar he was a loyal patriot who had supported war charities. Had he not given an entire day's takings to the Royal Navy after the loss of the *Hood*? He was a businessman, and although he admitted he had traded with both sides in the Spanish Civil War, it was his job to make money, so that was no betrayal. Increasingly he forgot that the principal case against him was based on evidence of his mixing with enemy agents in La Línea (albeit sometimes on behalf of the British), and more and more he convinced himself that the establishment in Gibraltar, the 'Rock Mafia' of rich families who ran everything, were trying to do him down.

Biagio D'Amato was an outsider, a poor Maltese boy who could not read and write, who started out with nothing, selling knickknacks from a bum-boat to tourists, but who had the brains and energy and business acumen to get a toehold in the food and drink and entertainment industry that serviced the Fortress. He did well, but, like Anthony Burgess, he always reckoned that vested interests and snobbery were against him. One member of the three-man Advisory Committee that judged his case, Mr Edward Baglietto Cottrell, the British vice consul in Algeciras, was also a director of the wine merchants Saccone and Speed, the D'Amato brothers' most powerful rival in Gibraltar's lucrative alcohol trade. Biagio D'Amato claimed his commercial rivals framed him because he was doing better than them, importing brands of Scotch and beer they did not have and then selling the empty bottles more profitably. D'Amato also suggested that Saccone and Speed had actually promised a rich reward for the right outcome to the then DSO, Lieutenant Colonel Medlam.

The case against D'Amato was already flimsy – there was no solid evidence of espionage, just circumstantial evidence of his being seen talking to people under suspicion, and three out-of-date Royal Navy signal sheets found in the D'Amato safe in July 1943 that seem to have just been scrap paper used to wrap notes or coins. In August 1945, D'Amato's lawyers in London issued writs against Edward Baglietto Cottrell as well as the other two members of the tribunal, Major Joseph Patron and Mr James Joseph Russo, alleging defamation of character and false imprisonment. Unfortunately, D'Amato now produced three letters as evidence of conspiracy against him, one each from Cottrell, Patron and Russo, denouncing D'Amato to the authorities in Gibraltar. But all three men denied writing the letters and all relevant branches of the Gibraltar bureaucracy adamantly denied receiving them. Paperwork mattered in Gibraltar and the government assiduously kept archives where such denunciations would normally be filed and minuted. Nor did the three letters themselves inspire any confidence. Their misspelling of proper names and slightly peculiar language suggest that the same hand may have forged them all.

D'Amato's best defence was the truth, that he was working for the Allies and that Desmond Bristow of SIS had asked him to spread the rumours to enemy agents. But this shrewd, uneducated businessman was so desperate to get back to Gibraltar that he may have fouled his own nest by falsifying evidence in order to prove his genuine innocence. Biagio D'Amato's case against the tribunal failed. The right even to visit Gibraltar was withheld until May 1950.

It was just another of the messes and unfairnesses of war. But all was not lost. Biagio D'Amato rebuilt his life and businesses across the frontier, contructing a four-storey hotel in La Línea in 1948, from where he could look across to the Rock, even though he was not allowed to go there.

What of the Indian boy and his cook, last seen in a life-raft made from oil drums after a British submarine torpedoed their ship in September 1940? Little Krishna Khubchand and Barsati Karya were picked up by the Germans occupying that part of France and interned with the other surviving British citizens. The first night they slept on blankets in a cinema in Bayonne. In the morning a German officer asked why a child was in with the men and ordered Krishna to be put with the Indian families, while Barsati stayed with the men. By November 1940, Krishna was being looked after by fellow vegetarians Mr and Mrs Khemchand in Royan. Hotu and Rukhmani Khemchand had pledged to drown together if their ship went down; neither could swim. But when they were torpedoed and found themselves in the water it was quite otherwise. Hotu felt weeds entangling his legs and, reaching down to free himself, found it was his pregnant wife's hair, which he grabbed hold of as he rose to the surface. Two months after being rescued they had a baby girl called Monica.

It took a long time for hard news of the Indians to get home. Worried relatives asked the Indian government what had happened to the *Kemmendine* en route to Rangoon, and what was this rumour of a German raider? Then a few garbled letters trickled out of France, sparking telegrams throughout the Sindhi merchant network. In October 1940, an employee of K. Chellaram called Vassumal sent a list of those who had perished and who had survived, with their firm's names. The survivors included 'Mr Barsati (Cook) and Kishin (child of 3 years) of Bulchand & Sons'. Another letter listed among the survivors 'Mr Valiram of Kishinchand and one son (9 years) of Mr Kubchand and his cook Chellaram'. A third, from Tarachand to Bhojraj, written in block letters and red-stamped in German *'GEPRÜFT'* ('scrutinised'), said, 'Please tell Mr Pohoomal firm that Sobhraj of Gibraltar died also sorry to write that Boolchan family is fully lost only one boy Kisha is left.'

By January 1941 the Gibraltar government had worked out that eighteen British Indians had been saved and eight lost, and Mr Chularam Bulchand, the brother of Krishna's father, was actively searching for his nephew, 'Krishin Khubchand Bulchand Daswani, 9 years old child, who is one of the survivors of the SS *Kemmendine*'. Via the American consul in Málaga, his requests ended up with the British Interests Section of the US Embassy in Paris. After the Germans had handed over a full list of the *Kemmendine* passengers, American consuls in Marseilles and Bordeaux helped to track down the Khemchands in the spring of 1941.

Mr and Mrs Hotu Khemchand, their baby daughter and an uncle, Mr Parsram Advani, together with Krishna and Barsati, were finally located at the Hotel Terminus in La Réole in the Gironde, where they had gone from Royan. Krishna was learning French and already forgetting his English and Spanish. With assistance from the Americans, they got visas to cross France and Spain and went by train down to Algeciras. There was the Rock, across the bay, and while the Khemchands put up at the Reina Cristina Hotel, Krishna took the ferry over to Waterport in Gibraltar. He was back home at 32 Irish Town for a couple of weeks of August 1941 until General Mason-MacFarlane ordered the fifty-two Indian shops to reduce their staffs to one Indian per shop. The rest had to leave for Tangier on the steam-packet *Rescue*. Krishna left with his cousin and his uncle, Mr Chularam Bulchand. Somehow though, Barsati Karya got scooped up by the British army and became a soldiers' cook in Glasgow. In Tangier, Krishna the Hindu boy attended the Christian Brothers school and only returned to his birthplace, the Rock, late in 1944.

Then, one day late in 1945, Barsati Karya turned up again in Gibraltar. The cook who once wore only pyjamas had become a dandy, arriving with twelve suits of different colours with shirts and ties and twelve pairs of shoes with socks. He drank and smoked heavily, and enjoyed women. When he got their Gibraltarian maid pregnant, Krishna's uncle Mr Bulchand had to settle a sum of money on her to get Barsati out of an unworkable marriage. But the maid kept the baby girl, and later she came round to Mr Bulchand's regularly for her pocket money.

During his adolescence, under the influence of Father Rapallo, Krishna wondered whether he ought to become a Roman Catholic like the other Gibraltarians. This wish to be a Christian stopped a wealthy Sindhi merchant from adopting him. Once, when Krishna told Barsati that he was going to church to pray, the little cook said: 'Why pray there? God is everywhere.'

Barsati Karya was only in his early thirties when he fell gravely ill. It was 1953. Krishna Khubchand was then twenty years old, but he spoke of it over sixty years later: 'I had him in my arms in his room in Irish Town. He had saliva in the mouth. He coughed and vomited . . . He drank and smoked too much, and he was not fully grown, a bit abnormal . . . But he was funny. He was a happy man. A very nice man.'

The brave little cook died in the arms of the youth he had once saved.

By the spring of 1944, the Gibraltar security situation was well under control; the Spanish had been embarrassed into pulling back their support for saboteurs; the executions of Cordon Cuenca and Muñoz at Moorish Castle were a deterrent, as was greater vigilance. The Security Intelligence Department, dubbed 'the OGPU' (after a forerunner of Russia's KGB), had their own office, the two-storey house with a terrace roof garden and a sunny patio at 10 Governor's Lane, across the road from the rear entrance to the Convent. David Scherr built a good team with Louis Bush and Billy Bulman, and together the three musketeers of the Security Intelligence Department (all now recruited into MI5) felt they had beaten off the enemy agents and Axis saboteurs who threatened Gibraltar. Their work had been greatly helped by the arrival in August 1943 of Subaltern (equivalent to Lieutenant) Betty Durnford of the Auxiliary Territorial Service or ATS, the women's branch of the army, who reorganised their records to cope with the huge increase in carding, copying and typing required.

In January 1944 Junior Commander (equivalent to Captain) Mollie Spencer came back to Gibraltar to become David Scherr's secretary. Reliable, accurate and serious about confidential work, now it was Spencer who was trusted to type the many reports to MI5 head office, to MI6, to Section V HQ and out-stations. She was busy socially. There were nurses at the hospital and WRNS at the 'Wrennery', but there were only four ATS on the Rock at that time, and as the most senior (and the most personable), Mollie Spencer was often called to the Convent to make up female numbers when the governor was entertaining important guests.

Security was now so tight on the Rock that Spanish agents of the German Abwehr began exporting their deadly wares to the UK instead. On 10 February 1944, Colonel Victor Rothschild, the head of MI5's anti-sabotage branch, BI(c), found himself dismantling yet another bomb sent from Spain. Rothschild was a biologist, used to dissecting the sperm and eggs of sea-urchins, so he was well able to micro-manipulate fuses and timers. As he settled down to take apart a suspicious crate of Spanish onions in a field near Northampton he dictated his actions into a field telephone for Miss Cynthia Shaw to write down, so that in the event of his being blown up, other bomb-disposal colleagues would not repeat the mistake. The transcript begins:

It is a crate in three compartments. The right-hand compartment has onions in it. The middle compartment also appears to have onions in it. The left-hand compartment has already had most of the onions taken out but I can see right at the bottom in the left-hand corner of the left-hand compartment one characteristic block of German TNT. Next to it is some material which looks rather like plastic explosive . . .

The transcript ends:

I am now going to start trying to take this plastic explosive to pieces. I see a primer inside one of them. I am going to try and take that out. I have taken the primer out and I can now see the detonator buried in the middle of the plastic.

It is a twenty-one-day Mark II German time clock. I have unscrewed the electric detonator from the Mark II delay so that one is safe. I am now going to look at the other piece of plastic.

I can just see the other Mark II delay inside the other piece of plastic.

I have taken the other primer off.

The other detonator is off.

All over, all safe now.

When Churchill got to hear of this, Victor Rothschild was awarded the George Medal. But, like its bombs, the Abwehr was coming apart. That same month, February 1944, Adolf Hitler abolished the organisation; all its foreign intelligence functions were taken over by Heinrich Himmler's metastasising SS. Wilhelm Canaris himself was arrested for alleged complicity in the July 1944 bomb plot against Hitler. Convicted of treason by an SS kangaroo court, the naked, white-haired, fifty-eight-year-old admiral was strangled by a short rope hung from an iron hook in Flossenbürg concentration camp on 9 April 1945.

Down in Gibraltar, in September 1944, David Scherr was awarded a Military Division MBE for his work. At long last, there was some time to relax, to have drinks at the Royal Gibraltar Yacht Club, to make excursions into Spain, sometimes for secret meetings and sometimes for picnics and swimming. Working together so closely, their initials typed together so often on the top of pages, DJS/MCS, it is not surprising that the boss, handsome David James Scherr, fell in love with his secretary, beautiful Mollie Clarke Spencer. But their business was secrecy; they were discreet.

The summer of 1945 was momentous. VE Day was 8 May, and the Labour Party general election landslide was on 26 July. (Churchill was out; Attlee was in; Burgess reckoned there were no Conservatives on the Rock of Gibraltar.) Newsreel pictures of the devastation of Hiroshima and Nagasaki emerged in August. Burgess said the 'ghastly flower' of the atomic bomb awed the men on the Rock.

'Nothing in the Army Bureau of Current Affairs or British Way and Purpose had prepared them for this.' VJ Day followed on 15 August. The war was over at last.

Three of the four enemies who menaced Gibraltar when the first bombs fell in 1940 were defeated: Hitler and Mussolini were dead (and Vichy's Pétain and Laval in jail, facing charges of treason). But General Francisco Franco, incredibly, had survived in Spain, though his regime continued the brutal repression of its own people. (In March 1945, the British cabinet were circulated a confidential minute from the Madrid embassy indicating that scores of people were still being shot every month, and the official attitude of HMG to the regime was held to be 'cold reserve'.) There was also no doubt that Franco had been helping the Nazi war effort by supplying Germany with vital minerals. Most important of these was tungsten/wolfram, the steel-hardening metal used in shells, armour and machine tools. When the Allies had offered to buy all his tungsten to stop it going to Germany, Franco merely doubled mining production and its price to the Allies, while continuing to sell tons of the better grade of the mineral in clandestine ways to Hitler's arms factories. In 1943 alone, the British bought over 2600 tons of inferior Spanish tungsten, paying at one point US$8000 a ton. (The price was so fabulous that the Portuguese began smuggling their own cheaper ore over the border into Spain in order to gain the same rate.) The British ended up paying Franco's regime in gold, nearly fifteen tons of it.

In 1944, SOE stuck a thumb in this optic. Refocusing now on economic warfare rather than sabotage (and disallowed by SHAEF from blowing up the French railway just north of Hendaye), SOE set a watch on just how the Germans were smuggling wolfram out of Spain via Irún and how they were substituting lead for wolfram in official stockpiles. On 28 May 1944, SOE offered convincing proof of forty tons of the mineral being smuggled illegally into German-occupied France.

But by then Churchill had given Franco a get-out-of-jail-free card. Just when the Americans and the British could jointly have been putting the squeeze on the Franco regime, their competitive rivalries for the Spanish market were driving them apart. In January 1944, the USA had stopped shipping petrol to Spain in order to force the Spanish regime to cease supplying wolfram to Nazi Germany. But Britain did not see the embargo through. In April 1944, Churchill authorised a deal ('which I shall be glad to sponsor') to restart shipping petrol to Spain, as well as allowing the Spanish to send sixty tons of wolfram a month to Nazi Germany, all in the rather shabby hope of gaining some commercial and trade advantage for the UK after the war. At its very weakest moment, on the brink of economic collapse, the Franco regime was shored up by what the Americans pointedly chose to call Winston Churchill's 'appeasement'.

On 24 May 1944, a fortnight before the D-Day landings, Churchill delivered a wide-ranging World Survey speech in the House of Commons in part of which he justified his attitude towards Franco's Spain. He looked back to June 1940 when Sir Samuel Hoare went to Madrid and when it seemed certain that Spain would join the Axis in the war against Great Britain. The Germans would then undertake 'the seizure of Gibraltar, which would then be handed back to a Germanized Spain. This last would have been easier said than done.'

Churchill continued, saying that 'if Spain had yielded to German blandishments and pressure' the burden would have been very heavy indeed. 'The Straits of Gibraltar would have been closed, and all access to Malta would have been cut off from the west. All the Spanish coast would have become a nesting-place of German U-boats.' But, he pointed out, the Spanish did not join the war. 'They had had enough of war, and they wished to keep out of it.'

The prime minister then moved on to Operation *Torch* in November 1942. 'At that moment, Spain's power to injure us was at its very highest.' The extended airfield at Gibraltar had sometimes held six hundred aircraft 'in full range and in full view of the Spanish batteries . . . However, the Spaniards continued absolutely friendly and tranquil. They asked no questions, they caused no inconveniences.' Churchill addressed himself to the Opposition benches and those supporters of the defunct Republic who detested Franco. 'I must say that I shall always consider a service was rendered at this time by Spain, not only to the United Kingdom and to the British Empire and Commonwealth, but to the cause of the United Nations. I have, therefore, no sympathy with those who think it clever, and even funny, to insult and abuse the Government of Spain whenever occasion serves.'

Perhaps a grateful Churchill felt he was settling a debt of honour to Franco, who in his way had helped Britain, but the prejudices of the old English aristocrat against the left were also reasserting themselves. Churchill feared a reversion to the blood and butchery of the Spanish Civil War if the status quo were changed. And in the finale of his 'kindly words about Spain', Churchill quashed the hopes of all those, including the Basques, the Catalans and the monarchists, who dreamed that an Allied victory might be extended to the Iberian peninsula, when he declared: 'Internal political problems in Spain are a matter for the Spaniards themselves. It is not for us – that is the Government – to meddle in such affairs.' Franco, the sly despot who hornswoggled both Adolf Hitler and Winston Churchill, carried a Spanish translation of this speech in his wallet for the last three decades of his dictatorship.

The *Generalísimo* soon wrote a grandiose letter to Churchill suggesting that Spain and Britain should unite against Russia, while querulously complaining that British agents had been interfering in Spain. Churchill rebuffed this approach, but the Americans did not. After the war, the USA signed a treaty with Spain to gain military bases, and US President Dwight Eisenhower duly visited the ageing tyrant in 1959.

But Franco had been trimming and tacking for years. When Sir Samuel Hoare paid his farewell ambassadorial visit in 1945, he saw that the pictures of Hitler and Mussolini on Franco's desk had already been replaced by those of the Pope and the President of Portugal.

★

Anthony Burgess wanted to compose music long before he thought of becoming a writer. In Gibraltar, on 21 August 1945, he completed his Sonata for Violin, Cello and Piano in G Minor. The second movement was entitled *For the Dead 1939–1945*.

Mollie Spencer and David Scherr, both in uniform, were married by the Very Reverend Dean Nason in the Moorish-looking Anglican Cathedral of Gibraltar on 25 August 1945, just three weeks after David's thirtieth birthday. Colonel Kirby-Green, the DSO, in morning dress, gave Mollie away, because her father had died not long before. Billy Bulman was best man and simply *everybody* was there, including HE the Governor and Lady Eastwood. There are 209 names on the guest list including thirty-five NCOs from the Field Security sections. There are Gibraltarians, Spaniards and Anglo-Andalusians, with names like Capurro, Carrara, Ferro, Hoare, Morro, Posso, Russo and Ryan; the double agent Charles Danino and his wife; the Gomezes, the Jimenezes. There are the WRNS, WAAFs and nurses whom Mollie knows; judges and journalists, consuls and coppers, engineers and administrators, family and friends. There are three officers from HMS *Spiraea* and three Spanish refugees, María, Petra and Alfonso, friends of Scherr's.

Everyone is smiling in the wedding photographs. The hot sun is shining. The long war is over. Hitler is vanquished. The Rock is safe, as is the all-red route. It is time for a honeymoon.

36

The Atlantic Outposts

The Second World War was the largest imperial war in human history, killing over fifty million people. As the Great War toppled thrones, so the Second World War smashed empires. The war destroyed Nazi Germany's slave empire, it destroyed Fascist Italy's African empire and it destroyed Imperial Japan's 'Greater Asia Co-Prosperity Sphere'.

The Second World War also blew apart the three-hundred-year-old British Empire. The dominions, the crown colonies, the protectorates, the mandates, the condominiums all mobilised to help 'the Mother Country', sending their people and their money to defeat Hitlerism. The British Empire and Commonweath made a glorious explosion of fireworks from 1939 to 1945, but when the show ended they all fell away. Exhausted casings, dwindling sparks, scorched sticks clattered back to earth. For the Imperial UK, victory was, in fact, defeat.

Two superpowers rose from the ash and rubble of the war: the USA and the USSR. As the Americans and the Russians began circling round each other in the Cold War, the British Empire looked old and burnt-out, and was breaking apart. Burma, Ceylon, India, Pakistan, South Africa went in 1947–8. Little fires flared briefly in the insurgencies, emergencies, and 'savage wars of peace' in hotspots like Aden, Borneo, Cyprus, Kenya, Malaya – but they too burned out. After the Suez operation failed disastrously in 1956, decolonisation and independence broke off more than two dozen lands. New nationalisms impelled what Harold Macmillan in 1960 called 'the wind of change'.

By January 1965, when the Thameside cranes bowed their heads to Sir Winston Churchill's coffin on its way up-river to the village churchyard by Blenheim Palace, the great mass of British hunting pink that once covered two-fifths of the globe in the atlases of pre-war schoolchildren was rubbed out. The British Empire had passed into history, and was now one with Nineveh and Tyre, 'the glory that was Greece, and the grandeur that was Rome'.

The British Commonwealth stood in its stead: exploitation slowly evolved into co-operation. The greatest legacy to the world of the British Empire was the English language. All that remains of the actual British Empire now are the dots of BOTs – the British Overseas Territories in Antarctica, the Atlantic and Indian Oceans, the Caribbean, and the peninsula of Gibraltar at the mouth of the Mediterranean.

There is a postscript to Gibraltar's stance on the world stage in the Second World War. On Christmas Eve 2015, *The Times* ran a full-page obituary of Rear Admiral John Mackenzie RN, who had just died, aged eighty-six. The obituary focused on Mackenzie's final command, living at the Mount as Flag Officer, Gibraltar. Mackenzie's historic moment came on 2 April 1982, when Argentina seized the British Falkland Islands in the South Atlantic by force, claiming sovereignty over *las islas Malvinas*. By chance, the bulk of the active Royal Navy fleet was at Gibraltar for naval exercise Springtrain, and the Rock suddenly became the vital staging post for the Task Force that embarked for the South Atlantic.

The people of Gibraltar were galvanised by the Falklands/ Malvinas crisis because they and their Chief Minister, the lawyer and ex-gunner Sir Joshua Hassan GBE KCVO LVO QC, understood the scenario exactly. An isolated British Overseas Territory, a tiny relic of empire, had been invaded by the Spanish-speaking neighbour, a military dictatorship seeking a popular victory over an outside enemy to cover up its own internal problems. It could easily have happened to the Gibraltarians in the Second World War, and could still threaten the Rock again one day.

When the Falklands/Malvinas war broke out in April 1982, the peninsula of Gibraltar had been cut off from the mainland for over a dozen years, and was almost as much an island as the ones in the South Atlantic. General Franco had closed the border at La Línea in 1969, severing the links between Gibraltar and Spain, including the telephone lines. Ironically, this amputation had the effect of making Gibraltar more British and less Spanish. The peninsula had also been forced to turn to Morocco for transport links, for food supplies and for workers, just as it had done during the sieges of the eighteenth century. More Muslims walked the old streets of Jebel-el-Tarik; they now make up 5 per cent of the population. Even though the aged Franco had died seven years earlier in November 1975 and the Socialist government then in power in Spain was hoping to join NATO and the EEC, the frontier would not open a crack until December 1982.

In London, the First Sea Lord, Admiral Sir Henry Leach, immediately grasped the situation. His father had been the captain of HMS *Prince of Wales* who went down with his battleship when Japanese aircraft sank it in December 1941, and the son was a fighter too. Leach had nearly been sacked for campaigning against the Conservative Defence Minister John Nott's cuts to the Royal Navy, and now he seized the opportunity to spurn defeatism and arrest further decline.

In full naval uniform, Leach went to Prime Minister Margaret Thatcher's office in the House of Commons. Although the Falkland Islands were nearly eight thousand miles away, he urged her to retake them: 'Since here was a clear, imminent threat to a British overseas territory that could only be reached by sea, what the hell was the point in having a navy if it was not used for this sort of thing?'

Mrs Thatcher's decision to send a task force of a hundred ships with eight thousand servicemen to liberate the Falkland Islands from illegal Argentine occupation was courageous because it was so risky. In the end, Operation *Corporate* cost the lives of 649 Argentines, 255 British military personnel and three Falkland Islanders, but it freed the eighteen hundred inhabitants from the Argentine military dictatorship and re-established their British sovereignty. On the

Nuremberg principle that acts of aggression like Argentina's were illegal, the British reaction to the invasion met the criteria of 'a just war'. It also helped topple the military junta in Buenos Aires, impelling the restoration of democracy in Argentina in 1983. This in turn enabled the National Commission on the Disappearance of Persons (Conadep) to investigate the Argentine dictatorship's many crimes, including kidnapping, murder, rape, theft and torture, as published in its distressing report *Nunca Más (Never Again)*.

The mission to free the Falklands was largely naval and 70 per cent of the casualties occurred at sea. The British task force was cobbled together for the seventy-four-day campaign: more than half the ships were requisitioned. The fighting head required a long tail and the old imperial outposts, Gibraltar and Ascension Island, became vital places for equipping, maintaining, manning, reorganising and protecting the men, ships and planes heading south. At the Rock, the nuclear submarines *Superb* and *Spartan* arrived, then disappeared towards the Atlantic; C-130 Hercules aircraft regularly landed, loaded and unloaded, and took off. But the problem was more than logistics.

Gibraltar was to rerun many Second World War scenarios. A combination of espionage, signals intelligence, cross-border police co-operation and direct political contact between friendly leaders stopped additional Exocet missiles manufactured in France from reaching Argentina. *Operación Algeciras*, an extraordinary plan for three Argentine *Buzo Tactico* frogmen (led by the 'turned' terrorist son of a former Decima Flottiglia MAS diver) to swim underwater and plant Italian limpet mines on a British ship in Gibraltar Bay, was discreetly thwarted.

Perhaps Gibraltar's most remarkable feat in April 1982 was the intensive dockyard work that transformed SS *Uganda* in four days flat from an educational cruise vessel to a thousand-bed hospital ship destined to treat men injured in the Falklands. This event stirred childhood memories in me.

I knew the *Uganda* when she was an almost brand-new passenger ship of the British India Steam Navigation Company, following the 'all-red route' to East Africa: London–Gibraltar–Malta–Port Said–Aden–Mombasa–Tanga–Zanzibar–Dar-es-Salaam–Beira. The *Uganda*, a black ship with two white stripes around the funnel, took the Rankin family from London to Kenya in April 1954. Our mother Peg, five months pregnant with my youngest sister Trina, was travelling with three other children under six years old. John was five, I was nearly four and Sarah was nineteen months old. We saw the Rock of Gibraltar by night and the Suez Canal by day. There was no air conditioning; it was hot; we were seasick. At Mombasa, our father was waiting on the dock, waving an *East African Standard*.

In Kenya Colony and Protectorate the Mau Mau rebellion – 'the Emergency' – was ratcheting up. General Erskine's troops swept through Nairobi that month, arresting thousands of Africans for screening, fingerprinting, issuing compulsory *kipande* or passes. It was the start of a happy childhood, in the midst of a violent colonial insurgency. But that is another story.

In time, our old passenger ship SS *Uganda* was converted into an educational cruise liner, taking hundreds of uniformed schoolchildren on learning trips around Scandinavia and the Mediterranean. In the spring of 1982, the kids on cruise no. 276 were hurriedly disembarked at Naples. The *Uganda*, now STUFT, a Ship Taken Up From Trade, steamed west to Gibraltar, and was nudged by three tugs into Dry Dock No. 2 for conversion into a hospital ship on Friday 16 April 1982.

The Conservative government's cuts to the Royal Navy, which, unwisely as it turned out, had included scrapping HMS *Endurance*, the South Atlantic patrol ship protecting the Falklands, meant that HM Dockyards at Chatham and Gibraltar were also scheduled for closure or privatisation. The Gibraltarian workers all had fresh redundancy notices in their pockets, but disappointment did not stop them from working round the clock on this job. The black funnel was painted white with two large red crosses added on either side.

Five more red crosses marked *Uganda* as a hospital ship protected under the 1949 Geneva Conventions.

It was a long, hard weekend, with all hands on all decks of *Uganda*, ripping out the cruise-liner fittings and reconstituting the ship, making a reinforced helicopter deck at the stern to land the wounded, installing full hospital facilities for traumatic injuries and wards with a thousand beds for casualties. They added water-distilling equipment and a satellite communications suite too.

Uganda sailed on Monday 19 April, staffed by 135 medics from the Royal Navy hospitals at Haslar and Stonehouse. Among the volunteers was sixty-nine-year-old Dr Bruce Cooper, who as a young man had been destined for entombment in Gibraltar's 'Stay-Behind-Cave' had the Germans invaded and conquered the Rock.

Hundreds of Gibraltarians turned out for the vessel of mercy as she sailed. Bilingual themselves, they were cheering a hospital ship that would treat each wounded combatant of either side equally under the sign of the red cross, whether he be a Juan López speaking Spanish or a John Ward who spoke English.

The Falklands/Malvinas war happened more than a generation ago, but if an older working man in Gibraltar should say '*yo trabajé en el Uganda*' – 'I worked on the *Uganda*' – he deserves, and receives, respect. It is a mark of pride and honour on the Rock, where the Union Jack still flies visibly. Once again, the Gibraltarians did their bit for the British Commonwealth of Nations, which they are part of and where they feel they freely belong, rather than under a neighbour with a history of dictatorship.

Notes

This book is dedicated to the memory of three of my best friends at Christ Church, Oxford: Ewen Gordon Frere Kerr, John Julian Somerset Hope and Nicholas Henry Adam Curtis, who were all born in 1950. The lines are from John Betjeman's poem 'In Memory of Basil, Marquess of Dufferin and Ava', written in 1945 for his own friend of college days, killed in Burma while serving with the Indian Field Broadcasting Units, which was founded and led by George Lowther Steer, another member of 'The House' who did not survive the war.

1 Enemies in the Dark

Winston Churchill's 18 June 1940 speech, using the phrase 'the Battle of Britain', and ending with '. . . this was their finest hour', was delivered first to Parliament, repeated for broadcast on the BBC and published in *Into Battle* (Cassell, 1941), pp. 225–34. His 14 July speech, 'The War of the Unknown Warriors', is on pp. 247–51. W. M. Thackeray's 1844 visit to Gibraltar is described in *Notes of a Journey from Cornhill to Grand Cairo*, first published under a pseudonym in 1846. 'Chattels of the military, slaves of the fortress' is from John Masters, *The Rock* (1970), p. 380. On the Gibraltarian civilian evacuations, see T. J. 'Tommy' Finlayson, *The Fortress Came First* (Gibraltar Books, 2000) and the collection of memorabilia *'We Thank God and England'* by Joe Gingell (Gibraltar Chronicle Printing, 2011). Edward Bridges's remark about evacuation as an industry is recorded in John Colville's diary, *The Fringes of Power*, on 31 May 1940. German numbers from Karl Ries and Hans Ring, *The Legion Condor*, translated by David Johnston (Schiffer Publishing, 1992), pp. 227–8. Benito Mussolini's declaration of war speech on 10 June 1940 is summarised in *Keesing's Contemporary Archives* (hereafter KCA), p. 4087A. Viscount Templewood records the mob outside the Madrid embassy on the first page of his memoir *Ambassador on Special Mission* (Collins, 1946). Franco's secret plan to attack the Rock is described in Manuel Ros Agudo, 'Preparativos secretos de Franco para atacar Gibraltar 1939–1941', in *Cuadernos de Historia Contemporánea* 23 (2001), and the slave-labour works to achieve it in José Manuel Algarbani ,'Los bunkers del estrecho y los prisioneros republicanos' in *Almoraima* 36 (2008), and *Los caminos de los prisioneros* (2013). The figure of 22,000 Gibraltarian civilians on the Rock on 18 July 1940 is from a letter to London by the Governor Lt-Gen. Sir Clive Liddell, in the 'General Mechanics of Evacuation 1940' file in the Gibraltar National Archives (hereafter GNA), as cited in *Gibraltar: The Making of a People* (2002) by Dr Joseph Garcia. The names of those killed in the air raid are from Dorothy E. Prior, *A Short History of Loreto in Gibraltar* (Doma, 2006); Gunner Leonard's details are on the Commonwealth War Graves Commission website. I interviewed Lt-Col. John Porral in October 2016.

2 Web of Empire

The Ashley Jackson quote comes from page 4 of *The British Empire: A Very Short Introduction* (2013). 'The greatest Thoroughfare' is from a 1743 pamphlet by George Burrington urging a war with France. On 'tectonic violence', see E. F. F. Rose and M. S. Rosenbaum, *Royal Engineer Geologists and the Geology of Gibraltar*, parts 1 and 2 (Gibraltar Museum reprint, 1990). In July 2016, the Gorham's Cave complex where the Neanderthals lived in Gibraltar was made a UNESCO World Heritage site. For the Moorish occupation of Gibraltar, see Tito Benady, 'The Founding of Gibraltar' and 'Moslem Gibraltar as Described in the Ancient Chronicles' in *Gibraltar Heritage Journal* 2 (1994), both reprinted in Benady, *Essays on the History of Gibraltar* (Gibraltar Books, 2014), pp. 3–17. The Trevelyan quote is from chapter 18 of *Blenheim* (Longmans, Green, 1931), which covers the taking of Gibraltar and the great victory of 'Marbrook' in 1704. For natural history see John Cortes and Clive Finlayson, *The Flowers and Wildlife of Gibraltar* (Gibraltar Books, 1988). Details of the taking of Gibraltar in 1704 come from Ignacio Lopez de Ayala, *The History of Gibraltar*, translated by James Bell (William Pickering, 1845), E. R. Kenyon, *Gibraltar under Moor, Spaniard and Briton* (Methuen, 1938), *No Peace without Spain* (The Kensal Press, 1991) by the late J. A. C. Hugill, Sir William Jackson, *The Rock of the Gibraltarians: a History of Gibraltar* (4th edn, Gibraltar Books, 2001) and Benady, *Essays on the History of Gibraltar.* The peculiar status of Jews and Moors in Gibraltar is discussed in Sir Joshua Hassan's essay 'The Treaty of Utrecht 1713 and the Jews of Gibraltar', originally a lecture given to the Jewish Historical Society in London on 15 May 1963, and published by them as a pamphlet in 1970. Richard Ford's description of Gibraltar is in volume 2 of the 1845 first edition of *A Handbook for Travellers in Spain, and Readers at Home*, buried in the chapter on Ronda and Granada. Thomas Gibson Bowles MP published his pamphlet *Gibraltar: a National Danger* in 1901. John Drinkwater's *A History of the Late Siege of Gibraltar* is reprinted by the Naval and Military Press, and James Falkner's *Fire over the Rock: The Great Siege of Gibraltar 1779–1783* (2009) is published by Pen and Sword. The Coleridge and Byron quotes (with many other gems) are from M. G. Sanchez, *Writing the Rock of Gibraltar: an Anthology of Literary Texts, 1720–1890* (Rock Scorpion Books, 2006). For more on 'little wars', see Charles J. Esdaile, *Fighting Napoleon: Guerrillas, Bandits and Adventurers in Spain 1808–1814* (Yale, 2004). Esdaile also edited the Duke of Wellington's *Military Dispatches* for Penguin Classics in 2014. More than a thousand books have been written about Horatio Nelson in the 250 years since his birth. The list of nicknames for the Rock come from Wilbur C. Abbott's *An Introduction to the Documents Relating to the International Status of Gibraltar* (Macmillan, 1934) pp. 3–4. Mrs Seacole in Gibraltar features in chapter 8 of *Wonderful Adventures of Mrs Seacole in Many Lands* (1857). Mark Twain's 'record of a pleasure-trip', *The Innocents Abroad*, was first published in 1869. 'The swing-door of the British Empire' is from D. R. Thorpe, *Eden* (Chatto & Windus, 2003), p. 101. For the Maltese contribution see E. G. Archer, *Gibraltar, Identity and Empire* (Routledge, 2006), p. 44. Details on the Hindu traders come from Claude Markovits, *The Global World of Indian Merchants, 1750–1947: Traders of Sind from Bukhara to Panama* (Cambridge University Press, 2000) and Richard J. M. Garcia, *A Quiet Voice That Would Be Heard* (L. B. Alwani Ltd, 2014). Stephen Constantine's book *Community and Identity: the Making of Modern Gibraltar since 1704* (Manchester University Press, 2009) is a fine study of the evolution of 'the Gibraltarian'. The March 1889 'Report on the Civil Population and Smuggling in Relation to Defence' is cited on p. 236, the number of Indian traders in 1938 on p. 247. On prostitutes see Philip Howell, *Geographies of Regulation: Policing Prostitution in 19th-Century Britain and the Empire* (Cambridge University Press, 2009). Global communications details are from *Signal! A History of Signalling in the Royal Navy* by Captain Barrie Kent and *Girdle round the Earth*, Hugh Barty-King's history of Cable and Wireless. The narrative historian Barbara Tuchman wrote about exercising sea power in *The Proud Tower: a portrait of the world before the war 1890–1914* (1966), p. 132, and about Mahan's making of history in *Practicing History: Selected Essays* (1981), pp. 26–7. Rudyard Kipling's poem welcoming the USA to the imperialist club first appeared in *McClure's* magazine in February 1899. Associate Professor Yu Wanli's article 'Re-thinking China's "Sea-Power" Strategy in Modern Times' appeared in *China-US Focus* on 14 February 2011. The saga continues: see 'China weaponises disputed islands', *The Times*, 29 March 2017, p. 27. Churchill to his mother is cited in Lawrence James, *Churchill and Empire* (Phoenix, 2014), p. 23. The Kaiser's manias are explored in John C. G. Röhl's three-volume biography *Wilhelm II* (Cambridge University Press, 2014). See also Christopher Frayling, *The Yellow Peril: Dr Fu Manchu and the Rise of Chinaphobia* (Thames & Hudson, 2014). On p. 250 of *The Naval Side of British History*, first published in 1924, Sir Geoffrey Callender (the founder of the National Maritime Museum) declared Captain Mahan as the progenitor of the German navy. Churchill's comments on Algeciras come from *The World Crisis*, vol. 1, *1911– 14*, pp. 19–20.

3 Rifts in the Rock

Winston Churchill's *Marlborough: His Life and Times* was first published by Harrap in four volumes between 1933 and 1938. Dr Gareth Stockey's book *Gibraltar: 'A Dagger in the Spine of Spain?'* (Sussex Academic Press, 2009), is a brilliant study of the Gibraltar–Spain frontier. Gordon Fergusson, *Hounds Are Home: the History of the Royal Calpe Hunt* (Springwood Books, 1979) is the classic account of Anglo-Andalusian fox-hunting. Wider social significance is teased out by Jennifer Ballantine Perera in 'Pablo Larios and the Royal Calpe Hunt as Markers of Transborder Activities', *Historia Contemporánea* 41 (2010), pp. 354–71. See also José Regueira Ramos, 'Los Larios en el Campo de Gibraltar', *Almoraima* 17 (1997) and Tito Benady, 'The Larios Family', *Gibraltar Heritage Journal* 1 (1993), pp. 53–8. Double-crowned Royal Calpe Hunt buttons are displayed in the Gibraltar Museum in Bomb House Lane. Charles Harington's autobiography is entitled *Tim Harington Looks Back* (John Murray, 1940), but his depressed quote is from Fergusson, *Hounds Are Home*, p. 276. The Henry Buckley quote is from *The Life and Death of the Spanish Republic* (I. B. Tauris, 2013 edition), pp. 173–4. Details about workers from La Línea are from Isaac Benyunes, 'Gibraltar during the Spanish Civil War', *Gibraltar Heritage Journal* 2 (1994) and Julio Ponce Alberca, *Gibraltar and the Spanish Civil War 1936–1939* (Bloomsbury Academic, 2015). 'Spain was open . . .' is from *Tim Harington Looks Back*, p. 187. Details on Freemasonry are from chapter 14 of Keith Sheriff, *The Rough Ashlar: the History of English Freemasonry in Gibraltar 1727–2002* (District Grand Lodge of Gibraltar, 2002) and chapter 3 of Ponce Alberca. General Franco visited Gibraltar briefly in March 1935 on his way to a military post in Morocco and imaginative speculations about his possible plottings feature in José Beneroso Santos and Belén López Collado, 'Gibraltar, Marzo de 1935. Diseño de una Conspiración', *Almoraima* 41 (October 2014). Captain José Larios, Marquis of

Larios, Duke of Lerma published his revealing *Combat over Spain: Memoirs of a Nationalist Fighter Pilot 1936–1939* in 1966. For an interesting reading of the Spanish Falange, see Wayne H. Bowen, *Spaniards and Nazi Germany: Collaboration in the New Order* (University of Missouri Press, 2000).

4 The Abyssinian Crisis

John Curry, *The Security Service 1908–1945* (HMSO, 1999), p. 396. Modern MI5 numbers from *The Times*, 9 January 2016, p. 20; 1930s numbers from F. H. Hinsley and C. A. G. Simkins, *British Intelligence in the Second World War*, vol. 4, p. 9. 'Imperial' quote from Arnold Holt-Wilson's lecture, cited in Christopher Andrew's introduction to Curry, above, p. 7. Kell's letter is in *German Espionage in Gibraltar (including Tangier and Morocco)* in the National Archives (TNA) under KV3/239. Major-General Strong's *Intelligence at the Top: Recollections of an Intelligence Officer* was published by Cassell/Giniger in 1968. Noel Annan describes Strong on p. 3 of *Changing Enemies: The Defeat and Regeneration of Germany* (HarperCollins, 1995). Biographical details of Admiral Wilhelm Canaris from Heinz Höhne, *Canaris* (Secker & Warburg, 1979). Canaris is not a German name: the Canarisi emerged near Italy's Lake Como in the sixteenth century. One branch went to Corsica (and gave some genes to Napoleon Bonaparte), another to Greece – where the initial C became K – and a third to Germany. Stanley Baldwin's evocation of 'that wonderful Jubilee summer' is from his speech 'On the Death of King George V', broadcast on 21 January 1936 and published in *Service of Our Lives: Last Speeches as Prime Minister* (Hodder & Stoughton, 1937), p. 12. 'No evidence of an affair' from Anne Sebba, *That Woman: the Life of Wallis Simpson, Duchess of Windsor* (Weidenfeld & Nicolson, 2011), p.127. On the AGNA, see John Weitz, *Hitler's Diplomat: the Life and Times of Joachim von Ribbentrop* (Ticknor & Fields, 1992), pp. 90–3 and Dr Paul Schmidt, *Hitler's Interpreter* (William Heinemann, 1951), pp. 32–6. 'Disastrous effects' from Sir Walford Selby, *Diplomatic Twilight 1930–1940* (John Murray, 1953), p. 49. Geoffrey T. Garratt's comments on Eden and Hoare are from *The Shadow of the Swastika* (Hamish Hamilton, 1938), pp. 156–7. F. E. Smith on Sir Samuel Hoare is quoted in Piers Brendon, *The Dark Valley: a Panorama of the 1930s* (Jonathan Cape, 2000), p. 270. Mussolini's Sardinian speech was reported in KCA 1680G. Christopher Andrew tells the story of the spy in the British Embassy in Rome in *Secret Service*, pp. 402–5. Differing views on war and peace and what to do about Ethiopia are explored in Daniel Waley, *British Public Opinion and the Abyssinian War 1935–6* (Temple Smith/LSE, 1975). The footnote about the Afghans comes from a 1932 letter that Samuel Hoare wrote to Stanley

Baldwin, reprinted in Viscount Templewood, *Nine Troubled Years* (Collins, 1954), p. 125. For a less cynical view of peace, and an attack on the 'Hawks' see Philip Noel-Baker, *The First World Disarmament Conference 1932–33, And Why It Failed* (Pergamon Press, 1979) and *The Private Manufacture of Armaments* (Victor Gollancz, 1936). Sir Samuel Hoare's July speech is reported in KCA 1719 and his September speech at Geneva (*'splendide mendax'*, said G. T. Garratt) in KCA 1788–1790. Mussolini's prison metaphor is quoted in Robert Holland, *Blue-Water Empire: The British in the Mediterranean since 1800* (Penguin, 2013), p. 213. The two Italian spies are identified in the Security Service report in TNA, KV4/259, p. 56 and Giulio Pistono's SyS file is KV2/3018. Helen Hiett's internationalist autobiography is *No Matter Where* (Dutton, 1944). Churchill's comment on encouragement of Abyssinian resistance is from his volume of speeches, *Step by Step, 1936–1939*, p. 22. Admiral Cunningham's thoughts on tackling the Italian fleet are in *A Sailor's Odyssey: the Autobiography of Admiral of the Fleet Viscount Cunningham of Hyndhope* (Hutchinson, 1951), p. 176. The 1935 Mediterranean fleet reinforcements are listed in KCA 1801A. Professor Arnold Toynbee's comment comes from the *Survey of International Affairs 1935, vol. II, Abyssinia and Italy*, p. 185. Sir John Dill's comment is recorded in *The Business of War: the war narrative of Major-General Sir John Kennedy* (Hutchinson, 1957), p. 3. Hoare on Laval from Viscount Templewood, *Nine Troubled Years* (Collins, 1954), pp. 167–8. The Duff Cooper quote is from *Old Men Forget* (Hart-Davis, 1953), pp. 192–3. Churchill's description of the Abyssinian war is from his speech of 17 April 1936, 'Where Do We Stand?' in *Step by Step, 1936–1939*, p. 24. The return of the Prince of Wales in 1928 is described in *A King's Story: the Memoirs of HRH the Duke of Windsor KG*, (Cassell, 1951), p. 224. The comments of Captain Morgan of HMS *Enterprise* come from FO 371/20197, quoted in Harold G. Marcus, *Haile Selassie I: the Formative Years 1892–1936* (Red Sea Press), p. 180. The 'weeded' file on the Emperor of Abyssinia is 14/1936 in the Gibraltar National Archives, and his visit was reported in the *Gibraltar Chronicle*, 1 and 4 June 1936. Leonard Mosley writes about the trans-shipping as a 'shabby ruse' on p. 239 of *Haile Selassie, The Conquering Lion* (Weidenfeld & Nicolson, 1964). Information on the emperor's shoe size is from John Lobb & Co in St James's St, London. Ras Kassa's comments on Gibraltar come from Bahru Zewde, 'Ethiopians Abroad', in *Proceedings of XVth International Conference of Ethiopian Studies* (Hamburg, 2003). Churchill's comment on the deposed Spanish monarch Alfonso XIII is from his *Great Contemporaries* (1941 reprint), p. 169. A photograph of the Duke of Gloucester's tall delegation appears opposite p. 76 of Wilfred Thesiger's *Danakil Diary: Journeys through Abyssinia 1930–34* (Flamingo, 1998). The

Addis Ababa hunt details are taken from G. L. Steer, *Caesar in Abyssinia* (Hodder & Stoughton, 1936), p. 403. King Edward VIII's reaction to receiving Haile Selassie is from p. 296 of *A King's Story* where he adds a malicious story about Stanley Baldwin's embarrassment re the Negus too. Keith Bowers's book *Imperial Exile: Emperor Haile Selassie in Britain 1936–1940* (Brown Dog Books, 2016) tells the whole melancholy story well. The Channon quote is from *Chips: the Diaries of Sir Henry Channon*, ed. Robert Rhodes James (Phoenix, 1993 edn), p. 63. David Lloyd George's speech about Abyssinia is reported in KCA 2153.

5 Rebellion of the Right

Julio Ponce Alberca's *Gibraltar and the Spanish Civil War, 1936–39: Local, National and International Perspectives*, translated by Irene Sánchez González, and published by Bloomsbury Academic in 2015, is outstanding. The Bowers story features in Reg Reynolds, *Gibraltar Connections* (Guideline, 1999), pp. 224–7. Mariola Summerfield, née Benavente, shared her memories with me in March 2016. Official documents from GNA file 240/1936 'Military Rising in Spain July 1936'. The Annual figures come from George Hills, *Franco: The Man and his Nation* (Robert Hale, 1967), p. 124. On the use of poison gas in Morocco see Sebastian Balfour, *Deadly Embrace: Morocco and the Road to the Spanish Civil War* (Oxford, 2002) and María Rosa de Madariaga and Carlos Lázaro Ávila, 'Guerra química en el Rif (1921–1927)', in *Historia 16*, no. 324 (April 2003), pp. 50–85. For a critique of their figures and conclusions see Colonel Jesús Albert Salueña, 'Armas químicas en el Rif', in *La Aventura de la Historia*, año 17, no. 199 (May 2015), pp. 16–22. The number of people Franco's rebels shot in Morocco on the night of 17/18 July is from Paul Preston, *The Spanish Holocaust* (Harper Press, 2012), p. 133, supported by detailed footnote 10 on p. 566. Proportion of forces the rebels controlled is from Sebastian Balfour, p. 271. The strategic importance of the Strait of Gibraltar is made clear in Michael Alpert, *La Guerra Civil Española en el Mar* (Crítica, 2008) and the key role of radio operator Benjamin Balboa is told in Daniel Sueiro's remarkable investigation *La flota es roja* (Argos Vergara, 1983; Ediciones Silente, 2009). *Cabo de Quilates* murders from G. L. Steer's masterpiece, *The Tree of Gernika: a Field Study of Modern War* (Hodder & Stoughton, 1938, and Faber Finds, 2009), pp. 79–80. Hugh Thomas figures from *The Spanish Civil War* (3rd edn, Pelican, 1979), p. 243. It is curious that British Vice Admiral Sir Peter Gretton's well-researched book on the Royal Navy in the Spanish Civil War, *El Factor Olvidado: la Marina Británica y la Guerra Civil Española* (Editorial San Martin, 1984) can only be read in

Spanish. For more on Major Hugh Pollard, see Peter Day, *Franco's Friends: How British Intelligence Helped Bring Franco to Power in Spain* (Biteback, 2011) and Ángel Viñas, *La Conspiración de General Franco* (Critica, 2011). Jay Allen's experiences are described in Gamel Woolsey, *Death's Other Kingdom: a Spanish Village on the Eve of the Civil War* (1939), pp. 24–6, Paul Preston, *We Saw Spain Die: Foreign Correspondents in the Spanish Civil War* (Constable, 2008), p. 299 and the *Gibraltar Chronicle*, 20 July 1936, p. 4. Details of units and early movements from Victor Hurtado, *Atlas de la Guerra Civil Espanola: La Sublevación* (Dau, 2011). La Línea incidents from the catalogue of the 2013 exhibition *Civilización y Barbarie: las metaforas de la Guerra Civil en el Campo de Gibraltar*, written by José Manuel Algarbani. He reckons 150 died in La Línea fighting; the contemporaneous *Gibraltar Chronicle* estimated 90. Povar's participation is cited in Larios, *Combat over Spain*, p. 24. Cross-border details in July 1936 from Cecilia Baldachino and Tito Benady, *The Royal Gibraltarian Police 1830–2005* (Gibraltar Books, 2005), pp. 42–5. F. Yeats-Brown's alleged crucifixions are in the 'Arriba España!' chapter of his ultra-rightist *European Jungle* (Eyre & Spottiswoode, 1939), p. 307. The royal view of *Potemkin* is from Kenneth Rose, *King George V* (Weidenfeld & Nicolson, 1983), p. 320. *The Somerville Papers* (Scolar Press, 1995), edited by Michael Simpson, are vol. 134 in the publications of the Navy Records Society. The description of the *Gibraltar Chronicle* is from George Orwell, *Diaries* (Harvill Secker, 2009), p. 80. The Carl von Clausewitz quote is from the 1993 Everyman's Library edition of *On War*, edited and translated by Michael Howard and Peter Paret, p. 100. Gamel Woolsey's description of arson is from chapter 5 of *Death's Other Kingdom*, Laurie Lee's from chapter 11 of *As I Walked Out One Midsummer Morning* (Andre Deutsch, 1969).

6 Death from the Air

Colonel Beattie's handwritten notes of the Kindelán–Brooks meeting are in the 'Military Rising in Spain, July 1936' file in the Gibraltar National Archives, GNA 240/1936. José Larios's admission that his sister Talia was working for Nationalist Intelligence is on page 124 of his book *Combat over Spain*. In the uncensored 1982 Planeta edition of his civil war memoir *Mis Cuadernos de Guerra*, Alfredo Kindelán says he was 'welcomed' ('*bien acogido por los ingleses*') in Gibraltar and that he telephoned 'an official account of the Movement' to Hitler, Mussolini and Alfonso XIII from the Rock. The mission to see Hitler is from Gerald Howson, *Arms for Spain* (John Murray, 1998), pp. 17–18 and Paul Preston, *Franco: a biography* (HarperCollins, 1993), pp. 158–60. The 'probable' presence of Admiral Canaris is alleged on page 32 of Ian Colvin, *Chief of Intelligence* (Victor Gollancz, 1951). For more on the enigmatic Wilhelm Canaris see Hugh Trevor-Roper's essay 'Admiral Canaris' in *The Philby Affair* (William Kimber, 1968) and Heinz Höhne's magisterial biography, translated by J. Maxwell Brownjohn, *Canaris* (Secker & Warburg, 1979), with his character admirably filleted by David Kahn in *Hitler's Spies: German Military Intelligence in World War II* (Hodder & Stoughton, 1978), pp. 226–36. The Félix Urtubi Ercilla story is from Håkan Gustavsson's website 'Air War in the Spanish Civil War 1936–39', http://surfcity.kund.dalnet.se/scw-1936.htm. Jay Allen's interview with Franco is described in Preston, *We Saw Spain Die*, p. 299. The names of executed Freemasons in La Línea are from Keith Sheriff, *The Rough Ashlar*, p. 254. Details of initial German weaponry supplied to Spanish rebels is from Raymond L. Proctor, *Hitler's Luftwaffe in the Spanish Civil War* (Greenwood Press, 1983) and Ries and Ring, *The Legion Condor*. For an overview, see chapter 6 of James S. Corum, *The Luftwaffe: Creating the Operational Air War, 1918–1940* (University Press of Kansas, 1997), pp. 182–223. Admiral Pipon's draft letter is in the 'Military Uprising' file in the Gibraltar National Archives; the Impartiality Ordinance was published in the *Gibraltar Chronicle & Official Gazette* (in both English and Spanish) on 10 August 1936. Joshua Hassan details from his political biography by Sir William Jackson and Francis Cantos, *From Fortress to Democracy* (Gibraltar Books, 1995). The numbers of people killed in Rio Tinto mining villages from Preston, *The Spanish Holocaust*, p. 151. The Trujillo to Hall quote is from David Avery, *Not on Queen Victoria's Birthday: the Story of the Rio Tinto Mines* (Collins, 1974), p. 374. Sterling figures from Duchess of Atholl, *Searchlight on Spain* (Penguin, 3rd edn, June 1938), p. 229. Hitler's comment about Spanish ore on 27 June 1937 was reported in the Nazi newspaper *Völkischer Beobachter*, KCA 2637D. Victor Gollancz published Arthur Koestler's *Spanish Testament*, with an introduction by the Duchess of Atholl, for the Left Book Club in 1937. Ian Gibson, *Queipo de Llano: Sevilla, verano de 1936* (Grijalbo, 1986) reprints the general's radio talks of July and August. Gerald Brenan's *Personal Record 1920–1972* (Jonathan Cape, 1974) tells the anecdote of Don Carlos Crooke Larios on p. 316. General Ritter von Thoma's 1945 talk with Basil Liddell Hart is in chapter 10, 'The Rise of Armour', in *The Other Side of the Hill* (Cassell, revised edition, 1951). In November 1942, General von Thoma of the Deutsches Afrika Korps was captured; see David Hunt, *A Don at War* (William Kimber, 1966), p. 141. On his flight back to England as a VIP PoW, he dined at Government House in Gibraltar. But while at Trent Park country-house prison with other senior German officers von Thoma was secretly bugged, revealing the names of Francoists who had maps and plans of Gibraltar Fortress. See *Tapping Hitler's Generals: Transcripts of Secret Conversations*

1942–45, edited by Sönke Neitzel (Frontline, 2013) and Helen Fry, *The M Room: Secret Listeners Who Bugged the Nazis* (Marranos Press, 2012). Neitzel and Fry also appeared in the Channel 4 docu-drama *Spying on Hitler: the Secret Recordings* (7 May 2013). Hugh Trevor-Roper drew on the transcripts of Thoma's eavesdropped revelations for his vivid sketch of Hermann Göring in *The Last Days of Hitler*. John Norris, *88mm FlaK 18/36/37/41* (Osprey New Vanguard 46, 2007) describes the famous gun. North American interest in new weaponry is noted in Kim M. Juntunen's MA thesis, 'US Army Attachés and the Spanish Civil War 1936–1939: the gathering of technical and tactical intelligence' (DTIC, 4 May 1990). Wesley K. Wark's essay 'British Intelligence and Small Wars in the 1930s', *Intelligence and National Security*, vol. 2, issue 4 (1987), points out the embarrassing British failure to learn from anything contradicting their own doctrines: new tactics were simply 'misuse'. On the 88 mm in North Africa see F. H. Hinsley *et al.*, *British Intelligence in the Second World War*, vol. 2 (HMSO, 1981), p. 707 and Omar N. Bradley, *A Soldier's Story* (The Modern Library, 1999), p. 41. On Spanish cryptologists, see Wladyslaw Kozaczuk, *Enigma* (Arms & Armour Press, 1984), p. 93, note 3. US supplies to Franco from Anthony Beevor, *The Battle for Spain* (Weidenfeld & Nicolson, 2006), p. 138 and Gerald Howson, *Arms for Spain: the Untold Story of the Spanish Civil War* (John Murray, 1998), pp. 73–4. Bland Line supplies from Gareth Stockey, *Gibraltar: 'A Dagger in the Spine of Spain?'* (Sussex, 2009), pp. 100–1. Pablo de Azcárate's memoir, *Mi embajada en Londres durante la guerra civil española*, with a prologue by Ángel Viñas, was republished by Ariel in 2012.

7 Deutschland über Alles

G. T. Garratt's *Mussolini's Roman Empire* was published as the second 'Penguin Special' in February 1938, two months after the first, Edgar Ansel Mowrer's *Germany Puts the Clock Back*. The Chamberlain quote is from *The Times* Parliamentary report, 26 June 1937, 8c. Churchill's plague-on-both-houses speech is in *Step by Step, 1936–1939*, pp. 95–7. Lord Halifax's defence of Non-Intervention is in *Documents on British Foreign Policy*, series 2, vol. 17, p. 541. J. B. Priestley's characterisation of the English is from *Rain upon Godshill: a Further Chapter of Autobiography* (Heinemann, 1939), p. 218. The Harington quotes are from *Tim Harington Looks Back*, pp. 191–4. Noel Monks describes Franco and the guns in the 'War in Spain' chapter of his autobiography *Eye Witness* (Frederick Muller, 1955). Randolph Churchill is quoted in Piers Brendon, *The Dark Valley* (Jonathan Cape, 2000), p. 301. I have drawn on Ries and Ring, *The Legion Condor*, Raul Arias Ramos and

Lucas Molina Franco, *Atlas Ilustrado de la Legión Cóndor* (Susaeta, n.d.), and Stefanie Schüler-Springorum, *La guerra como aventura: La Legión Cóndor en la guerra civil española 1936–1939* (Alianza, 2014). There is a huge literature on the bombing of Gernika. G. L. Steer's *The Tree of Gernika* and Herbert R. Southworth's *Guernica! Guernica! a Study of Journalism, Diplomacy, Propaganda and History* (California, 1977) are two of the best. Some recent books with new insights are Xabier Irujo's magisterial *El Gernika de Richthofen: un ensayo de bombardeo de terror* (Gernika Peace Museum, 2012), *Gernika: 26 de abril de 1937* (Crítica, 2017), and a vivid collage of Basque eyewitness and survivor accounts collected by William L. Smallwood, *The Day Guernica Was Bombed* (Gernika Peace Museum, 2012). Alberto de Onaindia described his experience in his autobiography *Hombre de paz en la guerra* (Ekin, 1973), cited on pp. 138–9 of Herbert R. Southworth's book. Aircraft carrier details from *Ark Royal: the Admiralty Account of her Achievement* (HMSO, 1942) and Viscount Templewood (Sir Samuel Hoare), *Nine Troubled Years* (Collins, 1954), p. 213. Naval construction figures and finance from Cabinet minutes, 17 February 1937, CAB/23/87. For the first cracking of Italian Enigma messages see Mavis Batey, *Dilly: The Man Who Broke Enigmas* (Dialogue/Biteback, 2009) pp. 59–64. José Ramón Soler Fuensanta *et al.*, 'Spanish Enigma: a History of the Enigma in Spain', *Cryptologia* 34 (2010), pp. 301–28 tracks the original machines that Franco bought from Germany, two of which, found in a cupboard, were handed over to GCHQ at a ceremony in the Spanish Army Museum in the Alcázar of Toledo in March 2012. Patrick Beesly's excellent *Very Special Intelligence: The Story of the Admiralty's Operational Intelligence Centre 1939–1945* was first published in 1977. The Greenhill Books reprint of 2000 contains a new introduction by W. J. R. Gardiner and a new afterword by Ralph Erskine. Churchill on 'red terror' in Málaga is in *Step by Step*, pp. 118–21. Antonio Bahamonde y Sánchez de Castro first published his shocking indictment *Un Año con Queipo* in 1938. It was translated as *Memoirs of a Spanish Nationalist* by United Editorial in February 1939. The invented atrocity story is also cited in K. W. Watkins, *Britain Divided: the Effect of the Civil War on British Political Opinion* (Nelson, 1963). Sir Ivone Kirkpatrick was Head of Chancery at the British Embassy in Berlin from 1933 to 1939 and knew all the top Nazis; the *Bengal Lancer* story is on p. 97 of his memoirs *The Inner Circle* (Macmillan, 1959). Details of the *Deutschland* funeral in Gibraltar and the *Admiral Scheer* visit are from Paul Baker, 'The Deutschland Incident', *Gibraltar Heritage Journal* 9 (2002), pp. 71–87. There are interesting photographs of the funerals in Roger James Bender, *Condor Legion: Uniforms, Organization and History* (RJB Publishing, 1992), pp. 47–57.

8 Guns over Gibraltar

The parliamentary debates about the guns over Gibraltar are drawn from *The Times*, Hansard and KCA. One of Churchill's speeches mentioning the guns is in *Step by Step*, pp. 155–8. The *Lepanto* incident is described in Luis Bolín, *Spain: the Vital Years* (Cassell, 1967), p. 175. A copy of the March 1938 *Madrid* story, with full translation into English, is in the GNA year files. Information about G. T. Garratt comes from his book jackets, the *ODNB* and a story in the October 2012 issue of *The Pioneer*, the journal of the Royal Pioneer Corps Association, marking the seventieth anniversary of the Pembroke Dock explosion. Admiral Rolf Carls on world war is in the Nuremberg Tribunal report, *Trial of the Major War Criminals*, vol. 19, p. 410, also in *Nazi Conspiracy and Aggression* (US Gov. Printing Office, 1946), vol. 4, pp. 828–9. Edmund Ironside as model for Richard Hannay is described in Janet Adam-Smith, *John Buchan: a Biography* (Rupert Hart-Davis, 1965), pp. 253–4 with further details from John C. Cairns's entry on the field marshal in the *Oxford DNB*. In *The Ironside Diaries, 1937–1940* (Constable, 1962), edited by Rory Macleod and Denis Kelly, the trip to Germany is on pp. 26–32. Hitler's Nuremberg speech is reported in KCA 2739D. Reichenau's directive is on pp. 209–10 of Martin Gilbert, *The Holocaust: a Jewish tragedy* (Fontana/Collins, 1987). See also p. 280 and footnote 710 of Sönke Neitzel and Harald Welzer, *Soldaten: On Fighting, Killing and Dying* (Simon & Schuster, 2013). Reichenau's July 1938 lecture at Leipzig (which was circulated to the British Cabinet) is in Hugh Thomas, *The Spanish Civil War*, p. 829. Ian Kershaw reports Hitler's 'Jewish-Bolshevik' speech in *Hitler 1936–1945: Nemesis* (Allen Lane/Penguin Press, 2000), p. 39. Ewan Butler's biography, *Mason-Mac: the Life of Lieutenant-General Sir Noel Mason-MacFarlane*, was published by Macmillan in 1973. Sir Nevile Henderson, *Failure of a Mission: Berlin 1937–1939* (Hodder & Stoughton, 1940) is interesting. Halifax encounters Hitler and Göring in chapter 9 of Andrew Roberts, *'The Holy Fox': the Life of Lord Halifax* (Weidenfeld & Nicolson, 1991). Von Fritsch was framed by the Gestapo as a homosexual and von Blomberg disgraced for marrying a prostitute. Five pornographic images of the latter's unblushing bride in lewd postures with a naked bald man are on page 348 of Max Williams, *Heinrich Himmler: a Photo History of the Reichsführer-SS* (Fonthill, 2014).

9 Scrabbling on the Brink

The Duke of Alba's protest about the reporting of Queipo de Llano's speech is from *The Times*, 3 February 1938, p. 13d. GNA file 116/1938 covers the same incident. Details about the German instructors at San Roque are from chapter 11 of Lucas Molina Franco and José-Maria Manrique García, *Soldiers of Von Thoma: Legion Condor Ground Forces in the Spanish Civil War 1936–1939* (Schiffer Military History, 2008). The book includes a photo of the La Línea parade on p. 149. The picture of the sixteen admirals is opposite p. 204 of *Tim Harington Looks Back*. Somerville's letter to his wife is from *The Somerville Papers*, p. 23 and details of the *Baleares* rescue, p. 26. The torpedo rumour is on p. 189 of Admiral Cunningham's *A Sailor's Odyssey*. Alfred A. Knopf first published William L. Shirer's *Berlin Diary: the Journal of a Foreign Correspondent 1934–1941* in 1941. The number of post-*Anschluss* suicides is from John Weitz's life of Ribbentrop, *Hitler's Diplomat* (Ticknor & Fields, 1992), p. 159. George Orwell's review of Hitler's *Mein Kampf* appeared in the *New English Weekly* on 21 March 1940 and is reprinted in the Everyman *Essays*, edited by John Carey in 2002, and also in *Seeing Things as They Are* (Harvill Secker, 2014), edited by Peter Davison. Geoffrey Household's autobiography is *Against the Wind* (Michael Joseph, 1958). *The Man Who Killed Hitler* was published by T. Werner Laurie in the UK and G. P. Putnam in USA, and its 'anonymous' authors were the American journalist Dean Southern Jennings, the German actress Ruth Landshoff-Yorck and the writer David S. Malcolmson. I am indebted to pp. 105–10 of Gareth Stockey's invaluable *Gibraltar: 'A Dagger in the Spine of Spain?'* for information about the *Baleares* memorial service, the pro-Republican rally that followed and the 'Burgos Office' party. The GNA file on that last embarrassing event is no longer in its box. Nationalist justifications are in Julio Ponce Alberca, *Gibraltar and the Spanish Civil War*, pp. 128–30. Pablo Larios funeral details from Fergusson, *Hounds Are Home*, pp. 301–2. The Marquesa de Povar's spying activities are discussed in the *German Espionage in Gibraltar* file in TNA, KV3/239, though her own GNA file is so thin as to have become almost non-existent. Czech crisis details from the relevant Keesing's Contemporary Archives; Sir Nevile Henderson's *Failure of a Mission*; Ewan Butler's biography *Mason-Mac*; chapter 12, 'The Road to Munich' of William L. Shirer, *The Rise and Fall of the Third Reich* (Secker & Warburg, 1960); chapter 5, 'Munich, 1938' of Ivone Kirkpatrick, *The Inner Circle* (Macmillan, 1959). An account of the whole year, month by month, is Giles Macdonogh, *1938: Hitler's Gamble* (Constable, 2009). A fascinating bilingual study of the wireless broadcasts then is David Vaughan, *Battle for the Airwaves: Radio and the 1938 Munich crisis/ Bitva o vilny: rozhlas v mnichovské krizi* (Cook Publications, 2014) which contains a CD with actuality in English, Czech and German. On the movements of his masterpiece, see *Picasso's Guernica* by Herschel B. Chipp (University of California Press, 1988), pp. 156–7. Churchill writes about Munich in *The Gathering Storm*, volume 1 of *The Second World War*; his superb 5 October 1938 speech is omitted from the collection *Step by Step, 1936–1939*, but was published in *The Speeches of Winston Churchill*, edited by David Cannadine (Penguin, 1990), pp. 129–43. Its howling down was witnessed by Douglas Dodds-Parker in his SOE book *Setting Europe Ablaze* (Springwood Books, 1984), p. 17. Anthony James's study of British government pamphlets, *Informing the People*, was published by HMSO in 1996. Ironside's arrival in Gibraltar, with the Hebrew Community and other speeches, is in GNA file MP 163/1938. For more eyewitness accounts of *Kristallnacht* see *The Night of Broken Glass*, edited by Uta Gerhardt and Thomas Karlauf (Polity Press, 2012). Kenneth Strong recalled the passport queue in *Intelligence at the Top: the Recollections of an Intelligence Officer* (Cassell/Giniger, 1968), p. 39. On the *José Luis Díez* incident see articles by Luis Romero Bartumeus in *Almoraima* 29 (2003), pp. 509–25 and Dennis Beiso in *Gibraltar Heritage Journal* 10 (2003), pp. 9–24. The Falangist letter to the *Gibraltar Chronicle* is quoted in chapter 3 of the *History of the Security Intelligence Department of the Defence Security Office Gibraltar 1939–1945*, TNA KV4/259. Ivan Maisky quote from *The Maisky Diaries 1932–1943*, edited by Gabriel Gorodetsky (Yale, 2015), p. 157. Ciano quote from *Ciano's Diary 1939–1943*, edited by Malcolm Muggeridge (Heinemann, 1947), p. 57. Roosevelt quote from Claude Bowers, *My Mission to Spain: Watching the Rehearsal for World War II* (Gollancz, 1954), p. 418. President Roosevelt also told his cabinet that the embargo on the Spanish Republic had been 'a grave mistake' on 27 January 1939; see Dominic Tierney, *FDR and the Spanish Civil War* (Duke University Press, 2007), p. 86. A short history of the Gibraltar Defence Force from 1938 to 1941 is in TNA, WO 176/167 and General Liddell's report on Gibraltar's defences is WO 32/ 11196. On MI5 worries about Sir Edmund Ironside see Stephen Dorril, *Blackshirt: Sir Oswald Mosley and British Fascism* (Viking, 2006) p. 469. German armaments production doubling from Adam Tooze, *Wages of Destruction: the Making and Breaking of the Nazi Economy* (Viking, 2007), p. 347.

10 The Disrupters

The Somerville Papers (Scolar Press/Navy Records Society, 1995), Michael Simpson's essay in the *ODNB* and Donald Macintyre, *Fighting Admiral: the Life of Admiral of the Fleet Sir James Somerville* (Evans Bros, 1961) are basic sources of information about this great sailor. For the history and dates of RDF/radar see J. G. Crowther and R. Whiddington, *Science at War* (HMSO, 1947), pp. 1–90. The Milch anecdote is from Peter Townsend, *Duel of Eagles* (1970), as quoted in the RAF Benevolent Fund booklet *A Short History of*

Royal Air Force Bentley Priory (1990). It also appears in Len Deighton's excellent *Battle of Britain* (Jonathan Cape, 1980). Udet revealing Rechlin is from A. Scott Berg, *Lindbergh* (Macmillan, 1998), p. 368. For more on the DMWD 'Wheezers and Dodgers', see Gerald Pawle, *The Secret War* (Harrap, 1956), introduced by Nevil Shute. Adam Sisman's *Hugh Trevor-Roper: the biography* (Weidenfeld & Nicolson, 2010) is superb. 'Sideways into S.I.S', Trevor-Roper's own account of his early days in MI8(c), was first published in Hayden B. Peake and Samuel Halpern, *In the Name of Intelligence: essays in honour of Walter Pforzheimer* (NIBC Press, 1994) and reprinted in Edward Harrison's anthology of Trevor-Roper's essays on intelligence, *The Secret World: behind the Curtain of British Intelligence in World War II and the Cold War* (I. B. Tauris, 2014). Harrison is also the author of a masterly essay, 'British Radio Security and Intelligence, 1939–43' in *English Historical Review*, vol. 124, no. 506 (February 2009) and 'Special Service in Germany and *The Last Days of Hitler*' in Blair Worden (ed.), *Hugh Trevor-Roper: the historian* (I. B. Tauris, 2016). The 'bum-sucking' quote is from Trevor-Roper's *Wartime Journals*, edited by Richard Davenport-Hines (I. B. Tauris, 2012), p. 73. W. N. Medlicott, *The Economic Blockade*, vol. 1 (HMSO, 1952), tells the story of contraband control, as does chapter 30 of *The Second Great War: a Standard History*, edited by Sir John Hamerton (Waverley Book Co./ Amalgamated Press, 1947). See also R. Hudson Smith, 'Contraband Control' in *Blackwood's Magazine*, no. 1920, vol. 318 (October 1975), pp. 289–305. First World War examples of evasions come from Carolina García Sanz, *La Primera Guerra Mundial en el Estrecho de Gibraltar* (CSIC, Madrid, 2011). On Sir Basil Clarke and breach of blockade in Denmark see chapter 10 of Richard Evans, *From the Frontline* (The History Press, 2013). Mollie Spencer's photo appears in the 2013 revised version of the illustrated talk her daughter Jennifer Scherr gave to the Friends of Gibraltar in Winchester on 16 October 2010, as recorded in *Rock Talk*, issue 5 (May 2011). The full *History of the Postal and Telegraphic Censorship Department 1938–1946* (2 vols, Home Office, 1952) is in the National Archives at Kew, DEFE 1/333 and 334. H. Montgomery Hyde, *Secret Intelligence Agent* (Constable, 1982) tells his part in the organisation in Liverpool, Gibraltar and Bermuda. Among his many books, Montgomery Hyde wrote a ground-breaking study following the 1967 Wolfenden Report: *The Other Love: an Historical and Contemporary Survey of Homosexuality in Britain* (Heinemann, 1970). John Verney's snippy observation is from his memoir, *Going to the Wars* (Collins, 1955), pp. 111–12. Alethea Hayter's *A Voyage in Vain: Coleridge's Journey to Malta in 1804* was published by Faber in 1973 and republished by Robin Clark in 1993. The 1940 convoy details come from Arnold Hague, *The Allied Convoy System 1939–1945: its Organization,*

Defence and Operation (Chatham Publishing, 2000), supplemented by
information from the comprehensive websites warsailors.com and uboat.
net. On Imperial Censorship in Bermuda, see Oliver Jensen, '800 Censors in
Bermuda', *LIFE*, 19 May 1941; H. Montgomery Hyde, *The Quiet Canadian:
the Secret Service Story of Sir William Stephenson* (Hamish Hamilton, 1962),
pp. 51–9; *This Week in Bermuda*, April 2010. Paul Einzig takes a critical
view of the early days of MEW in *Economic Warfare 1939–1940* (Macmillan,
1941) and Hugh Dalton's speech is from *The Penguin Hansard vol. 1, August
1939–May 1940*, pp. 98–105. Hugh Dalton's memoirs of 1931–45, *The Fateful
Years* (Frederick Muller, 1957) devotes two chapters to MEW and one to SOE.
Ben Pimlott's biography *Hugh Dalton* was first published by Jonathan Cape
in 1985 and David Dilks edited Sir Alexander Cadogan's diaries for Cassell
in 1971. The SOE Charter was first published in full in chapter one of Nigel
West, *Secret War: the Story of SOE, Britain's Wartime Sabotage Organisation*
(Hodder & Stoughton, 1992).

11 Fight and Flight

There is a large literature on the fall of France. Marc Bloch, *Strange Defeat:
a Statement of Evidence Written in 1940* (Norton, 1968, reissued 1999) is a
classic. Sir Alistair Horne's *To Lose a Battle: France 1940* (revised edition,
Penguin 1990) is a tremendous read. Horne praises Major-General Sir Edward
Spears's enthralling two-volume *Assignment to Catastrophe* (Heinemann,
1954) and dubs its ruthless and bilingual author 'the Suetonius of our times'.
Charles de Gaulle's war memoirs, *The Call to Honour 1940–1942* (Collins,
1955) can be read in conjunction with Winston Churchill's *Their Finest
Hour* (Cassell, 1949), augmented by Martin Gilbert, *Finest Hour: Winston
Churchill 1939–1941* (Heinemann, 1983) and David Reynolds, *In Command
of History: Churchill Fighting and Writing the Second World War* (Allen
Lane, 2004). Noel Monks's claim is on p. 25 of his *Fighter Squadrons: the Epic
Story of Two Hurricane Squadrons in France* (Angus & Robertson, 1941). The
twenty-first-century view is not so reliant on the idea of a decadent France,
as witnessed by William Shirer, author of *The Collapse of the Third Republic*
(Heinemann/Secker & Warburg, 1970). See Ernest R. May, *Strange Victory:
Hitler's Conquest of France* (Hill & Wang, 2000), Julian Jackson, *The Fall of
France: the Nazi invasion of 1940* (Oxford, 2003) and Philip Nord, *France
1940: Defending the Republic* (Yale University Press, 2015). Robert Gildea
has studied the aftermath brilliantly: *Marianne in Chains* (Macmillan, 2002)
examines the German occupation and *Fighters in the Shadows* (Faber, 2016)
comprehensively explores the French resistance. *Oberst* Rudolf Witzig wrote

an account of Fort Eben Emael in the 1966 Purnell part-work *History of the Second World War*, pp. 184–91. See also Gilberto Villahermosa, *Hitler's Paratrooper: the Life and Battles of Rudolf Witzig* (Frontline Books, 2010); Simon Dunstan, *Fort Eben Emael: the Key to Hitler's Victory in the West* (Osprey Fortress 30, 2005) and the interesting 1991 documentary film by Wolf Mauder and Sigrid Sessner, *The Attack on Fort Eben-Emael: Assault from the Air, 10 May 1940*. Heinz Guderian's *Achtung-Panzer: The Development of Tank Warfare*, translated by Christopher Duffy, appeared in Cassell Military Paperbacks in 1999. The importance of the Stuka is from James S. Corum's biography, *Wolfram von Richthofen: Master of the German Air War* (Kansas, 2008). 'Speed of attack' from William Stevenson's *A Man Called Intrepid*, as cited in Gordon Welchman, *The Hut Six Story: Breaking the Enigma Codes* (1982, reprinted by M. & M. Baldwin, 2005) on page 20, opposite the photograph of General Heinz Guderian's command vehicle with wireless and Enigma operators. On stimulants and 'uppers' to keep *Blitzkrieg* moving, see *Nazis on Speed: Drogen im 3. Reich* by Werner Pieper (2002) and Norman Ohler, *Blitzed: Drugs in Nazi Germany* (Allen Lane, 2016), especially chapter 2, '*Sieg High!* (1939–1941)', pp. 49–125. Hanna Diamond, *Fleeing Hitler: France 1940* (Oxford, 2007) is a vivid and poignant account of the exodus, also witnessed first-hand by C. Denis Freeman and Douglas Cooper in *The Road to Bordeaux* (The Cresset Press, 1940) and Helen Hiett in *No Matter Where*. A fine fictional account is 'Storm in June', part 1 of Irène Némirovsky's novel *Suite Française*, translated by Sandra Smith (Chatto & Windus, 2006). English Heritage had an informative exhibition at Dover Castle for the seventy-fifth anniversary of Operation *Dynamo*. David Woodward, *Ramsay at War* (William Kimber, 1957) tells the story of the indefatigable Admiral S... Bertram Home Ramsay. A. D. Divine, *Dunkirk* (Faber, 1945) is the classic account of the evacuation, and the Ramsgate 'Merrie England' quote is from p. 241. Nicholas Harman, *Dunkirk: the necessary myth* (Hodder & Stoughton, 1980) explores the propaganda side. Hugh Sebag-Montefiore, *Dunkirk: Fight to the Last Man* (Viking, 2006), Julian Thompson, *Dunkirk: Retreat to Victory* (Sidgwick & Jackson, 2008) and Sean Longden, *Dunkirk: The Men They Left Behind* (Constable, 2008) are vivid and poignant. Douglas C. Dildy, *Dunkirk 1940* (Osprey, 2010) gives a clear and comprehensive account. Frank and Joan Shaw, *We Remember Dunkirk* (1990) and David J. Knowles, *Escape from Catastrophe, 1940 Dunkirk* (2000) both contain graphic personal accounts. Hutchinson published Aileen Clayton's *The Enemy Is Listening: The Story of the Y Service* in 1980. Lt-Cdr Freddie Marshall RNVR records Admiral Somerville's May 1940 visit to the Dover naval intercept station in *They Listened in Secret*, edited by Gwendoline Page (George R. Reeve, 2003). *The Story of the Lost WRNS* is the sub-title of Paul Lund and Harry Ludlam's book *Nightmare Convoy* (Foulsham, 1987). The Roosevelt speech is quoted in Robert E. Sherwood, *The White House Papers of Harry L. Hopkins*, vol. 1 (Eyre & Spottiswoode, 1948), p. 145. Sybil Eccles's letter is on page 122 of *By Safe Hand. Letters of Sybil and David Eccles 1939–1945* (Bodley Head, 1983).

12 *Operation* Boomerang

The Herriot story is from *Épisodes* (Flammarion, 1950), quoted in a footnote on page 306 of *The Fall of France: June 1940*, vol. 2 of Maj.-Gen. Sir Edward Spears's *Assignment to Catastrophe* (Heinemann, 1954). Charles de Gaulle quote from page 88 of his war memoirs, *The Call to Honour 1940–1942* (Collins, 1955), and speeches from the adjoining volume *Documents*. The twenty-four-point French–German armistice terms are from KCA 4111A. Helen Hiett's dream is from *No Matter Where* (E. P. Dutton, 1944), p. 215. 'Claire case' papers are in TNA FO 1093/225, released in 2013. Keith Jeffrey adds more details in *MI6: the History of the Secret Intelligence Service 1909–1949* (Bloomsbury, 2010), pp. 404–7. Captain Raymond Dannreuther, *Somerville's Force H* (Aurum, 2005) is a good account of the Gibraltar-based fleet from 1940 to 1942. Duff Cooper in Gibraltar is from his autobiography *Old Men Forget* (Rupert Hart-Davis, 1953), p. 284. Brave Mandel is still a hero to some modern French politicians: see Nicolas Sarkozy, *Georges Mandel: le moine de la politique* (Bernard Grasset, 1994).

13 *'An Absolutely Bloody Business'*

On what de Gaulle called the 'hateful tragedy' of Mers-el-Kébir, see Andrew Browne Cunningham, *A Sailor's Odyssey* (Hutchinson, 1951), chapter 21; William L. Shirer, *The Collapse of the Third Republic* (William Heinemann/ Secker & Warburg, 1970), pp. 885–95; Warren Tute, *The Deadly Stroke* (Collins, 1973) and *The Reluctant Enemies* (Collins, 1989); *The Somerville Papers* (Scolar Press/Navy Records Society, 1995), pp. 37–121; David Brown, *The Road to Oran: Anglo-French Naval Relations, September 1939–July 1940* (Taylor & Francis, 2004); Colin Smith, *England's Last War against France: Fighting Vichy 1940–1942* (Phoenix, 2010), pp. 10–103. The story of the evacuation of civilians in Gibraltar is told by Finlayson in *The Fortress Came First* and Gingell in *'We Thank God and England . . .'* with details from Lourdes Galliano's excellent Second World War memoirs, *A Rocky Passage to Exile*. She also talks in the 2009 StraitVisions Productions DVD, *Evacuation: Cause and Effect*. I interviewed her in March 2016. Rear Admiral Sir Kenelm

Creighton's interesting *Convoy Commodore* was published by William Kimber in 1956, and Warren Tute's novel *The Rock* by Cassell & Co. in 1957. Samuel M. Benady, *Memoirs of a Gibraltarian (1905–1993)* describes the Gibraltarian protest in John Mackintosh Square on 11 July 1940. Joshua Hassan's memory of it is cited on page 21 of *From Fortress to Democracy* (Gibraltar Books, 1995). (In Tute's novel, *The Rock*, the event becomes an actual riot, with injuries.) Joseph Baglietto details from GNA file 474/1940 and family memories recorded in the 'Bordering on Britishness' oral history project run by Dr Andrew Canessa and Dr Jennifer Ballantine Perera. The names of the 18B prisoners and their ship are from GNA file 47/1940. The story of the Women's Voluntary Service in wartime is told in Charles Graves, *Women in Green* (Heinemann, 1948). Alberto Onaindia's letter to the archbishop's secretary is Onaindia 31-1(34) in his collected papers at the Sabino Arana Foundation in Bilbao. The text of Princess Elizabeth's first radio broadcast in 1940 to the children of the Empire is from volume 3 of *The War Illustrated*, p. 470, and also on the British Monarchy website.

14 *The Indian Boy and His Cook*

I interviewed Krishna Khubchand Daswani at his home in Gibraltar in May 2013 and then again in April 2015, a distinguished figure in his eighties, a former Justice of the Peace, a stalwart of the Rotary Club, and ex-President of the Hindu Merchants' Association. In between those meetings, the Alwani trust put up a plaque to his lost family in the monumental lobby of the old Exchange and Commercial Library building, now the Gibraltar Parliament. See also Percy Mañasco, 'The Tragic Evacuation of the Indian Community of Gibraltar in 1940' in *Gibraltar Heritage Journal* 6 (1999), pp. 7–19. The Henderson line sent many Scots on the road to Mandalay; their presence annoyed the Burmese policeman Eric Blair, giving him a lifelong anti-Scots prejudice: see Gordon Bowker, *George Orwell* (Little, Brown, 2003), p. 80. On HK *Atlantis*, see Wolfgang Frank and Capt. Bernhard Rogge's excellent *The German Raider Atlantis* (Ballantine Books, 1956) and Ulrich Mohr and A. V. Sellwood, *Phantom Raider: Nazi Germany's Most Successful Surface Raider* (Cerberus Publishing, 2004). On the significance of the *Automedon* 'pinch', see Peter Elphick, *Far Eastern File: the Intelligence War in the Far East 1930–1945* (Hodder & Stoughton, 1997) and Max Hastings, *The Secret War: Spies, Codes and Guerrillas 1939–1945* (William Collins, 2015), pp. 135–41.

15 Diplomatic Dandies

'Non-belligerent' from *By Safe Hand*, p. 126. The classic study is Denis Smyth, *Diplomacy and Strategy of Survival: British Policy and Franco's Spain, 1940–41* (Cambridge University Press, 1986), a superb book with admirable archival research. Richard Wigg's *Churchill and Spain: the Survival of the Franco Regime 1940–1945* (Sussex Academic Press, 2008) also rehabilitates the reputation of Sir Samuel Hoare, whose own memoir, *Ambassador on Special Mission* (Collins, 1946) assaults Francoism. Norman J. W. Goda, *Tomorrow the World: Hitler, Northwest Africa and the Path towards America* (Texas A&M, 1998) argues for a wider view of German strategy. Sir Alexander Cadogan's rude comments on Hoare come from pages 286, 287 and 326 of his *Diaries 1938–1945*, edited by David Dilks (Cassell, 1971). On some failures of SIS in the Spanish Civil War see Keith Jeffery, *MI6: the History of the Secret Intelligence Service 1909–1949* (Bloomsbury, 2010), p. 287. Alan Hillgarth's biography is by Duff Hart-Davis, *Man of War: the Secret Life of Captain Alan Hillgarth, Officer, Adventurer, Agent* (Century, 2012). Hillgarth's wartime memo, 'The role of the Naval Attaché in Spain', is in the appendix, pp. 353–87. There are details on Salvador Gomez-Beare in Eric Canessa, *They Went to War* (Gibraltar, 2004), pp. 99–103; Ben Macintyre, *Operation Mincemeat* (Bloomsbury, 2010) and Denis Smyth's book on 'the man who never was', *Deathly Deception* (Oxford, 2010). The 'Spanish Neutrality Scheme' to bribe Spanish generals, fronted by Juan March, is in TNA, FO 1093/233 and 234. That the original idea was 'C''s is recorded in Anthony Cave Brown, *The Last Hero: Wild Bill Donovan* (Times Books, 1982), p. 225. For those who read Spanish, Ángel Viñas, *SOBORNOS: De cómo Churchill y March compraron a los generales de Franco* [*BRIBES: How Churchill and March Bought Franco's Generals*] (Crítica, 2016) is quite unmatched. Few other Spanish historians have dug so deep in British archives. The unsigned memorandum of Vigón's meeting with Hitler is in the joint US Department of State and HMSO *Documents on German Foreign Policy 1918–1945*, series D, vol. IX, pp. 585–8. The fullest account of the bizarre episode of the Windsors in Iberia is Michael Bloch, *Operation Willi: the Plot to Kidnap the Duke of Windsor, July 1940* (Weidenfeld & Nicolson, 1984, ebook, 2012). The saga can also be traced through eighteen of the cables and messages in the *DGFP*, series D, vol. X (HMSO, 1957), and the battle to get those saved and published is described in Andrew Morton, *17 Carnations: the Windsors, the Nazis and the Cover-Up* (Michael O'Mara Books, 2015). See also chapter 34, 'Royal Interlude', of Martin Gilbert, *Finest Hour: Winston S. Churchill 1939–1941* (Heinemann, 1983), pp. 698–709; chapter 14, 'A Prince over the Water', of John Costello, *Ten Days to Destiny* (William Morrow & Co., 1991), pp. 352–74, and chapter 7

'Treachery', of Deborah Cadbury, *Princes at War* (Bloomsbury, 2015), pp. 161–90. Cadbury also revealed a damning intelligence report from German sources in the TV documentary *The Royal House of Windsor*, broadcast on Channel 4 in February 2017. Bermejillo's letter to Beigbeder is in *Documentos inéditos para la historia del Generalísimo Franco, Tomo II-I* (Azor, 1992), pp. 215–17, and much is made of it by Dr Karina Urbach in her path-breaking and brilliant study of upper-class supporters of the Nazis, *Go-Betweens for Hitler* (Oxford University Press, 2015). Beigbeder's report to Franco on his conversation with Canaris is on pp. 238–40 of *Documentos inéditos*. Hoare's account of dealing with Germans on the border is from *Ambassador on Special Mission*, pp. 52–4. Rosalinda Powell Fox's version is in chapter 20 of her interesting memoir *The Grass and the Asphalt* (J. S. Harter & Associates, Cádiz, n.d.). Mrs Fox is a key figure in María Dueñas's 2009 novel of love and espionage, *El tiempo entre costuras* (translated as *The Time In Between* in USA and *The Seamstress* in UK). Peter Kemp's report on his MI(R) mission to the Basque country in July and August 1940, stamped MOST SECRET, is in HS 6/921 in TNA; the episode is omitted from his 'secret warrior' autobiography *No Colours or Crest* (Cassell, 1958). For the War Trade Agreement, see David Eccles's letter of 22 June 1940 in *By Safe Hand*.

16 Digging In

'Erosion and harassment' from Michael Howard, *The Mediterranean Strategy in the Second World War* (Greenhill Books, 1993), p. 7. The naval action off Calabria is described in chapter 22 of Cunningham's autobiography, *A Sailor's Odyssey*. On Malta see Ernle Bradford, *Siege: Malta 1940–1943* (Hamish Hamilton, 1985) and Douglas Austin, *Churchill and Malta: a Special relationship* (Spellmount, 2014). RAF flying details come from Brian Cull and Frederick Galea, *Hurricanes over Malta, June 1940–April 1942* (Grub Street, 2001). General Liddell's 1941 report on Gibraltar is in TNA as WO/32/11196. Bernard Fergusson, *The Black Watch and the King's Enemies* (Collins, 1950) tells the story of the Scottish regiment in the Second World War, with some details on the 4th Battalion. Ian Reyes of the History Society Gibraltar gave me a personal ground tour of the Rock's wartime northeast defences, as well as much information from his war-diary research. Captain Galloway's George Medal citation is from Fortress Order No. 774, 17 December 1940 and all the names of the brave are in WO 373/66. 'The Shakespearean actor and film star Anthony Quayle's enjoyable autobiography, *A Time to Speak,* was published by Barrie & Jenkins in 1990. David Scherr quote from *History of the Security*

Intelligence Department of the Defence Security Office Gibraltar 1939–1945, TNA, KV4/259.

17 *Operation* Felix

Albert Speer's description of Adolf Hitler's visit to Paris is in 'The Descent Begins' chapter of *Inside the Third Reich* (Weidenfeld & Nicolson, 1970). Anthony G. Powell's translation of Erich von Manstein's *Lost Victories* was first published by Methuen in 1958. Hitler and Keitel's talk of Gibraltar is in *Ciano's Diplomatic Papers*, edited by Malcolm Muggeridge (Odham's, 1948), pp. 376–9. First mention of Spain in Franz Halder, *The Halder War Diary 1939–1942*, edited by Charles Burdick and Hans-Adolf Jacobsen (Greenhill Books, 1988), p. 227. Churchill's 14 July speech is in *Into Battle* (Cassell, 1941), pp. 247–51. For Hitler's Reichstag speech, see Kershaw, *Hitler: 1936–1945 Nemesis*, pp. 303–4; William L. Shirer, *Berlin Diary 1934–1941* (PRC, 1997), pp. 197–9 and *The Rise and Fall of the Third Reich* (Book Club Associates reprint, 1983). pp. 753–6, as well as Sefton Delmer, *Black Boomerang: an Autobiography, vol. 2* (Secker & Warburg, 1962), pp. 16–18. On the reconnaissance mission to Gibraltar, see chapter 1, 'To the Rock', of Charles B. Burdick, *Germany's Military Strategy and Spain in World War II* (Syracuse University Press, 1968); chapter 11, 'Tears for Heydrich' of Heinz Höhne's *Canaris*, and Alfonso Escuadra Sánchez, 'El Informe Witzig', in *Almoraima* 25 (2001), pp. 413–28. As well as having written the script for the Martin Nuza documentary film *Operation Felix: Hitler's Key to Victory* (Gold Productions 2013) Sr Escuadra is writing a large tome on the German plans to take Gibraltar. I attended his lecture on *Unternehmen Felix* at the Gibraltar Heritage Trust in John Mackintosh Square on 4 April 2016. He has also written on Franco's bunkers on the border, see Alfonso Escuadra Sánchez, 'Megalitos de Hormigón: la comisión Jevenois y el cerrojo fortificado del istmo' in *Almoraima* 29 (2003), pp. 543–59, as has José Manuel Algarbani Rodríguez, 'Los bunkers del estrecho y los prisioneros republicanos' in *Almoraima* 36 (2008), pp. 451–60. Churchill's dismissal of talks about Gibraltar is in Martin Gilbert, *Finest Hour*, p. 584. The movement of the four twelve-inch howitzers is noted in GNA secret file S61/1940. The statement that the Italian air raid was '*totalmente fortuita*' is from Alfonso Escuadra, *A La Sombra de la Roca: la segunda guerra mundial desde el campo de Gibraltar* (CajaSur, 1997), p. 109, and he confirmed the same to me in a personal communication. Baron von Stohrer's memorandum of 8 August 1940 was the first of fifteen incriminating documents, translated from German, Italian and Spanish into English and printed by the US Department of State in a March 1946 publication, *The*

Spanish Government and the Axis, which condemned the Spanish regime's links to German Nazism and Italian Fascism. It is also no. 313 in the US State Dept. and HMSO *DGFP*, series D, vol. X, pp. 442–5.

18 The Price of Dakar

Axis plans for economic hegemony and a return to the gold standard are reported in KCA 4291B, October 1940. Dorothy Baden-Powell, *Pimpernel Gold* (Robert Hale, 1978) and Robert Pearson, *Gold Run* (Casemate, 2015) describe the narrow escape of Norway's bullion. Maurice Hankey helped rescue some continental gold: see Stephen Roskill, *Hankey: Man of Secrets, vol. 3: 1931–1963* (Collins, 1974), p. 470. On the gold at Dakar, see Alfred Draper, *Operation Fish: the Race to Save Europe's Wealth 1939–1945* (Cassell, 1979); Arthur L. Smith Jr, *Hitler's Gold: the Story of Nazi War Loot* (Berg, 1989); *Nazi Gold: The London Conference* (FCO/HMSO, 1998). Churchill's role is described in Martin Gilbert, *Finest Hour* (William Heinemann, 1983). Correlli Barnett's comment is from *Engage the Enemy More Closely: the Royal Navy in the Second World War* (Hodder & Stoughton, 1991), p. 203. Huntziger's letter to Hemmens with gold information is No. 371 in the HMSO *DGFP*, series D, vol. X, pp. 516–20. The Dakar Expedition features in *Men at Arms* (1952), the first part of what would become Evelyn Waugh's *Sword of Honour* trilogy of Second World War novels. Commander Malcolm Saunders gives a clear account in Purnell's part-work *History of the Second World War* (1972), pp. 212–15. The three NCOs feature in Nick van der Bijl, *Sharing the Secret: a History of the Intelligence Corps, 1940–2010* (Pen & Sword, 2013), p. 73. Girard diary from William Mortimer Moore, *Free France's Lion: the Life of Philippe Leclerc, de Gaulle's Greatest General* (Casemate Publishers, 2011), p. 89. The Waugh quote is from *The Diaries of Evelyn Waugh*, edited by Michael Davie (Weidenfeld & Nicolson, 1976), p. 484. Unwise signal to PM from Bernard Fergusson, *Wavell: Portrait of a Soldier* (Collins, 1961), p. 53. For the case of Admiral Dudley North, see Noel Monks, *That Day at Gibraltar* (Frederick Muller, 1957); Arthur Marder, *Operation 'Menace': the Dakar Expedition and the Dudley North Affair* (Oxford University Press, 1976); Charlotte and Denis Plimmer, *A Matter of Expediency: The Jettison of Admiral Sir Dudley North* (Quartet, 1978).

19 Helen among the Trojans

The Randolph and Winston Churchill dialogue is from Martin Gilbert, *Finest Hour*, p. 358. For Edward R. Murrow's importance, see A. M. Sperber, *Murrow: His Life and Times* (Freundlich Books, 1986) and Philip Seib,

Broadcasts from the Blitz (Potomac Books, 2007). 'The papers of the admirable correspondent Helen Hiett Waller (1913–1961), including 'Ten Thousand Men and a Girl', are in the Sophia Smith Collection of Smith College, Northampton, Massachusetts, USA. Reporting the bombing of Gibraltar for NBC scooped her a National Headliner Award. Hiett's book *No Matter Where* was published by E. P. Dutton in 1944, and her sympatic piece on Russian PoWs being shipped back to Odessa was in the post-war anthology *Deadline Delayed* (Dutton, 1947). The Royal Engineers Library at Chatham has many specialised essays on the wartime tunnels of Gibraltar including those by Cave Cotton, Dale, Edmonds, Eley, Haycraft, Lander, D. M. Thomson, A. R. O. Williams and W. H. Wilson. Maj.-Gen. R. P. Pakenham-Walsh, *The History of the Corps of Royal Engineers, vol. VIII: 1938–1948* has an overview, pp. 322–31, and there is also a good account in the Gibraltar issue of *After the Battle* (No. 21, 1978). Details of the September bombing of Gibraltar from the GNA 'Air-Raids' file; Tito Benady, *The Royal Navy at Gibraltar* (Gibraltar Books, 2000), pp. 159–60; Peter Buttigieg, *We Weep No More* (Aquila Services, 1997), pp. 82–8; and Phil Smith and Darren Fa, *Underwater Gibraltar: a Guide to the Rock's Submerged Sites* (Aquila Services, 2004), pp. 70–3.

20 Dealing with Dictators

Serrano figures in *Ciano's Diary 1939–1943*, edited by Malcolm Muggeridge (Heinemann, 1947), pp. 99–100. Ramón Serrano Suñer describes his trip to Germany in his own book, *Entre Hendaya y Gibraltar* (Epesa, 1947). Details of the *Reichskanzlei* from Martin Kitchen, *Speer: Hitler's Architect* (Yale University Press, 2015), pp. 46–56. Paul Schmidt's notes of the Hitler–Serrano talk on September 17 were the fourth document in the 1946 US government file *The Spanish Government and the Axis*. Schmidt's account of the Ribbentrop–Serrano meeting is on page 190 of *Hitler's Interpreter* and Serrano Suñer's version on pages 181–3 of his book. Ángel Viñas is critical of Serrano Suñer in *SOBORNOS* (Crítica, 2016). For the Reich political plans to create an enormous German colonial empire in central Africa see *DGFP*, series D, vol. XI, pp. 483–91. Grand Admiral Raeder's and Admiral Dönitz's meetings with Hitler are recorded in *Fuehrer Conferences on Naval Affairs 1939–1945* (Chatham Publishing, 2005), which were originally sorted, translated and edited by Anthony Martienssen for the Admiralty and published in *Brassey's Naval Annual*. Martienssen also wrote *Hitler and His Admirals* (Secker & Warburg, 1948). On General Gonzalo Queipo de Llano's perversity, see Paul Preston's essay 'The Psychopathology of an Assassin' in *Mass Killings and Violence in Spain 1936–1952*, edited by Peter Anderson and

Miguel Angel Blanco del Arco (Routledge, 2014). On Serrano Suñer in Italy see *Ciano's Diplomatic Papers*, pp. 393–4 and *Entre Hendaya y Gibraltar*, pp. 195–8. The Brenner pass meeting is recorded on page 296 of *Ciano's Diary 1939–1943* and on pages 395–8 of his *Diplomatic Papers*, as well as in Hasso von Etzdorf.'s account in *The Halder War Diary 1939–1942*, pp. 262–6. Churchill's 8 October 1940 speech is in *Into Battle* (Cassell, 1941), p. 290. Serrano's letter to Ribbentrop is document 19 in *The Spanish Government and the Axis*. German military plans are in chapter 2 of Charles B. Burdick's *Germany's Military Strategy and Spain in World War Two* (Syracuse, 1968). For Spanish stocktaking in October 1940, see 'Disponibilades militares', no. 89 in *Documentos inéditos, Tomo II-I* (Azor, 1992), pp. 371–4. The Hispano-German secret police agreement is reproduced in Manuel Ros Agudo, *La Guerra Secreta de Franco* (Critica Contrastes, 2002), p. 182. For the register of Spanish Jews for the Gestapo, see 'La Lista de Franco para el Holocausto', *El País* Archivo online, 20 June 2010 and Giles Tremlett, 'Franco gave list of Spanish Jews to Nazis', *Guardian*, 21 June 2010. The two Britishers who did not stand for the German national anthem in the bullring were Tom Burns and Gerry Young, as described in Jimmy Burns, *Papa Spy* (Bloomsbury, 2009), pp. 133–5. The paper in the 7 May 2008 UCL *Bulletin of the History of Archaeology*, 'Relations between Spanish archaeologists and Nazi Germany (1939–1945)' by Francisco Gracia Alonso of Barcelona University is a fascinating look at Himmler's visit and the influence of *das Ahnenerbe* in Spain. In 2016, the National Archaeological Museum in Madrid was seeking to retrieve some of the archaeological items that Himmler took back to Germany. See 'A la caza del tesoro visigodo que los nazis se llevaron', *El País*, 28 August 2016 and 'Spain asks for return of Nazi gifts', *The Times*, 30 August 2016.

21 'Every Inch Must Be Pulverised'

'Fiasco' is from Elizabeth Wiskemann, *The Rome–Berlin Axis* (Collins: The Fontana Library, 1966), p. 283; 'torture' is from Wayne H. Bowen, *Spaniards and Nazi Germany* (Missouri, 2000), p. 93. Ian Kershaw describes the Hendaye meeting in *Hitler 1936–45: Nemesis*, pp. 329–30. Dr Paul Schmidt probably prepared the unsigned and incomplete memorandum of the Caudillo–*Führer* talk which appears as document 8 in *The Spanish Government and the Axis*, and in a slightly longer and more fluent translation as document 220 in the 1960 HMSO *Documents on German Foreign Policy*, series D, vol. XI, pp. 371–6. Schmidt's own account of the meetings is in *Hitler's Interpreter*, pp. 192–9 and in Leon Goldensohn, *The Nuremberg Interviews* (Pimlico, 2006), p. 444; Barón de las Torres's account is in Eduardo Palomar Baró, 'Entrevista entre Franco y Hitler' at www.generalisimofranciscofranco.com/historia/ hendaya01htm. Ramón Serrano Suñer admitted on page 284 of his second autobiography, *Memorias: Entre el silencio y la propaganda, la Historia como fue* (Editorial Planeta, 1977, two years after Franco's death), that Spain had secretly agreed, in principle, to join the Axis, and he prints the English version of the 'Hendaye protocol', taken from *DGFP*, D, vol. XI, pp. 466–7, twice in his book. 'Three or four teeth' is from *Ciano's Diplomatic Papers*, p. 402. For the classic overview of the dictators' encounter see Paul Preston 'Franco and Hitler: The Myth of Hendaye 1940' in *Contemporary European History*, vol. 1, issue 1 (1992), pp. 1–16. 'Führer Directive 18' is on pp. 80–7 of the 1966 Pan Books edition of *Hitler's War Directives 1939–1945*, edited by Hugh Trevor-Roper. Cunningham on Taranto from *A Sailor's Odyssey* (Hutchinson, 1951), p. 286. For the Fleet Air Arm influence on Japan, see Thomas P. Lowry and John W. G. Wellham, *The Attack on Taranto: Blueprint for Pearl Harbor* (Stackpole Books, 2000). Serrano Suñer details are from both *Entre Hendaya y Gibraltar* and *Memorias*. Schmidt's account of the Hitler–Serrano talks at Obersalzberg on 18 November 1940 is document no. 352 in *DGFP*, series D, vol. XI, and the following day's talk with Ribbentrop is document no. 357.

22 The Greatest Mistake

Ian Colvin's study of Canaris, *Chief of Intelligence* (Victor Gollancz, 1951) was the first book in English to wonder quite where the German admiral fitted along the axis (and near anagram) of patriot and traitor. In chapter 14, 'The Hendaye Tapestry', Colvin argues that Canaris discreetly helped Franco to thwart Hitler in Spain. Chapter 9 of Richard Bassett, *Hitler's Spy Chief: the Wilhelm Canaris Mystery* (Cassell, 2005) follows the same line of Canaris urging Spanish neutrality. The Vigón account of the Canaris/Franco interview is document 11 in the 1946 US State Dept publication *The Spanish Government and the Axis*. Details on Lt.-Col. Eleuterio Sánchez Rubio from his thick MI5 file in TNA, KV 2/3001. Lt-Col. Pardo's account of General Lanz's secret boat trip to survey Catalan Bay is no. 109 in *Documentos inéditos para la Historia del Generalisimo Franco, Tomo II-I*, and the Lanz reconnaissance is also described in Burdick, *Germany's Military Strategy and Spain in WWII*, pp. 105–13. Alan Hillgarth's conversation with Juan March is from MLBE 1/16 in the Churchill Centre Archives. Hillgarth's visit to London is described in Denis Smyth, *Diplomacy and Strategy of Survival* (Cambridge, 1986), pp. 161–4 and Duff Hart-Davis, *Man of War* (Century, 2012), pp. 207–8; *Sprinkler* and *Sconce* are on p. 214. Hillgarth's ten-page memo to Dalton is in FO 1093/233. The XX Committee's first meeting is from J. C. Masterman, *The Double-Cross System*

1939–1945 (Pimlico, 1995), p. 62. Dusko Popov describes questioning by Bill Cavendish-Bentinck about Canaris and Franco in *Spy/Counterspy* (Panther, 1976), p. 68. See also Kenneth Strong, *Men of Intelligence* (Giniger/Cassell, 1970), p. 119 and Patrick Howarth, *Intelligence Chief Extraordinary* (Bodley Head, 1986), pp. 145–9. Hitler's letter to Mussolini is from *DGFP*, series D, vol. XI, pp. 990–4, and Stohrer haranguing Franco and Hitler urging Mussolini are on pp. 1141–51. The Mussolini–Franco meeting at Bordighera is in *Ciano's Diplomatic Papers*, pp. 421–30, Serrano Suñer, *Entre Hendaya y Gibraltar*, pp. 262–7 and Preston, *Franco*, pp. 422–4, which also has the quote from Pétain. The Leahy citation is from Robert Sherwood, *The White House Papers of Harry L. Hopkins*, vol. 1, p. 296. On Hitler's regrets see François Genoud, *The Testament of Adolf Hitler: The Hitler–Bormann Documents February–March 1945*, trans R. H. Stevens (Cassell, 1961), p. 79. Ivone Kirkpatrick's two-hour talk with Hermann Göring is described on page 195 of his memoirs *The Inner Circle* (Macmillan, 1959). The lost prison interview with Göring was first published by Gilbert Villahermosa in the September 2006 issue of *World War II* magazine and is available online at historynet.com. Ralph Izzard's report of what Göring said is in MISC 49, Churchill Archives Centre Miscellaneous Holdings. Hugh Trevor-Roper's thoughts on Spain in 1940 are from his collection *History and Imagination* (Duckworth, 1981), p. 360.

23 Nosey Parker

Personal information on David Scherr and photocopies of some of his writing for *The Rock* are courtesy of his daughter Jennifer Scherr. Norman Lewis's *Jackdaw Cake* was first published by Hamish Hamilton in 1985, and the quotes are from pages 158 and 234 of the 2013 Eland edition. Geoffrey Household quotes come from the 'Soldier' section of his autobiography *Against the Wind* (Michael Joseph, 1958), pp. 123–30. Julian Evans on FSS is from *Semi-invisible Man: the Life of Norman Lewis* (Picador, 2009), pp. 193–4. Brown and Sidney's names are recorded on Panel 21, Column 1 of the Brookwood 1939–1945 Memorial in Surrey, which commemorates some 3500 Commonwealth land forces war dead who have no known grave. D. J. Scherr's *The History of the SID of the DSO Gibraltar 1939–1945* is held in the National Archives at Kew as KV4/259 and 260. Tito Vallejo's *The Yanito Dictionary* was first published by Panorama in 2001. Gibraltar referendums continue to deliver clear results: in June 2016, 96 per cent of an 84 per cent turnout voted to remain in the European Union, and were shocked to find they had lost. The M. G. Sanchez quote is from his 2016 post-Brexit essay, 'Fifty years of "Unbelonging"', written for the University of Basel. The Muriel

Spark dialogue is from *Curriculum Vitae: Autobiography* (Constable, 1992), p. 147. The Nick van der Bijl story is from *Sharing the Secret: a History of the Intelligence Corps 1940–2010* (Pen & Sword, 2013), pp. 72–3. Nicholas Monsarrat quote from *Three Corvettes* (Cassell, 1945), p. 40. Charles Causley's Main Street quote from his short story 'The Life and Death of Captain Exe' in *Hands to Dance and Skylark* (Robson Books, 1979), p. 15. Extracts from the poet's wartime diary are from Laurence Green, *All Cornwall Thunders at My Door: a biography of Charles Causley* (Cornovia Press, 2013), pp. 79–80. On homosexuality in the Second World War, see Emma Vickers, *Queen and Country: Same-Sex Desire in the British Armed Forces 1939–45* (Manchester University Press, 2013), a sensible, brave and pioneering work. Dr Vickers sent me the transcript of her July 2005 interview with the late Jimmy Jacques, who spent most of the wartime years in Gibraltar.

24 On the Run

A ground-breaking work on the escape system is Airey Neave, *Saturday at M.I.9: a History of Underground Escape Lines in North-West Europe in 1940–5* (Hodder & Stoughton, 1969). M. R. D. Foot and J. M. Langley, *MI9: the British Secret Service that Fostered Escape and Evasion 1939–1945 and its American Counterpart* (Bodley Head, 1979) was the first authoritative history of all the wartime 'ratlines' and the organisation behind them. A. J. Evans, author of *The Escaping Club*, interviewed many of those who got away and compiled *Escape and Liberation 1940–1945* (Hodder & Stoughton, 1945). Donald Darling's comment on gossipy Gibraltar is from *Secret Sunday* (William Kimber, 1975), p. 48. His sequel, *Sunday at Large: Assignments of a Secret Agent*, came out in 1977. Mistreatment of British prisoners in Spain from Allen Andrews, *Proud Fortress: the Fighting Story of Gibraltar* (Evans Bros, 1958), pp. 179–80, some of which is drawn from Gordon Instone's excellent *Freedom the Spur* (revised Great Pan edition, 1956). Vincent Brome, *The Way Back* (Cassell, 1957) tells the remarkable story of Albert Guérisse aka 'Pat O'Leary'. Harold Cole's MI5 files are KV 2/415–417 in TNA. In the same archive, Escape and Evasion reports are filed under WO 208. Antonio Téllez Solá, *La Red de Evasión del Grupo Ponzan: anarquistas en la guerra secreta contra el franquismo y el nazismo 1936-1944* (Virus Barcelona, 1996) tells how Spanish anarchists helped escapers and evaders. The classic account of wartime Polish resistance is Jan Karski's *Story of a Secret State: My Report to the World*, first published in the USA in 1944. The Penguin Classics edition of 2011 includes additional material from the 1999 Polish edition and notes from the 2010 French version. The Beevor quote is from his account of the

Lisbon mission in the Iberia section history HS 7/164. 'Marian Krajewski' features notably in Brooks Richards, *Secret Flotillas, vol. 2: Clandestine Sea Operations in the Western Mediterranean, North Africa and the Adriatic 1940–1944* (Pen & Sword, 2013). The remarkable story of Peter Musson's SOE 'smuggling fleet' is detailed in TNA HS 6/971. Incidents coinciding on 5 January are from Donald Darling, *Secret Sunday* (William Kimber, 1975), p. 45, and Airey Neave, *Saturday at MI 9* (Hodder & Stoughton, 1969), chapter 5. The escape from Colditz is described in chapter 7 of Airey Neave, *They Have Their Exits* (Hodder & Stoughton, 1953), pp. 78–92, and in chapter 13 of P. R. Reid, *The Colditz Story* (Pan Books, 1954), pp. 137–47. Airey Neave also wrote *Little Cyclone* (Hodder & Stoughton, 1954), the story of Countess Andrée de Jongh GM, the Belgian girl who started the Comet Line. The 2013 Biteback edition prints the names of all the members of the Comet Line killed in action. See also Paul Routledge, *Public Servant, Secret Agent: the Elusive Life and Violent Death of Airey Neave* (4th Estate, 2002). Derek Shuff's book, *Evader: the Epic Story of the First British Airman to Be Rescued by the Comète Escape Line in World War II* (Spellmount, 2003) tells Jack Newton's story. Bram van der Stok's obituary appeared in the *Daily Telegraph* on 1 July 1993; an article on him appeared in the *History Society Gibraltar Chronicle*, vol. 7, no. 3 (September 2016), and he features in Paul Brickhill's classic account, *The Great Escape* (Faber, 1951), pp. 232–5. (Elements of Bram van der Stok went into the character 'Sedgwick', played by James Coburn in the well-known 1963 Mirisch film, *The Great Escape*, written by James Clavell and directed by John Sturges.)

25 From the New World

Two interesting modern narrative histories of how America got into the war are Michael Fullilove, *Rendezvous with Destiny* (Penguin, 2013) and Marc Wortman, *1941: Fighting the Shadow War* (Atlantic Books, 2017). Robert Murphy tells his own story in *Diplomat among Warriors* (Doubleday, 1964). *The White House Papers of Harry L. Hopkins: an Intimate History* by Robert E. Sherwood were published in two volumes by Eyre and Spottiswoode in 1948–9. How Churchill laid out his script for broadcast can be seen in the Churchill Archive Centre, Churchill Papers, CHAR 9/1501/51, reproduced in Allen Packwood *et al.*, *Churchill and the Great Republic* (Library of Congress, 2004). The Courtauld's fire-sale is from Ron Chernow, *The House of Morgan: an American Banking Dynasty and the Rise of Modern Finance* (Grove Press, 1990), p. 462. William Donovan noting the '88' is from Anthony Cave Brown, *The Last Hero: Wild Bill Donovan* (Times Books, 1982), p. 133. A more recent biography by Douglas Waller, *Wild Bill Donovan: the Spymaster Who Created the OSS and Modern American Espionage* (Free Press, 2011), passes over this trip. The acerbic chapter on Donovan and OSS in Rhodri Jeffreys-Jones, *Cloak and Dollar: a History of American Secret Intelligence* (Yale University Press, 2002) is titled 'Hyping the Sideshow'. For 'determined interventionists' see Sallie Pisani, *The CIA and the Marshall Plan* (Edinburgh University Press, 1991), p. 3. Sir William Stephenson was the subject of H. Montgomery Hyde's *The Quiet Canadian* (Hamish Hamilton, 1962), whose US edition, with an introduction by Ian Fleming, is titled *Room 3603* (Farrar, Straus & Co., 1963). William Stevenson's lurid biography *A Man Called Intrepid* (Macmillan, 1976) is jolly exciting but largely untrue; Thomas F. Troy, *Wild Bill and Intrepid: Donovan, Stephenson and the Origin of CIA* (Yale University Press, 1996) is more scrupulous. Bill Macdonald, *The True 'Intrepid': Sir William Stephenson and the Unknown Agents* (Timberholme Books, 1998), though poorly edited and proofread, is full of fresh information. St Ermin's Press published *British Security Coordination: the Secret History of British Intelligence in the Americas 1940–1945,* with an introduction by Nigel West, also in 1998. Alex Danchev expertly edited *Establishing the Anglo-American Alliance: the Second World War Diaries of Brigadier Vivian Dykes* for Brassey's in 1990. Sir Samuel Hoare on Beigbeder's dismissal is in *Ambassador on Special Mission*, pp. 71–4, and his telegram to London of 22 October 1940, with the British military planners' response is in TNA PREM 3/405/1. The masterly Denis Smyth also discusses Hoare and Beigbeder's talks in *Diplomacy and Strategy of Survival*, pp. 105–8. There is an eight-page intelligence report on the activities of the German Armistice Commission's activities in Morocco in WO 204/12351, along with lists of persons whose sympathies were pro-Allied or pro-Axis. Herbert Richter's dispatch is on pp. 969–71 of *DGFP*, series D, vol. XI. Somerville on Donovan is from *The Somerville Papers* (Scolar/Navy Records, 1995), p. 235; his February letters to his wife on pp. 241–4. Neil Kemp's death is described in A. J. Smithers, *Taranto 1940: 'A Glorious Episode'* (Leo Cooper, 1995), p. 133. The Paramount News piece on *Cold Harbor* is on the Getty Images website, no. 502484783. Donovan's situation report is from *Establishing the Anglo-American Alliance*, p. 59. There is a good deal of Ian Fleming material in the ADM 223 series of Naval Intelligence files at TNA. The 'Stay-Behind-Cave' of Operation Tracer was rediscovered by the Gibraltar Caving Group on Boxing Day 1996. See the website discovergibraltar.com for more details. I visited it with Phil Smith of the Gibraltar Museum in April 2015. Hoare's briefing of Donovan is in *Ambassador on Special Mission*, pp. 107–10.

26 Helen's Return

Helen Hiett's comments, journalism, notes, letters and old menus are
from her papers at Smith College. Ship losses and casualties from *British
Vessels Lost at Sea 1939–45* (Patrick Stephens, 1976), a reprint of two 1947
HMSO publications, and Arnold Hague, *The Allied Convoy System 1939–45*
(Chatham Publishing, 2000). John Masefield quote from 'For All Seafarers', in
Merchantmen at War (HMSO, 1944).

27 Bloody War

J. R. Colville, *Man of Valour: the Life of Field-Marshal the Viscount Gort*
(Collins, 1972), is the standard biography. 'Lost soul' Gort is from Sir John
Kennedy's war narrative, edited by Bernard Fergusson, *The Business of War*
(Hutchinson, 1957), pp. 64–5. Details of Gort's first official visit to Muñoz
Grandes are in the GNA. The Crete casualty figures are from Martin Gilbert,
The Routledge Atlas of the Second World War (2008), p. 35. A portrait of
the amazing Kiwi soldier Charles 'Pug' Upham, 'A Modest Hero', is in
The Second World War: a World in Flames (Osprey, 2004), pp. 213–17.
Mountbatten's account of the sinking of HMS *Kelly*, given to his sister Louise,
Queen of Sweden, is in John Winton's anthology *Freedom's Battle: volume 1:
the War at Sea 1939–45* (Hutchinson, 1967), pp. 119–28. Sickbay Attendant
Wood's account of seeing the *Hood* sink is from Max Arthur, *Lost Voices of the
Royal Navy* (Hodder Headline, 2005), p. 297. Sigint details from Peter Jarvis,
The German Battleships (Bletchley Park Trust Report No. 2, 1997). US pilot
Lt. Leonard 'Tuck' Smith got the DFC for finding the *Bismarck*. John Moffat's
I Sank the Bismarck was published by Bantam Books in 2009. For the carnage
on board see chapter 12 of Ludovic Kennedy, *Pursuit: the Chase and Sinking
of the Bismarck* (Collins, 1974). The Warren Tute quote is on page 304 of *The
Rock*. Somerville on Gort, *The Somerville Papers*, p. 281. Churchill's letter to
Hoare about the Gibraltar airfield is quoted in the Gibraltar issue of *After the
Battle*, no. 21 (1978), pp. 10–11. For the secret information passed to Russia,
see Martin Gilbert, *The 'Golden Eggs': Churchill and Signals Intelligence*
(Bletchley Park Trust, 2008). Chapter 12 of Ewan Butler's *Mason-Mac* is about
the general's time in Russia. On the Anders Army, see Norman Davies, *Trail
of Hope* (Osprey, 2015). For Boris Kovalev's findings on the División Azul, see
Pilar Bonet, 'Violentos y ladrones, pero más humanos que los nazis', *El País*, 6
October 2015, p. 31. Figures from Gerald Kleinfeld and Lewis Tambs, *Hitler's
Spanish Legion: the Blue Division in Russia in WWII* (Stackpole Books, 1979).
Hitler's comments on the Spanish general Muñoz Grandes are in *Hitler's Table*

Talk 1941–1944, 3rd edition, edited by Hugh Trevor-Roper (Phoenix, 2000), pp. 693–4. Geoffrey Faulder Page featured in my *Churchill's Wizards: the British Genius for Deception 1914–1945* (Faber, 2008) because he experienced both the retreat from Mons in 1914 and the Dunkirk evacuation in 1940. He kept some papers from Operation *Substance*, which is also covered in ADM 223/519 in TNA, supplemented by *The Somerville Papers* and the Naval Staff History, published as *The Royal Navy and the Mediterranean, vol. II: November 1940–December 1941* (Whitehall History Publishing/Frank Cass, 2002). *Sea Devils* (Andrew Melrose, 1952) is the translation by James Cleugh of *Decima Flottiglia Mas* by its commander, Prince Julio Valerio Borghese. 'The Glorious Failure of Malta' is on pp. 96–113. Admiral Karl Dönitz on submarines from *Memoirs: Ten Years and Twenty Days* (Cassell Military Paperbacks, 2000), pp. 158–63. For more on the PBYs, see Ragnar J. Ragnarsson, *US Navy PBY Catalina Units of the Atlantic War* (Osprey Combat Aircraft series, 2006). Lawrence Paterson, *U-Boats in the Mediterranean 1941–1944* (Chatham Publishing, 2007) describes *U-81* sinking the *Ark Royal*.

28 Hands across the Sea

For Ian Fleming and John Godfrey in the USA see chapter 9 of Patrick Beesly, *Very Special Admiral: the Life of Admiral J. H. Godfrey CB* (Hamish Hamilton, 1980). On Roosevelt's note see Thomas F. Troy, *Wild Bill and Intrepid* (Yale University Press, 1996), pp. 128–31. H. V. Morton, *Atlantic Meeting* (Methuen, 1943) is an engaging account of Churchill's first meeting with Roosevelt on HMS *Prince of Wales*. On *Lady Hamilton* as propaganda, see James Chapman, *Past and Present: National Identity and the British Historical Film* (I. B. Tauris, 2005), pp. 43–4. José Antonio de Aguirre's reaction to the Atlantic Charter is from *Freedom Was Flesh and Blood* (Victor Gollancz, 1945), pp. 220–1, which is the British version of *De Guernica a Nueva York pasando por Berlin* (1942), following the American edition *Escape via Berlin* (1943). Churchill getting the news of the loss of two battleships is from Martin Gilbert, *Finest Hour* (Heinemann, 1983), p. 1273. Field Marshal Lord Alanbrooke reacts on page 210 of his *War Diaries 1939–1945*, edited by Alex Danchev and Daniel Todman (Weidenfeld & Nicolson, 2001). Juan March embarrassments from FO 1093/233 in TNA. Arcadia details from David J. Bercuson and Holger H. Herwig, *One Christmas in Washington: Churchill and Roosevelt Forge the Grand Alliance* (Phoenix, 2006). 'United Nations' from *The White House Papers of Harry L. Hopkins*, vol. 1, p. 455 and KCA 4957A.

29 The Clandestine Struggle

Commander Frank Slocum RN features in both volumes of Brooks Richards' magnum opus on clandestine sea operations in the Second World War, *Secret Flotillas* (Pen & Sword, 2012). 'Lifeline to Safety', part 4 of A. Cecil Hampshire, *On Hazardous Service* (William Kimber, 1974), is about HMS *Tarana*, whose last surviving crew member, Ronald Bruce Stephens, recalled his service on board in Sue and Andy Parlour's book, *HMS Tarana: In at the Deep End* (Serendipity, 2007). The SOE men out of Slaughter and May, apart from Quennell and Beevor (the father of the historian Anthony Beevor), included Alastair Hamilton, Hilary Scott, Harry Sporborg and Geoffrey Vickers, who was knighted for his work in Economic Warfare. The quote about Hugh Quennell's personality is from Laurie Dennett, *Slaughter and May: a Century in the City* (Granta Editions, 1989), p. 176. Quennell's SOE personal file is HS 9/1221/3 in TNA; his role in 'H' section is in the Iberian history HS 7/163 and 164, and the Algeciras ferry idea is in HS 3/203. On page 140 of Stephen Dorril's book *MI6: 50 years of Special Operations* (4th Estate, 2000), Quennell is called 'an insufferably arrogant and xenophobic Englishman'. Peter Kemp describes him on page 148 of *The Thorns of Memory* (Sinclair-Stevenson, 1990). Sir Samuel Hoare 'effectively vetoing' *Relator* is from Peter Wilkinson and Joan Bright Astley, *Gubbins and SOE* (Pen & Sword, 1997), p. 90. 'Explosive turds' from Carleton S. Coon's memoir, *A North Africa Story: the anthropologist as OSS Agent 1941–1943* (Gambit, 1980), pp. 30–1. Edward Wharton-Tigar describes the planting of the first Tangier bomb in chapter 5 of his autobiography *Burning Bright* (Metal Bulletin Books, 1987), an incident also covered by two FALAISE files in TNA: HS 6/950 and HS 6/951. Ralph Erskine is sceptical in 'Eavesdropping on Bodden: ISOS v. the Abwehr in the Strait of Gibraltar' in *Intelligence and National Security*, vol. 12, no. 3 (July 1997). Charles Causley's diary entry on the *Erin* explosion is from Laurence Green, *All Cornwall Thunders at My Door*, p. 85. The second Tangier bomb incident was brought to public notice by Superintendent Rob Allen of the Gibraltar Defence Police and ace reporter Brian Reyes, now the editor of the *Gibraltar Chronicle*; a plaque was put up to honour the dead police officers in the lobby of the Gibraltar Parliament on the seventieth anniversary in 2012. The 'weeded' SOE report with Gort's first cable and the description of the riot is HS 6/951 in TNA; the uncensored Colonial Office 'Enquiry into the explosion at Tangier of a diplomatic bag from Gibraltar' is CO 967/68. On 'limpet' mines see chapter 3 of Bernard O'Connor, *Churchill's School for Saboteurs: Station 17* (Amberley, 2014). The minutes of the enquiry into the despatch of explosives form part of the dossier of Mrs Isabel Curtis's post-war claim for a fairer widow's pension, at WO 258/138. The Top Secret

and Personal document is appended because the Governor of Gibraltar in
1947, General Sir Kenneth Anderson, fully supported the justice of her claim
that her husband PC Charles Curtis was 'improperly' sent to Tangier, that
SOE had been 'negligent' and that he had died more as a soldier than a
civilian. Decrypts of German Secret Service messages from Tangier in the first
half of February 1942 are in TNA HW 19/23. There is a good account of ISOS
and Section V in Kenneth Benton, 'The ISOS Years: Madrid 1941–43', with
an introduction by Christopher Andrew, *Journal of Contemporary History*,
vol. 30, no. 3 (July 1995) (Sage Publications). The remaining fragments of the
MI5 file on Hans Paul Krüger alias Kruse are in KV 2/525. GGG and 'Golfers'
information from the late Mavis Batey who worked with 'Dilly' Knox at
Bletchley Park. Tim Milne quote from *Kim Philby: the Unknown Story of
the KGB's Master Spy* (Biteback, 2014), pp.79–80 and R. V. Jones quote from
Most Secret War: British Scientific Intelligence 1939–1945 (Hamish Hamilton,
1978), p. 255. Admiralty discussions about possible action against 'Blake' and
the draft telegram to Sir Samuel Hoare are in the Naval Intelligence Division
file ADM 223/485, 'German Intelligence Service, Gibraltar Straits Area'.

30 Lighting the Torch

The Allied strategic decision for *Torch* is laid out clearly in Keith Sainsbury,
The North Africa Landings, 1942 ((Davis-Poynter, 1976), and the Axis threat
explained in Norman J. W. Goda, *Tomorrow the World: Hitler, Northwest
Africa and the Path toward America* (Texas A&M, 1998). Dwight D.
Eisenhower's own account of *Torch* is in *Crusade in Europe* (Heinemann,
1948), supplemented by Carlo D'Este, *Eisenhower: Allied Supreme
Commander* (Weidenfeld & Nicholson, 2002). Harry C. Butcher's *Three Years
with Eisenhower* (Heinemann, 1946) is an invaluable contemporaneous diary.
Kay Summersby, *Eisenhower Was My Boss* (Werner Laurie, 1949) gives the
driver's-eye view of life with Ike. Patton quotes from Carlo D'Este, *A Genius
for War: a Life of General George S. Patton* (Harper Collins, 1995), p. 419 and
Stanley P. Hirshson, *General Patton: a Soldier's Life* (Harper Perennial, 2003),
p. 267. On FDR's skilful tricksiness see Joseph E. Persico, *Roosevelt's Secret
War: FDR and World War II Espionage* (Random House, 2001). Thomas W.
Lippman's biography, *Arabian Knight: Colonel Bill Eddy USMC and the Rise
of American Power in the Middle East* (Selwa Press, 2008) is interesting. OSS
information from Michael Warner, CIA History Staff, Center for the Study
of Intelligence, May 2000. On Polish espionage see John Herman, 'Agency
Africa: Rygor's Franco-Polish Network and Operation Torch', *Journal of
Contemporary History* 22 (1987) (Sage Publications) and Major General

Rygor Slowikowski, *In the Secret Service: the Lighting of the Torch* (The Windrush Press, 1988). The Chiefs of Staff directive to SOE about North Africa is discussed in HS6/951 and OSS/SOE co-operation in Morocco in HS3/203. Carleton S. Coon's memoir, *A North Africa Story*, is revealing. The Abd el-Krim kidnap idea is in the SOE Morocco file HS 3/203 and Philip Jordan reprinted his piece in *Jordan's Tunis Diary* (Collins, 1943), pp. 13–17. The whereabouts of Eric Linklater's Gibraltar film script are unknown; his account of the trip, 'The Rock', is in *The Art of Adventure* (Macmillan, 1947), pp. 220–37. Churchill's visit to Stalin via Gibraltar and Cairo and back again is chapters 26–29 in *The Hinge of Fate*, vol. 4 of *The Second World War* (first published Cassell, 1951, in the Folio Society edition, 2000, pp. 367–422). It is also covered in chapters 7 and 8 of Brian Lavery, *Churchill Goes to War: Winston's Wartime Journeys* (Conway, 2007), pp. 121–53. Anthony Quayle's account of the prime minister's arrival on the Rock is in his autobiography, *A Time to Speak* (Barrie & Jenkins, 1990), pp. 237–9. Alec Cadogan's description of the last night in Moscow is in FO 1093/247. Mason-Mac's Gibraltar reports feature in the War Office file WO 106/2768, 'Operation TORCH in relation to Gibraltar'. There is an account of Operation *Pedestal* in Duncan Redford, *A History of the Royal Navy: World War II* (I. B. Tauris, 2014), pp. 167–9; real archive footage of the SS *Ohio* is used in the Alec Guinness/Jack Hawkins 1953 feature film *Malta Story*. The Begoña hand-grenade incident is described by Sir Samuel Hoare in *Ambassador on Special Mission*, pp. 165–6 and Preston, *Franco*, pp. 465–8, 470–1. Sundae appears in Nigel West's edition of *The Guy Liddell Diaries, vol. 1: 1939–1942* (Routledge, 2005), pp. 242–3, and on pp. 128–9 of Scherr's *History of the SID of the DSO Gibraltar*, TNA KV4/260. Donald Downes, *The Scarlet Thread: Adventures in Wartime Espionage* was published by Derek Verschoyle in 1953. In chapter 4 of Robin Winks, *Cloak and Gown: Scholars in America's Secret War* (Collins Harvill, 1987), which is about Downes, Professor Winks clearly identifies 'Alphonia' as Spain. *British Security Coordination: the Secret History of British Intelligence in the Americas 1940–1945,* which mentions Allied use of Basque agents, was published by St Ermin's Press in 1998. See also Persico, *Roosevelt's Secret War*, pp. 197–8. The kidnapping and elimination of Rodriguez (first drawn attention to in the National Archives by the assiduous Ángel Viñas) is from HS 7/254, SOE War Diary 33, Iberian Section, July–December 1942, pp. 39–43. Lt Clamorgan's plane crash is in FO 1093/227 and his SOE file is HS 9/318/5. The meeting of Murphy, Mast and Clark at Cherchell in Algeria is described in chapter 8, 'Fifth Column Activities in Africa', of Robert Murphy's *Diplomat among Warriors*, chapter 5, 'Secret Mission to Africa', of General Mark Clark's *Calculated Risk: his Personal Story of the War in North Africa and Italy*

(George G. Harrap, 1951) and chapters 2 and 3 of Terence Robertson's book about HMS *Seraph*, *The Ship with Two Captains* (Evans Bros, 1957).

31 The North African Landings

There is a good sketch of the great Admiral Sir Bertram Home Ramsay in Kenneth Edwards, *Seven Sailors* (Collins, 1945), pp. 11–80, and a biography by W. S. Chalmers, *Full Cycle* (Hodder & Stoughton, 1959). Admiral Cunningham's despatch about *Torch* was printed in a supplement to the *London Gazette*, 22 March 1949, pp. 1509–25. Life in RAF North Camp is well described by Jack Newman in *Erk on a Rock* (Merlin Books, 1984). Pete Grafton's *You, You & You: the People Out of Step with World War 2* was published by Pluto Press in 1981. The best book on Second World War deception is Thaddeus Holt, *The Deceivers* (Scribner, 2004). For a fuller account of Dudley Clarke's cross-dressing adventure in Spain, see my *Churchill's Wizards*, pp. 345–52. No-one has yet located Lord Gort's full report on Clarke. Dwight Eisenhower's surprise at commanding Gibraltar is from Carlo D'Este, *Eisenhower: Allied Supreme Commander*, p. 352. Eisenhower describes 'the most dismal setting' of his Gibraltar HQ and the awkward encounter with Giraud in chapter six, 'Invasion of Africa', of *Crusade in Europe* (Heinemann, 1948), pp. 106–27. William Mackenzie writes about 'Mallory' in *The Secret History of S.O.E. Special Operations Executive 1940–1945* (St Ermin's Press, 2000), pp. 324–5. Ian Reyes of the Fortress of Gibraltar Group and AquaGib superintendent Jose Luis Marzan helped me locate the two SOE wireless sites. See 'New discovery in Gibraltar', *Gibraltar Chronicle*, 4 Dec 2017, p. 4. Roosevelt's message to Franco is from Carlton Hayes, *Wartime Mission in Spain, 1942–1945* (Da Capo Press, 1976), p. 91. Operation Reservist features in chapter 2 of Rick Atkinson, *An Army at Dawn: the War in North Africa 1942–1943* (Little, Brown, 2003). Robert Murphy describes 7/8 November as 'A Frantic Night' in chapter 9 of *Diplomat among Warriors*. 'The Darlan "Deal"' is chapter 6 of General Mark Clark, *Calculated Risk*. Richard Crossman quoted in Anthony Sampson, *Macmillan: a Study in Ambiguity* (Allen Lane, 1967), p. 61. Harold Macmillan quote from *War Diaries: the Mediterranean 1943–1945* (Papermac, 1984), p. 3.

32 Underwater Gibraltar

A principal source on Decima Flottiglia MAS is *Sea Devils* (Andrew Melrose, 1952) by its commander, Prince Julio Valerio Borghese, translated from the Italian by James Cleugh. They also feature in Tom Waldron and James Gleeson,

The Frogmen: the Story of the War-time Underwater Operators (Evans Bros, 1950), Paul Kemp, *Underwater Warriors* (Brockhampton Press, 1999) and P. Crociani and P. P. Battistelli, *Italian Navy and Air Force Elite Units and Special Forces 1940–45* (Osprey, 2013). The discovery of the *Olterra*'s secret role and the sabotage operations carried out from her by human torpedoes prompted much British reporting and analysis, e.g. ADM 1/12534, ADM 1/12939, ADM 199/1812, ADM 223/583 and WO 204/12738. There is a good account (with illustrations) in David Scherr's *History of the SID*, KV 4/259 and 260. Giulio Pistono's MI5 file is KV 2/3018. See also Phil Smith and Darren Fa, *Underwater Gibraltar*. Desmond Bristow's *A Game of Moles: the Deceptions of an MI6 Officer* (Little, Brown, 1993) was written with his son Bill Bristow. The first book about Lionel 'Buster' Crabb was published four months after his disappearance in Portsmouth Harbour in April 1956, during an SIS-sponsored dive to examine the hull of the Russian cruiser which had brought Marshal Bulganin and Mr Khrushchev to Britain. Marshall Pugh's *Commander Crabb* (Macmillan, 1956) remains outstanding because the author had been working closely with his subject. Frank Goldsworthy also talks about the Crabb he knew in a 1990 oral history interview (Imperial War Museum no. 11245). Excitable books about Crabb include J. Bernard Hutton, *Frogman Extraordinary* (Neville Spearman, 1960), and two by Mike and Jacqui Welham: *Frogman Spy* (W. H. Allen, 1990) and *The Crabb Enigma* (Matador, 2010). Tim Binding plays with their ideas of Commander Crabb as not having died but been captured by the Russians and living out his days as Commander Korablov in an evocative and memorable novel, *Man Overboard*, published by Picador in 2005. Don Hale, *The Final Dive: the Life and Death of 'Buster' Crabb* (The History Press, 2007) detects the hidden hand of Admiral Lord Mountbatten. Nigel West debunks the myths in *Cold War Counterfeit Spies* (Frontline Books, 2016) pp. 86–93. The fullest official account – ordered by Prime Minister Anthony Eden – was only released to the National Archives in October 2015, nearly sixty years after the event. 'The Bridges Enquiry into the disappearance of Commander Crabb' is available online as CAB 301/121, 122, 123, 124 and 125.

33 Undercover and Underhand

A Freedom of Information request was unable to dislodge the José Estelle Key file HO 144/21846 from retention by the Home Office. It is, apparently, 'intended for future release/publication . . . at some future date'. The Treachery Act 1940 was passed in emergency to facilitate the prosecution of enemy spies who did not fall under the Treason Act 1695. See D. Seaborne Davies, 'The Treachery Act, 1940' in *The Modern Law Review*, vol. 4, no. 3 (January 1941), pp. 217–20. The classic account of the use of double agents by MI5 is J. C. Masterman, *The Double-Cross System 1939–1945* (Yale University Press, 1972, Pimlico, 1995). David Scherr describes the use of double agents in Gibraltar in his history, KV 4/259 and 260. The same files are rather hastily summarised in chapter 29, 'The ROCK', of Thomas Hennessey and Claire Thomas, *Spooks: the Unofficial History of MI5*, pp. 466–81. The credit for discovering the identity of 'NAG' (code-names were always written in capitals then) goes to Ian Reyes, a key member of the Gibraltar Fortress Group and a keen researcher of wartime Gibraltar. MI5's file on José Martin Muñoz file is KV 2/1162 and the joint file with Luis Lopez Cordon Cuenca is KV 2/2114. Albert Pierrepoint's autobiography, *Executioner: Pierrepoint*, was first published by Harrap in 1974. The Joshua Hassan story about the execution of the enemy spies is from the *Gibraltar Heritage Journal* 5 (1998), p. 17.

34 'The End of Poland'

The spring/summer 2006 issue 13 of *Everyone's War*, the journal of the Second World War Experience Centre, has seven interesting essays relating to Poland. *After the Battle* 20 (1978) contains an eighteen-page article with four dozen photographs on 'The Death of General Sikorski'. Anthony Quayle writes about the incident in his autobiography. 'Sikorski's Last Mission' is chapter 12 of Norman Davies, *Trail of Hope: the Anders Army, an odyssey across three continents* (Osprey, 2015). On the controversy: David Irving, *Accident: the death of General Sikorski* was published by William Kimber in 1967; *Soldiers: an obituary for Geneva*, a play by Rolf Hochhuth, translated by Robert David Macdonald, was published by Grove Press and André Deutsch in 1968, and Carlos Thompson's response, *The Assassination of Winston Churchill*, came out from Colin Smythe (Gerrards Cross) in 1969. D. D. Guttenplan, *The Holocaust on Trial: History, Justice and the David Irving Libel Case* (Granta Books, 2001) is a fine account of the complexities of the libel suit that the military historian David Irving brought in 2000 against the US historian Deborah E. Lipstadt because her 1995 Penguin book *Denying the Holocaust: the Growing Assault on Truth and Memory* accused him of distorting history. Irving lost his case; the judge called him a racist, anti-Semitic, right-wing pro-Nazi polemicist. In the 2016 feature film about the case, *Denial*, Irving is played by Timothy Spall, who had also starred in *Pierrepoint*. The Polish journalist Jan Strupczewski of Reuters helped me find and translate Professor Tebinka's words. The 10 April 2017 Reuters report from Warsaw was written by Marcin Goettig and Pawel Sobczak.

35 A Vision of Battlements

The author Anthony Burgess (1917–93), who was born John Wilson
in Manchester, wrote directly about Gibraltar in both volumes of his
autobiographical confessions, *Little Wilson and Big God* (William Heinemann,
1987) and *You've Had Your Time* (Heinemann, 1990); in his novels *A Vision
of Battlements* (Sidgwick & Jackson, 1965) and *Any Old Iron* (Hutchinson,
1989) and in journalism for the *Guardian* (1966), *Holiday* (1967) and the *Daily
Mail* (1985). In his three years stationed on the Rock, Burgess also began his
career as a critic, contributing a scathing review of soldiers' poetry to *The
Rock* magazine and twenty-eight film reviews for the *Gibraltar Chronicle* in
1946, which I located in copies held by the Garrison Library. The excellent
International Anthony Burgess Foundation in Manchester, established by
the writer's widow Liana Burgess in 2003, supplied me with Burgess's army
records, reviews of his books, and much more. Its director, Professor Andrew
Biswell, wrote *The Real Life of Anthony Burgess* (Picador, 2005). The other
British biography I have consulted, a tour de force of love/hate, is Roger Lewis,
Anthony Burgess (Faber, 2002). *The British Way and Purpose* (Consolidated
Edition) was prepared by the Directorate of Army Education in 1944. The
D'Amato brothers' story is pieced together from private family information,
the GNA box file S47/1940 and the Defence Regulation 18B detainee files HO
45/24147 and 25148 in TNA, Kew. What happened to Krishna Khubchand
also comes from family information and the 'Indians residing in Gibraltar'
file S.56/1939 in the Gibraltar National Archives. The Victor Rothschild field
telephone conversation is from chapter 3 of his autobiography *Meditations of
Broomstick* (Collins, 1977), pp. 29–32. Wolfram details from HS 7/164. See also
Joan María Thomàs, *La Batalla del Wolframio* (Catedra, 2010). The Spanish
section of Churchill's World Survey on 24 May 1944 is from *The Dawn of
Liberation* volume of war speeches (Cassell, 1945), pp. 88–91. Chapters 6 and
7 of Richard Wigg, *Churchill and Spain: the Survival of the Franco Regime
1940–1945* (Sussex Academic Press, 2008) explain the situation admirably.
The best book in Spanish on the period 1942–1945 is Carlos Collado Seidel, *El
telegrama que salvó a Franco* (Crítica, 2016) which is superbly researched. The
Spencer/Scherr wedding guest list was kindly supplied by Jennifer Scherr.

36 The Atlantic Outposts

The fifty or more books that I possess on the extraordinary Falklands/
Malvinas war of 1982 include Max Hastings and Simon Jenkins, *The Battle
for the Falklands* (Michael Joseph, 1983), Martin Middlebook, *Task Force: the*

Falklands War, 1982 (revised edition, Penguin, 1987), Lawrence Freedman and Virginia Gamba-Stonehouse, *Signals of War: the Falklands Conflict of 1982* (Faber, 1990), Nigel West, *The Secret War for the Falklands: the SAS, MI6, and the War Whitehall Nearly Lost* (Little, Brown, 1997), and Admiral Sandy Woodward (with Patrick Robinson), *One Hundred Days: the Memoirs of the Falklands Battle Group Commander* (3rd edn, Harper Press, 2012). The *guerra sucia* ('dirty war') crimes of the overthrown Argentine junta are exposed in *Nunca Más (Never Again)* (Faber, 1986). See also Marguerite Feitlowitz, *A Lexicon of Terror: Argentina and the Legacies of Torture* (Oxford University Press, 1998). The refitting of SS *Uganda* in Gibraltar is featured in the *Gibraltar Heritage Journal* 18 (2011) and 19 (2012), with articles by Orlando Bossino, David Sanchez and Malcolm Beanland. The names of Juan López and John Ward come from Jorge Luis Borges's poem about the South Atlantic conflict, in which two literate enemies who could have been friends end up in the same grave.

Acknowledgements

Gibraltarians have been exceptionally kind to a *guiri* on their terrain, an outsider retelling some of their stories. Thank you for what you have taught me. I am especially indebted to two great-hearted Gibraltarians who share the same surname. Although Brian Reyes and Ian Reyes are not related, they have both proved to be *reyes* – kings among men.

I am also deeply grateful to the following individuals and institutions for their help with the book. All mistakes and misunderstandings are mine alone.

Abebooks
Owen Adamberry
Hugh Alexander
José Manuel Algarbani
Michael Alpert
Amanda Baker
Paul Baker
Edward Baldwin
Jennifer Ballantine Perera
John Bassadone
Natasha Bassadone
The late Mavis Batey
Dennis Beiso
Sam Benady
Tito Benady
Yael Benady
Sam Benzaquen
András Bereznay
Andrew Biswell
Paul Blezard

Dr Mark Bolland
Joe Bossano
Keith Bowers
Anna Breen
Janine Button
Calpe Rowing Club
Andrew Canessa
Peter Canessa
Shireen Cantrell
Will Carr
Neville Chipulina
William Chislett
Stuart Christie
John Clink
Juan Collado
Jim Crone
John C. Culatto
Judith Curthoys
Jens Dahbi
Ed Davis

ACKNOWLEDGEMENTS

Amy Dimmock
Walter Donohue
Sally Dunsmore
Dover Castle (English Heritage)
Anna Edwards
Alfonso Escuadra Sánchez
Rebecca Faller
Clive Finlayson
Geraldine Finlayson
Tommy Finlayson
Fortress of Gibraltar Group
Cristina Galliano
Lourdes Galliano
Maggie Galliano
Adam Galloway
Marguerite Galloway
Richard Garcia
Gaby Garner
Rob Garner
Garrison Library
Gibraltar Chronicle
Gibraltar Heritage Trust
Gibraltar Museum
Gibraltar National Archives
Gibunco Gibraltar International
   Literary Festival
Joe Gingell
Iñaki Goiogana
Clive Golt
Michelle Gomez
Brian Gomila
Nicky Guerrero
John Charles Guy
Richard Harvey
Victor Hermida
Mike Hill
History Society Gibraltar
Thaddeus Holt
Imperial War Museum

International Anthony Burgess
   Foundation
Xabier Irujo
Pete Jackson
Robert Johnson
JSTOR
Kamlesh Khubchand
Krishna Khubchand
Cliff Kirkpatrick
Karen Kukil
Kevin Lane
Jean-Paul Latin
The late Solomon Levy
London Library
David Liebler
Julian Loose
Ben Macintyre
Graham Mark
Peter Martland
José Luis Marzan
Alice Mascarenhas
Ian McGhie
Peter McKay
Patrick Mifsud
Vin Mifsud
Clare Montado
Louise Napoli
National Archives, Kew
Navy News
Ingo Niebel
Tommy Norton
*Oxford Dictionary of National
   Biography*
Anthony Pitaluga
Grazyna Plebanek
John Porral
Mark Porral
Susan Préfol
Paul Preston

James Ramagge
John Rankin
Rosa Rankin-Gee
Eleanor Rees
Francis Richards
Jerry Robinson
The Rock Hotel
Barnaby Rogerson
Mike Rosner
Royal Engineers Museum, Library
  & Archive
Alfred Ryan
John Ryle
M. G. Sanchez
Lydia Segrave
Jennifer Scherr
James Scott
David Seed
Danielle Sellers
Sharp Printing
Michael Smith
Phil Smith

Robbie Spotswood
John Stagnetto
Gareth Stockey
Mathias Strohn
Jan Strupczewski
Mariola Summerfield
Chris Tavares
Michael Tavares
Juan José Téllez
Christopher Thompson
Ian Tidbury
TLS
Tito Vallejo Smith
Stephen Vassallo
Emma Vickers
John Waite
Kate Ward
Robert Wheeler
Julia Wilde
Edwin Williamson
Blair Worden
Delilah Yeo Smith

Special thanks for all her hard work to my beloved wife Maggie Gee, my patient first editor and constant encourager.

Permissions

The author and publishers are grateful to the following for the use of copyright material. Every effort has been made to trace and contact the copyright holders of material quoted in the text. The publishers would be pleased to rectify at the earliest opportunity any omissions or errors brought to their notice.

Patrick, Ramón and George Buckley for extracts from *The Life and Death of the Spanish Republic* by Henry Buckley.

Extracts from the work of Anthony Burgess, including *A Vision of Battlements*, published by Sidgwick & Jackson, *Little Wilson and Big God* and *You've Had Your Time*, published by Vintage, and journalism first published in the *Guardian*, *Holiday* and the *Daily Mail* by permission of David Higham Associates Limited on behalf of the International Anthony Burgess Foundation.

Extracts from the writings of Charles Causley by permission of David Higham Associates Limited.

Extracts from Sir Winston Churchill's speeches and books, including *The World Crisis*, *Great Contemporaries*, *Step by Step*, *Into Battle*, *The Second World War*, are reproduced with permission of Curtis Brown Ltd, London, on behalf of The Estate of Winston S. Churchill, © The Estate of Winston S. Churchill.

Artemis Cooper for extracts from *Old Men Forget* by Duff Cooper.

Extract from *The Art of Adventure* by Eric Linklater reprinted by permission of Peters Fraser & Dunlop (www.petersfraserdunlop.com) on behalf of the Estate of Eric Linklater.

Michael Hall and Islay Boeri for extracts from the writings of Lieutenant-General Sir Noel Mason-MacFarlane, K.C.B., D.S.O., M.C.

Index